# HENGISTBURY HEAD
## DORSET

VOLUME 2:
THE LATE UPPER PALAEOLITHIC
& EARLY MESOLITHIC SITES

R.N.E. Barton

With contributions from
D. E. Barton, C. A. Bergman, S. N. Collcutt, J. Cook,
J. Huxtable, I. Levi-Sala, R. I. Macphail, E. J. Rhodes, J. L. Ruiz,
C. Salter, R. Sanderson, R. G. Scaife, B. A. Tocher and R. Unger-Hamilton.

Oxford University Committee for Archaeology

Monograph No 34
1992

In Memoriam

IRENE LEVI-SALA

Copyright © Oxford University Committee for Archaeology and individual authors 1992

Published by the Oxford University Committee for Archaeology
Institute of Archaeology
36 Beaumont Street
Oxford

ISBN 0-947816-34-8
Designed and produced by Paradigm Design Ltd, Oxford
Printed in Great Britain

# Contents

# Acknowledgments

The Hengistbury Head Palaeolithic and Mesolithic Project was directed by the writer and formed the basis of his doctoral thesis research at Oxford University. The Project was sponsored by the Donald Baden-Powell Quaternary Research Centre under its director Dr Derek Roe who also acted as academic research supervisor. The initial setting up of the project owes much to the encouragement and active interest of Professor Barry Cunliffe of the Institute of Archaeology, Oxford who recognised this as an important adjunct of his own research on the headland. In terms of financial support the project could not have functioned without the help and involvement of many individuals and institutions. In particular, a special debt of gratitude is owed to the landowners, Bournemouth Corporation, for permitting the excavations and for remaining financially committed to the project over the five excavation seasons. Others acknowledged for their funding support include English Heritage, the Society of Antiquaries, the Prehistoric Society, the British Academy, Dorset Natural History and Archaeological Society, the Friends of the Red House Museum, the Wenner Gren Foundation, the L.S.B. Leakey Foundation, and one anonymous donor, who all gave generously to the project. In addition, English Heritage contributed a major part of the publication costs.

Many individuals must be thanked for their help and support in the various stages of the Project. During each season's fieldwork, considerable practical assistance was given to the excavations by the Bournemouth Parks Department through the kind offices of Mr Edward Hunt and Mr Mark Holloway, the ranger of Hengistbury Head. Special thanks must likewise be recorded to Mr Peter Hawes and Mr Ian Martindale for providing all kinds of facilities, free of charge, at the Marine Training Centre at Hengistbury and for their inexhaustible supply of useful distractions during enforced weather breaks. For arranging the loan of laser levelling equipment I am grateful to Mr Paul Prescott and Dr. Bulson, Ministry of Defence, Christchurch. I would also like to express my gratitude to Mr Norman Lindsey and Mr James Hooker of the City University's Department of Civil Engineering, for surveying work carried out during the 1983 season. Mr Michael Ridley, formerly of the Russell-Cotes Museum Bournemouth, is duly acknowledged for the close personal interest he took in the fieldwork, as is Mr Ronald Powell, who not only discovered one of the sites but found time between his other commitments to make site equipment and join the excavation team as a volunteer member.

My special thanks are reserved for all the volunteers who helped with the excavation and survey work. Apart from stoically putting up with gale-force winds, sand storms and the blazing heat (all experienced during the course of each summer !), they also had to endure the constant verbal reminders about keeping their spits horizontal and their sections straight. In this task I was ably abetted by my colleague Dr Christopher Bergman who helped supervise the team and taught many of its members (including myself) a great deal about flint technology. I would also like to express my personal gratitude to Dr Simon Collcutt, who was instrumental in my becoming involved in the Hengistbury Project and who, over the years, has provided much constructive support and valued criticism, not only in the field but also during the post-excavation work at the Donald Baden-Powell Quaternary Research Centre at Oxford.

Many individuals have helped in various ways with the post-excavation work and in bringing the report to its final stages of preparation. I would like to thank especially Mr James Knight for his Job-like patience in helping me in the later stages of the refitting programme and for his careful restoration of the drilled artefacts. I am indebted also to Ms Christine Wilson, Ms Hazel Martingell, Mr Jeffrey Wallis and Mr Rupert Cook for their truly magnificent artefact illustrations and to Mr Edward Roberts and Ms Anne Foster for their help in reproducing the site maps and the diagrams of refitted cores. Mr Paulo Scremin is also gratefully acknowledged for the high-quality photographs of the refitted cores, as are Mr Robert Wilkins, Mr Harold Edwards, Mr Simon Pressey and Mr Frank Schwartz who helped in the final preparation of illustrations and photographs. Finally, I am greatly indebted to Ms Alison Roberts and Ms Jill Cook of the British Museum, and to the staff of the Natural History Museum, for producing the Scanning Electron Photomicrographs used in this volume.

A number of my colleagues have seen earlier drafts of chapters and provided useful critical comments. They include Dr Mark Newcomer, Dr Derek Roe, Dr Roger Jacobi, Dr Andrew David, Dr Simon Collcutt, Mr Martin Street and Ms Alison Roberts. Ms Alison Roberts is also thanked for her considerable patience and expertise in editing the final version of the text. To each of these people I am extremely grateful but, as is wholly customary in these matters, the writer willingly concedes responsibility for any omissions or unforced errors which appear in the volume.

A sad footnote to the acknowledgements is to report the tragic death of one of the volume's contributors, Dr Irene Levi-Sala, who was killed in an aircrash in Chile in February 1991, before this publication went to press. This volume is thus dedicated to her memory and recognises the important contribution she made to microwear studies in her all too brief but highly productive academic career.

*Nick Barton*

# List of Illustrations

# List of Tables

*List of fiche illustrations*

# Addresses of contributors

Dr. R.N.E. Barton — Department of Archaeology, Saint David's University College, University of Wales, Lampeter, Dyfed SA48 7ED.

Prof. D.E. Barton — School of Mathematical Sciences, Queen Mary College, University of London, Mile End Road, London E1 4NS.

Dr. C.A. Bergman — Environmental Services Inc., 781 Neeb Road, Suite 5, Cincinnati, Ohio 45233, U.S.A.

Dr. S.N. Collcutt — Oxford Archaeological Associates Ltd., Lawrence House, 2 Polstead Road, Oxford OX2 6TN.

Ms. J. Cook — Department of Prehistoric & Romano-British Antiquities, The British Museum, Franks House, 38-46 Orsman Road, London N1.

Mrs. J. Huxtable — Research Laboratory for Archaeology & the History of Art, 6 Keble Road, Oxford OX1 3QJ.

Dr. I. Levi-Sala — (Late of) Institute of Archaeology, University of London, 31-34 Gordon Square, London WC1 OPY.

Dr. R.I. Macphail — Institute of Archaeology, University of London, 31-34 Gordon Square, London WC1 OPY.

Dr. E.J. Rhodes — Research Laboratory for Archaeology & the History of Art, 6 Keble Road, Oxford OX1 3QJ.

Mr. J.L. Ruiz — Department of Computer Science, Queen Mary College, University of London, Mile End Road, London E1 4NS.

Dr. C. Salter — Department of Metallurgy & Science of Materials, University of Oxford, Parks Road, Oxford OX1 3PH.

Mr. R. Sanderson — Geological Museum, Exhibition Road, London SW7 2DE.

Dr. R.G. Scaife — Department of Geography, University of Southampton, Southampton SO9 5NH.

Dr. B.A. Tocher — Institute of Earth Studies, The University College of Wales, Aberystwyth, Dyfed SY23 3DB.

Dr. R. Unger-Hamilton — Institute of Archaeology, University of London, 31-34 Gordon Square, London WC1 OPY.

# 1. Introduction to the Site Investigations

## 1.1 Introduction

There can be few promontories along Britain's southern coastline more spectacular than Hengistbury Head in Dorset. Carved by natural processes of marine and wind erosion over thousands of years, the headland today provides an impressive sight with its slightly tilted, pedestal form towering over the surrounding land and sea-scapes. The imposing nature of this landmark is further emphasised by the flat, low-lying land on either side, affording uninterrupted views of the headland for many miles around. On the seaward side the headland forms a major buttress overlooking the Isle of Wight and guarding the western approaches to the Solent Estuary.

Given its prominent position in the landscape, it is not hard to imagine why Hengistbury played such an influential role in the human settlement of this area in the prehistoric period. For, not only does it display a remarkable wealth and diversity in archaeological remains but it is also one of the very few open-air sites in Britain where an almost unbroken record of human activity can be traced from the Late Upper Palaeolithic to the Iron Age.

Although evidence exists of visits by hunter-gatherers of the Lower Palaeolithic, Hengistbury first appears to have been used intensively as a residential campsite about 12,500 years ago during the Late Glacial. The next evidence for occupation comes in the early Postglacial period about 9,700 years ago when the headland was exploited by Mesolithic hunter-gatherers. Later this was followed by settlement of the earliest farming communities who left behind evidence of their activities in the form of flint scatters and other artefactual debris. In the succeeding phases of the Bronze Age, the headland seems to have been treated as marginal land and during this time it became an important round barrow cemetery. Finally, in the first millennium BC the site was fortified and served as an international port for traders of the Iron Age.

This monograph is the second in the Hengistbury series and follows an earlier volume on the later prehistoric and Iron Age settlement of the headland (Cunliffe 1987). In this volume, the earlier prehistoric evidence is presented, with particular reference to the Late Glacial and early Postglacial occupation phases on Hengistbury Head. It presents in detail the results of the 1980–84 excavations at two sites: one Late Upper Palaeolithic, the other Mesolithic and evaluates this information against the background of previous research by Mace (1959) and by Campbell (1977).

The investigation of the Late Upper Palaeolithic and Mesolithic sites was conceived as an interdisciplinary project and relied upon the cooperation of a wide range of specialists in achieving its aims. The monograph incorporates the results of these specialist

reports, which it attempts to set out in a coherent and logical order. Following the introductory chapter, which deals with the overall methodology, the second chapter describes the contextual and chronological evidence of the Late Upper Palaeolithic and Mesolithic sites, with specialist contributions on the sediments, soils and flora. The next chapter deals with aspects of site taphonomy and the effects of post-depositional processes on site formation, particularly important in distinguishing natural from human influences in the spatial clustering of artefacts. Chapters 4 and 5 present the archaeological evidence from the Late Upper Palaeolithic site and the Mesolithic site, respectively. They concern the detailed descriptions of the lithic assemblages in terms of typological and technological analyses. These are supplemented by refitting studies, for interpreting manufacturing techniques and in elucidating site spatial evidence and human activity. At the end of the Late Upper Palaeolithic and Mesolithic chapters, each site is considered separately within its wider national and European context. Finally, Chapter 6 deals with management issues and the future conservation of the remaining archaeological resource, while Chapter 7 presents an archaeological glossary of terms employed in the monograph.

## 1.2 The archaeological sites in their setting

Hengistbury Head forms a narrow arm of land which projects into the English Channel close to the entrance of the Solent Estuary, near Bournemouth in Dorset (Fig. 1.2). The headland is about 1.5 km long and consists of an upland plateau known as Warren Hill which is separated from the mainland by a low-lying isthmus, a few metres above sea-level. The highest point of the headland, at 35 m OD, is located near the western end of the peninsula with the land shelving gently away south-eastwards and terminating in a sea-cliff about 14 m high. On the northern side of the headland is the large lagoonal estuary of Christchurch Harbour which is partially cut off from the sea by a barrier of sand dunes. A steep cliff characterises the southern edge of the headland, which overlooks the English Channel.

In terms of its setting, the Late Upper Palaeolithic site is situated towards the south-eastern tip of the headland. It lies within the 'Eastern Depression', a shallow trough-like feature which is the remains of a small north-south running valley now truncated by the sea cliff (Fig. 1.3). The main area of the site stands close to the present cliff path at about 14 m OD (Figs. 1.4, 1.5 and 1.6). The Late Upper Palaeolithic site is separated from the Mesolithic site by a distance of about 650 m. The latter is located further westwards on the upper slopes of Warren Hill and in recognition

1.1   *Aerial photograph of Hengistbury Head looking westwards towards Southbourne and Bournemouth. Both sites are on the southern cliff-edge.*
*(Photo: Kitchenham Ltd.)*

1.2  *The location of Hengistbury Head (Cunliffe 1987, Ill. 2).*

of its discoverer is referred to as the Powell Mesolithic site. Like the Upper Palaeolithic site it occupies a moderately sheltered position, in this case just below the crest of the hill between the coastal footpath and the cliff. Its general position may be located with reference to a round barrow (Barrow 9) which lies on the south edge of the footpath, roughly 35 m north west of the site (Fig. 1.17).

Today, both the Late Upper Palaeolithic and Mesolithic sites occupy positions close to the existing cliff-edge and, as such, it is hard to imagine them other than as coastal locations. In fact there are several clear lines of evidence to suggest not only that the shape of the headland was entirely different in the past but also, more importantly, that Hengistbury occupied an inland position rather than a coastal one.

To begin with, when the area was exploited by Late Glacial hunter-gatherers about 12,500 years ago, world sea levels were much lower than they are today and, at the time of occupation, were only gradually

1.3 *View of Eastern Depression looking south towards the cliff-edge.*

1.4 *View east across the Late Upper Palaeolithic site in 1980, with the edge of the Mace trenches just visible behind S.N. Collcutt.*

beginning to recover from a maximum basal depth of *c.* 90 OD (Jelgersma 1979). During this period, the flat coastal shelf would have been greatly extended southwards providing a major landbridge between Britain and Europe. In consequence, the ridge currently occupied by Hengistbury would have stood well inland and overlooked the now submerged valley system of the Solent. The Needles of the Isle of Wight are considered to be the remains of the south side of this valley. Thus, instead of a view of the English Channel, the Late Upper Palaeolithic site would have overlooked a major river (the so-called 'proto-Solent') flowing West-East between the present coastline and the Isle of Wight (Reid 1898). The rivers Avon and Stour, which presently flow just north of the headland, may also have followed slightly different courses, being either deflected across the narrow isthmus which connects

Hengistbury to the mainland, or joining the main proto-Solent river further to the east (for additional detail see Chapter 2.1.1). Even though the sea level gradually rose after 10,000 BP, the headland would have continued to be landlocked during the Early Mesolithic period. The postulated coastline at this time lay at least 20 km further south (Devoy 1982, 1987). Moreover, unlike the existing acid heathland, the vegetational cover of the headland in the Early Holocene would almost certainly have included light woodland (see Chapter 2.3). According to pollen evidence recovered from beneath the sea, the final separation of the Isle of Wight from the mainland may only have occurred as recently as 6,000 years ago (Devoy 1987).

Further major changes in the appearance of Hengistbury and the local landscape have continued into the recent historic period. For example, it is well-

1.5 *View west across the Late Upper Palaeolithic site in 1980 before excavation.*

known that extensive quarrying of ironstone in the nineteenth century cut into the main body of the headland and caused considerable damage. The effects of these operations, combined with marine and wind erosion, have had far reaching consequences not only at Hengistbury but in radically affecting areas further along the present coastline. The speed at which the seacliff continues to regress can be seen particularly clearly with reference to 18th century historical maps and sketches of the area (e.g. by Grose 1779 and by Murdoch Mackenzie 1785, cited in Cunliffe 1987)(Fig. 1.6). They show, amongst other things, that between 150–300 m of land on the south side of the headland has been lost to the sea over the past 200 years (see also Cunliffe 1978, 11). This has important implications for understanding the position of the Late Upper Palaeolithic and Mesolithic sites, both of which now stand right on the southern cliff-edge overlooking the sea.

## 1.3 The significance of the Hengistbury site discoveries

Upper Palaeolithic open-air occurrences are particularly rare in Britain and very seldom come from well-stratified primary contexts. Many of the existing collections consist of single finds or small assemblages of stray artefacts recovered during the course of commercial quarrying or ploughing activities. In such cases it is not unusual for the original provenance of the finds to have been lost, leaving only a rough impression of the geographical or contextual location. At the same time, the potential for finding sites of this kind is considerably hampered by the inaccessibility of Late Glacial landsurfaces which are often deeply buried under thick layers of alluvium or hillwash deposits. Each of these factors serves to underline the great value of a site like Hengistbury, which by virtue of its position close to the surface and its undisturbed strati-

graphic condition provide very considerable opportunities for archaeological investigation.

Historically, much of the early research work into the British Upper Palaeolithic concentrated upon caves and rockshelters, rather than open-air sites. This may be partly explained in terms of a long tradition of underground exploration activity which in the mid-nineteenth led to important archaeological discoveries at Kent's Cavern, Brixham Cave, Victoria Cave and many others, gaining caving further esteem and popularity and at the same time directly influencing the future course of Palaeolithic studies. Such endeavours were encouraged no doubt by the high visibility of caves as natural features making them obvious focal points for investigations of this kind. In consequence, when Dorothy Garrod presented the first major synthesis of the British Upper Palaeolithic in 1926, she was able to record 21 caves and rockshelters, easily surpassing open-air findspots by a ratio of over 3:1 (Garrod 1926, 195). In the intervening sixty years, since her work was published, many more sites of this age have come to light but this has not resulted in a nett shift in the overall balance and there continues to be an overwhelming bias towards caves in the archaeological literature. Such a view comes across very strongly, for example in the work of John Campbell, who noted only twelve open-air examples amongst a total of 47 findspots of Late Upper Palaeolithic age (Campbell 1977, 110–145). More recently, however, research by Roger Jacobi (1980) and by the writer (Barton 1986b), has demonstrated the hidden importance of open-air sites, especially in parts of S England. The reason for the new shift of emphasis is largely due to the recognition of many more artefacts of Late Upper Palaeolithic type in assemblages of mixed type. As a result, Jacobi has been able to suggest that 35 of 71 potential Late Glacial findspots come from open-air locations (1980). That this observation is likely to be only a conservative estimate is indicated by his latest

# HENGISTBURY HEAD, DORSET

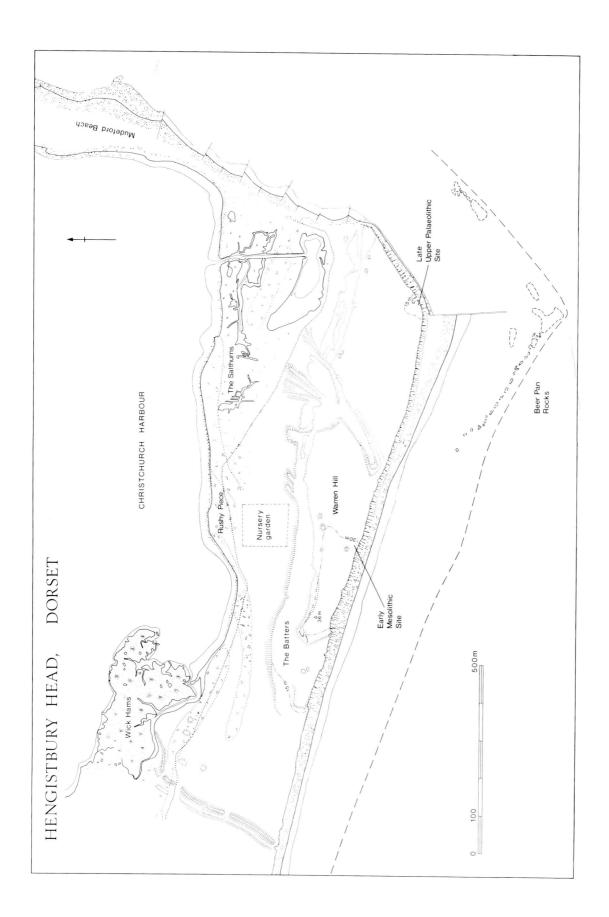

1.6  *General plan of Hengistbury showing the approximate position of the eighteenth century coastline, with the locations of the Late Upper Palaeolithic and Early Mesolithic sites (after Cunliffe 1987, Ill. 6).*

research which shows more than half of 150 possible Late Upper Palaeolithic findspots are from open-air sites (Jacobi pers. comm.). Further supporting evidence is provided in Barton (1986b), which reports as many as 60 open locations of 'terminal Glacial' age (additional to the figures cited by Jacobi). Significantly, the sites are heavily concentrated in south-east and central southern Britain, well away from the major outcrops of limestone containing caves and rockshelters. It should be recalled, however, that with the exception of one site, none has so far produced an assemblage of comparable size or typological complexity to that of Hengistbury.

In comparison with the Late Glacial locations, examples belonging to the early part of the succeeding Postglacial are considerably more common and probably reflect higher population densities of the British peninsula during this period. At a national level, Mesolithic finds have been extensively documented from open-air, cave and rockshelter sites throughout much of lowland and upland Britain (Clark 1932; Mellars 1974; Jacobi 1976; Wymer 1977; Woodman 1978), although there appears to be a clear preponderance of finds from open-air locations. Jacobi (1978) estimates an approximate total of 230 Early Mesolithic findspots from England alone, but in the past decade many more finds have been unearthed and the figure must now be revised significantly upwards. The relatively high visibility of Early Mesolithic occurrences in the British record, however, belies the fact that very few have been investigated according to modern scientific excavation techniques. The occurrence of the Early Mesolithic site at Hengistbury, and the immediate threat of cliff-erosion, therefore provided an exceptional and timely opportunity to investigate a site of this kind.

## 1.4 History of research at the Hengistbury sites

*The Late Upper Palaeolithic site:* Surface finds of flint artefacts have been made for many years at Hengistbury Head. Before World War I, a local antiquarian Mr Herbert Druitt paid two men, Mr Sidney Pester and Mr George Purdy to collect flint from the upper areas of the Headland. One of the most productive finds areas, intensively searched between January and March 1914, was "the SE corner of Hengistbury Head" where ploughing had taken place in preparation for a 'Scotch' Golf Course. Fortunately, plans for the eighteen-hole course were then dropped and the area reverted to its former natural state (Cunliffe 1978). After Druitt's death, his collection, which amounted to several thousand artefacts and included his field notebooks, went to the Red House Museum, Christchurch. Later, the finds were studied in detail by Mr. J.B. Calkin who recognised, amongst the main body of Neolithic and Bronze Age artefacts, material of Upper Palaeolithic type (Mace 1959; Calkin 1966).

Working with Druitt's diaries, Calkin was able to pinpoint areas near the SE corner of the headland where many of the Upper Palaeolithic finds had originated. In the 1950s he made several attempts to relocate the site by trial trenching parts of the shallow depression at the SE end of the Headland. His efforts were rewarded by the recovery of a handful of Upper Palaeolithic retouched tools (Mace 1959).

In 1957, Angela Mace, a Cambridge University graduate, carried out the first systematic investigation of the site. She had heard that Druitt "got all the flints from the north side of the footpath as the south side was not ploughed" (Mace 1959, 235). From her preliminary excavation work, Mace was able to conclude that the narrow strip of land south of the coastal footpath was indeed undisturbed and contained rich concentrations of Upper Palaeolithic finds. In all, she excavated more than 85 sq. yards, mostly on her own or with the aid of a local helper (Mace pers. comm.). Shortly after the excavations were published (1959), Mace left archaeology altogether and part of her collection was acquired by the British Museum. Her work represents an important landmark in British Late Upper Palaeolithic studies, confirming for the first time the existence of a major open-air site of this age and type in Britain.

No further work was undertaken at Hengistbury until 1968, when John Campbell, a doctoral research student at Oxford, re-examined part of the site. On the advice of Mace (Campbell 1977, 71 and *in litt.*), his excavations focused on the area east of hers near the cliff-edge. Campbell used a small team of helpers and the work was carried out over three short field seasons from April-May and June-July 1968, and in April 1969. A total of 136 sq. metres were investigated (Campbell 1977, 71). In his major review of the Upper Palaeolithic (1977) Campbell claimed that he had uncovered two discrete occupation levels at the same site at Hengistbury, one Mesolithic, the other Later Upper Palaeolithic. This was directly contrary to the earlier findings and cast considerable doubt over Mace's interpretation of the archaeology. Although Campbell's conclusions in this respect subsequently proved to be ill-founded, at the time the site came to be regarded as one of the few instances in Britain where Mesolithic and Upper Palaeolithic were found in secure stratigraphic relationship, one above the other.

Between Campbell's excavations in 1968–9 and the commencement of the new investigations in 1981 no further work took place at the site.

*The Powell Mesolithic site:* Although Mesolithic finds had been widely reported from Hengistbury Head (Rankine 1956; Palmer 1977; Wymer 1977) they had never been recovered in great enough density to indicate more than a background presence of such material. The chance discovery by Mr Ronald Powell in 1977 of a large number of Mesolithic artefacts eroding out of sand deposits on Warren Hill therefore provided a rare opportunity to investigate an *in situ* site of this period (Fig. 1.7).

1.7 *View eastwards from the Powell Early Mesolithic site in 1980, showing wind deflation surfaces along the cliff-edge. The site was identified from artefacts eroding out of the sands on the left.*

Before the 1977 discovery Mesolithic artefacts had been collected from a variety of places on the headland and adjacent areas. Many of these finds reside in personal collections (most notably those of the Marchese A. Nobili-Vitelleschi, Mr R. Atkinson, Mr. A. Cotton, Mr B. King and others) and are marked with locations such as 'Warren Hill', 'North Field', 'South Field' indicating only in very general terms where they were found. The existence of such material was reported by Palmer (in Wymer 1977) who also drew attention to "two axes and 30 microliths" from Warren Hill (Palmer 1977), although the whereabouts of the axes seems to be unknown. At about the same period, local interest was aroused by finds of Mesolithic artefacts near the summit of Warren Hill. These were identified by Mr M. Ridley (then of the Russell-Cotes Museum Bournemouth) and were found as a result of construction in 1975 of the new Coastguard's Hut. Apart from these isolated occurrences no other accounts existed of major Mesolithic finds from the headland.

The present site was discovered in the winter of 1977 by Mr Ronald Powell, an active amateur archaeologist, who noticed an unusually dense concentration of Mesolithic artefacts eroding out of a sandy area near the top of Warren Hill. The Russell-Cotes Museum was immediately alerted to the existence of the site and meanwhile Mr Powell continued very carefully to collect and record finds as they were exposed by the wind and rain. His frequent visits to the site enabled him to pinpoint the finds accurately and most of the artefacts were identified to location by an eight-figure map grid reference written on the back of each piece. Such details proved invaluable to the writer in linking this initial surface collection with the subsequently excavated assemblage.

By the time the writer's excavations had got underway in 1980, Mr Powell had already carefully catalogued well over 3,000 finds from this one location. It should be properly acknowledged that without his patient groundwork the site might never have come to the attention of the local museum or have been recognised for its intrinsic importance. It therefore appears singularly fitting that it should have become designated the Powell Mesolithic site, to distinguish it from the well-known Mace/Campbell site (then supposed to be a mixture of Upper Palaeolithic and Mesolithic artefacts) 650 metres further to the east.

## 1.5 The Hengistbury Palaeolithic and Mesolithic Project

Reference has already been made to the devastating effects of ground erosion at Hengistbury and the particularly disastrous consequences this has had for shallowly buried archaeological levels along the cliff-top. In recent years, the natural regression of the southern cliff has been accelerated by the effects of vegetation loss and subsequent wind deflation which in turn has led to major denudation of soils across the headland. Particularly at risk are the areas near the cliff edge which, once stripped of vegetation, become destabilised and highly prone to the effects of wind erosion (Fig. 1.7). As a result, any archaeological material in these areas will be much more susceptible to damage.

In recent times, the problem of erosion has steadily worsened and can be partially linked with the volume of visitor traffic to the headland which has visibly increased over the past few decades (see also Chapter 6). Apart from serving as a popular amenity for local walkers and birdwatchers, Hengistbury also attracts large numbers of people from the nearby tourist resort of Bournemouth. The heavy use of the headland was recently highlighted in a survey which showed that it

1.8 *Severe gullying along the cliff-edge by the Late Upper Palaeolithic site. Ironstone 'doggers' are visible in the Tertiary clays and on the beach.*

received more than a million visitors each year (May and Osborne 1981).

The problems of land erosion at Hengistbury have, of course, been apparent for many years. As early as 1976, the Department of the Environment's Inspectorate of Ancient Monuments (now English Heritage) recommended that a working party be established to investigate numerous problems relating to the archaeology of the headland. In parallel with this initiative Professor B. Cunliffe of Oxford University was invited by the landowners of Hengistbury Head, Bournemouth Borough Corporation, to advise them on the development of the area's archaeological resource, which resulted in the setting up of the Iron Age research project in 1978. At the same time the Hengistbury Head Management Committee drew up a series of initiatives for the positive management and upkeep of the headland. In 1980, following its recommendations, Professor Cunliffe, on behalf of the landowners, asked the writer and a colleague, Dr. (then Mr.) Simon Collcutt, to conduct a feasibility study in order to define the nature of threats to archaeological deposits, particularly along the southern cliff-edge and with special reference to the Upper Palaeolithic and Mesolithic sites. The subsequent report (Barton and Collcutt 1980) identified major areas of erosional damage and urged that immediate action be taken to rescue or record areas of the sites at the cliff-edge before they disappeared altogether into the sea.

As a result of these recommendations being accepted and formally approved, the landowners agreed to assist in funding rescue work at both of the sites concerned under the direction of the writer. Further grant-aid for the rescue excavations was made available by English Heritage, amongst other organisations.

*Project research design*
The overall aims of the project were four-fold:
(1) to investigate areas of the sites particularly under

threat from coastal erosion, including already damaged areas near the cliff-edge.
(2) to try to define the surviving spatial extent of both sites, with the possibility of preserving a representative sample of in situ deposits for future reference and research purposes.
(3) to obtain samples of well-stratified archaeological material and provide additional dating evidence and other contextual information, lacking in previous studies. This would also involve re-examining past conflicting interpretations of the Upper Palaeolithic site.
(4) to devise appropriate methods of excavation given the problems of (1) and the large numbers of artefacts involved.

## 1.6 Fieldwork programme

### 1.6.11 *Late Upper Palaeolithic site*

Four seasons' fieldwork were conducted at the Upper Palaeolithic site, between 1981–4 (Figs. 1.9 and 1.10). Each period in the field lasted approximately three weeks and employed, on average, 15–20 people, mostly drawn from British universities and the full-time professionals on the national excavation circuit. The project was organised from Oxford and was carried out with the permission and financial support of the landowners, Bournemouth Corporation. Because the site is a scheduled ancient monument, a permit of consent for digging needed to be obtained from the Historic Buildings and Monuments Commission, which also contributed a significant proportion of the project funding.

The excavation programme mainly concentrated its efforts on the area of the site near the cliff edge (Figs. 1.11 and 1.12). Between 1981 and 1984, an area of c. 96 square metres was excavated, including an exploratory area north of the coastal footpath (Fig.

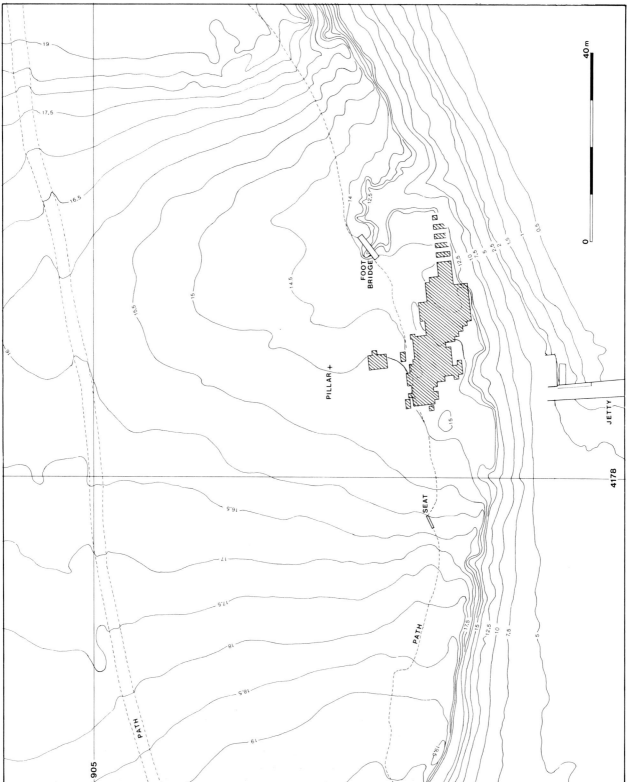

1.9   *The Late Upper Palaeolithic site excavation area. The concrete pillar  served as the datum point for the 1981-4  excavations.*

10

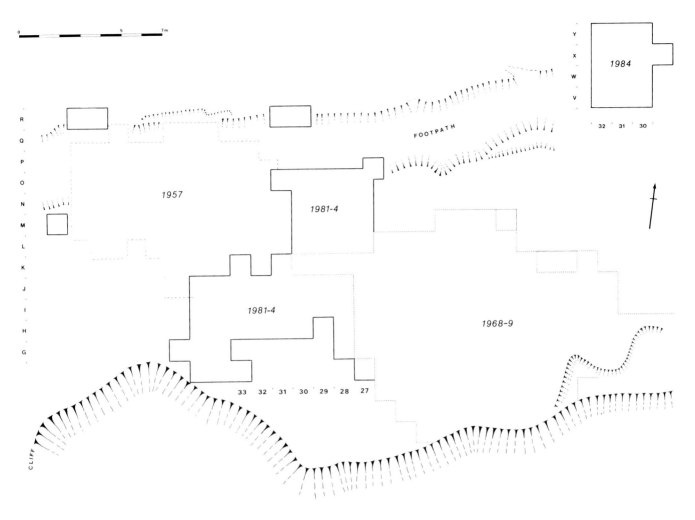

1.10 *Detail of the different areas investigated by Mace (1957), Campbell (1968-9) and Barton (1981-4). The location of 1984 N area is represented schematically. For its true position refer to the grid square numbers.*

1.9). In addition, a careful survey was undertaken of the deposits in the Eastern Depression.

## 1.6.2 *Ground survey north of the LUP site*

A special survey of the Eastern Depression was carried out during the 1983 season. Earlier studies, cited in Mace (1959), had suggested that the Upper Palaeolithic finds extended well inland of the coastal footpath beyond her excavations, but that the archaeological levels had mostly been ploughed away in that area. The aims of the survey work were therefore to map the extent of the archaeological deposits north of the Upper Palaeolithic site, and to use the opportunity to examine lower-lying areas near the base of the depression, to explore their potential for palaeoenvironmental evidence.

The survey of the main depression covered an area of 660 square metres and was preceded by a detailed mapping of the present land surface by electronic tachometer. Trial pits 25 x 25 cm were then systematically hand-dug at 10 metre intervals along prepared transects across the depression (Fig. 1.13). Sediments from the test pits were removed in 20–25 cm spits and sieved for small finds, before each profile was individually drawn and described. Copies of the survey archive

and results are lodged in the Pitt Rivers Museum, Oxford; a summary follows.

The results of the field survey revealed a dense concentration of Upper Palaeolithic artefacts just north of the footpath and not far from the main excavation area. The actual spread of finds also continued sporadically about 120 metres inland into the depression, but not all of the artefacts recovered were demonstrably of Palaeolithic type. It is clear for example that a significant admixture of Bronze Age material exists, especially towards the northern end of the depression. It was also noticeable that the total number of artefacts tapered off considerably in the central lower area of the depression, which today provides a natural conduit for surface run-off. The site itself is situated just west of the thalweg (the lowest point of the valley).

Data from the test pits revealed the superficial sediments to be thickest near the southern (seaward) end of the depression, with the sand deposits becoming thinner towards its northern perimeter. Not surprisingly, apart from the central cordon which was artefactually sterile, the finds also showed a tendency to diminish numerically further towards the back of the depression. No obvious signs of the 'ploughing' mentioned by Druitt (Mace 1959) could be recognised in the soil pro-

1.11 *View westwards of the Late Upper Palaeolithic excavations in 1984. The concrete blocks and rubble in the foreground belong to the coastal protection works also in progress at the time.*

1.12 *Close-up view of the Late Upper Palaeolithic excavations in 1982.*

files (see Chapter 2.1.4), though in some areas between the coastal and inland footpaths there were definite signs of bioturbation and disturbance. None of the recorded sediment structures, however, appeared to be consistent with those made by the plough (Collcutt pers. comm.).

A linear bank feature, clearly recognisable from aerial photographs (Fig. 1.14), was also investigated in

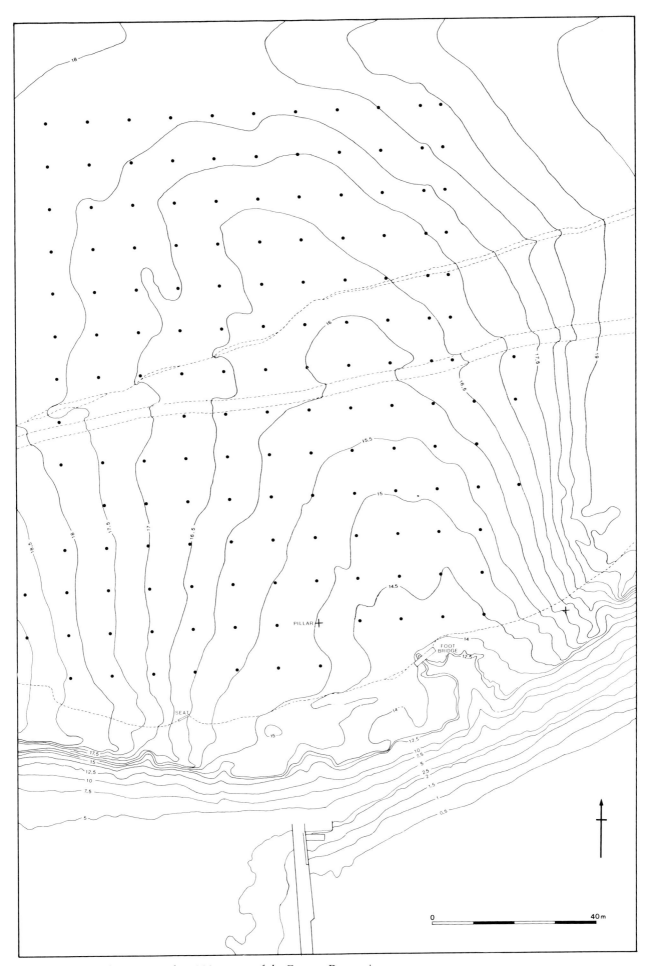

1.13  *Location of test pits in the 1983 survey of the Eastern Depression.*

1.14   *Aerial photograph of the headland with the bank and ditch feature visible as a lighter strip of vegetation running in a straight line (SE-NW) diagonally across the Eastern depression. (Photo: Cambridge Committee for Aerial Photography).*

some detail. The bank, just visible as a low hump at ground level, runs diagonally across the eastern depression on a north-westerly bearing for a distance of 170 metres from the cliff edge. It may be relevant that the bank appears to be aligned with two Bronze Age barrows perched conspicuously on the northern rim of the dry stream depression. It may therefore not simply be an isolated feature but part of a more complex prehistoric field boundary system, surviving in this area of the headland.

A section, dug across the linear feature at 'A' (Fig. 1.15), revealed a low bank covering an earlier buried soil horizon. On the western side, running parallel with the bank, was a U-shaped ditch roughly one metre deep by a metre wide. The results of the pollen and soil analyses of the bank and ditch sediments are presented in detail in sections 2.2.2 and 2.3.4. It is sufficient here to note that the results throw considerable light on the late Holocene vegetational history of the headland and provide indirect evidence for human activities at Hengistbury during the late prehistoric period. From combined pollen studies and direct dating of the sediments it is possible to infer an approximate Early Iron Age date for the construction of the bank and ditch.

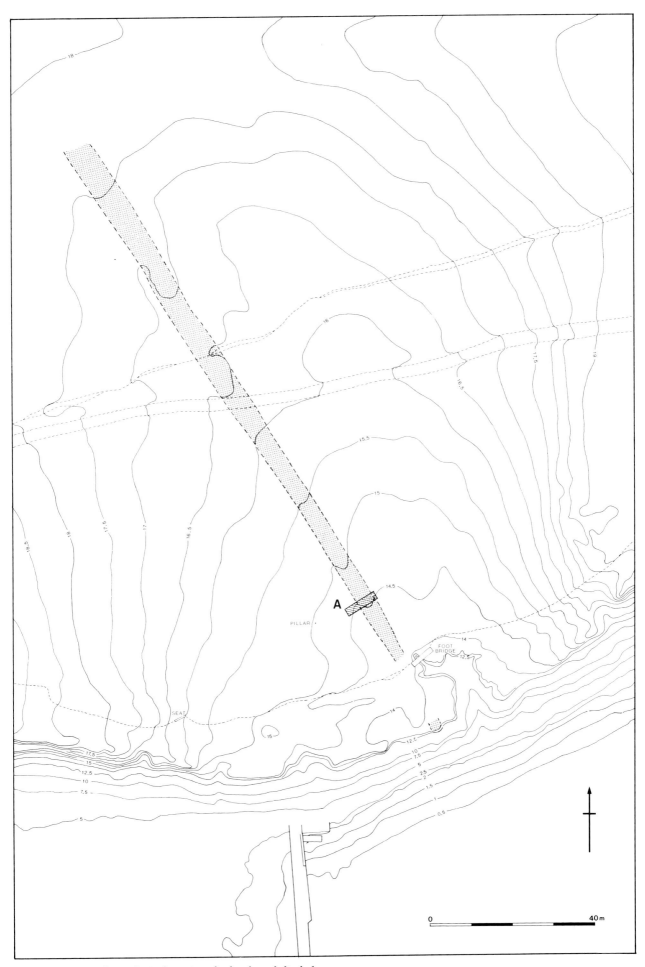

1.15   *Location of trench 'A' bisecting the bank and ditch feature.*

1.16 *View east across the Powell Mesolithic site during the 1982 excavation, with the Isle of Wight on the horizon.*

### 1.6.3 Powell Mesolithic site

The fieldwork at the Powell Mesolithic site was spread over four seasons 1980–1983, with an average of three weeks spent on excavations each season, generally overlapping with that at the Late Upper Palaeolithic site. The project employed approximately fifteen individuals per day, made up largely of university students, but including many full-time archaeologists and several colleagues from overseas. During the whole period, 78 square metres of the site were examined in detail, while a further area of approximately 50 square metres was covered by surface collection (Figs. 1.16 and 1.17).

In the first two seasons the excavation programme concentrated its efforts upon the area along the southern cliff-edge (Fig. 1.18) where the worst erosion damage was occurring, making rescue work an urgent priority. In addition, a long exploratory trench was cut northwards to establish how far the main flint scatter could be traced from the cliff-edge. Following positive indications of its existence northwards, the final season's work in 1982–3 was spent trying to locate the eastern edge of the main artefact scatter. During this work some of the highest concentrations of retouched tools and debitage were encountered, indicating a probable continuation of the site in this direction. The excavations confirmed that the Mesolithic evidence extended over an area of at least 40 square metres and represented a major focus of residential activity.

## 1.7 Field investigation techniques

At both sites, a conventional metre grid system was used and oriented with respect to compass north. The Mesolithic grid was established in 1980 and depth measurements were calculated according to two datum points (Fig. 1.17). The Late Upper Palaeolithic grid established a year later relied on a marked concrete pillar just north of the site for all artefact depths (Fig. 1.13). The horizontal grid at both sites consisted of one metre squares, each square being divided into eight rectangular sub-quadrants (of 50 x 25 cm). Hand excavating in these units proved quick and efficient and gave extra control in recording sieve finds. The sub-quadrant is the standard horizontal unit to which all artefacts from the sites are referable.

Because of the absence of recognisable geological layers, a vertical spit system of excavation was employed with the deposits being removed in successive two centimetre-thick slices (Fig. 1.19). In parts of the Mesolithic site which were overlain by a greater thickness of archaeologically 'sterile' sediments, the upper deposits were sometimes trowelled in 4 or 5 cm spits. This method of spit excavation proved to be a fast and accurate way of excavating material distributed over a wide vertical range. Where the windblown sands were already exposed on wind deflation surfaces near the cliff-edge, surface collection by metre squares preceded excavation.

Close vertical control was maintained throughout the excavations by taking height readings of the four corners of each square at regular intervals (usually following removal of several spits). A miniature builders' line-level resting on a metal strip served as a useful device for ensuring that a horizontal surface was maintained for each spit. Where possible, individual height readings were also taken for each artefact (with the aid of a AGA 300 laser level or an ordinary planar 'dumpy' level). In practice, however, this time-consuming process only proved possible in a systematic way at the Upper Palaeolithic site where most finds were given individual spot heights. The finds without spot heights are generally referable to a particular two centimetre spit.

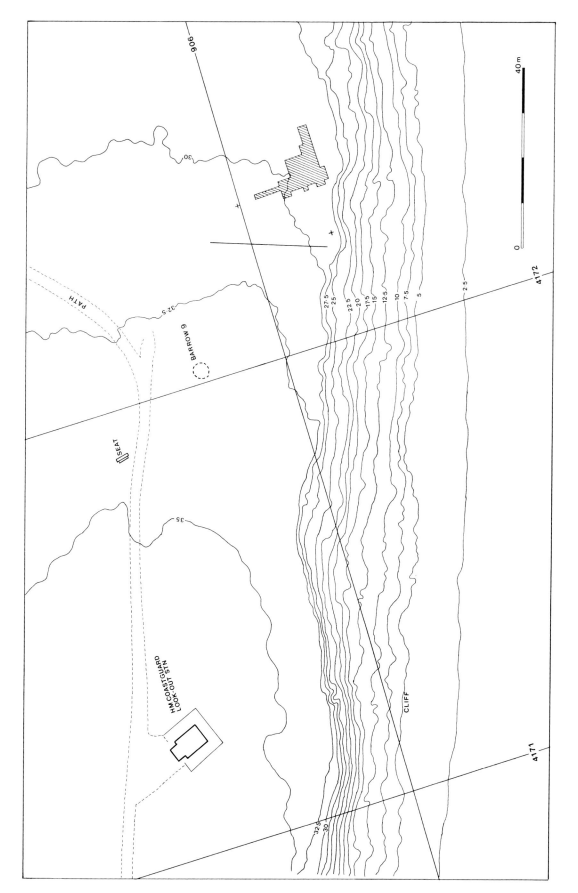

1.17 *Location of the Powell Mesolithic excavation trenches. The two crosses mark temporary site datum points, while the concrete base of the seat was used as a temporary bench mark.*

17

1.18 *Detail of the 1982 excavations, looking east. Note the lighter (Ea) horizons overlying the darker (Bh) horizons of the podzol. Most of the Mesolithic artefacts come from these horizons.*

1.19 *Excavation technique at the Powell Mesolithic site. Each metre square was sub-divided into rectangular units of 50 x 25 cm and excavated in 2 cm horizontal spits. Note the upper layer of interstratified modern sand and turf lines which seal the archaeological deposits.*

The horizontal position of each artefact larger than one centimetre was also mapped on millimetre graph paper and the details entered on a finds card which

accompanied the find (Fig. 1.21 for an example of the cards used). Again, because of time constraints and the sheer volume of flints at the Mesolithic site, mapping was not always feasible. Nowadays, it might be possible to employ more efficient means of recording large numbers of finds using a more automated computerised recording system but such facilities were not cheaply available at the time of excavation. We found the tandem methods of recording artefacts by mapping and entering details onto finds cards to be a useful means of cross-checking for any non-systematic errors.

Apart from details of square number, artefact number, x-, y- and z- (depth) measurements, other information was stored on the cards as well. This included the angle of dip and orientation of the pieces, which was of potential value in the study of artefact taphonomy (see Chapter 3). Sieved finds and those less than one centimetre long (unless retouched tools or tool debitage) were bagged according to sub-quadrant and spit level.

The decision to bag most finds individually was a precautionary measure and is now regarded as standard practice if edge-wear studies are to be undertaken. It is essential, for example, if such analyses are to be carried out, that any incidental damage to the artefacts such as abrasion caused by rubbing against other artefacts be avoided.

Systematic dry-screening or sieving of the sediments was carried out at both sites using 1.98 mm mesh sieves. Wider gauge mesh sieves (3.17 mm or eighth of an inch) used in the first season (at the Mesolithic site) were soon abandoned as they proved too coarse, resulting in the unnecessary loss of a significant proportion of the finer flint debris. In subsequent seasons, when this was remedied, it was found that the rate of recovery of some tiny retouched proximal ends and other

1.20 *View of metre squares under excavation at the Powell Mesolithic site in 1982. Note the very compact iron-manganese pan in the centre foreground in front of the wooden spirit level.*

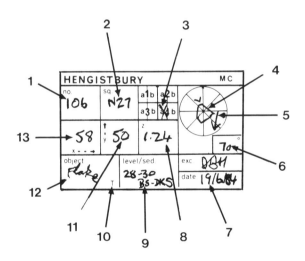

1.21 *Hengistbury finds card. Key: 1= find number; 2= square number; 3= sub-quadrant; 4= artefact orientation (arrow indicates proximal end and position of arrow outside outline shows the piece lay dorsal side up); 5= direction of dip; 6= degree of dip; 7= excavator's name and date of find; 8= depth below datum; 9= spit number and soil colour description; 10= burnt/unburnt (T is crossed out if the artefact is burnt); 11= Y-coordinate; 12= artefact type; 13= X-coordinate.*

debris from microlith manufacture had improved considerably. Overall, it confirmed that we were recovering many of the tiny chips of a size normally small enough to have been removed by the wind or other sorting processes (e.g. fluvial action). These observations were of particular importance in determining the extent to which the site may have been affected by post-depositional processes (see Chapter 3).

To provide a permanent record of the excavations, scaled section drawings and oblique photographs were made of a number of the soil profiles at both sites (see Chapter 2.1). In addition, rubber latex soil peels were made of several profiles at the Late Upper Palaeolithic site, for example where Campbell had reported the presence of a 'Mesolithic' channel feature (Fig. 2.6). The method involved spraying liquid latex directly on to the vertical section face using an ordinary garden spray gun. Once the latex was set (but not completely dry) scrim bandage was applied to the back of peel. This gives the latex extra rigidity and helps when removing the peel for storage. Once the latex was totally dry the peel was gently pulled away from the section leaving a thin veneer of sediments adhering to the latex surface. Although prone to shrinkage and some minor distortion, this method of recording soil profiles proved remarkably effective and practical in the field. Since the excavation the peels have been kept in storage away from direct sunlight, which degrades the latex. They have been housed temporarily at the Pitt Rivers Museum until more permanent storage facilities are found.

At the end of each field season the exposed trenches were lined with black plastic sheeting and then carefully backfilled using sediments dug from the spoil heap. Wherever possible the original grass and heather turves were also replaced to minimise the risk of further erosion damage and help stabilisation of the soil. Although the cliff will continue gradually to recede these simple measures have been shown to be highly effective in limiting the amount of surface soil loss along the cliff-top (see Chapter 6).

## 1.8 Post-excavation programme and methodology

### 1.8.1 *Analysis of the flint assemblages*

The flint artefacts from both assemblages were the subject of typological and technological studies. The first involves classification of the artefacts according to their morphological attributes, while the second is concerned primarily with elucidating the manufacturing process. These two approaches are essentially complementary, but whereas typology offers a 'static' view of the end-products (retouched tools and debitage), technological analyses seek to describe the set of procedures (or the 'dynamics') responsible for making a stone artefact and hence creating the evidence as found (Tixier *et al.* 1980). Studying technology relies not just upon observations of single artefacts but on those of more complete refitted flint reduction sequences, experimental studies and functional evidence.

As a necessary starting point in studying the collections, the flints were separated into two main artefact categories: a) debitage and b) retouched tools. In the case of debitage these products were further subdivided into flakes, blades, bladelets, crested pieces, core tablets, chips and cores following the guidelines supplied by Tixier (1963) and Newcomer (1972). The retouched tools were classified according to the Upper Palaeolithic type-list of de Sonneville-Bordes and Perrot (1953, 1954, 1955, 1956a, 1956b) and the Mesolithic type-list of Clark (1934a), for the respective sites.

*The debitage:* The study of the debitage was based upon the attribute lists and analytical methods adapted for Upper Palaeolithic assemblages by Tixier (1980), Bergman (1987a) and Ohnuma (1988). These approaches were modified in several respects for work on the Hengistbury collections (Barton 1986b). Measurements of the maximum length, breadth and thickness of the blanks made up the basic quantitative data. All of these measurements were taken at the maximum dimension on each artefact except for thickness. This last dimension was taken at the thickest point, excluding the bulb of percussion or the distal end where the distal end had 'plunged'. Measurements were recorded only on pieces larger than 5 mm; complete items of debitage under 5 mm were regarded as chips and simply counted (cf. Newcomer and Karlin 1987). In addition, the maximum breadths and thicknesses of butts were also recorded. Measurements such as these are useful for descriptive purposes, but they also reflect aspects of the flaking technology. For example, a non-marginal mode of flaking tends to produce a thicker blank with a larger butt than one where the blow falls extremely close to the core's edge (Bergman pers. comm.; also Bradley and Sampson 1986).

The qualitative attributes generally describe the condition of the blank as well as its shape. They include observations of: the blank's completeness (broken or unbroken); whether it is burnt or unburnt; the presence of butt abrasion; the presence or absence of cortex; the

patination; the direction of dorsal scars; and finally the profile of the blank. Also included under this category is the classification of butts. These were grouped according to the terminology of Tixier (1963, 1980): faceted, dihedral, plain and cortical. It was decided not to use the terms punctiform and linear for butt types, since these refer more to size than the type of platform preparation. The term dihedral is considered here to be the equivalent of 'dihedral faceted', as the Hengistbury examples usually result from faceting the core platform.

Cores were analysed in a similar manner to the rest of the debitage, with the maximum dimensions of each specimen measured. Because the cores as found are artefacts discarded at various stages of reduction, it was important to compare these data with the dimensions of fully refitted nodules to estimate the intensity of core reduction. At the Upper Palaeolithic site, for example, blade cores were often significantly reduced but, because of the differences in flint quality and requirements of blank size, a variety of core sizes are present. This contrasts markedly with the artefacts from the Mesolithic site, where the raw material is smaller and there is much less variability in the range of blank sizes. Qualitative attributes presented below, relating specifically to the technology, include the recording of the number and position of the platforms, as well as preparation (where present) on the flaking face and at the back of the nodule. The application of these data to characterising the assemblages both typologically and technologically is described under the relevant sections of the Late Upper Palaeolithic and Mesolithic assemblages.

*Retouched tools:* The retouched tools were treated in much the same way as the rest of the artefacts. After separating them into the relevant typological categories (e.g. end-scrapers, burins, backed blades etc.) the nature of the blank was recorded using qualitative and quantitative attributes as previously indicated. Following this stage the tools were catalogued according to the type and the position of retouch. For each major tool class a distinctive series of attributes was developed as illustrated in the following (see also the Glossary Chapter 7):

(1) *Backed blade*
    position of retouch
    type of retouch
    plan shape of backed edge
    special retouch types (e.g. anvil technique

(2) *End-scraper*
    position of retouch
    type of retouch
    plan shape of scraper edge
    scraper edge angle

(3) *Burin*
    position of burin edge
    type of spall removal surface
    number and position of burin facets
    retouch preparation of lateral edge

These analyses were supplemented by observations made on refitted examples of tools where it was sometimes possible to reconstruct various stages of manufacture not otherwise apparent on individual specimens.

## 1.8.2 Refitting and spatial analyses

Refitting studies contributed an essential part of the technological analysis of the Hengistbury flint assemblages, as well as providing important details on the spatial distribution of artefacts. By matching fragments of flaked material and joining them in sequence this method allows a strong relationship to be established between the manufacturing process and the pattern of artefact discard (Spurrell 1880; Leroi-Gourhan and Brézillon 1966, 1972; Van Noten 1978; Cahen *et al.* 1980). At Hengistbury, refitting was used in various ways to investigate:

### (1) *The methods of core reduction:*
This may be considered as the chain of events which begins with the selection of raw material and ends with the abandonment of the core, the utilised tool or other products (Cahen 1987). By using refitting evidence, technological features of the assemblage may be studied in much greater detail and the overall industry characterised more accurately than by studying individual artefacts in isolation. The identification of certain special groups of artefacts, such as intentionally broken segments, also became more evident once refitting had been employed (see Chapter 4.2).

### (2) *The spatial organisation of finds:*
When observations of a horizontal type are combined with the geological evidence they may then provide a better guide to the degree of site disturbance by natural post-depositional processes (Villa 1982). Thus, for example, using horizontal refitting evidence at Hengistbury, it was possible to rule out the influence of high energy geological processes in the overall distribution of artefacts. Refitted lithics revealed the existence of significant patterning in the artefact distributions, enabling a primary knapping cluster to be distinguished from a zone of mainly tool discard. The identification of these activities and the relationship between the different areas only became more evident once refitting work had been undertaken.

### (3) *The vertical distribution of artefacts:*
The analysis of the vertical distribution of the artefacts is equally relevant to the understanding of natural disturbance and other factors in site formation processes (Villa 1982; Schiffer 1987). In this case, the refitting of artefacts separated by some depth enabled the testing of certain claims made by Campbell (at the Late Upper Palaeolithic site) regarding the occurrence of different cultural levels. Some experimental work was also carried out to investigate the effects of post-depositional movements of artefacts in sands (see Chapter 3.2.5 and 3.2.8).

The practicalities of refitting have been described by various authors in detail elsewhere (e.g. Cahen 1987). It is sufficient here simply to state that some basic knowledge of typology and technology are required before undertaking such a task. Unlike pottery (South 1977; cf. also Schiffer 1987) and to a certain extent bone (David 1972; Poplin 1976), lithic materials require a more 'three-dimensional' approach, with the shape and size of the original nodule being less predictable. Most refitters begin by separating the material according to colour, texture and inclusions and by concentrating first on mending broken fragments (*viz.* proximal, medial and distal pieces). Only then does the task of joining dorsal to ventral surfaces and reconstructing reduction sequences become viable. Because the process of refitting is very time-consuming, it is essential that it should be carried out with particular questions in mind. The work on the Hengistbury collections, which took hundreds of man hours, was only justifiable in terms of the very specific aims of the research design.

## 1.8.3 Functional and microwear studies

Flint implements from the Hengistbury assemblages were subjected to microscopic analysis using both high-power (cf. Keeley 1980) and low-power (cf. Tringham *et al.* 1974) techniques. This relatively new area of research is still being developed and refined (see for example Cook and Dumont 1987; Roe 1985; Newcomer *et al.* 1986; Juel-Jensen 1988), but promises high potential for identifying tool-usage and thereby the nature of various activities at prehistoric sites. The importance of finding and interpreting wear traces on tools from Hengistbury, which would have great relevance to the evidence of artefact distribution, made their study a high priority.

The microwear analysis took the form of a pilot study (Morris in Bergman *et al.* 1983, 1987) to evaluate first whether or not the material was suitable for research purposes. Based on the initial promising results and the apparently excellent condition of the finds, further work was undertaken by Levi-Sala (1986a) and then by Unger-Hamilton on the Mesolithic and Late Upper Palaeolithic collections, respectively. Although their results differed from Morris's, they were able to demonstrate that polishes can and do survive even on artefacts that had undergone significant post-depositional surface modification. Amongst the more interesting conclusions to be drawn from the Hengistbury studies, however, is the positive contribution of microwear in reconstructing the taphonomic history of the artefacts and identifying the processes involved in site formation. This work shows that a more cautious approach should be developed especially when interpreting polishes on artefacts from sandy sites. The details of the methodology and the results are discussed and summarised in Chapters 4.5.5 and 5.3.6.

A second line of functional research is the analysis of

macroscopic wear-traces on artefacts. This type of modification, visible to the naked eye, was particularly informative at Hengistbury in determining how tools, such as the burins, were used. According to the location of damage and orientation of scars (and occasionally visible striations) it was possible to tell which areas of certain tools were employed, as well as the direction of use. Unlike microwear, these traces are apparently not masked by later surface modifications, at least not to any great extent. The results of functional analysis and supporting experimental studies (including the replication of tool use) are presented alongside the sections on the Late Upper Palaeolithic (Chapter 4.2 and 4.5) and the Mesolithic (Chapter 5.2) assemblages.

### 1.8.4 *Other post-excavation analyses*

In addition to the analyses mentioned above, other reports contained in this monograph refer to studies of the Late Pleistocene and Holocene palaeoenvironments (Chapter 2) plus specialist work on the non-flint materials found at both sites (see sections in Chapters 4 and 5). Special attention is also drawn to the dating evidence presented in these chapters, which places the Late Upper Palaeolithic occupation at 12,500±1150 years BP and the Mesolithic one at 9,750±950 years BP.

Finally, at the end of each of the main sections on the Late Upper Palaeolithic (4.10) and Mesolithic (5.5), is a synthesis of the results which reviews the main evidence and aims to place both sites in their wider setting. As a further guide to the reader, there is a summary of chapters at the end of the book as well as a selective Glossary of archaeological terms.

### 1.8.5 *Deposition of the archive and its contents.*

The site archive comprising the finds and field records of the excavations at the Late Upper Palaeolithic site (1968–9 and 1981–4) and the Powell Mesolithic site (1980–83) are to be deposited in the Russell-Cotes Museum, Bournemouth. A copy of the documentary archive will also be retained by the author and stored at the Donald Baden-Powell Quaternary Research Centre, Oxford.

The Campbell archive consists of cross-section diagrams of the deposits at the Late Upper Palaeolithic site and two notebooks containing a catalogue of finds from his excavations. A key to most of the notations used in these documents is provided in Campbell (1977). The five different datum points (I–V) employed by him are internally consistent and provide relative depths for most of his artefacts. Although the finds cannot be directly correlated to a permanent datum point, their absolute positions can be estimated vertically to within five centimetres, based on refitting evidence between the Campbell and the new collections.

Locational details of all finds from the 1981–4 Late Upper Palaeolithic excavations are mapped on site plans as well as being recorded individually on finds cards (the methodology is described in 1.6 above). This cross-referencing system enabled any locational errors to be identified at the post-excavation stage and corrected. The maplets are contained in the permanent archive, as are the finds cards which accompany each of the artefacts. Only one site datum was established (a concrete pillar marked with a horizontal red line) to which all depths can be correlated. The documentary archive contains drawings of the main site sections (including one through the later prehistoric bank and ditch, Fig. 2.11); the key sections and deposit descriptions are reproduced in this volume (see especially Chapters 2.1.4 and 2.2.2). There are three site notebooks, two of which provide day-to-day logs of excavations at the Late Upper Palaeolithic site and the Powell Mesolithic site. The third logbook contains general field notes covering the original evaluation (Barton and Collcutt 1980) and primary information on sediment samples, TL flint samples and the location of TL dosimeters at both sites. Spatial and technological data on the Late Upper Palaeolithic refitting artefacts and various of the tool categories are stored digitally as well as in hardcopy form. Copies of the disks and the finds sheets are stored with the rest of the archive. The software used for analysing the spatial information was written by Dr. Simon Collcutt and remains his copyright. Finally, there are number of photographs and slides of the sites held by the Russell-Cotes Museum, which are the copyright of the author.

The Powell Mesolithic site documentation includes the site notebooks mentioned above and general site plans. Due to time constraints, it was not possible to map artefact distributions for individual square metres, but spatial data is recorded on the finds cards which would allow such information to be reconstructed. In addition, although some depth data on finds was lost in the first season in 1980 (the result of faulty instrument readings), most artefacts can be ascribed relative depths within individual 20 or 50 mm spits (see 1.5.3).

### 1.8.6 *Note on the presentation of radiocarbon and thermoluminescence dates*

The radiocarbon dates which appear in the text are generally expressed in radiocarbon years before AD 1950 (years BP). In accordance with the recommendations of the International Radiocarbon Conference at Trondheim in 1985 (Kra and Stuiver 1986) the upper case letters 'BP' denote uncalibrated radiocarbon years before the present. Where calendrical years are occasionally referred to they are followed by the notation BC, and are likewise uncalibrated against tree-ring curve data.

The thermoluminescence dates for the Late Upper Palaeolithic and Mesolithic sites are presented as single age determinations. The ages are the weighted means of each group of dates, calculated according to the statistical methods described in Aitken and Alldred (1972).

# 2. Palaeoenvironmental and dating evidence from the Hengistbury sites

## 2.1 Physical setting and geology

### 2.1.1 General topography

Hengistbury Head lies about eight kilometres east of Bournemouth in Dorset (NGR SZ 175905; Figs. 1.2 and 1.6). It consists of a promontory, isolated on all sides by specific morphological features. To the south and east, the Head is bounded by sea cliffs with transitory but in part artificially stabilised littoral deposits (beach, sand dunes and spit sands/gravels) at their base. A former cliff line is represented by the submerged Beer Pan Rocks, out to sea some 300 m south of the present cliffs (see below). The sea area beyond Hengistbury referred to as the Solent Channel would have been part of the Solent River basin during periods of low Pleistocene sea level (Reid 1902). To the north, the Head overlooks minor 'saltings' (reed beds, marsh and mudflats) and, beyond these, the open water of Christchurch Harbour. The two major Wessex rivers, the Stour and the Avon, have their confluence just upstream of the harbour, and the whole area shows submergence morphology resulting from the Flandrian transgression. To the west, the Head is separated from the higher ground, with coastal cliffs, at Southbourne by a wide stretch of dry lowland (minimum c. 4 m OD).

The highland of the Head itself can be divided into a number of topographic areas, from west to east (Fig. 2.1). The highest point is at 37.5 m OD at the crest of Warren Hill. Eastwards, the hill drops away gently (3–5° slope) to c. 22 m OD. On the Eastern Head, the general surface is almost horizontal, reaching 19.5 m OD above the south-eastern cliffs. However, this surface is broadly dissected, but not breached on the north side, by a shallow valley-head, known as the Eastern Depression; the thalweg slopes c. 1.5° to the SSE, intersecting the cliff at c. 14 m OD, below which modern drainage has caused a steep nick-gully to form. In addition to the natural morphology, there are two prominent features caused by recent mining activities. The first is the Batters, a large scar and spoil terrace to the north and west of Warren Hill. The second is the Transverse Quarry, a deep trench, cut southwards but not quite reaching the cliff, at the break of slope below the eastern flank of Warren Hill (a feature which therefore serves to divide the Western from the Eastern Head).There are no permanent natural water bodies on the Head, although the impermeable Tertiaries (specifically, the Hengistbury Beds) cause seepage and gullying all around the periphery. The only damp area, with shallow standing water and sometimes temporary surface flow after heavy rain, is the Eastern Depression. The modern vegetation on the Head, showing a long and complex history of human interference, is described in Pepin (1985).

### Tertiary strata

The main body of the Head is composed of Middle to Late Eocene sediments, generally dipping gently (2–4°) towards the east-south-east. At this time in the Palaeogene, Hengistbury lay close to the maximum western extension of a series of major marine transgressions (cf. Anderton *et al.* 1979). The rather idiosyncratic deposits of the Head have since been physically isolated from other related outcrops and the condition of much of the contained fossil material is poor (cf. Hooker 1975 and 1977, for a discussion of the Tertiary palaeontology at Hengistbury). These factors have together made it very difficult to demonstrate regional chronocorrelation and to interpret the sedimentary facies. Nevertheless, there appears to be a growing consensus that the main sequence, as seen in the modern coastal cliffs, has cf. Boscombe Beds (Sands) (Selsey Formation, Bracklesham Group), overlain by Hengistbury Beds (partly Selsey Formation, partly Barton Formation), overlain by cf. Highcliff Sands (Barton Formation) (cf. Reid 1898; White 1917; Curry 1965, 1976; Melville and Freshney 1982; Plint 1983a). The cf. Boscombe Beds are dominantly tidal estuarine (Plint 1983b) but most of the rest of the sequence is composed of relatively near-shore marine and sublittoral facies. However, lagoonal, marsh and even deltaic environments have been variously proposed for some individual strata. Whatever the case, it would seem that neither land nor sea was ever very far away during this period.

The physical characteristics of these sediments show quite high lateral variability, a fact corroborated by a comparison of the descriptions of Prestwich (1849), White (1917) and Hooker (1975), each of whom studied slightly different natural sections during the recent history of cliff recession.

The cf. Boscombe Sands comprise a series of buff/grey fine to medium sands (with finer sands, loams and bituminous sands below the usual level of exposure) with rare light-coloured and hydrated flint pebbles; the most obvious structures are the burrows of large infauna (mostly decapods).

The Hengistbury Beds are composed mainly of grey/green/brown, often strongly glauconitic clays and silts, with some fine sand units and pockets of coarse sand; even within the short kilometre of exposure, there is a very clear westwards coarsening trend (both gradational, from clays to sandy clays, and also due to increasing content of purer fine sand lenses) at all levels within these strata. The Lower Hengistbury Beds contain seams of dark-stained, very hard chert (Cretaceous flint) pebbles and much plant debris, sometimes expressed as lignite lenses; laminations are often interrupted by relatively strong bioturbation. The finely laminated Upper Hengistbury Beds contain horizons of large (up to *c*. 3 m across) autochthonous sideritic concretions ('ironstone doggers') of variable internal structure and contents of iron and clastic silicates.

The cf. Highcliff Sands are yellow to almost white, well stratified medium to fine sands with some silt/clay laminae (especially near the base), showing parallel bedding or low angle cross-bedding; towards the top, the sands are commonly indurated with orange/red iron compounds.

It is noteworthy that, at Hengistbury itself, there are no significant Tertiary gravel bodies; even coarse sand is a minor component. However, moving westwards from Hengistbury towards the Palaeogene landmass, coarse clastics become increasingly abundant.

The Hengistbury Tertiaries are cut by an unconformity, developed in the cf. Highcliff Sands on the Western Head and in the Upper Hengistbury Beds on the Eastern Head; Pleistocene sediments immediately overlie the unconformity.

### 2.1.2  *Pleistocene sediments and processes pre-dating the Late Devensian*

Sediments of the earlier Pleistocene consist either of medium to coarse flint gravels, with minor sands and loams, or of diamicts with varying proportions of gravel and of fine material reworked from the underlying Tertiaries. No other lithologies (not even the 'sarsen' often occurring in similar sediments in the region) have yet been noted. Lateral, and even vertical, variability is extreme in these deposits. For example, a 2–3 m thick, structureless unit of very angular and sharp, medium gravel (shattered flint) is exposed on the western side of Warren Hill. At the Powell Mesolithic site (see below), on the eastern slope of Warren Hill, there is no trace of a gravel body above the cf. Highcliff Sands. At the Transverse Quarry, there are up to 2 m of interbedded medium to coarse gravels (with patches of matrix support), badly sorted gravely sands, and silty loams, above another 2–3 m of coarsely bedded to massive, slightly sandy, medium to coarse gravel. Around the margins of the Eastern Depression are coarsely bedded medium to coarse gravels in a sandy loam matrix whilst, along the central axis of the Depression, there are a series of clayey/silty diamicts with varying components of angular but edge-rounded flint gravel.

Cryogenic features are relatively common in all these deposits. Many units were clearly emplaced by mass movement, probably actual gelifluction in some cases; tongues of badly sorted wash material are often interbedded with mass movement deposits. Involutions are particularly well developed in silty/clayey units, with extreme cases showing amplitudes of up to 1 m. Many gravel bodies, especially those on the Eastern Head, are penetrated to a depth of up to 1.5 m by ice wedge casts, unequivocal indicators of at least sporadic permafrost (cf. the phenomena described by Lewin 1966, at a nearby site with comparable contexts). Truly patterned ground has not yet been recognised but zones with vertically oriented gravel are not uncommon. Nowhere on the Head is there any obvious evidence for several periglacial episodes significantly separated in time.

In the past, the Hengistbury gravels have been referred to a unit known regionally as the 'Plateau Gravel' and have been interpreted in terms of at least two 'terraces', usually assumed to be of fluvial origin (cf. White 1917; Green 1946); later authors have often repeated this claim (e.g. Campbell 1977; Cunliffe 1978; Lavender in Pepin 1979 and 1985). However, the sort of clear fluvial structures which are most definitely present in the gravels on the lowland immediately west of Warren Hill are totally absent from exposures on the Head itself. There would appear to be no surviving evidence of the original mode of deposition; littoral marine, fluvial or even large scale mass movement processes might have been involved. Large crescentic chattermarks are usually present on rounded pebble surfaces where these have survived, suggesting a high energy environment of transport (beach?), but this feature could have been inherited from any period since the Cretaceous. Altitudinal correlation of the Hengistbury gravels with other similar bodies in the region would thus seem premature, if not totally impossible. The only hints concerning the chronology of pre-late-glacial events at Hengistbury are provided by Macphail's observation (this volume, section 2.2.3) of disturbed palaeo-argillic features at the Mesolithic site which might date from a pre-Flandrian interglacial soil, and by a few finds of Lower/Middle Palaeolithic artefacts in disturbed contexts around the fringes of the Head (cf. Calkin and Green 1949; Roe 1981). The Eastern Depression was certainly initiated before the Late Devensian but this shallow valley has nothing to do with the purer gravel bodies around its margin, these being dissected, even older features.

By the beginning of the Late Devensian, most of the modern topography and deposit geometry had already been established. The Head had been isolated to the north and west by river valley incision at some point(s) in the earlier Pleistocene; indeed, the Stour and Avon valleys would probably have been significantly deeper than at present. The main difference would have been the absence of the sea to the south and east, an area that would then have been occupied by the Solent River basin (Reid 1902; Everard 1954; Melville and Freshney 1982). Historical records show that, only two centuries ago, the Head extended outwards in these directions for another 300 m (incorporating Beerpan Rocks). However, we do not know whether, in the Late Devensian and Early Flandrian, the Head graded down smoothly to the Solent Valley or whether it was bounded more abruptly by bluffs or even by an interglacial raised shoreline of pre-Flandrian age. In any case, it seems most likely that all the different sediment types, Tertiary as well as Pleistocene, discussed above would have outcropped in the immediate vicinity and would therefore have been available as potential sources for later deposits.

### 2.1.3 *Late Devensian and Flandrian sediments and processes*

*Pedogenic Effects:* The superficial sediments of interest here have all been subjected to strong pedogenic modification during the progression from brown sand soils to podzolic soils, as discussed in depth by Macphail (Chapter 2.2). Such processes as clay eluviation and biotic homogenisation will have obscured or even destroyed many of the fine sedimentary structures and other stratigraphic evidence that might once have existed. Nevertheless, a careful integration of the soil and sediment data will provide a useful general picture. For this reason, and also because pedogenic effects have sometimes been mistaken for primary sedimentary features at Hengistbury, the following deposit descriptions and section drawings will also include simple references to basic soil horizons (as observed in the field by SNC and other members of the excavation team). Sedimentary units from the two main archaeological sites will be numbered and labelled U(pper) P(alaeolithic) and M(esolithic) for ease of reference.

A note is necessary here concerning the Munsell soil colours reported by the various authors in the present volume. At any given location, different observers have recorded different damp (natural humidity) colours. This is not due to any disagreement or particular subjectivity; the colours simply do vary considerably, depending upon the weather at and prior to the time of observation, and no attempt has been made to standardise them in the text. Better correspondence between observations can be seen if the relative changes between units/horizons, rather than the actual colour designations, are considered, with hue and value (less affected by moisture) having more importance than chroma.

### 2.1.4 *Stratigraphy at the Late Upper Palaeolithic Site*

*Deposit Description:* The excavated part of the Late Upper Palaeolithic site (centred at SZ 17839043) lies in the Eastern Depression, just west of the modern thalweg (i.e. where the opposite slopes meet at the bottom of the valley), at an altitude of *c.* 14.5 m OD (Fig. 2.1). The site has been laterally truncated to the south by recent cliff recession. The surface slope within the site has components of 3–4° both along bearings of 60° (towards the thalweg) and 150° (parallel to the thalweg), giving a maximum slope of *c.* 5° along a bearing of 105°; this slope is generally reproduced by the podzolic horizons developed in the underlying sediments. However, judging from the distribution of Late Upper Palaeolithic artefacts, the palaeoslope during the Late Devensian would have had a maximum of *c.* 1.5° along a bearing of 150°. The cross-valley component was either negligible or very slight (*c.* 0.5°) along a bearing of 240°, suggesting that the floor of the Depression was almost flat and/or that the thalweg has drifted eastwards and steepened its slopes during the Flandrian. On the other hand, during an earlier phase in the

Pleistocene the thalweg appears to have followed more or less its modern course. Cross-sections from the site are presented in Figures 2.2–2.5; Macphail also provides a detailed description of the pedological phenomena (Chapter 2.2).

Not shown in the sections, but present at depth throughout the site, are finely bedded clays with silt laminae, referable to the Eocene Upper Hengistbury Beds. Also, perched around the periphery of the Depression, there are gravel bodies of earlier Pleistocene age. Both these sediment stocks have contributed to the rest of the sediments at the Late Upper Palaeolithic site.

*Unit UP5* is a massive deposit of badly sorted clay/silt/sand, with common fine to coarse gravel particles supported by the matrix. It appears to be a diamict derived from all possible local sediment stocks, although it is perhaps slightly poorer in clays than might have been expected, given the proximity of the Upper Hengistbury Beds. Thus, despite the slight to moderate stickiness, this deposit is still very significantly permeable. Orientation of coarser particles and the highly convoluted shape of the sharp upper boundary suggest that the unit was cryoturbated after it had been buried by an appreciable thickness (at least 30 cm) of younger deposits. No firm evidence for dating is available but, on simple stratigraphic grounds, the unit is considered to be of an unspecified earlier Pleistocene age (cf. 2.1.2 above); there is no reason to suspect the presence of a significant diastem between this and younger deposits.

*Unit UP4* is basically a 75–100 cm thick fine to medium sand body; Late Upper Palaeolithic and later artefacts occur within it, as do the horizons of a podzolic soil. The pedogenetic features make it very difficult to decide whether or not meaningful sedimentary subdivisions can be defined; there are certainly no depositional structures or even diffuse boundaries within the sands. However, within the zone below the main illuvial horizons of the podzol, there is a slight downward increase in clays and silts and, within the unit as a whole, there is a slight downward increase in dispersed fine gravel; neither the clay/silt nor the gravel component ever rises to more than c. 15–20%. This unit also contains a variety of well defined, biogenic disturbance features which, when followed during excavation, were always found to originate either at the modern surface or, most commonly, at or about the interface between units UP3 and UP2; these features will be discussed further below.

*Unit UP3* consists of a heterogeneous and discontinuous complex of small scale sedimentary and erosional features stratified between units UP4 and UP2; these features are seldom more than 8 cm thick. First, there are wavy spreads of material, similar to UP4 and often having very diffuse boundaries with UP4, but which appear enriched in coarse sand and fine gravel; these features are probably very minor lag deposits resulting

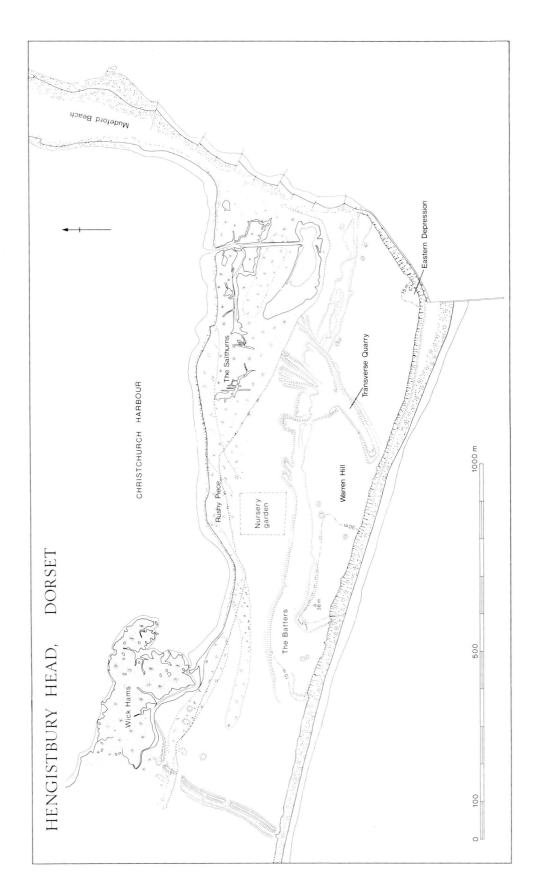

## HENGISTBURY HEAD, DORSET

Muneford Beach

CHRISTCHURCH HARBOUR

Wick Hams

Rushy Piece

Nursery garden

The Saltburns

The Batters

36 m

30 m

15 m

15 m

Warren Hill

Transverse Quarry

Eastern Depression

15 m

0    100    500    1000 m

2.1  *The main topographic features of Hengistbury Head (after Cunliffe 1987, Ill. 6).*

2.2 *Late Upper Palaeolithic site: N-S section, interface 29/30 in N-O.Typical section showing podzol development. Metre scale.*

from the winnowing of the top of unit UP4. Second, there are shallow channels filled with silty clay and minor organics, interspersed with tiny patches of sand and rare, isolated particles of very fine gravel; when followed during excavation, these channels can be seen to form a winding, branching pattern and are in all respects very similar to the minor drainage channels functioning today in some damper parts of the Depression. The two types of feature described here are in fact end-members of a continuum, with sinuous clayey lags occupying a middle position. These clear signs of erosion can be compared with Macphail's suggestion (Chapter 2.2.2) that 20 cm or more seem to be missing from the top of the podzolic profile within this site; indeed, at some points, there is no sign of an Ah horizon.

*Unit UP2* consists of lenses of finely divided or peaty organics, with some lenses of organic sand and zones with rooting systems referable to heathland. The relatively common occurrence of fine gravel suggests that organic deposition was often accompanied by continued erosion of the underlying mineral sediments. There are even occasional asymmetrical erosion channels, with a near-vertical 'bank' (up to *c.* 6 cm high) and filled with organics rich in fine gravel. Unit UP2 is itself truncated in a few places, although the mechanism is not apparent.

Given the signs of erosion in units UP3 and UP2, and also the discontinuous and/or lenticular geometry of the many individual components, both erosion and deposition may well have been quite significantly time-transgressive. If the suggestion, made above, that the thalweg drifted eastwards during the Flandrian is correct, one would expect units UP3 and UP2 to get younger more or less regularly in that same direction.

*Unit UP1* is a series of wavy, interstratified sand and organic lenses and laminations, with disseminated, extremely fine gravel; some true turflines are present but at no point is the deposit well compacted. A band, *c.* 1–2 cm thick, of particularly clean sand usually occurs at the base of the series.

### 2.1.5   *Previous stratigraphic interpretations*

Mention must be made here of the interpretations of the stratigraphy offered by previous excavators at the Late Upper Palaeolithic site. Mace (1959) recognised the podzol developed in unit UP4 and concluded, as do we, that the horizons do not have the stratigraphic significance of sedimentary units. However, Campbell (1977), whilst recognising the presence of a podzol, felt that true sedimentary units were involved, some of the boundaries of which coincided with the soil horizons. Such a proposition was apparently supported by his interpretation of his pollen and artefactual data (see Chapters 2.3.1 and 4.2.4), an interpretation which we feel is open to a serious charge of circular reasoning. In addition, Campbell identified ice wedge casts, hearths, stake holes and other supposed archaeological structures, all of which are questioned here.

The linchpin of Campbell's stratigraphic argument is his layer B2, a zone which corresponds more or less exactly to the organic-rich illuvial horizon (the upper part of the Bhs) of the podzol recognised during the present campaign. Campbell felt that this was a 'solifluction' deposit because of its contorted morphology and the *c.* 6% 'gravel' component (mostly in the 15.4–100 mm size range). He stated (1977, 73): "Layer B2 also includes a discontinuous series of fairly hard iron-pans, but rather than being mostly iron derived

28

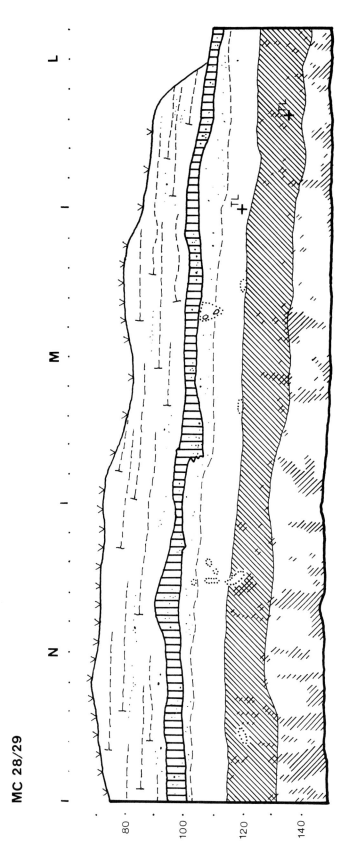

2.3 *Late Upper Palaeolithic site: N-S section, interface 28/29 in O-L. TL = Thermoluminescence dosimeter capsules. The sediment key appears in Fig. 2.5.*

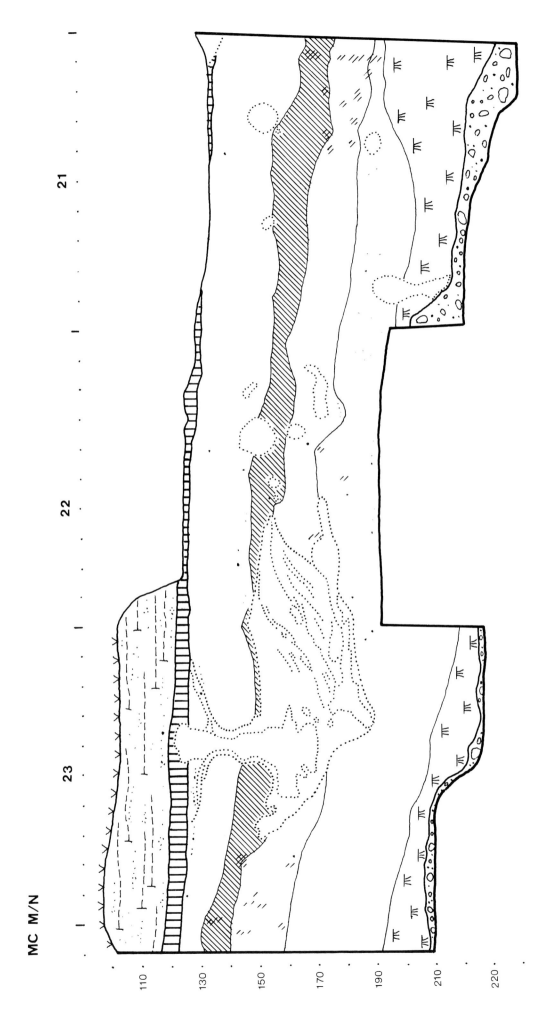

2.4  *Late Upper Palaeolithic site: W-E section, interface M/N in 23-21. The sediment key appears in Fig. 2.5.*

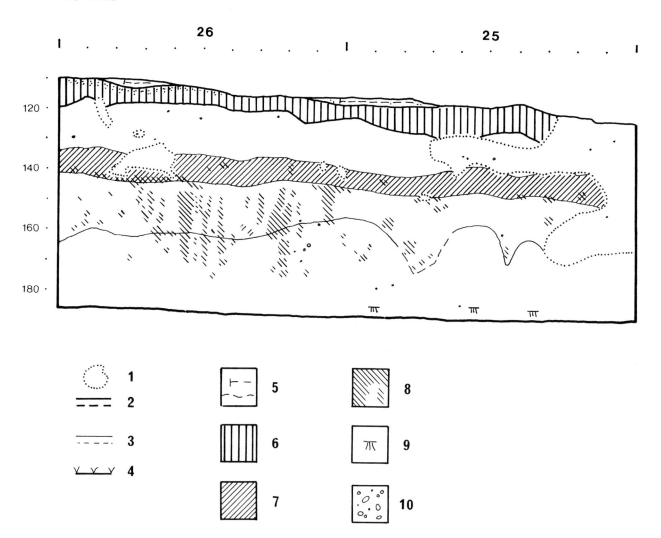

2.5 *Late Upper Palaeolithic site: W-E section, interface L/M in 25-26. Sediment key: 1= recent disturbance (roots, burrows etc.); 2= geological boundaries (solid- sharp, dashed- diffuse); 3= pedological horizon boundaries (solid- sharp, dashed- diffuse); 4= vegetated surface; 5= wavy interstratified sand and organic lenses and laminations; 6= lenses of finely divided, or peaty, or ganics; 7= organic-rich illuvial Bh and Bhs horizons; 8= as 7, but with strong iron concretions; 9= clay, silt, sand diamict; 10= flint gravel.*

from subsequent humic formations above, most appears to have come from the highly ferruginous layers and bedrock below and elsewhere on Warren Hill by a process of wind-derivation of fine particles and solifluction of coarser elements." It appears that Campbell was referring to material thought to be ironstone clasts from the Upper Hengistbury Beds; nowhere did he make a claim for the presence of significant flint gravel.

First, we cannot agree that the iron concretions in unit UP4 are dominantly or even significantly composed of derived Tertiary material. The nodular concretions are sometimes superficially more similar to the Tertiary ironstone than they are to the more massive Flandrian iron pans formed in better drained areas of the Head, but they are still demonstrably *in situ* pedogenic features (cf. Chapter 2.2.2). For one thing, the nodules often contain very fine and angular flint debris

(as does the host sediment body) whilst the Tertiaries never have such a component. On the other hand, true clasts of Tertiary ironstone have indeed been recovered, in small numbers, from unit UP4 during the present campaign. Even ignoring the direct proof of the use of iron compounds by man at this site, we would have no hesitation in recognising these objects as manuports. Everywhere in the Eastern Depression the Tertiaries are covered by thick earlier Pleistocene deposits with abundant flint gravel and very little if any ironstone, and nowhere in or near the Depression do the ironstone doggers occur, even buried, at or above the altitude of the Late Upper Palaeolithic site. There is simply no possible geological mechanism which could have introduced ironstone without adding large amounts of medium to coarse flint gravel as well, material that in fact is absent. If we remove the 'gravel' component from Campbell's layer B2, and we make due

2.6   *Late Upper Palaeolithic site: channel feature ('gutter') at interface 11/12 in G. Centimetre scale on photographic board.*

and reasonable allowance for the effects of gley pod-zolisation, there is absolutely no basis for recognising a discrete sedimentary unit at this level.

Campbell also recorded a number of supposed ice wedge casts at the boundary between his layers B2 and the underlying B1; from his section drawings, these features were 10–25 cm deep, were never wider than *c.*5 cm, were filled with his layer B2 material, sometimes occurred in quite dense groups with pairs as little as 5 cm apart, and were never sufficiently continuous in plan to appear in sections one metre apart. From a theoretical viewpoint alone, it is extremely unlikely that features with such dimensions, morphology and distribution were ice wedge casts or even sand-filled frost cracks (see, for example, the detailed discussion by Washburn 1979). In none of the squares dug into unit UP4 during the present campaign were cryogenic wedges found. Unfortunately, most of the sections with wedge-shaped features illustrated by Campbell were excavated away before the end of his campaign. However, his sections defining the northern limit of his excavation area survive; all illustrated wedge-shaped features are in fact unequivocal pedogenic features associated with the penetration of tree roots in the past.

None of the hearths claimed by Campbell survive in section. However black organic-rich lenses and subsurface accumulations are common throughout the site at the same levels within the soil profile. Much burnt flint and tiny particles of charcoal were recovered during the present campaign, but no organised hearth features were recognised. The spatial plot of burnt flints from Campbell's excavations shows no overall relationship with the positions of his supposed hearths.

Towards the eastern end of the site, Campbell (1977, 76) recognised a structure, defined by "fairly clear stake-holes" and external 'gutters', at the boundary between his layers A1a and A1b (at or about the transition between UP4 and UP3–2 in our terminology). The stake holes were "filled with what appeared to be the ordinary peaty sand of the overlying layer A1b" and they penetrated to a depth of only 12 cm. It seems likely that they too were root penetration features. One of the 'gutters' is still in section (Fig. 2.6) and proved to be a perfectly natural erosion channel, just like the others occurring elsewhere in the site in units UP3 and UP2; in this specific case, peat formation had commenced before the cutting of the channel.

Finally, Campbell recognised a deep basin-like feature (1977, Fig. 42), filled with material referred to his layer A1b, material which supplied the pollen for his reconstruction of the whole of the first half of the Flandrian. The section survived and a new drawing was made, presented here as Figure 2.4. The whole phenomenon is a good example of a structure formed by the rotting of a major tree stump and its root sys-

2.7  *Late Upper Palaeolithic site: biogenic disturbance feature on right hand side of photograph. W-E section, interface L/M in 25-26 (cf. Fig. 2.4). Metre scale.*

tem; the tree was growing on a surface high up within unit UP2. Similar features are recorded in section and in plan elsewhere on the site (Figs. 2.7 and 2.8)

It has been necessary to criticise Campbell's interpretations, point by point, in order to dispel any misconceptions which would interfere with a proper understanding of the archaeology. However, Campbell only made one basic error in that he failed to give full consideration to geological, pedogenic and biogenic modification of existing sediment; once this mistake was made, overinterpretation of the observed textural and colour changes would follow more or less automatically. In Chapter 3.1 below, we will present further data which suggests that it would have been impossible for anything but the most solid and substantial structure, sedimentary or archaeological, to survive for long within unit UP4.

### 2.1.6 *Stratigraphy at the Powell Mesolithic Site*

The Powell Mesolithic site (centred at SZ 17239058) lies on the eastern flank of Warren Hill, at an altitude of *c.* 30 m OD (Figs. 2.1 and 1.17). The site has been laterally truncated to the south by recent cliff recession. The general slope in this area is *c.* 3–5° to the east; there is also a modern component to the slope towards the cliff edge (south) but, judging from the relatively restricted exposures available, this would probably not have been the case in the earlier Flandrian. Cross-sections from the site are presented in Figs. 2.9–2.10; Macphail also provides a detailed description

of the pedological phenomena (section 2.2.3).

Not shown in the section drawings, but present at depth at various testing points throughout the site, are finely bedded sands with the bedding planes picked out by bright red iron compounds. These sands are referable to the Eocene cf. Highcliff Sands, deposits which probably provided much of the sediment for the overlying sequence.

As has been noted above, there is no gravel body of earlier Pleistocene age at this site, although such gravels begin to appear only a few metres further upslope to the west. Individual gravel-sized particles do occur, however, becoming more common in a rough trend up through the sequence, suggesting derivation from the nearby gravel bodies as the latter became subject to erosion.

The rather diffuse upper boundary of the lowest defined sedimentary unit, *Unit M5*, coincides roughly with the upper limit of the illuvial soil horizons. There are sometimes relatively modern burrows (probably rabbit) at and just above this boundary but, even so, the boundary seems to have been quite irregular. The sediment of M5 is composed mainly of a homogeneous coarse silt and fine sand, with a minor clay content (up to *c.* 10% of material below 2 mm diameter) at depths below the strongest influence of podzolisation. Altered sideritic clasts (Tertiary) are present in small quantities in all sand grades at levels within this unit below the effects of podzolisation. Material coarser than 2 mm is very rare. The firmly indurated soil horizons (Bh and Bhs) are of sedimentary importance since, near the cliff, they have acted as a modern erosion base, with gravel

2.8  *Late Upper Palaeolithic site: The dark stain marks a biogenic disturbance feature, probably a rotted tree stump, in square M20.*

and artefacts from formerly overlying units having been let down as a coarse lag onto the exhumed 'iron pan'.

*Unit M4* is very similar to the material below, save that there is a significant proportion of fine to medium gravel-sized particles dispersed throughout the sediment.

The boundary between units M4 and M3 is often marked by a discontinuous stone line (including particles up to small cobble size) but the transition in the fine matrix is gradual and difficult to appreciate on site; both units are well compacted. The sediment of *Unit M3* is broadly similar to underlying deposits, with fine sand remaining dominant. However, a minor coarse sand and fine to medium gravel component is irregularly present, giving a degree of textural heterogeneity on a small spatial scale; only towards the top of the unit does the coarse component begin to wane.

*Unit M2* is a very thin organic deposit, sometimes merely a richly organic-impregnated sand but sometimes a true buried turfline. At least in places, this unit must represent the Ah or even H horizon of the underlying podzolic soil (cf. section 2.2.3). However, especially towards the south and east, this unit clearly truncates the underlying sequence (cutting into the Ea1 horizon of Macphail at a few points). Also, M2 was sometimes itself truncated or even removed by the emplacement of overlying deposits. *Unit M2* is therefore best considered to be time-transgressive, probably significantly so.

The sequence is capped by *Unit M1*, a series of slightly wavy, only moderately compacted clean sand lenses and laminations, often with organic partings (extremely weak 'turflines').

Mesolithic and probably Bronze Age artefacts occur mainly in *Unit M3* but with a smaller number of specimens in *Unit M4*; the spatial distribution of artefacts is of considerable interest and is discussed in more detail in Chapter 3.

### 2.1.7  *Stratigraphy on the periphery of an Early Bronze Age barrow (Warren Hill) and of the linear bank and ditch feature (Eastern Depression)*

*Barrow 9:* Barrow 9 is an Early Bronze Age feature lying on the eastern flank of Warren Hill (SZ 17209062), some 50 m upslope of the Powell Mesolithic site (Fig. 1.17). The barrow is one of those excavated in 1919 by St. George Gray (Cunliffe 1978). In 1982, a metre square sounding was dug, 5 m along a bearing of 119° from the highest surviving point of the small barrow. The reasons for this sounding were, first, the need to assess the possibility of pollution of the Mesolithic site by Bronze Age flint artefacts (cf. Chapter 5.1.1) and, second, to recover stratigraphic information concerning the history of sand mobility on the Head. The sounding was carefully placed far enough away from the barrow so as not to disturb any remaining unexcavated part of the feature itself, but close enough so as to pick up the 1919 tip and any peripheral stratigraphic features dating from the Early Bronze Age.

The section of this sounding (not illustrated here)

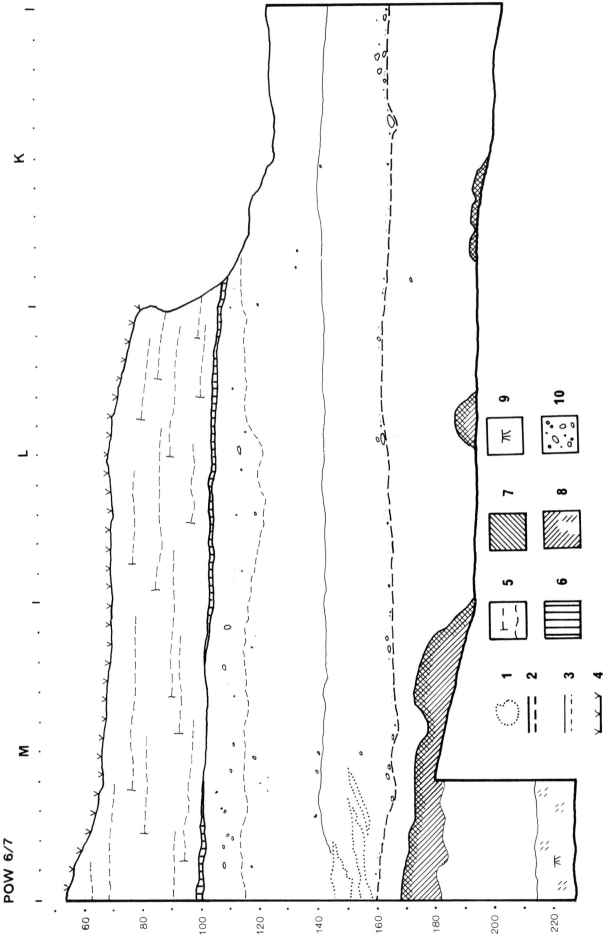

2.9   Powell Mesolithic site: N-S section, interface 6/7 in K-M. Sediment key: 1= recent disturbance (roots, burrows etc.); 2= geological boundaries (solid- sharp, dashed- diffuse); 3= pedological horizon wavy interstratified sand and organic lenses and laminations; 6= lenses of finely divided, or peaty, organics; 7= organic-rich illuvial Bh and Bhs horizons; 8= as 7, but with strong iron concretions; 9= clay, silt, sand diamict; 10= flint gravel.

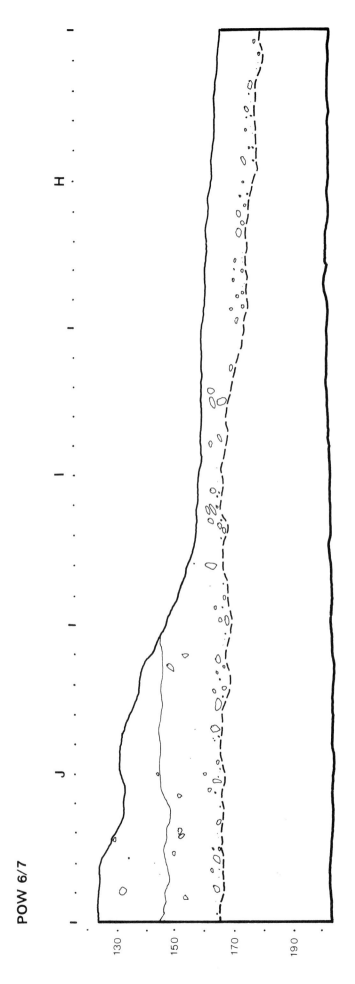

POW 6/7

130

150

170

190

2.10  *Powell Mesolithic site: N-S section, interface 6/7 in H-J. The sediment key appears in* Fig. 2.9.

shows a truncated palaeosol of a weak podzolic type in the lower part of the sequence. Note, however, that a little clay is present throughout, even in very small proportions in the eluvial horizon. There is no true turfline at the top of this palaeosol and the succeeding deposit is a mottled sand with all the characteristics of 'tip' derived from the underlying sediments. Flint debitage, of a type often associated with Early Bronze Age sites in the region (cf. section 5.1.1), was present from just below and from above this 'tip' but was extremely rich within the tip itself; rare charcoal was also noted. It therefore seems reasonable to interpret these phenomena as general peripheral disturbance consequent upon the building of the barrow. Above the Bronze Age disturbance there is a fine sand unit capped by a buried turfline (of heathland type) and again showing weak podzolic organisation. The youngest unit, here as in many other areas on the Head, is composed of thin interbedded lenses and laminations of clean sand and peat/turf. Stratified within this last unit is the 1919 tip, identified by its content of iron nails, wooden pegs with attached steel wire, strongly altered animal bone, and disturbed lumps of sediment from all underlying deposits including the Eocene cf. Highcliff Sands (naturally present here at a depth of *c*. 2 m below the modern surface).

*Ditch and Bank:* The Eastern Depression is crossed obliquely by a ditch and bank feature, the line of which is clearly visible on aerial photographs (Fig. 1.14) but more difficult to see on the ground. The ditch outcrops in the cliff just east of the Late Upper Palaeolithic site and Campbell (1977) noted it there and also in short trenches behind the cliff. A trench was dug across the ditch and bank further north into the Depression (Fig. 1.15) during the present campaign. The palaeosol and pollen profile buried under the bank are discussed in detail by Macphail and Scaife (Chapters 2.2 and 2.3); they also provide evidence that the feature dates from the Late Bronze Age/Early Iron Age (rather than from the Neolithic/Bronze Age as suggested by Campbell).

A section from the recent trench is provided in Fig. 2.11 and a description of the entire sequence is given by Macphail (Chapter 2.2.2). Of interest here is the 20–30 cm of sandy material, with podzolic characteristics, overlying the bank (Fig. 2.12 and 2.13). Such material is totally absent from the section at the cliff edge; instead, the organic-rich ditch fill is there capped by 15–20 cm of interstratified sand and turf/peat lenses and laminations.

*The Late Historical Period*
During a twenty-five year period starting in 1848, large scale mining of ironstone doggers was carried out on and around the Head (for details see Lavender in Pepin 1985), an expansion of an exploitation pattern which had begun on a smaller scale at least a century earlier (White 1917). Ironstone was removed not only from the landward side (from the Batters and the Transverse Quarry) but also from the sea cliffs, causing some 300

m of cliff recession, until 1938 when the Long Groyne (Breakwater) was built, slowing but not completely arresting erosion. Much of the huge quantities of fine sediment liberated was carried north-eastwards by the sea but very significant amounts would have become available for localised wind transport.

Mace (1959), relying upon the unpublished notes of a local collector, Mr. H. Druitt, suggested that the Head (including all of the Eastern Depression save for a narrow strip near the cliff) had been ploughed in 1913 in preparation for a golf course. Mace drew in the boundary of the supposed ploughed area on her plan and implied that evidence of ploughing was found in the single sounding which she dug north of the boundary. Calkin (1960) stated that Upper Palaeolithic finds had come to light during preparations for the golf course in 1914, but Cunliffe (1978, 16) notes: "There followed an abortive scheme for the construction of a golf course, but after some preparation of the low-lying areas in 1912, involving extensive ploughing, the syndicate collapsed (Calkin 1966, 8)". During the present campaign, we have carried out a systematic survey of the Eastern Depression, with observations from small soundings and from the 'banks' of minor erosional features. On many occasions, superficial sequences of peaty lenses and water-laid sand/silt/clay laminae were noted that must have taken more than 70 years to form. Even below such stratified sequences, or where they were absent, we could find absolutely no evidence of recent ploughing. If such ploughing did in fact take place, we can only suppose that the disturbed sandy 'tilth' was almost immediately removed by wind and water erosion. The only fact that might support this last suggestion is the very weak development or, more commonly, absence of an uppermost interstratified turf/sand unit in areas within the Depression away from the cliff edge.

During WWII, the Head was used as an artillery range, with guns mounted on Warren Hill aimed at the eastern end of the Head. Several shell craters are visible, one in the Eastern Depression being particularly obvious due to the bracken growing on the well-drained gravel pulled up from depth. It is possible that this and other military activities on the Head would have disturbed vegetation sufficiently to cause increased sand mobility.

Since the war, increasing visitor pressure has encouraged erosion and sand mobility, although this is now being controlled by such measures as the laying of imported (exotic) gravel on paths.

### 2.1.8 *Discussion: The origin and modification of Late Devensian and Flandrian sand deposits on the headland*

As has been noted in earlier sections, the deposits which contain the archaeological material studied during the present project are basically fine sand bodies. In the past, the sand has usually been interpreted as aeolian material: Mace (1959) believed that all the sand was 'wind-blown', Campbell (1977) considered that

EP DITCH

EAST ————→

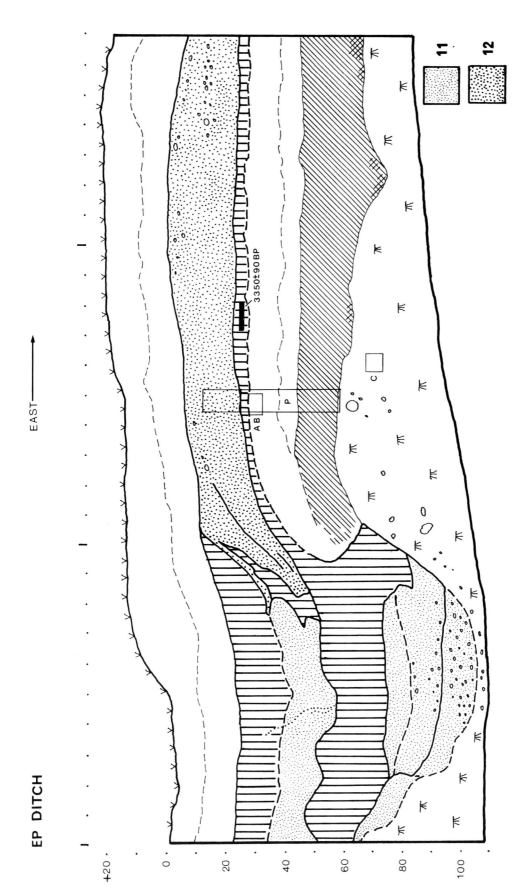

2.11 Bank and ditch feature, Eastern Depression: W-E section at 'A' (Fig. 1.15). Sediment key (see Fig. 2.9): 11= fine stratified sediments; 12= mixed humose sediments; the junction between these and the buried land surface below possibly consists of a layer of inverted turves. Note position of soil samples (A, B and C) and pollen column (P).

37

2.12 *Bank and ditch feature, Eastern Depression: W-E section, view of ditch. Scale in six inch bars.*

2.13 *Bank and ditch feature, Eastern Depression: W-E section, detail of ditch. Scale in six inch bars.*

much of it was, and the same general opinion has been held during the present campaign. However, the aeolian hypothesis has not until now been discussed in detail. The issue is of great importance, not only for the obvious palaeoenvironmental reasons, but also because of the radical implications for the artefact taphonomy (see Chapter 3 below).

Samples of sand from various levels and locations have been prepared both by the present author and by Macphail (see Chapter 2.2), who has kindly allowed the graphic presentation and discussion of some of his results in this section. Samples have been analysed using standard techniques, with $H_2O_2$ or NaOH pre-

treatment to remove soluble organics. Particle distributions are shown in Figure 2.14 and summary statistics are reported in Tables 2.1 and 2.2. The logarithmic phi scale of diameters has been used throughout since this best characterises the size distributions of these types of sediment (phi = -$\log_2$ mm diameter; thus, -1 phi = 2 mm, 0 phi = 1 mm, 1 phi = 0.5 mm, 2 phi = 0.25 mm, 3 phi = 0.125 mm, 4 phi = 0.0625 mm, etc.). The bell-shaped frequency (BSF) and sigmoid cumulative frequency (SCF) graphs in Figure 2.14 need no explanation, but the linear-segmented, gaussian-transformed cumulative frequency (GTCF) graphs will not be so familiar.

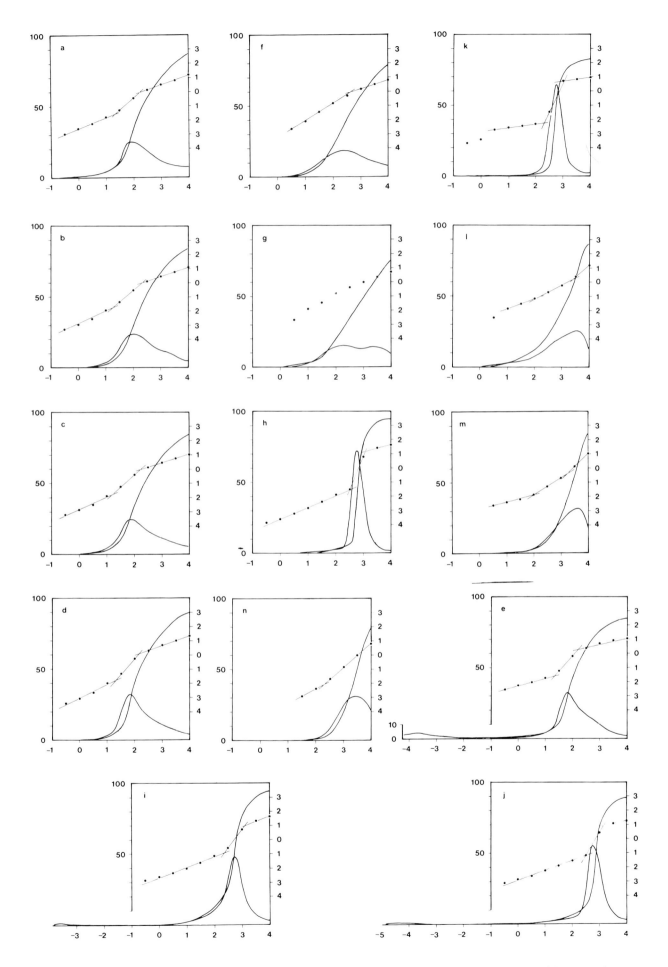

2.14   *Particle size distributions of Late Devensian and Flandrian sands. The key to these graphs is in Tables 2.1 and 2.2.*

*Table 2.1 Summary statistics of Late Devensian and Flandrian sands.*

| Sample | Mz | So | Sk | Ku | Mo | (Mz-Mo) |
|--------|------|------|-------|------|------|---------|
| M/C2   | 2.59 | 0.80 | 0.32  | 0.75 | 1.90 | 0.78    |
| S4     | 2.72 | 0.71 | 0.18  | 0.63 | 2.02 | 0.70    |
| S1     | 2.68 | 0.74 | 0.20  | 0.63 | 1.90 | 0.78    |
| M/C35  | 2.50 | 0.60 | 0.01  | 0.69 | 1.82 | 0.68    |
| M/C27  | 2.58 | 0.61 | 0.20  | 0.52 | 1.81 | 0.77    |
| RM6    | 3.12 | 0.83 | 0.17  | 0.56 | 2.36 | 0.76    |
| RM8    | 3.13 | 0.90 | 0.04  | 0.68 | 2.25 | 0.88    |
| P1     | 2.87 | 0.13 | 0.01  | 0.57 | 2.77 | 0.10    |
| P6     | 2.69 | 0.26 | −0.02 | 0.49 | 2.73 | −0.04   |
| P8     | 2.96 | 0.20 | 0.05  | 0.44 | 2.72 | 0.24    |
| P11    | 3.22 | 0.26 | 0.20  | 0.29 | 2.75 | 0.47    |
| RM20   | 3.22 | 0.55 | −0.30 | 0.77 | 3.55 | −0.33   |
| RM21   | 3.41 | 0.41 | −0.05 | 0.66 | 3.60 | 0.19    |
| RM24   | 3.55 | 0.30 | −0.09 | 0.44 | 3.45 | 0.10    |

These measures are graphic statistics expressed in phi units (phi = $-\log_2$ mm), calculated from cumulative frequency plots of material finer than −1 phi (2 mm) diameter (see Fig. 2.14).

The phi values at various percentiles (p) are read off the graphs to give the following simple statistics:
Median     Mz   = (p16 + p50 + p84)/3
Sorting      So   = (p75 − p25)/2
Skewness   Sk   = [(p25 + p75) − 2p50]/2
(positive values indicate fine tails, negative values, coarse tails)
        Kurtosis   Ku   = (p75 − p25)/(p84 − p16)
(low values indicate material concentrated in a central peak and in extreme coarse and/or fine tails, high values indicate material concentrated in a broad, ill-defined central part of the distribution)
Also, Mode (Mo) is the most common particle size, and (Mz -Mo) is a measure of modal skewness.

The sediment samples are as follows:
M/C2     Upper Pal Site, Square M24, unit UP1.
S4        Upper Pal Site, Square V20 (pathside bank),
          upper middle unit UP4.
S1        Upper Pal Site, Square V20 (pathside bank),
          middle unit UP4.
M/C35   Upper Pal Site, Square I32, lower middle unit UP4.
M/C27   Upper Pal Site, Square M24, unit UP5.
RM6     Bank & Ditch, Eastern Depression, Profile 1 (Macphail),
          horizon bEa.
RM8     Bank & Ditch, Eastern Depression, Profile 1 (Macphail),
          horizon bB(t)sg.
P1        Meso Site, Square N6, Unit M1.
P6        Meso Site, Square N6, lower unit M3.
P8        Meso Site, Square N6, unit M4.
P11     Meso Site, Square N6, lower unit M5.
RM20    Meso Site, Profile 4 (Macphail), horizon Ea1
          (= lower unit M3).
RM21    Meso Site, Profile 4 (Macphail), horizon Ea2 (= unit M4).
RM24    Meso Site, Profile 4 (Macphail), horizon B(t)sg
          (= lower unit M5).

Sediments which have been affected by a reasonably coherent energy regime tend to be composed of a number of subpopulations of particle sizes, due to mechanically different but more or less simultaneous modes of transport; the main divisions are the rolling (surface) subpopulation, the saltation ('bouncing') subpopulation and the suspension (in air or water) subpopulation. An estimate of the nature and importance of subpopulations can be gained by plotting phi values against gaussian-transformed cumulative percentage (cf. Visher 1969). Usually, this involves plotting the cumulative percentages on probability paper, an awkward unequal-interval method. However, Collcutt (1984) has suggested the use of z-values representing cumulative areas under the Normal Standard Curve (tabulated in most statistics textbooks), so that an equal-interval scale results without changing the form of the 'curve' in any way. Z-values (symmetrically distributed about zero) are shown on the right of the graphs in Figure 2.14, but readers merely wishing to ascertain a cumulative percentage value can do so by reading the point on the ordinary cumulative (SCF) graph which is vertically above or below the point of interest on the gaussian-transformed 'curve' (GTCF). The technicalities can be set aside for the moment; the important thing is that, when strongly differentiated subpopulations with individual distributions approximating to statistically normal distributions (a general tendency in nature) are present, they can be estimated by fitting straight-line segments to portions of the GTCF 'curve'. The recognition of subpopulations of specific types can give considerable insight into the depositional and modificational environments involved; for instance, aeolian sands very rarely include a significant suspension subpopulation, saltation being the dominant mode of transport. Further details are given in the captions to Figure 2.14 and Table 2.2.

First, the argument concerning mass movement, already raised in 'previous stratigraphic interpretations' (above), must be formalised here. Sample M/C27 (Fig. 2.14, e) is a classic mass movement deposit, which has also suffered cryoturbation, from the base of the Late Upper Palaeolithic site sequence. Apart from the overall irregularity of the size distribution (best seen in the BSF curve), the sediment contains a most significant proportion of gravel (even plotted up to only -4 phi, that is, 16 mm diameters). Even though little or no fine gravel or coarse sand is present, sample RM8 (Fig. 2.14, g), from the base of the sequence further north in the Eastern Depression, also seems to have suffered geological mass disturbance, seen in the badly sorted, irregular distribution with no sign of discrete subpopulations. No amount of later pedogenic modification would suffice to hide the true nature of such deposits. Yet, nowhere do deposits known to contain archaeological material display such characteristics.

As a general principle, it can be said that it seems highly unlikely that significant geological disturbance could occur in the Late Devensian/Flandrian deposits of the Head without an extreme climatic control (such as factors inducing permafrost). Slopes are generally low, and the dominantly sandy (permeable and porous) texture of strata over appreciable thicknesses would not respond en masse to merely transitory cryogenic stresses – these types of sediment are simply not greatly susceptible to ice segregation (cf. Linell and Tedrow 1981). Any suspicion that important fine fractions of the sediments have been destroyed by subsequent podzolisation is allayed by the low percentages (c. 5–20%) of clays and silts in the unaffected subsoil, material which still shows high permeability and high interparticle friction (resistance to bulk plastic deformation). In order to illustrate this resistance to deformation, sediments in the Late Upper Palaeolithic site were field test-

Table 2.2 Subpopulations within the Late Devensian
and Flandrian sands.

| Sample | A-sort | A-% | A-FT | B-sort | B-% | B-FT | C-sort (approx) |
|---|---|---|---|---|---|---|---|
| M/C2 | mod | 9 | 1.35 | good | 48 | 2.25 | mod |
| S4 | poor | 5 | 1.25 | good | 40 | 2.31 | good |
| S1 | poor | 5 | 1.20 | good | 41 | 2.24 | good |
| M/C35 | poor | 6 | 1.31 | good | 43 | 2.15 | good |
| M/C27 | mod | 7 | 1.31 | mod | 45 | 2.42 | poor |
| RM6 | | | | ?mod | 45(A+B%) | 2.62 | good |
| RM8 | (subpopulations not well defined) | | | | | | |
| P1 | poor | 6 | 2.47 | good | 71 | 2.98 | mod |
| P6 | poor | 21 | 2.33 | good | 59 | 3.07 | mod |
| P8 | mod | 12 | 2.48 | good | 63 | 3.13 | good |
| P11 | mod | c.2 | 2.31 | good | 71 | 3.05 | mod |
| RM20 | mod | 12 | 2.17 | mod | 45 | 3.42 | mod |
| RM21 | mod | 3 | 2.03 | good | 35 | 3.42 | good |
| RM24 | mod | 2 | 2.26 | | >77(B+C%) | | good (B+C) |

Subpopulations, A the coarsest, B the middle range and C the finest, are defined by visual fitting of straight-line segments to graphs of material finer than −1 phi, plotted with phi units against gaussian-transformed cumulative percentages (see Fig. 2.14 GTCF 'curves' and text). An estimate of sorting (poor, moderate, good) is given for each subpopulation and, for A and B, the percentage representation and the fine truncation (FT, the point of intersection in phi units with the next finer subpopulation). Thus it is estimated, for instance, that Sample M/C2 has a well sorted B subpopulation, which represents 48% of the total sample (finer than −1 phi) and which contains particles with diameters lying between 1.35 phi (the FT of the coarser A subpopulation) and 2.25 phi.

The sediment samples are those defined in Table 2.1.

ed with a cone penetrometer (cone angle, 30°; base area, 3.23 cm$^2$; base diameter, 2.03 cm; cone height and chosen penetration, 3.8 cm) and a Torvane shear strength indicator. Values for the eluvial Ea horizon (almost clean sand, highly resistant to plastic deformation) and for the sediment below the main illuvial horizons (but within the gleyed zone) showed no significant difference in any given vertical profile (penetrability varied in the range 88–156 newtons, shear strength in the range 33–49 kilopascals). When compared with these figures, the slightly clayier material at the very base of unit UP4 showed a drop in penetrability of 15–35% and in shear strength of only 0–10%, whilst unit UP5 (the basal mass movement deposit) showed a drop in penetrability of c. 40% and in shear strength of c. 20%; these lowest deposits were much damper than the sands above at the time of testing. Therefore, none of these sediments can be described as easily deformable and certainly not as plastic.

Mass movement can be ruled out as a significant source for the Late Devensian and Flandrian sands, as can true fluvial processes (on the general grounds of sediment type, deposit geometry, and local topography). This leaves aeolian processes and wash processes as possible emplacement mechanisms. Again on theoretical grounds, major wash transport seems unlikely because the sediments are so permeable; only when the water table is exceptionally high or is perched near the surface due to ground ice or the build-up of organic material (as in parts of the Eastern Depression today) will wash and minor channel flow become significant, and then mostly as erosive, rather than depositional, agents. Aeolian deposition would therefore seem to be

the only available mechanism to account for the bulk of the sands. However, we can do much better than this argument by mere elimination.

It is important that the meaning of the term 'aeolian' be unambiguous here: all that is implied is a wind transport system. The climatic overtones associated with regional loess sheets and coversands do not apply as the sands on the Head bear no resemblance whatsoever to such sediment types. Nor is there any sign of dune development on top of the Head; traces of dune bedding would certainly have survived even strong pedogenesis, especially in thicker sand bodies. There is every reason to believe that an extremely local sedimentation pattern (on a scale of hundreds of metres at the most) was involved throughout the period of interest. No detailed mineralogical analysis has yet been carried out, but the observed presence of glauconitic and sideritic grains, and even rare mica platelets, within the sands at several locations proves an input from the local Tertiaries. The underrepresentation of coarse and even medium sands, in the Late Devensian and Flandrian deposits just as in the Tertiaries, is also highly suggestive. There is no reasonable justification for looking any further afield for the dominant sand source, particularly as the Head is and was almost surrounded by river valleys which would have constituted a major barrier (water and denser vegetation) to saltating allochthonous grains. Since many observers (e.g. Sharp 1966) have reported that it requires 10–15 km of saltation transport for classic aeolian sand size distribution characteristics to be developed, we should not expect the sands on the Head to show particularly good sorting. Even a moderate silt and clay content need not be surprising because, over short distances, sand-sized aggregates of fines ('pellets' and desiccation flakes) can be carried intact by the wind.

If the sands at Hengistbury are the result of local factors, we cannot use simple comparison with the published data usually derived from large scale sedimentary systems. A local model is required, based upon deposits which are beyond doubt of aeolian origin. This model is provided most satisfactorily by the body of interbedded clean sands and turf lenses which caps the sequence in many areas of the Head (see specifically *Units* UP1 and M1).

The sand/turf body is of very recent origin. Close to the barrow on Warren Hill (Barrow 9, see above), tip from the archaeological excavations of 1919 is stratified deep within the sand/turf body and, at the Late Upper Palaeolithic site, a George V penny was found, again well within the unit. This massive rise in sand mobility was caused by the quarrying and other major disturbances mentioned earlier. A combination of recent date and point sedimentation rates fast enough to swamp turf cover over and over again indicates that this sand cannot have been significantly modified by pedogenesis; the particle size distributions are therefore original and no structures defined by clay/silt particles can have been destroyed. Yet, compaction of the sands is usually low and nowhere are there any clay/silt laminae or channel-like features. The unit blankets the Head, irrespective of topography, and internal stratification, defined by turflines, often indicates gently undulating or hummocky accretion surfaces, often with roughly parallel upper and lower sand subunit boundaries of significant lateral extent. These sands are therefore of exclusively aeolian origin and their characteristics should accurately reflect local conditions.

The particle size distributions of this sand/turf body (after removal of organics) at the Late Upper Palaeolithic (sample M/C2) and Powell Mesolithic (sample P1) sites are shown in Figs. 2.14, a and 2.14, h, respectively.

First, it should be noted that both samples show positive skewness (fine tails), a feature common to most aeolian sands and thought to be due to the limiting effect of well defined maximum wind velocities. Also, both samples show the presence of three subpopulations within the sand grades (Table 2.2). The minor A subpopulation in each case is referable to rolling transport. The major B and C subpopulations both appear to reflect saltation transport, since the relative coarseness of the C material precludes true air suspension at anything but exceptional wind velocities (the boundary between saltation and suspension in air transport is normally close to 4.3 phi, rarely coarsening to an extreme of 3.5 phi; cf. Reineck and Singh 1980). The presence of two saltation subpopulations is most interesting as this suggests rhythmically changing wind speeds and/or direction (in the case of these recent sands, the cause is probably the diurnal sea breeze cycle but longer, even annual cycles would produce a similar

effect). This characteristic cannot have been inherited from a Tertiary source; even if such subtle features of an earlier particle size distribution could have survived just the slightest wind transport, which is very unlikely, the fining westwards trend in the recent sands is the opposite of that in the Tertiaries.

Having looked at the similarities between samples M/C2 and P1, we may now turn to the marked contrasts. Compared with the recent sands in the Late Upper Palaeolithic site, those in the Powell Mesolithic site show a finer median and mode (and a corresponding shift in the limits of the sand subpopulations), much better sorting, a dominant B saltation subpopulation (response to a clearer dominant wind pattern), a smaller rolling (A) subpopulation, and a smaller proportion of silts and clays. These contrasts are predictable when the topographic differences between the sites are considered: the Late Upper Palaeolithic site is in a relatively sheltered depression at 14 m OD, whilst the Mesolithic site is in an exposed position near the brow of Warren Hill at 31 m OD. The pattern confirms the suggestion that we are dealing with an extremely localised sedimentary system. Further, it provides a test for assumptions about older sand bodies. If local topographic factors are so important now, there is every reason to expect that they would have been important in the past; the same general pattern as in the recent aeolian sands should occur in presumed aeolian sands even as old as the Late Devensian.

The reader is now asked to consider the data in Figure 2.14 and Tables 2.1 and 2.2 for the main sand body on the Head, that which contains both the Late Upper Palaeolithic (samples S4, S1, and M/C35) and the Powell Mesolithic (samples P6, P8, RM20 and RM21) artefacts. The overall pattern is remarkably similar to that established for the recent aeolian sands, right down to the dual saltation subpopulations. Even sample RM6, from a slightly less sheltered position within the Eastern Depression, shows a shift towards finer sands, although sorting is poor largely due to the marked rolling subpopulation to be expected in what is still a dominantly sediment catchment rather than source area. The general pattern can be confirmed all over the Head, although the trends can sometimes be rather patchy in response to extremely small scale variations in topography (witness the differences between P6/P8 and RM20/RM21 derived from sampling columns only a few metres apart).

However, there is one very significant anomaly between the upper sands in the Powell Mesolithic site and the model based on the recent aeolian sands. Samples P6, P8, RM20 and RM21, whilst retaining enough of the expected characteristics not to cast serious doubt upon the hypothesis of aeolian deposition, nevertheless show a tendency towards negative skewness and a build-up of the rolling/sliding subpopulation. The presence of minor stone lines and coarser lenses has already been noted in Chapter (2.1.6 above). Furthermore, angular flint clasts above *c.* 2 mm in diameter show extreme edge-rounding, even resembling sand blasting on some of the largest particles. All these features strongly suggest that, rather than being an area exclusively subjected to sand deposition, the higher slopes of Warren Hill have been the site of alternating deposition and erosion by wind deflation (wind winnowing), although net accretion was clearly the rule during most periods. Again, this aspect of the pattern is predictable from simple topography. Far from weakening the overall aeolian hypothesis, the recognition of deflation as an important process in exposed areas lends a time dimension to the model which could not be provided by data derived only from the recent sands with their artificially extreme sedimentation rates.

Finally, a word of caution against overinterpretation of minor fluctuations in the reported data is necessary. The discussion has centred around the dominant sand fraction in order to avoid being misled by later pedogenic effects. However, it should not be forgotten that even the coarser particles have not escaped a significant degree of biogenic mixing and perhaps even minor biogenic sorting (see Chapter 3.1); such effects will to some extent have blurred the original sedimentary details.

### 2.1.9 *Reconstruction of the sedimentary history of the headland*

The Eocene marine deposits were eventually capped by gravels, although the mechanisms involved are as yet unknown. Then, the whole sequence was carved into the recognisable topography of Hengistbury Head by valley incision at various points during the earlier Pleistocene. Thus, highly diverse stocks were made available for later sedimentation but, at the same time, the physical isolation of the Head would severely restrict the range of sedimentary processes which could take effect.

At the beginning of the Late Devensian, the dominant set of processes was still that associated with a markedly cold climate. Local relief had probably been rounded and smoothed by significant mass movement. For instance, the floor of the Eastern Depression would have been generally rather flat or hummocky, as opposed to the modern situation with a shallow basinal form and a developing thalweg. During drier seasons, very local movement of sands by wind contributed material which would later be caught up in such deposits as *Unit* UP5. However, as the cold waned a threshold was reached because of the permeable nature of the sediments and the physical isolation of the Head. Deprived of sufficient effective water, cryogenic processes would very quickly have ceased to produce major geological effects and aeolian processes would have taken over as the dominant sedimentary mode. This does not necessarily imply an absolutely drier climate, merely a reactivation of subsurface drainage consequent upon the degradation of ground ice. There is no evidence for the re-establishment of significant ground ice at any time after Late Devensian Zone Ia;

the cold of Late Devensian Zone III might have been extreme enough but it was not sustained long enough to reverse the local trend.

From early in the Late Devensian (Late Glacial) Interstadial up until the present day, wind has been the main depositional mechanism acting upon the local sediments of the Head, more or less irrespective (except perhaps with regard to rate) of the prevailing climate. At different points, the aeolian sands have been found to contain Late Upper Palaeolithic, Early Mesolithic, (scattered) Neolithic, and Bronze Age artefacts; aeolian sands overlie the Early Bronze Age barrow and the Late Bronze Age/Early Iron Age bank and ditch, whilst recent sand mobility is ubiquitous. Any break in the vegetation cover would lay bare incoherent sand, any closing in the vegetation cover would trap the sand once again. The vegetation and soil patterns have certainly changed many times during this period (see Chapters 2.2 and 2.3). However, the only condition which might have been able to shut off sand mobility, namely a really well established and dense woodland cover, would have had little chance to develop on top of the Head itself. Light soils, poor base (nutrient) status, the danger of edaphic drought, increasing salt input from the encroaching Flandrian sea, and the ever present wind would have limited the maximum size of trees and would have caused quite rapid turnover. Even if only as small patches, sand sources would have been continually uncovered by such processes as treefall, minor slope failure, natural burning, animal burrowing and, of course, various types of human interference.

Sedimentation was not uniform across the whole headland. Lower, more protected areas, and especially the Eastern Depression, would have been dominantly sites of deposition throughout most of this period. On the other hand, more exposed areas nearer the top of Warren Hill would have been subject to much greater point fluctuations between deposition and deflation; the importance of deflation grew as leaching of the topsoil intensified. This contrast is of great importance to the history of burial and exhumation of artefacts (see especially Chapter 3.1.6).

During the later prehistoric periods, human interference increased to levels that significantly modified the sedimentation patterns. At least localised clearance may have occurred as early as the Neolithic, space had to be found for the construction of the Early Bronze Age barrows, and more or less the whole Head appears to have been cleared by the beginning of the Iron Age (see Chapter 2.3.4). Open areas would have been very quickly scoured by wind deflation; it seems most likely that the major truncation at the top of *Unit* M3 in the Powell Mesolithic site was at least initiated in this way. Also, the combined and partially interrelated effects of human activity and the progression towards acidic podzolic soils allowed the build-up of organic matter in the topmost soil horizons; this reduced the permeability of the sediments and caused more surface drainage which, in turn, encouraged yet more organic build-up (see Chapter 2.2.2 and 2.3.3). In low lying areas, such as the Eastern Depression, true peats developed in places, associated with winding and constantly shifting drainage channels. Because the organics produced local catchments of low permeability, average rainfall infiltration rates would have been lowered so that concentrated and moving surface water would have been present for long enough to erode even the permeable sands at the base of the peat. Thus, tens of centimetres were removed from the top of the main sand body in the Late Upper Palaeolithic site. Even on the much drier flanks of Warren Hill, sheet erosion and rilling may have become significant, although this suggestion cannot now be tested because of the destruction of any wash apron around the base of the hill itself by recent ironstone quarrying. Again, this increased truncation effect is of the greatest relevance to the artefact taphonomy.

Erosion initiated, accelerated or totally created by man has continued to the present day. As a direct result, both Late Upper Palaeolithic and Mesolithic artefacts were first discovered by surface collection and the rescue rationale for the present project was established. However, if erosion continues at recent rates, it will not take very long for all primary archaeological occurrences on top of the Head to be utterly obliterated.

## 2.2 Late Devensian and Holocene soil formation

### 2.2.1  Materials and methods

At Hengistbury Head parent materials include sediments of various textures of the Bracklesham Beds (Eocene) and superficial deposits (gravels, sands and diamicts). For convenience, the Hengistbury study area is divided into the Eastern Depression (with the Late Upper Palaeolithic site, Fig. 2.1) where sediments have often been reworked from solifluucted head deposits, and Warren Hill (the Powell Mesolithic site) to the west where probable blown sands occur over superficial gravels. The area was examined by an auger survey and at quarry, gully and cliff sections. Four soil profiles were studied. These are, in the Eastern Depression, Profile 1 (Fig. 2.15 and Table 2.3) – the buried soil (and pollen profile) beneath a probable Late Bronze Age/Early Iron Age bank; Profile 2 (Fig. 2.16 and Table 2.4) – the Mace/Campbell Late Upper Palaeolithic site; and Profile 3 (Fig. 2.17 and Table 2.5) – the Transverse Quarry with its well-drained podzol on cryoturbated gravelly head; and on Warren Hill, Profile 4 (Fig. 2.18 and Table 2.6) – the Powell Mesolithic site.

Soils were described (cf. Hodgson 1974) and selectively sampled for micromorphology (cf. Avery and Bascomb 1974) and analyses of grain size, pH, organic carbon, iron, aluminium and nitrogen (C, Fe, Al and N data from Dr Peter Loveland, Soil Survey England and Wales, Rothamsted). Ten large (5 cm x 6–13 cm) thin sections prepared at the Institut National

2.15  *Bank and ditch feature, Eastern Depression: typical gley podzol beneath bank (Field Profile 1). Pollen sample column and thin sections A/B and C; buried H horizon dating to 3,350 ± 90 BP.*

Agronomique, Grignon, France, were described according to Bullock *et al.* (In press); Murphy et al. (1985) and Courty *et al.* 1989). Only the summarised data are presented here. For more detailed descriptions of the thin sections the reader is referred to Fiche 1. A3–12.

### 2.2.2  Eastern Depression (Late Upper Palaeolithic site)

*The Late Glacial:* The Late Upper Palaeolithic (12,500±1150 years BP) artefacts occur in the lower Ea and upper Bh horizons of the present day cover of (nodular) gley podzols (Table 2.4 and Fig. 2.16) developed in reworked Bracklesham Beds. The lowest deposits below the artefacts are mainly coarse (sandy loams, sands and gravels) and poorly sorted (Table 2.7, sample 24), and when seen in gully and quarry sections show evidence of cryoturbation. In the upper metre of the soil, however, later mixing and Flandrian soil

*Table 2.3  Profile 1: Bank and buried soil beneath the bank feature.*

Profile 1: (Fig. 2.15)

*Slope*: 6° South.
*Relief*: centre of low ground in the Eastern Depression c. 30 m from present-day cliff; both receiving and shedding site.
*Vegetation*: 'wet' *Callunetum*.
*Parent Material*: (mainly) fine and medium sands derived from the Eocene Beds (sands, clays and gravels), Tertiary.
*Altitude*: *c.* 14 m OD.
*Soil Type*: (buried) typical gley-podzol (Avery 1980).

Horizon, depth cm

*Bank*

| | |
|---|---|
| L.F.H.<br>5–0 | Wet Mor horizon; shallow litter of *Calluna* leaves and flower heads; includes c. 20% sand; many medium and abundant fine roots. |
| Ah<br>0–20 | Black to dark reddish brown (5YR 2.5/1–3/2) moderately weak fine and medium (bleached) sand; coarse angular blocky; few small stones (flints); very humose; many medium and fine roots; clear, irregular boundary. |
| Ea<br>20(24)–<br>43 | Discontinuous reddish brown (5YR 4/3) loose to weak structureless sand; few small flints; moderately humose; few fine roots; broken, irregular boundary. |
| Bhsg/Ah<br>(mixed<br>dump)<br>20(24) | Mixed; common black (5YR 2.5/1) coarse blocky, moderately weak, very humose Ah, associated with areas of common fine and medium roots; common very dark grey (5YR 3/1) weak, humose Bhs material, (possibly also stained Ea); few yellowish red (5YR 5/.6) moderately firm 'Bsg' nodules somewhat leached; at the base Ah material is present, the junction with the OGS possibly being a layer of inverted turves; sharp smooth boundary. |

*Old Ground Surface*

| | |
|---|---|
| bH<br>43–<br>44(46) | Dark reddish brown (5YR 3/3) weak Mor (5% sand); medium blocky, stone free; very humose ('peaty'); few fine roots; clear smooth boundary. |
| bAh<br>44(46)–<br>56 | Very dark grey (5YR 3/1) weak fine and medium sand; coarse blocky; few small flints; humose; very few fine roots; wavy boundary. |
| bEa Light<br>56–61 | Reddish brown (5YR 5/3) loose to weak structureless fine and medium sand (Table 2.1) with reddish brown (5YR 5/3) humic stains; few stones; no roots; clear, irregular boundary. |
| bBhs<br>61–<br>66(96) | Dark reddish grey (5YR 4/2) weak fine and medium loamy sand (Table 2.1); weakly massive; few small flints; moderately humose; clear very irregular (patches of 'clayey' involutions?) boundary. |
| bB(t)sg<br>66(96)–<br>106+ | Pinkish grey (7.5YR 6/2) sand and reddish yellow (7.5YR 7/8) sandy loam (bulk analysis as loamy sand; Table 2.1); weak; reddish yellow areas moderately plastic; massive/poorly developed medium prisms; clay coatings present; 'inclusions' of common small to very large flints; few pores; common 'old' medium roots with associated 'washed in' humus. |

development has obscured such features if they ever existed. Also the soil itself is better sorted comprising mainly fine and medium sand (Table 2.7, samples 6, 7 and 8) and lacking significant gravel. At depth the soil also includes patches of sandy loam associated with argillic features (Avery 1980) (Fiche 1.A14; Table 2.8).

2.16  *Late Upper Palaeolithic site: typical (nodular) gley podzol (Field Profile 2). Note the layer of recent sand and humic lenses by the trowel. The hole in the subsoil marks the position of the soil radioactivity measurements by gamma spectrometer.*

*Table 2.4  The Upper Palaeolithic site soil description.*

Profile 2: (Fig. 2.16)

*Section*: Mace-Campbell.
*Slope*: 4° South.
*Relief*: low ground in Eastern Depression c. 3–4 metres from present-day cliff; both receiving and shedding site.
*Vegetation*: 'wet' *Callunetum*.
*Parent Material*: (as Profile 1)
*Altitude*: *c.* 13 m OD.
*Soil Type*: Typical (nodular) gley-podzol.

Horizon, depth cm

Superficial cover of *Calluna* turf and 8 cm of bleached blown sand.

| | |
|---|---|
| Ah<br>0–7 | Dark reddish brown (5YR 2.5/2) and reddish grey (5YR 5/2) weak sand; medium angular blocky; few small stones (flints); humose; common fine and very fine roots; clear, wavy boundary. |
| Ea<br>7–20 | Reddish grey (5YR 5/2) very weak sand; structureless; few small flints; few fine roots; clear, wavy boundary. |
| Bhs<br>20–<br>46(55) | Mainly dark reddish brown (5YR 3/2) with patches of black (5YR 2.5/1) moderately weak sand; massive; few small flints; (few strong brown Bsg nodules at 30 cm depth); few fine roots; generally, clear irregular boundary. |
| B(t)sg<br>6(55sg)<br>–80 | Pale brown (10YR 6/3) and brownish yellow ) (10YR 6/8) weak sand (also areas of sandy loam); massive with weakly prismatic structure; few small flints; possible clay coatings in areas of finer soil. |

Early soil fabrics were identified at the well drained southern end of the Transverse Quarry (Profile 3; Fig. 2.17). These are specific periglacial features preserved where the base of the present day podzol meets the cryoturbated parent material. These features described in thin section (G) as silt and clay pans, caps and link cappings, are referred to elsewhere as 'silt droplets and cappings' because of their mode of origin (Romans *et al.* 1966; Romans and Robertson 1974 see thin section G). This silt and clay pan microfabric at a contemporary depth of 125 cm is very strong and continuously formed (Fiche 1.B2 & B3) and shows no sign of being disrupted by later periglacial activity (Romans pers. comm.). A survey of this fabric type in alpine and upland soils across the British Isles has shown that fabrics dating to the Pre-Boreal (Zone IV, Flandrian Ia) occur at increasingly higher altitudes and decreasing depth, with distance from the Scandinavian ice sheet (Romans and Robertson 1974). In addition, such fabric types of this date were only weakly and patchily formed in the southern periphery of the British Isles (e.g. Brecon Beacons) because the cold climate at this time was modified by maritime influences (Romans *et al.* 1980).

In short, the link cappings at Hengistbury Head are both too deep and too well formed to be Pre-Boreal in origin. Rather they seem to relate to the extreme desiccation of the soil through freezing under a continental climate, spring ice melting of the surface causing abrupt slaking and translocation of unsorted fine soil into the bone-dry subsoil. As the soil water was rapidly absorbed into the dry soil the transported load was suddenly deposited to form very sharp edged (top) and strong pans and cappings. Thus, these freeze-thaw features probably pre-date the Late Upper Palaeolithic occupation, occurring early in the Late Devensian Interstadial (Zones Ia, Ib and II), or possibly earlier in the Devensian (Romans pers. comm.).

The presence of these pans at the Transverse Quarry also shows that at this time the area was acting as an well-drained convex slope to Warren Hill, because these features do not form on low slope, poorly drained areas.

Romans and Robertson (1974) also suggest the general disruption or removal of these freeze-thaw fabrics by the effects of the intense cold conditions of Late Devensian Zone III. The preservation – intact – of these earlier freeze/thaw fabrics in the Transverse Quarry at Hengistbury Head indicate that these were protected by deep burial, mostly under successive solifluced layers. This interpretation in part stems from the analysis of Late Devensian freeze-thaw fabrics in subsoils at Chysauster, Cornwall (Macphail 1987b). Here earlier strongly formed Late Devensian silt pans had been fragmented by periglacial activity in Zone III, and a weakly developed silt pan and massive fabric of Zone IV date superimposed upon them. Such findings compare well with those of Romans and Robertson (1974 and Romans pers. comm.) for the British Isles as a whole.

2.17 *Transverse Quarry: truncated humo-ferric podzol covered by recent blown sand (Field Profile 3).*

As noted earlier the Late Upper Palaeolithic artefacts themselves occur in better sorted sediments (Table 2.7, sample 6,7,8) than those produced purely by solifluction (Table 2.7, sample 18). A continued accretion of the former deposits, probably by local aeolian activity (see Chapter 2.1.8) during the Late Devensian Interstadial may have to be envisaged to bury them deeply enough to survive at least since Zone IV, until the development of the depression threatened them. In fact, the subsoil microfabric at the Mace/Campbell site (Profile 2; Fig. 2.16) still shows relic continuous massive structure and silt and sand segregations (thin section D), but these are unfortunately not diagnostic of any particular Late Devensian period.

*The Early Flandrian:* The effects of Flandrian pedogenesis have also to be considered. For example, those moderately sorted sands associated with the Late Devensian period and Late Upper Palaeolithic occupation have also been influenced by soil formation later than the Pre-Boreal which would have been for instance responsible for the loss of any fine material,

*Table 2.5 Profile 3: Transverse Quarry soil description.*

Profile 3: (Fig. 2.17)

*Slope*: 2° North East.
*Relief*: gently sloping ground between Warren Hill and the Eastern Depression, *c*. 30 metres from present cliff.
*Vegetation*: 'dry' *Callunetum*.
*Parent Material*: Sands and gravels derived from the Eocene Beds.
*Altitude*: *c*. 1 8m OD.
*Soil Type*: humo-ferric podzol.

Horizon, depth cm

| | |
|---|---|
| L.F.H. | Highly rooted, black very humose; bleached sand. |
| Ah/Ea 0–51 | Dark grey (5YR 4/1) and light reddish brown (5YR 6/3) very weak sand; weakly blocky to structureless; few small flints; moderately humose; many medium and fine roots; clear, irregular boundary. |
| Ea2 51–70 | Reddish brown (5YR 5/4) moderately firm sand; structureless to massive; very few flints; low humus; rare medium roots; clear to sharp, irregular boundary. |
| Bh 70–74 | Very dark grey (5YR 3/1) firm sand; massive; many small to large flints; few medium roots; very humose; clear, irregular boundary. |
| Bhs 74– 97(105) | Dark reddish brown (5YR 3/3) very firm sand; massive; many small to large flints; rare roots; moderately humose; gradual, irregular boundary. |
| Bsx/Bx 97(105) –140 | Strong brown (7.5YR 4/6) firm sandy loam (Table 2.1); massive; many small to large flints; rare roots; becoming more brown (7.5YR 5/4) with depth; dark red (2.5YR 3/6) iron pans isolating greyish zones – convolutions and lenses. |
| C 140+ | Cryoturbated Pleistocene Head. |

especially clay, from the upper soil. Early pedogenic effects active even in the Late Glacial were decalcification, weathering and biological homogenisation (Catt 1979). In theory (Macphail 1987a, 335–336), with warmer conditions and the eventual establishment of a forest cover (see Scaife this Chapter 2.3), well-drained and poor Eocene sediments rapidly weather (erdefication; Conacher and Dalrymple 1977) to produce , at first a Bw horizon (Avery 1980; see Warren Hill for further evidence). Under the effects of organic leachate from the forest canopy, fine clay mobilised in the upper soil is translocated down profile into the Bt horizon (Duchaufour 1982; Fedoroff 1982). Clay translocation, but of a more coarse and dusty type, also continues if the forest is disturbed by human activity (Scaife and Macphail 1983; Macphail 1986). Micromorphological evidence at Profiles 1(C) and 2(D) in the Eastern Depression and at the Transverse Quarry (Profile 4, J and K) shows that Bw horizon formation and clay – including dusty clay – translocation occurred in the early Holocene, forming an argillic brown sand soil with a Bt horizon (Fiche 1.A14). These findings complement the pollen evidence (see Scaife this volume) of a postglacial deciduous forest which was extant until the later Flandrian.

Although water tables at this time were perhaps lower (see below) than at present, it is believed that the soils were not droughty because of the underlying loamy sands maintaining a perched water table, as now. The micromorphological evidence may also suggest rather poor root penetration into the subsoil when the soil was a brown sand. Thus the site has a long history of imperfect soil drainage to the present, which indicates that contemporary measurements of soil moisture for thermoluminescence dating on the site (see Fig. 2.16) may accurately reflect past soil water conditions, although surface runoff has probably accelerated as the cliff encroached.

*The Late Flandrian:* There is ample field and micromorphological evidence of the progressive leaching and acidification (leading to podzolisation) of the soils of the Eastern Depression during this period. This is provided by the buried soil (Profile 1) beneath the Bank feature; by the present day soil (Profile 2) 20–25 metres downslope at the Late Upper Palaeolithic site, with which it is locally compared; and by the freely draining podzol at the Transverse Quarry (Profile 3). These profiles have already been used to describe early Flandrian soil formation from their relic microfabrics. Attempts to date later pedogenic and environmental events at Hengistbury Head rest on two c14 dates. One from the H(Oh) horizon from the buried soil (Profile 1), and one from the cemented Bhs horizon of a modern podzol (Profile 3).

At the Bank and Ditch feature, which runs North/South across the Head, more than 40 cm of overburden, comprising dumped soil derived from a gleyed podzol (similar to the buried soil and those now locally present), buries a gleyed podzol with a 2–3 cm thick H horizon. This buried Mor humus horizon, which was sampled for radiocarbon dating, was well sealed by possible turves overlain by subsoil overburden, and was thus unlikely to be contaminated by more recent organic matter. We know from the pollen column (see Fig. 2.15; and see Scaife Chapter 2.3) and from the microfabric analysis (Fiche 1.A13) that the buried soil formed under oak woodland and that the H horizon represents a mainly *vertical* accumulation of (coprolitic) Mor humus, little affected by biological activity, similar in some ways to a peat (Fiche 1.A3–13 Moderate ultra violet light fluorescence also indicates good preservation of pollen. Therefore, when interpreting the radiocarbon date the Mor humus horizon accumulation was regarded first as a fossil deposit, and secondly generally free of residual or older organic matter (Guillet 1982; Macphail 1987a, 360). Thus the date of 3350±90 BP (*c*. 1400 BC uncalibrated) (HAR – 6186) is interpreted as suggesting that the Bank and Ditch feature was constructed in Late Bronze Age/Early Iron Age times. Other evidence presented below tends to support this conjecture.

Scaife (Chapter 2.3.4) suggests from his two pollen profiles (one from the buried soil, the other from a nearby shallow valley-head peat) that Bronze Age forest clearances accelerated peat formation in this headward sapping valley, an erosion process which was active until later coastal cliff recession reduced the catchment. Decrease of evapotranspiration after primary clearance not only may have encouraged peat formation, a phenomenon common to southern English mires through anthropogenic disturbance (Moore and Wilmott 1976), but also raised the already high (see above) water table sufficiently to produce progressive surface erosion of the Eastern Depression. This mechanism may account for the present lack of Late Upper Palaeolithic finds east of the present site, along a zone close to the thalweg.

In addition to shallow peat formation, hydromorphism is reflected in the morphology of the podzols through the leaching of microfabrics and the deposition of (nodular) amorphous iron (Fiche 1.A14; Table 2.8, Profiles 1 and 2). Pollen shows that woodland, dominated by oak, regenerated and was extant up to the construction of the bank. Since the bank buries a typical gley podzol (Profile 1) and is itself composed of dumped soil from such a podzol (nodular Bsg horizon material being present in the overburden) it indicates that podzolisation had occurred under an oak woodland cover, by the date suggested earlier. Similar instances of podzols formed under an oak cover, without a history of heath, can be cited from Woodhall Spa, Lincolnshire, by the Atlantic period (Valentine and Dalrymple 1975), from Black Down, Dorset, by the Bronze Age (Dimbleby in Thompson and Ashbee 1957), from Caesar's Camp, Keston, Kent, by the Iron Age (Dimbleby 1961) and from the New Forest, by the present (Dimbleby and Gill 1955). The Mean Residence Time (MRT) date of 1,700±90 BP (HAR-6185) obtained from a Bhs horizon at Hengistbury Head possibly indicates podzolisation by the later Bronze Age, in contrast to earlier dates similarly obtained from podzols influenced by Mesolithic (Scaife and Macphail 1983) and Neolithic (Perrin *et al.* 1964) activities. Woodland regeneration at Hengistbury, however, would have been aided by a lack of droughtiness, of the type which affects many lowland heaths.

Oak woodland on poor parent materials produces an acid organic leachate which progressively acidifies soils, which at Hengistbury were already being leached of cations and clay whilst still argillic soils. Decreasing pH caused the disappearance of earthworms and irreversible soil acidification, further acidifying the oak woodland leachate and initiating the podzol process (Dimbleby 1962). Clay is actively destroyed by acidity in the upper soil as organic chelates mobilise and translocate sesquioxides (Al and Fe) downprofile (de Coninck 1980; Duchaufour 1982; Mokma and Buurman 1982). Organic matter is also translocated downprofile into the Bh horizon, eventually leading to the development of humic Ah, bleached Ea and dark brown Bh and Bs horizons typical of podzols.

We can compare the buried Late Bronze Age/Early Iron Age podzol formed under oak woodland, with the nearby present day podzol (Profile 2). The former can be regarded as a well-sealed buried soil, even whilst it is

likely that its subsoil has continued to be influenced by hydromorphic processes. In contrast, the latter, although now truncated and buried by bleached sand had however continued to develop under *Calluna* probably until the 20th century disturbances noted by Collcutt (Chapter 2.1).

Both gley podzols are severely leached (Table 2.8, Nos 1–13) but, because of hydromorphic effects, they have illuvial horizons only weakly enriched in organic carbon and sesquioxides. The large quantities of amorphous nodular iron seen in the soil profile and in thin section (D) are associated with concentrations of 'residual non-podzolic' (Bascomb 1968) dithionite extractable iron. Relic argillic features (C and D) have also been influenced by podzolic leaching and hydromorphic depletion (Fiche 1.A14). Both profiles contain quantities of iron in their Ah horizons (Table 2.8, samples 4, 5 and 6) which is linked to their original surface organic matter (Macphail 1979; Mokma and Buurman 1982). However, Profile 1 beneath the bank contains significantly greater amounts of aluminium, which is presumably still mobile because of anaerobic burial (Scaife and Macphail 1983). This is possibly as a result of the oak woodland raw humus being richer in aluminium than that under *Calluna* Mor (as at Profile 2) which has existed across the headland since the bank construction (Scaife Chapter 2.3.4). Other differences between the character of Mor humus developed under oak woodland and under *Calluna* were noted in thin section. Ah horizons developed under *Calluna* have very low levels of biological activity (Duchaufour 1982) and this is reflected in both well-drained and wet buried Ah horizons from, for example, the Experimental Earthwork at Wareham, Dorset and West Heath, Sussex (Scaife and Macphail 1983; Fisher and Macphail 1985). At Hengistbury Head, the wet H and Ah horizons (sample A and B) developed under oak woodland are moderately perforated by biopores (Fiche 1.A13), possibly because soil conditions under oak were less acid than under heath (Simmons and Tooley 1981). This difference in pH is not clear at Hengistbury Head, although at the Iron Age Caesar's Camp, Keston in Kent, the buried podzol which formed under oak woodland (Dimbleby 1962) has a generally higher pH and a possibly more biologically worked Ah horizon than the overlying podzol formed under *Calluna* on the rampart (Cornwall 1958; Macphail 1985).

Examination of the microfabric of the Hengistbury H and Ah horizons by Ultra Violet Light showed almost all the organic matter to be amorphous and although derived from coprogenic residues (as 'mobile' organic matter) actual excrements are generally absent, hence it is an H layer rather than an F layer. The moderate fluorescence of the layer apparently relates to the presence of much residual pollen and whereas most were coated by organic precipitates some individuals, including oak (Fiche 1.A13) and the spore *Polypodium*, showed up clearly (Van Vliet *et al.* 1983). The age character of buried organic matter has been commonly described (Babel 1975; Fisher and Macphail 1985; Macphail 1985), and shows that the biopores at Hengistbury were contemporary with the oak woodland.

As a comparison with the gley podzols formed in the centre of the Eastern Depression we can describe the well-drained, well developed humo-ferric podzol present in the nearby Transverse Quarry (Profile 3). Here, strongly formed illuvial Bh and Bhs horizons (Table 2.8, samples 15 and 16); thin sections E and F) have developed under a present cover of *Calluna*. This profile is a type P (or Plateau) humo-ferric podzol (Macphail 1979, 1983a), the best expressed podzol at Hengistbury Head, formed by dominant vertical eluviation and illuviation. Thus, this profile was the best choice for a radiocarbon assay of illuvial organic matter in Bh horizons as a means of dating the onset of podzolisation on the heath (Perrin *et al.* 1964; Guillet 1982). In theory a Mean Residence Time (MRT) date (which differs from the 'fossil' date obtained from Profile 1) gained by radiocarbon dating of a Bh horizon occurs as a result of a supposedly constant input of poorly biodegradable organic matter, especially under acidophilic heathland. Bh horizons formed beneath woodland, which tend to give rather younger dates in Righi and Guillet (1977) and de Coninck (1980), have shown that the oldest dates occur in cemented monomorphic fabrics. Thus, the Bhs horizon (thin section F; Fiche 1.B1) was selected for analysis although it in fact contained less organic matter than the overlying Bh horizon. For the analysis the organic matter was not chemically fractionated, and so the MRT date must be regarded as an average of all the organic components (Guillet 1982).

The MRT date of 1,700±90 BP (HAR-6185) was obtained from the Bhs horizon at Profile 3. This date may be interpreted as suggesting that major podzolisation at Hengistbury Head began in the Late Bronze Age, about the same time as on many other heathlands in Southern Britain (Cornwall 1958; Dimbleby 1962; Macphail 1987a). For example, it can be compared with MRT dates of 3,770 BP (Scaife and Macphail 1983) and 1,580–2,800 BP (Perrin *et al.* 1964) for Bh horizons at heathland sites associated with known Mesolithic and Neolithic woodland disturbances, respectively. At West Heath, Sussex, the MRT date was associated with the early appearance of *Calluna* (Scaife and Macphail 1983) and it may be that at Hengistbury this 'short' date of *c.* 1,700 BP may relate to *Calluna* coming in later, perhaps in the Late Bronze Age. Guillet (1982), for example, found in the Vosges (France), that a series of well developed podzols produced a correlation between the dates of the appearance of *Calluna* (established by palynology) and the age of organic matter in the Bh horizons of these profiles, thereby suggesting that the MRT 'apparent ages' are about half that of the establishment of heathlands responsible for the formation of podzols. This in turn may suggest that the construction of the bank and ditch feature at Hengistbury, which has an interpreted Late Bronze

Age/Early Iron Age date, led to final woodland clearance and the establishment of *Calluna* heath and this continued the podzolisation already begun under the oak woodland cover, but produced a better developed and less biodegradable Bh horizon (Guillet 1982). In terms of its archaeological significance, the bank and ditch feature at Hengistbury can probably be regarded as a land boundary, typical of the Bronze Age (Balaam *et al.* 1982).

More recently, surface disturbance of the heathland, probably due in part to 19th century ironstone quarrying and later gunnery practice in World War II, have caused shallow erosional features and shallow buried humic horizons which are unrelated to the prehistoric archaeology of the Headland (Macphail 1982).

### 2.2.3 *Warren Hill (Powell Mesolithic site)*

The parent material at Profile 4, in which the Powell Mesolithic artefacts occurs (in the Ea2 horizon), is less coarse (i.e. less medium sand) and better sorted than in the Eastern Depression. On Warren Hill these sands often occur over superficial gravels which themselves rest on Bracklesham Beds deposits. However, at the Mesolithic site the sands directly overlie the Tertiary series, and are dominated by very fine and fine sands (Table 2.7, samples 21-23; thin sections I and J) suggesting these have a windblown origin, presumably relating at least in part to Late Glacial conditions (Catt 1979). Although some fine material in the deeply underlying B(t)sg horizon (Table 2.7, sample 24; thin section K; Fiche 1.B2–3) is illuvial, the pre-soil parent material may still only have contained little silt and clay. Such a wind sorted and deposited parent material was no doubt easily disturbed during the Mesolithic occupation (TL dated to 9,950±950 BP), although the degree of soil development in a period ranging from the Pre-Boreal to the Boreal must be conjectural. Certainly the artefacts appear still to be in the upper part of the soil, mainly in the Ea2 horizon, although also occurring throughout the overlying 60 cm of Ea1 and Ah/Ea horizon material which can be rather more poorly sorted (Table 2.7 samples 19–20; thin section H; Fiche 1.B4–5).

*Flandrian soil formation:* A soil history similar to that of the Eastern Depression can be described from Warren Hill, but in more detail because the sub-soil levels at the Powell Mesolithic site (Profile 4) have been much less affected by podzolic and hydromorphic depletion. The present day soil is a humo-ferric podzol as demonstrated by soil ignition and other analyses (Table 2.8 samples 19–24); thin sections H-K; Fiche 1.B5). In addition, its subsoil horizons show traits of an earlier brown soil origin (Fiche 1.B6). Grain size (Table 2.7) and microfabric analyses (K) suggest that most of the clay that is present in the subsoil is argillic (Avery 1980). It coats sand size skeletal grains including weathered glauconite. A possible sequence of a Bw microaggregate (erde) fabric, succeeded by primary

2.18 *Powell Mesolithic site: (Field Profile 4). The trowel marks the top of the dark grey Ah and Ea horizons. The Mesolithic artefacts are concentrated near the top of the lighter (pinkish) grey Ea2 horizon.*

*Table 2.6 The Powell Mesolithic site soil description.*

Profile 4: (Fig. 2.18)

*Slope*: 5° South.
*Relief*: plateau edge area of Warren Hill, *c.* 3 metres from present-day cliff; mainly shedding site.
*Vegetation*: 'dry' *Callunetum*.
*Parent Material*: very fine and fine sands, derived from Eocene Beds.
*Altitude*: *c.* 30 m OD.
*Soil Type*: humo-ferric podzol.

Horizon, depth cm

30–40 cm of 'recent' moderately humic 'grey' blown sand, with few thin 'turf' lines.

| | |
|---|---|
| Ah & Ea 0–23(25) | Very dark grey (5YR 3/1) moderately weak very fine and fine sand (Table 2.1); generally structureless; few small and medium flints; moderately humic; rootlets; gradual irregular boundary. |
| Ea1 23(25) –58 | Mainly pinkish grey (5YR 7/2) with few very dark grey (5YR 3/1) and very few reddish brown (5YR 4/4) moderately weak sand (Table 2.1); structureless; stone-free in upper part, becoming moderately stony with medium flints; very low humus; gradual, irregular boundary. |
| Ea2 58– 69(82) | Pinkish grey (5YR 7/2) loose very fine and fine sand (Table 2.1); stone-free, contains (50%) coarse very firm Bh mottles; broken, clear boundary. |
| Bh 69–82 | Dark reddish brown (5YR 2.3/2) very firm sand (as Ea2); massive; very humose; clear, irregular boundary. |
| Bhs 82–102 | Reddish grey (5YR 5/2) in upper part, and yellowish red (5YR 4/6) very firm sand; massive; stone-free; repeating thin Bh pans; gradual and clear, irregular boundary. |
| Btsg 102– 125+ | Mainly light yellowish brown (10YR 6/4) moderately firm sand with strong brown (7.5YR 5/8) firm sandy loam (both bulked as loamy sand, Table 2.1), and pinkish grey (7.5YR 7/2) 'clay' bands; massive/weakly developed medium prisms; possible old roots; clay coatings present in finer areas. |

limpid clay translocation and later dusty clay translocation can be recognised. This fabric, representing brown sand/brown argillic sand soil formation, has been preserved from podzolic leaching by depth (1 m) and also by later ferruginous cementation of the soil peds relic of this early brown soil phase.

Elsewhere, limpid clay followed by dusty clay illuviation has been tentatively associated with early Mesolithic woodland disturbance, for example at Selmeston, Sussex (Scaife and Macphail 1983) and at High Rocks, Kent (Macphail *et al.* 1987). It is therefore a possibility that, by disturbing the early Flandrian forest, the Mesolithic occupation at Warren Hill produced the fabric types described above. Alternatively, these could relate to Late Bronze Age clearances identified in the pollen record (Scaife Chapter 2.3.5 and pers. comm.).

At a number of Mesolithic sites in Southern England it has been conjectured that human interference on poor soils produced localised acidification and podzolisation, for example, at the Sussex sites of Iping Common (Keef *et al.* 1965) and West Heath (Scaife and Macphail 1983). These cases may therefore suggest that at Hengistbury Head localised podzolisation may have occurred on poor, coarse substrates, such as blown sand, although at Warren Hill there is no positive data to suggest this. On the other hand evidence from the Eastern Depression clearly indicates a probable Bronze Age date for the general podzolisation of the Headland.

### 2.2.4 *Soil and vegetational history of the headland*

Although well south of the Devensian ice sheet the superficial deposits and Bracklesham Beds sediments at Hengistbury Head were strongly affected by periglacial conditions, mixing original sedimentary layers and producing a number of cryoturbated features including involutions and ice wedges, typical of those seen over a wide area of South-East England (Catt 1979). The soils in which the prehistoric artefacts occur were however further reworked during the Late Glacial, with a trend towards better sorting of the upper sediments. For example, the well-drained conditions on the eastern slopes of Warren Hill and the Powell Mesolithic site allowed strongly formed and continuous clay and silt link cappings (silt droplet fabric; Romans *et al.* 1966, Romans and Robertson 1974) to develop under freeze-thaw conditions during the Late Devensian Interstadial (Zones 1b, Ic and II). Layering of this fabric could also relate to regular successive solifluction episodes. Similar fabrics of this date, but often reworked by later Zone III and Flandrian pedogenesis have been noted across the British Isles (Romans and Robertson 1974). The sands of the Late Upper Palaeolithic occupation are better sorted than the purely soliflucted material, probably by local wind sorting (Collcutt pers. comm. and Chapter 2.1.8).

As the freeze-thaw microfabrics are so well preserved by later soil burial from reworking by the harsh conditions of Zone III it is possible that the artefacts deposited by Late Upper Palaeolithic man at a level only now exposed by the development of the Eastern Depression, were similarly buried and little disturbed.

The Powell Mesolithic flints at Warren Hill occur in very well sorted sands containing over 50% very fine sand and indicate a probable windblown origin. Such a deposit could relate to aeolian activity under periglacial conditions (Catt 1979) at this site possibly during Zone III/Zone IV. The broad dating of the Mesolithic artefacts suggests the site may have been occupied at any time within Pre-Boreal or Boreal times, when such windblown sediments were undergoing primary pedogenesis in the form of decalcification and weathering (Ball 1975; Macphail 1987a), allowing raw mineral soils to develop into brown soils. Deep sub-soil horizons at the site below the present day podzol contain microfabric evidence of Bw and Bt horizon (Avery 1980) formation of brown sands (Dalrymple 1962; Conacher and Dalrymple 1977) and argillic brown sands (*Sol lessivé*, Fedoroff 1982). In addition, the concentration of flint artefacts in the Ea2 horizon, besides relating to a possible deflation surface (lag deposit), may have occurred through earthworm working while the soil was still brown, thus necessarily pre-dating acidification. Other examples of pre-podzol earthworm working can be cited from Mesolithic sites at Oakhanger, Hampshire (Rankine and Dimbleby 1960), West Heath, Sussex (Drewett 1976) and the Neolithic site of Rackham, Sussex (Dimbleby and Bradley 1975). At Hengistbury Head, then, perhaps the soil acidification which occurred under oak woodland was initiated by the known primary Bronze Age clearance.

In the Eastern Depression it is known that oak woodland regenerated at the same time as the area was being progressively eroded by a larger valley (now removed by coastal cliff recession) advancing headwards and upslope. It is possible the peat in this valley head may have formed during the Atlantic period (Scaife 2.3.4). While peat growth may have been encouraged by the wet climate, its development was no doubt accelerated by primary forest clearance in the Bronze Age which further raised the water table in this already imperfectly drained area. Contemporary surface water flow may even have accelerated the erosion of this depression removing Late Upper Palaeolithic artefacts upslope and east of the present site. This area is today notably devoid of any occupation evidence.

| Dates kyr BP | Pollen Zones | | Soils | Archaeology |
|---|---|---|---|---|
| Late Devensian | I | a b | Solifluction & Freeze-thaw soil formation | |
| | | c | | Late Upper Palaeolithic occupation |
| 11.8 | | | | |
| | II | | "Sedimentary" burial of Zone I/II surfaces | |
| 11.0 | | | | |
| | III | | ?Blown sand deposition across headland | |
| 10.0 | | | | |
| | IV | | Primary soil formation | Mesolithic occupation |
| 9.6 | | | | |
| | V | | Brown sand & argillic b.s. soil formation under developing forest | |
| | VI | | | |
| | VII | | ? Forest clearance, increased surface soil wetness (East Depression). Peat initiation. | |
| | VIII | | Progressive soil acidification —— Podzolisation under Oak woodland regeneration. | Neolithic/Bronze Age artefacts |
| | | | Final woodland clearance; creation of *Calluna* heath; podzolisation continues. | Late Bronze Age/ Early Iron Age Bank & ditch |

Continuing poor drainage and increasing acidity under the oak woodland cover produced gley soils in the Eastern Depression. The inferred history of development of the Hengistbury soils and flora is presented in Figure 2.19.

## 2.3    The vegetational history

### 2.3.1    *Introduction*

We are fortunate that Central Southern England now has a substantial corpus of data on Late Devensian and Flandrian vegetational and environmental changes. This is largely due to the earlier pollen works of Seagrief at Wareham in Dorset, Nursling in Hampshire (Seagrief 1959) and Cranes Moor, Hampshire (Seagrief 1960). More recent analyses are those of Haskins (1978) in the Poole Harbour and Wareham region of Dorset; Scaife (1980) in the Isle of Wight; and Waton (1982a, 1982b) across the southern counties. From these studies it is possible to obtain a good insight into the likely environments of Hengistbury Head during the Late Devensian (Zones I-III) and Early Flandrian (I) when the headland was occupied during the Late Upper Palaeolithic and succeeding Mesolithic periods. Site specific data for Hengistbury relates only to the later prehistoric periods (Flandrian III). It relies upon two new pollen analyses of the peats in the Eastern Depression (Fig. 2.1) and of a palaeosol (buried land surface) underlying a field bank boundary in the same depression, which cuts across part of the Late Upper Palaeolithic site. In the absence of direct evidence for the earlier periods at Hengistbury I have summarised where possible the available environmental evidence for the Late Devensian and Early Flandrian based on various locations in the Hampshire Basin and surrounding areas. In some instances these are only a few kilometres from the archaeological sites and may give a fairly reliable indication of the contemporary environment.

One other possible source of pollen data, the analyses of Campbell (1977) from samples taken within the Late Upper Palaeolithic site, remains highly problematic. The following points give cause for concern:

(1) The contexts sampled by Campbell show very different histories of oxidation and acidity, and thus of preservation potential.

(2) The identification of certain taxa (e.g. *Betula nana*) reported by Campbell might be difficult to accept given the techniques he was using.

(3) Campbell's diagram is a composite deduced from horizontally dispersed contexts in no demonstrable stratigraphic sequence. In addition, the one surviving context, upon which Campbell based his reconstruction of the whole of the Holocene, appears to Barton and Collcutt to be a major tree-fall feature; (cf. Fig. 2.4).

(4) Data presented in this section and in Chapter 3 suggests that many of the contexts sampled by Campbell would have been subjected to strong biotic homogenisation.

Given these difficulties, I am unable to integrate my own data and interpretation of the site with Campbell's pollen results, and the latter will not be discussed further here.

### 2.3.2 *Late Devensian background*

This period which begins around 13,000 BP includes the main period of the Late Upper Palaeolithic occupation on the Headland. Organic, waterlogged sediments suitable for pollen analysis spanning this time are rare in southern England. Perhaps the best insight into the region's vegetational characteristics comes from the Lea Valley plant beds, Hertfordshire (Allison *et al.* 1952; Reid 1949; Reid and Chandler 1923) and from Colney Heath, also in Hertfordshire (Godwin 1964). The former have radiocarbon dates attributable to the Pleniglacial B (full glacial) at 28,000±1500 BP. The latter has been dated to 13,560±210 BP and thus within the Late-Devensian proper. These sites show a remarkably similar floristic component with a predominance of cold tolerant heliophytes of arctic and sub-alpine character and a marked sparsity or absence of trees. At

West Drayton, Middlesex, comparable results have been forthcoming from plant-bearing levels within the Colne floodplain (Gibbard and Hall 1982). Although radiocarbon dates of 11,230±120 BP and 13,405±170 BP from these levels suggest the possibility of interstadial conditions, the macrobotanical evidence indicates otherwise. Instead the absence of birch woodland and the presence of cold tolerant herbs illustrates once again that the environment at this time was one of more open herbaceous vegetation. Outside the Thames valley and its tributaries, data pertaining to the Late-Devensian are few. Tentative results obtained from pollen from Brook, Kent (Lambert, in Kerney *et al.* 1964) show that similar open conditions existed during this period with only small quantities of tree pollen.

Slightly better evidence for the Zone II Allerød Interstadial (*c.* 12,000–11,000 BP) has been obtained from closer to Hengistbury at Morden 'A' in Poole Harbour (Haskins 1978) and from Gatcombe Withy Bed and Munsley Bog, Isle of Wight (Scaife 1980, 1982). Analyses of the two Isle of Wight sites (Scaife 1980, 1982) show a rich and varied heliophilous herbaceous component and indicate environments of open woodland character. Seagrief and Haskins argue from the presence of herbaceous plants that similar conditions prevailed in Hampshire and Dorset (Scaife 1980, 1982) at this time. Seagrief (1959), Seagrief and Godwin (1960), Haskins (1978) and Scaife (1980) all record that Betula woodland was growing in the region from the Allerød onwards. The relatively greater percentages of both *Pinus* and *Betula* in these areas may in part be a function of the earlier pollen diagrams being calculated as a percentage of arboreal pollen rather than the more representative total land pollen. It may be argued therefore that the Allerød shows the presence of open *Betula* woodland in S. Britain (identified by Seagrief (1956) as *Betula pendula* from macroscopic fossil remains). *Pinus* seems unlikely to have been widely present at any Southern British site during the Late Devensian. Its appearance in small percentages may be explained either by highly localised and sporadic pine stands or, as seems more likely, by long distance wind dispersal.

Marked changes in the flora of southern England occur at the beginning of Zone III. In spite of certain problems in reconstructing whole plant communities from pollen evidence (Moore 1980), it is possible to recognise a number of plant community types which were present during the Younger Dryas (Zone III) on the Isle of Wight (Scaife 1980, 1982, 1987). They include five basic types: A) Shrub communities, composed of *Juniperus*, ericoid taxa, *Betula nana* and *Hippophaë rhamnoides;* B) Short turf communities, with *Helianthemum* and *Dryas octopetala* which are characteristic indicators and are typical of those communities growing today in Upper Teesdale, in the North of England. C) Tall herb communities; in moister environments these are evidenced by the characteristic taxa *Thalictrum, Sanguisorba officinalis, Filipendula, Polygonum bistorta* type (including *P.*

*viviparum*), *Polemonium caeruleum*, *Valeriana*, *Scabiosa*, *Succisa*, and *Trollius europaeus*. D) Disturbed soils; intense periglacial activity and resulting soil instability are reflected by the presence of *Chenopodium* type (including *Atriplex*), *Polygonum convolvulus*, *Plantago major* and *Artemisia* species. E) Wetter topographic situations of valley fen and mire would have supported sedge and *Sphagnum* communities, whilst more eutrophic conditions of spring flushes would have contained floristically rich reed swamps.

On the basis of this evidence it can be suggested that in S Britain this period was harsher climatically than previously postulated. This is also expressed in beetle studies which have shown that the rapidly declining temperatures in Zone III annihilated the earlier, more thermophilous elements of the Zone II fauna (Osborne 1971, 1972, 1974). It may be significant that none of the occupation evidence from Hengistbury dates from this period. Indeed, this observation can be extended to other parts of the region where the more or less total absence of archaeological evidence from well-dated Zone III contexts may be linked to the colder climatic conditions (but see Barton 1989).

### 2.3.3 Flandrian Ia-Ic background (Pre-Boreal/sub-Boreal, Godwin's pollen zones IV-VI)

Rapidly rising temperatures at 10,000 BP initiated the successional rise to dominance of the Flandrian forest. The period from 10,000–7,500 BP, within which the Hengistbury Mesolithic settlement occurs, is one of dynamic vegetational change throughout Western Europe. Initially, pollen evidence suggested that rising temperatures in the early Postglacial period saw the gradual development of woodland elements in response. Coleopteran analyses, however, demonstrate that the rise in mean annual temperatures may have occurred very rapidly shortly after 10,000 BP (Osborne 1974), reaching fully temperate conditions similar to those of today by about 9,800 BP (Atkinson *et al.* 1987). Distinct vegetational changes evidenced from central southern England (Seagrief 1959; Seagrief and Godwin 1960, Haskins 1978, Scaife 1980, 1982, Kerney *et al.* 1980) therefore reflect a complex response of plant communities to changing environmental conditions and especially to competition and dispersal factors, and, maturation of soils. During this rise to dominance of arboreal elements can be seen a diminution of those herbaceous plant communities referred to above.

The commencement of Flandrian temperature amelioration is marked in the first instance by the expansion of *Juniperus* representing a transitional period of dynamic vegetation between the open vegetation of the Late Devensian and the first appearance of true pioneer *Betula* woodland. The early rise in juniper has been evidenced from the Isle of Wight (Scaife 1980, 1982, 1987), Poole Harbour (Haskins 1978) and Surrey (Carpenter and Woodcock 1981); from this it can be

shown that mean July temperatures of greater than 12° Celsius had been reached by 9,970±50 BP (SRR–1433: Scaife 1980, 1982). Subsequent to the *Juniperus* expansion, *Betula* rapidly becomes the dominant woodland element in the Preboreal (Flandrian Ia (FIa) = Godwin's pollen zone IV). *Pinus* pollen values also increase in the immediately post-*Juniperus* stage showing sustained growth in the region, as opposed to sporadic appearances which might be due to long distance transportation.

The Powell Mesolithic site at Hengistbury dates to the first part of the 10th millennium BP and, judging by the mean date of *c.* 9,750 BP, falls within this early phase of *Betula* dominance. By FIb (Godwin's pollen zone V), *Pinus* becomes widespread in southern England (Haskins 1978; Scaife 1980), ousting birch woodland in most areas. Although the spread of pine is the most outstanding feature of the early Boreal, local continuation of birch is recorded in some pollen diagrams (Haskins 1978). The massive spread of *Corylus* throughout Britain at this time is also an event widely recognised and with *Pinus* is regarded as synonymous with the true Boreal forest expansion. From numerous radiocarbon dates now available, a markedly non-synchronous expansion of *Corylus* across Britain is indicated (Smith and Pilcher 1973). This is thought to be due to differing refugia providing sources for its migration. In the Hampshire basin a relatively early date for its growth is apparent, after which it maintained its importance initially with *Betula* and *Pinus* and subsequently with *Quercus* and *Ulmus* (in FIc = Godwin's pollen zone VI)

### 2.3.4 Palynological results from the Eastern Depression

All the results presented here derive from samples taken in the Eastern Depression (Fig. 2.1). This covers an area of about one hectare at the southeastern end of the headland, forming an elongate, U-shaped basin which runs out to the cliff-edge. Apart from sands the depression contains a superficial deposit of black highly humified and structureless peat which is in places 65 cm deep. Two areas of relevance to this study are 1) the deeper parts of the depression itself, closest to the cliff-edge, which contain the thickest peat, and 2) an artificial bank and ditch feature of later prehistoric age, the latter of which is infilled with a highly humified, structureless peat deposit. The profiles from these locations have been designated Hengistbury 1 and Hengistbury 2 respectively.

It is thought likely that the Eastern Depression forms the head of a truncated dry stream valley, once a tributary of the Solent river system (Everard 1954; Mace 1959; Wooldridge and Linton 1933). Today, the depression runs out to a low sea-cliff at 14 m OD which is unstable due to active coastal erosion. At what stage it became occupied by a valley/topogenous mire is not known but similar peat-filled depressions are found on the SW coast of the Isle of Wight, where their fossilised character has long been realised (Clifford 1936; White 1921) and where a possible Atlantic age for the peats can be inferred (Clifford *op. cit.*; Scaife 1980 and unpublished data).

The Depression now contains a relatively dry heathland flora although some *Erica tetralix, Molinia* and *Juncus spp.* remain from what must once have been a damper, wet heath community. This fact is evidenced in the fossil pollen record which includes a number of taxa of damp ground and mire. This record includes that of *Radiola linoides*, a rare but characteristic plant of wet sandy heaths and pond margins. It is thought that truncation and reduction of the valley mire on the south side by coastal erosion may have been responsible for this subsequent dehydration.

### (1) *The central Eastern Depression*

During the excavation season of 1983, test pits were dug throughout the area of the Eastern Depression as part of the archaeological survey. One of these pits, east of the bank and ditch feature, was selected for pollen analysis and expanded so that a continuous sequence of samples at 4 cm intervals could be obtained. Samples were prepared using standard techniques for the extraction of sub-fossil pollen and spores (see 1.A14). The results of the analysis are presented in diagrammatic form (Fig. 2.20) with pollen calculated as a percentage of the arboreal pollen sum and herbs as a percentage of this sum. Spores are shown as a percentage of total pollen plus spores. A number of changes in the stratified pollen record are evident and have been designated as local pollen assemblage zones (HH: 1–3). These are given from the base at 62 cm upwards to the contemporary land surface. The pollen zones and stratigraphic changes are described and discussed below:

*HH: 1 62–53 cm.* Characterised by relatively high values of the pollen of *Ulmus, Tilia, Fraxinus,* and Gramineae and spores of *Dryopteris* type, *Pteridium aquilinum* and *Polypodium.* The zone is dominated by high values of *Quercus* (80%), *Alnus* (75%), *Betula* (15%) and *Corylus* type (37%) (Not relative percentages). Also noted are small quantities of *Erica, Calluna, Filipendula* and a peak in *Rumex.*

*Commentary:* It is apparent that the environment was locally dominated by *Quercus* and *Alnus*, and it is likely that the latter was growing in the wetter areas of the depression. Low Cyperaceae percentages and the presence of *Alnus* suggest that the deposit accumulated in a carr woodland environment with fringing woodlands comprising *Quercus* and *Corylus*. Other arboreal elements probably only occurred in small numbers or, as is quite likely, the pollen may be of allochthonous origin. The high percentages of spores may be due to differential preservation in the basal mineral sediments but the well-preserved nature of the pollen suggests that Sporophytes were an important element of the vegetation at this time. Dating of these basal sediments

is problematic (see below), since the peats, being highly humified, compacted and penetrated with rootlets, precluded reasonable sampling for radiocarbon assay. In view of the changes which occur in the ensuing zone (HH: 2) two possible interpretations exist: Either (A) this zone represents the period prior to the widely recognised *Ulmus* decline at c. 5,000 BP, or (B) it represents a period sometime before the largely asynchronous phenomena of the *Tilia* decline in southern Britain, placed variously between 4,000–3,000 BP.

*HH: 2 53–25 cm.* This zone is delimited at its base by declining values of *Ulmus, Tilia*, Gramineae and spores, and by increasing importance of *Betula* and *Ilex.* Within HH: 2, two pollen assemblage sub-zones have also been recognised: 2a (37–53 cm) and 2b (25–38 cm). 2b is distinguishable by its increasing values of *Quercus, Ulmus,* Gramineae and *Pteridium.* Peaks of Gramineae and *Plantago lanceolata* also occur. *Betula* (up to 50%), *Quercus* (70%), *Alnus* (20–25%) and *Corylus* remain the dominant pollen taxa.

*Commentary:* The vegetation throughout this zone remains dominantly *Betula, Quercus* and *Corylus* as in the preceding zone. Again, few herbs are present, with the exception of Gramineae which increase markedly at the top of HH: 2a and throughout HH: 2b. Cereal–type pollen is consistently present in the whole of HH :2 and it is possible that this zone represents a period of increased anthropogenic activity on the headland. It is within sub-zone HH: 2b that the pollen assemblage from the buried land surface beneath the bank feature (see below) may be correlated. The pollen from the buried feature appears to reflect activity dating to the Bronze Age.

*HH: 3 25–0 cm.* This zone is delimited by the massive increase of heathland taxa. These include, *Erica, Calluna* and *Empetrum. Potentilla* type, *Rumex, Plantago* spp. Gramineae and *Pteridium* may also be related to such a heathland ecosystem although. The pollen of *Radiola linoides* mentioned above occurs within this assemblage zone. Total arboreal pollen declines sharply, although increases in *Pinus, Ulmus* (25–17 cm), *Corylus, Fagus* and *Salix* are evident. Herbaceous diversity also increases sharply.

*Commentary:* This zone represents a major ecological and environmental shift from conditions of deciduous woodland to its current status of open heathland. The heathland/ericaceous taxa noted above have low pollen production and/or dispersal characteristics and these attest to their autochthoneity. The preceding zone HH:2 has indications of increasing anthropogenic activity with the rise in herbs, whilst the presence of *Ilex* indicates some opening of the woodland canopy. No truncation of the peat profile was noted and the smooth, continuous pollen 'curves' for a number of taxa further confirms the absence of a stratigraphic

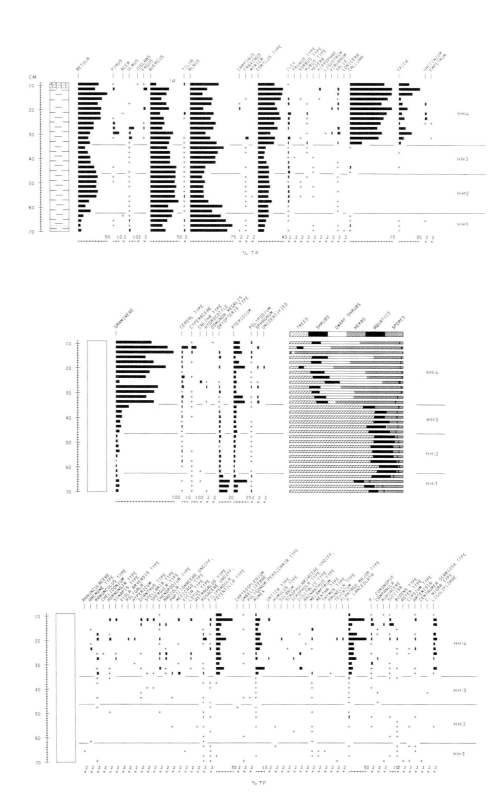

2.20  *Eastern Depression: Total pollen (TP) and Arboreal pollen (AP) percentages for pollen profile Hengistbury 1.*

break with the underlying zone containing woodland taxa. It seems extremely likely, therefore, that this change may be directly attributable to widespread forest clearance on the headland. If this is true, however, it post-dates the youngest levels of the soil pollen profile dated at 3,350±90 BP (HAR- 6186) for the humic horizon. The lowest levels of HH:3 show a peak of *Pteridium* which was perhaps a response to this clear-

ance by fire or to soil deterioration as a consequence of soil leaching. It is also noted that this is accompanied by relatively higher frequencies of cereal pollen and weeds typical of disturbed ground.

### (2) Buried land surface under the bank

Pollen analysis was carried out through the bank and old land surface from 30–59 cm (Fig. 2.21). Samples

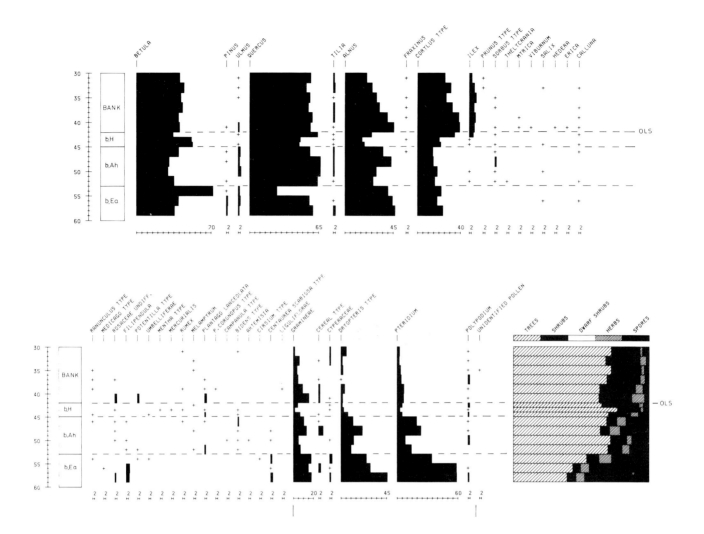

2.21 *Bank and ditch feature, Eastern Depression: TP and AP percentages for pollen profile Hengistbury 2 from buried surface under the bank.*

below 59 cm extending into the b-BHs and b-Bsg horizons were also processed. Absolute pollen frequency (APF) calculations were made using the addition of known quantities of exotic pollen and normal techniques were used for the removal of organic and inorganic detritus (see Fiche 1.B7). Pollen was, however, only found to be present in sufficient quantities from the middle of the b-Ea at 57–59 cm upwards. This is thought to be due to the effects of repeated groundwater fluctuations occurring in the lower soil horizons (Macphail pers. comm.).

In the buried ground surface three broad horizons are recognisable which correlate with the primary pedological divisions recorded by Macphail (this volume), and the spectrum represented by the overlying bank sediment. From top to bottom they comprise:

(i) *b–H: 44–42 cm.* The uppermost humic horizon has been radiocarbon dated to 3,350±90 BP (HAR–6186; see MacPhail 2.2.2). These levels produced remarkably high absolute pollen frequencies (up to 22 million grains per gram) with preparations resulting in pure pollen of well-preserved character. A dominance of

woodland genera is indicated by *Betula*, *Quercus*, *Alnus* and *Corylus* with few herbs represented. *Ilex* is present becoming increasingly important (2%).

*Commentary*: The unusual richness of pollen is undoubtedly due to the acid nature of the raw humus horizons. Comparably high pollen frequencies have been recorded from similar situations elsewhere (Dimbleby pers. comm.). Since this horizon has apparently not been truncated it can be postulated that these levels are representative of the vegetation at the site at the time of construction of the bank. The rare presence of *Ilex* within the deciduous woodland taxa is important because it is usually grossly under-represented in pollen diagrams due to its entomophilous character and low pollen production. Its overall significance is discussed below.

(ii) *b–Ah 44–53 cm.* The five levels of this zone show similarly high values of arboreal pollen (*Betula*, *Quercus*, *Alnus* and *Corylus* type with some *Ulmus* and sporadic occurrences of *Tilia*). This and the overlying humus (b-H) have the highest representations of

56

Table 2.7    Soil grain size

| Sample | Soil | Clay | FZ | MZ | CZ | Silt | VFS | FS | MS | CS | VCS | Sand | TSS No. |
|---|---|---|---|---|---|---|---|---|---|---|---|---|---|
| | *Profile 1* | 2 | 6 | 20 | 50 | 2–50 | 100 | 200 | 500 | 1000 | 2000um | | |
| 6 | bEa | No data | – | – | – | – | 17 | 33 | 31 | 2 | 0 | 83 | |
| 7 | bBhs | 8 | 0 | 6 | 3 | 9 | 18 | 32 | 30 | 3 | 0 | 83 | |
| 8 | bB(t)sg | 8 | 0 | 4 | 5 | 9 | 25 | 28 | 27 | 3 | 0 | 83 | C |
| | *Profile 3* | | | | | | | | | | | | |
| 18 | lower Bsx/Bx | 16 | 2 | 7 | 3 | 12 | 1 | 28 | 20 | 4 | 1 | 72 | G |
| | *Profile 4* | | | | | | | | | | | | |
| 19 | Ah/Ea | No data | – | – | – | – | 40 | 32 | 5 | 3 | 1 | 90 | |
| 20 | Ea1 | No data | – | – | – | – | 40 | 37 | 14 | 3 | 0 | 94 | H |
| 21 | Ea2 | No data | – | – | – | – | 53 | 37 | 5 | 1 | 0 | 95 | I |
| 22 | Bh | 1 | 1 | 3 | 2 | 6 | 55 | 35 | 4 | 1 | 0 | 94 | J |
| 23 | Bhs | No data | – | – | – | – | 55 | 37 | 1 | 0 | 0 | 92 | |
| 24 | B(t)sg | 8 | 1 | 3 | 2 | 6 | 47 | 37 | 2 | 0 | 0 | 86 | K |

Table 2.8    Chemistry of soil samples

| Sample No. | | pH | Org C | C | Pyro Fe | Al | Dith Fe | N | TTS No. |
|---|---|---|---|---|---|---|---|---|---|
| | *Profile 1* | | | | | | | | |
| 1 | Ah | 4.4 | | | | | | | |
| 2 | dump Bsg/Bhs | 4.7 | | | | | | | |
| 3 | dump Ah/H | 4.6 | | | | | | | |
| 4 | bH | 4.7 | 5.35 | 2.0 | 0.19 | 0.56 | 0 | 0.23 | A |
| 5 | bAh | 4.7 | | 0.1 | 0.01 | 0.14 | 0 | 0.03 | B |
| 6 | bEa | 4.7 | | 0.1 | 0.00 | 0.02 | 0.0 | – | |
| 7 | bB(hs) | 4.8 | | 0.5 | 0.01 | 0.11 | 0.03 | – | |
| 8 | bB(t)sg | 4.8 | | 0.1 | 0.02 | 0.10 | 0.09 | – | C |
| | *Profile 2* | | | | | | | | |
| 9 | Ah | 4.8 | | 0.6 | 0.13 | 0.04 | 0.02 | 0.12 | |
| 10 | Ea | 4.6 | | 0.0 | 0.01 | 0.0 | 0.00 | – | |
| 11 | Bhs | 4.4 | | 0.2 | 0.16 | 0.10 | 0.04 | – | |
| 12 | Bhsg | 4.8 | | 0.7 | 0.20 | 0.18 | 0.37 | – | |
| 13 | B(t)sg | 5.1 | | 0.1 | 0.06 | 0.08 | 0.16 | – | D |
| | *Profile 3* | | | | | | | | |
| 14 | Ea2 | 4.5 | 0.27 | 0.0 | 0.06 | 0.01 | 0.52 | | |
| 15 | Bh | 3.8 | – | 1.6 | 1.19 | 0.15 | 0.57 | | E |
| 16 | Bhs | 4.1 | – | 1.2 | 0.78 | 0.15 | 0.53 | | F |
| 17 | upper Bsx/Bx | 4.5 | 0.22 | | | | | | |
| 18 | lower Bsx/Bx | 4.9 | 0.17 | | | | | | G |
| | *Profile 4* | | | | | | | | |
| 19 | Ah/Ea | 4.5 | 1.33 | | | | | | |
| 20 | Ea | 4.6 | 0.05 | | | | | | H |
| 21 | Ea2 | 4.6 | 0.07 | | | | | | I |
| 22 | Bh | 5.1 | 0.69 | | | | | | J |
| 23 | Bh | 5.5 | 0.74 | | | | | | |
| 24 | Btsg | 5.2 | 0.07 | | | | | | K |

NB   Pyro. :   Pyrophosphate Extractable (Avery and Bascombe 1974)  
     Dith. :   Dithionite Extractable

57

*Quercus* (up to 65% AP). Shrubs are also represented with *Ilex* and *Sorbus* type (including *Crataegus*). Total quantities of herbs are low in frequency and diversity. Gramineae are present in higher value than in the b-H although still in relatively small quantities (up to 7% Total Pollen and Spores). Cereal-type pollen is also present, here being defined as Gramineae of size >50μ with large pore and annuli and relatively coarse columellate structure.

*Commentary*: It is clear that the vegetation of these upper soil horizons reflects a woodland ecosystem unusually growing on acid podzolic soils. Such a phenomenon has previously been discussed by Dimbleby (Dimbleby and Gill 1955) and is further amplified below.

(iii) *b–Ea 59–53 cm*. This is the basal zone of the soil pollen sequence. Vegetation of this zone shows a predominance of shrub and arboreal pollen, including *Quercus, Betula, Alnus* and *Corylus*. Herbaceous pollen are few with *Filipendula* and Gramineae being the only significant occurrences but at relatively low frequencies (10% and 2% TP, respectively). Values of spores of *Dryopteris* type and *Pteridium* are high (40% TP).

*Commentary*: The existence of high frequencies of spores in the basal levels of soil profiles has often been noted in such pollen studies and, as shown by analyses of the absolute pollen frequencies, is often due to the effects of differential preservation in their favour. However, the high values of *Pteridium* (especially *P. aquilinum*), although difficult to interpret for this reason, may here represent the initiation of soil acidity which allowed the preservation of subsequently deposited pollen. This is important and is likely to be the first indication of soil deterioration. It may in fact be due to the initial effects of anthropogenic activity or to the natural processes of soil deterioration on sandy soils through the build-up of raw humus and contained polyphenols.

Part of the bank overlying the buried land surface was also sampled for pollen analysis. Work concentrated on the lower 12 cm of the bank which displayed a substantial humic content. As with the buried soil sequence, the pollen spectra are dominated by arboreal pollen, the only exceptional feature being the noticeable increase in *Ilex*. Because it is often underrepresented in the pollen spectra it can be implied that it was an important constituent in the local flora or at least in the area from which the the soils were obtained in constructing the bank. It should be noted that the uppermost level of the *in situ* b–H horizon has a similar value of *Ilex*. This level undoubtedly was the contemporary landsurface and indicates the bank was constructed of scraped material, not all of which came from the ditch itself.

The presence of *Ilex* is of special interest, since it seems to indicate the opening of the forest/woodland canopy in the period even *prior* to the construction of the bank. *Ilex* today forms an important understorey shrub to *Quercus* and *Fagus* woodland in the New Forest, Hampshire and Parkhurst Forest, Isle of Wight. In situations of dense wood canopy and low light input flowering is sparse but increases markedly with canopy opening. This may have been the case at Hengistbury with deforestation being caused by a change of landuse and the building of visible field boundaries.

Local variability in the structure of the Hengistbury woodland, around the time of clearance, may be indicated by subtle differences in the pollen from the bank and the underlying buried land surface. Slightly higher values of *Corylus* (22%) and *Alnus* (15–30%), and slightly lower values of *Betula* (15–25%) and *Quercus* (20–30%) are recorded in the bank profile. No direct evidence can be found for the use of turves in the construction of the bank, as suggested by Macphail (Chapter 2.2, above). However, their apparent absence need not be surprising. For example it is possible that soil disturbance during the building of the bank and the markedly high pollen frequencies in the sediments may have masked any evidence of such structures visible to the palynologist. This effect has been noted elsewhere (Scaife 1988).

Due to the highly disorganised nature of the peaty sediments, no samples were taken from the ditch immediately adjacent to the sampled bank (Fig. 2.11). The ditch, which runs along the western side of the bank is clearly visible in aerial photographs (see Fig. 1.14). It shows up as a linear feature which runs diagonally across the Eastern Depression and is truncated by the sea cliff. A peat-filled channel presumed to be an extension of the same ditch and visible in the cliff section was sampled in 1981 by Sue Colledge (Birmingham University). Preliminary pollen results showed that the peats were rich in arboreal pollen, but no further sampling was undertaken.

### 2.3.5  *Summary and discussion*

It is unfortunate that the peats sampled from the Eastern Depression are of such a highly humified, degraded character and contain modern rootlets which make them unsuitable for radiocarbon dating. In view of the constant character through time of the forest as represented in both pollen sequences (Central Eastern Depression and the Bank), this poses some problems in the dating and the interpretation of the pollen spectra and of the individual pollen assemblage zones. Pollen analyses of the two profiles are however informative in showing clearly that the headland was forested almost throughout the whole of the later prehistoric period.

The relative decline in *Ulmus* and *Tilia* values noted in the pollen assemblage zones of the Central Eastern Depression and the Bank remain enigmatic. Actual dating evidence for this decline is scanty and depends on the correlation between HH:2 and b-H horizon of the buried land surface. Since the latter can be dated to *c.* 3,350 BP, it seems that the fall in *Ulmus* and *Tilia* values is unlikely to have occurred much after this time (in the 4th millennium BP). Without better dating evidence, however, it is impossible to say whether the assemblages (particularly HH: 1) relate to a period just prior to the well-known *Ulmus* decline at *c.*5,000 BP or whether the fall in *Tilia* points to a much later period of reduction. Unlike the elm decline, the decrease in *Tilia* appears not to be a synchronous event in Southern Britain. For example, whereas its decline has been dated to the late Neolithic at Boreham Farm, Isle of Wight (Scaife 1980) the same does not occur in Epping Forest, Essex until the Saxon period (Baker *et al.* 1978). In the Hampshire Basin a marked reduction in *Tilia* seems to occur within the middle Bronze Age (Scaife 1980, 1987). However, it is the author's opinion that at Hengistbury the decline may have occurred at a slightly earlier date than elsewhere in the Hampshire Basin. The main arguments for this may be summarised as follows:

(a) The diagram from the buried land surface shows no continuously high values of *Tilia* and *Fraxinus* although the top of the sequence has been dated to 3,350 BP. If the middle/late Bronze Age decline had taken place it might be expected that *Tilia* would be represented in the profile especially in the lowest levels of the b-Ea where *Tilia* would preserve well in the poorer preserving conditions of the sandy Ea.

(b) A marked secondary *Ulmus* regeneration is clearly seen in pollen diagrams throughout the region and which relates to middle or late Neolithic regeneration (Whittle 1978; Scaife 1980, 1988). This is not seen in the Hengistbury pollen diagrams and indicates therefore a date later than this for both pollen spectra.

(c) *Tilia* was widely dominant on sandy soils during the Atlantic period and after, until its demise through anthropogenic activity. At *c.*5,000 BP when *Ulmus* declines in many pollen stratigraphical sequences, *Tilia* often remains important until its decline in the late Neolithic or Bronze Age after which it displays only sporadic records. It is, however, accepted that because of its entomophily and poor and local representation, any discussion of this taxon must remain site specific. Here, *Tilia* declines at the HH:1/HH:2 boundary from what are relatively low percentages to sporadic occurrences and which probably relate to growth not in very close proximity to the site.

(d) *Fraxinus*, whilst undoubtedly a constituent of the Atlantic forest, tends to show an increased response and more consistent record subsequent to the first Neolithic activity which is generally associated with the Neolithic *Ulmus* decline at *c.*5,000 BP. This is due to the opening of the forest canopy allowing better pollen representation, or due to its recolonisation of areas previously occupied by *Ulmus*. At Hengistbury, *Fraxinus* is present at the base of HH:1 in low frequencies but

subsequently declines rather than expands, which may therefore be construed as increasing human activities in the pollen catchment with clearance of areas of woodland.

(e) Pollen of cerealia type is present in all zones to the base of the buried land surface. Whilst there is some evidence of pre-*Ulmus* decline cereal pollen (Edwards and Hirons 1984) this is by no means unquestionably the case in southern England where the first cereal pollen records occur in close correspondence with the *Ulmus* decline (Scaife 1988). Pollen assemblage zone HH:1 is therefore likely to post-date the first introduction of arable agriculture in the Neolithic.

In summary, it seems highly probable based on the evidence above that the HH:1/HH:2 pollen assemblage zone boundary does not represent the classic *Ulmus* decline, but a much later decline in *Ulmus* and other taxa. The cause of this decline may have been anthropogenic or due to natural factors such as a rather generalised deterioration in soil base status, possibly affecting areas at some distance from the site. The very highly humified nature of the peats in the Eastern Depression and the correlation with the sub-bank soil pollen spectra imply that the 37 cm of peat in zones HH:1 and HH:2 are a compacted and relatively long sequence which according to the reasoning above may extend back to the middle or late Neolithic.

The soil pollen sequence of the sub-bank land surface may be correlated with pollen assemblage zone HH:2 in showing the dominance of woodland prior to the construction of the bank and ditch at or just after 3,350±90 BP (1,400 BC uncalibrated). Within the soil pollen diagram there is little indication of the major environmental change to the heathland ecosystem which is represented in its entirety in HH:3. This change must have occurred after 3,350 BP and therefore the Hengistbury heathland is of relatively recent origin when compared to similar environments elsewhere in southern England (Dimbleby 1962, 1974). For example some areas of the Tertiary sand in the Hampshire basin saw expansions of ericaceous heathland communities during the Mesolithic, as shown at Iping Common, West Sussex (Dimbleby in Keef *et al.* 1965) and Oakhanger Warren, Hampshire (Rankine and Dimbleby 1960). A rather later and more massive expansion of heathland is also seen at Oakhanger during the Bronze Age (Dimbleby 1961; Scaife and Macphail 1983; Scaife 1988). At Hengistbury, the radiocarbon dating of the buried soil 'H' horizon provides only a *maximum* age for this expansion. It is likely, however, that the construction of the late Bronze Age bank marks the initiation of forest clearance. Progressive soil deterioration occurred and then continued through the late Bronze Age and into the Iron Age, no doubt accelerated by the extensive, anthropogenic activity which is known to have taken place on the headland in these periods.

## 2.4 Thermoluminescence (TL) dating of burned artefacts from the Hengistbury sites

### 2.4.1 *Introduction*

Thermoluminescence (TL) is the emission of light when a mineral is heated. This light is additional to the ordinary red-hot glow; usually it occurs at a lower temperature. The TL represents the release of energy that has been stored in the crystal lattice of the mineral. The stored energy is in the form of trapped electrons which have been excited by exposure to a weak flux of nuclear radiation. The radiation comes from the naturally occurring radioelements (potassium 40, thorium and uranium) present in samples and soil.

The basic tenet of TL dating is that at the time of the event being dated the latent TL of the sample was reset to zero by some method: then during the burial period the TL re-accumulates so that the intensity measurable today is related to the age. The erasure of geologically acquired TL at the time of the archaeological event is by heating in the case of burnt flint; a temperature of around 400° is necessary.

The basic age equation is

$$\text{Age} = \frac{\text{\textit{Archaeological dose}}}{\text{Annual dose}}$$

The archaeological dose (AD) is evaluated from laboratory measurements of the TL accrued over the burial period (NTL) and the sensitivity of the sample.

$$\text{AD} = \frac{\text{\textit{NTL}}}{\text{TL per unit dose of radiation}}$$

The annual radiation dose is determined by laboratory and on-site measurements. It is made up of two parts: the internal dose taken from the sample and the external one from the surrounding burial soil (up to a distance of 0.3 metre from the sample). For flint and calcite this latter component may be as much as 80% of the total annual dose and so the reliability of the age depends on an accurate evaluation of it.

The annual dose is influenced by the water content of sample and soil during burial. An upper limit to the effect is obtained by measuring the saturation water content, and the as-dug content can also be measured. Uncertainty about water content over the burial period is one of the chief factors limiting the accuracy available.

### 2.4.2 *Flint artefacts*

Six flint artefacts from the Late Upper Palaeolithic site were dated in 1982, two others were rejected because they had not been burned sufficiently to eliminate their geological signal. The dating method is described in detail in Huxtable and Jacobi (1982).

The ADs for the flints ranged from 0.6 to 0.9 krad

and their 'a values' from 0.07 to 0.18. The environmental dose rates were initially assessed by on-site gamma spectrometer measurements in Squares L26 and M21. Then calcium fluoride dosimeters were buried on the site and left in place for more than a year before retrieval and measurement. The internal dose rate was assessed by thick source alpha counting and flame photometry. The environmental dose rate was approximately 80% of the total dose rate to the flints.

Individual ages calculated in years BP for flint artefacts are as follows:

| | |
|---|---|
| a1–O31 | 14,300±2,430 |
| a2–N30 | 10,800±1,900 |
| a4–J33 | 12,800±1,970 |
| a5–L29 | 10,400±1,420 |
| a11–R30 | 11,900±1,290 |
| a12–I33 | 13,000±1,920 |

The error limit quoted for all the dates is the total error (systematic plus random) at 68% level of confidence. The average age is calculated according to the statistical scheme of Aitken and Alldred (1972).

On the basis of these figures, the average age of this site is 12,500±1150 years BP (OXTL 707a). In the age calculations it has been assumed that the wetness of the burial soil has been (0.75±0.25) of saturation for the whole of the burial period. If the soil had been entirely saturated for the whole period then the flints would be older by about 2%. On the other hand, total dryness of the sites for the whole burial period would make the flints younger by about 10%.

### 2.4.3 *Sandstone Cobbles*

Three fragments of fractured sandstone cobbles (X, Y and L) were submitted for laboratory examination. The two from the northern sector (squares X and Y) belonged to two individual cobbles reconstructed from several shattered pieces found close together (Figs. 4.31 and 2.22) and were submitted in 1984. The third (from square L29/30), which was submitted in 1987, came from a fragmented cobble in the main area south of the footpath and appears not to belong to either of the other cobbles. The aim of the laboratory work was to see if any or all of the stones had been heated in antiquity. The excavator did not wish to have a TL age determination done, as this would have destroyed too much of the material.

Samples were taken from X30/80, X29/47 (refitting pieces), Y30/96 and L29/37 with a diamond impregnated corer. The TL signals from the stones were good and they had been drained to at least 500°C in antiquity: that is, all the stones had been burned.

The AD for the stones X and Y was approximately 2.5 krad and their internal dose rates were measured using thick source alpha counting and flame photometry. This, combined with the average environmental gamma dose rate from the site, showed that the burn-

2.22 *Sandstone cobble fragments from excavation squares X29/X30/Y30, north of footpath. Note the bioturbation features visible in the standing section. 2 m scale.*

ing of the stones was consistent with an Upper Palaeolithic date.

The AD for stone L was approximately 1.5 krad but there was not enough material to estimate its internal dose rate. All one can say for this stone was that it had been burned in antiquity, most probably in the period 5,000–25,000 years BP.

### 2.4.4 *TL dating of burned flints from the Powell Mesolithic assemblage*

The methodology has been referred to above. Five flaked artefacts (all cores) from the site were dated in 1982, one was rejected because it still contained a geological signal.

The ADs for the flints ranged from 0.5 to 0.8 krad and their 'a values' from 0.08 to 0.15. The environmental dose rate was assessed using calcium fluoride dosimeters buried in the site and left in place for a year. Again, it was approximately 80% of the total dose rate.

The individual ages expressed in years BP are:

| | |
|---|---|
| C1–I9 | 9,320±1,260 |
| C2–G11 | 7,000±1,140 |
| C3–F14 | 12,300±1,670 |
| C7–D14 | 8,880±1,000 |
| C9–G11 | 10,750±1,500 |

The same error limits and soil moisture content apply here as above.

On the basis of these figures the average age of the Powell Mesolithic site is 9,750±950 years BP (OXTL 707C). The average age is calculated according to the statistical methods stated in Aitken and Alldred (1972). A slightly wider scatter of individual ages was produced for the site than had been predicted by the statistics. Unfortunately, there is no way of ascertaining on present TL dating evidence whether the site was visited once or many times during the Mesolithic period. On the other hand artefact studies including refitting evidence (see Chapter 5.1.1) now suggests the likelihood of closely related flaking episodes perhaps all deriving from a single period of occupation.

## 2.5 Optical luminescence dating of sediments at the Late Upper Palaeolithic Site

### 2.5.1 *Introduction*

In recent years several new techniques have been developed for use in the dating of archaeological sites. However, as many archaeological and geological sites do not have suitable material available for dating (e.g. charcoal, bone, shell, pottery etc.), techniques which measure directly the age of the sediments have been developed. The new technique of Optical Dating is closely related to Thermoluminescence (TL) dating; the event dated is the last exposure of the sediment grains to sunlight, during transportation and deposition (Huntley *et al.* 1985).

Several sediment samples were measured from the Late Upper Palaeolithic site (Fig. 2.23), primarily for comparing Optical Dating with other well established dating techniques. Preliminary results have been published in Rhodes (1988). Here, finalised values based on further measurements are presented, followed by a brief outline of the technique.

### 2.5.2 *Technique*

Although Optical Dating is still at an experimental stage in its development it is thought likely that within a few years the technique will become a powerful and widely used tool in the dating of Late Pleistocene and Holocene sediments. A main advantage that it is hoped

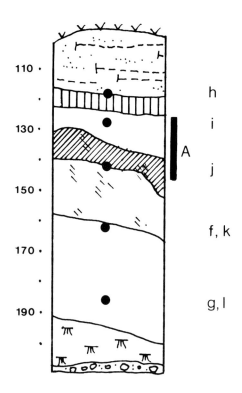

2.23 *Schematic section at interface 24/23 in M showing the positions of the five OSL samples (h-l), two TL samples (f-g) and the approximate range of depths of the six TL-dated Late Upper Palaeolithic flints (A). The depth scale is in cm below the site datum. The sediment key is shown in Fig. 2.5.*

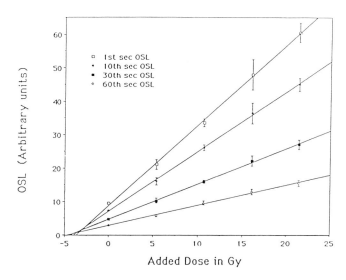

2.24 *Optically-stimulated luminescence dating results. Regenerated OSL growth curves (using linear fits) plotted for the integrated OSL measured in the 1st, 10th, 30th and 60th seconds of laser exposure after removal of the natural OSL signal by a 90 second laser exposure (at a power of 5 mW cm-}) and 10 minutes of solar simulator lamp exposure. Sample 707i11.*

Table 2.9 *Summary of sample data and Optical TL dates*

| Sample ref. | Depth (cm) | Total Dose Rate(Gy/Ka) | Equivalent Dose (Gy) | Age (Ka) |
|---|---|---|---|---|
| 707h11 | 22 | $0.77 \pm 0.10$ | $1.4 \pm 0.2$ | $1.8 \pm 0.3$ |
| 707i11 | 31 | $0.77 \pm 0.05$ | $4.2 \pm 0.2$ | $5.5 \pm 0.5$ |
| 707j11 | 44 | $0.87 \pm 0.05$ | $9.9 \pm 2.0$ | $11.4 \pm 2.4$ |
| 707k11 | 65 | $0.84 \pm 0.08$ | $15.5 + 3.2/-2.2$ | $18.5 + 4.2/-3.2$ |
| 707l11 | 88 | $0.87 \pm 0.06$ | $20.4 + 2.6/-2.4$ | $23.4 + 3.4/-3.2$ |

Table 2.10 *Radiocarbon dates from Hengistbury.*

| Lab No | Sample | Site data | Date (BP) | Ref. |
|---|---|---|---|---|
| OxA-398 | Charcoal | X30 2b/117/23-24 | $8,590 \pm 120$ | 1 |
| OxA-399 | Charcoal | Y32 2a/105/24-25 | $4,770 \pm 180$ | 1 |
| OxA-411 | Charcoal | X30 2b/100/15-16 | $7,690 \pm 110$ | 1 |
| OxA-412 | Charcoal | Y31 2b/105/16-17 | $8,140 \pm 120$ | 1 |
| OxA-413 | Humic extraction of OxA-412 | | $7,910 \pm 140$ | 1 |
| GrN-6220 | Organic sand extract | | $2,765 \pm 70$ | 2 |
| GrN-6221a | Peaty sand extract | | $3,355 \pm 85$ | 2 |
| GrN-6221b | Peaty sand | | $3,150 \pm 335$ | 2 |

Lab: OxA= Oxford accelerator facility; GrN= Groningen; Reference: 1= Gillespie *et al.* 1985, 2= Campbell (1977, Table 4).

this technique will have over related methods such as TL dating of sediments is the complete (or virtually complete) zeroing of the signal at the time of deposition.

The technique of Optical Dating is very closely related to TL dating (see above); in both cases, after being reset to zero, the luminescence signal accumulates due to exposure to ionising radiation from naturally occurring radionucleides in the burial environment. In the TL dating of burnt material the signal is zeroed by heating to a temperature in excess of 400°C. The resetting of unburnt sediment TL relies on bleaching by natural sunlight during the transportation of the sediment grains immediately prior to burial. However, because of the presence of a component of the TL which is not bleachable, the signal is not reduced to zero even by long sunlight exposure, leaving a residual TL component. In consequence, there is a large error associated with the determination of the size of this residual TL component in the laboratory, causing the overall accuracy of the technique to be reduced. In Optical Dating only the light sensitive part of the TL signal is measured. This signal is zeroed very rapidly by sunlight (down to <1% in around 10 minutes) and so for most sediments no residual signal would be expec-ted.

In collecting the dating samples it is important that they receive no light exposure either during collection (in steel or plastic cylinders), transportation or preparation.

Actual measurement of the luminescence is carried out while quartz grains separated from the sediment

are exposed to bright monochromatic green light from a laser. Blue glass filters placed before the detector cut out the green laser light allowing blue luminescence from the grains to be measured.

Measurement of the natural environmental radioactivity is made both on-site and in the laboratory. At Hengistbury, portable multichannel NaI gamma spectrometer measurements, taking around one hour per sample, were made in the position of each sample at the time of collection. Samples were collected to measure the present-day water content and for calculating the maximum possible water content of the sediments through time. In the laboratory each sample was measured using the technique of high resolution gamma spectrometry, and alpha counting and flame photometry measurements were made on two of the samples as a cross-check.

### 2.5.3    Dating results

The error limits quoted above are the total error, both random and systematic, at the 68% confidence level. Some asymmetry is introduced into the error on the equivalent dose by non-linear growth characteristics of the luminescence signal.

As with the Hengistbury Head Late Upper Palaeolithic site, initial results from other sites are proving extremely encouraging. At present it is envisaged that the technique will be most useful in the range 10–100 ka (10,000–100,000 years Before Present) to an accuracy of around 10–15%, although both the range and the accuracy are dependent on the level of environmental radiation, water content and sample characteristics.

## 2.6    Radiocarbon dating evidence from the Late Upper Palaeolithic site

Excavations north of the footpath at the Late Upper Palaeolithic site (Fig. 1.10) yielded far higher densities of burnt flint artefacts than elsewhere on the site. Associated with these finds were several broken sandstone (sandrock cf. 2.4.3) cobbles, which were shown by thermoluminescence tests to have been thermally fractured in antiquity (2.4.3 and 4.2.2). The burnt flints included examples of backed blades, burins and end-scrapers and there was no doubt that this represented a continuation of the Late Upper Palaeolithic site area. Apart from the burned artefacts there were also many fragments of charred wood in the surrounding sediments and at the same depth as the sandstone cobbles. When taken together these elements provided strong circumstantial evidence for the existence of a hearth feature.

Amongst the charred wood fragments were several small sub-rectangular pieces about 5 mm long which were fairly compact and appeared to be suitable for accelerator dating purposes. Because of the highly degraded condition of the charred fragments it was not possible to obtain a detailed identification of the wood prior to submission. Each of the samples was prepared and underwent special cleaning in the laboratory according to the pre-treatment methods described in Gillespie et al. (1984). The results are presented in Table 2.10 together with those of an earlier attempt to produce conventional radiocarbon dates for the site (Campbell 1977).

Although it is clear that the measurements are far too young and cannot date the Late Upper Palaeolithic occupation, it is difficult to interpret their true significance. In the first place the dates lack internal consistency, with OxA–399 being significantly younger in age than the rest. It should also be stated that although the charred material was found in apparent relation to the archaeology, the association is not totally unambiguous and the wood could be intrusive. In this respect it is noteworthy that various attempts to date charcoal from Late Palaeolithic sites in podzolised sands have resulted in similarly young ages and charcoal dates from sandy environments should always be treated with caution (Gowlett et al. 1987). If the Oxford results are taken at face value, they would appear to date events much later than the principal occupation. The most economical explanation is that the charcoal was introduced from a higher level as a result of bioturbation .

Campbell (1977) made a similar attempt to radiocarbon date organic materials from the site but used bulked material instead of individual samples. From the Groningen results (Table 2.9) he concluded that the samples were contaminated by humic acids associated with more recent soil formation. Thus, in his opinion the dates reflected the latest period of podzolisation, rather than the true age of the occupation itself (Campbell 1977, 72).

# 3. Site formation processes at the Hengistbury sites

## 3.1  The effects of non-anthropogenic phenomena on artefact taphonomy

### 3.1.1  Introduction

The Hengistbury sites occur in locally derived wind-blown sands which have been modified by a series of pedological and biological processes (Chapter 2.1.3, 2.2, and 2.3). Geologically, the sands are massive and would appear to contain no subunit boundaries. No formal archaeological structures or 'living surfaces' have been recovered. Instead, the occupation evidence occurs as a diffuse band of artefacts, on average 20–50 cm thick but occasionally reaching 80 cm in thickness. If refitting material is taken to be the remains of original knapping scatters, there has been a horizontal dilation in linear dimensions in the order of 500–600%. Furthermore, there is a low, but persistent, occurrence of later prehistoric material which intrudes into otherwise Mesolithic or Upper Palaeolithic contexts.

The present chapter contains a discussion of the main geological and biological processes which might have contributed to the observed spatial distribution of the Hengistbury artefacts. Drawing upon taphonomic theory and upon environmental data from Hengistbury itself, an attempt will be made to assess the likely significance of each process and, where possible, to predict the effects upon the artefact distribution. Two models of site formation are presented based on the observed data from the Late Upper Palaeolithic and Mesolithic sites.

Figure 3.1 is a simple diagram showing the broad groupings of processes which might be expected to be of potential taphonomic significance in middle latitudes (outside the glaciated zone), at low altitude, and given a range of climates. Most of the headings are self-explanatory but further details will be introduced below where necessary. The majority of the processes listed can involve some movement of stone artefacts, whilst a few can inhibit movement. The special cases of burning (2 and 12) and frost shattering (11) are included, not because significant movement is produced directly, but because thermally induced total or incipient fractures can alter the size, shape and surface texture of a flint at any point after the fracture event, thus altering the flint's response to other taphonomic processes. Anthropogenic effects are included in the diagram for the sake of completeness but these will be discussed in section 3.2 of this chapter.

Some of the processes on the general list can be ruled out of the analysis on geological grounds (cf. Chapter 2.1). Processes involving the build-up of significant ground ice (9, 13, 18, and 19) are very unlikely in this situation and there is no available evidence that flints have been disturbed in these ways. However, less extreme cryogenic effects are theoretically possible and cannot be ignored. Processes dependent upon relatively high sediment plasticity (14, 16, 20 and 31) will

have been at least severely restricted at Hengistbury; the conditions for debris flow would have been completely absent. Disturbance by flowing water (6, 7 and 30) would have been minimal but this case will need further discussion below. The topography on the Head itself has been low throughout the period of interest, so that the effects of all those surface processes driven by the downslope component of gravity would have been relatively weak.

The body of this section will be divided into two parts, dealing with horizontal and vertical aspects of taphonomy, respectively. This division makes discussion much easier but it is, nevertheless, artificial. Ultimately, the results of taphonomic systems are three-dimensional.

### 3.1.2  Processes affecting the horizontal distribution of artefacts

*Wind action:* The effects of wind upon the horizontal distribution of objects has been widely studied by geoscientists (cf. Bagnold 1941; Warren 1979; Reineck and Singh 1980). In general terms, particles *c.* 1 mm in diameter move by saltation at wind speeds (measured at 2 m above the surface) of 36 km/h (*fluid threshold*), or 27 km/h if momentum can be conserved by progressive bombardment (*impact threshold*). Bombardment can result in the movement of a new grain six times the diameter of the incoming grain. Particles *c.* 2 mm in diameter move by rolling or surface creep in winds which have reached 40 km/h; to keep a 2 mm particle suspended in the air would require a wind lift component of 18 km/h. These broad considerations would suggest that wind deflation (the removal of sand and the concentration of coarser particles; see below) is the only process likely to affect stone artefacts to any significant degree.

However, the geoscientist is concerned with *average* effects which, cumulatively, produce predictable results over relatively large areas. More unlikely and quirky events at the coarse end of the particle size distribution in wind transport systems are just not significant in this context. But such events are precisely the ones which should interest an archaeologist concerned with the lateral disturbance of a flint scatter on a sandy surface. Artefacts of surprisingly large size do move in the wind, sometimes with archaeologically significant results (cf. Shelley and Nials 1983). This movement is not easily predictable from theory; a variety of wind tunnel experiments would be necessary to give some idea of the general pattern. From observation of experimental material at Hengistbury and elsewhere, it would appear that artefact shape and exact disposition

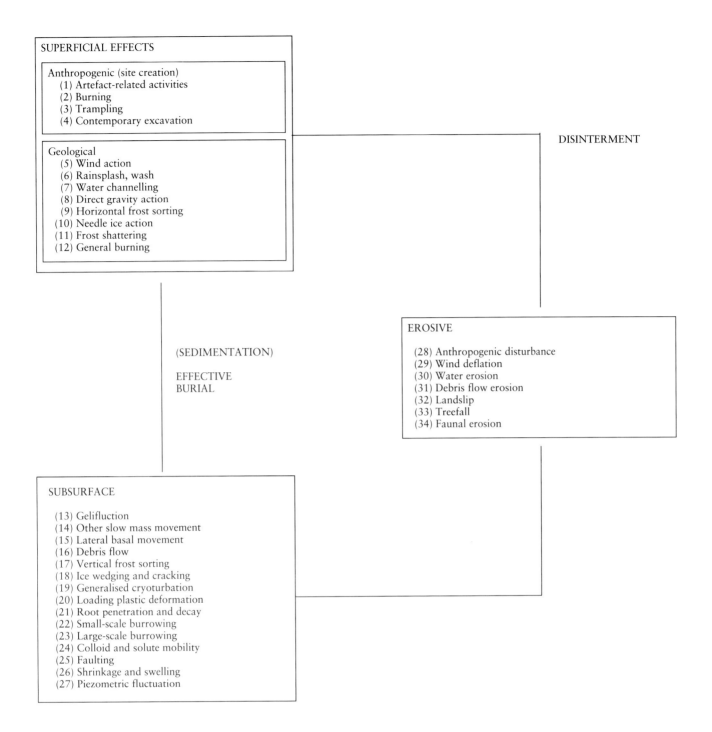

```
┌─────────────────────────────────────┐
│ SUPERFICIAL EFFECTS                   │
│  ┌──────────────────────────────────┐ │
│  │ Anthropogenic (site creation)     │ │
│  │   (1) Artefact-related activities │ │
│  │   (2) Burning                     │ │
│  │   (3) Trampling                   │ │
│  │   (4) Contemporary excavation     │ │
│  └──────────────────────────────────┘ │
│  ┌──────────────────────────────────┐ │        DISINTERMENT
│  │ Geological                        │ │
│  │   (5) Wind action                 │ │
│  │   (6) Rainsplash, wash            │ │
│  │   (7) Water channelling           │ │
│  │   (8) Direct gravity action       │ │
│  │   (9) Horizontal frost sorting    │ │
│  │  (10) Needle ice action           │ │
│  │  (11) Frost shattering            │ │
│  │  (12) General burning             │ │
│  └──────────────────────────────────┘ │
└─────────────────────────────────────┘
```

(SEDIMENTATION)

EFFECTIVE
BURIAL

**EROSIVE**

(28) Anthropogenic disturbance
(29) Wind deflation
(30) Water erosion
(31) Debris flow erosion
(32) Landslip
(33) Treefall
(34) Faunal erosion

**SUBSURFACE**

(13) Gelifluction
(14) Other slow mass movement
(15) Lateral basal movement
(16) Debris flow
(17) Vertical frost sorting
(18) Ice wedging and cracking
(19) Generalised cryoturbation
(20) Loading plastic deformation
(21) Root penetration and decay
(22) Small-scale burrowing
(23) Large-scale burrowing
(24) Colloid and solute mobility
(25) Faulting
(26) Shrinkage and swelling
(27) Piezometric fluctuation

3.1  *General taphonomic processes relating to stone artefacts.*

on the ground are very important. Quite large flakes can be flipped over if they lie with an edge protruding into the wind. Pieces perched on other artefacts are similarly vulnerable. High-standing pieces may plough forward very slowly or roll, depending upon their general shape. It even seems likely that lift can be generated by wind passing over a smaller flake lying with its curved ventral surface upwards (like an aircraft wing). Raindrop impact (see below) might provide another mechanism for tipping at least lighter pieces into a more effective airstream. Wind action at the time of a knapping episode will obviously provide a potential for dispersal even before the debitage hits the ground. During the trampling experiment carried out at

Hengistbury (Chapter 3.2.6), it was noticed that many of the tiny chips (<1 cm) were removed by wind action, a process actually witnessed during the emplacement of the scatter.

On the negative side, ground texture and especially vegetation cover can inhibit or at least complicate movement; Chepil and Woodruff (1963) have shown that the slowing of wind and the eventual thickening of a more or less dead air zone are directly proportional to a combination of the height of obstacles and their closeness of spacing, whilst Bressolier and Thomas (1977) have demonstrated a complex interaction between plants and airflow.

Another inhibiting mechanism might be a factor of

time. It has been noticed in the Hengistbury experimental scatters that, once the edge of a piece becomes even slightly buried by sediment, further movement by wind is rare. Very little horizontal change has been observed in the experiments, set up at Hengistbury over eight years ago (Barton and Bergman 1982), and those in soft dunes retain their overall integrity. It is noteworthy that although the scatters are periodically uncovered and partially reburied by the wind, only the smallest chips seem to have been removed by wind action. I suggest that smaller artefacts recently dropped on a surface are vulnerable to wind action. On the other hand, artefacts that are beginning to be covered by sediment, or formerly buried artefacts partially uncovered by deflation, will be part of what might be called a wind/obstacle equilibrium and they will be less susceptible to horizontal disturbance. That the response of artefacts to various taphonomic processes might change as they 'settle' into their new environment is a proposition which will need thorough testing by longer term experimentation.

It can be demonstrated that wind will affect artefact scatters, both during and after knapping. For larger artefacts, the effects will probably be limited to a maximum general dilation in the order of 100–200%. Some size sorting and preferential orientation might develop, but surface (ground) irregularities and variability in wind direction could easily disrupt the patterns. The only effect which might be predicted with some confidence would be the removal of significant proportions of the finest debitage from the immediate vicinity of knapping scatters, although such winnowing could of course be due to factors other than wind. Conversely, a scatter containing approximately the original amount of fine debris could be considered more or less undisturbed.

*Channelled water flow, wash and rainsplash:* The effects of surface water are likely to have been relatively minor at Hengistbury. This can be illustrated by a consideration of the physical parameters.

Let us assume truly torrential rainfall at 100 mm/h (approximately the maximum observed in Britain under present conditions; cf. Rodda 1967). Ignoring the fact that potential infiltration rate (estimated by site experiment) is in the region of 500 mm/h for the leached sands and even 150 mm/h for the clayiest material below the main podzol horizons, let us assume that there is zero loss from infiltration, transpiration and evaporation. Now, being rather generous, the Eastern Depression represents a catchment of *c.* 40,000 sq m and the area of Warren Hill above the Powell Mesolithic site represents a catchment of *c.* 25,000 sq. m; these figures are reasonable maxima for any time in the past 15,000 years.

First, let us consider channelled flow. The critical water erosion velocity for sands at 0.1 mm diameter is *c.* 0.45 m/sec. Therefore, a channelled flow of *c.* 2.5 sq m cross-section could efficiently drain the Eastern Depression, and one of *c.* 1.6 sq m could drain the area

of the Powell Mesolithic site. These theoretical cross-sections would be halved if we allowed a speed high enough to erode particles of *c.* 2.5 mm diameter, quartered with a speed high enough to erode particles of *c.* 12 mm diameter. Of course, such high speeds would cause the channels to entrench almost instantaneously right through the main sand body.

Second, let us consider undifferentiated wash. The flow speed would be considerably slower than the threshold of *c.* 0.1 m/sec below which all particulate erosion ceases; even the transportation of clays eroded by some other mechanism would be unlikely. However, such undifferentiated flow is in fact most implausible in a natural situation and rilling would very soon develop. Observation on the Head of *puddle fans* composed of sediment derived from rilling of compacted gravel paths on relatively long (*c.*30 m) slopes of up to 10° shows muddy fine sands with no flint debris above 2 mm diameter. This contrasts with observations of one of the experimental scatters located on a hard substrate of clay and gravels, which has altered its shape significantly since it was originally knapped. The circular scatter has become elongate and orientated in the same direction taken by surface waters when the site is flooded from time to time. Since the scatter is located in the dunes below the Head itself, at a point where the water table is often at or above the surface, this apparently contrary observation only serves to strengthen the argument presented here.

If we now restate the improbability of zero infiltration, transpiration and evaporation, it can be seen how inadequate the catchments are to generate major erosion and transport by flowing water. This impression is reinforced by the observation that even the modern gullies cutting the cliffs around the Head die out extremely fast inland. Such gullies, which always erode down to the underlying Tertiary strata, owe their existence to the high hydraulic gradient near the recent cliffs and are therefore unrepresentative of former conditions. In any case, at least the basal portions of ancient features of this type could hardly escape detection.

Although it is clear that, throughout the period of interest, the Head has been drained by dominantly subsurface routes, some surface water erosion indeed occurred at the top of the main sand body. It was argued in Chapter 2.1.9 that this was primarily due to a build-up of organics in certain areas, which drastically lowered the infiltration rates. Even though artefacts found at this erosion surface might therefore have been disturbed, the great bulk of the artefacts in both the Late Upper Palaeolithic and Mesolithic sites lay well out of reach. As a further control, I have excavated a stretch of one of the minor erosion channels in the Late Upper Palaeolithic site in order to assess the potential for artefact disturbance. Natural flint fragments and the few artefacts which lay this high in the sands had been concentrated just outside the channel boundaries; they had not even been organised into a lag at the channel bottom. The sediment of the channel itself contained only extremely rare flint debris with maximum dimensions never exceeding 4 mm.

One final situation in which significant overland flow might be generated involves the sealing of the ground surface by ice (see below). It has already been demonstrated that, with zero rainfall infiltration, the catchments are not large enough to produce widespread flow capable of disturbing anything but the smallest artefactual debris. The discharge would be increased if snowmelt were added to torrential rainfall. In order to double the discharge, roughly a 60 cm thickness of snow would need to melt in one hour, an unrealistically high figure. Although the rate of thaw is obviously highly dependent upon many local factors, most observers report that winter snow cover (averaging 1 m in thickness) in arctic to subarctic regions takes 10–20 days to melt given underlying frozen ground (cf. Embleton and King 1975; French 1976). Allowing a rate of thaw of 1 m/5 days, in order to compensate for the lower latitude of Hengistbury, and allowing that melt might be restricted to 8 hours in a day, the peak increase in rainfall equivalent would be only 3.75%.

A more detailed discussion of transport by flowing water of stone debitage, including the results of flume experiments, is given by Schick (1986). It is clear that artefacts, especially when they are anomalously large with respect to the natural sediment size distribution, may move more easily than theoretical Hjulström/Sundborg models, the normal yardstick in sedimentology, would suggest. However, significant movement of anything larger than stone chips did not occur in Schick's flume tests at flow velocities below *c.* 0.3 m/sec, with a water depth of 20 cm and a smooth bed.

If surface water flow can be assumed to have had no major effect on the Hengistbury artefacts, the same may not be true for rainsplash, a mechanism which is independent of catchment. Storm intensity raindrops can hit the ground with a momentum as high as *c.* 60.0 gf, although average drops have a momentum of nearer 0.2 gf (Pettersen 1958). Disturbance of stones up to 5 cm in diameter during experiments is reported by Kirkby and Kirkby (1974). Rainsplash is unlikely to have anything more than a very minor random dilation effect on artefact scatters on level ground but, given even a gentle slope, there is a potential for directed movement. However, if the surface were vegetated, rainsplash would be largely inhibited as a transport agent. If, on the other hand, the surface were composed of a bare sandy material, there would be a tendency for larger objects to be buried by rainsplashed sand, except on higher angle slopes.

Since it is most unlikely that large scale steep slopes existed on the Head in the vicinity of the archaeological sites, the maximum potential effects of rainsplash would probably be restricted to lateral reorganisation of artefacts over a few centimetres or decimetres. Certainly, no size or shape patterning which might have resulted from this process is now detectable amongst the Hengistbury artefacts.

*Cryological processes:* It was noted above that the significant build-up of ground ice would have been unlikely in the sandy Hengistbury context, even during colder phases at the end of the Pleistocene; this suggestion is supported by the lack of major subsurface cryogenic structures young enough to have affected the archaeological material. Most if not all forms of patterned ground (cf. French, 1976; Washburn 1979) can therefore be ruled out as mechanisms for displacing and sorting the artefacts.

However, ice will form at and close to any damp surface given air temperatures below about -2° Celsius, although accumulation of ice is still restricted if the topsoil is not moderately loamy (cf. Gradwell 1954; Washburn 1979). Since ice is preferentially formed at points of greatest heat loss, it may build up quite spectacularly under stones (as needle ice and nubbins) and, after several freeze-thaw cycles, a significant lateral displacement may occur; objects weighing as much as 15 kg can be lifted clear of the ground in this way (Mackay and Mathews 1974).

The direct observations of Bowers *et al.* (1983) on the displacement of stone artefacts in a periglacial environment demonstrate the potential. Although these authors are aware that some directionality and sorting would be caused by certain combinations of surface slope, other factors causing 'lop-sided' freezing and/or thawing (e.g. wind or oblique solar radiation), and heterogeneous surface texture and humidity, they observed essentially random creep (with respect to direction and intrinsic artefact properties such as weight) averaging *c.* 4 cm/year for individual artefacts in their experiments. The exact figure will of course depend upon the particular environment (the observations cited were made in Alaska at altitudes of around 800 m) but the order of magnitude seems applicable, probably as a maximum, to periglacial situations with low slopes. Bowers *et al.* also report a stochastic computer simulation, based upon the field observations and using a map of a replica knapping scatter as the starting point. After '100 years', the scatter had been almost homogenised and, judging from the published diagrams, general dilation had reached *c.* 20%; after '1000 years', dilation had reached *c.* 55% and there was no obvious trace of the original knapping patterning.

It is of interest here to note that no unequivocal signs of frost shattering post-dating manufacture have been observed on any of the Hengistbury flint artefacts so far recovered.

*Other natural processes:* A number of other natural process, such as treefall or burrowing, could have affected the horizontal distribution of the Hengistbury artefacts. Such processes will be discussed in detail below, with respect to their possible contribution to vertical dispersal. It is difficult to define the role of these processes in the horizontal plane, especially in situations close to the surface, beyond the suggestion that significant disturbance would probably be more patchy than uniform. Some of the refitted scatters from the Late Upper Palaeolithic site were recovered from an area which I will argue below was affected by treefall, yet they are not any more dispersed than those not apparently disturbed in this way. There is no sign at Hengistbury of any subsurface process which would have produced horizontal dispersal of greater magnitude than the observed vertical dispersal (70 cm maximum), save in probably rare and unpredictable cases involving large burrowing animals. With respect to assemblages rather than individual artefacts, I would suggest that the processes grouped here would not have caused horizontal dispersal on a significantly greater scale than would have been the case for wind action or rainsplash.

### 3.1.3    *Discussion of horizontal dispersion*

A number of natural processes have been considered above which might have helped to produce the degree of horizontal disturbance noted at Hengistbury. Mechanisms such as wind action and rainsplash seem to be good candidates in this respect. On the other hand, it has also been suggested on good theoretical grounds that these processes, either individually or in combination, would be most unlikely to have produced disturbance of significantly greater magnitude than that actually observed.

It therefore seems justifiable to reverse the point of view and suggest that natural disturbance is unlikely to have obscured all traces of the original anthropogenic spatial organisation of the sites. In addition, it may be suggested that the excavated material represents reasonably unbiased samples of the original stone artefact assemblages; it is unlikely that natural processes have been responsible for sorting or differential removal by size or shape, except sometimes in the case of the finest knapping debris.

Further evidence may be brought forward to support this view. In many cases, in both sites, refitted knapping scatters overlie one another, yet the details of each distribution *are* significantly different. Consider, for example, the centroid diagrams in Figure 3.10 (Chapter 3.2.3). Cores A and B appear to be knapping scatters which have been 'stretched' whilst maintaining some of the original internal relationships. Core H shows a more homogeneous distribution, and Core J bears little resemblance to a 'classic' knapping scatter. It is also the case that these overlapping scatters have significantly different overall shapes and orientations of the axis of elongation. What natural process, acting upon the same space which contained all these groups, could have differentiated between group members to produce such variation?

However, these arguments cannot be pushed too far. It has been noted (see Chapter 5.5.5) that there is good reason to suppose that the Powell Mesolithic site represents a restricted range of activities, most probably carried out over a short length of time. Such clear evidence is not present at the Late Upper Palaeolithic site, which seems to represent a rather more complex set of activities (Chapter 4.10.6). What if the overlapping refitting scatters mentioned above were laid down at different times (different seasons or even different years)? Each new scatter would be affected by conditions at the time, whilst older scatters might have had a chance to 'settle' into their environment better. This supposition highlights both the limitations of the data and the pressing need for further careful and longer term experimentation on low energy taphonomic processes.

In most of this section I have tended to treat the Mesolithic and Late Upper Palaeolithic sites jointly. This is because no really major, qualitative differences between the types of horizontal distribution pattern in the two sites have yet been identified, despite the fact that their demonstrably different ages and the slightly different physical setting might lead one to expect some contrast. The main problem lies in ensuring comparability between data on refitting scatters from each site, since the smaller size of artefacts, their greater density and the type of raw material at the Powell Mesolithic site all make refitting programmes very much more arduous than with the Late Upper Palaeolithic material. There is a suspicion, for example, that the Late Upper Palaeolithic knapping scatters may be more diffuse than the Mesolithic ones; if this could be proven in the future it would be of some significance, especially since the Mesolithic material, being composed of smaller objects on the average and having been originally deposited on slightly higher surface slopes, ought to have been a little more susceptible to movement under low energy conditions.

One of the few absolute difference which has been reported by the excavators is the considerable underrepresentation of fine debitage at the Late Upper Palaeolithic site, a pattern not repeated at the Powell Mesolithic site. It seems most likely that this contrast is due to differing wind effects. This is logical given the probability that the Palaeolithic environment was much more open than the Mesolithic one. However, geological data (cf. Chapter 2.1.6) show that the sediments in the Powell Mesolithic site have been modified by wind deflation whilst there is no such suggestion for the Palaeolithic site. This apparent contradiction might be explained by the concept of temporal increase in stability through environmental integration, mentioned on several occasions above. I put forward the hypothesis that the Mesolithic artefacts were able to 'settle' into their environment so that, during a later deflation event, they reacted as elements in overall dynamic equilibrium as part of the sedimentary context. At the Late Upper Palaeolithic site, however, I suggest that the artefacts were affected by wind whilst they still represented anomalies in the natural environment; in addition to greater wind exposure or actual windiness, it is even possible that the Late Upper Palaeolithic artefacts remained on the surface for longer, perhaps due to a frozen substrate or simply to lower sedimentation rates. It is interesting to speculate upon the degree to which trampling, by quickly integrating the artefacts into the sediment, might modify the susceptibility of an assemblage to horizontal disturbance mechanisms other than the trampling itself. Clearly, such conjecture cannot be pursued with the information presently available. However, I see no reason why this sort of question may not be approached in the future, with both improved analyses of the archaeological material and more detailed and controlled experimentation.

Simply because of the geometry involved, horizontal dispersal in low energy systems is likely to be the cumulative result of a number of different processes, rather than of a single dominant one. In the light of the above discussion, it is suggested that no process which appears possible in the Hengistbury context would be sufficient on its own to account for the observed distribution, nor can any possible process be ignored since it will probably have been at least a minor contributor to the overall pattern.

### 3.1.4 *Processes affecting the vertical distribution of artefacts*

*Slow mass movement, plastic deformation and faulting:* As was noted above and in Chapter 2.1, processes dependent upon high sediment plasticity, high slopes, common ground ice or combinations of these are most unlikely to have been active in the sandy deposits at Hengistbury. Thus, solifluction (and gelifluction), convolutions and other major plastic responses will not have affected the artefacts, a proposition which is supported by the lack of major sedimentary structures which would inevitably have resulted from such processes. Even if slopes had been locally sufficient to allow some form of creep, the resulting vertical profile would show an upward increase in artefact size (cf. Culling 1963), a trend which is the exact opposite of that which I have actually observed, not to mention lateral size sorting (cf. Rick 1976).

However, a degree of basal deformation, in those sediments which are relatively rich in fine material and well be'ow the archaeological zones, is a theoretical possibility. Such basal movement, whether dominantly vertical or lateral, would automatically have caused faulting in the overlying sands, material which, even before strong podzolisation, would almost certainly have been able to respond only in a brittle manner. No faulting of the pedogenic horizons has been observed on the Head, except very close to recent cliffs and where heavy vehicles have been brought into the Eastern Depression. Any faulting pre-dating maturing of the podzolic horizons might now be invisible as such, but no major disjunction of the artefact bands has yet been observed.

It is therefore concluded that plastic deformation and faulting played no significant role in the development of the vertical spread of artefacts at Hengistbury, although minor basal movement might have produced very low amplitude and low frequency warping of the sites as a whole.

*Chemical and ground water processes:* Chemical processes are most unlikely to have affected directly the Hengistbury artefacts but pedological processes, involving colloid and solute mobility, would certainly have acted as secondary controls to other movement mechanisms. Broadly, upper horizons would progressively lose colloids, and thus plasticity and water-holding capability, whilst lower horizons would be slowly indurated, mostly by iron compounds. Apart from mechanical changes, overall nutrient status would decline, reducing biological activity.

Ground water would also have formed a part of the pedological/biological system. In addition to capillary and adsorbed water, the local water table would probably be subject to marked fluctuation over much of the period of interest. Apart from acting as an adhesive when scarce and a lubricant when common, water under pressure might cause some dilation of sediments.

Repeated shrinkage and swelling (the *argilliturbation* of some authors) is usually caused by a combination of chemical and ground water processes. Moeyersons (1978) has demonstrated through detailed experimentation that some movement of artefacts can be brought about by this mechanism (but see below). However, the effect will only be marked when the sediment contains significant quantities of hygrophilic colloids and expanding clay minerals; in extreme cases such as in gilgai, stones are usually expelled upwards and a reverse grading may develop (cf. Johnson and Hester 1972). Within the sediments of the Head, shrinkage and swelling would have been a very minor process, even before the onset of podzolisation; the clayier subsoil does not now show macroscopic shrinkage cracks when left to dry.

The total contribution of chemical and ground water processes to vertical movement of artefacts at Hengistbury is rather difficult to assess. It seems probable that, overall, such processes would never have been highly significant and that, through time, a slight tendency towards facilitating movement would have shifted to a growing tendency towards inhibiting movement.

*Cryological processes:* As has been noted at several points in the preceding text, the main sand body on the Head is not now, and most probably never was, anything more than very marginally frost-susceptible. Violent subsurface disturbance associated with the segregation of ground ice is therefore most unlikely.

However, freezing without significant segregation would certainly have occurred, at least at the end of the Pleistocene. With very coarse approximations of the relevant parameters, using values quoted by Washburn (1979) and Linell and Tedrow (1981), and employing the formula of Yong and Warkentin (1975), the depth of maximum freezing to be expected in a generalised sandy sediment under conditions similar to those on the present-day Norwegian coast at the Arctic Circle would be *c.* 1.9 m. It can therefore be tentatively suggested that weak vertical frost sorting might theoretically have been possible in the Hengistbury sands. Such effects have received considerable attention in the general archaeological literature (cf. Williams 1973; Johnson and Hansen 1974; Johnson *et al*. 1977; Wood and Johnson 1978; Rolfsen 1980).

Two separate processes, frost-pull and frost-push, may be involved (cf. Washburn 1979) but the effects are inseparable in practice. The critical parameter is effective height, the dimension of the object parallel to the maximum heat loss gradient (often roughly at right angles to the ground surface); the greater the effective height, the greater the potential for movement of the object towards the surface. Furthermore, effective height of elongated objects is maximised by frost-pull since this process tends to rotate such objects to orientations nearer the upright. Subsurface frost sorting should therefore produce a clearly recognisable vertical artefact distribution, with size (represented by weight given a uniform raw material), length and dip all inversely proportional to depth. I have observed that the Hengistbury artefact distributions show the opposite trends to those expected under the frost sorting hypothesis.

*Wind deflation*: Wind deflation is a process which counteracts most of the other processes discussed here. When an artefact assemblage has been dispersed in the vertical plane by any combination of mechanisms, the removal of the finer sediment matrix by wind erosion reconcentrates the assemblage at the new surface, together with any natural larger particles that lay within the deflated material (cf. Wood and Johnson 1978). Deflation has been a process of considerable importance at Hengistbury, especially at the Powell Mesolithic site, as can be demonstrated by geological methods (see Chapter 2.1.6 and 2.1.8). Theoretically, once artefacts have been re-exposed at a surface, direct wind action can again come into play (see above).

*Large scale biological processes:* Two different sets of biological processes are discussed here: treefall and large scale burrowing.

*Treefall*: can occur at quite a wide range of energy levels. At one extreme, a tree may die and its subsurface tissue may decay *in situ*, producing only minor and very localised disturbance of artefacts contained within the surrounding sediment. I have recognised examples of the resulting structures at the Late Upper Palaeolithic site (see Chapter 2.1.5). At the other extreme, a healthy tree can be uprooted by high wind, giving rise to a relatively large area of disturbance. If the process is repeated in an area with relatively cohesive sediments, irregular cradle-knoll topography may result.

Newell (1981) has collated data on treefall (windthrow) features, citing horizontal maximum dimensions between 1.7 m and 7.62 m with an average of around 3m, and maximum depths between 0.2 m

and 1.9 m with an average of around 0.5 m. However, these figures do not take into account differences in tree size and species (rooting pattern), in ground water conditions, or in sediment/soil type (cf. Woodman, 1985), parameters which must have a very considerable effect upon the eventual extent of disturbance. Wood and Johnson (1978) give a more detailed discussion of this topic and, amongst other things, they cite figures which suggest that disturbance (measured either areally or by volume) is roughly linearly proportional to tree diameter. Many observers have noted that most windthrow depressions are elongated in plan and asymmetrical in the vertical plane, with the steeper side in the direction of treefall. In addition to overall disturbance, there appears to be a tendency (not yet confirmed by widespread observation) for a certain degree of size sorting in the eventual backfill of windthrow depressions; larger objects may remain trapped for longer in the exposed uplifted roots, whilst smaller objects are quickly redeposited, thus giving an upward coarsening trend. In addition, treefall, especially in sandy soils, may accelerate wind deflation and therefore may help to concentrate artefacts at or near the new surface.

At Hengistbury, I have not yet recognised features with the classic characteristics of treefall depressions, a rather surprising state of affairs, since the Head was lightly wooded during at least the earlier part of the Flandrian. In Chapter 2.1.9 and 2.3.3 it was argued that trees on top of the Head would have been rather small. It was also suggested that considerable sand overburden was removed from above both the Late Upper Palaeolithic and Powell Mesolithic sites by wind erosion after woodland clearance in later prehistory. It is therefore possible that the artefacts of interest always lay below the zone of greatest treefall disturbance. However, it is also possible that treefall features have been masked by later podzolisation; the only remaining trace might then be a rough upward increase in artefact size (assuming no later redistribution by other subsurface processes). Such a trend would be counter to the general upward decrease actually observed at the sites, although there is one interesting case in the area fully excavated by Campbell at the Late Upper Palaeolithic site. In six metre squares (F24, F23, G24, G23, H24 and H23), there is certainly no downward increase in artefact size and there is a slight suggestion that there might even be a reverse tendency. Campbell (1977, Fig. 46) records, in G of his Section 23/24, a '?hearth' below a 'disturbance feature' set in a basin shaped pocket of his Layer A1b, a 'layer' which my observations of extant sections have consistently shown to be composed of organic-rich disturbed material. It seems likely that these three stratigraphic features should be grouped and seen as an intrusive depression which, together with the size trend, would constitute an anomaly that would be strongly suggestive of a treefall effect.

It is therefore concluded that, whilst individual treefall disturbances may have affected artefacts in a few places, the dominant characteristics of the present vertical distribution result from other mechanisms.

*Animal burrowing*: The second set of processes of interest here involve the burrowing activities of animals which are quite large in relation to the size of the artefacts; the majority of the artefacts would thus be vulnerable to falling into burrows or to being directly displaced by the digging itself. Worldwide, the variety of large burrowing animals is considerable (cf. Hole 1981) and most environmental settings will have at least two or three species. Thus, Rolfsen (1980) reports artefacts being brought to the surface as well as being carried down to the lowest parts of burrows by voles in Norway, whilst Erlandson (1984) discusses similar bidirectional effects due to the pocket gopher in the USA. Given heavy bioturbation of this sort in an environment with stable, non-accreting surfaces, an originally discrete artefact horizon might be split into two bands, one above the other, separated by a sterile zone or at least by one where artefacts were significantly rarer. It should be noted that even arid dune fields may suffer considerable large to medium scale faunalturbation (cf. Ahlbrandt *et al.* 1978).

At Hengistbury, the most obvious burrowing animal is the rabbit. Burrows are today found wherever low banks provide a roughly vertical surface from which excavation can begin; burrows then run inwards for 4–5 m at most, before turning upwards towards a high level 'back door'. Burrows are common on better drained slopes but very rare in the damper Eastern Depression. Features of rabbit dimension have disturbed the artefacts in a few cases, especially at the dry Powell Mesolithic site where recent cliff recession has produced a suitable bank. However, all burrows of this type are very clear (sharp contacts and dark, organic-rich fill); there are no features with increasingly diffuse and leached characteristics, suggesting that rabbit disturbance is a relatively recent effect. Other burrows, probably produced by small rodents, rarely penetrate more than 10–15 cm into the top of the sands. One last class of rare unbranching burrows, 2–3 cm wide with long vertical and horizontal sections joined more or less at right angles, have been observed to penetrate right through the sand body and into the clayier subsoil; the animal responsible has not been identified but it seems possible that a reptile is involved.

The lack of altered and thus relatively old burrows of any type at either of the archaeological sites suggests that larger scale burrowing has not been a significant factor in the development of vertical artefact distributions, at least since the podzolic soils approached maturity 3–4 thousand years ago. However, within part of the Mesolithic site, the artefact distribution is split into two higher density bands, one above the other, with refits between the bands, a pattern which might be due to large scale bioturbation although there are absolutely no signs of burrows today. The difficulty here is that other processes (e.g. wind deflation) can produce a similar bimodal pattern. Data is not yet available on the size and shape sorting, if any, produced by large scale burrowing, a fact which seriously hinders deductive analysis.

*Smaller scale biological processes*: Again, two sets of processes are discussed here, those dependent upon soil mesofauna and those dependent upon biologically active plant roots. However, due to the small size of these agents in relation to the majority of artefacts, the end result is likely to be similar, whether fauna or flora are involved.

There is a very large literature on soil mesofauna in various environmental settings (cf. Hole 1981); in most cases, the activity of this fauna has been observed to have a marked effect upon the vertical distribution of larger objects within the soil. The groups which have been studied most thoroughly include ants (cf. Baxter and Hole 1967; Wiken *et al.* 1976), termites (cf. Nye 1955; Ruhe 1959; Williams 1968; Lee and Wood 1971; Pomeroy 1976), beetles (cf. Brussaard and Runia 1984; Kalisz and Stone 1984) and earthworms (cf. Satchell 1983). Research into marine bioturbation has also produced much data on basic mechanisms, of interest even in the terrestrial setting, including work on lugworms (cf. Hylleberg 1975) and callianassid shrimps (cf. Tudhope and Scoffin 1984).

The group which has perhaps received most attention from archaeologists in temperate environments comprises the earthworms. Atkinson (1957) has publicised the extraordinarily detailed observations of Darwin (first appearing in 1881 but more readily available in the 1883 edition) concerning earthworms (and lugworms). Darwin concentrated upon those species which ingest soil material at depth and then cast at the surface; he noted that objects become progressively buried in this way. However, Darwin also observed:

"The specific gravity of the objects does not affect their rate of sinking, as could be seen by porous cinders, burnt marl, chalk and quartz pebbles, having all sunk to the same depth within the same time [15 years]."(1883, 160).

It is of crucial importance that Darwin was reporting an observed real situation involving relatively heavy loamy soils and small objects (less than one inch in diameter). Cornwall added further detail:

"One effect of the bringing by worms of their castings to the surface is to sink into the soil, and eventually bury, any body lying on it which is too large to be swallowed by them. This sinking is assisted by the collapse, below, of old worm-tunnels and the falling in of the subsoil which has been penetrated by them. The resultant rate of sinking of stones and other bodies is commensurate with the surface accumulation and may amount to as much as 1/5 inch annually." (1958, 52).

The concept implied by both Darwin and Cornwall involves the letting-down of objects by removal of sediment from below and its accumulation above; the word 'sink' does not appear to imply differential movement between objects and the bulk of their matrix. This concept is probably the cause of such statements as that of Barker:

"[...] it is most unlikely that the vertical stratigraphic relationship of objects will be reversed by earthworm action; that is, objects will rarely overtake one another so that a later object finishes up below an earlier one in the same series of layers." (1977, 120).

I reject this last statement as an improper generalisation; stratigraphic reversals may be rare (although by no means impossible) in stiff, clayey sediment but, in sandier deposits, any such assumption is most dangerous, as will be demonstrated below.

That the simple 'excavation below/redeposition above' model proposed by Darwin and others was unacceptable, at least in sandier deposits, appeared likely in the present context from the start. Accordingly, a very simple experiment was set up: if absolute downward movement of artefacts required actual removal of sediment from below, the mere creation and destruction of voids below artefacts should have no overall effect. Stein appears to accept this proposition when she writes: "They [earthworms] may not necessarily affect the position of larger objects, but will definitely disturb material less than 2 mm in diameter." (1983, 286). Since my experiment was informal and qualitative, I will not quote exact dimensions here.

A vertical cylinder, wide enough that the sides should not interfere with movement of moderately sized flint artefacts, was filled with Hengistbury sand. Pairs of artefacts, of similar shape but differing size (weight), were placed on the sand surface. Small holes around the base of the cylinder were used to introduce a long needle into the sand well below the artefacts, gently by hand; the needle was kept horizontal and each entry hole was used in rotation, again and again. The experiment was repeated over various durations and with different pairs of artefacts. Artefacts always sank into the sand quite quickly and, in the majority of cases, the larger artefact sank faster. Coloured grains set initially in a continuous marker band between the artefacts and the zone of needle penetration suffered both upward and downward displacement, suggesting that the whole sand volume was reacting to the void creation/destruction; no coloured grains reached the surface, even when an artefact had sunk to the original level of the marker band. The effect described was quickly slowed, but not changed qualitatively, by moistening the sand although, when the sand became truly wet, the effect again accelerated.

Without making any exaggerated claims for the validity of this experiment, I do feel that it demonstrates the possibility that the artefacts themselves can play an *active* role in dispersal and that the characteristics (weight, shape, etc.) of individual objects may be very important.

Moeyersons (1978), experimenting with a sandy loam (a clayier sediment than the Hengistbury sand would ever have been), noted the importance of weight and shape factors to the pattern of vertical dispersal under conditions of gentle wetting and drying and other forms of mechanical consolidation. He noted that heavier stone artefacts sank faster than lighter ones but that the dispersal effect dropped off rapidly as the sediment compacted. Moeyersons's shape experiments do not appear to me to be truly valid because he used wooden blocks instead of stone, claiming that weight is unimportant once an object is well buried; I feel that valid observations can only be made if objects have a significantly higher density than the bulk density of the matrix. The aim of these experiments was to elucidate the conditions which had separated refitting artefacts by over a metre vertically in the Central African archaeological site of Gombe (cf. also Cahen and Moeyersons 1977). It is Moeyersons's conclusions that have caused me to cite his work at this point:

"The experiments show that vertical dispersion of artefacts can be expected in a consolidating [...] mantle. However, it is evident that the high degree of vertical dispersion of artefacts, as recorded at Gombe, can only be explained by a high number of reiterations: in other words, consolidation and destruction of structures should have occurred repeatedly at Gombe.
It is [...] strongly suggested here that the activity of termites and worms can lead to recurrent or maybe continuous consolidation of the mantle. Indeed, galleries, holes and burrows are partly the result of the biogenic removal of particles from the inner part of the mantle. [...] Their consecutive collapse finally will transform the soil, which was consolidated before, into a loose mantle, ready to reconsolidate under the weight of the overburden" (1978, 126).

Combining Moeyersons's observations and a number of other relevant points of information, a series of general propositions may be constructed concerning the effects of small scale biological activity on vertical artefact distribution.

First, it may be said that small scale biological activity causes a dilation of the sediment. Earthworms (and some marine worms) transport fine sediment (usually particles <1–2 mm in diameter) within their gut. Some species cast this sediment upon reaching the surface but many other species cast immediately or cast in existing underground voids (cf. Stein 1983). In addition, many animals, especially insects of various sorts, carry fine sediment in their mouthparts or roll aggregates, and redistribute the material often nearer the surface. Granted that sedimentation rate is low compared with biological activity, the overall result of differential particle size translocation in a variety of environments (by casting, carrying or more unusual methods such as water-jetting) is known to be normally graded bedding (cf. Rhoades and Stanley 1965; Warme 1967; Pomeroy 1976; Tudhope and Scoffin 1984); in such stable sedimentary situations, the graded bed is often underlain by a stone-line, marking the lower limit of activity. On the other hand, if sedimentation rate is fast, irregular or even negative, or if subsurface environmental parameters (temperature, moisture, etc.) fluctuate significantly, a decreasingly well marked pattern, or no pattern at all, will result.

However, earthworms also force their way through sediment without ingesting that sediment. Clearly, many other types of soil mesofauna do this as well, as do growing roots (cf. Rolfsen 1980). The potential importance of roots in connection with void creation is illustrated by Dickinson's (1982) suggestion that, on semi-permanent grassland in Staffordshire today, there is total growth-decay turnover of the rooting system in only one year.

Biological activity therefore dilates the deposit, whether or not sediment is actually transported to higher levels. With sufficient time, the effect might reasonably be expected to become more or less uniform wherever environmental parameters are uniform. However, earthworms and other soil mesofauna preferentially undermine stones (cf. Rolfsen 1980), presumably for microenvironmental reasons, thus increasing the potential for subsidence of these larger objects.

Counteracting the biological dilation, overburden pressure causes a compaction of the sediment, the two sets of processes being coupled to give almost a 'seething' quality to the deposit through time. The effect will diminish with depth, because the sediment will be more compacted overall and biological activity will be less extreme.

Nearer the surface, a stone artefact, which will be markedly denser than the surrounding sediment, will represent a heavier overburden with respect to voids immediately underlying it. The extent of the 'zone of influence' of an artefact will depend mostly upon the characteristics of the sediment. I expect from theory that the greatest zone of influence would develop in a dry, well rounded sand or in a strongly plastic material but, given time, the tendency should develop in any deposit where the extra pressure exerted by the artefact is enough to overcome cohesive and frictional forces. Conversely, I would expect that the density differential might not be enough to produce significant movement in highly cohesive sediments which are able to spread the overburden load more evenly, thus explaining the normal absence of really diffuse bands of artefacts in sites with heavy soils, even when these soils have suffered small scale bioturbation.

I therefore suggest the concept of a threshold for a given combination of mechanical sediment properties and of individual artefact characteristics; below the threshold, the artefact is not 'forceful' enough to overcome the resistance of the sediment but, above the threshold, the sediment yields. This concept has several logical consequences.

Small artefacts may not represent sufficient density anomalies to initiate sinking and I would expect them to play a more passive role. Earthworms and many other types of soil mesofauna deliberately shunt or carry in their mouthparts, not only fine particles, but also particles which are too large to ingest (the actual maximum size of particle depends upon the size of the animal and the shape of the particle; European earthworms certainly carry objects at least as large as 4

mm). These larger particles may be redeposited anywhere but they are sometimes used as structural elements within the burrow system (e.g. material to floor sleeping chambers or to act as trapdoors in certain passages). Also, active growth of roots will displace small artefacts more easily than larger ones. Rather than being left behind at the top of a dispersion band, I would expect the distribution of small artefacts to be a function of biological patterning which, given time and a number of different biological agents, might give a random result overall.

Unusually large objects might also prove more resistant to movement than the general trend might suggest. Although such objects are heavy, there must come a point where the size differential between object and underlying voids is so great that a high concentration of voids would be necessary, simultaneously present below most parts of the object, before the object could overcome the cohesive and frictional forces. Darwin, speaking of prehistoric standing monuments, noted that the "sinking [of great fragments of stone] does not appear to have been sensibly aided by their weight, though this was considerable" (1883, 161).

The density of a material such as flint is sufficiently uniform for the more easily measured parameter of weight to act as a substitute for size during analysis. However, cortical flint is a little less dense and, more importantly, the surface is very much rougher than interior flint, suggesting that movement of cortical pieces might be relatively inhibited. It is interesting that Salazar-Jimenez et al. (1982) suggest that the degree of surface ornamentation of shells affects their susceptibility to displacement during marine bioturbation.

Stone artefacts are not regular objects. Any inequality of weight distribution will produce torque, whilst inequalities of shape will tend to give realignment during movement to minimise friction. However, these parameters and their various possible combinations are extremely difficult to evaluate. I observed twisting of descending artefacts, both in my sand cylinder experiment (reported above) and in another informal experiment involving bringing a sand column containing artefacts to quick conditions by gently increasing upwards water through-flow. The twisting behaviour of a given artefact was not accurately predictable and seemed to be very sensitive to the initial orientation of the piece. However, in the great majority of cases, I did observe in both experiments that the further an artefact descended, the greater became its principal component of dip. The downward pressure exerted by a platy object is increased if its weight acts upon a smaller area (i.e. if the dip of the object is increased). The main exception to this trend would be expected if biological activity stops or shifts its focus upwards for some reason. Uninterrupted compaction at this deep level would then tend to reduce dip again, as would lateral shear at any level.

If factors such as weight, shape and surface roughness are indeed important as controls of artefact dispersal, then possible subsurface modification of these factors cannot be ignored. Even flint artefacts are not immutable, particularly in the case of heavily burnt pieces. It appears likely that severe thermal fractures might be vulnerable to total failure, due to minor but repeated moisture, temperature or pressure changes in the sediment matrix, long after the initial burning episode. Thus, a heavily burnt piece might undergo a significant period of subsidence as a *large* artefact, but might then break up into several *small* artefacts. The fact that a severely burnt surface will produce increased frictional resistance to movement must also be considered; if the ratio of smooth unburnt surface to hackly surface changes during the burial period, a most complex distribution pattern might arise.

At Hengistbury, conditions governing the effects of small scale biological activity have changed significantly since the formation of the Late Upper Palaeolithic and Mesolithic sites. At earlier points (but later than periods of significant sediment freezing), the soil conditions would have been much more favourable to biological activity of all types but, at the same time, the sediments would have been more cohesive and less responsive to individual artefacts. Later, increasing podzolisation would have reduced overall biological activity concomitantly with reduction in sediment cohesion. However, even podzols are by no means biologically sterile. Today, earthworms are very rare in the sand body but ants and burrowing wasps are significantly present, at least in the upper zone; beetles and rootlets, although nowhere abundant, penetrate right through the sand body into the clayier subsoil. Ahlbrandt *et al.* (1978) note the surprisingly high biomass of soil mesofauna in aeolian sands in general, even in arid dune fields. Downward artefact displacement would never have been rapid at Hengistbury but, given the very long periods available, it seems highly probable that low to moderate small scale biological activity coupled with continual sediment compaction will together have constituted the dominant artefact dispersal mechanism. Furthermore, the potential for differential movement according to intrinsic artefact characteristics (weight, shape, etc.) is clear.

I believe that further laboratory experimentation to demonstrate more precisely the effects of small scale biological activity is within present capabilities. Using forced population concentrations (of earthworms, for example), deeply buried nutrient sources and artificially accelerated diurnality/seasonality, I would expect significant vertical patterning of artefacts to develop, at least in sandier sediments, within a period of about five years. A mechanised version of my sand cylinder would also be helpful to investigate the more complex effects of artefact shape.

### 3.1.5 A model for a site in a dominantly depositional sedimentary environment: the Late Upper Palaeolithic site

I start with the proposition (discussed elsewhere in this volume) that the overwhelming majority of the artefacts are referable to a single Late Upper Palaeolithic occupation or, at most, to a series of such occupations in very close spatial and temporal proximity. Within relatively small areas, the original living surface had negligible vertical relief when compared with the total vertical spread in artefacts observed today. Trampling would have resulted in artefacts being variously buried (dependent upon the exact state of the surface at the time) but, again, the maximum depth of trampling effects would have been very much less than the current lower limit of dispersal. At the time of abandonment, artefacts would have been present in a relatively narrow band, at and just under the surface; it is assumed that within relatively small areas this band was more or less horizontal.

Aeolian sedimentation continued to bury the artefacts more deeply, until some time in the Neolithic or Bronze Age when net deposition switched to net erosion (see Chapter 2.1.9). In some areas of the Eastern Depression Late Upper Palaeolithic material may have been disinterred and dispersed by erosion but, within the main excavated areas, the erosion front stopped before significantly affecting the artefact distribution. Vertical dispersal was therefore a subsurface phenomenon, with no massive reversals or recycling.

The dominant processes producing vertical dispersal of the artefacts were various types of biological activity. Larger scale effects, such as those resulting from major burrowing and treefall events, were localised and may be recognised by particular distribution patterns and by sedimentary features. It was the smaller scale effects, cumulated over relatively long periods, which caused the general vertical distribution pattern to develop. Such effects can be divided into two main categories: (1) direct displacement of at least the smallest artefacts by biological agents; and (2) the creation of small (millimetre scale) voids in the sandy sediment by biological agents followed by the collapse of these voids, allowing differential movement of artefacts, movement powered by gravity but governed by the intrinsic properties of individual pieces.

Artefacts dating from periods later than the Upper Palaeolithic will often be recognisable as such, not only due to intrinsic factors, but also because they entered a system with essentially cumulative effects at a later stage; such intrusive objects will occupy anomalous ('immature') positions within the general vertical distribution pattern.

If this model approximates to the real taphonomic history of the Late Upper Palaeolithic site, a number of predictions concerning the artefact patterning can be made:

*Basic Model*: 1. There will be a significant increase in size (weight) with depth of burial; 2. There will be a significant increase in artefact dip with depth of burial, except in the lowest zone where dominant compaction of sediment should cause a reversal of the trend; 3. Any measure which combines the properties of artefact weight, shape and dip in such a way as to reflect the vertical component of force exerted by the artefact under gravity will show a better correlation with depth than any one of the properties considered in isolation.

*Refinements:* 4. The smallest artefacts will not show a weight/depth correlation but will show a random weight distribution, probably with a mode in numbers nearer the centre of the vertical spread; 5. Cortical pieces will show frictional retardation in proportion to the relative amount of cortical surface (theoretical considerations would suggest that the relationship is likely to be curvilinear); 6. Heavily burnt artefacts will show a very complex vertical distribution pattern and not the general weight/depth correlation expected in sound unburnt flints. Since progressive comminution would result in smaller pieces occurring too low but increases in the proportion of hackly surface would result in frictional retardation, prediction of the distribution pattern for this class of object would be extremely difficult; 7. Intrusive (significantly younger) artefacts will show the same dispersal pattern as the population as a whole when considered separately but, in absolute terms, their pattern will be immature. Intrusive artefacts will therefore appear to lie too high when compared with the overall pattern of dispersal.

*Anomalies:* 8. Marked divergence from the above model should be localised in the horizontal plane if the general reasoning concerning the Late Upper Palaeolithic site is correct. When a different and well developed pattern can be firmly demonstrated (e.g. reverse size grading, bimodal spatial or weight distribution in the vertical plane, etc.) more than one mechanism could be responsible; data on associated sedimentary structures will be needed to differentiate between the possibilities deduced from spatial distribution of artefacts.

*Data:* Two different sorts of data batch could be used to test these predictions. First, the total assemblage from a small number of contiguous excavation squares could be chosen. This approach would have the advantage of providing a large enough sample in a small area, so that one would not have to rely too heavily upon the assumption of original horizontality; the disadvantage is that artefacts dating from different periods might be included.

Second, one or more refitted groups could be chosen. This approach would have the advantage of providing samples of demonstrably contemporary artefacts (at least, within each refitted group); the disadvantage is that a much larger number of contiguous squares would be need to provide large enough samples, putting more strain upon the assumption of original horizontality.

### 3.1.6 *A model for a site in a variable sedimentary environment involving both deposition and erosion: the Powell Mesolithic site*

Essentially the same basic model is proposed for the Powell Mesolithic site as for the Late Upper Palaeolithic site. However, at the former, four special circumstances arose which greatly complicated the final vertical distribution pattern: (1) the presence well below the level of the original Mesolithic occupation surface (or trampling band) of a diffuse deflation lag, including in places relatively large cobbles; (2) continued deflation of the sand body after the Mesolithic occupation, perhaps reaching a maximum during woodland clearance in later prehistory; (3) the possible activity of an undefined burrowing animal at some time far enough in the past for pedological processes to have destroyed visible traces of burrows in the sediment; and (4) the addition to the system, probably during the Bronze Age, of a small number of artefacts, but including some relatively large pieces (e.g. cores). The predicted trajectory of finds through time is outlined in Figure 3.2.

Shortly after the Mesolithic occupation, the artefacts were concentrated in a shallow trampling band near the surface (Fig. 3.2, 1). The most likely vegetation would have been light woodland with a relatively important understorey. Soils would probably still have been at the brown earth stage and subsurface biological activity would have been vigorous.

The artefacts then drifted downwards and size sorting began to occur, due to the continual collapse of small scale biogenic voids, the mechanism already discussed in detail in above (Fig. 3.2, 2). The cobble lag deep in the sequence was only slightly affected, both because it lay in compacted sediment below the zone of greatest biological activity and because the lag was sometimes dense enough to interfere with movement of its own elements and with the passage of biological agents. The vegetation cover was still essentially open woodland, although soil conditions were becoming more acidic and subsurface biological activity had passed its maximum.

A major clearance phase occurred. From this point onwards, there was to be little if any woodland regeneration and biological activity on and within an already podzolic soil would change both qualitatively and quantitatively. The Mesolithic artefacts continued their downward drift, although the rate of drift decreased as biological activity declined. The larger pieces began to interact with the cobble lag (Fig. 3.2, 3), although real site observation shows that this lag was not present in all areas and, even when present, it was sometimes too deep for the artefact drift to reach it. A small number of, say, Bronze Age artefacts were deposited at the contemporary surface (Fig. 3.2, 4). Unequivocal later prehistoric artefacts have, of course, been identified in the dominantly Mesolithic assemblage.

Subsequent development may have proceeded along a number of different paths.

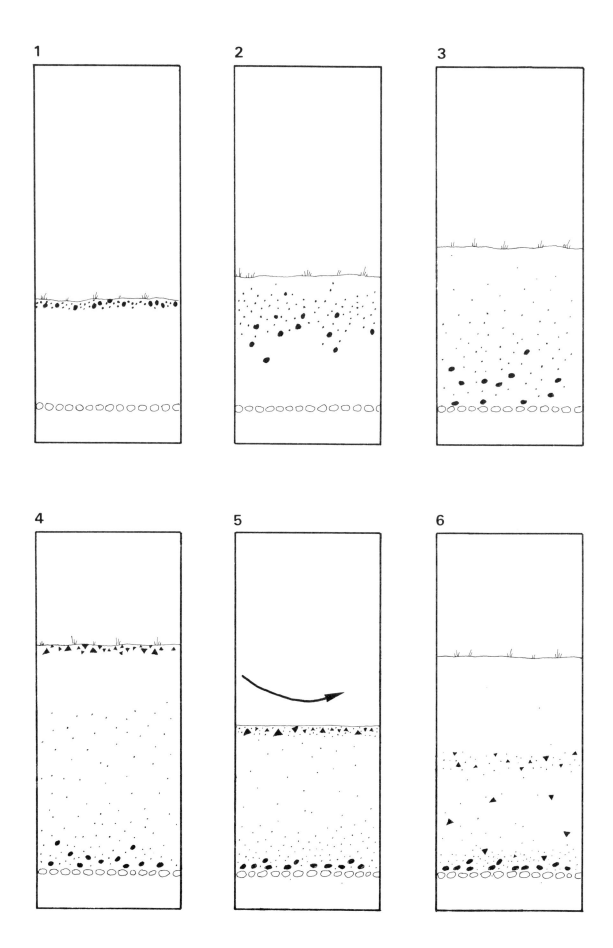

3.2   *Hypothetical stages of site formation at the Powell Mesolithic site (after Barton 1987). Key: 1= site shortly after abandonment; 2= downward drift and size sorting of artefacts; 3= downward drift slows down and larger pieces affected by cobble lag deposit; 4= Bronze Age occupation at surface; 5= wind deflation produces some mixing of Bronze Age artefacts with the upper part of Mesolithic distribution; 6= subsequent build up of sands resulting in the bimodal distribution of artefacts, as excavated.*

The simplest path merely involved continued deposition. The resulting vertical distribution pattern would have been very similar to that developed at the Late Upper Palaeolithic site. The main divergence would have been due to the effect of the cobble lag, where present, which would have caused the dispersal pattern to dense up again near the base and would have allowed only relatively small artefacts to penetrate through it. The accumulation of artefacts near the lag would have had a negative feedback effect, since biological activity would have been further inhibited.

A second possible path would have involved erosive processes (Fig. 3.2, 5), and especially wind deflation, reaching the artefact distribution. Those Mesolithic artefacts which previously lay highest in the sands (that is, the generally smaller ones) would have been disinterred and concentrated upon the degrading surface; some lateral displacement and reorganisation of these pieces might have occurred whilst they were exposed. These disinterred Mesolithic artefacts were now brought into close spatial association with the Bronze Age pieces. Note that there is indeed strong geological/pedological evidence for a truncation surface, most probably caused by wind deflation, at the top of the artefact distribution at the Powell Mesolithic site.

The timing of wind deflation events at the Mesolithic site is not clear. The real sediment parameters suggest that at least minor deflation was probably quite frequent during much of the Flandrian. Deflation events might have happened, on a local scale (localised clearance, treefall, natural fires, etc.), before the arrival of farming communities. However, the most economical use of the data would suggest that the presence of Bronze Age people, widespread clearance and major deflation of the disturbed surface would have followed closely and causatively one upon the next.

Given a little more vertical drifting of artefacts, a double-banded artefact distribution would eventually have resulted after major wind deflation (Fig. 3.2, 6).

A third possible path involves a population of unspecified larger burrowing animals digging into the archaeological deposits. Apart from disturbing objects in the vicinity of burrows, the creatures brought sediment, containing artefacts, back up to the surface. Older burrows were gently choked with fine sediment and organic matter and any remaining voids were closed by bulk subsidence. In this way, a middle zone depleted in artefacts developed.

It is reiterated that there is no independent evidence that this burrowing mechanism has indeed affected the Mesolithic site. No trace of burrows, other than obviously very recent ones, now survives. If larger scale burrowing did occur, it must have taken place several thousand years ago so that soil processes would have had a chance to obliterate the sedimentary structures. Of course, there is no clue whatsoever as to what type of animal might have been involved and mammals are not the only permissible candidates. However, even with this lack of hard evidence, I do not feel justified in ignoring this generally plausible possibility.

Given a little more vertical drifting of artefacts, a double-banded artefact distribution would eventually have resulted after major burrowing. The pattern would be very similar, if not identical, to that produced by wind deflation; no particularly convincing criteria have yet been discovered to distinguish between the effects of these two mechanisms. Note that, in some squares in the Mesolithic site, an extremely distinct double-banded distribution is indeed present, and that the two bands are linked by artefact refits.

Finally, it should be noted that not all possible combinations of process and timing have been covered (e.g. burrowing, followed by deflation, followed by more burrowing, etc.), nor have other possible processes, such as treefall, been considered.

If this model approximates to the real taphonomic history of the Powell Mesolithic site, the complexity of the situation would render most predictions concerning the fine details of the artefact patterning at least premature, if not impossible.

The only substantial prediction which can be derived from most, if not all 'versions' of the model is as follows: Those mechanisms suggested above as complicating the picture at the Powell Mesolithic site (cobble lag, wind deflation, burrowing animals, Bronze Age input and, perhaps, treefall as well) are most unlikely to have been equally influential in all parts of the site, so that laterally variable and patchy vertical distribution patterns ought to have resulted, probably on a horizontal scale of about 2–4 metres or even less. Such patchiness is certainly a feature of the sediments at this site.

### 3.1.7 Discussion of vertical dispersion

The relatively more simple model for the Late Upper Palaeolithic site is the more satisfactory in logical terms. Even given the facts that the real-world situation will inevitably include much random 'noise', and that many of the parameters which have actually been measured can only be approximations to the complex physical attributes of the artefacts, it is reasonable to expect that the clear predictions of the model can be tested statistically against the observed data to produce an unequivocal answer, one way or the other.

I have carried out an informal statistical analysis of detailed information for total artefacts recovered from two excavation squares at the Late Upper Palaeolithic site. The approach involved the calculation and optimisation of a non-parametric correlation coefficient, using stepped constraints increasingly close to the total model suggested above. For instance, the simple correlation between weight and depth was poor but, as each minor adjustment involved in the total model was made, the correlation coefficient became increasingly high (and statistically significant in non-parametric statistical terms). I am satisfied that the Hengistbury data (for these two squares, at least) fit all aspects of the model closely. A separate statistical approach is reported in section 4.4 below. The results were negative. I would suggest the following reasons: a) parametric statistics involve basic assumptions which are demonstrably false for the the data used; b) each sample extended over many excavation squares, putting extreme strain upon the assumption of an originally horizontal surface; and c) only part of the model was tested in isolation. The best statistical approach to this problem would involve either multivariate analysis (taking into account all the relevant parameters) or a more rigorous stepwise approach (similar to that already carried out). The multivariate approach has the disadvantage of being strictly simultaneous, with little chance to observe the individual effects of each part of the model. The stepwise approach allows interim observations. Taking an example from my own analysis, by iterative removal of the smaller artefacts to optimise the correlation between weight and depth in the remaining larger artefacts, I arrived at a cut-off weight which falls within the range reported by various authors under modern conditions for the largest objects subject to essentially random direct displacement by small scale biological processes.

At the Powell Mesolithic site, the vertical distribution appears to be very much more complex. Nevertheless, a plausible qualitative model has been proposed and the low-level prediction of strong but extremely variable patterning can be statistically tested.

The models for vertical dispersion for each of the two sites have the following general characteristics: (1) the models are plausible (or are even the most plausible ones available) given the acquired data on physical context; (2) the models are not inconsistent with the premise of dominant assemblage integrity, Upper Palaeolithic at one site, and Mesolithic at the other; and (3) the models do not resort to processes which would involve major horizontal disturbance as well as vertical dispersal (nor have any processes, both likely to have caused major horizontal dispersal and probable in these physical contexts, been ignored).

## 3.2 Anthropogenic effects on artefact taphonomy

### 3.2.1 Introduction

Various cumulative processes can affect the horizontal and vertical distribution of artefacts at archaeological sites (Schiffer 1987). In the last section attention was focused on natural post-depositional processes and the degree to which these may have affected the finds distributions at Hengistbury. In this section we assess the influences of human activities on the spatial patterning of artefacts at the Late Upper Palaeolithic and Mesolithic sites. One of the main propositions put forward here is that once post-depositional agencies can be identified and their cumulative influences on an individual site accurately assessed, they can effectively be removed from the site formation model, thus allowing patterns left by human activity to be more easily

interpreted. In other words, it is suggested that by quantifying the natural effects it is possible to reset the clock to the time that a site was abandoned and to observe spatial clustering of artefacts before many of the post-depositional processes had the time to take effect. In this way it is considered that patterns of anthropogenic activity can be identified even at sites where significant levels of natural disturbance are known or are suspected to have occurred.

In considering anthropogenic patterning at prehistoric sites like Hengistbury it is important to recognise the likely range of variation possible from artefact distributions in the horizontal and the vertical planes. For example, a reasonable starting point for any vertical distribution model is the fact that human activity takes place at or relatively close to the surface of the ground. The same parameters do not apply to the horizontal distributions where there is little guidance in defining the original spatial pattern or its physical boundaries. Moreover, the horizontal surface scatter is almost invariably several orders of magnitude greater than the vertical spread (even at sites in primary geological context). In consequence it is usually much more difficult to decide whether or not human action was involved in minor lateral displacements of artefacts than it is with a similarly moderate displacement in the vertical plane.

A further problem in interpreting horizontal distributional patterns is that anthropogenic and other processes working on or near an exposed surface are highly likely to be influenced by a variety of cumulative effects, whereas vertical distributions tend to reflect fewer or only single dominant taphonomic processes. Despite the inherent difficulties in reconstructing and interpreting the various taphonomic effects, we believe that the horizontal distribution of artefacts at Hengistbury contains spatial information on human activities at the site, which can be positively identified and separated from the background effects of post-depositional processes.

### 3.2.2 Flint artefact scatters at Hengistbury

The great value in studying lithic artefact scatter patterns is that the production processes involved are relatively uncomplicated and often leave highly distinctive patterns of residue (Cahen 1987). For a single nodule, the process of reduction may take no more than a few minutes and a single reduction episode can thus be seen as an activity of strictly limited duration. The resulting waste material left 'as flaked' may also closely reflect the actual methods of production, down to the working position of the flintknapper and sometimes even indicate the nature of percussive instruments used (Newcomer and Sieveking 1980). Unless affected by wholesale removal (collecting and dumping of waste cf. Gallagher 1977), any movement of individual pieces away from a primary production zone (by whatever means) will be referable to the original flaking scatter. This provides the archaeologist with a useful uniformitarian model and an important starting point for analysing spatial patterns and site structure.

A high proportion of the material recovered from the Late Upper Palaeolithic and Mesolithic sites at Hengistbury consists of flint knapping debitage, resulting from the production of blanks for tool manufacture. Because we are concerned here with general processes (anthropogenic effects on artefact scatters in sands) we have deliberately avoided dealing with the total horizontal distribution of artefacts at each site. Instead, we focus on a number of individual core reduction episodes which are then compared first with spatial data from experiments and then with comparable information from other archaeological flake scatters. The evidence is considered under the following sub-headings:

- The size and distribution of the Hengistbury refitted scatters
- The spatial distribution and size of experimental scatters
- Data on artefact scatters from archaeological sites in sands
- Other anthropogenic factors affecting horizontal distributions.

### 3.2.3  The size and distribution of the Hengistbury flint scatters

The South Central area of the Late Upper Palaeolithic site excavated by Campbell is characterised by a considerable concentration of blade and flake debitage plus associated blade cores (Fig. 3.3). Of particular interest is the apparent lack of overlap with the main concentration of retouched tools which lies further to the North West of the same area. The implications of this spatial clustering are discussed in more detail below (Chapter 4.4.4 and 4.10.6) but it is sufficient here to note that the accumulation of debitage in the South Central area is consistent with the expected pattern of a primary knapping zone where blanks were manufactured and the better pieces retained for use elsewhere. Some confirmation of this interpretation is provided by the refitting evidence which shows that amongst the more completely refitted core sequences noticeable gaps are present. Although positive proof is still lacking, it is clear that the missing elements include highly regular blades which are comparable in size to tools found in other parts of the site.

From the refitting evidence it is apparent that, in addition to the horizontal overlapping of different core episodes, each of the flint scatters appears to be of more or less uniform size and shape, being roughly sub-circular with a diameter of about 400–500 cm (Figs. 3.4–3.6). In some of the lesser scatters it is not as easy to identify an overall shape (Figs. 3.7–3.8). The one major refitted flint core at the Powell Mesolithic site is similar in shape to the larger Palaeolithic scatters (Fig. 3.9).

Different ways may be used for expressing the dimensions of the flint scatters. At the Late Upper Palaeolithic site, the distribution centres of each refitted core group (av(x), av(y)) were calculated with radii represented by the sum of the standard deviations (sd (x) + sd (y)). As a result the scatters can be shown to have the following radii: Core A= 306 cm; Core B= 243 cm; Core H= 286 cm and Core J= 360 cm (Fig. 4.52 and Table 4.23). These figures describe the maximum dimensions of the refitting clusters; they do not, for example, take into account areas of greater density within each scatter.

An alternative method of presenting these data is illustrated for four of the reassembled cores. An explanation of the method, which expresses the scatters with respect to a 'centroid', is provided below (Fig. 3.10). Although some experience is required in interpreting these diagrams, in practice it allows the area of the densest part of the scatter to be calculated. This enables rapid comparison with other scatters and the method has the potential for revealing subtle differences between distributions which may not be so readily apparent in simple two-dimensional scatter plots.

According to the density or 'centroid' diagrams, there would seem to be some subtle contrasts between the various different Upper Palaeolithic scatters. For example, in the plots of the centroids (Fig. 3.10) cores A and B appear to be knapping scatters which have 'stretched' whilst maintaining some of the original shape. On the other hand core H shows a more homogeneous distribution (note the position of the core some distance from the rest, showing as a well-separated peak) while core J apparently bears little resemblance to any of the others. In this respect, it may be significant that Core J includes two retouched tools, a fact which could have influenced the shape of the distribution, particularly if tool activity resulted in displacement of these and other pieces. Such events may help to explain the more 'dilated' appearance of this flint scatter. Apart from minor variation in their shape, there may also be very slight variation discernible in terms of the axis of the orientation of elongation of the scatters (Figs. 3.4–3.6).

Such minor divergences suggest that natural processes were not the agencies responsible for the accumulation of the artefact clusters or for the occasional removal of artefacts from core groups, except sometimes in the case of the finest knapping debris (see *wind action*, Chapter 3.1.2). Given the contrasting weight profiles of flakes and blades making up the individual flint clusters it is also hard to envisage post-depositional processes which could produce such a relatively high degree of uniformity in the overall shape and orientation of the observed scatters, without producing other very distinctive effects (cf. Schick 1986).

Although there is clearly no doubting the human hand behind the Hengistbury artefact scatters, much less certainty surrounds the original appearance of the knapping clusters and the degree to which these may or may not have been affected by subsequent activities or natural movements within the sediments. In order to assess how the scatters might have appeared when freshly knapped and to identify features associated

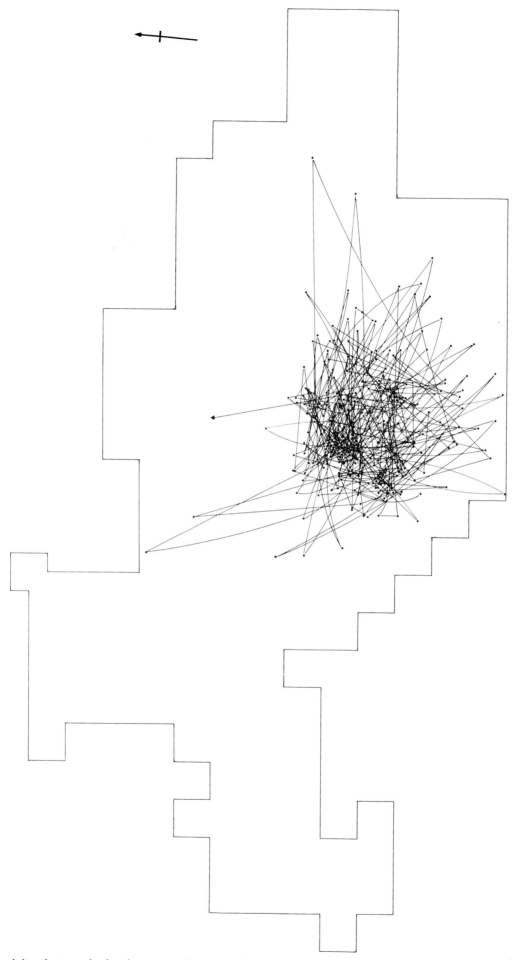

3.3 *Horizontal distribution of refitted cores (combination of cores A, B and H) at the Late Upper Palaeolithic site in Campbell's South Central area. The cores are indicated by solid triangles.*

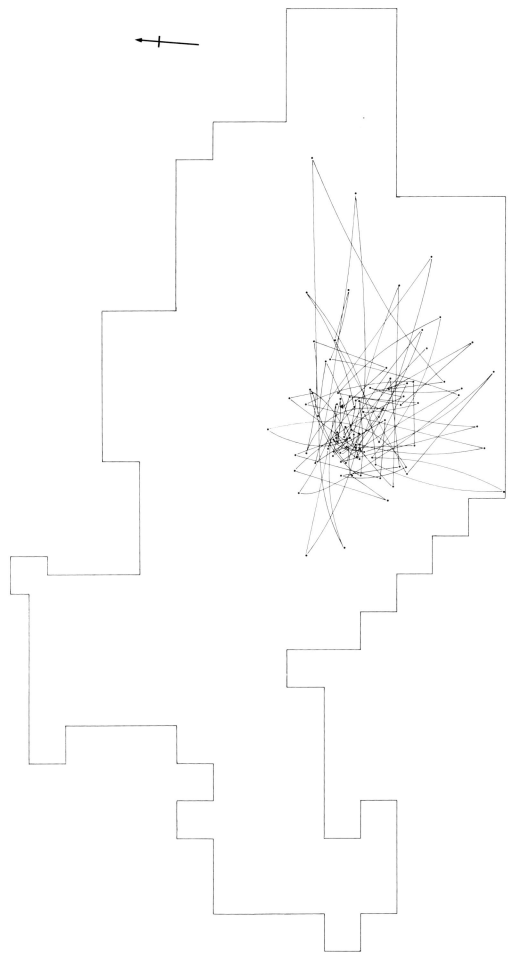

3.4  *Horizontal distribution of refitted core A at the LUP site. The core is indicated by a solid triangle.*

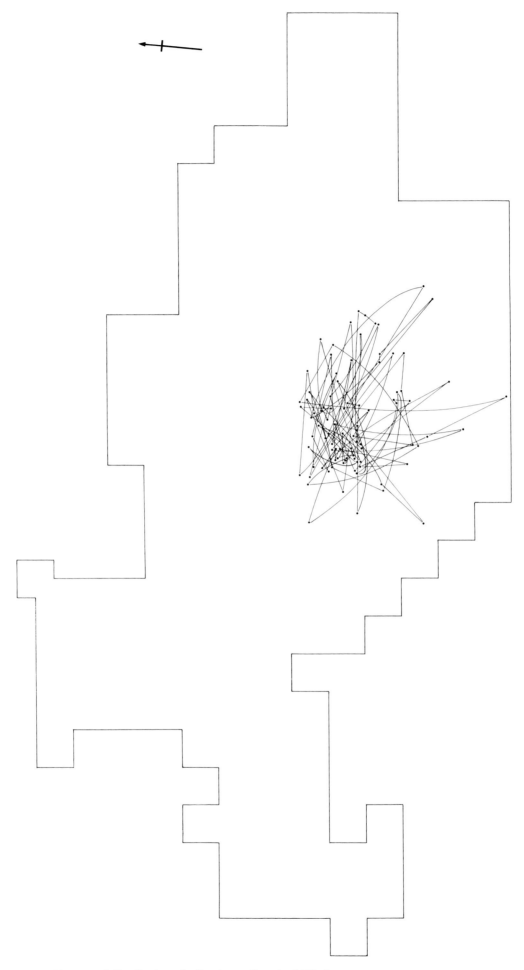

3.5 *Horizontal distribution of refitted core B at the LUP site.*

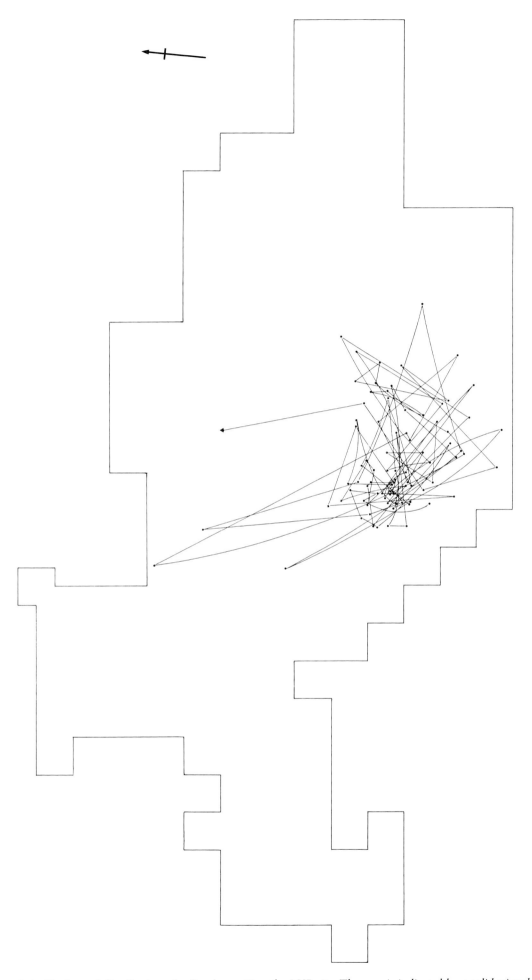

3.6  *Horizontal distribution of refitted core H at the LUP site. The core is indicated by a solid triangle.*

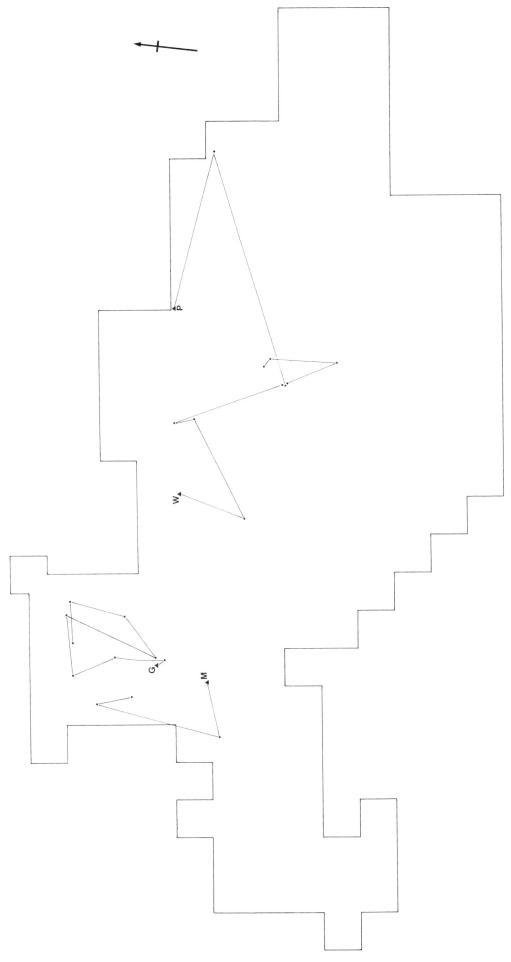

3.7   *Horizontal distribution of smaller refit groups (G, M, P, W) at the LUP site. The cores are indicated by solid triangles.*

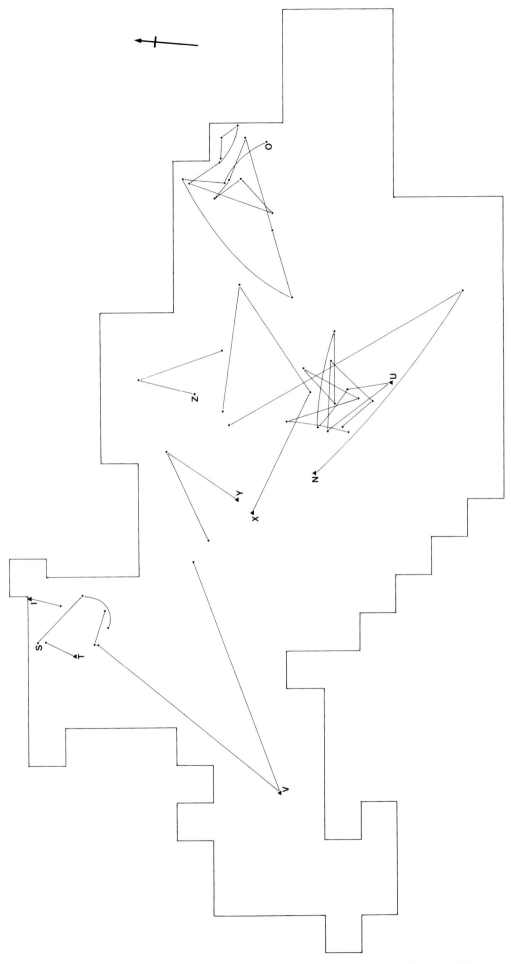

3.8   *Horizontal distribution of smaller refit groups (I, N, O, S, T, U, V, X, Y, Z) at the LUP site.*
*The cores are indicated by solid triangles.*

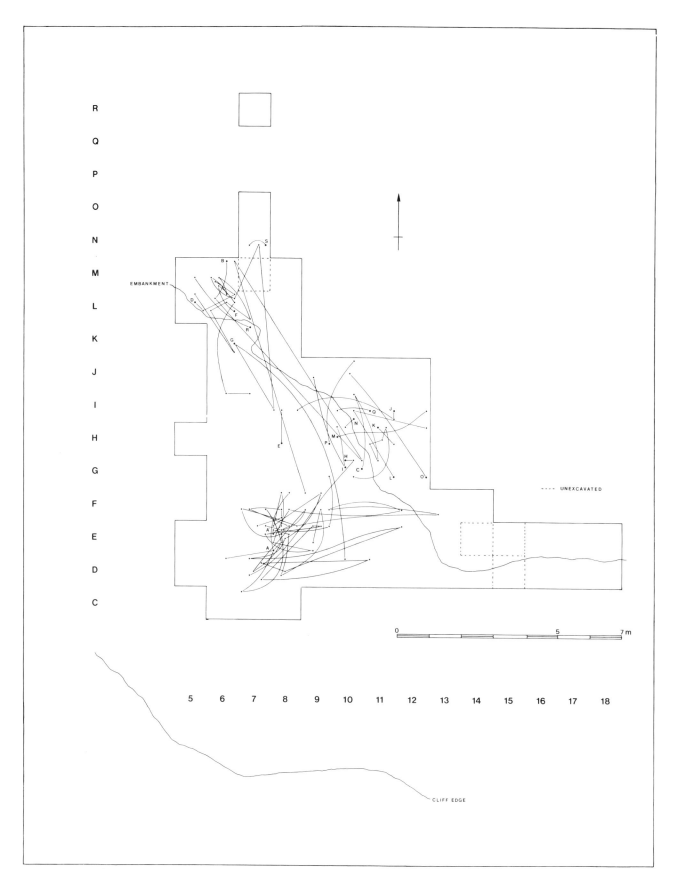

3.9 *Horizontal distribution of refitted cores from the Powell Mesolithic site.*

with human displacement, it is necessary to turn next to the comparative data of experimental studies and evidence derived from excavated scatters at other archaeological sites.

### 3.2.4 *Spatial distribution and size of experimental scatters*

Modern flaking experiments provide an important yardstick for studying the horizontal distribution of prehistoric flint scatters. Experimentation shows for example that the size of scatters may be influenced by a number of common factors most of which are applicable to the prehistoric record. Table 3.1 shows the results of some recent flaking experiments. Since we are concerned principally with the shape and size of the scatters at Hengistbury, the data are organised so as to allow easy inter-comparison with the archaeological examples. The information relies upon fairly crude measurements of overall scatter dimensions taken from published diagrams and supporting text.

On the basis of these experimental data two general propositions may be put forward regarding the overall dimensions of the scatters. First, it would seem reasonably obvious that scatter size is partly dependent on the amount of material flaked. Thus for example five flaking episodes superimposed one upon the other, generally speaking, will produce a wider spreading of material than say the products of a single episode. A second and perhaps more significant variable relates to the working position of the flintknapper, whether standing up or seated on or near to the ground (Newcomer and Sieveking 1980). This is very clearly illustrated by comparing the dimensions of a scatter flaked from a standing position with several executed sitting down (Table 3.1 and Fig. 3.11).

Other factors which appear to influence the scatters, though to a lesser degree, are the ways in which the core was held by the knapper and the method of percussion (Newcomer and Sieveking 1980). Newcomer has pointed out that the use of some punch techniques can produce a considerable dispersal of debitage and this has also been demonstrated in blade making experiments by Tixier (1972). The same observation has been made by Hansen and Madsen (1983) who describe the results of making a thin-butted axe. In the experiment the punch produced a considerable throw of material, covering an oval area of approximately 400 x 200 cm. Not all indirect methods of percussion, however, produce the same widely dispersed pattern of flakes. For example, several knappers have noted that when the punch is aimed downwards the scatter can become much more restricted in area. At Hengistbury, there is no technological evidence to support the suggestion that specialised punch techniques were employed in blade making. Indeed, it is far more likely that a method of direct percussion was used instead.

On the basis of these observations it is possible to make a reasonable approximation of the expected size of newly knapped scatters. Leaving aside specialised techniques (e.g. use of the punch) and the adoption of unlikely knapping postures, we suggest that undisturbed scatter dimensions might vary by a factor of about five, and that maximum dimensions would rarely exceed 200 x 200 cm and often lie below 100 x 100 cm.

From the point of view of shape, the experimental examples can be described as mostly circular when flaked close to the ground. When flaked from either an elevated or standing position they show a tendency to

Table 3.1 Selected experimental flint scatters: horizontal dimensions

| Position of knapper | Action | No. of nodules | Scatter size, Max. dimensions (cm) | Source |
|---|---|---|---|---|
| Seated on ground | BM | 1 | 40 x 40 | 1 |
| Seated on ground | AM | 1 | 60 x 40 | 2 |
| Seated on ground | AM | 5 | 75 x 50 | 5 |
| Raised seat (30 cm)* | BM | 1 | 60 x 50 | 4 |
| Raised seat (45 cm) | BM | 1 | 100 x 50 | 2 |
| Raised seat (30 cm)* | BM | 5 | 110 x 70 | 4 |
| Raised seat (40 cm) | BM | 15 | 175 x 150 | 3 |
| Standing | AM | 1 | 250 x 200 | 2 |

*Indirect percussion  BM= Blade Manufacture; AM= Axe Manufacture

Sources: 1- Barton & Bergman 1982, Plate 15; 2- Newcomer & Sieveking 1980; Figs. 3, 7 & 8; 3- Fischer *et al.* 1979, Fig. 6; 4- Boëda & Pelegrin 1985, Fig. 12; 5- Hansen & Madsen 1983, Fig 5.

become slightly more elongated. Occasionally, variations may be produced, for example when a seated knapper performs the flaking using the outside of the thigh. This can result in a distinctive bipartite distribution, with the knapper's leg dividing the scatter into two halves (Newcomer and Sieveking 1980; Boëda and Pelegrin 1985).

Finally, although the Hengistbury scatters exhibit an internal consistency in their shape, they are much more dilated than the experimental examples mentioned in this section.

### 3.2.5 Comparative data on flint artefact scatters from Hengistbury and other sites in sands and finer sediments

As has already been mentioned, one of the most effective methods of studying the spatial arrangement of flint scatters is via refitting groups of finds, an approach which allows recognition and separation of individual flaking episodes. Despite recent advances in site spatial analyses, comparatively few Late Upper Palaeolithic and Mesolithic sites have been subjected to this detailed level of study. All the examples provided in Table 3.2 involve blade technologies and in most instances the data is from refitted cores. The size of scatter in each of these cases has been determined by measuring length and breadth axes of the main area of refitted sequences. Inevitably, because there is a certain amount of subjectivity in making these measurements, the scatter sizes can only be regarded as best estimates. Only in two cases (Trollesgave and Avington VI) has extensive refitting not been carried out. However in both of these examples the scatters seem to represent fairly intensive and probably short-lived activity episodes; they are thus broadly comparable to the rest of the refitting data.

Whereas the sizes of scatters may vary considerably from site to site, most of the them can be described as sub-circular or oval in shape. The broadest scatters come from Hengistbury Head and the Late Palaeolithic sites of Meer II (Belgium) and Oldeholtwolde

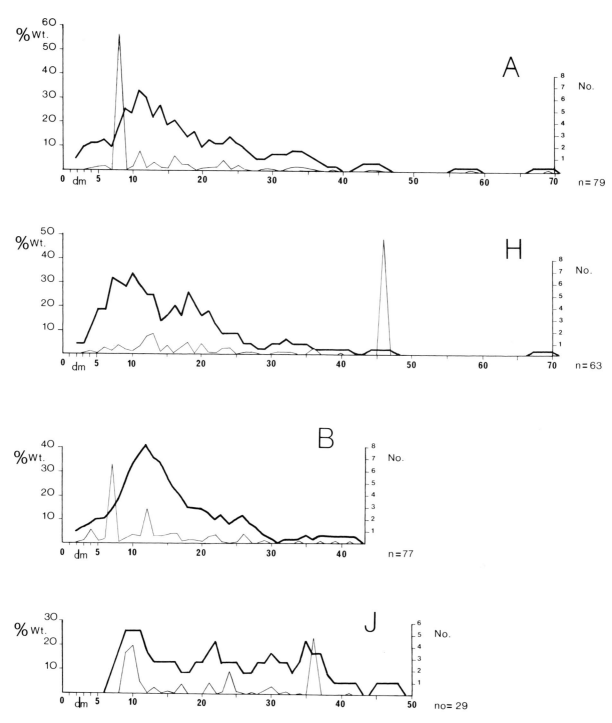

3.10 *Centroid diagram of main refitted core scatters. A centroid is first defined by the two points that are the mean measurements of the X and Y coordinates for all the individual group members. (If standard deviations of the X and Y coordinates are also calculated they provide an expression of the approximate size of the denser part of the scatter). Once the centroid is known, each member is then represented by its linear distance from the centroid, irrespective of the bearing of the line, thus reducing the original two-dimensional data to a single dimension. The two diagrams for each group have an abscissa calibrated in decimetre (10 cm) classes, the centroid lying at the origin to the left. The ordinates show first (thick line) a running mean (over four decimetre classes) of counts of pieces occurring in each class, a smoothing procedure to bring out the main characteristics; and, second (thin line), percentage by weight of pieces occurring in each class. The diagrams show subtle differences between distributions that are not easy to see in simple two-dimensional dot plots.*

(Netherlands). By contrast, some of the tightest and smallest groupings occur at the Paris Basin Late Magdalenian sites of Marsangy and Pincevent. Although the range in sizes may well be due to a combination of factors (e.g. the number of refits in each scatter; the diminishing success rate for longer distance refits etc.), it is noteworthy that all the larger scatters come from sites in sands. Most of the smaller refitting scatters (i.e. the four from Avington VI, Marsangy, Pincevent and Verberie) originate from sites in cohesive finer-grained sediments. This pattern is not a simple or linear one. For example, there are sites in relatively

3.11 *Knapper seated on ground with experimental flint scatter.*

*Table 3.2 Selected archaeological flint scatters: horizontal dimensions.*

| Site | Scatter size, max. dimensions in cm | Source |
|---|---|---|
| Hengistbury Upper Palaeo. | 500 x 400 | – |
| Hengistbury Mesolithic | 400 x 300 | – |
| Oldeholtwolde | 400 x 300 | 1 |
| Neerharen-de Kip | 300 x 200 | 2 |
| Trollesgave | 400 x 200 | 3 |
| Meer IV | 350 x 250 | 4,5 |
| Avington VI | 150 x 150 | 9 |
| Pincevent | 130 x 75  to 20 x 15 | 5,6 |
| Marsangy | 150 x 120 to 25 x 25 | 7 |
| Verberie | 75 x 75 | 8 |

Sources: 1- Stapert *et al.* 1986, Fig. 58; 2- Lauwers & Vermeersch 1982, Figs. 16-18; 3- Fischer & Mortensen 1977, Fig. 5; 4- Van Noten 1978, Planche 89; 5- Cahen *et al.* 1980, Fig 4.; 6- Karlin & Newcomer 1982, Fig. 1; 7- Schmider & Croisset 1985, Fig.1; Audouze *et al.* 1981, Figs. 7 & 8; Barton & Froom 1986, 80

fine-grained deposits where refitting has demonstrated both relatively diffuse scatters and ones with tighter distribution patterns (Bergman and Roberts 1988). However, we have been unable to find unequivocal examples of densely packed flintknapping clusters from any site in sand deposits.

The fact that scatter patterns of widely contrasting sizes may occur at the same site is well-illustrated at Pincevent where scatters vary in dimension from small, tight examples of 20 x 15 cm (Karlin and Newcomer 1982) to more diffuse ones with a surface area of 130 x 75 cm (Cahen *et al.* 1980). A similar range has been noted at Marsangy (Schmider and Croisset 1985). At Pincevent this degree of variability has been interpreted

as reflecting different types of human activity at the site. Thus, for example, while some of the smallest scatters occur well away from the main debitage zones and have been interpreted as 'dumps' (Karlin and Newcomer 1982), other less densely packed clusters appear to be associated with blank production activity around limestone knapping seats (Leroi-Gourhan and Brézillon 1966, 263–285). Seating of a comparable type has also been identified at the Danish Upper Palaeolithic site of Trollesgave (Fischer and Mortensen 1977). Unlike Pincevent this is a site in sands but the artefact horizon appears to be undisturbed and is sealed beneath a deposit of organic mud. The refitted scatter is of slightly greater dimension than the larger Pincevent examples, covering an area of roughly 400 x 200 cm. The variability in scatter sizes between sites warns us not to make spuriously exact or uniform assumptions about the appearance of undisturbed knapping scatters even when the circumstances of preservation are good. On the other hand the measurements provide a reasonable guide to the range of dimensions which might be expected in scatters which have been left 'as flaked' and not modified by further human activity.

Although generally bigger, the scatters from sites in sands do not, as a group, appear to share any great uniformity, except that they tend to be sub-circular or slightly elongate in shape. In terms of size, there is a marked gradation between the larger groupings at Hengistbury (Palaeolithic and Mesolithic) and Oldeholtwolde, and the Mesolithic clusters from Neerharen-de Kip, where several groupings, including those with refits, fall into the 300 x 200 cm size category (Lauwers and Vermeersch 1982). At Meer II, although scatter CIV (Van Noten 1978; Cahen *et al.* 1980) fits within the larger size range for sites in sands, it includes a slightly denser sub-circular cluster of 50 blanks (350 x 250 cm) within the main refitting group.

The degree of variability in the size of the scatters may in some cases be due to natural post-depositional processes causing dilation and some blurring of original shape. However, the large size of an artefact scatter in sands does not automatically imply wholesale dispersal or disturbance by natural agencies. A good illustrative example is provided by Oldeholtwolde where a flint scatter lies adjacent to an intact hearth feature. The lined hearth pit measures about 35 x 50 cm with some stone slabs of the hearth lining also lying in a restricted area immediately surrounding the hearth pit. The associated flint scatter covers a fairly large surface area (400 x 300 cm) with the core separated from the cluster by a distance of some 600 cm. Since the hearth structure is clearly *in situ*, with the loose stones surrounding it probably evidencing successive hearth cleaning episodes (Stapert *et al.* 1986), there is little reason to suppose that the flint scatter has been greatly disturbed *by natural agencies*. In other words, the spatial arrangement of the artefacts and the hearth stones probably reflects an original distribution pattern arising from human activity around the fire. A similar horizontal separation between a core and the main scatter of refitting debitage has been recorded at Hengistbury (Core H). Here, the absence of obvious signs of lateral mass movement in the sediments, implies that the core was physically removed from the scatter, rather than a major displacement of the whole grouping. Both of these examples provide a useful reminder that scatter configurations may still retain important human behavioural information even in the cases where some post-depositional movement is suspected.

Another way of detecting the presence of significant disturbance by natural processes involves the recognition of the smaller by-products of debitage. Here it is worth noting that tiny millimetre-size chips and flint dust are found within the flint scatters both in sandy sites (e.g. Oldeholtwolde) and those in finer and more cohesive sediments such as Avington VI; there is therefore no reason to suspect that substrate type may be automatically linked to the disappearance of fine debris. The Hengistbury Late Upper Palaeolithic site contained rather lower densities of chips than might otherwise have been expected given the quantities of flake and blade debris. In this case the loss of material can most probably be attributed to wind action, perhaps implying that the occupation surface remained unburied for some time.

### 3.2.6    Other anthropogenic factors affecting horizontal distributions

*Artificial structures:* Pits, stake holes or other man-made features such as hearths can affect the horizontal distribution of artefact scatters. For example, at the Late Magdalenian site of Pincevent, hearth-emptying activities have resulted in clear patterning of artefacts dispersed in a fan-shape around the fire. In other areas of the same site, the edges of scatters are so clearly defined as to suggest the existence of an impenetrable barrier such as a tent wall (Leroi-Gourhan and Brézillon 1966, Fig. 78).

At Hengistbury, Campbell's claims for the existence of artificial structures and stake-holes can generally be discounted on sedimentological and pedological grounds (see Chapter 2.1.5). In consequence, most of the 'features' he reported can be ascribed to purely natural phenomena. For example the so-called artificial parallel gullies flanking the Mesolithic 'tent-base' (Campbell 1977, 76) are no different from natural gullying which can be observed over many areas of the headland today. The superficial channelling appears to be linked to surface drainage processes.

The apparent absence of humanly constructed features at Hengistbury and other sites is no guarantee that these were not originally present. Indeed judging from the large number of burnt artefacts and imported blocks of quartzite recovered at the Late Upper Palaeolithic site, it seems highly probable (as is argued in Chapter 4.2.3 and 4.10.6) that lined hearths or fire scatters were present within the occupation area. We therefore take the minimal view that, while there is no direct evidence for large-scale structures (such as major pits), smaller-scale features like shallow depressions or flat stone-lined hearths would have caused only minor disturbances. Given the nature of the post-depositional processes at work at Hengistbury (see 3.1.3) it is extremely unlikely that any superficial features of this kind will have survived in their original form.

*Trampling:* Experiments have shown that people or animals walking over a site can move artefacts significant distances from their original positions by foot-scuffing (Gifford and Behrensmeyer 1977; Gifford-Gonzalez *et al.* 1985; Villa 1982; Villa and Courtin 1983). Since this might have important implications for the horizontal appearance of the archaeological scatters, it was decided to carry out a series of trampling experiments in order to provide data for comparative purposes.

In one experiment a small oval-shaped flint scatter about 30 x 20 cm was laid down on a bare sandy surface not far from one of the excavations (Fig. 3.12). It was deliberately placed so the artefacts could be numbered and later retrieved. The scatter simulated the shape of material knapped from a position seated on the ground (Newcomer and Sieveking 1980; Barton and Bergman 1982) and consisted of pieces in the <10 to 60 mm size range. The sands were made up entirely of sediments taken from the excavation sieving pile; they were about 50–75 cm deep, overlying a gravel substrate. Prior to the experiment, the sands were compacted by walking over them and the surface flattened with a shovel. Once the scatter was laid down it was subjected to frequent passes by people in soft-soled shoes or bare feet over a period of one week.

The results were somewhat surprising. Contrary to our expectations very little change occurred in the overall horizontal distribution of finds. Although, the scatter had become slightly more diffuse and elongated (40 x 25 cm) along the axis of the main pathway, surprisingly few pieces had been kicked or scuffed very far from their original positions (Fig. 3.13). One explanation for the apparent stability of the scatter is the fact that the artefacts were quickly pressed into the soft, relatively moist sand. This served to anchor them partly into the sediment and prevent much further movement.

Examination of the literature on experimental trampling suggests that a broad generalisation can be made concerning the substrate type and its effect on artefact movement. Horizontal dispersal by scuffing is generally more marked with harder (more coherent) substrates than softer ones; in the case of the former, artefacts remain exposed at the surface and are thus more susceptible to further shifts through time. It might be argued that our experiment using Hengistbury sediment was not a good test, since a much harder surface would be produced by soil development and even light vegetation. On the other hand, we are well aware from informal observations that lateral movements of artefacts can be slowed down significantly by the presence of even minimal turf cover which traps the flints and prevents them from being moved. With all these factors

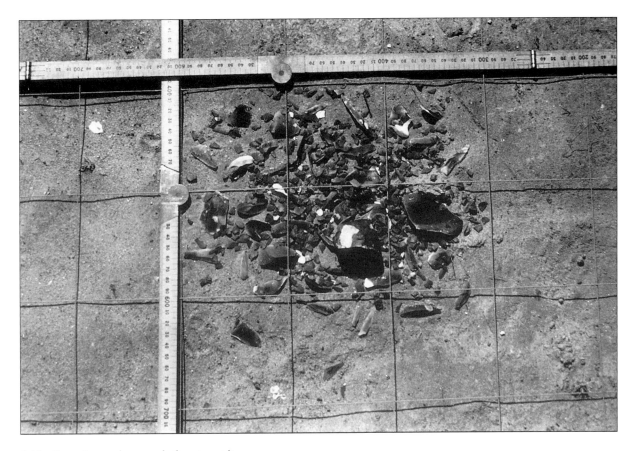

3.12 *Experimental scatter before trampling.*

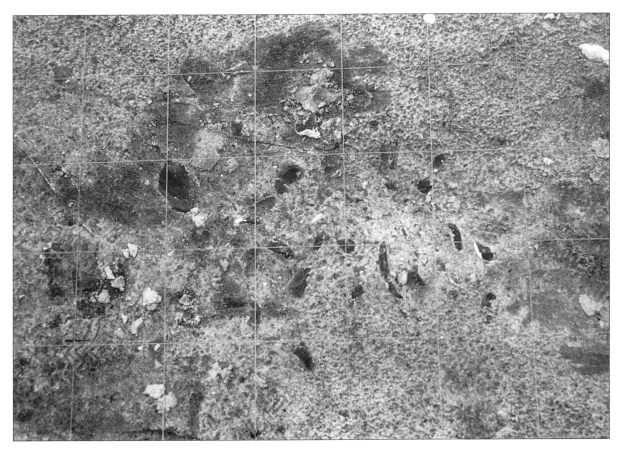

3.13 *Experimental scatter after one week's trampling.*

taken into consideration we do not believe that trampling could by itself have produced much more than a
25–50% dilation of the Hengistbury archaeological
scatters. In our experience, therefore, this mechanism
cannot be more than a minor contributory factor in the
dispersal of artefacts.

### 3.2.7 Discussion of archaeological horizontal distributions

In summary, the refitted scatters from both the Late
Upper Palaeolithic and the Powell Mesolithic sites consist of horizontal groupings of debitage with maximum
dimensions of 500–600 cm. If experimental flint scatters, knapped at ground level, are taken as a logical
starting point, then this shows that the archaeological
clusters have been affected by linear dilation factors of
between 500–600%. In comparing the Hengistbury
scatters with other archaeological examples we have
noticed that there is a tendency for greater increase in
the dilation factor in sandier sites than in ones with
firmer substrates. On the other hand, it has also been
observed that on both types of substrate there are significant differences in the size of debitage scatters
which might sometimes be attributed to human patterns of activity (hearth cleaning, the dumping of
waste, tent walls etc.). Although all or some of these
arguments can be applied to Hengistbury, most of the
refitted scatters seem to be of a similar size (but see 4.4)
and we would therefore suggest that perhaps half or
even more of the dilation factors at Hengistbury must
be the result of natural processes. Fortunately,
although causing a significant blurring in the record,
these post-depositional factors have not obscured all
trace of human activity and distinctive spatial patterning of the original occupation is still discernible at the
Late Upper Palaeolithic site (see Chapter 4.10.6).

### 3.2.8 Vertical distribution patterns of artefact scatters from Hengistbury and other sites

The range of anthropogenic factors which can influence the vertical distribution of artefacts overlaps substantially with those described above for the horizontal
plane.

The archaeological data presented in Table 3.3
shows that the vertical scatter of finds can vary quite
considerably from site to site. The most marked differences occur between Pincevent, a site in loamy, coherent sediments and the Powell Mesolithic site at
Hengistbury which lies in sands. The closest parallels
to Pincevent are provided by Verberie and Avington
VI, both of which are also stratified in fine grained sediments. Unlike the above, most of the other sites occur
in sands or coarser grained material. The only major
exception to this pattern is Meer II which although
showing a superficially similar vertical distribution pattern to other sand sites, is in fact stratified in slightly
different deposits being made up of fine and medium
grain sands. The sediments may also not be quite as

Table 3.3 *Vertical distributions of archaeological flint scatters.*

| Sites | Estimated vertical spread of finds (cm) | Source |
|---|---|---|
| Hengistbury Upper Palaeo. | 40-50 | – |
| Hengistbury Mesolithic | 50-70 | – |
| Oldeholtwolde | 20-30 | 1 |
| Neerharen-de Kip | 50-60 | 2 |
| Weelde-Paardsdrank | 20-50 | 5 |
| Trollesgave | 20-25 | 3 |
| Meer IV | 20-45 | 4 |
| Avington VI | 5-10 | 9 |
| Pincevent, Sect 36 | 3- 5 | 6,7 |
| Verberie | 10-15 | 8 |

Sources: 1- Stapert *et al.* 1986, 189; 2- Lauwers & Vermeersch
1982, 22; 3-Fischer & Mortensen 1977, Fig. 5; 4- Van Noten 1978,
Fig. 13; 5- Huyge & Vermeersch 1982, Fig. 14 15; 6- Karlin &
Newcomer 1982, Fig. 1; 7- Leroi-Gourhan & Brézillon 1972, 15-
17; Audouze *et al.* 1981, 105; 9- Barton & Froom 1986, 80.

homogeneous as at Hengistbury or at the other Belgian
sites of Neerharen-de Kip and Weelde-Paardsdrank
(Lauwers and Vermeersch 1982; Huyge and
Vermeersch 1982).

An interesting feature of one of the sand sites,
Trollesgave in Denmark, is the relatively narrow vertical band of artefacts. One factor which might have
influenced this distribution pattern is the organic mud
deposit immediately overlying the sands. Depending on
when this deposit formed, it could effectively have
sealed the site and inhibited the more pronounced post-
depositional processes evidenced in the distributions
from other sites in sands.

As with the horizontal distribution, we may therefore make the general observation that the vertical dispersal of artefacts usually appears 'greater' in sandy
sites than in sites with more coherent substrates. Unlike
horizontal movements, however, we suggest that in
most cases vertical dispersal is due predominantly to
natural processes rather than anthropogenic ones (see
Chapter 3.1.5 and 3.1.6).

### 3.2.9 Anthropogenic factors affecting vertical distributions

*Artifical structures:* The absence of convincing evidence
for pits, post holes and other excavated structures at
Hengistbury, has already been mentioned above. These
features in any case might only have caused localised
disturbances in the depth distributions. Nothing of this
kind is apparent at either the Powell Mesolithic or Late
Upper Palaeolithic sites where the artefacts are stratified in bands of more or less even thickness (see Figs.
3.14 and 3.15). In passing, it should be noted that this
is also largely true of the other archaeological occurrences listed in Table 3.3.

*Trampling:* The only other obvious anthropogenic process likely to have been of significance is that of trampling. It will be recalled that Mace (1959) originally
suggested this mechanism to account for the observed
dispersed banding in the distribution of artefacts at the
Late Upper Palaeolithic site.

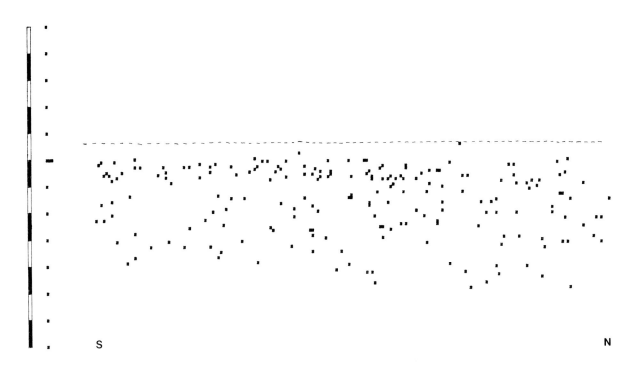

3.14 *Vertical distribution of artefacts from the Late Upper Palaeolithic site (squares N29-029). Dotted line marks the geological boundary between the recent deposits and the underlying sands. Scale in 10 cm.*

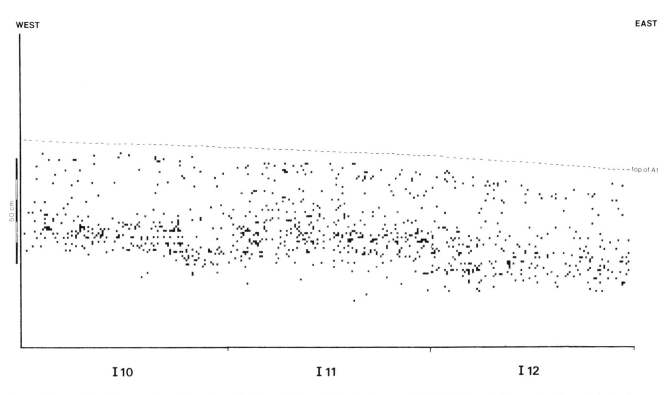

3.15 *Vertical distribution of artefacts from the Powell Mesolithic site (squares I10-I12). Dotted line marks the pedological boundary between the Ah and the (underlying) Ea1 soil horizons.*

The effects of trampling on the vertical distributions of objects have been considered in detail by many archaeological and palaeontological experimenters. Most people seem to agree that trampling can cause marked changes to the vertical arrangement of finds, especially in coarser sediments (Stockton 1973; Villa 1982; Villa and Courtin 1983; Gifford-Gonzalez et al. 1985). While we would not necessarily disagree with

the findings of such work, the results of our own trampling experiments offer a slightly different perspective on the same problem.

In addition to the need to assess the likely depth to which casual trampling would move material vertically, our experiments were designed to examine the possibility that repeated occupations at one site over a relatively long period could leave stratigraphically discrete bands of artefacts, with no intermixing. The latter was prompted by the belief that two levels of flints, separated by as little as 5 cm of sand, would *not* in fact remain unmixed after trampling. A previous experiment by Stockton (1973) had also suggested that trampling would result in size sorting, with the heavier finds being left higher than the lighter pieces.

As in the horizontal experiment reported above, a scatter 30 x 20 cm in size was laid down on a bare sandy surface not far from one of the excavations; it consisted of flints in the <10 to 60 mm range. The scatter was trampled for one week. Then a covering of 5 cm of sterile sand was placed immediately above the the first scatter and a second flint scatter (this time sprayed with red paint to aid identification) was placed on the new surface. Trampling was resumed for a further seven days before the 'site' was excavated.

Contrary to our expectations, flints from neither the lower nor the upper scatter had drifted more than a centimetre or two downwards from their original positions and, although the scatters were slightly closer, they remained totally discrete.

One clue as to the apparent lack of drift may lie in the slightly damp feel to the sediments noted as they were being re-excavated. Indeed higher moisture levels were also recorded 6–8 cm below the surface in Gifford-Gonzalez's experiment; she concluded that the consolidating effect prevented the further downward migration of the artefacts (Gifford-Gonzalez *et al.* 1985, 810). Such an explanation seems a reasonable one but, in the absence of information regarding prehistoric humidity levels at Hengistbury (which must have varied considerably even on a diurnal basis), it is impossible to calculate the exact significance of this parameter. It should be noted that the Mesolithic and Late Upper Palaeolithic occupation surfaces may well have been vegetated, a factor which would also have hindered vertical movement from the surface downwards. In addition, apparently similar sands may have slightly different size-sorting and grain-shape characteristics which can radically effect their resistance to penetration, thus casting doubt upon the comparability of published data. In future it might be useful to report penetrometer readings together with the observations of such experiments.

A second feature noted in our experiments, was the absence of the diagnostic size sorting observed by Stockton and others. Admittedly, this would have been difficult to recognise due to the fact that very little movement had taken place. Nevertheless even when the smaller chips were taken into consideration, there was nothing to suggest more than just a random weight distribution of finds throughout the artefact scatters, as trampled.

Although the results of the trampling experiments revealed few direct comparisons with the archaeological data, they did provide some insight into the potential effects such activity might cause to artefact distributions. At Hengistbury the archaeological scatters are spread vertically over depths of 40–50 cm and sometimes substantially more. If we assume a maximum migration of 10 cm due to trampling, it is very clear (*pace* Mace) that whatever the process or processes responsible for the archaeological distribution, they would have swamped the trampling effect totally. On present evidence, therefore, although trampling may have added to the overall distribution of finds, its contribution should not be over-estimated.

### 3.2.10  *Conclusions*

The results of the above analysis and those presented in the previous section have shown that certain broad generalisations can be offered regarding the site formation processes at Hengistbury. The fact that contextual studies of this kind are now widely recognised as essential elements in the interpretation of archaeological data amply justifies the time and effort spent on this work.

The main conclusions of Chapter 3.1 and 3.2 regarding the taphonomic studies can be summarised as follows:

(1) Both the Powell Mesolithic and Late Upper Palaeolithic sites contain a single dominant lithic assemblage. Any minor intrusive elements can be identified, if not directly (as in the case of individual flakes), then by inference based upon site formation models proposed for the two sites (3.1.5 and 3.1.6). These are further clarified and elaborated with reference to technological and typological arguments presented in later sections (see especially 4.2.3, 4.3.3 and 5.1.2).

(2) The study of post-depositional processes in sands has provided coarse estimates of the likely contribution of natural agencies in the formation of the Hengistbury sites. These have served to eliminate factors of mass-movement from the list of potential geological processes affecting the artefact distributions. Although it seems unlikely that any major non-anthropogenic dispersal mechanism has been overlooked, should this not prove to be the case, we believe that the structure of our approach would make the integration and assessment of any new data relatively easy.

(3) Despite the acknowledged effects of biological processes in the formation of the Hengistbury sites, these are only moderately disruptive to the artefact distributions and have not erased all evidence of the original patterning. These observations are confirmed in the refitting of core groups and the spatial clustering of finds (see also 4.4 below).

(4) Taking the above factors into account it is suggested that recognition of human patterning in the spatial clusters of artefacts is feasible if undertaken at the appropriate scale. Thus, at neither site should horizontal associations between any two objects less than 2 m apart be considered *automatically* to be a reflection of an original artefact discard pattern. For spatial associations involving reasonably large groups of artefacts

(e.g. refitted scatters) this limit could probably be significantly reduced, but in no case, to a separation measured on a scale of less than one metre.

(5) Application of these criteria to the Late Upper Palaeolithic site (where fairly extensive refitting has been undertaken) has revealed the presence of clear structuring in the spatial distribution of finds. The interpretation of these data is discussed below (4.4 and 4.10.6).

# 4. The Late Upper Palaeolithic site

## 4.1 The finds: debitage and cores

This section deals with the artefacts recovered from the 1968–1969 and the 1981–1984 excavations. The data are presented in two groups, for convenience: 1) flakes and 2) blades and bladelets. In order to study the debitage a list was devised composed of a series of quantitative and qualitative attributes which would best describe the flaking technology. The quantitative attributes include the maximum length and breadth of each piece as well as the dimensions of its butt. The thickness of each blank was also measured according to its thickest part (excluding the bulb). The qualitative attributes include aspects of the distal ends, the direction of the dorsal scars and the type of profile (as in Marks 1976, 372–3; Bergman 1987a, 278–283). Also in the list is the category 'unidentifiable' for cases where it was difficult to distinguish a specific technological feature due to problems such as breakage, burning, patination and so forth. The main technological features noted are listed in the table below, while the definitions of some of the attributes appear in the Glossary.

(1) Overall dimensions
    (a) Length
    (b) Breadth
    (c) Thickness
(2) Butt dimensions
    (a) Length
    (b) Breadth
(3) Butt type
    (a) Faceted
    (b) Dihedral faceted
    (c) Plain
    (d) Cortex/Natural surface
(4) Flaking mode
    (a) Hard hammer
    (b) Soft hammer
    (c) Unidentifiable
(5) Distal termination
    (a) Blunt/feathered
    (b) Hinge fracture
    (c) Plunging
    (d) Unidentifiable
(6) Profile
    (a) Straight
    (b) Curved
    (c) Unidentifiable
(7) Dorsal scars
    (a) Unidirectional
    (b) Bidirectional opposed
    (c) Crossed
    (d) Multidirectional
    (e) Unidentifiable

In the following analysis only complete pieces of debitage were considered since broken artefacts by their very nature frequently preserve only partial information. This has decreased the sample size to almost 900 pieces or 15% of the 6,081 flakes, blades and bladelets. We believe, however, that the sample is still fully representative of the assemblage as a whole.

One feature worth commenting upon before discussing the debitage is the high number of burned pieces in the collection. Out of a total of 13,419 artefacts examined from the site 6,001 or 45% are thermally fractured or altered in some way by heating. The number of burned pieces caused difficulties when analysing the debitage and contributed significantly to the inflated percentage of unidentifiable attributes. A range of Hengistbury blade and flake debitage is illustrated in Figure 4.1.

*Flakes:* Out of 3,815 flakes, 590 complete pieces in the 1968–9 and 1981–4 collections were analysed. The unbroken flakes represent 15.5% of the total. The complete examples have mean dimensions of 32 x 25 x 6 mm. The standard deviations for these measurements are 17, 13 and 4 mm, respectively (Table 4.3 and Fig. 4.2). The butts of these pieces are generally quite large averaging 10 x 4 mm, with standard deviations of 7 and 3 mm (Table 4.2 and Fig. 4.3).

The butts are usually plain (83%) and less often faceted (13%). The number of flakes detached with

Table 4.1 *Debitage from the 1968-9 and 1981-4 collections*

| Artefact Class | n | % |
|---|---|---|
| Flakes | 3,815 | 28.4 |
| Blades/Bladelets | 2,266 | 16.9 |
| Chips | 3,260 | 24.3 |
| Unclassified | 4,078 | 30.4 |
| Total | 13,419 | 100.0 |

Table 4.2 *Flakes: length, breadth & thickness measurements*

Main dimensions (mm)

| | | Length | Breadth | Thickness |
|---|---|---|---|---|
| Total | = | 469 | 556 | 558 |
| Range | = | 7-114 | 8-91 | 1-30 |
| Mean | = | 32.3 | 25.4 | 5.9 |
| Standard Deviation = | | 16.7 | 12.7 | 4.3 |

Butt dimensions (mm)

| | | | |
|---|---|---|---|
| Total | = | 380 | 380 |
| Range | = | 1-36 | 3-15 |
| Mean | = | 10.7 | 4.0 |
| Standard Deviation = | | 7.1 | 3.0 |

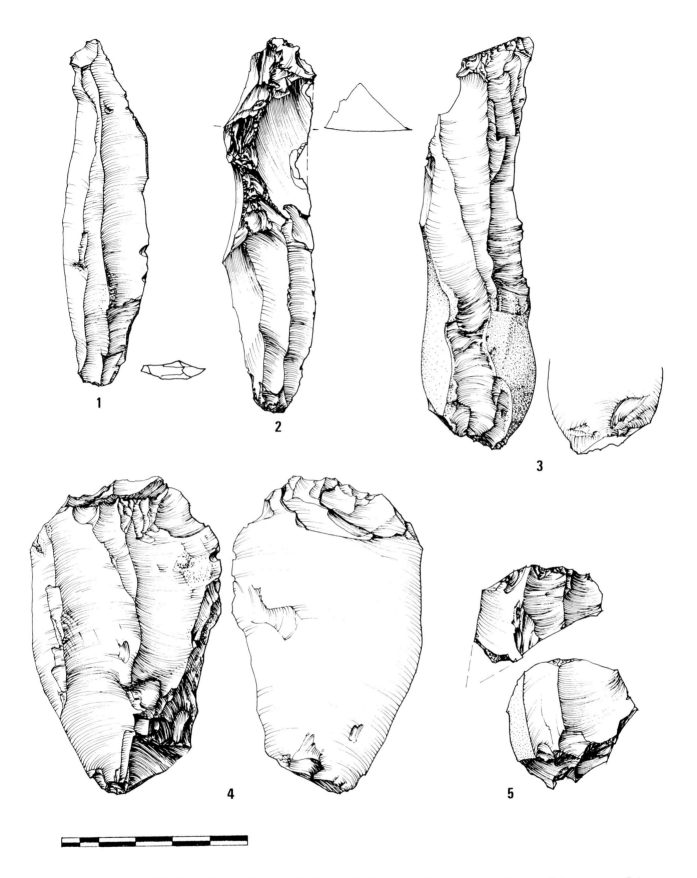

4.1 *Selected examples of blade and flake debitage. 1-3= blades (2 showing unidirectional cresting); 4= flake core on a flake; 5= core tablet. Centimetre scale.*

soft hammers (153) is slightly greater than the number which were hard-hammer struck (113). Platform abrasion, which is used to prepare the core's edge for the percussive blow, is found on roughly one quarter of all flakes (26%). The distal ends of the flakes are usually blunt (44%) or have hinge fractures (23%). In profile they are curved (65%) or straight (18%). The dorsal scars are overwhelmingly dominated by the unidirectional pattern (55%). Crossed and multidirectional scars together account for 28% of the total. These observations are summarised in the Table 4.3.

*Blades*

The 307 blades and bladelets which were measured represent 13.6% of the total of 2,266. They have mean dimensions of 55 x 19 x 6 mm, with standard deviations of 28, 8 and 4 mm, respectively (Fig. 4.4). The butts tend to be plain (85%) and are smaller than those on flakes; they have average measurements of 8 x 3 mm (SD = 5 and 2 mm)(Fig. 4.5)

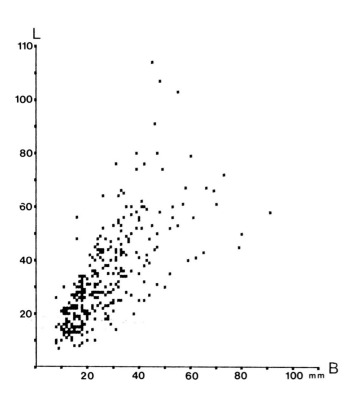

4.2 *Scatter diagram of flake length x breadth dimensions.*

Table 4.3 *Flakes: qualitative attributes*

|  | n | % |
|---|---|---|
| *Butt type* |  |  |
| (a) Faceted | 29 | 7.2 |
| (b) Dihedral faceted | 22 | 5.4 |
| (c) Plain | 338 | 83.4 |
| (d) Cortex/Natural surface | 16 | 3.9 |
| *Platform Abrasion* | 153 | 25.9 |
| *Cortex* | 348 | 59.0 |
| *Flaking mode* |  |  |
| (a) Hard hammer | 113 | 19.2 |
| (b) Soft hammer | 153 | 25.9 |
| (c) Unidentifiable | 324 | 54.9 |
| *Distal terminations* |  |  |
| (a) Blunt/feathered | 259 | 43.9 |
| (b) Hinge fracture | 134 | 22.7 |
| (c) Plunging | 9 | 1.5 |
| (d) Cortex/Natural surface | 96 | 16.3 |
| (e) Unidentifiable | 91 | 15.4 |
| *Profile* |  |  |
| (a) Straight | 108 | 18.3 |
| (b) Curved | 383 | 64.9 |
| (c) Twisted | 1 | 0.2 |
| (d) Unidentifiable | 98 | 16.6 |
| *Dorsal Scar Pattern* |  |  |
| (a) Unidirectional | 325 | 55.1 |
| (b) Opposed | 33 | 5.6 |
| (c) Crossed | 85 | 14.4 |
| (d) Multidirectional | 78 | 13.2 |
| (e) Unidentifiable | 69 | 11.7 |

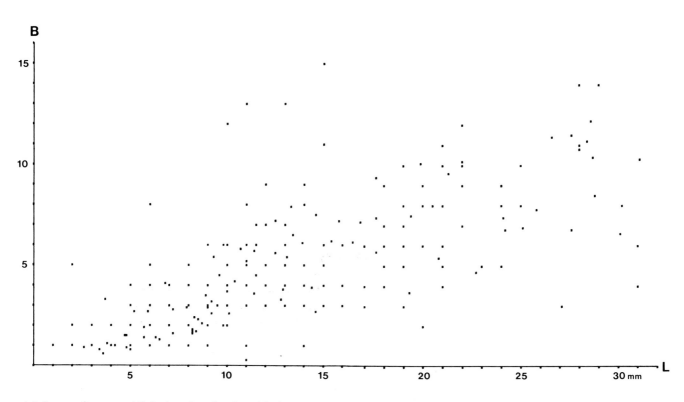

4.3 *Scatter diagram of flake butt length x breadth dimensions.*

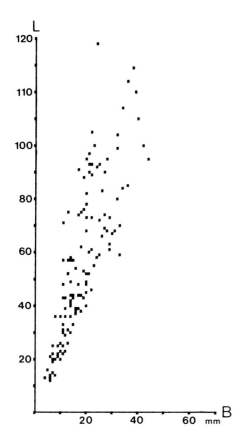

4.4 *Scatter diagram of blade length x breadth dimensions.*

The tiny size of some of the butts is due to the fact that the blow which detached the blank was aimed quite close to the core's edge (cf. marginal flaking) and removed only a small fraction of the striking platform. In order to carry this out successfully the striking platform must be carefully prepared and it is worth noting that platform abrasion occurs on 41% of the blades and bladelets. Some of the butts were even more heavily modified and and this also shows on the core platforms which were sometimes abraded to the point of being ground.

When compared with flakes it can be seen that fewer blades and bladelets have cortex, which occurs on 38%

Table 4.4 *Blades and bladelets: length, breadth &*
*thickness measurements*

| Main dimensions (mm) | | Length | Breadth | Thickness |
|---|---|---|---|---|
| Total | = | 192 | 272 | 272 |
| Range | = | 8-138 | 4-44 | 1-21 |
| Mean | = | 54.8 | 18.9 | 5.6 |
| Standard Deviation = | | 28.0 | 8.0 | 3.5 |
| | | | | |
| Butt dimensions (mm) | | | | |
| Total | = | 165 | 164 | |
| Range | = | 1-28 | 0.8-17 | |
| Mean | = | 7.7 | 2.9 | |
| Standard Deviation = | | 4.9 | 2.3 | |

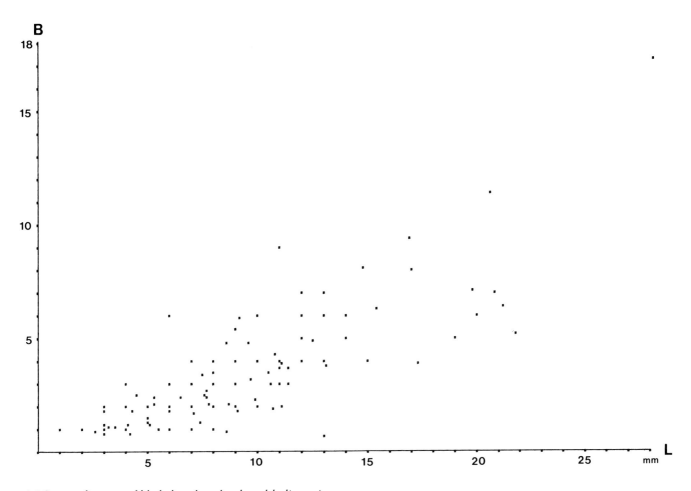

4.5 *Scatter diagram of blade butt length x breadth dimensions.*

of all laminar blanks. This is not particularly surprising since much of the cortex is removed in the initial stages of core preparation, before blade debitage begins. Most of the blades and bladelets were detached with soft hammers. Of the 100 pieces for which the flaking mode could be determined (cf. Newcomer 1975; Ohnuma and Bergman 1982), 80 were soft-hammer struck. The distal terminations of the blanks are often blunt (51%), while hinge fractures occur less commonly (13%) when compared to flakes. In profile the blades and bladelets are usually curved (62%) and less frequently straight (13%). The dorsal scars are again characterised by uni-directional removals (56%). Opposed scars occur more often on blades and bladelets than on flakes. The above data are summarised in the following table:

*Table 4.5 Blades and bladelets: qualitative attributes*

|  | n | % |
| --- | --- | --- |
| *Butt type* |  |  |
| (a) Faceted | 19 | 11.5 |
| (b) Dihedral faceted | 4 | 2.4 |
| (c) Plain | 141 | 85.4 |
| (d) Cortex/Natural surface | 1 | 0.6 |
| *Platform Abrasion* | 126 | 41.0 |
| *Cortex* | 107 | 38.4 |
| *Flaking mode* |  |  |
| (a) Hard hammer | 20 | 6.5 |
| (b) Soft hammer | 80 | 26.1 |
| (c) Unidentifiable | 207 | 67.4 |
| *Distal terminations* |  |  |
| (a) Blunt/feathered | 156 | 50.8 |
| (b) Hinge fracture | 41 | 13.3 |
| (c) Plunging | 11 | 3.6 |
| (d) Cortex/Natural surface | 15 | 4.9 |
| (e) Unidentifiable | 84 | 27.4 |
| *Profile* |  |  |
| (a) Straight | 41 | 13.3 |
| (b) Curved | 191 | 62.2 |
| (c) Twisted | – | – |
| (d) Unidentifiable | 75 | 24.4 |
| *Dorsal Scar Pattern* |  |  |
| (a) Unidirectional | 171 | 55.7 |
| (b) Opposed | 54 | 17.6 |
| (c) Crossed | 22 | 7.2 |
| (d) Multidirectional | 40 | 13.0 |
| (e) Unidentifiable | 20 | 6.5 |

As can be seen from the above statistics, certain differences exist in the two major classes of debitage from the Late Upper Palaeolithic site. A noticeable feature, for example, is the clear relationship of butt size to blank thickness with flakes having larger butts and thicker cross-sections than the blades. Blades and bladelets also show more frequent signs of platform abrasion, than their counterparts. This is related to the fact that blades and bladelets are detached by a blow aimed close to the core's edge, making it essential to prepare the platform carefully by removing any obstacles or overhangs. Another divergence is in the frequent occurrence of cortex on flakes, a feature not shared by blades since fewer of these come from the initial stages of core preparation.

The distal ends of blades and bladelets are generally blunt. In profile these blanks are straight or curved, while pieces with twisted profiles are virtually absent. The dorsal scar pattern is dominated by unidirectional removals. This provides an apparent contrast with the evidence from the cores where two opposed platform cores are most common. Refitting evidence, however, provides an explanation: it shows that flaking usually took place from one platform with the second platform playing a subsidiary role for correcting accidents, such as hinge fractures, and for maintaining the shape of the flaking face. At Hengistbury the knappers do not appear to have employed each platform alternately.

Although, the kinds of flaking tools probably varied, soft percussors were often used to detach flakes, blades and bladelets. In the majority of cases, however, it proved difficult to determine conclusively which hammer-type was preferred. There seems to be a grey area between blanks which were clearly hard hammer-struck and those which were soft-hammer struck. Experiments by both authors have shown that this may be due to the use of soft stone hammers which leave ventral features similar to, but not quite so diffuse as, those produced by antler hammer (cf. Ohnuma and Bergman 1982). In general, it seems whereas hard hammer flaking was employed during the early stages of preforming the core, softer hammers were used in the later stages of blade production.

*Crested pieces:* There are a total of 111 crested pieces from the three excavated collections. Since cresting is most frequently used to prepare cores for blade production it is hardly surprising that crested pieces generally have blade dimensions. Out of 82 examples from 1968–9 and 1981–4 excavations 78% are on blades, while the remainder (18 or 22%) consist of crested flakes. In the three collections the majority are made up of unidirectional crests (82.9%) with lesser frequencies of bidirectional crests (17.1%). This is an interesting observation because, in conjunction with the refitting evidence (see Chapter 4.3), it demonstrates that bidirectional cresting was not the preferred technique even in the case of blade cores (Fig. 4.1, 2).

Much of the crested debitage is either broken or burnt. Statistics from the 1968–9 and 1981–4 samples show that 74.4% of pieces are broken, while 32.9 % are thermally altered (Table 4.7).

*Core tablets:* Sixty eight core tablets (Fig. 4.1, 5) have been recorded from the site and the majority of these (45.6%) come from Campbell's 1968–9 area. This also coincides with a rich zone of debitage where most of the refitted material comes from. As with the crested pieces many of the core tablets are broken (Table 4.7). Of those counted in the 1968–9 and 1981–4 collections 66% have breaks, with a lesser proportion burnt (32%).

In terms of the overall distribution pattern, the blade and flake debitage is widely scattered across the site (Fig. 4.6). Slightly higher concentrations are discernible

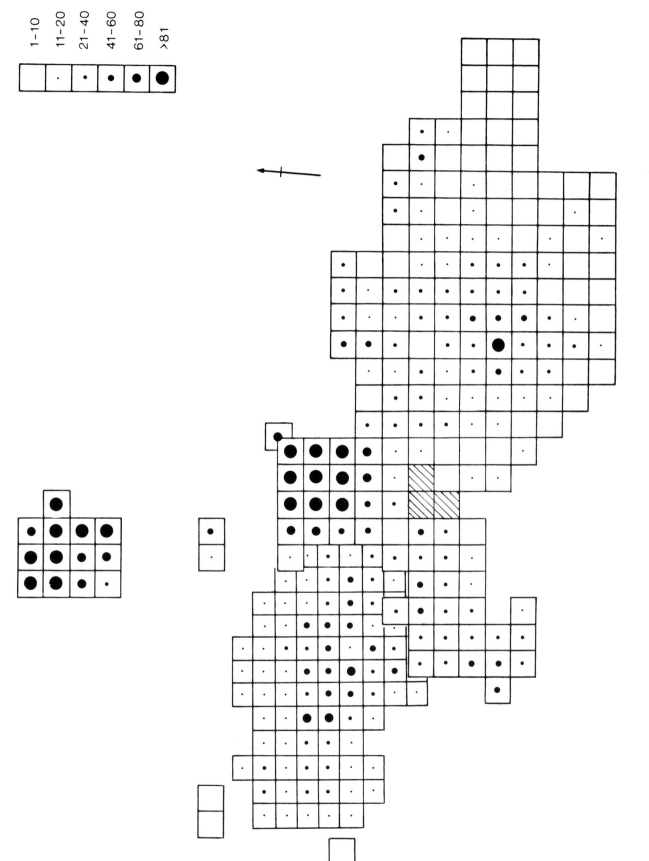

4.6 *Horizontal density distribution of flakes, blades and bladelets. The cross-hatched squares were not systematically excavated.*

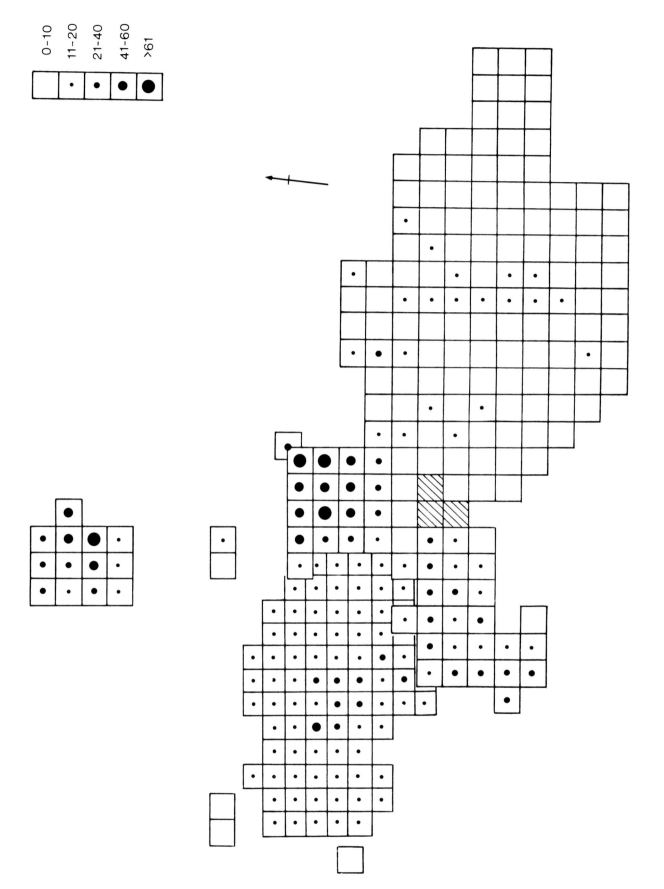

4.7    Horizontal density distribution of burned flakes, blades and bladelets. The cross-hatched squares were not systematically excavated.

Table 4.6 *Crested pieces & core tablets from the three excavations.*

|  | 1957 | 1968-9 | 1981-4 |
|---|---|---|---|
| Unidirectional crest | 23 | 38 | 31 |
| Bidirectional crest | 6 | 8 | 5 |
| Core tablets | 15 | 31 | 22 |

Table 4.7 *Crested pieces & core tablets: broken and burnt artefacts*

|  | Unbroken/broken | | Unburnt/burnt | | Total |
|---|---|---|---|---|---|
| Crested pieces | | | | | |
| 1968-9 | 11 | 35 | 31 | 15 | 46 |
| 1981-4 | 10 | 26 | 24 | 12 | 36 |
| Core tablets | | | | | |
| 1968-9 | 13 | 18 | 24 | 7 | 31 |
| 1981-4 | 5 | 17 | 11 | 11 | 22 |

in the 1981–4 areas, but there are also localised densities of flaked material in the Campbell area (e.g. centring on Square G23). A clearer contrast occurs north of the footpath where some of the highest concentrations of flints have so far been recorded. A further trend can be recognised in the increase of burned artefacts in the north and western areas of the site (Fig. 4.7), with much lower totals in the south central area. We believe these differences are important and have significant implications for interpreting site activities. The question of burnt flint is a subject we shall return to at the end of the chapter (see 4.10.6).

Before concluding this section it is worth briefly commenting upon the debitage recovered by Mace in 1957. According to the published data (Mace 1959, 239), over 1,700 flakes and blades were recorded along with 785 fragments and 'chips' less than 15 mm long. Superficially this suggests slightly lower densities of artefacts than were uncovered in the adjacent areas. However, it is evident from an examination of the material housed in the British Museum that a significant element of the smaller debitage is missing. Such differences may be due in part to the nature of the recovery methods used. For example, since no systematic sieving was employed in the 1957 work, it is highly likely that a proportion of the debitage, including the waste from retouching tools, is under-represented. Apart from these slight anomalies, it is quite clear that in terms of raw material, technology and composition the the debitage from all three excavations is substantially the same.

A surface collection made by Druitt in 1914 in the area north of the excavations also yielded a substantial assemblage of Upper Palaeolithic artefacts. Amongst the flints are quantities of mostly broken blade fragments (362), morphologically similar in type to those from the area further south. The collection also contains many flakes, but individually these are less easy to distinguish from Bronze Age finds also known to occur in the same area. In addition to the simple blade and flake debitage are 27 unidirectionally crested pieces, 9 bidirectionally crested artefacts and nine core tablets. All of these are very similar to the examples in the excavated collections and indicate a northwards continuation of the site. The survival of further deposits containing Late Upper Palaeolithic artefacts north of the footpath was also confirmed in the 1983 ground survey of the Eastern Depression (1.5.2).

*Cores:* Out of a total of 88 cores from the three excavated collections, 25 are flake cores and 63 are blade cores. This figure does not include over 40 substantial core fragments and one large core preform (Fig. 4.51), recovered from the 1968–9 excavations.

*Blade Cores:* The majority of cores recovered from the three excavations are blade cores. These can be divided into single platform cores (38%), two platform cores (57%) and multiplatform cores (5%)(Figs. 4.8 and 4.9). The commonest type of core from the site is the opposed platform blade core of which there are 30 examples. Excluded from this class, but probably closely related to it, are 12 single platform cores with remains of bidirectional scars. The scar direction shows they had opposed platforms at an earlier stage in their reduction. The blade cores vary greatly in size depending upon the shape of the original nodule and the amount of reduction involved (see section on refitting 4.3). The mean length for this group is 72 mm with a standard deviation of 26.8 mm. Width dimensions vary for the same reasons; they show an average measurement of 46±16.4 mm.

In terms of overall morphology, most of the blade cores can be described as prismatic (68%), with relatively few pyramidal examples (8%) and the rest being made up of irregular or unclassifiable forms (Table 4.8). Nearly all the examples are made from nodules but there is one blade core on a frost-fractured flake.

The technique of preparing and flaking the blade cores is discussed in detail in a following section (Chapter 4.3). Not surprisingly the uniformity of the reduction techniques used is reflected in the shape of the abandoned cores. Thus, although there may be an important size disparity, the cores are virtually similar in all other respects. The reason for the variation, particularly in size, appears to be linked to the quality of

Table 4.8 *Blade cores from the three excavated collections*

|  | Prismatic | Pyramidal | Irregular |
|---|---|---|---|
| One Platform | 2 | 5 | 7 |
| Two Platforms, opposed | 27 | – | 3 (1) |
| Two Platforms, crossed | 4 | – | 2 |
| Multiplatform | – | – | 3 |
| (1) core on a flake | | | |

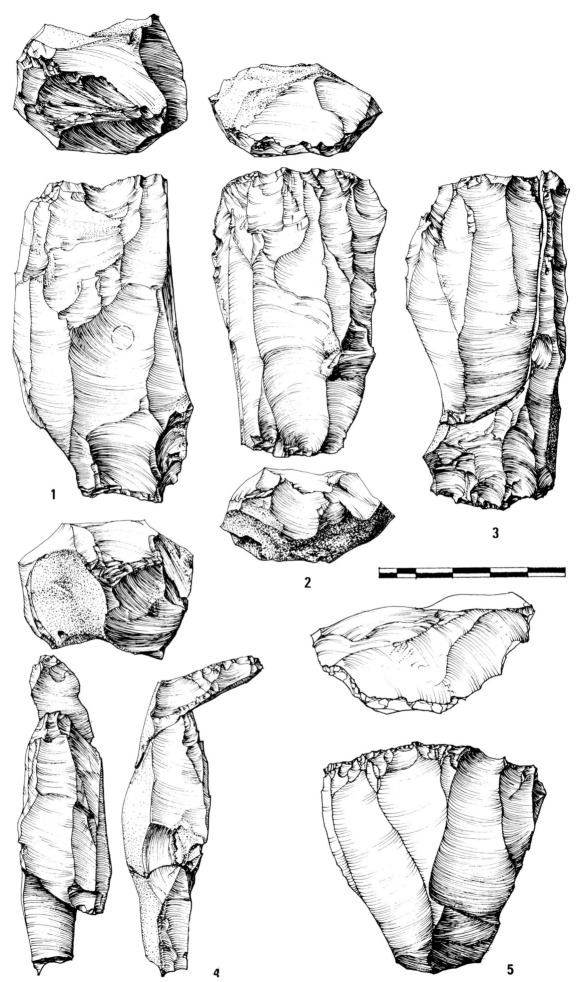

4.8   *Late Upper Palaeolithic blade cores. 1-4= opposed platform cores (3 with plunging blade refit, 4 core N with core tablet refit); 5= single platform pyramidal core. The broken circle on 1 indicates a drilled sample hole for flint sourcing purposes. Centimetre scale.*

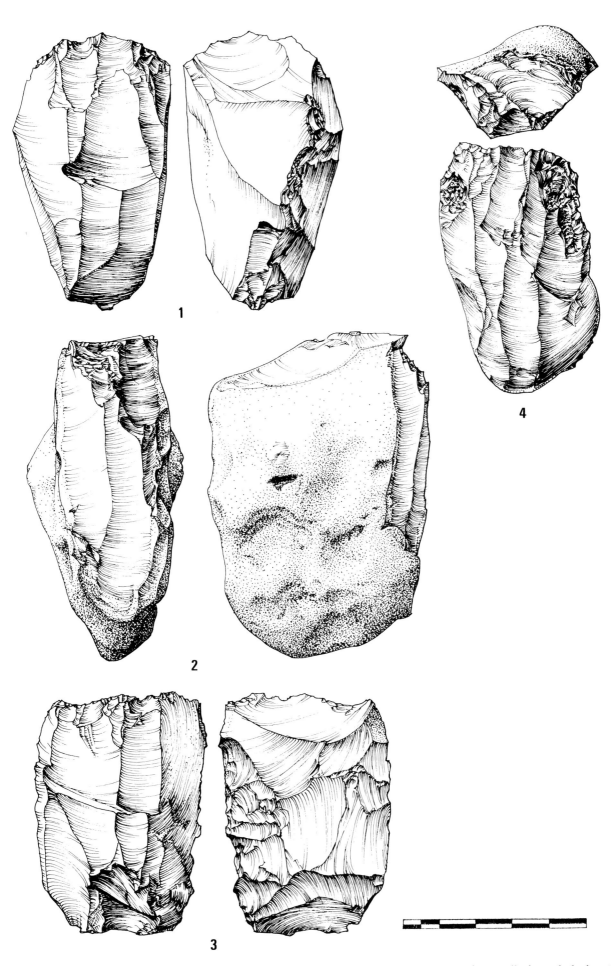

4.9   *Late Upper Palaeolithic blade cores. 1-2 and 4= single platform prismatic cores (4 with partially faceted platform); 3= opposed platform prismatic core. Centimetre scale.*

the raw material. For instance, a major flaw in the flint could lead to abandonment early in the reduction process. As a result there is a relatively even spread of sizes from the largest to the most reduced example (a variation in length of 200–36 mm).

Most of the blade cores display some part of their original cortical exterior; only 14% are devoid of all cortex. This indicates the influence of the shape of the raw material which is mainly in the form of flattish, oval flint cobbles (Fig. 4.9, 2). It also suggests that no major preforming of cores took place away from the site, a fact which is further confirmed by the refitting evidence (see Chapter 4.3).

The production of blades generally involved careful preforming of the cores. Signs of preparation can be found on the platforms, on the flaking face and sometimes at the back (Fig. 4.9, 1) and on the side margins of the core (Fig. 4.9, 3). Typically, the striking platforms were prepared and rejuvenated using two techniques: faceting and core tablet removal. The former method leaves small overlapping flake scars on the platform (Fig. 4.9, 4); these are often confined to the front of the platform and would best be described as partial faceting (cf. Bordes 1967, Fig. 6). While signs of faceting are found on a significant proportion of core platforms (25%), plain examples resulting from the removal of a single flake or core tablet are much more common (66%). It is noteworthy that the majority of blades also have plain butts. The rest of the core platforms are unclassifiable either due to burning, breakage or both. The above percentages are based on the number of platforms examined (n= 98) and make allowance for the fact that on eleven examples one platform was faceted while the other was plain. Whether the figures accurately reflect the relative frequency of each platform type is debatable, especially in the light of refitting data which shows that blades with plain butts and those with faceted butts were sometimes detached from the same end of the core (for example, Core H, Plate 4.40). The two techniques seem to have been used quite interchangeably.

Preparation of the core frequently involved careful abrasion of the striking platform in order to strengthen it against crushing (4.8,5). The degree of modification ranges from minimal chipping along the outer periphery to the extensive rubbing or grinding of the core's edge. That preparation of some kind was more often than not employed is indicated by its presence on 55% of all blade cores. Significantly, it is absent on most of the faceted platforms. Refitting evidence shows that in these cases the percussive blow was generally delivered well back from the platform edge.

Preparation of the back of the core seems to have depended largely on the shape and size of the original nodule. Cresting (bidirectional or unidirectional) is present on 14% of cores (Fig. 4.9, 1), whilst occasionally, flat, invasive flaking was employed (9%). The more usual method was to leave the back of the core either cortical or only partly modified (44%). In some cases, when flaking had extended around the whole of the

*Table 4.9 Blade core platforms*

|  | Plain | Plain/Faceted | Faceted | Other |
|---|---|---|---|---|
| One Platform | 14 | – | 6 | 4 |
| Two Platforms | 20 | 11 | 4 | 1 |
| Multiplatform | 1 | – | – | 2 |

*Table 4.10 Blade cores: preparation to the back of the core.*

|  | Cortical | Crested | Flat flaking | Other |
|---|---|---|---|---|
| One Platform | 10 | 2 | 4 | 8 |
| Two Platforms | 18 | 7 | 2 | 9 |
| Multiplatform | – | – | – | 3 |

core's periphery, it was impossible to tell whether there had been any modification at all. Some of the results of core preparation are reflected in the cross-sections of the cores. In 25% of examples the cores have round cross-sections, 19% are triangular, 8% are trapezoidal while the rest (48%) are irregular. Included in the triangular forms are most of the cores with posterior cresting.

Cresting is not limited to the back of the cores. From the refitting work it is clear that it was often employed at the front of the core to initiate a series of blade removals; cresting was also utilised from time to time to repair the flaking face and traces of such modification can be seen on 6% of the blade cores. Cresting occurs along the sides of 11% of the cores and here it may be associated with changes in flaking direction, as for example shown in refitted Core B (see 4.3.2). In no case is cresting on the sides accompanied by cresting on the back or front of the core.

Finally, a relatively high percentage of blade cores from the excavated areas show evidence of burning (25%). But, since the affected pieces do not form a concentrated cluster (Fig. 4.10), there is little obvious reason to associate them with a special localisation of activities as for example around a central hearth. On the other hand, it will be argued in the final section of this chapter (4.10.6), that the dispersed scatter of burnt flints in the NW part of the site (including mainly tools) may perhaps be linked to hearth emptying activities. In this respect it is noticeable that slightly higher frequencies of burnt cores were also recovered from this same area.

The Druitt surface collection referred to above contains numerous examples of blade (43) and flake cores (20), predominantly in unburnt condition. The blade cores are characterised by prismatic types, a feature also observed in the excavated collections (Table 4.8). Refitted examples of blade debitage to a few of these cores implies that knapping activities also took place further north of the main excavated area of the site. This provides further confirmation that Late Upper

Table 4.11  Blade cores from the Druitt surface collection.

|  | Prismatic | Pyramidal | Irregular |
|---|---|---|---|
| One Platform | 5 | 7 | 6 |
| Two Platforms, opposed | 18(1) | – | 3 |
| Two Platforms, crossed | 2 | – | – |
| Multiplatform | – | – | 2 |
| (1) core on a flake | | | |

Table 4.12  Flake cores from the three excavation collections

|  | Globular | Irregular |
|---|---|---|
| One Platform | – | 8 (1) |
| Two Platforms, opposed | – | 2 |
| Multiplatform | 1 | 14 |
| (1) core on a flake | | |

Palaeolithic activity extended well beyond the recently excavated areas, into the northern parts of the Eastern Depression.

*Flake Cores*: Amongst the 25 flake cores in the excavated assemblage (Table 4.12), over half are multiplatform types (60%), with eight single platform cores (32%) and two examples with opposed platforms (8%). Most of the cores are small, cortical and highly irregular in shape and are therefore probably not the remnants of discarded blade cores. There is one example of a core on a flake. The mean length and breadth of all measured specimens is 56 x 41 mm with standard deviations of 10.3 and 8.7 mm, respectively.

Nearly all of the flake cores have a major area of cortex on their exterior surfaces. This is an interesting attribute which indicates that the final form of the flake core probably corresponds quite closely the original shape of the nodule. The reduction method seems to have been fairly haphazard with minimal preparation to the striking platforms and new platforms often occupying the scars of previous flake removals. This suggests a different technique of debitage from the blade cores. The fact that the flake cores were clearly intended for the production of small flake blanks is demonstrated by several of the refits. In one example (Core K, Fig. 4.44) the detached flake blank was made into an end-scraper.

The morphology of the flake cores is highly irregular, due to the opportunistic method of flaking which also does not rely on much platform preparation. In 48% of cases the platforms are plain; whilst only one of the 25 cores shows evidence of faceting. Signs of repair of the flaking face are present on only a single example, a multiplatform core. In addition, relatively few (20%) of flake cores have abraded platforms.

It may be significant that eleven of the cores are on

small beach cobbles and seven of these display clusters of incipient percussion cones on their platforms. Such features are especially characteristic of post-Palaeolithic artefacts identified from other sites on the headland. It is therefore possible that the cores in question are Neolithic or later in age. The minimal intrusion of this material is discussed in Chapter 3.

A so far unique occurrence at the site is that of a flake core on a flake (Fig. 4.1, 4). Typologically it resembles cores described in Newcomer and Hivernel-Guerre (1974). In the Hengistbury example the platform was created at the distal end by an inverse truncation before a small series of flakes was detached down the central, dorsal arête. From the small number of removals, it is difficult to see how this piece could genuinely have been intended as a core. It is possible that the flakes were detached as a form of tool preparation or as a method of thinning the blank cf. a Kostienki knife (*sensu* Otte, 1980). The artefact belongs within the refitted group of Core J (see 4.3.2), which has also produced a dihedral burin.

Finally, there is nothing in the size range of either the blade cores or the flake cores to suggest the presence of more than one major assemblage at the site (*pace* Campbell 1977). As we shall see in the section on refitting (Chapter 4.3) there are perfectly valid reasons why one should expect to find cores in various stages of reduction; in many cases it is even possible to identify the actual cause of discard. The evidence put forward by Campbell (1977, Fig. 174) in support of his arguments is based upon differences in mean length measurements between smaller 'Mesolithic' cores and larger 'Upper Palaeolithic' ones. The figures quoted for the smaller cores (58.6±12.2 mm for 12 cores in his area and 61.4±12.2 mm for 30 in the Mace area) in fact show a considerable overlap with 14 larger examples from his area (90.9±34.7 mm). The coefficient of variation (standard deviation/mean) for the 'Palaeolithic' cores is also twice that of the 'Mesolithic' examples. In short, the data presented by Campbell is simply not strong enough to support his model of size division.

*Discussion*: From the high proportion of blade cores found it is evident that blade blanks were the main object of lithic production at the Late Upper Palaeolithic site . It is also clear from the type of debitage recovered that all stages of core reduction are represented in the assemblage from the initial roughing-out stages to the discard of exhausted or broken cores. An important implication of this observation, is that the majority of cores were brought to the site as whole nodules and not specially prepared or in a 'preformed' state. The significance of this fact, in terms of human behaviour, is that the weight of the nodules was not greatly reduced before they were transported (?carried) to the site, a distance of at least 12 km.

Although, the horizontal distribution of the flint debitage reveals some tendency towards clustering, as revealed by the refitting data (see 4.3.3), there is no evidence for the preferential concentration of cores by size or weight, as suggested by Campbell. Instead, the cores, which occur in low densities, seem generally to coincide with the slightly denser distributions of the blade and flake debitage (Figs. 4.6 and 4.10). This would indicate that the cores were subject to very much the same processes as those affecting the rest of the debitage. There is therefore nothing in the spatial distribution of cores or other finds to suggest the highly structured circle of 'tent weights' claimed by Campbell (1977, Fig. 51).

Previous claims have been made at Hengistbury for the utilisation of cores as burins and also as scrapers (Mace 1959). In our experience such claims are rarely justified, and in any case are mostly very difficult to prove. In most instances more economic explanations may account for the appearance of 'retouch', such as abrasion of the core edge to prepare the striking platform. One exception is provided by Core V (Figs. 4.49 and 4.50). Here, a large opposed-platform blade core 200 mm long shows very heavy crushing along one edge. It is conceivable that the damage scars were the result of some heavy form of use, such as chopping (cf. Barton 1986a). This is the only core from the site with evidence that it might have been used as an *ad hoc* tool.

## 4.2 The retouched tool assemblage

### 4.2.1. *Introduction and typology*

The material presented here comes from three major artefact collections from the Late Upper Palaeolithic site. The finds derive from three different excavations undertaken in 1957 (Mace 1959) in 1968–69 (Campbell 1977) and between 1981–4 (Barton and Bergman 1982; Barton 1983a, 1983b; Barton and Huxtable 1983). It is clear from the restricted area of the finds and the contiguous nature of the excavated distributions that the artefacts belong to a single Late Upper Palaeolithic assemblage (see Chapter 3.2). Finds from a large surface collection made by Druitt and others in adjacent areas of the headland are also summarised (Table 4.14). These have been described in detail elsewhere (Mace 1959) and illustrate the extent of Upper Palaeolithic occupation at Hengistbury.

The retouched tools from the three excavated collections have been treated together and the total counts have been amalgamated. To aid comparison between the three data sets, summary tables of the tool classes by excavation are provided in table 4.13.

The various tool types have been roughly grouped according to the type-list created by de Sonneville-Bordes and Perrot (1953, 1954, 1955, 1956a and b.) for describing Upper Palaeolithic tools. A selection of definitions relevant to Hengistbury Head is also provided in the Archaeological Glossary. Due to the fact that we believe a simple type list provides adequate information, as well as being easier to interpret (Azoury and Hodson 1973; Doran and Hodson 1975, 257–264), we have tried wherever possible to avoid

*Table 4.13 Retouched tools from the excavated collections.*

|  | 1957 | 1968-9 | 1981-4 | % |
|---|---|---|---|---|
| End-Scrapers | 39 | 42 | 66 | 22.7 |
| Composite tools | 1 | – | – | 0.2 |
| Piercers/Becs | – | 3 | 1 | 0.6 |
| Burins | 36 | 14 | 16 | 10.2 |
| Truncations | 2 | 5 | 7 | 2.1 |
| Notches/Denticulates | 4 | 2 | 6 | 1.8 |
| Backed blades/bladelets | 143 | 51 | 130 | 49.9 |
| Shouldered Points | 7 | – | 1 | 1.2 |
| Tanged Points | – | – | 2 | 0.3 |
| Retouched Flakes | – | – | 2 | 0.3 |
| Microliths | – | – | 4 | 0.6 |
| Miscellaneous | 16 | 5 | 27 | 7.4 |
| Broken tangs | 6 | 1 | 10 | 2.6 |
| Totals: | 254 | 123 | 272 | 99.9 |

*Table 4.14 Retouched tools from the surface collections.*

|  | Druitt 1914 | Calkin 1950 | Others |
|---|---|---|---|
| End-Scrapers | 21(1) | –(1) | 1 |
| Composite tools | – | – | 1 |
| Piercers/Becs | 2 | – | – |
| Burins | 12 | 1 | 2 |
| Truncations | 2 | – | – |
| Notches/Denticulates | – | – | – |
| Backed blades/bladelets | 20(2) | 3 | 6 |
| Shouldered Points | 1 | 1 | – |
| Tanged Points | 2 | – | – |
| Retouched Flakes | 1 | – | – |
| Microliths | – | – | – |
| Miscellaneous | 4 | – | – |
| Broken tangs | 1 | – | – |
| Totals: | 66(69) | 5(6) | 10 |

(Brackets= totals including missing tools figured in Mace 1959)

creating numerous sub-categories of tool-types. Under this simplified scheme tools are grouped according to their main morphological characteristics, with any variation being discussed under each category.

The total excavated collection consists of some 649 retouched tools including 147 end-scrapers, 66 burins and 324 backed blades and bladelets. There are a small but significant number of tanged pieces and tanged points (19) and shouldered points (8) as well as 14 truncations. By contrast, all other types are poorly represented, and except for 48 miscellaneous retouched items account for less than 2% of the tool assemblage. The following section presents data on each of the main individual tool groups.

*End-Scrapers*: This group is composed of 147 end-scrapers including 35 fragmentary examples. Of the 112 complete or nearly complete tools, 78 are made on flakes and 32 on blades. There are 15 scrapers which are made on crested pieces or core tablets.

The collection is dominated typologically by the simple end-scraper with 97 examples. There are nine tools made on retouched blanks (Fig. 4.11, 8–9), while the remaining four circular scrapers (cf. de Sonneville-Bordes and Perrot 1954, 330) are all atypical (Fig.

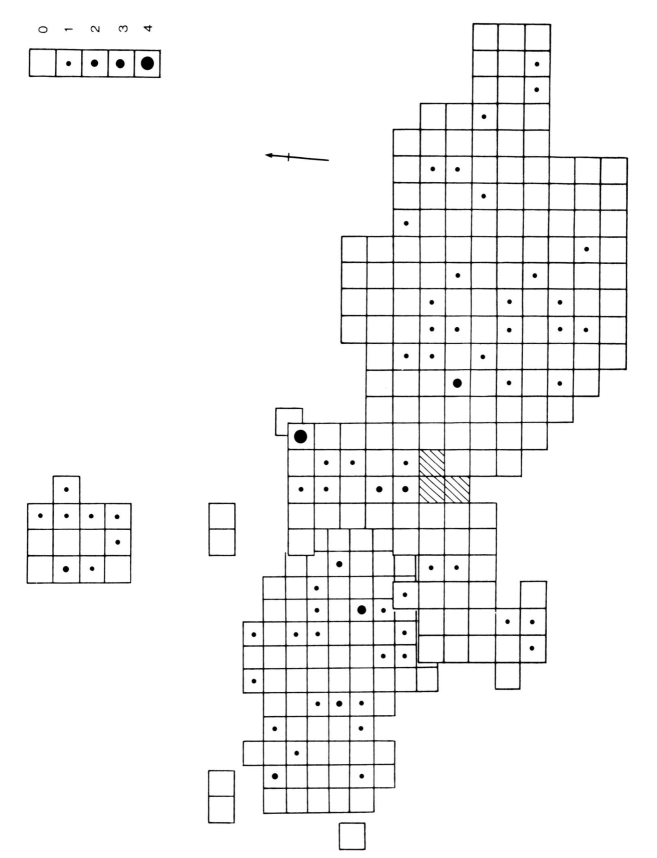

4.10 *Horizontal distribution of cores. Number of cores per metre square. The cross-hatched squares were not systematically excavated.*

*Table 4.15 End-scraper typology (Total=147)*

|                                   | n  | %  |
|-----------------------------------|----|----|
| Simple end-scraper                | 97 | 66 |
| End-scraper on a retouched blank  | 9  | 6  |
| Atypical circular scraper         | 4  | 3  |
| Double end-scraper                | 2  | 1  |
| Broken/unidentifiable scrapers    | 35 | 24 |

4.12, 3). There are three double end-scrapers of which two come from excavated contexts and the third, not counted here, comes from the surface collection (see Mace 1959, Fig. 10).

The flake end-scrapers are generally made on small blanks, with a mean length of 41 mm and a standard deviation of 12.2 mm. The average width and thickness of these pieces is 34 mm and 10.5 mm, with standard deviations of 8.5 and 3.6 mm, respectively. Most end-scrapers made on flakes (72%) have some cortex on their dorsal surfaces (Fig. 4.12, 2 and 4), while the remainder are characterised by multidirectional or unidirectional scars. The fact that blanks selected for scraper manufacture come from the earlier stages of core reduction is suggested both by the frequent presence of cortex and from examples refitted to cores. In one case (Core V), three scrapers have been refitted to a blade core, which was abandoned at an early stage of reduction. Two out of three tools have cortex on their dorsal surfaces (4.11.9–10), while refitting shows that the third (Fig. 4.12, 5) must also have had a cortical area. Another example (Core K) has an end-scraper made on a flake detached from the outer part of the nodule. The blank is partly cortical and the negative flake scar reveals that about 6 mm of the original distal edge was removed by retouch (Fig. 4.44).

There are 32 end-scrapers made on blades. The mean length of the complete pieces is 55 mm with a standard deviation of 13.2 mm. Not surprisingly, they are narrower and thinner than those made on flakes, averaging 23 mm and 9 mm, respectively. The majority of these tools are broken (63%), which contrasts with the lower figure of 43% for end-scrapers made on flakes. The greater percentage of broken blade tools may be due to the fact that they are longer and thinner, making them more susceptible to breakage during retouching, sharpening or use.

The morphological features of the scraper edges appear to be fairly uniform. The edge is almost always semi-circular in plan and placed at the distal end of the blank, although 12% of the scrapers (n= 115) are retouched proximally. The edge is usually formed by semi-abrupt retouch (cf. Tixier *et al.* 1980, 89) which is always direct. The edge angles vary but the majority are between 40–70°. Occasionally the scraper-edge has abrupt retouch probably as a result of sharpening (Fig. 4.12, 5).

Morphological differences in the edge angles of certain end-scrapers have been put forward by Campbell (1977, 180) as evidence for mixing in the assemblage.

He suggested that 'Mesolithic' examples had slightly lower edge angles than 'Upper Palaeolithic' ones. However, based on our own experiences in making stone tools we believe that edge angle may be influenced by a number of factors such as the particular task to hand and the degree of tool use. It is quite common, for example, for the working edge of the tool to become progressively steeper as a result of several resharpenings. Another reason we do not find Campbell's argument convincing is based on the refitting evidence. A good illustration of the problem is provided by Core V (Fig. 4.50) onto which three end-scrapers have been refitted. The scraper fronts of two of the tools (the third is broken) have edge angles of 50 and 80° respectively. If Campbell's criteria had been applied rigorously the two scrapers would have been classified as belonging to separate assemblages.

From a functional point of view, one of the end-scrapers displays pronounced rounding at its edge which is consistent with working a hard material such as stone (cf. Van Noten 1978; Newcomer 1981). Microscopic striations on this piece show that the tool was used in a direction perpendicular to the scraper edge (Fig. 4.13), confirming the expected motion of tool use. Figure 4.13 also shows two experimental scrapers used to work stone and hide, respectively. Less well-developed rounding of a similar kind has also been observed on several other examples, but these are the exception rather than the rule. In profile, many of the scraper blanks (80%) are slightly curved, with a concave ventral surface (Fig. 4.12, 5). On some scrapers this feature seems to have been deliberately accentuated since the tool's edge is located near the maximum point of curvature and gives the scraper a hooked appearance. The exact purpose of this feature is unclear but it might be linked to a special use in hide-working (Nissen and Dittemore 1974).

The fact that scraper retouch chips have been found at the site (see below) and in one case actually refitted to a scraper edge (Fig. 4.12, 7) offers direct evidence that tools were made and/or sharpened on site. On some specimens the retouch removals making up the scraper-edge have a lamellar appearance with regular, parallel scars (Fig. 4.11, 5). This kind of retouch is probably produced by pressure flaking. Pressure flaking may have been used in preference to percussion since it allows greater control and ease in maintaining the desired semi-abrupt edge angle.

The spatial distribution of end-scrapers shows a general scatter of these tools across the site, with a slight decrease in numbers in the south central area and towards the cliff-edge (Fig. 4.14). The number of scrapers in both the Mace and Campbell areas never reaches more than three scrapers per square metre while in the northern sector as many as five end-scrapers have been recorded from a single metre square. Overall, it is difficult to document any significant clustering of these tools, although it is noteworthy that two of the three scrapers which refit to Core V were found less than a metre apart. The absence of scrapers near the aban-

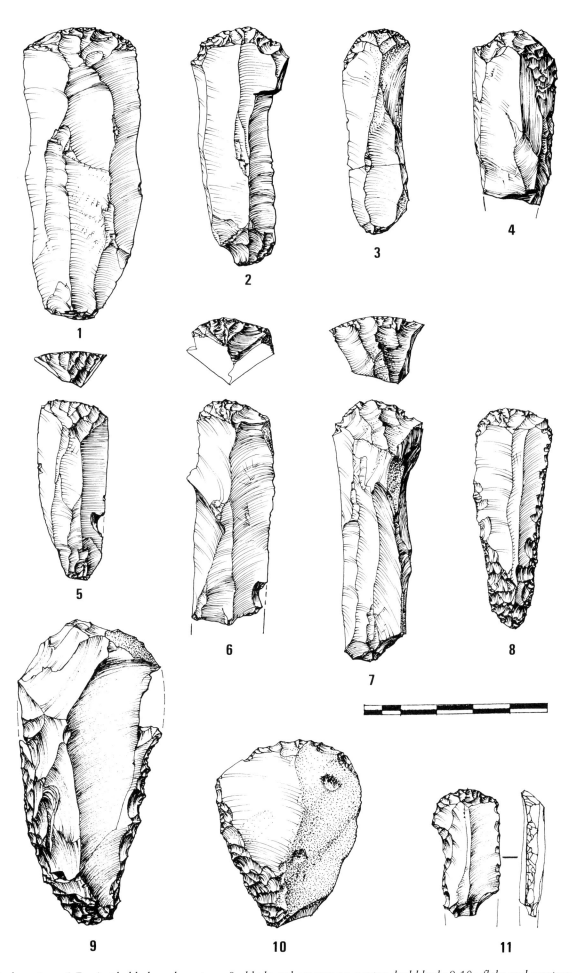

4.11 *End-scrapers. 1-7= simple blade end-scrapers; 8= blade end-scraper on a retouched blank; 9-10= flake end-scrapers on retouched blanks; 11= blade end-scraper on a retouched (shouldered) blank. Centimetre scale.*

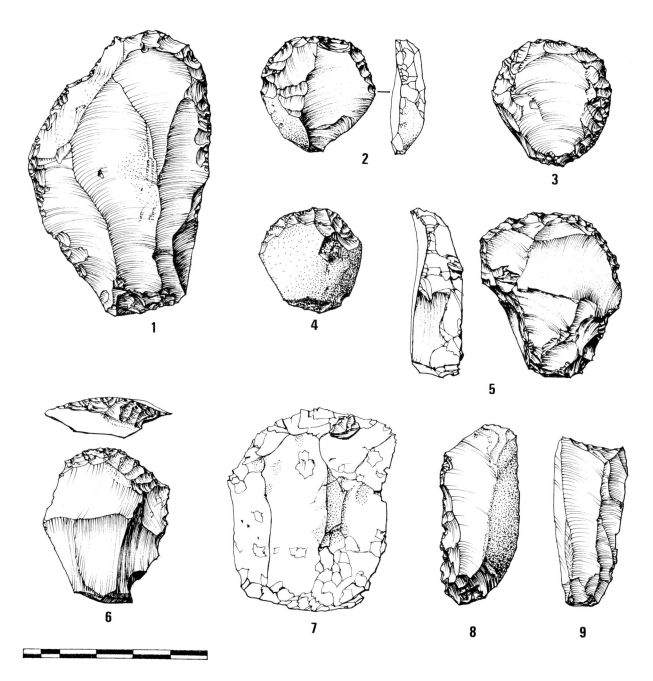

4.12 *End-scrapers and other retouched tools. 1-2 and 4-7= simple flake end-scrapers (7 burnt example with unburnt refitting retouch chip); 3= atypical circular scraper; 8= denticulate; 9= concave truncation. Centimetre scale.*

doned core may suggest a separation of activities (manufacture and use) or at least a separate discard pattern for the core and the tools. It should be noted in passing that except for the end-scrapers no further refits were found for this core (for further discussion of Core V see 4.3.2 and 4.3.3). As with some of the other tool categories, the end-scrapers include a relatively high proportion of burnt pieces (53%). This is an observation we shall return to at the end of the section (4.2.3).

*Composite Tools:* The only composite tool from the excavations is made on a blade and combines a burin on truncation and an end-scraper (Mace 1959, Fig. 6). There is one other example from the surface collection (Vitelleschi pers. comm.) which consists of a truncation

burin on a tanged support. It is possible that this artefact represents a re-cycled tanged point (Fig 4.18, 6).

*Piercers/Becs:* There are four examples of this class in the excavated sample, plus two from the surface collection. Two are made on blades, one is on a flake, while the last two examples are made on burin spalls. One of the burin spalls has been refitted to a burin on lateral retouch. There are two multiple tools combining becs. The largest simple bec is made on a retouched blade and measures 93 x 27 x 8 mm (4.15,1). Its tip, which is offset to the main axis, has been formed by direct, abrupt retouch converging from both lateral edges. Minor signs of utilisation are visible on the ventral surface of the tip in the form of minute flake scars.

Another bec, which is also offset, has macroscopic polish and rounding at its tip. One of the two double becs is made on an intentionally broken blade fragment (Fig. 4.15, 3), the other is made on a burin spall. Unlike the previous examples, neither of the multiple tools shows any sign of damage due to use.

*Burins*: Of the total of 66 burins 33 are dihedral (Figs. 4.16 and 4.17) and 24 are on truncation (Figs. 4.18 and 4.19) while nine were too badly broken or burned for such a distinction to be made. The number of burins made on flakes (29) and blades (25) is roughly equal. The mean length and width of these pieces is 50.1 x 28.4 mm (standard deviations = 16.8 and 11.0 mm, respectively). They tend to be rather thick with a mean of 10.8 mm and a standard deviation of 4.7 mm. Over 50% of the burins are partly corticated.

From Table 4.16 it can be seen that there are 33 dihedral burins which make up one half of the burin assemblage. The most numerous example of this type is the burin on a break (accidental and intentional) with 13 examples (Fig. 4.17). The five multiple dihedral burins have the following combinations: dihedral symmetrical/dihedral symmetrical (1), dihedral angle burin/burin on a break (1) and burin on a break/burin on a break (3). The last group includes two tools made on intentional breaks; one of these has two *tranchet* blows struck from the same distal break (Fig. 4.17, 6). Finally, there are two dihedral angle burins.

The truncation burins make up 36.3% of this tool group. The most common types are burins on oblique and concave truncations (Fig. 4.18) with 12 and eight examples, respectively. There is one burin on a convex truncation (Fig. 4.18, 3) and one burin on abrupt lateral retouch (Fig. 4.18, 1). One of the two multiple truncation burins combines burins on oblique truncations, while the other has straight truncations.

The burins from Hengistbury Head are simple with only two examples having more than three facets forming the burin edge. There is no tendency towards multi-faceted burins and, not surprisingly, flat-faced facets (i.e. facets on the ventral surface) are rare with 11.8% of a total of 76 burins having this feature (inclusive of multiple tools). The burin edges have a mean width of 6.3 mm (standard deviation = 2.6 mm). It is noteworthy that this is significantly smaller than the blanks' thicknesses. The burin edges are also generally square in shape with 68.4% examples of this type (see Ronen 1965; Newcomer 1972, Fig. 9). Finally, these tools are more often made at the distal end (36) than at the proximal end (19).

Unless an artefact could definitely be identified as a burin spall it was regarded as an ordinary blank. In many cases it was possible to refit spalls to burins clearly establishing them as the by-products of the burin blow technique. Some of these pieces were atypical and not regarded as spalls until they were placed back on a burin. Over 100 burin spalls were examined from the site and various technological features noted.

As can be seen from Table 4.17 there is an equal distribution of primary and secondary spalls. A number of spalls show signs of retouch preparation prior to the delivery of the burin blow (Fig. 4.17, 2). This retouch helps to regularise the edge, in a manner analogous to cresting, and ensures the successful removal of a long spall. There are seven plunging spalls of which two removed opposed truncation burins, while a third example removed a truncation (Fig. 4.19, 1).

The relationship between burins to burin spalls is illustrated in Table 4.18. From the data presented it is clear that a considerable disparity exists between the 1957 sample and the more recent collections. Whereas over half the total number of burins from the site come from the 1957 sample, relatively few burin spalls were recovered, giving a burin to burin spall ratio of 1:0.5. This contrasts with the 1968–9 and 1981–4 collections where the ratio is 1:2.4 and 1:4.1, respectively. We believe this reflects real distributional differences between the excavated areas, especially since very small burin spalls (<10 mm long) were recovered by Mace. Furthermore, the densest burin distribution occurs in the eastern end of the 1957 excavation (Mace 1959, Fig. 3), and lies directly adjacent to the 1981–4 area which yielded 65 spalls. Clearly, further work on refitting between the 1957 and 1981–4 collections would be desirable in order to prove the relationship.

Refitting of a small sample of the burin spalls has provided useful information about the sequence of tool-use and re-sharpening, as well as the spatial relationship between the tools and their by-products. Tool use is well-illustrated, in one instance, by a group of four refitting burin spalls, detached from a truncation burin (Fig. 4.18, 5). One of the spalls (the third to be detached) shows significant edge-damage along the facet, demonstrating that the tool was either only utilised at this stage or there was a change in function. The latter might have involved the use of a much harder material resulting in visible edge-damage. From the limited refitting evidence (Fig. 4.20) it is also possible to suggest that the burins were used and re-sharpened near the same spot and that they were not heavily curated tools.

Refitting has also been informative in testing the observations of Campbell who recognised two distinctive burin groups (amongst his own collection as well as the Mace sample), which he separated on morphological and metrical grounds. In contrast to Campbell, we could find no such ambiguity in the metrical or morphological data (one of his burin groups was represented by only five tools), and this was substantiated by the refitting programme. One striking example involves two burins and a plunging spall from the same blank (Fig. 4.19). The mid-section consists of a burin on a break described by Campbell as 'Mesolithic'. The two end sections, by contrast, are made up of a burin on truncation and plunging spall both regarded as 'Upper Palaeolithic'. On the basis of this observation (and backed up by many more examples of refitted cores and debitage) there can be little doubt that all the

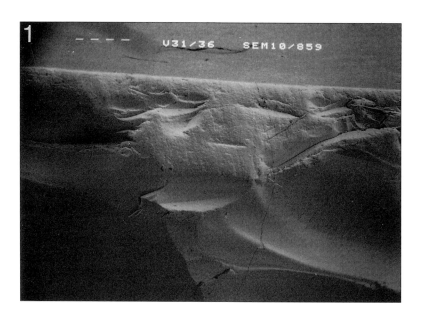

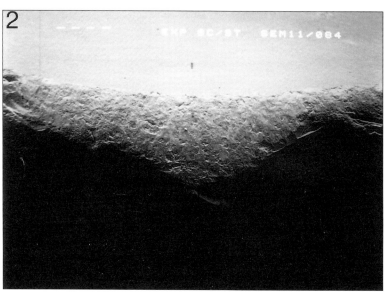

4.13 SEM photomicrographs of Hengistbury scraper V31/36 and experimental examples. 1 and 4= archaeological tool (x27 and x120); 2 and 5= experimental tool used to scrape stone (x27 and x120); 3 and 6= experimental tool used to scrape soaked

*fallow deer rawhide treated with yellow ochre additive (x27 and x150). Bar on extreme right of scale= 0.1 mm. (Photo: Natural History Museum)*

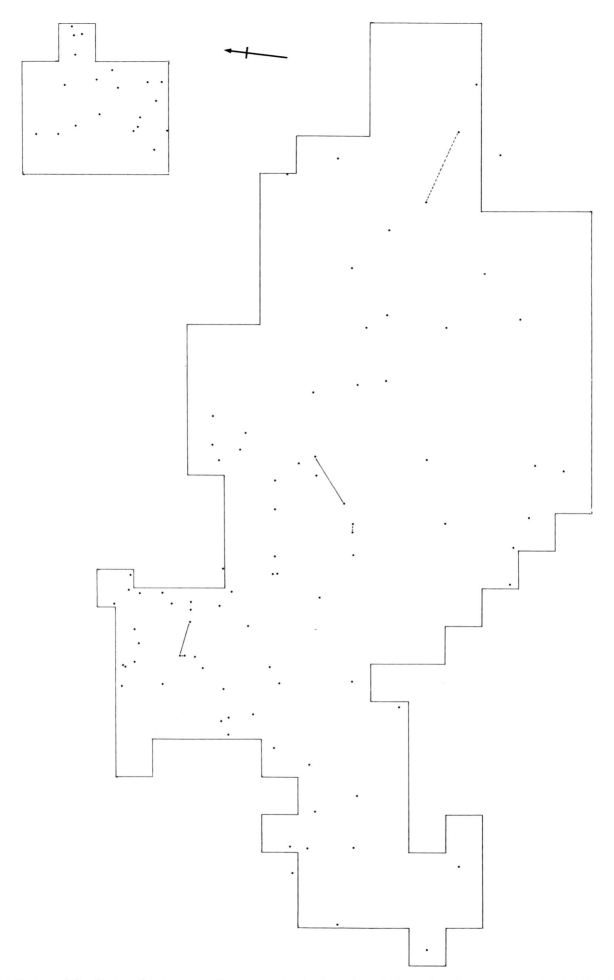

4.14 *Horizontal distribution of end-scrapers. Dorso-ventral refits shown by solid lines; dashed lines represent break refits. Scale 10 mm = 1 m. For the true spatial relationship of the Northern squares (in box) see Figure 4.6.*

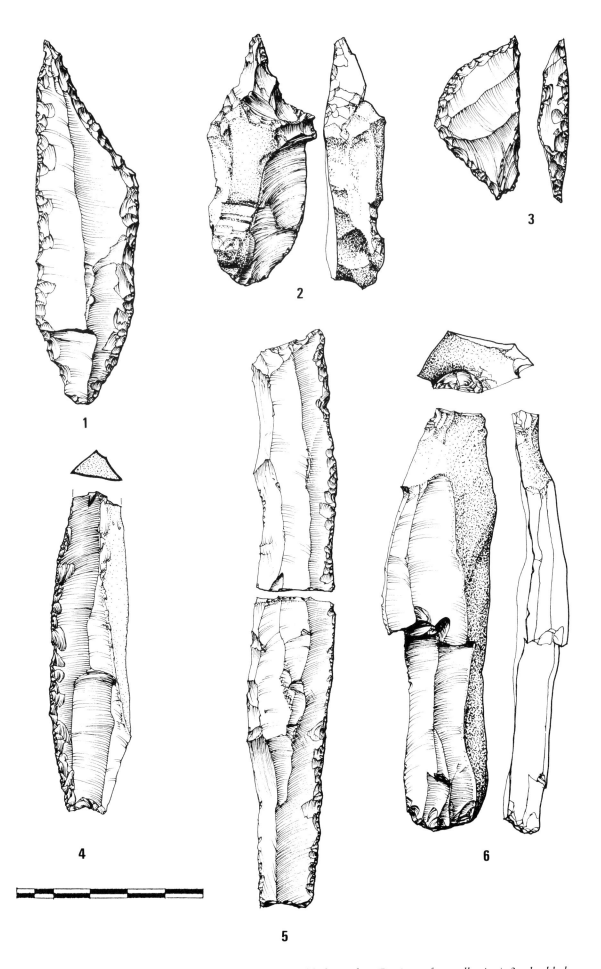

4.15  *Piercers, becs and truncations. 1= bec on retouched blade; 2= bec (Druitt surface collection); 3= double bec; 4-5= concave truncations on blades; 6= straight truncation on a large blade. Centimetre scale.*

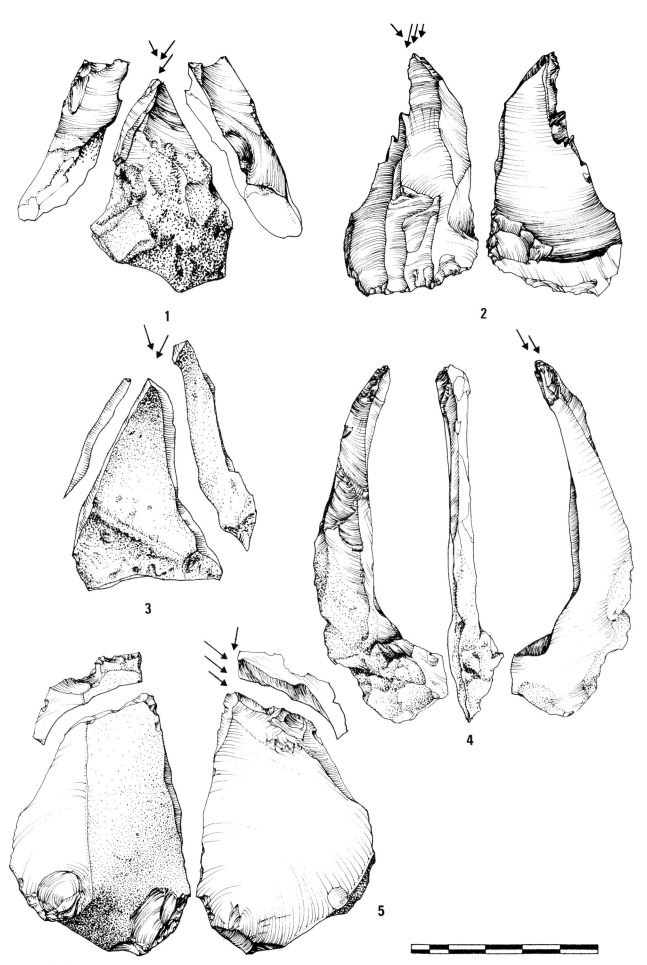

4.16 Dihedral burins and spalls. 1= dihedral symmetrical burin; 2-3= dihedral asymmetrical burins; 4= secondary spall from a dihedral burin; 5= dihedral asymmetrical burin with a refitting spall showing earlier distal truncation. Centimetre scale.

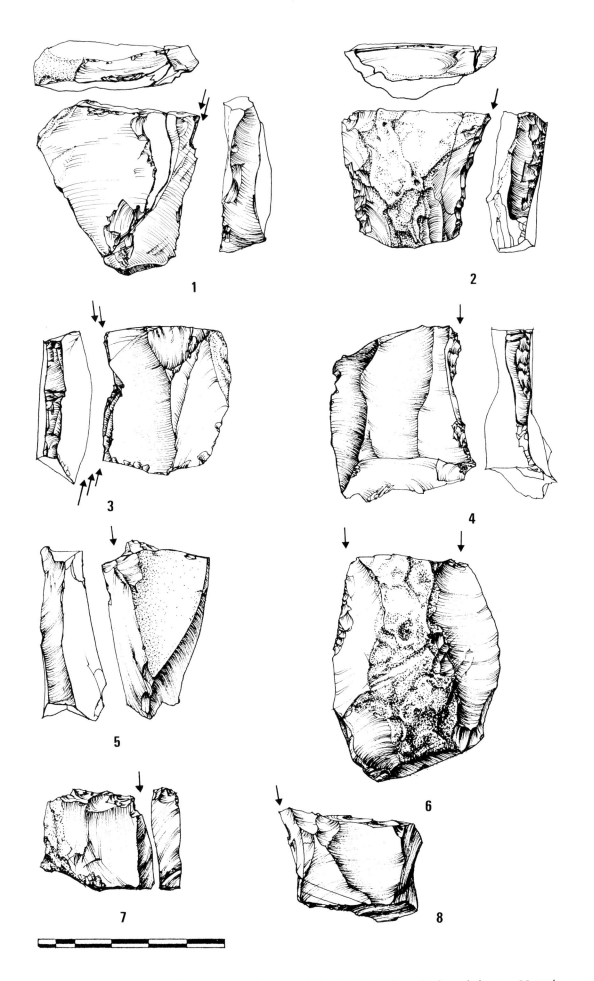

4.17 *Dihedral burins on intentional breaks. 1-2, 4-5 and 7-8= angle burins; 3 and 6= multiple angle burins. (Note the post spall removal edge damage on the facets of 1-2, 4 and 6). Centimetre scale.*

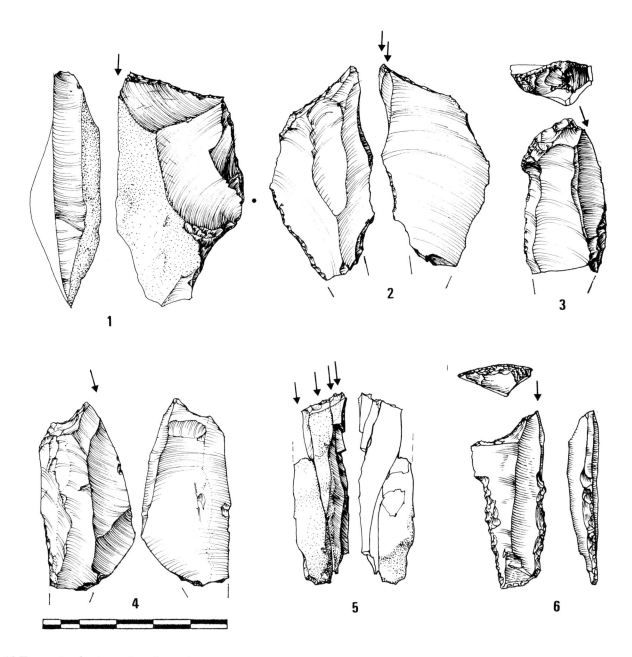

4.18 Truncation burins and spalls. 1= burin on a lateral truncation; 2 and 4= burins on concave truncations; 3= burin on a convex truncation (with heavily rubbed end); 5= a series of burin spalls probably from a burin on straight truncation; 6= composite tool consisting of a concave truncation burin on a tanged support (re-used tanged point ?). Centimetre scale.

Table 4.16 Burin typology (total=66)

|  | n | % |
|---|---|---|
| Burin on a break | 13 | 19.7 |
| Burin on a natural surface | 3 | 4.6 |
| Dihedral asymmetrical burin | 6 | 9.1 |
| Dihedral symmetrical burin | 4 | 6.1 |
| Dihedral angle burin | 2 | 3.0 |
| Multiple dihedral burin | 5 | 7.6 |
|  |  |  |
| Burin on a straight truncation | – | – |
| Burin on an oblique truncation | 12 | 18.2 |
| Burin on a concave truncation | 8 | 12.1 |
| Burin on a convex truncation | 1 | 1.5 |
| Burin on lateral retouch | 1 | 1.5 |
| Multiple truncation burin | 2 | 3.0 |
|  |  |  |
| Broken/unidentifiable burins | 9 | 13.6 |

pieces are in fact contemporary and the result of Late Upper Palaeolithic activity.

There is little information relating to the function of the burins from the site. Unger-Hamilton's results (4.5.4) indicate that most of the sample is unsuitable for microwear analysis due to post-depositional surface modification or other inhibitory factors (e.g. 45% of specimens were burnt). However, several tools have macroscopic damage which may provide clues to their use. A common type of damage occurs on the burin facets of 13 pieces. This takes the form of discontinuous retouch and edge crushing. The retouch is typically composed of short flake scars with expanding edges which terminate in hinge fractures; in some cases it is quite heavy and also occurs on refitted spalls (see

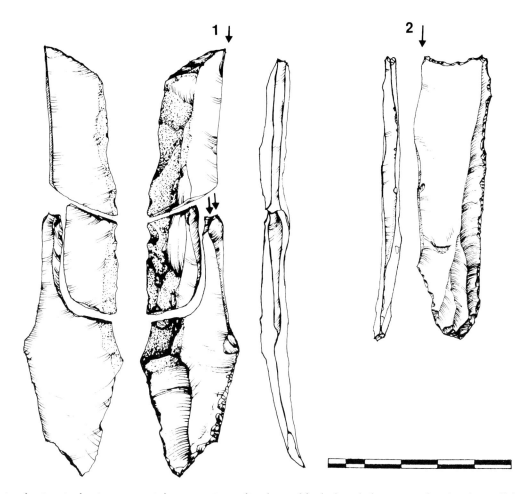

4.19 *Truncation burins. 1= burin on a straight truncation refitted to a dihedral angle burin on a break. The spall from the burin on a break plunged and detached the distal truncation. 2= burin on a concave truncation. Centimetre scale.*

Table 4.17 *Burin spalls*    (total= 118)

|  |  | n | % |
|---|---|---|---|
| (a) | Primary spalls | 60 | 50.8 |
|  | Secondary spalls | 58 | 49.2 |
| (b) | Spalls from dihedral burins | 12 | 10.2 |
|  | Spalls from truncation burins | 18 | 15.3 |
|  | Unidentified | 88 | 74.6 |
| (c) | Evidence of retouch preparation prior to the burin blow | 41 | 34.7 |
| (d) | Plunging spalls | 7 | 5.9 |

Table 4.18 *Burin: Burin spall ratios*

|  | 1957 | 1968–9 | 1981–4 |
|---|---|---|---|
| Burins | 36 | 14 | 16 |
| Burin Spalls | 20 | 33 | 65 |
| B:BS ratio | 1:0.5 | 1:2.4 | 1:4.1 |

above). If this damage is functional, as opposed to accidental, it indicates that the burin facet was the working edge of these particular tools. Burin facets have been used experimentally by the authors for scraping and shaping the surfaces of bone and antler tools (Bordes 1965; Newcomer 1974; Bergman 1987b). A rarer form of damage is the visible rounding which occurs on one burin edge (Fig. 4.21).

Burins are scattered over much of the site with no obvious finds concentrations. As with other tool types there is a tendency for the number of finds to increase from east to west across the site, as well as in the northern sector. Another recurrent feature is the very low density of tools from the south central part of Campbell's site (Fig. 4.20), the area which corresponds to a clearly defined zone of debitage. Finally, refitting shows that there is rarely any great distance between a burin and its spalls, suggesting that the tools were sharpened, used and discarded in more or less the same spot.

*Truncations*: This group consists of 14 tools from the three excavations. They comprise five straight truncations, four oblique truncations, three concave truncations and three multiple truncations (oblique/oblique, oblique/concave and concave/ concave).

All the truncations are made on blades or bladelets by direct semi-abrupt or abrupt retouch. Nine of them are broken and six of these are also burnt. One of the

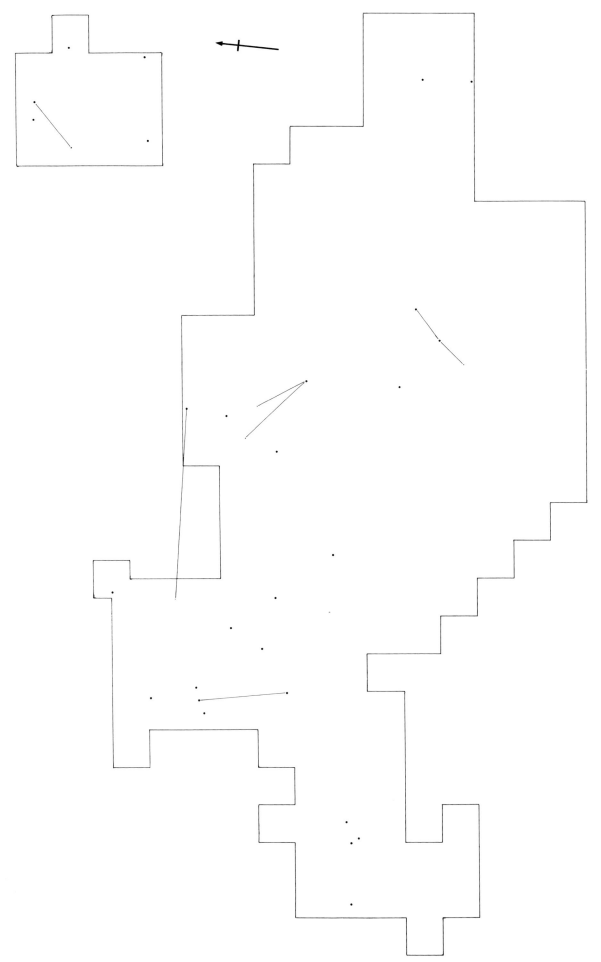

4.20 *Horizontal distribution of burins and refitting burin spalls. The spalls are represented by the smaller dots. Scale 10 mm = 1 m. For the true spatial relationship of the Northern squares (in box) see Figure 4.6.*

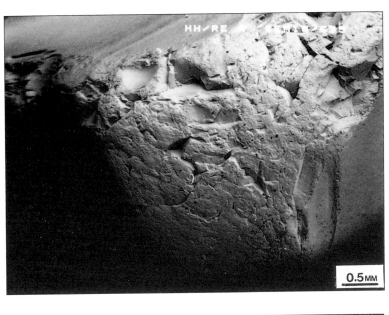

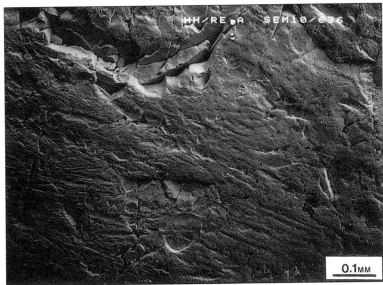

4.21 SEM photomicrographs of the burin on a convex truncation with a heavily rubbed end (Fig. 4.18.3). Close-up view of the distal tip at increasing magnifications. Note the orientation of striations indicating the direction of tool-use. (Photo: Natural History Museum)

Table 4.19 Truncations (total= 14)

| | Single Truncation | | | Multiple Truncation | |
| | Straight | Oblique | Concave | Oblique | Mixed |
| --- | --- | --- | --- | --- | --- |
| Proximal | 2 | 2 | 1 | 1 | 1 |
| Distal | 3 | 1 | 3 | 1 | 1 |

pieces is made on an intentional break. The largest artefact measures 151 x 22 x 6 mm (Fig. 4.15, 5). Four of the tools are truncated proximally, seven are truncated distally (Fig. 4.12, 9) while three have truncations at both ends (Table 4.19). The function of these tools is unknown, but in some cases they might be unstruck burins. In three of the concave examples there are signs of additional lateral retouch to the blanks. Retouch has also been noted on the edges of several burins and seems to have been associated with regularising the edge prior to the removal of the burin spall. The lateral retouch on other truncations can sometimes be highly elaborate, as in the case of two truncations made on blades (Fig. 4.15, 4–5) with direct, stepped and scaled retouch that resemble *lames magdaléniennes du Morin* (de Sonneville-Bordes and Deffarge 1974).

*Notches/Denticulates*: There are nine denticulates and three notches. Some of these tools display irregular Clactonian notches (cf. Bordes 1961) along one edge and may be accidental forms of damage. For example Figure 4.22 illustrates an intentionally broken flake; the denticulations could have been produced if the blank was accidentally moved whilst being segmented on an anvil. In other cases (Fig. 4.12, 8) the denticulation seems to have been quite deliberate. Also included in this sub-category are at least two specimens which appear to be post-palaeolithic in date. One is a flake with a microdenticulated edge. It bears some resemblance to the microdenticulates from the Mesolithic site, except that the modified edge is convex in shape. The second is on a flake with beach chattered cortex, quite unlike most of the artefacts from the site. It displays contiguous notches on the ventral surface and numerous dorsal incipient cones. All these features are consistent with artefacts of Neolithic or later age from the Headland.

*Backed blades and bladelets*: Backed blades and bladelets make up the single largest component of the retouched tool assemblage. There are 324 backed pieces, mostly broken, of which 119 are in very fragmentary condition. A typical example from the site has a relatively straight back formed by direct, abrupt retouch (Fig. 4.22). The retouch removes a significant part of the width of the piece, but this may vary and a small number (22) of tools display only marginal retouch. Morphologically, most of the pieces have simple outlines. Classified with backed blades are 14 backed points, of which half are broken. Amongst the complete tools are two curve backed points and two angle backed points.

The backed blades and bladelets show a considerable range in size and there is no clear distinction between the two classes on metrical grounds. Lengths of complete pieces vary between 33–78 mm with a mean of 5.2 mm and a standard deviation of 1.3 mm. The blanks selected for making these tools average 3.5 mm in thickness with a standard deviation of 1.3. This is slightly thinner than the mean measurement for unretouched blades which is 5.6 mm with a standard deviation of 3.5 mm. Although it is difficult to assess the original widths of the blanks selected for backing, a comparison with the unretouched blades and bladelets suggests that between 5–7 mm of the edge was removed by retouch. Given a mean backed width of 11.2 mm (sd.= 3.6 mm) this would place most of them in the backed blade class and indicate that more or less a third of the original width had been removed by retouch. Unlike some of the other tool classes (e.g. endscrapers), a slightly higher proportion of backed pieces have flat, rather than curved, profiles (54%). The blanks selected are nearly always non-cortical, only 5% of the backed pieces have areas of cortex.

There appears to be no strong lateralisation in the distribution of retouch on these tools. The retouch occurs on the right edge in 103 cases, while 145 tools are retouched on the left side. Sometimes a lateral edge has only partial retouch, which seems to be due to the fact that the original blank had a naturally abrupt edge and needed little modification. There are 9 double backed pieces with the retouch occurring on both edges, one of these is a burin spall. The use of an anvil to produce the retouch is relatively rare, although it is used most notably on some of the thicker tools (Fig. 4.23, 10 and 14). Nineteen pieces with an average thickness of 5.3 mm (SD = 2.3 mm) show the characteristic bidirectional retouch scars. This compares with a mean thickness of 3.4 mm (SD = 1.0 mm) for the rest of the sample (n=210) where anvil retouch is absent (for further definition see 'anvil retouch' in the Glossary of Archaeological Terms).

Two thirds (65.4%) of the backed blades and bladelets are burned (see also Mace 1959, 239) which partly accounts for the large number of broken pieces in this category. There are several underlying factors which might explain their presence and these are discussed in detail in Chapter 4.3. One likely explanation, however, may be the accidental or deliberate incorporation of artefacts into the hot embers of a fire. If so, the high percentage of burnt pieces may reflect an association with activities around a hearth, perhaps involving the heating of plant resin adhesives for replacing broken or worn tools in their hafts. Some evidence for retooling activities of this kind is provided from Late Upper Palaeolithic sites on the European mainland where burnt and often broken artefacts are concentrated around such features. At the French Late Magdalenian site of Pincevent these observations have been supplemented by the recent find of a composite projectile tip near a hearth (Leroi-Gourhan 1983). This tool consists of a grooved reindeer antler point into

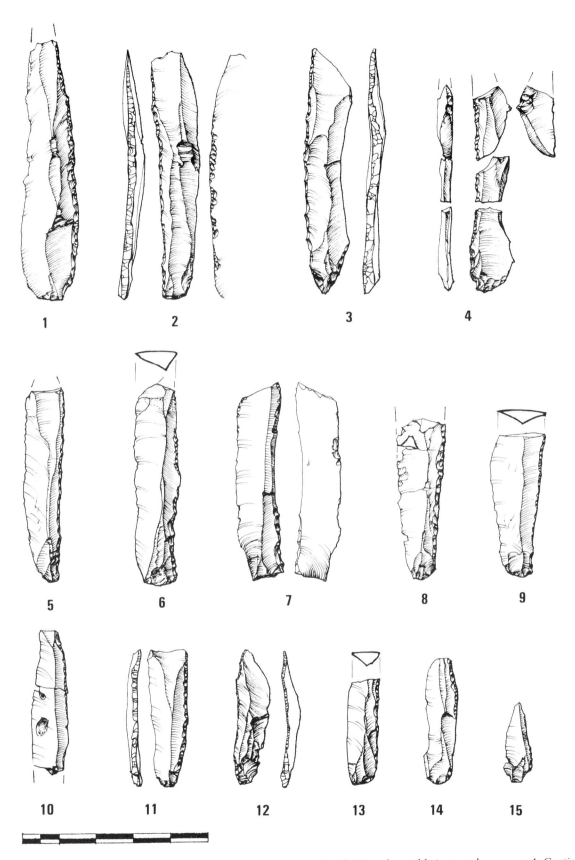

4.22 *Straight-backed blades and bladelets. Note the edge damage on 2 and 7-8 and possible impact damage on 4. Centimetre scale.*

which bladelets have been inserted and presumably fixed with resin. So far the only hint that backed pieces from Hengistbury were hafted comes from a partially burnt tool. The blade shows intense reddening at one end with a sharp transverse boundary between the burnt and unburnt portions (Fig. 4.23, 11), perhaps indicating partial embedding in a haft.

Although thermal fracture accounts for most of the

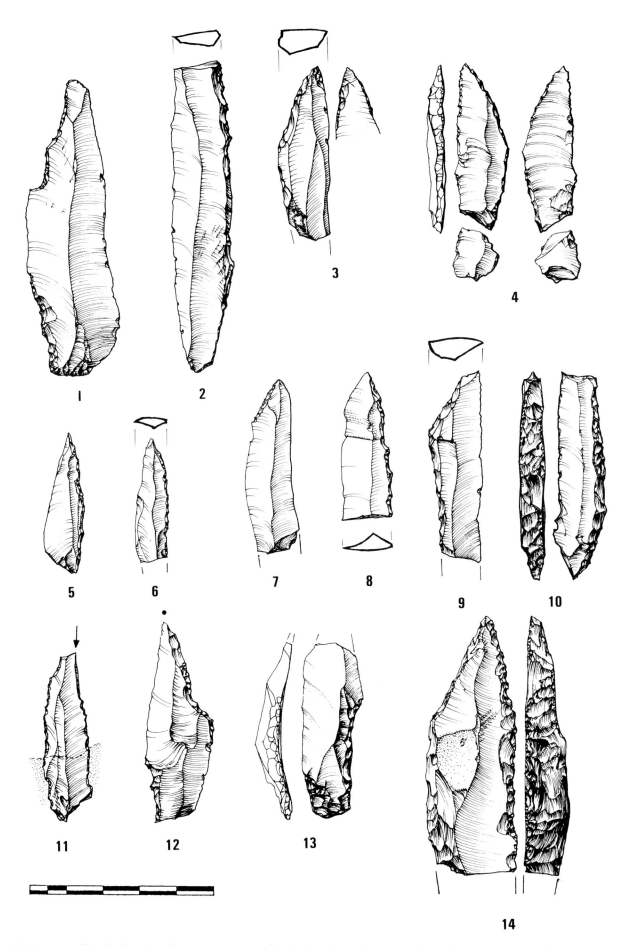

4.23 *Selection of backed tools and truncations. 1= unfinished tool; 2 and 14= large backed tools; 3-4= curve-backed points (4 is similar to a Creswell point, also note edge damage prior to removal of the proximal end) ; 9= Creswell point; 5-6 and 8= backed points; 7= truncation; 10= curve-backed blade with straight distal truncation; 11= backed tool (dotted zone marks burnt end); 12= backed and truncated tool; 13= shouldered blade. Centimetre scale.*

breakage among the incomplete tools, a number of the backed blades have breaks due to torsion or flexion. One example (Fig. 4.22, 4) has been fragmented into three pieces probably as a result of impact (Barton and Bergman 1982; Bergman and Newcomer 1983, Fig. 2). Simple snaps and flexion breaks can also occur during the course of manufacture and this type of accident is likewise represented in the archaeological sample. Another form of breakage is a side snap which occurs on a small number of pieces.

Discontinuous, scalar retouch has occasionally been noted on the ventral surface of backed blades and bladelets (Fig. 4.22, 2 and 7). Since it is confined to the edge opposite the backing it is considered to have resulted from use. Scalar edge damage has been replicated on experimental backed blades used by the authors as knives, for example in scraping away the periosteum of bone, as an initial stage of marrow extraction. However, this form of use mainly resulted in bifacial damage along the flint edge, a feature not present on the Hengistbury pieces. The localisation of damage strongly suggests the archaeological tools were held at a steep angle to the material being worked.

The distribution of backed blades and bladelets shows a definite concentration of material in the western half of the site. Much lower densities of these tools occur in the Campbell area, and these are found well away from the zones where much of the refitted debitage was concentrated (Fig. 4.22). This seems to indicate, once again, that areas where blanks were manufactured differ from those where tools were discarded. By far the richest concentration of backed material occurs in the northern sector, where densities reach 15 per sq. m; totals approaching this level have also been recorded in the Mace area in the north-west. The horizontal distribution between mainly broken refitting pieces varies greatly, but it is noteworthy that some long distance refits occur between Mace and the other areas. Refits of this kind are unlikely to be due simply to post-depositional drift within the sands.

Finally, it should be noted that apparent differences in the tools cited by Campbell (1977, Table 52 and page 194) as evidence for two separate cultural groupings is not supported by the present analysis. First, his argument is based on the mean width measurements of artefacts from the 1957 and 1968–9 excavations ('Upper Palaeolithic'= 16.6±6.3mm; 'Mesolithic' (mainly Mace)= 11.7±3.1mm ) and it is clear from these figures that there is a significant statistical overlap in the range. In the second place, new measurements based on a much bigger sample show a figure altogether closer to the original one for the Mace collection (11.2±3.6 mm). In short, there is little reason to doubt that the assemblage is not entirely homogeneous.

*Shouldered points*: There are five shouldered points and three point fragments in the excavated collection (Fig. 4.25). Several other tools of this type have been recovered from the surface. The mean measurement of the five complete specimens is 55 x 16 x 5 mm. The

tools, which are always on blades, are made by direct, abrupt retouch forming a distinctive shoulder at the proximal end. The tip is usually modified into a point by an oblique distal truncation. Sometimes the tools display additional retouch near the base, on the edge opposite the shoulder.

The Hengistbury shouldered pieces are typologically identical to the Hamburgian points from Northern Germany (Schwabedissen 1954). No particular preference is shown for the side selected for shouldering. Four of the eight examples are shouldered on the right edge, the rest are modified on the left side. Unlike the German examples, however, there are no points with inverse retouch or showing a small projecting 'spur' at the proximal end. This small sample is discussed in more detail in 4.10.6. Points recovered from the Hamburgian levels at Stellmoor were believed to have been used as projectile tips (Rust 1943), although the precise grounds for believing this have been questioned (Clark 1975). No definite function is proposed for the Hengistbury shouldered points except to note that they can make very effective projectile heads as demonstrated in archery experiments (by Christopher Bergman). It may also be significant that despite the general absence of lateral edge damage, a minute 'burin facet', which may have resulted from impact, occurs at the distal end of one of the artefacts (Fig. 4.25, 9).

*Tanged points*: Of the 19 artefacts recovered from excavated contexts, only three are more or less complete tanged points (Fig. 4.25). A further two points derive from surface collections made at the beginning of the century near the site (Mace 1959). The points are large and have mean dimensions of 60 x 23 x 7 mm. Characteristically, the tools consist of an axial tang at the proximal end formed by direct, abrupt retouch. The distal end may be retouched to make the tip more pointed. Also included here are 17 proximal fragments of tangs (Fig. 4.25, 5–6). In some cases it is possible to see where the retouch terminates in a double 'shoulder', while in other examples only the base remains. The width and thickness of these fragments is entirely consistent with the tangs of complete specimens. Many of the fragments likewise show the straightness of profile found on the complete forms.

If the tanged points served as projectiles, as seems probable, the broken ends may represent fragments brought back to the site in their shafts for replacement (cf. Gramly 1982). The authors' experiments have shown that tanged points such as these sometimes break on impact at the intersection of the tang and the main body of the tool (see also Madsen 1983; Fischer *et al.* 1984). The base is often held firmly in the shaft especially if sinew is used as the hafting agent. As observed above (under '*Composite tools*') one truncation burin occurs on a tanged support (Fig.4.18, 6); this may be a tanged point which had been re-used after a hunting breakage (cf. Madsen 1983).

*Retouched flakes*: There are only two retouched flakes,

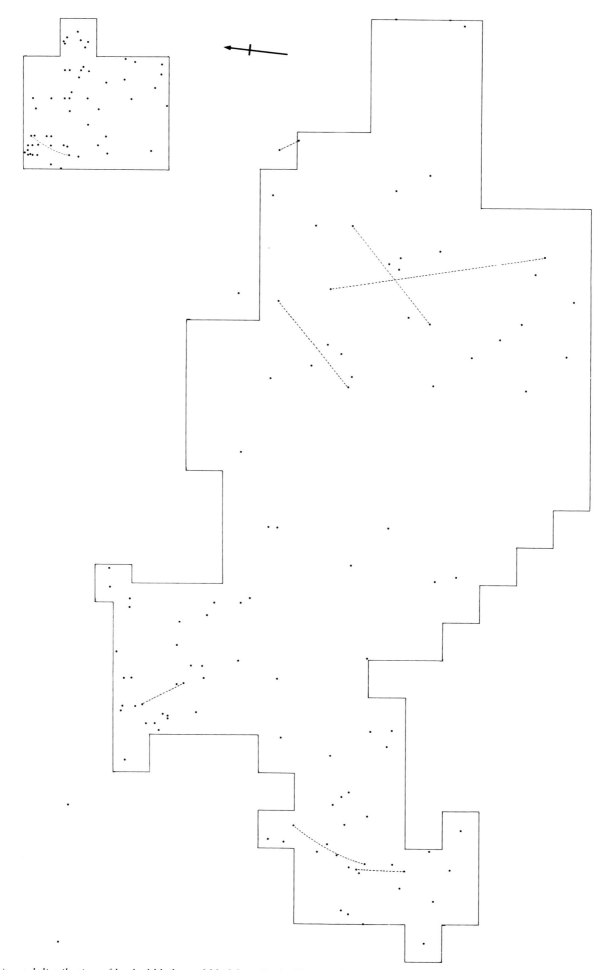

4.24 *Horizontal distribution of backed blades and bladelets. Dashed lines indicate break refits. Scale 10 mm = 1 m. For the true spatial relationship of the Northern squares (in box) see Figure 4.6.*

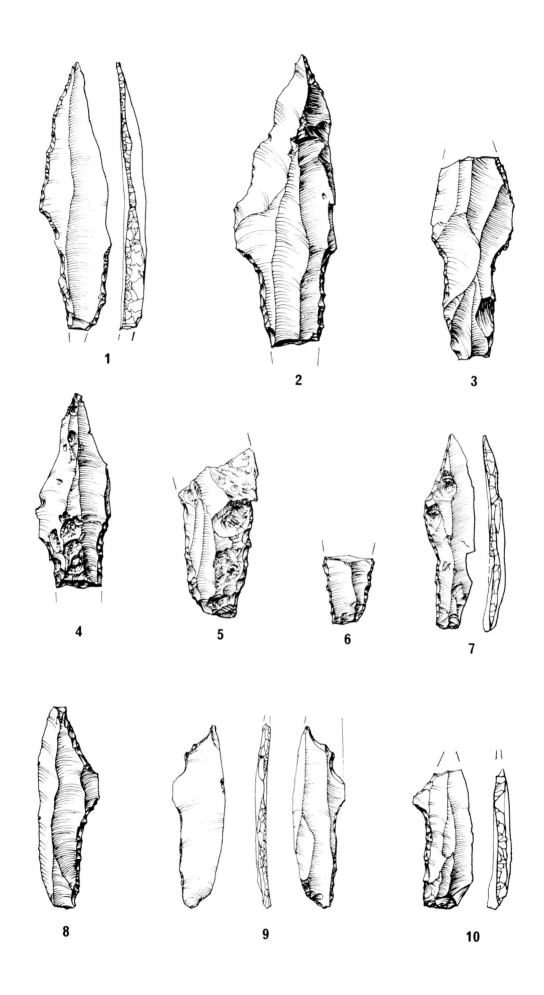

4.25   *Tanged points and shouldered points. 1-4= tanged points (2 from Druitt Collection); 5-6= broken tangs; 7-10 shouldered points.  Scale = 1:1.*

one of which (Fig. 4.63, 3) is partially cortical and has continuous abrupt retouch down one lateral edge.

*Microliths*: The small number of microliths recovered from the site include three scalene triangles and one minuscule non-geometric B-type microlith (backed bladelet). Although microliths can occur in North European Upper Palaeolithic toolkits (Rust 1937, 1943; Taute 1968) it is virtually certain that these pieces are intrusive to the site and are post-palaeolithic in age. It is also significant that the finds mostly occur on the periphery of the densest artefact distribution and are of a slightly different patina from the rest of the assemblage. Typologically, the microliths most closely resemble material found at the nearby Late Mesolithic site of Mother Siller's Channel (Palmer 1977).

*Miscellaneous tools and tool fragments*: This group comprises some 48 pieces which are retouched but do not fit easily into any of the above categories. They are mainly pieces which are badly broken and have some retouch which is usually marginal and discontinuous. A relatively high proportion of the pieces are also burnt (50%). In a few cases it is probable that they represent broken fragments of formal tools which are now unrecognisable. Eleven of the artefacts occur in association with intentional breaks (see below). Two artefacts in the miscellaneous class are made on very small, narrow flakes, with a triangular cross-section, and displaying a series of tiny lamellar removals at one extremity. They resemble tools attributed to the Wehlen group of the Federmesser Complex (sensu Schwabedissen 1954, Tafel 53; Veil pers. comm.).

*Intentional breaks*: Attention has already been drawn to this aspect of the assemblage (Bergman et al. 1983, 1987) and only a few relevant points will be discussed here. At Hengistbury an intentional break involves the snapping of a flake or blade which results in two or more substantial pieces. The breaks are transverse to the long axis of the artefact and have no pronounced concavity (Fig. 4.26). Depending on the requirements of the knapper, the blank could be broken into one or more pieces to be used directly, or modified by retouch or burin blow technique into a tool. Since this action is clearly separated from primary blank production and involves transforming the artefact by deliberate breakage, they should properly be regarded as intermediate tool forms.

A number of characteristic features appear on the broken flakes under consideration which can be grouped as: 1) 'contact features' and 2) features which result from flexion (Bergman *et al.* 1983, 1987). The first group can be identified according to attributes that are the direct result of the percussive blow. These include the presence of points and cones of percussion, incipient cones and dorsal ridge crushing. The second group includes conchoidal fracture marks, lips and wedge-shaped fracture lines. These are not necessarily diagnostic of intentional breakage since they can also occur on accidental breaks.

The 176 artefacts believed to have been intentionally snapped form a remarkably consistent group in terms of their morphology. The segments are rectangular in shape and have mean dimensions of 24.3 x 25.8 x 7.2 mm with standard deviations of 9.4, 6.8 and 2.4, respectively (Table 4.20).

A comparison with the data for blade debitage shows that the intentionally broken pieces have a slightly greater mean thickness. In terms of breadth these pieces compare most closely with the flake sample. Cortex occurs on 37% of these artefacts but it usually covers less than half of the dorsal surface. The most common type of segment is mesial (72) followed by distal (40) and proximal (24). Almost one third of these pieces are burned.

As mentioned above there are a number of features resulting from percussion which are diagnostic of intentional fracture. In our sample over 50% of the artefacts believed to have been deliberately snapped display these 'contact features'. They are not necessarily confined to the break but can occur on either the ventral or the dorsal surface. An additional 10% do not have contact features but have been refitted to breaks where these are present.

As can be seen from the table below 36.4% of the sample have neither percussion features nor can be refitted to ones that do. This group of 64 artefacts is composed of break surfaces which display only attributes due to flexion (wedge-shaped fracture lines, lips etc.). The artefacts were tentatively classed as intentional breaks because of their regular form and straight break surfaces. While these features occur during intentional breakage they may also result from knapping accidents. An example of this is when a blade snaps into several segments as it is detached from the core. Such pieces rarely if ever display contact features

Table 4.20  *Intentional breaks: overall dimensions (mm) of unretouched segments*

|  |  | Length | Breadth | Thickness |
|---|---|---|---|---|
| Total | = | 134 | 134 | 131 |
| Range | = | 6–70 | 13–47 | 4–15 |
| Mean | = | 24.3 | 25.8 | 7.2 |
| Standard Deviation | = | 9.4 | 6.8 | 2.4 |

Table 4.21  *Intentional breaks.*  (Total= 176)

|  | *n* | % |
|---|---|---|
| Pieces with contact features on the break (point, cone of percussion etc.) | 84 | 47.7 |
| Pieces with surface contact features only (Dorsal ridge crushing and incipient cones) | 10 | 5.7 |
| Pieces without contact features refitted to artefacts where these are present | 18 | 10.2 |
| Pieces without contact features or refits, but with straight breaks | 64 | 36.4 |

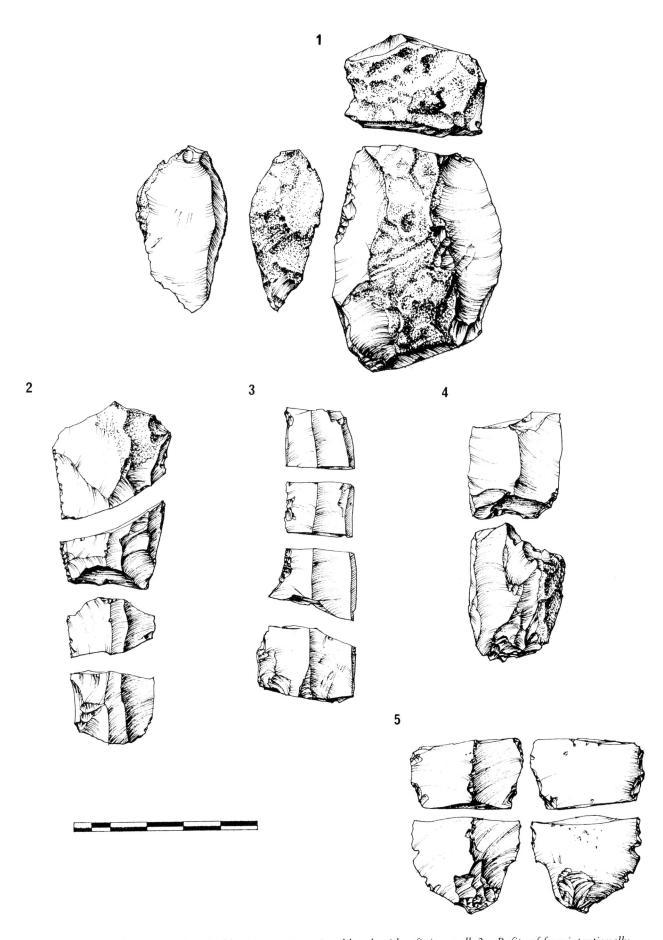

4.26 *Intentional breaks. Key: 1= A typical burin on an intentional break with refitting spall. 2 = Refits of four intentionally broken pieces forming part of the original blade. 3 = Similar refitted blade; first segment and third from top show burin-like breaks along edges. 4 = Refitting intentional breaks with spontaneous notch on lip. 5 = Refitted intentional breaks with incipient cones (ventral) and dorsal ridge crushing. Centimetre scale.*

but it must be recognised that a considerable grey area exists between intentional and accidental breakage. Indeed in our experiments, 25% of over 300 percussively broken blanks failed to show points and cones of percussion, dorsal ridge crushing or incipient cones (Bergman *et al.* 1983, 1987).

At Hengistbury, the majority of the intentionally broken artefacts are unretouched segments (146 or 82.9%). Just over 56% of these have contact features which is roughly the same proportion as in the entire sample. Although most of the pieces display no visible macroscopic traces of use there are a few examples with edge damage. Most notable is one intentionally broken flake refitted to a burin on a break. Both the burin facet and the break surface display identical edge damage. This indicates that some of the segments were used without being modified into recognisable tools.

There are 30 pieces which have been intentionally broken and are also retouched tools. Ten of these are burins made on breaks, where the break surface serves as a platform for detaching the spalls. There are also two burins which have had their burin edges removed by an intentional break. This was presumably done to create a new burin edge as well as a platform to detach additional spalls. The other tools consist mainly of partially retouched pieces, and those with denticulated or notched edges (16). In some cases the retouch might be attributed to spontaneous effects, as for example in Figure 4.26,4, where we suspect the retouch occurred accidentally during the snapping of the flake. The remaining tools consist of two rubbed end pieces, one truncation and one double bec. No other tool occurs on a blank with unequivocal contact features. It is possible that several end-scrapers with transverse breaks were intentionally broken. However, since the entire scraper edge was removed in the process, leaving a steep edge angle, it is unlikely that this was done for re-sharpening purposes.

The 176 intentionally broken pieces form a small but significant portion of the Late Upper Palaeolithic assemblage. Although they make up only a fraction (2.9%) of the total flake, blade and bladelet debitage, they represent a highly recognisable and distinctive feature of the flint industry. This is an unusual characteristic, and one which does not appear common at other British Upper Palaeolithic sites. It would be interesting to know, for example, whether this method occurs at European sites or other British ones especially where there is a scarcity of large, good quality flint raw material in the immediate area.

In terms of their horizontal distribution these artefacts cluster towards the western half of the site, being mainly concentrated in the 1957 and 1981–4 areas (Bergman *et al.* 1983, 1987, Fig.3.9). There are 24 groups of refitted intentional breaks, each consisting of two or more rejoined artefacts. Ten of the groups are made up of three or more refits. Aside from one group without contact features, most of the refits occur over shorter distances of between two to three metres. A more precise analysis of the spatial information is not possible because many of the refits are from the 1957 area where accurate distributional data is lacking.

*Utilised Pieces*: Within the three collections there are a number of pieces which cannot be classified as implements in the formal sense but which exist under the separate category of *a posteriori* tools (*sensu* Bordes 1970). These are defined as artefacts with little or no deliberate modification, but which show distinct signs of utilisation.

*(A) Rubbed ends*: Among these pieces are 15 artefacts which display heavily rounded or rubbed ends (Fig. 4.27 and 4.28). The rubbed areas are confined to either the tip or the butt end, and are concentrated on corners or projecting high points, such as a dorsal ridge. Macroscopically the ends have a smooth and polished appearance, and are frequently associated with discontinuous retouch or edge-damage. Identical rounding occurs on at least one of the burins (see above).

Only the ends of substantial flakes and blades appear to have been selected for use, the largest of these is on a blade 100 mm long. Most of the artefacts of this type display rubbing at one end (usually proximal), whilst only one blade is rubbed at both ends (Fig. 4.27, 2). A careful inspection of the pieces shows that the blanks were sometimes modified prior to their use, for example by inverse or direct retouch (Fig. 4.27, 4). In other instances an unretouched end, such as the ventral side of the butt, was utilised (Fig. 4.27, 2). Figure 4.28 shows an SEM micrograph of an artefact's rubbed extremity (Campbell 1060). Striations running parallel with the rounded edge indicate the direction of use. The tool was probably held edge downward and used in a back and forth motion. Occasionally edge damage is found contiguous to the rubbed area, but also partially covered by it (Fig. 4.27, 5). For these pieces in particular it may be possible to suggest several stages in the development of wear beginning with edge damage and culminating in the heavy grinding partly overlying the damage scars. This is an area where future experiments would prove especially fruitful.

*(B) Edge-damaged artefacts*: There are a fairly large number of artefacts with discontinuous retouch along one edge. However, in most cases it is difficult to separate these with any confidence from accidental effects, such as spontaneous retouch or trampling damage. In a few examples, where well-developed signs of 'retouch' occur along breaks or deliberately modified edges it is possible to be more certain. Figure 4.27, 3 shows a proximally snapped blade with invasive scalar retouch on the ventral surface. In the authors' opinion this is unlikely to be the result of spontaneous damage. The break edge seems to have been utilised as a tool.

*(C) Hammerstones*: There is one flint cobble with a heavily battered cortical surface. It weighs 125 gm and may have been used as a hammerstone (Fig. 4.29).

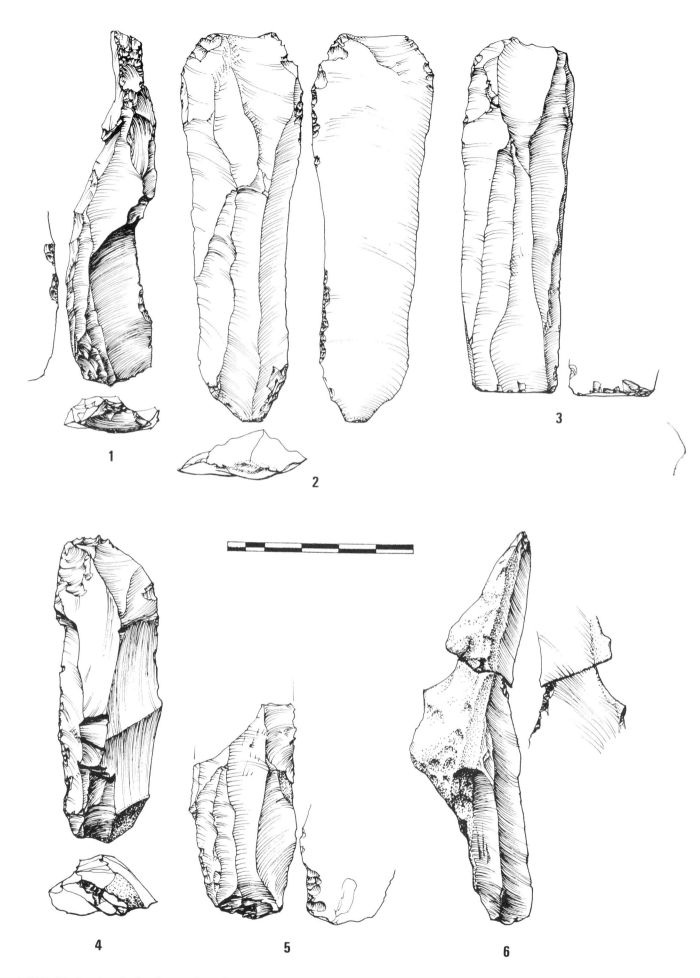

4.27 Rubbed end and edge damaged artefacts. 1-2 and 4-5= rubbed pieces; 3= blade with proximal edge damage; 6= snapped blade with edge damage. Centimetre scale.

133

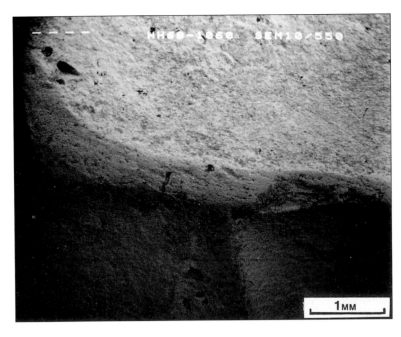

*4.28 SEM photomicrographs of rubbed end tool (HH68 1060) at increasing magnifications. (Photo: Natural History Museum)*

## 4.2.2 Retouched tool debitage

*Burin spalls (see under Burins).*

*Retouch flakes*: Numerous tiny 'chips', detached during the course of tool-making, have been recovered from the excavations. Many of them are quite curved and probably come from the manufacture of tools such as end-scrapers. One unburnt retouch flake of this type has been refitted to a burnt end-scraper (Fig. 4.12, 7). It was found only a short distance from the tool, suggesting that the scraper was sharpened, used and discarded near the same spot.

*Krukowski microburin*: Only one example of this type of tool waste has been recovered from the site. The vir-

tual absence of this by-product of backing may coincide with the scarcity of anvil retouch on backed blades at the site.

*Microburins and microburin miss-hits*: Two microburins and one miss-hit come from the excavations. The existence of these pieces can probably be attributed to a low level post-palaeolithic presence at the site, although it is not inconceivable that one of the larger examples is the accidental result of backed blade manufacture (Bordes and Fitte 1964).

## 4.2.3 Non flint materials

Apart from flint other materials recovered from the

4.29 *Flint hammerstones. Left= experimental; right= archaeological. 10 cm scale.*

4.30 *Refitted sandstone cobble from L29/O30. 10 cm scale.*

occupation area include a number of fragmented sandstone cobbles and pieces of red ochre.

The sandstone cobbles come from two areas of the site. From south of the footpath, centring on squares L29 and 030, were found several fragments which refit to form a block 11.2 x 9.0 x 3.6 cm in dimension (Fig. 4.30). The pieces show evidence of fire cracking and it is possible the block was used to line a hearth. Mace

4.31 *Refitted sandstone cobble from X30/Y30. 10 cm scale.*

also reported two lumps of sandstone "lying a few feet from one another" (1959, 254) in the adjacent area but sadly these items are now lost.

A second group of broken sandstone fragments was recovered in the area north of the footpath (squares X30/29 and Y30). Refitting shows they belong to two cobbles, one of which weighs more than 2 kg (Figs. 4.31 and 4.67). Like the pieces from the southern area, these fragments were thermally fractured in antiquity as demonstrated by thermoluminescence tests (see Chapter 2.4.3). All the sandstone pieces must have been carried to the site, since no material of this kind is known from the Headland.

Considerable numbers of red ochre fragments have been found scattered throughout the occupation area, ranging from fist-size lumps to tiny flecks the size of a pinhead. The ochre ranges in colour from deep brown to bright pink and is similar in appearance and texture to some of the ironstone which occurs in the geological deposits of the headland (see Chapter 4.7). Only a few pieces of red ochre are obviously altered or show clear signs of utilisation. One of these is an ochre 'crayon' about 20 mm long which is slightly pointed at one end (Fig. 4.32). The sides of this object are also noticeably rounded and are marked by groups of striations which run lengthways back from the pointed end (Fig. 4.33). The abrasion along the edges was probably caused by grinding against a hard material such as stone although there is no evidence of ochre staining on any of the flint artefacts or the sandstones. The presence of smaller pieces of the pigment suggests that as well as grinding,

the ochre might have been deliberately fragmented as part of the processing.

### 4.2.4 *Summary and discussion*

There are 649 retouched tools from the Hengistbury site, making it the largest extant collection of lithic finds from any Late Upper Palaeolithic site in Britain. Previous doubts expressed over the homogeneity of the assemblage can now be firmly discounted. The metrical data on cores shows no formal division of the sample according to size, and there is no clear size differentiation in the burins or the backed blades, as suggested earlier by Campbell (1977). Similarly, the differences in end-scraper edge angle, previously regarded as significant, can be explained much more economically in functional terms. Supporting confirmation in this case is also provided by the refitting evidence (discussed in 4.3.3).

The Late Upper Palaeolithic tool assemblage is dominated by backed blades and bladelets. These pieces tend to have straight backs formed by abrupt retouch. As a class they exhibit a wide size range, but are mostly of blade dimensions (cf. Tixier 1963). This feature immediately separates them from the Late Magdalenian assemblages of Northern France (e.g. Pincevent, Verberie, Marsangy) which are typified by the presence of backed bladelets (*lamelles à dos)*. The question of the Hengistbury assemblage and its wider continental affinities is discussed in detail in a later section (4.10.5). The other main components of the

*4.32 Red ochre 'crayon'. 5 mm scale.*

retouched tool assemblage are simple end-scrapers, and burins which are divided more or less evenly between dihedral and truncation types. Most of the other tool classes including composite tools, becs and piercers are only poorly represented. Amongst the more distinctive elements of the tool inventory are large tanged points, shouldered points and several *lames magdaléniennes du Morin*.

In terms of their spatial distribution, the backed blades form a noticeable cluster in the northern and western parts of the site (Fig. 4.24), where there may be as many as 15 finds per square metre. Much lower densities of these tools occur in the south central (Campbell) area. A high percentage of the tools are also burnt and in fragmentary condition. By analogy with some European Late Upper Palaeolithic sites this may

reflect re-tooling activities around a hearth, although no definite evidence of this kind has yet been identified at Hengistbury. It is conceivable, however, that the remains of such a structure are represented by a scatter of sandstone blocks reported by Mace (1959, 254), and other burned blocks in the adjacent NW area of the site.

With the exception of one other artefact type, none of the lithic tool groups displays any obvious signs of horizontal clustering of the kind exhibited by the backed blades. Rather they form a generally diffuse scatter across much of the site with a tendency to thin out towards the eastern fringes of the excavated area (Figs. 4.14 and 4.20). The exception is provided by the intentionally broken segments whose focus of distribution partly coincides with the densest concentration of

*Table 4.22 Totals of burned retouched tools and other artefacts*

|  | burnt | unburnt | % burnt |
|---|---|---|---|
| End-Scrapers | 78 | 69 | 53.1 |
| Burins | 30 | 66 | 45.4 |
| Backed Blades/Bladelets | 197 | 301 | 65.4 |
| Intentional Breaks (unretouched segments) | 46 | 100 | 31.5 |

backed tools (in the Mace area and around its edges).

The distribution of the intentional breaks is particularly interesting when compared with the data on the condition of these and other artefacts. As can be observed in Table 4.22 unlike the major tool groups, the intentionally broken segments show relatively low incidences of burning. A similar pattern can also be seen with the debitage which displays a relatively high percentage of thermally altered pieces (41.9% in the 1968–9 and 1981–4 areas; although not formally quantified the percentage is even higher in the Mace area). Such observations are brought more sharply into focus by the fact that the area of greatest concentration of segmented blades overlaps substantially with that of the backed tools. If it is assumed that the taphonomic history of the artefacts is the same (as the writers strongly believe), it is likely that the condition of the artefacts results from very different activities performed in the same area of the site. This could also be explained by events separated by relatively short time intervals, for example during and after the use of an individual hearth.

The general nature of activities performed at the Late Upper Palaeolithic site can partly be reconstructed from functional and morphological analyses of the artefacts and also by comparison with other Late Glacial assemblages. The functional study of tools is dealt with in detail in a later section (4.5), as is the comparative evidence from contemporary Late Glacial sites (4.10.6). From the size and composition of the lithic inventory it is possible to speculate that the Hengistbury toolkit covered a wide range of activities associated with maintenance and processing tasks. The probability that end-scrapers functioned as hideworking tools is supported by the characteristics of edge morphology, while macroscopic edge damage on the burins is consistent with their use on bone and antler materials. In addition, it appears that stoneworking (Fig. 4.13) and drilling of harder objects also occurred at the site, according to damage patterns recorded on some of the artefacts. The interpretation of the toolkit and other wider aspects of the assemblage are discussed in detail in the final section of this chapter (4.10).

## 4.3 Refitting and reduction sequences

### 4.3.1 *Introduction*

The refitting of stone artefacts essentially involves the exact reversal of the flintknapper's craft. For instead of reducing a block of flint by striking a succession of flakes, the refitter begins with a jumbled pile of flakes and tries to fit them back in the correct order of removal. Obvious analogies have been drawn with the jig-saw puzzle, but this underestimates the complexity of refitting. To begin with, the stone artefact 'puzzles' rarely have all the pieces present, they are frequently composed of a mixture of different refitting sets and finally, of course, they are intrinsically more difficult in being three-dimensional.

Nowadays, widespread use is made of refitting, on a variety of archaeological materials, including stone, bone, antler, ivory and pottery, as well as on metals. The advantage of using the technique on flaked stone is that because of the method of removal and the unique identifying properties of each piece, the lithic fragments can be related to others in order of sequence. This is important because it establishes a clear frame of reference for a set of operations which begins with the selection of a nodule and finishes with the abandonment of the tool and the discard of any unwanted by-products. Equally, the flaking operation usually leaves distinctive patterns of residue and, in consequence, there often exists a strong link between the actual flaking process and the spatial distribution of artefacts (Cahen 1987). Refitting also allows a more sophisticated methodological approach to the study of natural geological processes and how these might affect artefact scatter patterns at archaeological sites (Villa 1982). At the root of all these studies is the desire to interpret human activities and behavioural patterns from the evidence as excavated.

The idea of refitting is, of course, not new to archaeology and much has been written about its history (Cahen *et al.* 1980; Cahen 1987, for recent summaries). As early as the nineteenth century it was realised that the conjoining of artefacts could be used to show the contemporaneity of flaking events and the process by which stone tools were made. Early published accounts are those of F C J Spurrell (1880) and W G Smith (1884, 1894), as well as the work of lesser known contemporaries, such as the Reverend King (Anon 1862). These accounts were followed by the studies from the continent by Munck (1893) and most interestingly by Commont (1909, 1916) who used refitting evidence in an innovative way to prove the undisturbed nature of some Palaeolithic deposits.

Despite early recognition of the technique and its applications to archaeological data, the full potential of refitting studies continued to go largely unnoticed for more than half a century. Its rediscovery as an analytical tool and general revival from obscurity over the past two decades owes much to the emergence of the 'new Archaeology' (cf. Isaac 1971). Today, refitting is regarded as an established technique for studying human behavioural patterns and is widely employed in the analysis of residues from Palaeolithic sites (Leroi-Gourhan and Brézillon 1966, 1972; Van Noten 1978).

Although the previous excavators of the Late Upper Palaeolithic site at Hengistbury acknowledged their awareness of artefact refitting studies, neither of them used the technique extensively. Angela Mace merely mentioned the subject to confirm her impression that the artefacts had been laid down in soft sand, whilst efforts by L H Keeley to refit artefacts were not pursued beyond a preliminary stage (Campbell pers. comm.). When our work began at the site in 1981, it soon became apparent that many of the flints could be fitted together and, by then, the usefulness of studying sites in this way had become more widely accepted. The particular reasons for undertaking the refitting programme are set out in the introduction (Chapter 1.5).

In this section we examine the application of refitting work to the study of the flaking technology at the Late Upper Palaeolithic site. For the purposes of this volume, the study of technology deals with the methods of lithic production and refers to the full set of actions associated with core reduction. At Hengistbury, this process (as demonstrated by refitting) begins with the initial selection of the flint nodule, followed by the various stages of preforming and preparation before the main reductive episode in which blade and flake blanks are detached from the core. The reduction process may finish at the blank production stage or continue through further modification of the blanks into tools. The advantage of this method of study is that it allows the entire process to be analysed and not just the end-products. In this way it is possible to describe and characterise each assemblage in terms of its broader 'technological pattern' (*sensu* Cahen 1987). As such it provides a further classificatory tool when describing variability between different assemblages. This has important implications for assessing the Hengistbury assemblage and setting it in its wider European Upper Palaeolithic context (4.10.5).

### 4.3.2 *Individual refitting sequences*

Over 30 refitting groups of artefacts have been recorded from the site, of which 23 involve the joining of flakes, blades and bladelets to cores. Described below are fifteen of the more substantial reconstructions plus a few of the less extensive refits which illustrate particular technological features of the flint assemblage.

*Core A: G22/1317*: This blade core with two, opposed platforms consists of over 90 refitting artefacts (Fig. 4.34). Amongst the debitage are 36 flakes and 26 blades, most of which are broken. There are five core tablets. The longest blade in the sequence measures 138 mm. The rest of the blades range in size from 95–44 mm; relatively few of them fit into the bladelet class. Just under half the blades (nine) are partly cortical. The stages of reduction can be summarised as follows:
— Selection of a flattish, oval-shaped flint cobble measuring approximately 200 x 120 mm. The cobble displays a smooth, but slightly abraded cortical exterior.

— Removal of cortical flakes around some of the perimeter, producing bidirectional flake scars around both ends and one edge of the nodule. In effect, this gave the block a trapezoidal outline, with a crested ridge running down the longest axis of the nodule.

— The removal of both ends of the nodule to produce opposed striking platforms. Some of the interlinking pieces are missing but it would seem that the platform shown in Figure 4.34 was clearly intended to be used first.

— A crested blade was detached from the main platform. The crested blade itself is absent, but the negative scar extends halfway down the long axis of the block and it is obvious that the removal was not entirely successful. It may be that at this stage the second platform, at the opposite end of the core was utilised to detach the remaining portion of the central crest.
— A series of perhaps a dozen blades was then detached from the first platform (Fig. 4.35). Towards the end of this sequence the core was turned 180° and the second platform was used interchangeably with the first. This is indicated by the direction of dorsal flake scars on the detached blanks. Judging by the presence of hinge terminations on these pieces it seems reasonable that the second platform was mainly used to correct such faults and reshape the flaking face. No signs of repairing the core (e.g. by re-cresting) are present, although fairly frequent rejuvenation of the second platform is evidenced by at least five refitting core tablets. This is in marked contrast to the first suite of blades which were all removed from the same unmodified platform; all the butts are plain and show signs of heavy preparatory abrasion. Despite the apparent suitability of the blanks for tool manufacture, no refitting examples could be found.

— The core was finally abandoned due to a natural flaw in the flint. In this final stage the core weighed 501 gm, which is significantly less than the 1.5 kg of the reassembled core.

*Core B: G23/203:* Core B is an opposed-platform blade core made up of 90 refitted artefacts, mostly fragmented and showing ancient break surfaces. According to Campbell's classification of individual artefacts 62 are 'Palaeolithic', 25 'Mesolithic' and 4 are 'unclassified'. When the broken pieces are rejoined they produce 34 complete flakes and 27 blades, including five crested blades and one crested flake. There is a single core tablet. The blades range in length from 105–30 mm, with bladelets fairly well represented in the sample. The majority of blades have plain butts; some of them display pronounced platform abrasion at the proximal end, which resembles heavy grinding. Two thirds of all the blade blanks are non-cortical and this category includes the smaller sizes. The one tool in this refitted cluster is a retouched blade with an oblique distal trun-

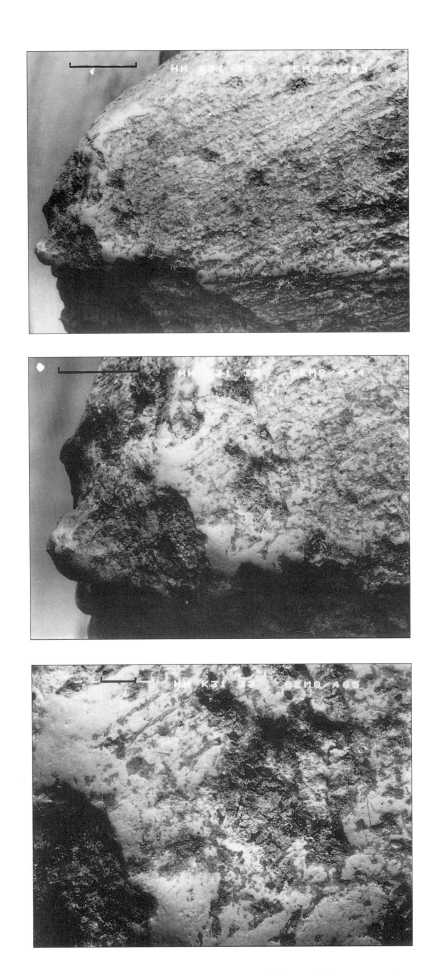

*4.33 SEM photomicrographs of ochre 'crayon'. Top: scale bar= 1 mm; middle: scale bar= 0.5 mm; bottom: scale bar= 0.1 mm. (Photo: Natural History Museum)*

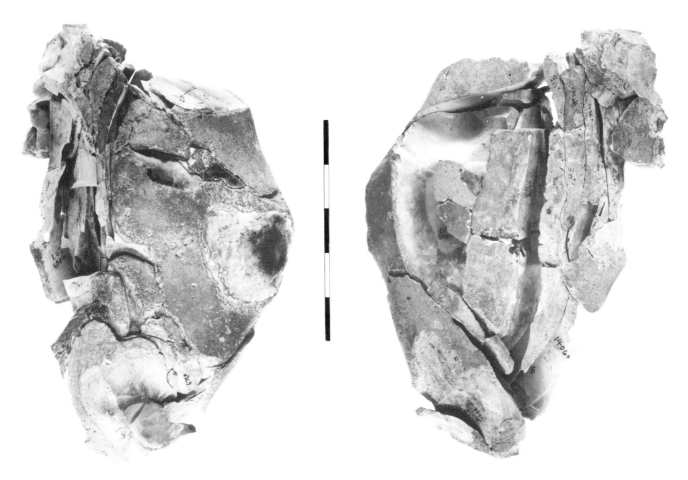

4.34 Core A. 10 cm scale.

cation (Fig. 4.36). The reconstruction of the core suggests the following reduction sequence:

— As in other examples from the site, a fairly flat, elongate flint nodule was selected for flaking. The reassembled form shows that it had a smooth, thin cortical surface and measured approximately 190 x 90 mm.

— After the initial removal of cortical flakes and blades from one of the flat sides, a large tablet was detached from the top of the nodule. Despite the mediocre quality of the first blades, the only refitted tool was made on one of these blanks. The removal of the core tablet left the main axis of percussion orientated down the broader side of the nodule. This would have made the shape of the flaking face awkward to control, particularly for making blades (a keel-shape is generally preferable). One option was simply to re-orientate the flaking face along the narrower sides of the nodule; the cresting of both lateral edges at this point shows that this was indeed the intention of the flintknapper.

— The reduction continued with the removal of a second core tablet which corrected the platform angle and aligned it above one of the crested edges. At about the same time an opposed platform was created and the original flaking face (on the broader side) underwent re-shaping. Here, the versatility of employing two crests can be seen: first in creating a central ridge to direct the percussive blow and second in controlling the shape of the core. In this instance several long flakes originating from the crest travelled almost as far as the other crest; they served to maintain the 'keel-shape' of the core.

— A further stage saw the removal of a bidirectionally crested blade followed by a series of long, partly cortical blades. During this stage several of the blades hinged. As a result the flaking face was re-crested and debitage restarted from the opposite platform. More blade removals followed, first from one platform then the other. It is not possible to tell whether the platforms were used alternately, because of gaps in the reduction sequence. The refitted blades from this stage measure between 80–40 mm.

— The core was finally discarded due to a deep diagonal flaw across the flaking face, which had been responsible for accidental breaks in the last blade removals. The abandoned core weighed just 193 gm, as compared to the 710 gm of the refitted block.

CORE C: D23/290 and E23/152: This reconstructed

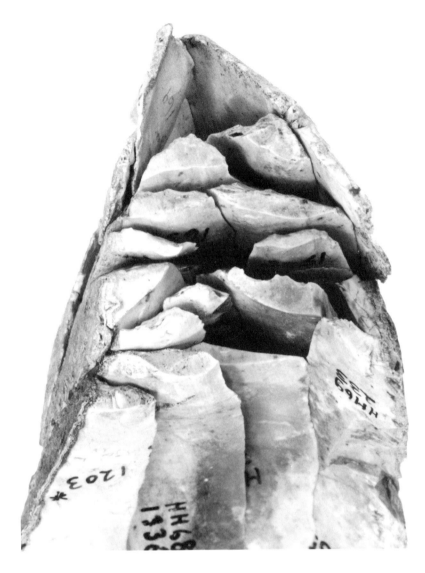

4.35 *Suite of refitting blades from core A, showing mainly plain butts.*

block is made up of two blade cores (Fig. 4.37): a single platform example (D23/290) and a two (non-opposed) platform example (E23/152). Although, only 12 artefacts can be refitted to the block, this is enough to show that cresting was not used to prepare either core for blade production. The only preparation appears in the form of faceting (minor flake removals to adjust the platform angle) which is present on one of the cores (D23/290). In all, seven flakes and five blades can be rejoined to the cores. The largest blade is 90 mm long.

— In its original form, the flint nodule was perhaps 150 mm long, and had an elongated, but slightly globular shape. Its outer surfaces reveal a smooth, slightly weathered cortex.

— At a very early stage in reduction the nodule was broken into two substantial fragments. The break surface follows a natural fracture plane and it is quite likely the block was broken accidentally during initial testing.

— The single platform core shows extensive preparation and reduction; it also has a faceted platform. In contrast, the second core has plain platforms and the butts of the refitting flints are also unmodified.

— The two-platform core was abandoned after only a few cortical blades had been detached. This core doubtless could have been rejuvenated and further reduced but, possibly because of its small size, was rejected early on. The single platform core, on the other hand, was made on a larger fragment and underwent greater reduction. This core also has a more or less triangular cross-section and therefore required very little preparation. In comparison with other cores, the refitting sequence shows many gaps and it is these which represent pieces which were removed to another part of the site. Unfortunately positive proof of this is so far lacking. The biggest blade from this core was a plunging removal 90 mm long; the other blades are considerably smaller and narrower, and may have provided suitable blanks for backing.

— The one-platform and two-platform cores weighed 240 and 320 gm respectively; the combined weight of the refitted block was 668 gm.

*CORE D: N27/104*: Although this is not a substantially reconstructed core (Fig. 4.38), its main interest lies in the method of core preparation and reduction. In contrast to some of the larger blade cores from Hengistbury (e.g. Cores A, B and H), this block displays no dorsal crest; the back of the core is totally cortical and unmodified. Judging by the cylindrical shape of the nodule any extensive preforming was simply not necessary. The slightly weathered appearance of the cortex and its thickness is typical of many of the cores from the site.

The overall size of the core was probably not much longer than its present length of 91 mm. Only fifteen fragments have been refitted, mostly to one end of the core and belonging to the final stages of reduction. Due to their broken and burnt condition it is only possible to identify one blade, although it is clear from the dorsal scars that a number of thick blades and flakes had been detached in the earlier stages. The proximal ends of the artefacts show heavy platform abrasion. Towards the end of the flaking sequence the top of the core broke away. Surprisingly, several attempts were made to continue flaking from the break surface before the core was finally thrown away.

Two observations can be made about the condition of this group of artefacts. First, as can be seen from Figure 4.38, some are more heavily patinated than others, whilst the patina can also vary between broken ends of the same piece (cf. J30 1127 and J30 86). This is in contradistinction to Campbell's argument that the assemblage could be split into two groups according to factors such as patination (see Chapter 3). A second interesting feature concerns the burnt condition of at least four of the artefacts. These come from metre squares adjacent to the core but the core itself is unburnt. It is intriguing that burning (perhaps scorching from a nearby hearth) could be so localised as to affect only the debitage and not the core.

*CORE G: L29/40*: A single platform flake core made on a spherical nodule with a very worn, beach-chattered cortex (Fig. 4.39). Four flakes and four unclassifiable fragments ('chunks') have been refitted to the core. Apart perhaps from a few of the earlier removals, many problems were evidently encountered in flaking the nodule. A core tablet to rejuvenate the striking platform plunged and removed much of the block; several of the flakes reveal natural internal fractures in the flint, while the core itself shows a relatively high proportion of flake scars with hinge terminations. This refitted group is unusual since it shows reduction continued even after it became clear that the material was badly flawed. It is extremely doubtful whether many usable flakes were detached from this core.

*CORE H: J22/1634*: This is an opposed platform blade

core which has been almost completely reassembled from 86 refitting artefacts (Fig. 4.40). There are 46 flakes and 28 blades, including three crested blades. In terms of Campbell's classification of the artefacts 64 are attributable to the 'Palaeolithic', 17 to the 'Mesolithic' and the rest are 'unclassified'. One possible tool also belongs to this core. Although minor flakes from platform rejuvenation are present, there is only one typical core tablet. The majority of the blades (22) are cortical but there are many gaps, especially in the later stages, which show that the non-cortical blade blanks are heavily under represented. The blades range in size from 129–52 mm; they show a variety of butt-types including plain and faceted forms (Fig. 4.41). The plain butts are generally smaller than the faceted kind, and unlike the latter, are also abraded at the proximal ends. Substantial refitting of this block has allowed a fairly complete reduction sequence to be described:

— Initial selection of a large oval flint cobble measuring c. 300 x 150 mm. The size of cobble and smooth texture of the cortex are quite unlike any of the locally occurring flint on the headland.

— Striking platforms were prepared at opposite ends of the nodule and the longer edges of the block were crested. The cresting at the back of the core is only partial. The frontal crest displays several very large negative flake scars but, since none of the corresponding cortical flakes could be found, it is likely that some preliminary work took place away from the main flaking area.

— A bidirectionally crested blade was removed from the front of the core. It did not travel the whole length of the core and the remaining portion was detached from the opposite platform. Flaking continued from this platform with a suite of cortical blades. In between removals, minute adjustments were made to the platform angle, as evidenced by small flakes which can be refitted to the platform.

— After about 20 blades and flakes were detached, the core was rotated 180° and four or five blanks removed from the opposite platform. Flaking then continued from the initial platform, although the opposite platform was used more frequently to correct faults. It appears the second platform served mainly to regulate or repair the main flaking face. From the refits, it is possible to reconstruct five rotations of the core.

— Despite its still substantial size, the core was abandoned before it became 'exhausted'. This was probably due to crystalline inclusions in the flint and a deep transverse fault. From its reconstruction, the nodule must originally have weighed more than 2500 gm. When it was discarded it weighed just under 1040 gm.

*CORE HH: L29/42*: An opposed platform blade core with only a few of the final removals refitted (Fig. 4.42). These consist of a core tablet and two broken blades. Owing to the incompleteness of reconstruction, it is impossible to tell the original size of the nodule. However, like the smaller cores from the site, it displays no dorsal crest. The cortex on the back of the core is smooth and is not similar to the cortical exteriors of the local Hengistbury flint. The small size of the core (49 mm) and the presence of negative scars suggest that the blanks produced in the final stages were small but fairly broad flakes and blades.

*CORE J: 123/939*: This refitted group consists of two cores, a burin and 32 other artefacts (Fig. 4.43). The cores comprise an opposed platform blade core and a core on a flake; the tool is a dihedral burin with two refitting spalls. Amongst the unretouched artefacts are 5 blades and 22 flakes including two core tablets. There is one partially crested piece. From the reassembled artefacts it is possible to describe part of the reduction sequence as follows:

— Refitting suggests that the original block of raw material was globular in shape, measuring not much more than 130 x 100 mm. The nodule has a very smooth, thin cortical exterior. There are no signs of cresting across the back of the core.

— As with other cores, both ends of the block were removed to create opposed striking platforms. This is shown by several very large negative flake removals at either end of the nodule. Interestingly, none of these big flakes could be found in the assemblage.

— Cortical flakes were then removed from the sides of the block. No attempt was made to create a crest, probably because the shape of the nodule made this difficult or unnecessary. Most of the removals derive from one of the platforms.

— After rejuvenating the platform by removing a large core tablet, further flakes were detached, including one later used as a core. As can be seen in Figure 4.14, this flake was inversely truncated at the distal end before several removals were made down the dorsal side. Whether this is a true core, or a tool in a preparatory stage, or a finished implement is discussed in the section on cores. The piece shows certain similarities with the Kostienki knife.

4.36a   *Core B. 10 cm scale.*

144

4.36b  *Core B, reverse view. 10 cm scale.*

— Reduction of the main core continued after rotating the nodule first 90 then, 180°. It is interesting to note that at this stage the core was a multiplatform example. One of the larger flakes from the group was subsequently modified (by removal of several spalls) into a dihedral burin (Fig. 4.16, 3).

-— Absent from the sequence are many of the blanks belonging to the main reduction episode. Because of this it is difficult to reconstruct the transition from a multiplatform to an opposed platform core. It seems clear, however, that cresting was not employed and that after the removal of cortical flakes most of the shaping was achieved by detaching large non-cortical blanks from either side of the main flaking face. A refitting fragment to the top of the core shows no preparation to the platform other than abrasion of the edge.

— Debitage continued from both ends of the core, although it is evident that the knapper encountered major problems owing to a large crystalline inclusion in the flaking face. After one further rejuvenation

involving the partial cresting of the flaking face, the core was abandoned. Since much of the core is missing it is difficult to calculate the original weight of the nodule, but it must have been considerably more than the existing refitted assemblage (510 gm). When it was finally discarded the core weighed just under 100 gm.

*CORE K: O27/148:* This small multiplatform flake core consists of a refitting end-scraper and an unretouched flake (Fig. 4.44). The block, which is almost complete, is globular in shape and may have broken off a larger nodule. It appears the small nodule underwent minor reduction, perhaps sufficient to produce just one or two usable blanks. A large proportion of the core is covered in cortex of a thin, rolled type very different from the battered condition of the gravel flint in the local Headland deposits. The distribution of scars on the core and refitting flakes does not suggest any careful preparation or preforming stage. With the aid of refitting it can be shown that the edge of the scraper was cortical prior to its modification. Judging from the

145

4.37 Core C. 10 cm scale.

4.38 Core D. 10 cm scale.

146

*4.39 Core G. 10 cm scale.*

negative flake scar, up to 6 mm of the original edge was removed by semi-abrupt, direct retouch.

*CORE M: K29/2691*: A group of three laminar blanks which fit back to a two-platform blade core. There is no cortex on the core and the indications are that this is the end-product of a much reduced nodule. The remains of unidirectional cresting are present on the back of the core.

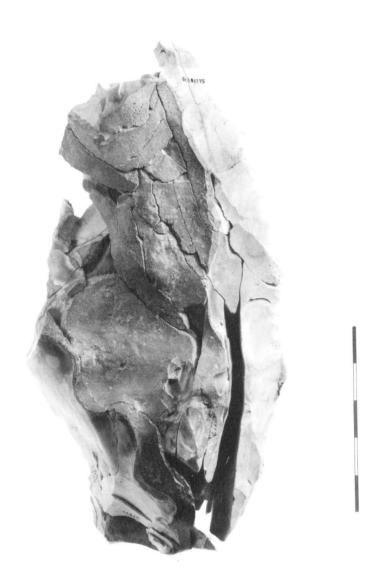

4.40  *Core H. 10 cm scale.*

*CORE N: H24/1480*: An opposed platform bladelet core with a refitting core tablet and broken flake fragment (Fig. 4.8, 4). As with other cores of this type, the back of the core is covered in cortex. Originally, this might have been part of a much larger nodule but it is impossible to tell from its present reduced state. The gap between the edge of the core tablet and the existing flaking face shows that a large number of blades and bladelets are missing from the sequence. The fact that this was not interrupted by further rejuvenation (other core tablets) suggests a highly successful reduction episode. A large crystalline inclusion on one side was eventually responsible for the core's discard.

*CORE O*: Although the core itself is missing from this group of four flakes and 11 blades, enough of the refitted sequence remains to provide useful information on the reduction strategy. The refits show that several cortical flakes were removed from the front of the block to create a bidirectional crest (Fig. 4.45). This was followed by a crested blade removal and a series of blades from one end of the core. Six of the latter have been

refitted. The core was then rotated 180° and at least two further blades were detached from the opposite end, before the core was again turned around and a blade struck from the first platform. The longest blade from the refitted sequence measures 83 mm. There is no indication that the core was abandoned at this stage; it is possible that it was removed for further reduction elsewhere on the site.

Several observations may be made about the reduction method. In the first place, the opposite platform was most probably of secondary importance and served principally to reshape the flaking face. Apart from the crested examples, most of the blades from the first platform have small plain butts which are heavily abraded. The fact that minor adjustments were also made to this platform is apparent from one or two of the larger butts which show signs of faceting; this feature is otherwise 'invisible' on the smaller, punctiform butt (Fig. 4.46). Only by refitting a sufficient number of blades does the faceting become evident.

*CORE R: O29/104*: This is an opposed platform blade

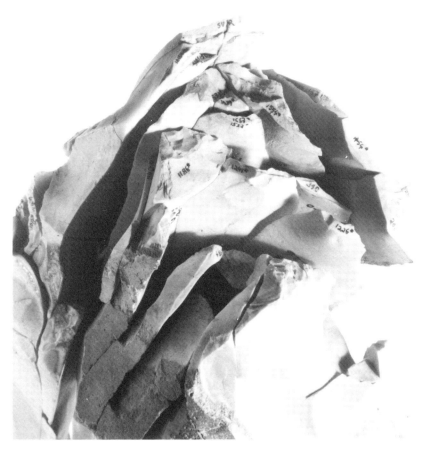

4.41   *Suite of refitting blades from core H, showing partially faceted and plain butts.*

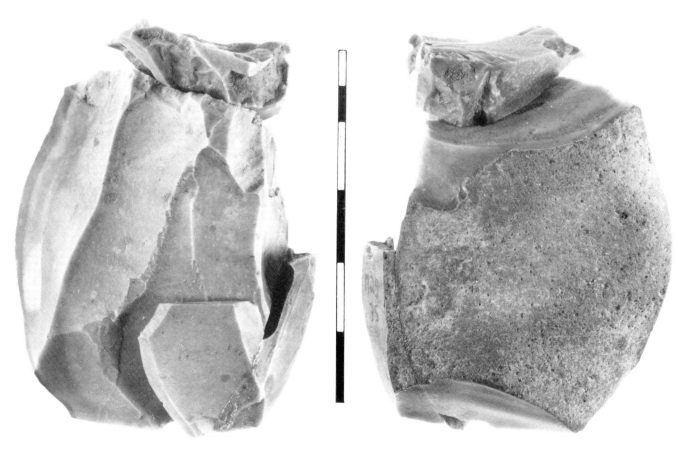

4.42   *Core HH. 5 cm scale.*

149

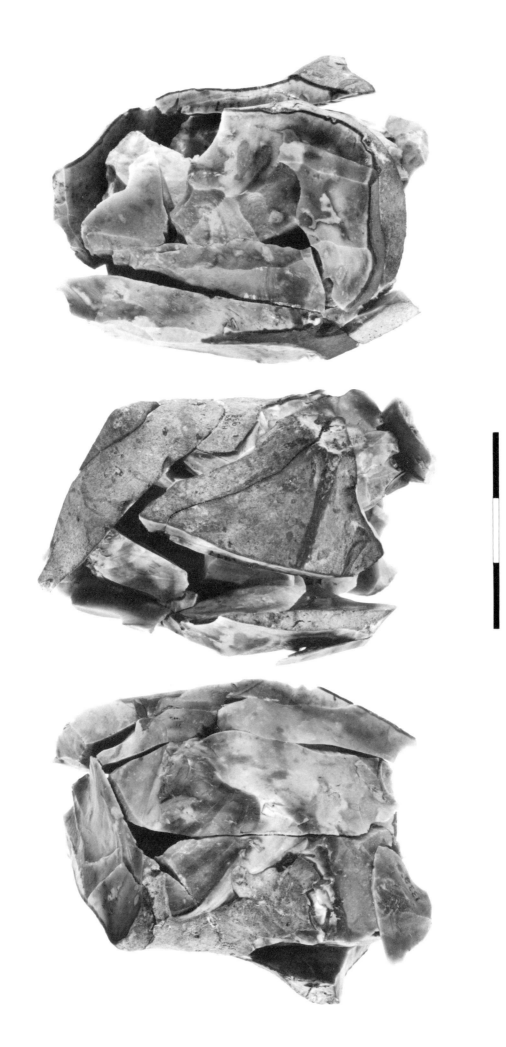

4.43   *Core J. Refitted burin shown on central view, middle foreground. 6 cm scale.*

4.44 *Core K. Refitted end-scraper shown on right view beneath flake N27 164. 5 cm scale.*

core made up of 15 refits, of which eight are flakes and five are blades. There is one core tablet. Enough of the nodule has been reassembled to show it was originally cylindrical in shape and over 130 mm long (Fig. 4.47). The outer surfaces are characterised by a thin iron-stained cortex which is heavily rolled.

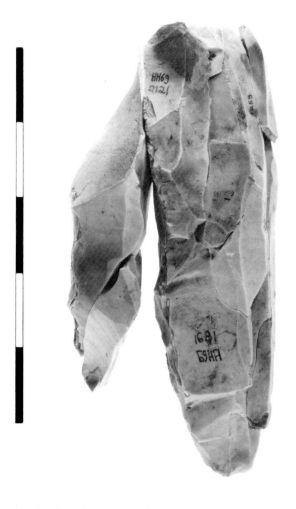

4.45   *Core O. 10 cm scale.*

Given the cylindrical shape of the nodule, its reduction seems to have followed a highly regular and predictable pattern. After the removal of both ends of the block, blanks were struck from the opposed platforms. Although it is difficult to be certain, it is unlikely that the core was ever crested. Certainly, the back of the core is wholly unmodified and a blade from near the beginning of the reduction sequence shows none of the signs of an earlier crested removal (transverse flake scars). This cortical blank measures 88 mm and is also the longest refitted blade. In the early stages, both striking platforms appear to have been rejuvenated by faceting, but later alteration of one platform involved the removal of a large core tablet. The narrow cross-section of the core suggests that further removals were impossible; the core was discarded because it was exhausted.

*CORE U: F21/484:* Seven flakes and four blades can be fitted to this opposed platform blade core, which was abandoned in the early stages of reduction (Fig. 4.48). The original block was irregular in shape but probably measured over 150 mm long and about 100 mm wide. The relatively thick cortical exterior is rolled but does not display extensive chattermarks and is therefore distinctly different from the local flint sources. From the refits the following sequence can be reconstructed:

— Preparation began with the removal of flakes around the periphery of the block, forming a characteristic bidirectional crest along part of one edge. The crest was not intended to guide a series of blade removals; rather it seems to have been designed as an ancillary aid at the back of the core for controlling the angle of the striking platforms.

— A few large flakes were detached to prepare opposed striking platforms. No attempt was made to

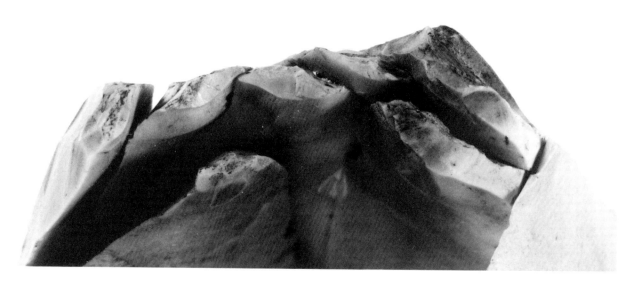

4.46   *Suite of blades from core O, showing partially faceted and plain butts (also note heavy platform abrasion).*

152

4.47 *Core R. 10 cm scale.*

crest the front of the core; instead, several flakes were removed in succession down the front using one of the prepared platforms. These removals are all cortical and short.

— The core was then rotated 180°, and flaking continued from the opposite platform. None of the flakes travelled far enough to meet the scars left by earlier removals and efforts to continue flaking seem to have been prevented by a coarse inclusion in the flint.

— The core was again rotated and this time the previous flaking face was used as a platform. A few flakes were then detached but the whole block was discarded soon afterwards. The core was probably abandoned because of the flaw mentioned earlier.

*CORE V: 132/87*: This very large opposed platform blade core consists of only three refits, all them being end-scrapers on flakes (Fig. 4.49). The refitted block weighs *c.* 1;900 gm and is by far the largest nodule recovered from the site. A surprising feature of this core is that it was certainly capable of further reduction, but for reasons outlined below flaking was halted at an early stage.

Despite the fact that all of the earliest removals are lacking, it is clear that reduction followed a broadly similar pattern to the other Hengistbury cores. It began with preparation of striking platforms at opposite ends of a nodule. From the residual cortical surfaces we can guess that the block of flint was probably fairly flat and more or less oblong in shape. The exterior surfaces reveal a thin, rolled cortex but without the 'chatter-marks' typical of the locally obtainable flint. Like Core B, the opposed platforms were not orientated towards the edges, but to the flatter sides of the block. This may have been in order to remove the cortex and 'thin' the nodule bifacially before proceeding further. Judging from the size of the negative flake scars, some of these preparation flakes must have been quite large and it is surprising that none was found in the immediate vicinity of the core or the scrapers. This leads us to suspect that the preparatory work was undertaken in another area or possibly away from the site.

Once sufficient flakes had been removed from the broader sides, two bidirectional crests were probably prepared along the lateral edges although the existence of one of them can only be surmised from remnant flake scars. At this point one might have expected the platforms to be re-orientated and for debitage to con-

4.48  *Core U. 10 cm scale.*

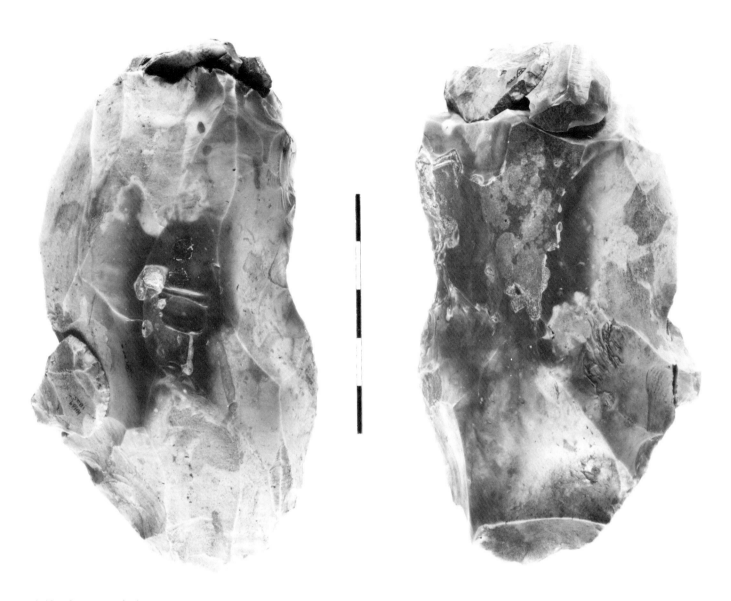

4.49  *Core V with three end-scraper refits. Note the heavy scalar damage on the concave edge of the core. 10 cm scale.*

tinue down the lateral edges. This decision was never taken and flaking effectively ceased.

The three tools belong to the early stages of reduction. Two of them are made on successive flakes associated with platform preparation. Typologically, the two are quite dissimilar: one has added lateral retouch and is curved in profile, the other is only retouched distally and owes its straighter profile to extensive distal modification (Fig. 4.11, 9–10). Both of them are burnt in contrast to the third end-scraper which was found a few metres away (see 4.2 *End-scrapers* for further discussion). This third scraper is made on a thick flake detached from the lateral edge of the core; a large part of the distal end has been removed by retouch. The scraper fronts of two of the tools show markedly different angles of 50 and 80 degrees respectively. According to criteria developed by Campbell (1977, 80) these should fall into separate cultural categories (see conclusion below). Based on similarities in the cortex several other scrapers are strongly suspected as coming from this core, but because the intervening refits are missing this is impossible to prove.

An intriguing question about this core is why it was discarded at such an early stage, when there were no obvious flaws and, as mentioned above, the block could easily have been further reduced. A possible explanation may lie in the unusual appearance of the crested lateral edge (Fig. 4.50), which on closer inspection shows evidence of crushing in addition to flaking (Newcomer pers. comm.). The presumed need for heavy-duty tools, for woodworking and other tasks, has been remarked upon elsewhere (Barton 1986a) and it is possible that this core served some such purpose. It is also interesting to note the worn appearance of the arêtes along the flatter sides of the core; these may also have been a result of utilisation.

CORE ROUGHOUT: HH68 1040: This is a flattish cobble, oval in shape and measuring 165 x 130 mm with a weight of 1,551 gm. The nodule is mainly cortical with a few flake scars around its edge; only a few of the original flakes have been refitted (not shown in Fig. 4.51). The nodule appears to have suffered thermal (possibly frost) fracture which may have been the cause

4.50  Core V. Note heavy crushing on the concave edge of the left view. 10 cm scale.

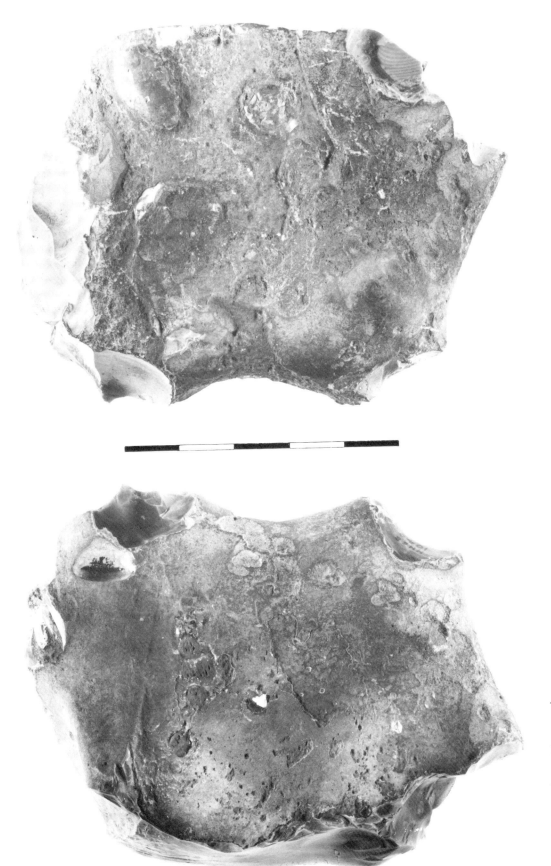

4.51  *Core roughout. 10 cm scale.*

157

of breakage during the initial flaking and the reason for its abandonment. The flaking around the periphery suggests the preliminary stages of bi-directional cresting. The first stage was probably never fully completed because of the breakage.

### 4.3.3 *Summary and discussion*

The refitting of flint debitage at the Late Upper Palaeolithic site has enabled us to study the reduction process in detail, from the first stages of preparing the nodule to the last stages of core rejection and abandonment. At Hengistbury, reduction appears to have been aimed principally at the preparation of suitable blanks, mainly blades, for tool manufacture. The latter involved a further stage of modification in which the blanks were reduced by secondary chipping or by deliberate snapping. By refitting, we have been able to observe each of these separate stages and provide a better basis for assessing the technological characteristics of the flint assemblage.

Of the 30 refitted sequences, 23 involve the joining of artefacts to actual cores but only a minority consist of more or less complete reconstructions. Given this relatively small sample how can we assume that what we are describing is in any way 'typical' of the whole assemblage ? This may be answered in three ways: first, refitting enables us to recognise various stages in the reduction process and these observations can be applied to partially refitted (and sometimes even unrefitted) cores; secondly, judging from the total evidence, the range of variability in the reduction techniques used is relatively narrow and not difficult to define. Finally, underlying these arguments is the assumption that each flaking episode will have been borne out of actions repeated many thousands of times in a flintknapper's lifetime. As a result there is a strong element of predictability in flaking of this kind.

The main characteristics of core reduction and debitage can be separated into the following simplified stages: raw material selection, preforming the core (cresting and preparation of striking platforms), blank production and core discard.

*Raw material selection*: An important factor in any lithic technology is the nature of the raw material used for flaking. In order to make the longer blades required at Hengistbury it was obviously necessary to start with relatively large cobbles of flint. As we have seen at this site, great care went into the selection of the raw material. We think for example that most of the flint did not derive from the local gravels, as these do not provide suitably-sized nodules. Apart from their small size, the presence of incipient fracture planes (caused by frost) in the local flint gravels (e.g. core G) may have been another reason why they were disregarded by the Upper Palaeolithic flintknappers. From the refitting evidence it is possible to demonstrate a preference for generally elongate cobbles, either oblong or globular in shape. With few exceptions (notably core H) these

rarely exceeded 200 mm, but are all appreciably larger than the fist-size cobbles available locally. The nearest alternative source of larger material lies at least 12 km away to the south-east (Isle of Wight), but it is possible that more distant sources were exploited. Judging from the weathered surface appearance of some of the nodules, the flint was probably not quarried directly from the chalk.

*Preforming the core*: Generally speaking, the preparation of blade cores at Hengistbury involved the removal of both ends of a flint nodule so that blades could be extracted from the longer sides. In practice the initial shaping was a more complicated process and was largely determined by the shape of the original nodule. Two methods appear to have been used principally: 1) if the nodule was fairly flat and oblong, the flint block was bidirectionally 'crested' along its periphery. The cresting of an edge served to make it more regular and guide the early blade removals. Preparation of this kind is illustrated on Core H (Fig. 4.40) and on an abandoned core roughout (Fig. 4.51); 2) If the nodule was cylindrical or globular in shape, cresting was generally not employed. The latter technique, in which blanks were removed lengthways down an unprepared edge, is shown on Core C (Fig. 4.37).

*Cresting*: In the larger reassembled blade cores it is apparent that two crests were prepared, one at the front of the core and one at the back. Whereas the frontal crest was created to guide the initial blade removals, the rear crest served as an ancillary to guide the run of core tablet removals as well as helping to shape the core's sides (Newcomer pers. comm.). Both crests also functioned to moderate the shape and thickness of the core. Core B illustrates how flakes struck from the posterior crest helped restore the 'keel-shape' of the core. Another variant of this technique involved the production of a single frontal crest. This method was rarely used in the initial stages and may have been used instead for rejuvenating the flaking face, as in Core J.

A number of refitted blade cores show that cresting was not always used in the initial stages of preparation. This is particularly apparent on cylindrical nodules where blanks could just as easily be removed down the unprepared, curved sides of the block. In such cases (e.g. core R) hardly any preparation was necessary beyond the creation of platforms at either end of the nodule. Reshaping of the main flaking face was sometimes achieved with the help of several large removals from one of the platforms. Many of the cores on more cylindrical blocks (not all refitted) show one major flaking face with an entirely cortical backing or with a combination of cortex and some flat, invasive flake removals.

*Preparation of striking platforms*: In both the cylindrical and flatter, oval nodules the preparation of two (opposed) platforms was considered the norm. From the reassembled cores, it is possible to show that while the main removals frequently originated from one end of the core the second platform served mainly to correct accidents and regulate the shape of the flaking face. This is particularly well illustrated in the examples of cores A, B and H.

During reduction it often became necessary to rejuvenate the striking platforms. This involved adjusting the platform angle either by partial faceting (multiple removals of smaller flakes) or by detaching single core tablets. Interestingly, neither method was used to the exclusion of the other. In fact, refitting has shown that blades with faceted butts can be rejoined to blades with plain butts, indicating that minute adjustments were made between removals at the same end of the core (e.g. Core H, Fig. 4.41). Blades with punctiform butts were sometimes struck from faceted core platforms (e.g. Core O), an observation impossible to confirm without access to refitting. Faceting was also occasionally employed on cylindrical blocks (e.g. Core R), although judging from the majority of core platforms in these cases the removal of larger tablets seems to have been the more usual method.

*Blank production*: From the relatively high proportion of blade cores at the site it is clear that flintworking was principally aimed at blade and bladelet manufacture. This is also confirmed by the preponderance of tools made on such blanks.

The refitted sequences illustrate a great diversity in size of the blanks detached, with no real indication of which types were regarded as suitable for toolmaking. Blades ranging in length from 138–44 mm have been refitted to single cores (e.g. core A). Some examples, such as core H, show gaps left by larger blades implying these were removed by the flintknapper for use elsewhere. In other cases, blades of regular length and thickness, which would otherwise have made good supports for backed tools or end-scrapers, were apparently ignored altogether (e.g. refitted group O). Finally, as illustrated by core B, small blades were occasionally used for toolmaking. Surprisingly, the example in question was made on a blank of mediocre quality and belonged to an earlier part of the reduction sequence; again other apparently suitable examples from this core seem to have been ignored.

When assessed together, these features seem to suggest a generally opportunist approach to the manufacture and selection of tools. An exception, however, may be identified in the case of Core V, where three end-scrapers can be fitted to a single block. In this example we suspect that several other end-scrapers also belong to the same core, but this cannot yet be positively demonstrated. Clearly, it would be interesting to know whether the core was pre-selected for making supports for end-scrapers perhaps with an immediate processing task in mind. Other potential examples of this kind have been observed elsewhere in the Late

Palaeolithic of NW Europe (Van Noten 1978; Moss 1983).

*Core discard*: The reasons for discarding cores at Hengistbury can usually be attributed to simple breakage, internal faulting within the flint or to obstacles caused by inclusions or a combination of these factors. In their final form, the blade cores are sufficiently diverse in appearance to suggest that they were abandoned at various stages of reduction. Several were discarded in the very earliest flaking stages, as for example core U, whilst others appear more or less worked out (cores D and HH). Measurements of the larger refitted examples suggest they underwent a 60–75% average weight loss due to flaking. A noticeable feature of a few of the reassembled cores is the apparent absence of the earliest flake removals. Judging by the size of the negative flake scars these would have been large cortical flakes and therefore easily identifiable amongst the rest of the debitage. The fact that none was recognised for cores H, V or the large core roughout (HH68 1040) suggests that some testing of material could have taken place at the raw material source. In one instance the core itself is missing (e.g. refitted cluster O) and it remains an open question whether the core was removed to another area of the site or away from Hengistbury altogether. It is unlikely that the blades from this particular reduction episode were brought in from elsewhere because the block consists of crested and cortical debitage.

Finally, reference has been made in the above text to Campbell's original classification of artefacts into either 'Upper Palaeolithic' or 'Mesolithic' types. Analysis of two of the refitted cores (B and H) shows a mixture of flakes and blades of both 'types' on each of the cores. Moreover, given that Palaeolithic artefacts often fit above and beneath supposedly Mesolithic ones it is now quite clear that these cultural attributions are meaningless and should therefore be firmly discounted. Similarly, refitting has shown that Campbell's original separation of the Hengistbury end-scrapers into 'Upper Palaeolithic' and 'Mesolithic' types on the basis of edge angles (1977, Fig. 171) is also groundless. End-scrapers fulfilling the criteria of both cultural types can be shown to fit to the same core (Core V). In short, refitting evidence supports the general view that the assemblage is entirely homogeneous and is of one Late Upper Palaeolithic type.

This concludes the section on core reduction at the Late Upper Palaeolithic site. Using refitting evidence it has been possible not only to identify the recurrent technological features of the assemblage, but also to provide some measure of explanation of the reduction methods used. For further discussion of raw material procurement and comparisons of flaking techniques with other British and NW European assemblages, the reader is referred to the final section (4.10) of this chapter.

## 4.4  A spatial analysis of refitted artefacts

### 4.4.1  *Introduction*

The analysis concerns 29 refitting sequences from the Late Upper Palaeolithic site with the number of artefacts in each group varying from two (Core I) to 79 (Core A). The total sample consists of 385 individual flakes and blades belonging to 25 cores and four sets of refits where the core is missing. The artefacts derive from Campbell's 1968–9 area and from the recent excavations 1981–4.

A preliminary sort through the data indicated that the refit groups could be shown to form two larger units, a north-western one (NW) and one in the south central (SC) area of the site. These were defined as two discrete artefact clusters several metres apart which do not overlap and show no interconnecting refits.

For the purposes of the analysis the NW cluster was divided into two arbitrary samples consisting of roughly equal numbers of refitted artefacts (Groups 1 and 3), and based upon the presence or absence of particular core-types. Group 1 (refit groups D, L, H2, I, R) consisted of 37 artefacts while Group 3 (refit groups E, F, G, K, M, S, T, V) had a total of 36 artefacts. The same principle was applied to the other major cluster (SC). Here six groups of refits were defined which consisted of reassembled cores A, B, H and J (with 79, 77, 72 and 28 refits respectively) and two smaller groups (2 and 4). Group 2 (core groups N, U, X, Y) was made up of 21 artefacts while Group 4 (O, P, W, Z) comprised 28 flints.

### 4.4.2  *Synopsis of variables*

For each of the 385 artefacts basic measurements were used which defined location (x -eastings, y -northings and z -depths), size information (length, breadth, thickness and weight data) plus attributes of order (position in the refitting sequence) and posture (angle of dip, as excavated). The latter eventually had to be discarded because observations of dip had only consistently been recorded in the 1981–4 excavations (for which there were relatively few refits).

### 4.4.3  *Analysis*

The data sample consisted of some 3,000 observations relative to 385 artefacts. One of the problems encountered in the analysis were numbers of missing values for individual artefacts. In some cases these related to an absence of either x or y coordinates or depth measurements (in the Campbell data), but weights were sometimes missing also (due to the fact that the artefacts had been refitted before weighing).

An analysis of refitting data was carried with two aims in mind. First, to map the spatial distribution of artefacts in order to examine whether this would reveal further patterning in the horizontal plane and secondly, to investigate the vertical relationship between refitted finds. In particular it was hoped to test some of the taphonomic models concerning site formation set out in Chapter 3.1. For example, one expectation was that measurable trends might be visible in the depth/weight ratios of the flint artefacts. Such information would have important implications for understanding how artefacts had become vertically dispersed since the time of the Late Upper Palaeolithic occupation.

### 4.4.4  *The horizontal distribution of refits*

On the x and y plane the artefacts appear to fall into two distinct flint scatters (NW and SC). This is illustrated in Figure 4.52 by the distribution of core groups 1/3 and 2/4, which are separated by a minimum distance of at least 2.5 metres and demonstrate no interconnecting refits. Also within the SC cluster are core groups A, B, H and J which overlap spatially with groups 2/4, but do not impinge upon the area of the NW cluster. The SC cluster forms the largest grouping and contains 70% of the total number of refitting artefacts. The smaller NW cluster contains 17% of the sample, all of which are associated with core groups 1/3.

Means, standard deviations and correlation coefficients were calculated for the x and y values in each of the eight groups for individual artefacts. No significant correlation could be detected between the two variables. This indicates that there are no preferred directions of scatter in the x and y axes so that the groups can be summarised by circles to show their dispersion. In Figure 4.52 one circle is drawn for each group: centres correspond to distribution centres (av (x), av (y)), and radii are represented by the sum of the standard deviations (sd (x) + sd (y)).

These circles help demonstrate the discrete nature of the two main flint clusters described above. About 87% of pieces are found inside their corresponding circles. Group 4 is the one with the largest radius (437 cm), while Group 1 is the most compact example with a radius of 195 cm (Table 4.23).

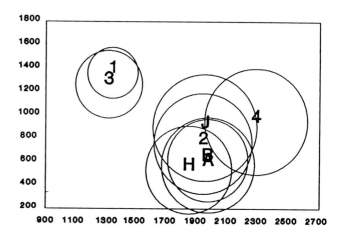

4.52 *Mapped distribution of main core refit groups. The circles represent the approximate horizontal spread of each group. The centres of each group (mean (x,y)) are identified by numbers and letters. 2 m scale units.*

*Table 4.23    Horizontal data for refitting core groups (cm)*

| Refit Groups | No. | x variable Mean | SD | y variable Mean | SD | Radius |
|---|---|---|---|---|---|---|
| A | 79 | 1932.56 | 169.47 | 573.37 | 136.86 | 306.33 |
| B | 77 | 1931.7 | 38.36 | 615.23 | 105.15 | 243.51 |
| H | 74 | 1838.59 | 144.85 | 533.56 | 140.78 | 285.63 |
| J | 29 | 1943.93 | 166.33 | 893.58 | 193.9 | 360.23 |
| 2 | 22 | 1931.22 | 162.06 | 757.32 | 194.79 | 356.85 |
| 4 | 28 | 2280.32 | 316.7 | 945.0 | 120.67 | 437.37 |
| 1 | 34 | 1338.19 | 86.01 | 1361.41 | 109.5 | 195.51 |
| 3 | 35 | 1314.71 | 115.94 | 1264.71 | 143.9 | 259.84 |

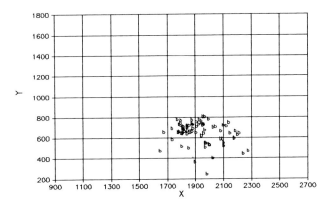

4.54  *Map of refit group B. b= artefacts, B= core. 2 m scale units.*

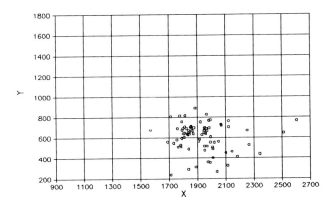

4.53  *Map of refit group A. a= artefacts, A= core. 2 m scale units.*

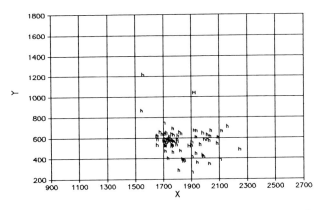

4.55  *Map of refit group H. h= artefacts, H= core. 2 m scale units.*

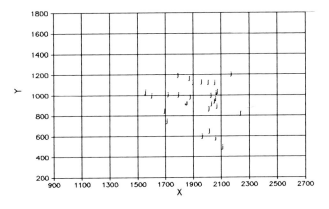

4.56  *Map of refit group J. j= artefacts, J= core. 2 m scale units.*

The distance (on the x-y plane) from each piece to its core was computed for Groups A, B, H and J. The resulting average distances are 189, 156, 502 and 250 cm, respectively. It can be seen from Figures 4.53, 4.54 and 4.56 that in most cases the cores are relatively close to their centres of distribution (absolute centres of circles). The main exception is Group H where the core is several metres from the main cluster of finds (Fig. 4.55). It may be significant that of all artefacts in the refitting groups Core H is also the largest.

Lastly, information plotted (but not shown here) on the removal order of each artefact in the refitting sequences showed no discernible patterning in horizontal terms. Nevertheless in a future study it might prove interesting to calculate the distances between successive removals to see whether these differ substantially from the average refit distances within each scatter group. This could provide a useful additional parameter in judging the relative 'disturbance' of each scatter and also possibly of the site as a whole.

### 4.4.5    The vertical distribution of refits

*Depth*: Artefacts belonging to all refitting groups are found at depths in the range of 16–122 cm. Half of them are in the interval 70–95 cm, that is occurring in a band roughly 25 cm thick. About 4% of flints occur at or below 100 cm, while 18% are found between 50–16 cm. This is illustrated in Figures 4.57–4.60 which shows the distribution of depth measurements for each of the groups.

In terms of the individual groups, cores A and B have their central mean depths at about 80 cm with standard deviations of around 10 cm. These two groups, together with group J (sd = 12), are the ones with the least variable depths. Mean depths of groups 2 and 4 are 80 and 77 cm, but they are more variable with standard deviations of 12.3 and 17.3 cm respectively. Lying slightly deeper than A and B is group H with a mean depth of 86 cm but again this group also shows a greater vertical dispersal (sd= 16). Finally, and most surprisingly, Groups 1 and 3 have mean depths of 44 and 41 cm with standard deviations of 12.4 and

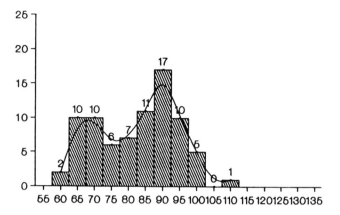

4.57 *Depth histogram and trend of group A. X axis= depths below datum at 5 cm intervals, Y axis= absolute frequency of artefacts.*

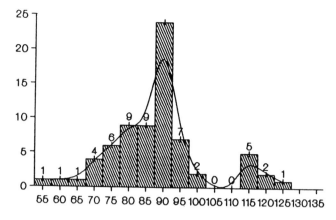

4.59 *Depth histogram and trend of group H. X axis= depths below datum at 5 cm intervals, Y axis= absolute frequency of artefacts.*

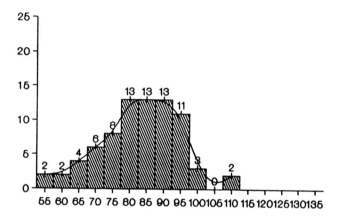

4.58 *Depth histogram and trend of group B. X axis= depths below datum at 5 cm intervals, Y axis= absolute frequency of artefacts.*

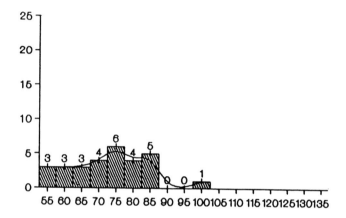

4.60 *Depth histogram and trend of group J. X axis= depths below datum at 5 cm intervals, Y axis= absolute frequency of artefacts.*

11.9. A summary of the depth results is presented in Table 4.24.

From the above table it is apparent that artefacts in the groups 1 and 3 have average depths of 43 cm and are therefore considerably shallower than flints from the other refitting groups which have average readings of 80 cm. This may well be related to the fact that groups 1 and 3 are separated horizontally from the other core groups, forming a cluster several metres north-west of the main distribution. Although the distances involved are relatively small, the average depths of artefacts suggest the possibility of a gently undulating surface which could explain the vertical disparity between the two groups.

*Weight*

The weights of most of the flint artefacts were recorded. The results are presented in decigrams (dgm). Since the weight and the size of the artefacts are proportional it follows that the heaviest artefacts will also be the largest ones. All weights were measured for artefacts from groups A, B and J; but only 63 (out of 74 were available for group H). Not all of the weights for groups 1, 2, 3 and 4 were available.

In all relevant cases the heaviest piece within each

*Table 4.24 Mean depths in cm of core groups and absolute depths of cores*

| Refit Groups | Mean Depth | Stan Dev | Core Depth | Stan Error | No. of Refits |
|---|---|---|---|---|---|
| A | 81.4 | 12.0 | 83 | 1.35 | 79 |
| B | 80.7 | 12.6 | 85 | 1.44 | 77 |
| H | 86.2 | 16.2 | 82 | 1.91 | 72 |
| J | 70.1 | 12.1 | 83 | 2.25 | 29 |
| 2 (NUYX) | 79.7 | 12.3 | 92 92 67 77 | | 21 |
| 4 (POWZ) | 77.1 | 17.3 | 68 50 | | 28 |
| 1 (DLH2IR) | 43.7 | 12.4 | 46 50  64 48 | | 37 |
| 3 (EFGKMSTV) | 41.5 | 11.9 | 31 59  48 44 | | 36 |
| | | | 48 53 | | |

group is its core, which can sometimes be many times larger than any of the reassembled artefacts. Because this could potentially obscure any weight-depth correlation the cores were excluded from the calculations.

The mean weights of artefacts (excluding cores) are presented in Table 4.25.

In groups A and B mean weights are 52 and 61 dgm. Groups H and J follow with mean measurements of

Table 4.25 *Mean weights in decigrams of refits excluding cores*

| Refit Groups | Core Weight | Total Wt(-core) | Mean Weight | Stan Dev | Number (-core) |
|---|---|---|---|---|---|
| A | 5015.0 | 4033.5 | 52.4 | 83.2 | 77 |
| B | 1926.0 | 4644.3 | 61.1 | 85.0 | 76 |
| H | >9999.9 | 10685.3 | 172.3 | 189.3 | 62 |
| J | 996.8 | 3886.6 | 143.9 | 222.8 | 27 |
| 2 | | 2166.2 | 114.0 | | 19 |
| 4 | | 3130.3 | 107.9 | | 29 |
| 1 | | 3229.9 | 97.9 | | 33 |
| 3 | | 4696.6 | 167.7 | | 28 |

172 and 143 dgm respectively. Average weights for groups 1, 2, 3 and 4 are not much different, varying from 167 (group 3) to 98 dgm (group 1).

A significant feature of these figures is the fact that although Group 1/3 (located in the NW) is not markedly different in terms of weight, it is much higher (less deep) than any of the other refits.

*Weight vs. depth*
Statistical regression analysis (details not given here) shows there is no immediately obvious correlation between weight and depth, although it is possible that some subtle differences may exist which are not apparent in the present results. It should be noted for instance that about 10% of the refitted sample had to be omitted for insufficiency of data. In addition it was not possible to test all the variables suggested in Chapter 3.1.5

### 4.4.6  *Conclusion*

The horizontal data broadly confirm earlier observations made in Chapter 3.2. Most of the refitted artefacts derive from the south central (SC) area of the Campbell excavations. By comparison efforts to refit material in other parts of the site resulted in relatively fewer groups of refits and of these many represent only partially reassembled cores. The separation of the SC cluster (mainly cores with large numbers of refits) from the NW cluster (cores with less refits and 'floating' sequences with missing cores) may reflect actual horizontal separation of site activities. For example, whereas retouched tools are sparsely distributed in the SC area, the NW cluster overlaps with substantial concentrations of tools. It is suggested below (4.10.6) that the SC cluster represents a knapping zone where blanks were prepared for toolmaking but tool-using and discard occurred in other parts of the site including the northern area.

In terms of the vertical distribution of refits, it can be stated in most cases that the heaviest pieces (the cores) lie significantly deeper than the mean level of their constituent refits. However, the prediction of a clear correlation between weight and depth of artefacts, according to the theoretical model proposed in Chapter 3.1.7, is not borne out by this present study. The reasons for this are difficult to ascertain but may be due to number of potential error factors, including differences in the nature of the data-sets analysed (refitted *versus* unrefitted artefacts), the standard of information (Campbell's records in this analysis *versus* data from the recent excavations in Collcutt's work), and the underlying assumption that the original ground surface of the occupation site was relatively flat. As such there may be some justification for the vertical model outlined in Chapter 3.1.7, but further testing will be necessary to provide definitive proof.

## 4.5  A functional analysis of selected flint artefacts

### 4.5.1  *Introduction*

The flint assemblage from Hengistbury Head consisted of implements which, when examined with the naked eye, appeared to be in good enough condition for use-wear analysis. However, the implements were evidently affected by gloss patina, and some by white patina (cf. Keeley 1980). Several microwear analysts had examined artefacts from this assemblage but opinions varied as to whether or not a 'high-power' microwear analysis based on Keeley's method (1980) was feasible. The aim of this type of analysis is the identification of past tool use with particular emphasis paid to the contact materials. This method entails the comparison of the 'use-wear traces', or surface alterations in the form of micro-polishes and striations on archaeological implements, with those on experimental implements, using a light microscope at magnifications of 50 to 400x. That such use-wear traces can be destroyed or masked by white patina has generally been accepted (Keeley 1980, 29). However, Keeley's suggestion that use-wear traces are preserved and discernible on implements with natural gloss patina remained to be investigated.

Whereas Morris (in Bergman *et al.* 1983, 1987) reported use-wear polishes on intentionally broken blades from Hengistbury, other analysts (e.g. Levi-Sala) came to the conclusion that because of the gloss-patina a microwear analysis of the material would be unsuccessful. The problem was of particular interest as the presence of gloss patina on many flint assemblages from Upper Palaeolithic Northern Europe sites has been reported by Stapert (1976) and others.

The aims of this analysis were threefold:

(1) to determine to what extent the implements from Hengistbury had been affected by natural surface modifications, and whether use-wear polishes could be identified on glossy flint implements.

(2) to assess the potential value of microwear analysis in the

study of the post-depositional history of the flint assemblage.

(3) to investigate alternative sources of information regarding past tool use when microwear polishes could not be reliably identified.

### 4.5.2   Method

The Hengistbury implements were studied microscopically for information about the post-depositional history of the assemblage, as well as for their suitability for a microwear analysis. The high power microwear study was based on the method developed by Keeley (1980), but with some differences (Unger-Hamilton 1984a, 139–40). During the course of the work on the Hengistbury artefacts, the emphasis changed from the study of micro-polishes to the observation of other functional attributes: for example experimental evidence had consistently demonstrated that tools of particular morphology could only be used for certain tasks (Wilmsen 1968; Unger-Hamilton 1984a). It had also demonstrated that edge 'abrasion' and 'micro-flaking' (Tringham et al. 1974; Odell and Odell-Vereecken 1980; Unger-Hamilton 1984a, 36–48) were indicative of tool action, and to a certain extent, of the nature of the contact material, provided the implements were unaffected by general edge damage due to factors other than use. This appeared to be the case with the Hengistbury assemblage.

The archaeological tools were mainly selected from artefacts excavated in the Northern Section (1984), but also included several others from the 1981 excavation south of the footpath and the Mace 1957 collection now housed in the British Museum.

A reference collection of flint artefacts was used for comparative purposes, which included replicas of Late Upper Palaeolithic tools made by Bergman out of S English flint, similar to that occurring at the site. The implements were flaked with stone or antler hammers and in some instances pressure flaked with an antler tine. The worked materials included fresh and seasoned wood of deciduous and coniferous trees, fresh, cooked and dry bone of various ungulates, several species of fish, fresh, dry and soaked hide of several species of deer, horn, several types of stone and a large number of plant species (Unger-Hamilton 1984a, 84–104). Both the experimental and the archaeological implements were cleaned with ammonia-free detergent and then with distilled water for ten minutes in an ultrasonic cleaning tank. The implements were kept in separate plastic bags. They were examined with an Olympus Vanox microscope at M 50–200x, and photographed with Ilford FP4 film.

### 4.5.3   Condition and suitability of the assemblage for microwear analysis

The raw material in the Hengistbury assemblage is fairly homogeneous: the flint is of fine to medium grain size and has a beige to brown colour. Broken examples show that the original colour was blue/black or brown and is typical of the Cretaceous flint which occurs in much of S England.

Microscopic study of the glossy artefacts showed the areas with weak macro-gloss to be evenly distributed micro-polishes (Fig. 4.61, 1). Areas with strong gloss patches corresponded to bright flattened polishes, probably phenomena similar to 'white spots' (Moss 1983, 81–3) and 'friction gloss' (Shepherd 1972; Stapert 1976). Also revealed were random striations resembling Stapert's 'soil scratches' (1976). These traces looked identical to traces from experiments (Unger-Hamilton 1984a, Plate 7 a, c and e) in which stone and water had been rubbed against flint. Most interestingly, the deep scores (Fig. 4.61, 3) which often occurred uniformly distributed on the ancient implements (for instance on burin spalls, see below) were created in experiments (Fig. 4.61, 4) in which Bergman and I trampled ten flint artefacts in sand for five minutes. The scores which I had assumed at first to be use-related were therefore probably of natural origin.

The experimental evidence then suggests that contact with stones, water and soil caused some of the surface modifications on the Late Upper Palaeolithic assemblage. The lack of general edge damage, however, indicates that the alteration process had been quite gentle (see Levi-Sala, this volume).

The microscopic analysis of the artefacts using Keeley's 'high-power' method, revealed in most instances wear traces which were superficially compatible with the results (see below) of the functional analysis based on tool morphology and edge damage. Four of the five burins with flaking at the burin edge had polish and striations parallel to the facets, consistent with a grooving motion, while the burins with retouch on their facets had polish streaks perpendicular to the facets, consistent with retouch or a scraping motion. One of the burin spalls had deep scores perpendicular to the long axis of the tip. Scrapers had superficial striations and/or deep scores on their ventral aspects running obliquely from the scraper edges. The micro-polishes (Fig. 4.62, 1) concentrated on many of these edges did look like experimental hide scraping polishes (Fig. 4.62, 2), and like the photograph of a 'hide-scraping' polish on a scraper from Meer II (Keeley 1978, Plate 55, 3). It was perhaps this kind of observation which led Morris (Bergman et al. 1983, 1987) to assume that use-wear polishes could be identified on the Hengistbury implements. However, similar polishes (cf. Fig. 4.61, 2) were discovered on the ridges and the bulbs of the same pieces, and other tools from Hengistbury. It appeared improbable that all these parts had been used in the same way, namely to scrape hide, and two possibilities remained: either all the polishes were due to natural agencies, or a use-wear polish similar to some experimental hide polishes was preserved on the working edge and looked indistinguishable from natural polishes.

Levi-Sala (1986a, 1986b and this volume) has demonstrated in her experiments that gloss and polish

4.61 *Microwear polishes. 1= HH72 end-scraper, general polish (probably natural)(x200); 2= HH72 end-scraper, dorsal view of unretouched lateral edge (x50); 3= HH17/2/IV showing scores (x200); 4= experimental point showing scores after trampling (x200).*

concentrations on flint edges can be caused by natural processes. On the other hand, Rottlaender's hypothesis (1975) that gloss patina inhibits the formation of white patina by closing the gaps in the flint which are open to chemical attack, led me, like Keeley (1980, 29), to speculate that perhaps use-wear polish would have the same effect, because it also demonstrably smoothes the flint surface (Unger-Hamilton 1984b). This process may well lead to the preservation of use-wear polishes on some patinated flint tools.

Whatever the case, the existence of such potentially confusing micro-traces indicated to me (*contra* Keeley 1980, 29) that a distinction between natural and use-wear polishes on the Hengistbury implements was impossible, and that therefore a functional analysis of this material using microwear traces alone would not be productive.

### 4.5.4 Selected artefacts from the Late Upper Palaeolithic assemblage

*End-Scrapers*: End-scrapers have received attention by functional analysts since the 19th century (Moss 1983, 38–43; Unger-Hamilton 1984a, 161–3). According to ethnographic evidence (Gould *et al.* 1971), as well as evidence from 'low-power' (e.g. Brink 1978) and 'high-power' microwear analyses scrapers have been used as scrapers of hide and other materials, as wood-adzes, choppers and saws, as well as grooving tools (for further references see Unger-Hamilton 1984a).

An important feature in the functional analysis of scrapers proved to be the edge angle (Wilmsen 1968; Gould *et al.* 1971; Keeley 1978, 75; Hayden 1979b, 124; Broadbent and Knutson 1975); an acute angle of 46–55° seemed optimal for hide-scraping, a steeper edge of 66–75° optimal for hide-softening and for wood-and bone-scraping. However, one problem for the functional analyst is the fact that edge angles could be increased considerably by retouch (Wilmsen 1968; Broadbent and Knutson 1975), and wear traces could be removed (Hayden 1979a, 207), by resharpening.

A factor crucial to hide-working appeared to be the curving (in plan) of the scraper edge which gives it a hooked appearance (Nissen and Dittemore 1974; but see Kamminga 1978, 137).

*Experiments and results*: Sixty-two experimental scrapers were used to scrape, cut and chop a wide range of materials (for details see Unger-Hamilton 1984a, 163–9). Some of the scrapers were used inserted longitudinally in wooden hafts.

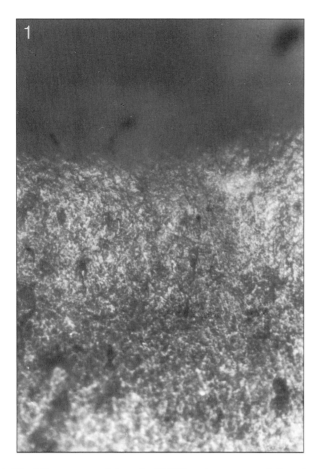

4.62   *Microwear polishes. 1= HH80 end-scraper, polish and striations on ventral side of scraper edge (x200); 2= experimental end-scraper (hide) on ventral side of scraper edge (x200).*

The experiments demonstrated that an acute angle, and a curved profile, of the active edge proved important for scraping hide (C. Bergman pers. comm.), but not for scraping less yielding materials, such as stone. Hafting increased the efficiency of hide scrapers (see also Broadbent and Knutson 1975, 116; Semenov 1964, 87).

The edge damage patterns resulting from different actions (scraping, cutting and chopping) were distinct. All scraping tools, regardless of the worked material, showed edge 'abrasion' (Tringham *et al.* 1974) which was not seen on scrapers used as cutting or chopping tools. However, the degree of edge damage differed according to the hardness of the material scraped (see Unger-Hamilton 1984a, 41–3, Table 1).

*End-scrapers in the assemblage*: Of the thirteen scrapers examined from Hengistbury nine were blade end-scrapers (four of which were broken at the distal end), three were flake-scrapers and one was a flake scraper with steep retouch at the distal, as well as on one lateral edge. They ranged in length from 20 to 65 mm, in width from 12 to 39 mm and in thickness from 4 to 14 mm. All the edges with scraper retouch (Fig. 4.63) were slightly convex in plan. The edge-angles (45 to 90°) were mostly abrupt due to severe undercutting of the

scraper-edges, presumably from resharpening. Nevertheless, most of the scrapers had originally had an overhang (useful for hide-scraping). Despite the very steep edge angles it appeared that the scrapers had been used after resharpening, judging by the evident abrasion of nearly all the scraper edges. This abrasion suggested that the tools had been used to scrape rather than for chopping or cutting.

The lack of microscopic edge-flaking (Tringham *et al.* 1974) and the very slight degree of abrasion of the scraper-edges was consistent with the experimental hide-scrapers, as well as of scrapers used to scrape soaked antler. If use had been of short duration (unlikely in view of the exhaustion of most scraper edges) then the slight abrasion of the scraper edges could have been evidence of the scraping of unyielding materials such as stone or shell. Such a hierarchy of possible worked materials may seem vague, but it is necessary, and it is equally advisable in a 'high-power' microwear analysis (Vaughan 1981, 382; Unger-Hamilton 1984a, 174).

Two of the archaeological end-scrapers' lateral edges had, in contrast to other edges, fine retouch, possibly the result of utilisation on a soft material or deliberate modification to facilitate handling. One other scraper had a steep irregularly retouched lateral edge. It was not abraded and had therefore presumably not

166

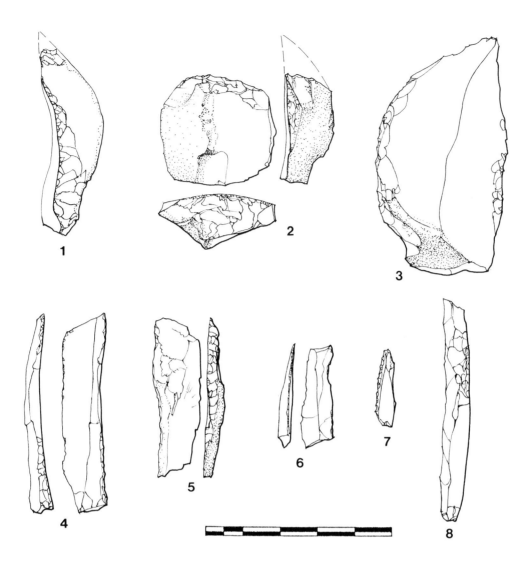

4.63 *Selected tools examined for microwear. 1–2= end-scrapers; 3= retouched (backed) flake; 4-7 backed blades and bladelets; 8= burin spall. Centimetre scale.*

been used to scrape. Perhaps the retouch made it easier to haft or to hold the implement.

*Backed blades and bladelets*: Various uses could be envisaged for backed blades, bladelets and flakes. Such tools have been classified according to ethnographic and experimental evidence (see Moss 1983, 43–6; Unger-Hamilton 1984a, 186–98 and 226–81) as rasps, scrapers, grooving tools (with the truncated ends), plant and meat knives (Semenov 1964, 101–13; Frison 1979) and saws. Backed bladelets at Pincevent, France, were probably used as side barbs and projectile points (Moss 1983, 115–6).

*Experiments and results*: Various backed blades, bladelets and flakes were used on a wide variety of materials (for details see Unger-Hamilton 1984a, 188–90). The tools were used to cut, saw, whittle, de-scale (fish) and groove. The tools were used unhafted, or else hafted in wooden or antler handles and secured with a mixture of resin and wax. In addition I studied the wear-traces on bladelets used as projectile points and barbs (Barton and Bergman 1982) and on hafted backed blades and bladelets which had been used to cut meat and wood (Moss and Newcomer 1982), as well as the wear traces on a blade used by Bergman to incise flint cortex. Incised flint cortex had been excavated at Hengistbury (Chapter 4.6).

Acutely-angled blades with unretouched cutting edges could be used for cutting hide and meat, whittling wood and scaling fish, as well as cutting thin-and soft-stemmed plants. A large chunk of meat was best cut with unhafted long blades or with hafted bladelets.

Different types of action (whittling and cutting) caused different patterns of edge damage (Unger-Hamilton 1984a, 42–3). The degree and pattern of edge damage also differed according to the hardness of the material worked. The edge of a blade used to incise flint cortex, for instance, was abraded rather than flaked. Hafted cutting tools showed more evenly distributed edge damage than did unhafted tools (Unger-Hamilton 1984a, 103).

*Backed blades and bladelets in the assemblage*: The length of the thirteen backed blades and bladelets examined ranged from 25 (a fragment) to 74 mm, the width from 8 to 36 mm and the thickness from 2 to 18 mm. Nine of the backed pieces had one or two snapped and/or truncated ends. The fine bifacial edge damage (Fig. 4.63, 4) seen on the sharp edges on most blades suggested that they had been used as cutting implements, for neither the edge rounding characteristic of whittling or scaling tools, nor the concentration of edge damage typical of grooving tools was found. The acute edge angles and the low level of damage seen on these blades suggested that they may have been used to cut a soft material such as meat or hide. Plant-gathering activities tend to leave a visible gloss confined to the active edges of the flint blades (Unger-Hamilton 1984a, 101) which was not found on any of the blades from the Hengistbury site. Had such a gloss existed, it would probably have been preserved despite the patination (Unger-Hamilton 1984a, 266).

The exceptions were a backed flake and a blade with strong and regular unifacial retouch at the proximal end of one lateral edge. The precise function of these pieces however remains unclear.

According to my experiments hafting of some of these implements may be inferred from the morphology and the edge damage of tools: nine blades had snapped and/or retouched ends, eight of the blades had a thickness of between 4–5 mm. The removal of the ends and the uniform thickness, as well as the even distribution of the edge damage along the blade edges suggested that these blades were standardised and suitable for hafting (Fig. 4.63, 6). Several of the tools displayed 'impact fractures' and this may be taken as indirect evidence that they were hafted. On the other hand two of the backed pieces, one a 18 mm thick flake (Fig. 4.63, 3), the other, a blade curved in section, could not in my opinion have been hafted. The latter had a shallowly retouched notch on the steep edge which might have provided a more comfortable finger grip.

*Burins*: Burins have several possible working edges and can be used in a variety of ways. Newcomer (1972, Appendix 3) discussed several uses of burins: for instance to groove hard organic materials such as bone, or for scraping, boring, drilling (cf. Semenov 1964, 66 and 98–9) or for engraving purposes. Low-power studies of burins by Seitzer (1978) have shown a statistically significant relationship between function (as indicated by edge-wear) and various burin types. Using high-power microwear analyses more specific functions have also been put forward including the grooving or boring of bone and antler (Keeley 1978; Unger-Hamilton 1984a).

*Experiments and results*: Twenty-one burin edges were used to groove and perforate a variety of materials (see Unger-Hamilton 1984a, 212–3). In addition, burin facets were used as cutting and scraping edges. The location of edge damage varied according to the action

(see Unger-Hamilton 1984a, 213–4), while the form and severity of edge damage varied according to the hardness of the worked material.

*Burins in the assemblage*: Two truncation burins and ten dihedral burins from the 198l to 1984 excavations, as well as three burins from the Mace excavations and stored in boxes in the British Museum were examined.

The burins selected from the 1981–4 excavations ranged in length from 24 to 81 mm, in width from 14 to 35 mm and in thickness from 5 to 17 mm. Five of the burins (Fig. 4.17, 4) showed strong micro-flaking (Tringham *et al.* 1974) at the burin-edge. The location and extent of the edge damage suggested to me at first that the burins had been used as groovers rather than as perforators; the severity of the micro-flaking matching only that produced by experimentally grooving dry bone (cf. Keeley's results, 1978, 81). However, Bergman has pointed out that most of the burin-edges were too wide to be easily used in this manner. Alternatively, though most unlikely in this assemblage, the burins may sometimes have functioned as cores for producing drill bits (on burin spalls, cf. Newcomer 1972). Two burins had strong unifacial edge damage developed along the facets. This suggested that these facets were used for scraping.

Of the three burins housed in the British Museum one was a truncation burin (50 mm long) which had a 9 mm wide burin-edge with very little edge damage. Regular unifacial retouch was found not only at the distal but also on the lateral edge below the burin facet abutting a proximal break. Two burins on breaks were each 45 mm long, consisted of several refits and had burin facets and adjoining lateral edges with unifacial retouch forming angles of 50 to 90°. One of these (Fig. 4.17, 2) had a matching retouched spall. The continuous nature of the retouch from the spall to the lateral edge suggested that the retouch had been made in preparation to spall removal (the same appeared to be the case with the two burins mentioned above). Beneath the spall, irregular retouch was present on the burin facet and could have been produced by use, such as scraping or whittling. No edge damage in the form of micro-flaking or abrasion was found on the ventral aspect of the facet. This indicated that the material scraped or whittled was probably not very hard. The concave shape of the facet suggested a worked material of convex shape.

Altogether, two burins had apparently been used as scrapers, and one burin as a scraping or whittling tool on a medium-hard material of convex shape. Five burins may have been used with their facets as grooving implements, and another six may have been unused.

*Burin spalls*: Burins are created through the removal of a burin spall by burin-blow technique (Newcomer 1972, 26). In some cases burin spalls were simply resharpening products (Keeley 1978), in other cases (Betts pers. comm.; Tosi and Piperno 1973) burin spalls had apparently been used as drills. Semenov (1964, 744–83) examined perforated shell and stone objects and illustrated (1964, Fig. 25) various methods of boring: by hand, with a stone drill inserted in a wooden rod and rotated between the palms of the hand, and with a bow-drill.

*Experiments and results*: Several piercers, borers, and hafted drills, some made from burin spalls, were used to perforate a variety of materials (Unger-Hamilton 1984a, 177–9).

In order to be used as drills and borers, the tools had to be symmetrical about a longitudinal axis. Mechanical bow-drilling (Unger-Hamilton *et al.* 1987) was always easier and more effective than was boring by hand. Different actions led in most instances to different location of edge damage (Unger-Hamilton 1984a, 179–181). The micro-flaking from manual movements tended to be much stronger than the micro-flaking from mechanical drilling which also appeared to cause most abrasion, in some instances (the drilling of wood, stone, and with abrasives) producing macro-gloss.

*Burin spalls in the assemblage*: The fourteen burin spalls examined were between 12 and 38 mm long and between 2 and 8 mm thick. Six of these (Fig. 4.63, 8) were curved or irregularly shaped and were either unre-touched or else partially retouched on one dorsal ridge. These were probably resharpening spalls and were not straight enough to be drills.

The other eight burin spalls were straight, and four of these had retouch along one ridge and two along one edge. Two spalls were retouched at the tip, one at both ends. They had tips which were abraded (one more so) and had probably been used as perforators. The tips were certainly too blunt and/or evenly abraded for the spalls to have been projectiles, grooving tools or piercers of materials like hide, and the shape of these tools ruled out other uses.

The absence of gloss (on one abraded tip) and the presence of gloss (confined to the other abraded tip and therefore most likely from use) were of interest: gloss had been found on the tips of experimental drills used to drill stone, wood or a material with the addition of abrasive (Unger-Hamilton *et al.* 1987). However, drilling shell and bone (when drilled without abrasive) did not produce glossy drill-tips. It is therefore conceivable that shell or bone had been drilled with one of the burin spalls from Hengistbury Head and that stone, wood or a material with the addition of abrasive had been drilled with the other. However, no drilled objects have been recovered from the site. The two spalls which had probably been used as perforators were so small that they could not have been used efficiently without a haft. It is therefore likely that the spalls were used in a drill, but whether a fast rotary drill was involved is impossible to say.

### 4.5.5 *Summary and conclusions*

The gloss-patinated flint implements from Hengistbury Head had microscopic evidence of natural surface modifications in the form of general sheen and polish concentration on all edges. The fact that microwear traces on the tools from Hengistbury were often similar to use-wear traces, together with previous, similar observations, leads me, like Keeley (1980, 29) to speculate that use-wear traces are preserved despite patination. An in-depth study of polishes on patinated tools might prove useful in future microwear analyses of patinated assemblages. Nevertheless, the presence of the post-depositional surface modifications (see also Levi-Sala 5.3) suggested to me that a 'high-power' use-wear analysis of the gloss-patinated implements from Hengistbury would, in the present state of our knowledge, be impossible. The same is thought to apply to all gloss-patinated flint implements.

A 'high-power' microwear analysis of experimental pieces yielded some results relevant to the post-depositional history of the assemblage. The experimental evidence suggested that the natural surface modifications of Hengistbury artefacts had originated from contact of the flint with stones, water and soil. The lack of general edge damage on the implements nevertheless implied that the alteration process had been a gentle one.

Despite the fact that the tools from Hengistbury were obviously affected by gloss-patination, and despite the fact that use-wear polishes could not be confidently identified, the functional analysis of the tools appeared to yield some positive results. Factors other than the polishes, namely tool shape, retouch and edge damage in the form of micro-flaking or abrasion, provided evidence of use. Examination of these features revealed in several cases how the tools were used, whether they had been hafted, and on which broad category of contact material they had been used. Previous blind tests had demonstrated that this method is not all that inferior to high-power microwear analysis (Newcomer *et al.* 1986). In the case of polish identification basic assumptions also have to be made: although polishes do not appear to change greatly after full development, before this stage (which has yet to be precisely defined) they go through considerable visual changes: the beginning of plant polish can look like meat polish, and so on. Similarly, polishes do not always divide neatly into categories of contact materials. In these cases several alternative contact materials therefore have to be allowed for. It is in my opinion only rarely that the limitation of variables and the near perfect preservation of tools allow one to come to more confident and precise conclusions.

As far as the Late Upper Palaeolithic assemblage is concerned it seems that the 13 scrapers examined had been used to scrape hide or softened antler, and that most had been used in hafts. The lateral edges of two scrapers may have been used to cut soft material. Of the 13 backed blades in the sample, nine appear to have been hafted and functioned as cutting tools on softer materials, such as hide or meat. Two bladelets may have been used as projectile points. Fifteen burins were also examined from the recent excavations and the Mace sample. Three of them appeared to have been modified in advance of spall-removal. Two burins appeared to have been used as scrapers, and in one case a burin had probably been used to scrape or whittle a medium-hard material of convex shape. Five burins may have been used with their facets as grooving implements, and another six burins may have been unused.

Of the retouched tool debitage examined, six of 14 burins spalls were simple waste products. The function, if any, of six others with retouch on one edge or ridge remains unclear. The final two spalls which were modified by retouch at the tip had apparently been used hafted to drill shell or bone in one instance, and stone, wood or a material with the addition of abrasive in the other. Despite these indications, however, it should be pointed out that no drilled or perforated objects have yet been recovered from the Late Upper Palaeolithic site.

As a postscript it is noted that several artefacts examined by Dr Hamilton were subsequently mislaid and are at the time of publication still missing from the collection (RNEB).

## 4.6 Artefacts with engraved cortex

### 4.6.1 *Description and microscopic analysis*

Two flint artefacts in the Late Upper Palaeolithic assemblage have engraved cortical surfaces which appear to be the result of deliberate alteration rather than accidental damage or natural modification.

The artefacts consist of a small multi-platform core 57 x 56 mm and weighing 171.8 gm, and a flake measuring 108 x 31 x 12 mm. They both display small areas of smooth cortex, less than 1 mm thick, while the flaked surfaces have a beige to light tan patina typical of the lithic assemblage. Like the rest of the artefacts the flint is also unabraded and in very fresh condition. The flake can be joined to the core across a narrow band of cortex. The refit shows that the flake was removed quite early in the reduction sequence, and can be classified as a core tablet. The two pieces were found relatively close together, in squares O29 and O26/P27, just south of the footpath during the 1981–4 excavations. Despite efforts to locate other possible refits to the core none was found.

The cortical surfaces of both artefacts are scored with fine, intersecting incisions (Fig. 4.64). Although they are less than 1 mm wide, these incisions are distinct and clearly visible to the naked eye. The majority of them extend across 35 mm of the two joined pieces, and are truncated at the edges formed by other artefact removals from the core. This clearly indicates that the incisions originally covered a larger surface and, more importantly, that they were made prior to the flaking

of the core. The lines may be generally described as straight, although they exhibit slight irregularities where gritty inclusions occur in the cortex (Fig 4.65, 1). They originate from different directions and intersect to form a cross-hatched pattern.

Observation of the surviving intersections suggests that one set of lines were incised from a single direction prior to the scoring of overlapping marks from a different direction. These macroscopic observations indicate that the cortex was incised as a result of deliberate human action, rather than any natural process. To obtain more information about the purpose of the incisions and the manner in which they may have been produced, the cortical surfaces were examined (by JC) under a Scanning Electron Microscope (SEM) and compared with marks made during replication experiments.

Observed at low magnification (x15–x25) in the SEM, the lines have U-shaped cross-sections and maintain an even width and depth despite irregularities on the bottom of the grooves and along the sides (Fig. 4.65, 1). These irregularities are caused by numerous silica inclusions which give the cortex its gritty texture. The absence of internal features such as striations within the grooves may also be due to the texture of the cortex although some signs of smoothing of the grain surfaces (Fig. 4.65, 2) are visible at higher magnifications (up to x150). The incisions do not penetrate beneath the cortical exterior of the flint and there are no signs that the grooves have been incised more than once.

In an attempt to replicate the macroscopic and microscopic characteristics of the incisions, a number of experiments were carried out (by NB and CB). In these experiments, unretouched flint blades with fine, sharp edges less than 1 mm thick were used to produce incisions on flint nodules with relatively thin cortical surfaces. In one set of experiments, distinct, thin incisions were produced on the cortex by using sharp unretouched 'corners' of blades, for example at the intersection of a lateral edge and a broken distal end of a blank. To the naked eye, the incisions appeared to resemble those on the archaeological specimens. Microscopically, the symmetrical U-shape of the groove cross-section (Fig. 4.65, 3) is similar but the experimental examples also exhibit internal striations which run parallel to the length, along the centre bottom of the incisions (Fig. 4.65, 4). The internal surfaces of the experimental incisions are also much smoother than those observed on the archaeological specimens. However, these differences could easily be related to variation in cortex texture rather than distinct modes of production. The cortex on the experimental pieces contains fewer silica inclusions and probably provided a more even, less resistant surface than that of the Hengistbury artefacts. As cortex texture and thickness can vary considerably even between flint nodules derived from the same source, this is a difficult variable to control for satisfactorily in experiments. Consequently, it is also difficult to assess the exact rel-

4.64 *Core and refitting flake with engraved cortex. 10 mm scale.*

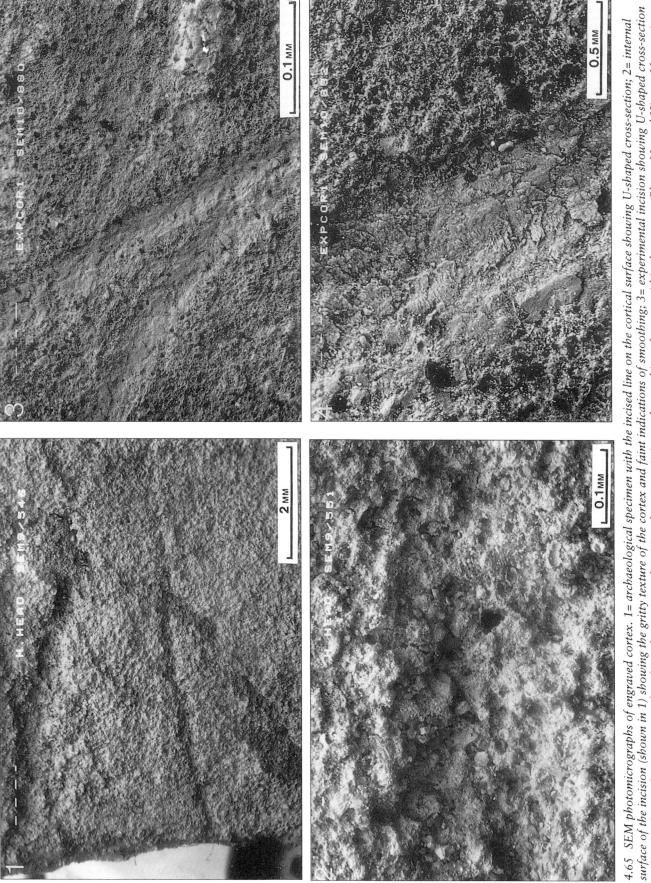

4.65 SEM photomicrographs of engraved cortex. 1= archaeological specimen with the incised line on the cortical surface showing U-shaped cross-section; 2= internal surface of the incision (shown in 1) showing the gritty texture of the cortex and faint indications of smoothing; 3= experimental incision showing U-shaped cross-section and internal smoothing; 4= internal surface of experimental incision showing striation and smoothing of cortex within the groove. (Photo: Natural History Museum)

evance of the similarities and differences observed in the marks. Nevertheless, gross mark morphology and the occasional instances of smoothing within the archaeological examples suggest they may have been made in the same manner as the experimental marks. In the same set of experiments, attempts were also made to accentuate the incisions by going back over them but this resulted in the lines being widened and made less distinct, a feature not observed on the archaeological pieces.

In a second set of experiments, a flatter flint nodule was used as a 'working surface' on which meat was cut into strips using an unretouched blade. This action produced a series of parallel and sometimes criss-cross incisions on the cortex, similar to those which may be seen on a well-used kitchen 'cutting-board'. However, the lines differ from those on the archaeological specimens as they are uneven in depth and sometimes overlapped or are double-cut.

Both the observed characteristics and the insights provided by the replication experiments indicate that the incisions present on the cortical surfaces of two artefacts at Hengistbury Head were probably made by using a stone artefact directly on the cortical surface. The resulting cross-hatched pattern appears to be a schematic design. Similar designs have also been noted on the cortical surfaces of artefacts from other Late Upper Palaeolithic sites in Britain and on the continent.

### 4.6.2 Engraved stones from other British and European Late Upper Palaeolithic contexts

Apart from Hengistbury only one other British Late Upper Palaeolithic site has so far yielded unambiguous evidence of engraved stonework. The site of Gough's Cave, Somerset has produced two engraved artefacts within occupation levels dating to around 12,400 BP (see Tables 4.27 and 4.28). The first is a flint flake with a series of lines engraved on the corticated dorsal surface (Jacobi pers. comm.), but the restricted nature of the working makes any precise comparison with the Hengistbury examples difficult. The second artefact is a slate *retouchoir* engraved on one side with a series of sub-horizontal lines recut by a single vertical line (Jacobi 1988). As with the Hengistbury example the motifs on both artefacts are abstract rather than naturalistic in design. Examples of hare tibiae and mammoth ivory decorated with incised groups of lines have also been recovered from the same cave (Tratman 1976, Charles 1991).

Evidence for decorated and engraved stones occurs throughout the Upper Palaeolithic of Europe (Leonardi 1988) and may occasionally be represented by earlier examples also (cf. Commont 1916). In French Late Upper Palaeolithic contexts, stone artefacts with schematic decorations are most frequently linked with a style of artwork occurring in the Late Magdalenian VI (Sieveking 1987). A review of the evidence by Ann

Sieveking has shown that many of the objects are characterised by scribbly schematic or geometric designs. Such objects are not confined to caves but occur at many open-air sites as well. Amongst recorded examples of naturalistic engravings are those on artefacts from the Paris Basin. The best known include representations of horse engraved on the corticated surface of a burin from Pincevent (Brézillon 1977a) and on a sandstone *plaquette* from Cepoy (Allain 1976). One of the geographically closest finds to Britain comes from the cave site at Gouy, on the outskirts of Rouen in Normandy, and consists of geometric designs carved in chalk (Martin 1972). Further south, but of potential chronological relevance to Hengistbury, is the engraved cortex of flints from Roc-aux-Sorciers (Angles-sur-l'Anglin) found within an atypical Late Magdalenian lithic assemblage containing tanged points and Hamburgian shouldered points (Saint-Mathurin and Pincon 1986). In eastern France, schematic engravings have been noted on pebbles from Latest Magdalenian and 'epi-palaeolithic' (or Azilian) levels at Rochedane, ranging in age from 11,090–10,730 BP (Thévenin 1982). Elsewhere, criss-cross patterns and other abstract decoration also figure prominently in Azilian mobiliary art of SW France and the Pyrenees (cf. Chollot 1964; Sieveking 1981).

In Belgium, scratched rectilinear designs have been identified on cortical artefacts from apparently Late Upper Palaeolithic contexts at Lommel (Verheylewegen 1956), and from Presle (Dewez 1987). The latter assemblage, presumed to be of Pre-Allerød age, contains lithic finds of very similar type to those of the British Creswellian (cf. Gough's Cave). Further north in the Netherlands, flint artefacts with engraved surfaces have been recorded from a number of Federmesser sites including De Fransman I (Wouters 1984), Oostelbeers-Dennendijk (Van der Lee 1977), Drunen (Span 1983) and De Baanen (Arts 1988). All of these items bear abstract or geometric designs but so far none derives from a securely datable context. In passing, it is noteworthy that of all the decorated objects so far mentioned, the criss-cross relief on the artefact from De Baanen displays the most striking resemblance to the Hengistbury example.

Despite the general absence of well-documented examples from N Germany, stylistic representations on stone objects and artefacts are known from several locations from the central Rhineland. These include the numerous engraved items of artwork (mainly naturalistic but including highly stylised representations) on *plaquettes* from the Late Magdalenian site of Gönnersdorf (Bosinski and Fischer 1974; Bolus *et al.* 1988). Abstract engravings have also been identified on an arrowshaft-smoother from the nearby, but slightly later, Federmesser site at Niederbieber (Loftus 1982). In S Scandinavia, artefacts with engraved cortical surfaces, considered to be deliberately incised, have been recovered from the Late Palaeolithic Bromme site of Segebro in S Sweden (Salomonsson 1964). Although artefacts with cortical markings have also been recorded from as far east as Poland, these are not believed to be of intentional workmanship (Schild pers. comm.).

Given the widely scattered geographic distribution of engraved stone artefacts in the European Late Upper Palaeolithic it is not surprising that examples should occur on the outermost fringes of this area, in Britain. However, because few such items are likely to have been overlooked in museum collections it is equally obvious that they represent extremely rare occurrences especially when viewed in terms of the totality of such finds from Europe as a whole.

## 4.7 An analysis of red ochre samples

### 4.7.1 *Introduction and methodology*

Eleven pieces of ochre/ironstone were examined from the Late Upper Palaeolithic site and small samples were cut from ten of them using a 0.3 mm thick alumina slitting wheel. Whilst cutting the samples, it was noted that the freshly cut surfaces of all the objects except number 209 showed a bright red coloration, and all these samples produced a characteristic cherry red streak typical of the iron mineral hematite. Object 209 was a 'limonitic' brown colour, which is also the colour of the majority of the ironstone nodules ('doggers') found in the geological strata of the headland (Fig. 4.66). Six of the samples were found to be attracted to a small hand magnet (see Table 4.26). This suggested that these samples also contained the iron minerals magnetite or possibly maghemite which are both magnetic. It is unusual, although not impossible, for these minerals to form naturally under sedimentary conditions.

The samples were then mounted in transparent acrylic resin, ground flat, polished, then carbon coated for examination in the Cameca Camebax Electron Microprobe Analyser. This allowed the rapid analysis and identification of detrital minerals present (mainly quartz), and determination of the hafnium oxide to zirconium oxide concentration ratio of the zircon grains found in some of the samples. The Absorbed Current Image from the Camebax EMPA was processed using the Intellect 200 Digital Image Analysis equipment, which allowed the rapid determination of the relative proportion of the clastic mineral grains to the iron-rich matrix in the section. The results from these studies are also presented in Table 4.26.

### 4.7.2 *Discussion*

The brown colour and high proportion of clastic minerals to the matrix material found in sample 209 distinguishes it from the other palaeolithic examples. Its colour and high sand content are typical of the majority of the ironstone nodules found in the strata of the headland. Ironstones of hematitic red colour and low sand content are rare. Nevertheless, during a cursory survey of the headland by the author, some surface enriched doggers found at the base of the cliff immediately south of the transverse quarry (NGR SZ 174907) were more like the material from the Late Upper Palaeolithic site. During the same survey it was also noted that the average iron content of the nodules seemed to increase eastwards, reaching a maximum in the region of the nineteenth century ironstone quarry (the so-called Transverse Quarry), mentioned above, and near the Late Upper Palaeolithic site. Therefore, if the source of these stones was local, it is more than likely they came from the region and strata with the highest iron content. Reconstructing the landscape, it is probable that the position of the nineteenth century quarry marks the region of richest iron ores, and judging by the slope, the ironstone doggers would have come to the surface on the northern (inland) side of Warren Hill. Unfortunately, the quarrying activity has removed any nodules in this region, and the sea has destroyed any possible exposure to the south. Even so, some of the thin enriched exterior shells from the nodules in the quarry were very similar in grain size and shape, and proportion of silica grains to matrix material, to the ten hematite red samples from the archaeological site.

A number of differences were, however, observed between the archaeological and geological samples. For example, the ironstone nodules from the quarry section and around the base of the cliff show considerable variation in colour within, and between, individual doggers, ranging from light yellow to dark red-brown

*Table 4.26 The ochre/ironstone samples*

| Sample No | Weight gs. | Colour | Magnetic | % area Silica | No of Zircons | HfO$_2$/ZrO$_2$ in Zircons | Mean of larger grain size μm. | Lab No |
|---|---|---|---|---|---|---|---|---|
| K31 33 | 0.095 | red | no | 0.5 | 0 | | X | 0X381 |
| H31 Sieved | 1.355 | red | yes | 18.5 | 3 | 0.017 | 81 | 0X383 |
| 14 | 0.137 | red | yes | 12.1 | 0 | | 60 | 0X382 |
| 34 | 0.926 | red | no | X | 0 | | X | 0X388 |
| 43 | 15.163 | red | yes | 21.0 | 0 | | 85 | 0X390 |
| 50 | 1.815 | red | yes | 17.0 | 0 | | 49 | 0X387 |
| 54 | 4.25 | red | no | 0.0 | 0 | | X | 0X384 |
| 62 | 3.459 | red | no | 57.4 | 0 | | 291 | 0X385 |
| 67 | 7.124 | red | yes | 10.2 | 1 | 0.016 | 60 | 0X386 |
| 83 | 8.241 | red | yes | 7.8 | 5 | 0.015 | 78 | 0X389 |
| 209 | 347.0 | brown | no | 55.1 | 0 | | 217 | 0X391 |

X = Not determined

4.66 *Ironstone 'doggers' on the beach at Hengistbury.*

colour over a few millimetres. By contrast the archaeological specimens were fairly uniform in colour. Another difference between the modern and Palaeolithic ironstones was that the modern geological specimens contained an occasional bright green grain (probably the mineral glauconite), whereas these were not seen in the archaeological samples. However, electron microprobe analysis showed that some of the archaeological samples contained small regions with elevated concentrations of potassium and aluminium. It is likely that these regions represented the decomposition products of the glauconite grains seen in fresh rock. The $HfO_2$ to $ZrO_2$ ratios for both the modern ironstone nodules and the Late Upper Palaeolithic samples fell into the 0.015–0.017 range. Thus all the available evidence strongly suggests that the 'hematite' red ochre/ironstones were obtained from a local source on Warren Hill.

A possible explanation as to why no geological samples were found with iron contents as high as those from the archaeological material, is that when the ironstone nodules are exposed to oxidising conditions they tend to undergo a series of chemical changes which result in the surface layers of the nodules becoming enriched in iron. Such processes can be relatively rapid: for example, an enriched zone 4–5 mm thick was formed on sideritic ironstone nodules in a Lincolnshire quarry in 12 years. Also, the migration of iron salts can result in the formation of massive 'hard pans' or 'bog-ores' where the acidity of the ground water or the oxygen potential of the ground water decrease. Thus, rocks with iron contents as high as those noted in the Late

Upper Palaeolithic samples either could have formed due to the natural surface enrichment of the ironstone doggers in the Upper Hengistbury Beds (geological formation) when exposed to surface or sub-surface weathering, or they could have formed as a hard-pan formation. However, the presence of decomposed glauconite grains in the archaeological material would seem to rule out the hard-pan mode of formation, because the mineral is thought to form only under marine conditions.

Some interesting observations may be made concerning ironstone recovered during the excavation of the Iron Age site on the north-western side of Hengistbury Head (Cunliffe 1987). Here a large number of blocks, some 150 mm thick, were found to be of the same high quality ironstone as found at the Late Upper Palaeolithic site. As was noted above, none of the geological specimens collected was magnetic, but one piece from the Late Upper Palaeolithic site and over half (by weight) of the ironstone from the Cunliffe excavation showed some degree of magnetism (Salter 1987). A number of the latter also showed clear signs of fire cracking. It was therefore concluded that the magnetic properties of the ironstone had been induced by the conversion of some of the iron containing minerals into the magnetic iron oxides, magnetite or maghemite. It was found, experimentally, that the geological material will become magnetic when heated to relatively modest temperatures (270–300°C), for quite short periods (20 minutes). The magnetic effect induced by such mild heating, however, decays within a couple of years. As a result, it was decided to determine the X-ray diffraction patterns from samples of the 'hematitic' red ironstone from the Cunliffe excavation. These produced weak quartz, siderite and hematite lines, suggesting that most of the iron oxide is in an amorphous or poorly-crystalline form. The same material when mildly heated and left to return to the non-magnetic state showed only the quartz and hematite lines.

A second experiment was carried out, heating the rock to higher temperatures (around 700°C). It was found that if heating was very rapid, the rock would shatter explosively. This was probably due to the trapped moisture being converted to steam. However, if the initial heating stage was carried out more gently, the rock would withstand being heated to 700°C without any significant change in shape or loss of mechanical strength. If the conditions were mildly reducing, the sample became magnetic. The X-ray diffraction patterns from the magnetic sample suggests that both the minerals maghemite and magnetite were present as well as hematite. Such a sample would retain its magnetism. The exact degree of conversion would depend on the temperature, the reducing capacity of atmosphere, and the duration of the heating period employed. However, the conditions found within a camp fire would be sufficiently reducing to impart some magnetic properties.

The original rocks were likely to have had a colour similar to sample 209 (a brownish colour), and a mild oxidising roast would have converted them to a bright red colour, easily used as a pigment. It is, therefore, quite reasonable to suppose that these rocks were deliberately heated. Because of the relatively poor control over the process in an open camp fire, it is hardly surprising that some of the samples experienced the slightly reducing conditions necessary to induce their magnetic properties.

### 4.7.3   Conclusion

All the samples are consistent with an origin within a few hundred metres of the Late Upper Palaeolithic site. It is certain that six of the archaeological samples had been heated, and it is probable that four of the remaining 'red' samples had been similarly treated. As there were no signs of fire cracking on the Late Upper Palaeolithic samples, it was originally considered unlikely that the samples had been heated deliberately. However, considering how very heat resistant this type of rock has proved to be during experimental firings, it is now thought probable that the samples were subjected to deliberate heating to improve their colour.

## 4.8 Flint sourcing using palynological methods

### 4.8.1   Introduction

In an attempt to determine the provenance of flint implements from the Late Upper Palaeolithic site, a palynological analysis was undertaken. This involved the examination of a number of small drilled samples from flint artefacts (various blade cores) using standard palynological processing techniques.

The only previously published account of a palynological examination of flint artefacts is that by Valensi (1960) who described a dinoflagellate cyst assemblage from flint implements of the Magdalenian period in France. This work merely described the cysts and gave a rough geological age (late Cretaceous), but did not attempt to discover the provenance of the flints themselves.

The flints used in the present study all showed a chalk cortex. Since this cortex is normally lost in flints from a derived geological context (e.g. river gravels, beach deposits), its presence suggests that they may have been quarried or collected from some *in situ* context. It was hoped that a palynological analysis would provide an assemblage of organic-walled microfossils which could be correlated with those present in flinty chalks which are exposed in Hampshire and Dorset at the present day. The expectation of success was based on the work of Clarke and Verdier (1967) who described Upper Cretaceous dinoflagellate cysts from the Isle of Wight; these however were not obtained directly from flints, but from so-called 'flinty chalk'.

### 4.8.2   Methodology

A small series of Palaeolithic artefacts (including cores C, H and V) were cored using a hollow diamond encrusted drill bit. Several specimens were removed from each artefact and afterwards care was taken to plug the holes with an inert filler (the refilled holes are just visible in Figs. 4.8,1 4.40, 4.49 and 4.51). The samples consisted of small tubular core specimens roughly 3–4 mm in diameter and 20 mm long. In order to provide samples of a comparative nature several control specimens were included from freshly quarried flint at Alum Bay on the Isle of Wight (the nearest outcrop of flint visible from Hengistbury today) and from Tarrant Rushton and Purbeck (both on the Dorset mainland and within relatively close reach of the Headland).

Once removed, the drilled samples were cleaned in distilled water and then a weak concentration of hydrochloric acid (HCl), sufficient to remove any adhering chalk. Next, the washed samples were placed in individually labelled polypropylene beakers (250 ml), and left to dry in a cabinet for 24 hours. When dry the samples were crushed and 30 gm of material was separated from each specimen.

Stage two involved the removal of silicates from the crushed flint by covering the samples with 40–60% Hydrofluoric acid (HF) and placing them in a fume cupboard. After stirring the samples the beakers were capped and left for 24 hours. The solution was then decanted from the beakers and distilled water used to rinse the samples repeatedly, until they became neutral (this usually entailed 5–6 washes).

The last stage involved placing the residues in a centrifuge for 3–5 minutes at 3,000 rpm. Finally, 1–2 drops of concentrated residue from each sample were mixed with an equal amount of warm glycerine jelly and mounted on a glass slide for microscopic examination.

### 4.8.3  *Results*

Regrettably, all of the samples processed were barren of organic matter and therefore do not allow any useful correlations to be made at present. However, investigations are continuing and it may be possible at some stage to delineate intervals in the chalk succession which are similarly barren of palynomorphs. In this respect it is interesting to note that the three modern samples from Dorset and the Isle of Wight all showed similar absences of microfossils.

## 4.9  Non-flint rock materials in the assemblage

Samples taken from one of several thermally fractured rocks at the Late Upper Palaeolithic site (Fig. 4.30) were examined under a light microscope at the Geological Museum, London. The samples which consisted of a very friable quartz aggregate (sandrock), may be identified under the more popular term 'Sarsen'. Historically, this term was used by laymen to describe any large or inconvenient boulder, but, it was gradually taken over by nineteenth century geologists to indicate specifically the pale grey sandstone blocks which littered much of SE England. Today, areas of the Salisbury Plain and the Marlborough Downs are well-known for the occurrence of these rocks.

The stones as a group are secondarily cemented sandstones and flint conglomerates (Summerfield 1979). Three types are recognised: Grain Supported (GS) fabric; Floating (F) fabric and Conglomerate (C) fabric. The Hengistbury samples represent the GS fabric type.

The presence of erratic blocks of sarsen in the Bournemouth area have been known for a long time and several examples were formally identified by the Geological Survey (White 1917). They are (or were) most common towards Wimborne Minster, north of Bournemouth, where it is believed they occurred within the Plateau Gravel deposits. Large free-standing sarsens have also been recorded in a number of Bournemouth gardens (Pleyder 1895; Solly 1910).

Despite these observations, it seems that no sarsens have been reported as being unequivocally *in situ*. They probably represent remains of deposits of various ages from the mid-Palaeocene to Oligocene. The date of silicification may be even later.

## 4.10  The Late Upper Palaeolithic site in its wider perspective

### 4.10.1  *Introduction*

This section deals with the Hengistbury site and its affinities with contemporary Late Glacial material in Britain and the NW European mainland. It also examines the question of site structure and intra-site variability comparing the Hengistbury assemblage with data from selected British and continental sites. To begin with, however, it is necessary to consider the Late Upper Palaeolithic occupation of Hengistbury in the context of the changing climatic conditions at the end of the Ice Age. This review is necessarily of a fairly general nature because of the wide error margin associated with the thermoluminescence dating of the site (12,500±1200 BP). Despite the lack of precision, the evidence suggests that the occupation should be placed sometime after the early thermal maximum which marks the first part of the Late Glacial interstadial.

### 4.10.2  *Late Glacial environments*

*Prior to 13,000 BP*: At its maximum, around 18,000 BP, the late Devensian ice sheet covered much of Britain north of a line stretching from the Pembrokeshire coast to the Wash in East Anglia (Boulton *et al.* 1977). Eustatic effects of the ice meant that world sea levels were at least 100 m to 130 m below that of the present day (Lowe and Walker 1984). By 14,000 BP the sea level had risen significantly but still lay at least 60 m (Fairbridge 1961) and perhaps 90 m (Jelgersma 1979) below its present level. This left a landbridge between Britain and Europe which was not to be fully broken until after 10,000 BP (Devoy 1982). Before 13,000 BP many parts of S Britain were affected by severe periglacial conditions (Atkinson *et al.* 1987). Winter temperatures were on average between –20 and –25°C, while in the warmest summer months they barely rose above 10°C. Such a thermal regime was accentuated by the landlocked position of eastern Britain (with no North Sea buffer) and the proximity in winter, on the western side, of Atlantic sea ice (Ruddiman and McIntyre 1981). Pollen and beetle evidence from N Wales (Coope and Brophy 1972) and NW England (Coope and Pennington 1977) shows that such conditions prevailed in the British Isles until at least 14,500 BP.

The transition from fully glacial to interstadial conditions seems to have occurred over a remarkably short period in NW Europe (Lowe and Walker 1984). This is indicated by the dramatic shift northwards of polar waters from a position off the coast of Ireland at 13,300±700 BP (Duplessy *et al.* 1981; Ruddiman and McIntyre 1981) to somewhere north-west of Scotland by 13,000 BP (Lowe and Walker 1984). The rapidity of such change is not reflected uniformly in the terrestrial record, with some indicators (beetles) reacting far more quickly to climatic events than others (plants). For example in S England plant macrofossils indicative of cold climate conditions have been radiocarbon dated to 13,405±170 BP (Gibbard and Hall 1982) from Colnbrook in Buckinghamshire, whereas a similar date (13,560±210 BP) from nearby Hertfordshire (Colney Heath) on peats with a beetle fauna suggest temperate conditions not much different from those of today

(Pearson 1962; Godwin 1964). To complicate matters vegetation patterns throughout this period show strong regional differentiation (Pennington 1977b). Despite these problems it is clear that the climate in W Britain (Pennington 1977a), in SE England (Godwin 1964) and possibly North Wales (Seddon 1962) had improved sufficiently for tall herb communities and dwarf shrub heath to colonise large areas of the country between 14,000 and 13,000 BP.

There are few well-dated British vertebrate faunas from this period. Suspected as being absent from Britain, however, are many of the larger mammals characteristic of the Mid-Devensian, such as woolly rhinoceros, musk ox, lion and spotted hyena (Stuart 1977, 1982). Others, like the mammoth and bison may have survived in NW Europe but in much diminished numbers, as hinted by isolated radiocarbon dates from Britain (Coope and Lister 1987), Scandinavia (Andersen 1988) and Germany (Bolus *et al.* 1988). Vertebrates typical of open habitats, such as horse, reindeer, arctic fox are thought to have been much in evidence.

*13,000–12,000 BP: The pre-Allerød stage of the Late Glacial Interstadial.:* At approximately 13,000 BP a major thermal improvement is indicated by insect faunas and the localised spread of birch woodland. It marks the beginning of the oscillation termed either the 'Lateglacial Interstadial' (*sensu* Lowe and Walker 1984) or the 'Windermere Interstadial' (*sensu* Coope and Pennington 1977). Various problems are acknowledged over the dating of deposits at the type-site and for this reason some authors would prefer suspending the term Windermere in favour of alternative regional strato-types (Lowe and Walker 1984). While the interstadial might be correlated with the NW European Bølling oscillation (Pennington 1975), there are few convincing sites in England where two distinctive phases of woody plant dominance (Bølling and Allerød) can be recognised. To avoid any of the existing ambiguities the term 'Late Glacial' interstadial is preferred by the writer.

In southern England the climatic amelioration is signalled by beetle assemblages typical of arctic environments being replaced by those of a distinctively more temperate aspect around 13,000 BP (Atkinson *et al.* 1987). The evidence suggests that temperatures rose by 25°C in winter and by 7–8°C in summer to a level not that much different from that of the present day. A slightly cooler thermal regime is indicated for N England and SW Scotland (Coope 1977).

Pollen evidence from this period indicates that open habitats were colonised by shrub vegetation including juniper (*Juniperus*) and willow (*Salix*), and in the more oceanic western regions, by the crowberry (*Empetrum*). Birch woodland subsequently developed in many areas of central and southern England (Lowe and Walker 1984). This birch phase probably occurred as early as 12,500 BP in parts of W Britain (Switsur and West 1975) and may account for the early appear-

ance of elk in the faunal record (Hallam *et al.* 1973; Stuart 1982). However, not all parts of the country displayed the same vegetation patterns for it appears that birch woods were less well-developed in eastern Britain (Newey 1970; Turner and Kershaw 1973; Bennett 1983) while Scots pine (*Pinus sylvestris*) featured prominently in the woodlands of SE England (Godwin 1975b). The relative scarcity of birch in some areas may have been due to a combination of local edaphic factors and exposure to cold easterly winds blowing across the dry North Sea Plain (Lowe and Walker 1984) or to prolonged summer drought (Coope and Joachim 1980). It has even been suggested that some of the chalkland areas remained more or less unwooded until the Postglacial period (Bush 1988).

Considerable diversity is also exhibited in the mammal faunas of the Late Glacial period, but this need not reflect environmental differences at a regional level, as too little is known about the specific preferences and adaptations of many of the animals concerned. Thus the woolly mammoth (*Mammuthus primigenius*), traditionally regarded as a creature of the open steppe, appears to persist well into the Interstadial (Table 4.27) as indicated by dated records from caves in the N Midlands and as far west as Devon and Somerset (Coope and Lister 1987; Gillespie *et al.* 1985; Currant 1987). Similarly late records of the mammoth occur elsewhere in N Europe (Delpech 1975; Poplin 1976). Other contemporary elements in the British faunal record include horse (*Equus ferus*), mountain or arctic hare (*Lepus timidus*), arctic fox (*Alopex lagopus*) as well as more temperate adapted species such as elk (*Alces alces*), red deer (*Cervus elaphus*) and aurochs (*Bos primigenius*). All of these species have been found at human occupation sites and were therefore part of the potentially exploited fauna. Indeed, except for elk every one of these vertebrates is recorded from Gough's Cave in SW England (Currant 1986). One Late Glacial species which does appear to have closely defined preferences for open steppe environments is the saiga antelope (*Saiga tatarica*) and it has been suggested that its re-appearance in S and SW Britain around 12,500 BP coincides with an increased aridification of the climate (Currant 1987).

In summary, the above data imply that by 12,500 BP the climate in many parts of Britain had become as warm as the present day, with birch woodland being present, at least locally. These conditions may not have prevailed throughout eastern areas which may have been drier and more open. It is during this period that the earliest evidence of the re-settlement of England can be reliably documented (see below).

*12,000–11,000 BP: The Allerød stage of the Late Glacial Interstadial*: The rapid climatic warming appears to have been followed by a period of reduction in average annual temperatures. Unlike the amelioration, this cooling phase seems to have been less dramatic and to have taken place gradually over a period of perhaps a millennium (Atkinson *et al.* 1987). During

| Lab No | Sample | Findspot (County) | Date (BP) | Ref. |
|---|---|---|---|---|
| OxA–466 | *red deer | Gough's Cave (Somerset) | 12,800±170 | 1 |
| OxA–621 | red deer | Misbourne (Berks) | 12,530±200 | 2 |
| OxA–1563 | red deer | K. Arthur's Cave (H&W) | 12,210±120 | 7 |
| OxA–1562 | red deer | K. Arthur's Cave (H&W | 12,120±120 | 7 |
| OxA–801 | red deer | Aveline's H. (Somerset) | 12,100±180 | 7 |
| OxA–1021 | mammoth | Condover (Shrop) | 12,700±160 | 3 |
| OxA–1455 | mammoth | Condover (Shrop) | 12,400±160 | 7 |
| OxA–1456 | mammoth | Condover (Shrop) | 12,330±120 | 7 |
| OxA–1316 | mammoth | Condover (Shrop) | 12,300±180 | 7 |
| OxA–1204 | mammoth | Pin Hole (Derbys) | 12,460±160 | 3 |
| OxA–320 | mammoth | Robin H's Cave (Derbys) | 12,320±120 | 7 |
| OxA–464 | *horse | Gough's Cave (Somerset) | 12,470±160 | 1 |
| OxA–465 | *horse | Gough's Cave (Somerset) | 12,360±170 | 1 |
| OxA–1200 | arctic fox | Gough's Cave (Somerset) | 12,400±110 | 3 |
| OxA–150 | elk | Poulton-le-Fylde (Lancs) | 12,400±300 | 1 |
| OxA–463 | saiga | Gough's Cave (Somerset) | 12,380±160 | 1 |
| OxA–1464 | saiga | Soldier's H. (Somerset) | 12,100±140 | 7 |
| OxA–1616 | *arctic hare | Robin H's Cave (Derbys) | 12,600±170 | 7 |
| OxA–1617 | *arctic hare | Robin H's Cave (Derbys) | 12,420±200 | 7 |
| OxA–1618 | *arctic hare | Robin H's Cave (Derbys) | 12,480±170 | 7 |
| OxA–1619 | *arctic hare | Robin H's Cave (Derbys) | 12,450±150 | 7 |
| OxA–1670 | *arctic hare | Robin H's Cave (Derbys) | 12,290±120 | 7 |
| OxA–1467 | *arctic hare | Pin Hole (Derbys) | 12,350±120 | 7 |
| OxA–735 | arctic hare | Church Hole (Notts) | 12,240±150 | 2 |
| OxA–1122 | reindeer | Aveline's H (Somerset) | 12,480±130 | 5 |
| BM–524 | brown bear | Sun Hole (Somerset) | 12,378±150 | 6 |
| OxA–1471 | bovid | Pin Hole (Derbys) | 12,400±140 | 7 |
| OxA–1615 | bovid | Pin Hole (Derbys) | 12,480±160 | 7 |
| OxA–1121 | *bovid | Aveline's H (Somerset) | 12,380±130 | 5 |
| OxA–588 | bovid | Gough's Cave (Somerset) | 12,030±150 | 4 |
| OxA–813 | aurochs | Gough's Cave (Somerset) | 11,900±140 | 2 |
| OxA–1203 | aurochs | Kent's Cavern (Devon) | 11,880±120 | 3 |
| BM–570 | bovid | Kent's Cavern (Devon) | 11,570±410 | 3 |
| OxA–1493 | *reindeer | Fox Hole Cave (Derbys) | 11,970±120 | 7 |

* humanly modified bone/antler.

References: 1= Gillespie *et al.* 1985; 2= Gowlett *et al.* 1986b; 3= Hedges *et al.* 1988; 4= Gowlett *et al.* 1986a; 5= Hedges *et al.* 1987; 6= Campbell 1977; 7= Hedges *et al.* 1989.

this time no appreciable southwards movement occurs in the Atlantic polar waters, but elsewhere changes in terrestrial environments indicating a fall in mean annual temperatures are recorded. According to beetle remains the decline in annual temperatures probably began as early as 12,500 BP, with an average drop of about 3–4°C by 12,000 BP (Bishop and Coope 1977; Lowe and Walker 1984). At this time temperatures of the coldest winter months had fallen to –5°C, while summer levels may have remained more or less constant (Atkinson *et al.* 1987).

Pollen data suggest a major expansion of birch woodland, which may have been linked to the thermal decline (Coope and Joachim 1980). The rise in birch did not occur in a fully synchronous manner across the country and in some places it never became the dominant tree species. For example, in SE Britain the change from open to wooded conditions seems to have occurred relatively gradually (West 1977) with mixed birch/pine forest being recorded around 11,900 BP (Kerney *et al.* 1964). A more dense spread of pine woodland is identified from contemporary pollen diagrams from Dorset and Hampshire (Haskins 1978), although factors of long distance pollen transport may

have exaggerated its presence locally (Scaife and Macphail 1983).

From 11,400 BP onwards summer temperatures appear to have cooled considerably (Atkinson *et al.* 1987). Pollen extracted from organic deposits in SE Britain (Gibbard and Hall 1982) shows a return to more open conditions by 11,230±120 BP with the only wooded vegetation certainly present being willow (Scaife 1987). From Hockham Mere in East Anglia a date of 11,160±190 BP (Bennett 1983) marks the occurrence of a windblown sand deposit. The sediments reflect possibly drier, colder conditions, but apart from a slight reduction in juniper evidence of the climatic deterioration is not manifested in the pollen profile.

Faunal evidence for this period indicates the presence in SW England of temperate woodland species, such as bovids (Kent's Cavern: OxA–1203 11,880±120 BP and BM–2168R 11,800±420 BP) but reindeer may have continued to thrive in certain upland areas. Records of reindeer from Fox Hole in N England at this time, however, need not imply the existence of fully open conditions since these animals are also known to exploit forests and high ground south of the tundra belt (Currant 1986). Local factors influencing

Table 4.28 Selection of Late Upper Palaeolithic dates from Britain

| Lab No | Sample | Findspot (County) | Date (BP) | Ref. |
|--------|--------|-------------------|-----------|------|
| OxA–466 | red deer metapodial (cut) | Gough's Cave (Somerset) | 12,800±170 | 1 |
| OxA–587 | horse phalanx (cut) | Gough's Old Cave(Somerset) | 12,530±150 | 2 |
| OxA–150 | elk metapodial (barbed point) | Poulton-le-Fylde (Lancashire) | 12,400±300 | 1 |
| OxA–1500 | large herbivore diaphysis (cut) | Three Holes Cave (Devon) | 12,350±160 | 4 |
| OxA–1789 | bone piercer | Kent's Cavern (Devon) | 12,320±130 | 4 |
| OxA–535 | human ulna | Sun Hole (Somerset) | 12,210±160 | 2 |
| OxA–1494 | antler rod fragment | Fox Hole Cave (Derbyshire) | 12,000±120 | 4 |
| OxA–1493 | reindeer antler bevelled rod | Fox Hole Cave (Derbyshire) | 11,970±120 | 4 |
| OxA–1950 | antler point | Leman & Ower (North Sea) | 11,740±150 | 5 |
| OxA–1946 | antler point | Porth y Waen (Shropshire) | 11,390±120 | 5 |
| OxA–517 | bone point | Sproughton (Suffolk) | 10,910±150 | 2 |
| OxA–518 | antler point | Sproughton (Suffolk) | 10,700±160 | 2 |
| OxA–811 | red deer vertebra associated with cut ribs | Elderbush Cave (Staffordshire) | 10,600±110 | 3 |
| OxA–803 | reindeer antler artefact | Earls Barton (Northants) | 10,320±150 | 3 |

References: 1= Gillespie *et al.* 1985; 2= Gowlett *et al.* 1986a; 3= Gowlett *et al.* 1986b; 4= Hedges *et al.* 1989; 5= Bonsall & Smith 1989.

the distribution of this species in the Allerød might have included the existence of deep enough snowcover to inhibit predators during spring calving (Jacobi 1981b). No other components of the contemporary fauna have yet been satisfactorily dated, but based on NW European parallels it is likely that other forest animals such as elk, (*Alces alces*), beaver (*Castor fiber*) and wild pig (*Sus scrofa*) inhabited lowland areas of Britain at this time.

### 4.10.3 Dating evidence for human occupation during the Late Glacial Interstadial

Current dating estimates suggest that re-settlement of the British Isles after the Last Glacial Maximum did not begin until the onset of climatically warmer conditions around 13,500 BP. Evidence for earlier commencement is based on a solitary radiocarbon date published by Campbell (1977) for the 'Black Band' at Kent's Cavern, Devon (GrN–6203 14,275±120 BP). Although from within a unit containing artefacts, the date originates from an unmodified brown bear bone and its association with human activity therefore cannot be substantiated (Jacobi 1980). A recently dated bone tool (Table 4.28) from the same layer may provide a more realistic indicator of the Late Upper Palaeolithic use of the cave. The evidence for a more delayed recolonisation of the British peninsula than previously predicted (for example in Campbell 1977; Kozlowski and Kozlowski 1979) is also supported by the radiocarbon record which shows no sustained occupation in NW Europe north of the Loire or west of the Oder until the 14th millennium BC (Jacobi 1980; Otte 1988).

So far the most complete series of British radiocarbon dates for this period comes from Gough's Cave, Cheddar Gorge in Somerset, where the earliest date of 12,800±170 BP, is on a cut bone of red deer (Jacobi 1986 and see Table 4.28 above). There are now over fifteen dates from the cave spanning the period c. 12,800–12,100 BP and these place the occupation within the pre-Allerød stage of the Late Glacial Interstadial. Similar dates have now been obtained

directly on human bone from Sun Hole in the Cheddar Gorge and on modified animal bone from Aveline's Hole, Somerset, and the four N English sites of Fox Hole, Pin Hole and Robin Hood's Cave, Derbyshire and Poulton-le-Fylde, Lancashire (Table 4.28). These are in broad agreement with the Gough's Cave dates and, together with the thermoluminescence determinations from Hengistbury, provide the beginnings of a more realistic dating framework for the British Late Upper Palaeolithic.

In contrast to the relatively well-documented pre-Allerød finds, evidence for human activity during the succeeding Allerød phase is extremely sparse. The few published dates either fall at the the very beginning or at the end of this period. The early Allerød evidence is so far limited to one bevelled antler projectile head (*sagaie*) from Fox Hole, Derbyshire (Jacobi pers. comm.) and an antler barbed point dredged from the North Sea (Table 4.28). At the very end of the interstadial there are also a pair of dates on bone and antler barbed points from Suffolk in Eastern England (Cook and Barton 1986) and on an antler point from Porth y Waen in Shropshire (Bonsall and Smith 1989). The paucity of well-dated finds from this period, however, does not preclude sustained human occupation of the British peninsula at this time. Certainly, on the basis of dated NW European occurrences there is little reason to suppose that settlement did not extend across the North Sea plain into eastern Britain for some if not all of the Late Interstadial period.

### 4.10.4 Late Upper Palaeolithic technologies of the Late Glacial Interstadial: Typological and technological variability

#### The Creswellian cave assemblages

This grouping was first formally described by Dorothy Garrod (1926), and is defined typologically according to the presence of the Creswell point, an elongated trapezoidal tool. Creswellian assemblages are known almost exclusively from cave and rockshelter locations and despite the existence of isolated findspots, no large scale open-air sites are yet recorded in Britain

(Campbell 1977; Jacobi 1980). The radiocarbon record (see above) suggests that the bulk of these assemblages probably fit within the pre-Allerød stage of the Late Glacial Interstadial. More evolved forms of the Creswellian may belong to the Allerød or subsequent stadial (Campbell 1977) but this view is based on typological arguments rather than actual dated occurrences.

In addition to the angle-backed trapezoidal forms, an important identifying characteristic of the British Creswellian is the total absence of straight-backed blades and bladelets of the type found within contemporary Late Magdalenian assemblages of NW Europe (Collcutt 1979). In the largest Creswellian collection of its kind from Gough's Cave, Somerset, the retouched lithic equipment is typified by trapezoidal pieces (mainly bi-truncated Cheddar points), shouldered points, scrapers on the ends of mostly long blanks, composite tools and piercers, including amongst them true *Zinken* (cf. Brézillon 1977b, and see Glossary definition in Chapter 7). The toolkit is also characterised by a very slight predominance of burins over scrapers (Jacobi pers. comm.). Collections with similar combinations of tools include those from Sun Hole and Soldier's Hole (both in the Cheddar Gorge near Gough's Cave), Kent's Cavern (Devon) and the southern Welsh site of Hoyle's Mouth (Burleigh *et al.* 1985; Jacobi 1986).

Also sharing this Creswellian technology are the eponymous cave assemblages from the Creswell Crags (Nottinghamshire and Derbyshire), which demonstrate a similar predominance of angle-backed forms and an absence of straight-backed blades and bladelets. New radiocarbon dates on cut bone and antler from Robin Hood's Cave, Pin Hole (Jacobi pers. comm.) and one item from Fox Hole (Hedges *et al.* 1989, Table 4.28), suggest contemporary human exploitation of SW, central and northern Britain during the early part of the Late Glacial Interstadial.

Despite the fact that typological analyses have been undertaken of the retouched tool assemblages, no systematic study has yet been made of the flint debitage from the British Creswellian. Like their Late Upper Palaeolithic European counterparts the British assemblages are all based on blade production, with the majority of tools being made on blade blanks. A small sample of blades from Gough's Cave (spits 9–17) was examined by the writer for comparative purposes. This revealed that the blanks were detached from opposed platform blade cores, prepared by cresting. Some of the larger blades also reveal heavy abrasion at their proximal ends (for definition see Glossary). Special attention to preparation of the platforms is also reflected in the morphology of butt types. A high percentage of blade butts examined (n=104) from the site were faceted (49.5%), while most of the others were either tiny plain (punctiform) or plain (37.9%)(see also Table 4.31). Strictly speaking, most of the faceted examples should be described as being *partially* faceted, with the butt surface characterised by one major scar and a few tiny, subsidiary flake removals. The intention here seems to have been to adjust the angle of the striking

platform, rather than to isolate individual platforms. Few of the butts, for example, fall within the category of *talon à éperon* as described for typical Late Magdalenian assemblages (e.g. Karlin in Leroi-Gourhan and Brézillon 1972). However, according to Jacobi (in litt.) the technique does appear to have been used more extensively at the site according to the analysis of tool butt morphology. If not interpreted entirely in stylistic terms, there may be other good reasons why faceting of the butts was employed. For example, it may reflect a conscious effort on the part of the flint-knappers, to optimise the raw material, given the fact that the nearest source of flint lay over 40 miles to the east (Jacobi pers. comm.).

Evidence for the use of the lithic toolkit comes from associated faunal remains at Gough's Cave and other sites in Cheddar Gorge. Amongst the potentially exploited animals recorded at these locations are large game such as horses, red deer and wild cattle, and also smaller mammals like the mountain hare, as well as birds and wildfowl (Burleigh *et al.* 1985; Harrison 1986, 1989). At Gough's Cave evidence from cut-marked horse and deer bones shows that the animal carcasses were skinned and butchered with the aid of lithic tools (Parkin *et al.* 1986). The bones also show clear signs of meat filleting, while processing of the lower limbs (of horses) included the removal of tendons (possibly sinew for supplying raw materials in bow making or net weaving). The actual methods of hunting can only be guessed but the restricted nature of the gorge bottom suggests that animals may have been trapped in small numbers rather than in large herds. Single horse kills could have coincided with the period of the reproductive cycle when mares separate from the main herd in late spring and early summer in search of more isolated places to foal (Mohr 1971). A reconstruction of the likely period of occupation at Gough's Cave has been attempted on the basis of tooth eruption and dental growth patterns on the faunal specimens. The study of immature red deer jaws indicates the cave was probably used over the winter (Parkin *et al.* 1986). On the other hand incremental studies on the cementum of horse teeth and one of red deer show some animals were killed in the summer (Beasley 1987). Although hard to interpret, such lines of evidence would seem to imply repeated visits to the site at different times of the year.

Associated with the Creswellian lithic toolkits are various bone, antler and ivory artefacts. The assemblages are not considered rich by north-west European standards but the equipment is sufficiently standardised to suggest they could all belong to one broadly related technology. Thus, double-bevelled antler *sagaies* occur at Fox Hole (Bramwell 1977), Victoria Cave, Kinsey Cave (N Yorks), (Campbell 1977), and ivory articles of the same type from the Pin Hole (Creswell) and from Gough's Cave (Currant *et al.* 1989). Sewing equipment in the form of eyed bone needles has been found at Kent's Cavern and Church Hole (Campbell 1977), and the presence of similar items can be implied at Gough's Cave by needle-blank cores (Burleigh *et al.* 1985). Awls made of hare tibiae are documented from Gough's Cave and are duplicated at Creswell Crags (Jacobi pers. comm.). The ornamental perforated (drilled) fox teeth beads at Gough's Cave may also have parallels at King Arthur's Cave, but the latter are not well enough documented to be certain of their dating.

Broader European comparisons have been drawn between British bone and antler artefacts and those of the Late Magdalenian (Garrod 1926). In particular, the two *bâtons percés* from Gough's Cave (recently augmented by the discovery of a third in September 1989), the biserial harpoon from Kent's Cavern and the engraving of a horse's head from Robin Hood's Cave, are frequently cited as each having closest parallels with items of Late Magdalenian equipment from France and Belgium (Garrod 1926; Campbell 1977). To these might be added the eyed bone needles and bevelled rods (*sagaies*) mentioned above (Currant *et al.* 1989), although the latter have also been recorded from other non-Magdalenian contexts in the European Late Upper Palaeolithic (Rust 1943).

Notwithstanding these similarities, other features would suggest at least some divergence from the typical Late Magdalenian. Thus, for example, evidence for the use of the groove-and-splinter technique, occurring throughout the Upper Palaeolithic and considered typical of the French and Belgian Late Magdalenian (Dewez 1987), is all but absent at British sites. This may however be due to some specific local factor such as the absence or otherwise of suitably dense winter antler for toolmaking (Jacobi pers. comm.). Other differences of possible significance include the relatively infrequent use of red ochre, which is found in large quantities (as thin scatters of powdered material and hematite blocks) at many Late Magdalenian occupations. In this respect, the British cave locations seem to compare more closely with the Belgian Creswello-Tjongerian ones (see below), which unlike their local Magdalenian counterparts rarely display any extensive spreads of red colorant (Dewez 1987). It may also be relevant that whereas the Late Magdalenian groups of N France and Belgium tended to utilise fossil shells from the Jurassic beds of the Paris Basin, the Belgian Creswello-Tjongerian assemblages contain sea shells from the Atlantic shoreline (Dewez 1987). Similar imports, sometimes supplemented by North Sea amber, are recorded at Gough's Cave (shells and amber) and Robin Hood's Cave (amber).

### Late Upper Palaeolithic open-air site assemblages from Titchwell and Brockhill

A second group of Late Upper Palaeolithic assemblages, probably overlapping chronologically with the Creswellian, has been identified at a number of open-air locations in S Britain. Except for Hengistbury, the assemblages are not well-dated and their identification rests largely on typological and technological comparisons. The main distinguishing feature of the lithic tech-

nology is the presence of straight-backed blades which heavily outnumber all other backed forms including trapezoidal elements. There are also considerable technological differences in the debitage. Apart from Hengistbury, the largest collections potentially of this type come from Brockhill, Surrey and Titchwell, Norfolk. Although the sites are not located close together, they occur well away from the upland areas of limestone geology associated with the typical Creswellian occurrences. Because of their relevance to Hengistbury, the Brockhill and Titchwell assemblages are described below.

#### Brockhill, Surrey
*Location and stratigraphic context*: This assemblage is of particular significance since it offers the closest typological and technological parallels with the Hengistbury material. The assemblage contains 194 retouched tools and over 1,500 other artefacts (Cox 1976) making it one of the richest Late Upper Palaeolithic reference collections available from S. Britain. The Brockhill site lies a few kilometres NW of Woking in Surrey, on a slight rise overlooking the Parley Brook. It owes its discovery to Mr H P Lawson who collected artefacts from ploughed fields in the early 1920s (Smith 1924; Hooper 1933).

From contemporary descriptions it appears that the finds occurred in sands, above lower Bagshot (Tertiary) sands (Smith 1924). As at Hengistbury, the sands are heavily podzolised, and according to Smith (1924) the flints came from within a concreted iron pan which lay 1 ft 6 in to 2 ft 6 in beneath the contemporary landsurface.

In recent years attempts by the Mayford History Society and the British Museum to re-locate the site (Bonsall 1977) have shown that a large part of the original area has been destroyed. A detailed report of the finds is still awaiting full publication (Bonsall in prep) and what follows only briefly summarises some of the main characteristics of the assemblage as they relate to Hengistbury.

*Debitage*: The flint collection consists predominantly of blade and flake debitage with very few cores. There is no indication whether this is a factor of site function

*Table 4.29 Brockhill: retouched tools in the BM collection (nominal totals).*

|  | No | % |
|---|---|---|
| End-scrapers | 50 | 25.9 |
| Composite tools | 3 | 1.5 |
| Piercers/becs/*Zinken* | 7 | 3.6 |
| Burins | 49 | 25.2 |
| Truncations | 19 | 9.8 |
| Notches/denticulates | (?)3 | 1.5 |
| Backed blades/bladelets | 40 | 20.7 |
| Shouldered points | 4 | 2.1 |
| Retouched flakes | 9 | 4.6 |
| Miscellaneous retouch | 10 | 5.2 |
| Total | 194 | 100.1 |

or due to some form of collecting bias, but it is note-worthy that a significant number of the blades and flakes are cortical, and belong to the earlier stages of reduction. The presence of crested pieces and core tablets also provides ample evidence for local core reduction episodes. In this respect it is relevant that over half of the cores are much reduced multiplatform examples.

A small sample of 110 blades and bladelets was examined by the writer for their butt features. This revealed a high percentage of plain and punctiform types (70.9% and 13.6%, respectively), with lesser frequencies of faceted (7.3%), linear (5.4%), dihedral (1.8%) and cortical (0.9%) types. A high proportion of butts also display signs of heavy platform abrasion. These technological attributes are very similar to the ones observed in the Hengistbury collection (Table 4.31).

*Retouched tools: comparisons with Hengistbury*: The British Museum collection consists of a nominal total of 194 retouched tools, although many other flakes and blades have notches or discontinuous areas of retouch consistent with the effects of modern plough damage.

4Of the 50 end-scrapers, most are made on flakes (40), nine on blades and one is on an unidentifiable fragment. Typologically, the majority of examples are simple end-scrapers, and are comparable to those recovered from Hengistbury. Over two thirds of the simple flake end-scrapers are on short blanks, less than 40 mm in length. Other types include thumbnail and atypical forms but these are relatively uncommon. There is one double end-scraper. A dissimilarity with Hengistbury is the apparent absence of end-scrapers on retouched blades.

Burins make up a large proportion (25.2%) of the retouched tool assemblage. Of the total of 49 burins, 17 are dihedral burins, 19 are truncation burins, while there are six multiple mixed burins. The remaining seven examples are too broken to classify. The burins are generally simple with one facet making up the burin edge in the majority of cases. Like Hengistbury, the tools are made on fairly thick blanks (over two thirds of them being thicker than 10 mm) and are characterised by wide burin facets. The fact that ten burin spalls have also been recovered and one can be refitted (onto an asymmetrical dihedral burin) shows that tools were made and re-sharpened on site.

Together with burins and end-scrapers, backed blades and bladelets comprise some of the most important elements of the tool assemblage. There are 40 tools in this group. Although many of them are broken (over 50%) sometimes making identification difficult, very few of the complete pieces are curved in profile or end in points. Typologically, the tools can be described as straight-backed blades, very similar to those found at Hengistbury. The blanks are fairly thin being less than 6 mm thick, but are mostly made on broad pieces over 9mm wide, placing them within the backed blade cate-gory (see Glossary for size definition). The retouch on the tools is nearly always direct and abrupt, and located down the whole of one edge.

There are four backed and truncated pieces which are similar to 'Creswell points' and three backed tools with straight distal truncations. Two other pieces are retouched down both edges; one of them is a very large backed knife measuring 87 mm long. It very closely resembles one of the Hengistbury tools (Fig. 4.23, 14). The collection also includes four shouldered points, which are also truncated and are paralleled in the Hengistbury assemblage (cf. Fig. 4.25). An unusual feature of one of the tools is the presence of cortex on its left edge. A flexional snap at the distal end of this tool resembles an impact fracture.

There are nineteen single truncations and two bi-truncated pieces (not to be confused with Cheddar points). With the exception of one tool all of the truncated pieces are made on relatively wide supports ranging from 14–29 mm with thicknesses varying between 4–8 mm.

Despite obvious parallels with Hengistbury, there are also several points of divergence between the two assemblages. In the first place the Hengistbury collection contains very few piercers or becs and no examples of *Zinken*. At Brockhill seven tools may be classified in this group and all of them are single examples. They include four simple *Zinken* (cf. Schwabedissen 1954; Brézillon 1977b), only one of which may be regarded as typical (see Glossary for definition). The other tools consist of two piercers and a bec. One of the piercers is less than 35 mm long and resembles a *microperçoir* (cf. Leroi-Gourhan and Brézillon 1972, Fig. 28). A further significant difference is in the absence at the Surrey site of intentionally broken artefacts or tools made on flake or blade segments. As we have seen, these form a recognisable element in the Hengistbury assemblage. Finally, whereas the burins and some of the becs at Hengistbury display signs of heavy use, these are generally lacking on the Brockhill tools. If this is not merely the result of the Brockhill tools being unused, it might point to considerable contrasts in site activities and in tool function.

*Titchwell, Norfolk*
*General details*: The second large collection of Late Upper Palaeolithic material derives from an eroding shoreline on the north Norfolk coast, overlooking the Wash. The site has been visited since the early 1980s by two experienced flint collectors (Mr G Drown and Mr T Sharman) who between them have collected more than 500 flint artefacts, including about 46 retouched tools of Late Glacial type. Limited fieldwork, subsequently undertaken by Mr J Wymer of the Norfolk Archaeological Unit, has now added important details relating to the stratigraphic context of the finds. The results of this work are currently being prepared for publication (Barton and Wymer in prep).

*Location and stratigraphic context*: The area concerned is a 2–3 km stretch of beach on the North

Norfolk coast at approximately (NGR) TF 756450, more or less equidistant between the village boundaries of Titchwell and Thornham. The beach and tidal flats are composed of sand and shingle deposits which form a gently sloping shelf extending several kilometres beyond the coast into the North Sea.

Most of the flint artefacts have been picked up on the gravelly beach at low tide in the intertidal zone. Recent fieldwork by Mr J Wymer has shown that the finds probably originate from within a Late Devensian clay deposit overlain by a series of Holocene peats (Wymer pers. comm.). Up until now only very few *in situ* finds have been recorded, but these include a large opposed platform blade core and a backed blade, both clearly of Upper Palaeolithic type. These finds were embedded in the top of the clay, which is weathered and has the appearance of a palaeosol (Wymer pers. comm.). The only relevant radiocarbon and pollen dating evidence so far to emerge relates to the formation of the organic deposits overlying the archaeological horizon. This suggests that the peat began to form in the period of the Zone V–VI transition (*c.* 9,000 BP), and gives only *a terminus ante quem* for the underlying flint industry. It is possible, therefore, that the Titchwell assemblage is considerably younger than either that of Hengistbury or Brockhill.

### The artefact assemblage
*Raw material*: The artefacts recovered are all made of flint derived from the local Cretaceous Chalk bedrock, which outcrops in the vicinity of the site. The flint used is the same high-quality raw material available throughout much of East Anglia. The fact that the raw material is available in large nodules presumably accounts in part for the large size of the blade industry.

*Debitage*: Among the artefacts represented in the collection and examined by the writer are blade cores with blade and bladelet debitage. The unretouched waste also comprises flakes and the products of core rejuvenation such as crested pieces and core tablets.

The majority of cores are of opposed platform prismatic type (10 out of 19). They range in size from 39–188 mm in length and include several bladelet cores (Fig. 4.67, 3). The prismatic cores are typified by plain striking platforms with other examples of preparation (e.g. faceting or partial faceting) being relatively uncommon. This is reflected in the blade butts which also show fairly low percentages of faceted examples (Table 4.31). Cresting modification which is found on many of the backs and/or sides of the Hengistbury blade cores is more or less absent.

A sample of blades measured by Wymer show a broad spread in lengths ranging from 26–207 mm. Mean maximum length x breadth x thickness dimensions are 72±29.3 x 22±8.2 x 8±3.4 mm, respectively (n=99). As in the Hengistbury assemblage there is no clear separation between blades and bladelets with one size of blank naturally grading into the other. The blades are typically straight and relatively narrow. A

Table 4.30    *Titchwell: retouched tools in the Kings Lynn Museum collection (nominal totals).*

|  | No | % |
|---|---|---|
| End-scrapers | 26 | 53.0 |
| Composite tools | 1 | 2.0 |
| Burins | 9 | 18.4 |
| Truncations | 4 | 8.2 |
| Backed blades/bladelets | 3 | 6.1 |
| Microliths | 1 | 2.0 |
| Retouched blades | 2 | 4.1 |
| Miscellaneous retouch | 3 | 6.1 |
| Total | 49 | 99.9 |

study of the butts by the writer revealed a clear predominance of plain (60%) and punctiform (17%) types (n=161). A smaller proportion of pieces displayed faceted butts (9.3%), whilst linear (5.3%), dihedral (2%) and cortical (0.6%) examples were all but absent (Fig. 4.32).

Bulbar surface features indicate that the hard hammer flaking mode was apparently seldom used in the production of blades. Fairly commonly represented are the characteristic stigmata of the soft hammer (18%) or a presumed soft stone alternative (31%), but many of the bulbar surfaces (45%) were undiagnostic.

*Retouched tools:* At the time of writing the assemblage consists of under 50 retouched tools. Nevertheless this figure will doubtless continue to rise as more material is collected from the beach. The tools are all characterised by the same black-staining which typifies the Upper Palaeolithic blade debitage. Not included is a small but significant number of Neolithic and Bronze Age artefacts which can be distinguished typologically and by the lesser degree of surface discoloration. The Upper Palaeolithic collection consists of end-scrapers, burins, backed blades and truncations. Also tentatively included are a microlith and several miscellaneous retouched pieces (Table 4.30).

End-scrapers, which are the most common tool form, are made on both blade (13) and flake (10) supports, with the rest being double end-scrapers. The relatively high proportion of scrapers made on the ends of blades is not a feature shared with either the Hengistbury or Brockhill assemblages, where the majority are made on flakes. At Titchwell this may simply have been in response to the plentiful supplies of high quality raw material.

The nine burins in the collection consist of three burins on truncation and six dihedral examples. The tools are generally made on thinner blanks than those from either Hengistbury or Brockhill. Most of them appear on blade supports with average length x breadth x thickness dimensions of 70±24.1 x 28±7.7 x 14±7.2 mm.

Numerically speaking, backed blades (3) are too poorly represented to allow more than a few general observations. They consist of two broken mesial fragments (one with a possible 'impact fracture', Fig. 4.67, 4)

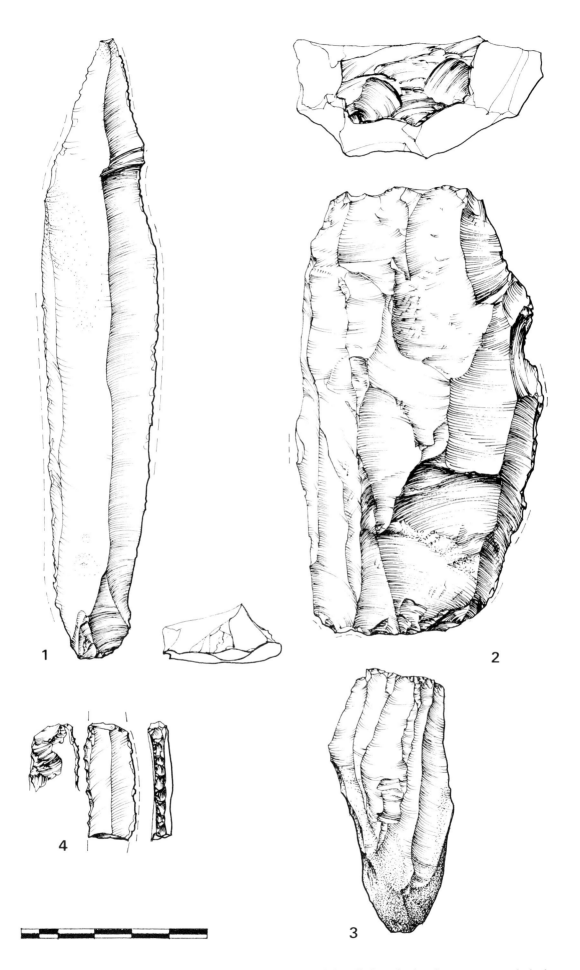

4.67  *Titchwell: debitage and retouched tools. 1= unretouched blade (slightly rolled) with plain butt; 2= opposed platform blade core with faceted platform; 3= single platform bladelet core; 4= backed blade. Centimetre scale.*

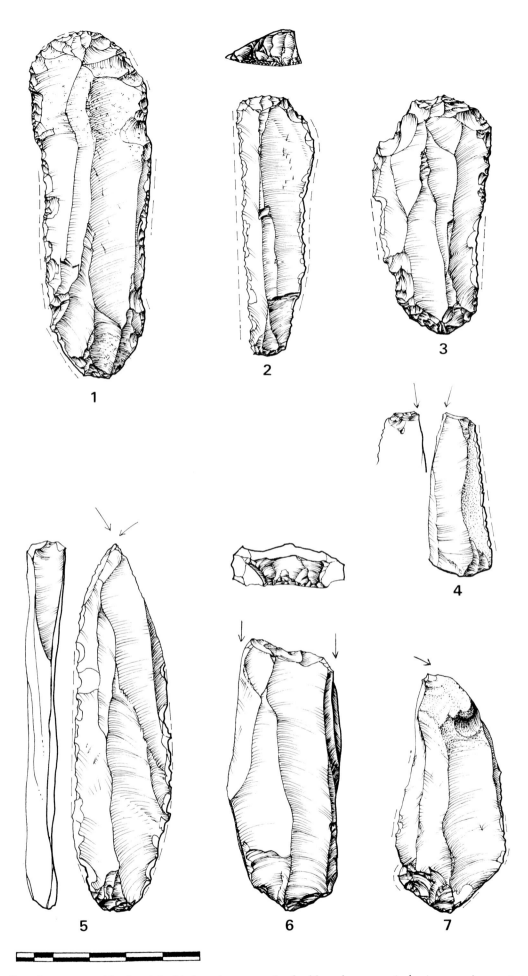

4.68   *Titchwell: end-scrapers and burins. 1-2= blade end-scrapers; 3= double end-scraper; 4= burin on an inverse proximal truncation; 5= symmetrical dihedral burin; 6= multiple burin on a concave truncation; 7= dihedral transverse burin.*

and an angle-backed piece snapped at the proximal end. The latter was the only backed item to have been found *in situ*. It comes from the top of the clay and is typologically similar to a Creswell point (Campbell 1977; Jacobi 1980). Such tools are known from various open-air findspots (Jacobi 1980), including Hengistbury and Brockhill.

There are four tools with single truncations, of which three are oblique and one is straight. The straight truncation is made on the distal end of a large flake. One of the oblique truncations occurs at the distal end of a blade blank but is otherwise comparable to an obliquely blunted microlith (cf. Clark 1934a).

Finally, there are two blades with scalariform bilateral retouch similar to that which occurs on *lames magdaléniennes*. One of the blades is snapped at a point just below the tip and it is possible that the retouch converged to form a bec which was subsequently broken.

*Discussion*: Neither the Brockhill, nor the Titchwell lithic assemblages come from well-dated contexts. Nevertheless, on typological and technological grounds they show much closer similarities to Hengistbury than to any of the Creswellian cave assemblages. In particular, Brockhill with its straight-backed blades, shouldered points and burins made on thick blanks offers the closest analogies with Hengistbury. Although the retouched tool inventory from Titchwell is largely devoid of any backed material, it is noteworthy that the only angle-backed piece so far recorded is not a trapezoidal Cheddar point. The debitage from this collection also displays few parallels with the Creswellian assemblages. The continued absence of any large open-air assemblages with Cheddar points may be a reflection of a distribution pattern more apparent than real. For example, such finds are known to occur in poorly stratified open-air collections in the Netherlands (Bohmers 1960). It would therefore not be surprising if assemblages containing these forms, but accompanied by blade technologies distinct from those of Hengistbury type, were eventually to come to light in lowland Britain.

Perhaps the clearest contrast so far to emerge between the cave and open-air assemblages is in different styles of lithic debitage (Table 4.31). This is best illustrated in the methods of core reduction and platform preparation identified, on the one hand in the Gough's Cave assemblage, and on the other in lithic collections from open-air sites such as Hengistbury. In particular the blades from the Cheddar Gorge site show a relatively high percentage of faceted butts which can be contrasted with a predominance of plain and punctiform types at each of the open-air sites reviewed. This feature need not simply be a response to raw material constraints, as the examples of Titchwell (local sources) and Hengistbury (non-local sources) would appear to show. The differences in the blade butt morphology also suggest that the presence or absence of tool-types such as straight-backed blades

Table 4.31 *Comparisons between British Late Upper Palaeolithic sites: blade butt indices (percentages)*

| | Plain/ punctiform | Faceted | Dihedral faceted | Cortical | Linear |
|---|---|---|---|---|---|
| Hengistbury | 85.4 | 11.5 | 2.4 | 0.6 | – |
| Brockhill | 84.5 | 7.3 | 1.8 | 0.9 | 5.4 |
| Titchwell | 82.8 | 9.3 | 2.0 | 0.6 | 5.3 |
| Gough's Cave | 37.9 | 49.5 | 5.3 | 0.0 | 7.4 |

and trapezoidal points is not simply a result of functional variability between the open-air and cave locations. If the open-air occurrences are contemporary with the Creswellian ones, as seems possible, it indicates a much greater diversity in the British Late Glacial record than previously acknowledged.

*Other open-air findspots in Britain*: At least 30 related Late Upper Palaeolithic open-air findspots are known, mostly from Southern Britain (Campbell 1977; Jacobi 1980). The artefacts concerned are generally isolated examples and derive from surface collections, so the main basis for comparison often rests on observations of typological similarity alone.

Amongst diagnostic finds from the open-air sites are retouched tools such as large tanged points and shouldered points, although the latter as noted above also occur in Creswellian contexts and should therefore be interpreted with caution. Except for Hengistbury, tanged and shouldered tools appear in combination at only one other open-air site at Cranwich in Norfolk, although the tanged artefact is considered by some, including myself, to be of Post-Palaeolithic type (Wymer 1971; Jacobi and Martingell 1980; Jacobi 1980).

Individual examples of large tanged points have been found at various sites in Essex. These include ones at Widford Brickpit, Chelmsford, Stone Point near Walton-on-the-Naze, and from an unprovenanced location near Manningtree (Jacobi 1981a) and one from Bolton and Laughlin's Pit, Ipswich (Moir 1932; Jacobi 1975, Fig. I.13). Other tanged points are recorded from Sussex at Newhouse Farm, Buxted (Woodcock 1978; Jacobi 1981a) and from Hampshire at Headley and at Oakhanger Site VII (Jacobi 1980), the latter showing a completely different patina from the rest of the predominantly Mesolithic assemblage. The most northerly open-air occurrence of a large tanged point apparently comes from Brumby Woods in Humberside (Jacobi 1980).

Shouldered points similar to the Hengistbury ones are documented from more numerous findspots, some of which are shown in Figure 4.69. Geographically closest to Hengistbury are the finds from Rush Corner Cemetery, Bournemouth (Campbell 1977) and Long Island, near Portsmouth Harbour in Hampshire (Draper 1962; Campbell 1977). A further Hampshire

4.69 *English open-air findspots of larged tanged points and shouldered points (after Jacobi 1980, with additions). Key: Solid circles= shouldered points; open circles= large tanged points; Split circles= shouldered points and large tanged points. 1= Hengistbury Head; 2= Cranwich; 3= Oakhanger site VII; 4= Headley; 5= Brumby Wood; 6= Newhouse Farm; 7= Widford Brickpit; 8= Manningtree; 9= Stone Point; 10= Bolton and Laughlin's pit; 11= Brockhill; 12= Rush Corner; 13= Long Island; 14= Fir Hill, Kingsley; 15= Stonewall Park; 16= Oare; 17= Shoeburyness; 18= Wandsworth; 19= Wallington; 20= Salmonby.*

example was found at Fir Hill, Kingsley (Jacobi 1980). Individual shouldered pieces have also been recorded from Kent (Stonewall Park and Oare), Greater London (Wallington and Wandsworth), Essex (Shoeburyness), Suffolk (Oat Hill, Wangford) and Norfolk (Cranwich),

all of which are cited in Jacobi (1980).

Apart from these finds there are a several small artefact collections from the Bournemouth area which are probably of Late Upper Palaeolithic type and individually bear certain similarities to the material from

4.70 *Late Upper Palaeolithic open-air findspots in the Bournemouth area. 1= Hengistbury Head; 2= the Hengistbury bird sanctuary; 3= Tuckton; 4= Iford; 5= Rush Corner cemetery; 6= Little Down Common, Pokesdown; 7= Bendigo Road; 8= Bosley; 9= Ensbury Park; 10= Dudsbury; 11= Ameysford, Ferndown; 12= Lower Close.*

Hengistbury (I would like to acknowledge Roger Jacobi's part in drawing to my attention some of this material). Most notable amongst these collections are the straight-backed blade and blade debitage finds from Ameysford, Ferndown; a shouldered piece from Ensbury Park; and at Hengistbury itself various backed artefacts in the area of the 'Nursery' on the low-lying northern side of the Headland. To these findspots can probably now be added several others (Fig. 4.70) which have produced well-made blades of the same size range as the Hengistbury debitage and displaying many resemblances in the butt characteristics.

### 4.10.5 *Hengistbury Head and its continental affinities*

*Introduction:* During the last glacial maximum much of Europe north of the Loire and west of the Oder seems to have been humanly deserted (Hahn 1979; Gamble 1986). Indeed, across much of the NW European land area, population levels may have dropped so low that signs of human activity appear to be practically invisible before about 14,000 radiocarbon years ago (Jacobi 1980). The increase in the num-

ber of recorded archaeological occurrences in these areas after this time seems to have been partly a response to the climatic amelioration referred to in 4.10.2 above. It is therefore reasonable to suppose that the British peninsula only became more permanently resettled once population levels had risen significantly on the NW European mainland. In consequence, it is to these areas of the neighbouring mainland that our search now turns for possible antecedents of or parallels with the British Later Upper Palaeolithic.

The occurrence of specialised hunting economies during the Late Glacial is characterised in NW Europe by two broad technological groupings: the Late Magdalenian (de Sonneville-Bordes 1960; Leroi-Gourhan and Brézillon 1966) and the Hamburgian (Rust 1937). For many authors, these are regarded as closely related technologies which co-existed from the first phase of the Late Glacial Interstadial (*c.* 13,000 BP). Also now suspected of being present at this time are a number of other technologies which overlap geographically with the Late Magdalenian and the Hamburgian, but in many ways are distinctive from these groupings. Some hint of a dichotomy in the archaeological record is provided in France, Belgium and the Netherlands where sites of Late Magdalenian type occur alongside ones of a more British Creswellian type. Similarly, in N Germany there would appear to be a temporal and spatial overlap between Hamburgian assemblages and those often described as 'early Federmesser' type. In each of these areas, therefore, there seems to be evidence for different technological responses to the contemporary Late Glacial environment. By the same token, a similar diversity might also reasonably be expected in the indigenous lithic assemblages of the British Isles.

*Late Magdalenian*: The Late Magdalenian is considered to have its antecedents in the Upper Palaeolithic traditions of SW France (de Sonneville-Bordes 1969). The Hamburgian although previously regarded as having an eastern origin (Rust 1937, 1943), is today considered to be more closely related to the Magdalenian (Bohmers 1960; Burdukiewicz 1981). On the other hand, few still believe that the two technologies are so closely connected that they represent merely seasonal variants of the same social grouping (cf. Sturdy 1975).

Various distinctions may be drawn between the Late Magdalenian and Hamburgian on the basis of the lithic equipment and flaking technology. Some divergence can also be recognised, though to a lesser extent, in the methods of bone-and antler-working. The open-air sites of the Paris Basin (Leroi-Gourhan and Brézillon 1966, 1972; Audouze 1987) are regarded as highly representative of this Late Magdalenian technology. The retouched tools are characterised by straight-backed blades and bladelets, piercers, burins (usually on truncation), end-of-blade scrapers, truncated blades and *pièces esquillées*. There is also a tendency for burins to outnumber end-scrapers. Similar combinations of forms have been found northwards into Belgium (Vermeersch 1981; Vermeersch and Symens 1988) and the Netherlands (Arts and Deeben 1987) and eastwards across the Rhine Valley (Bolus *et al.* 1988) into East Germany and Czechoslovakia (Desbrosse and Kozlowski 1988). These assemblages are not just confined to open-air stations, but occur in the caves of limestone regions from the Ardennes in Belgium (Arts and Deeben 1987; Dewez 1987) to the Swabian Alb (Albrecht 1979).

The Late Magdalenian lithic debitage reflects a high degree of standardisation in blank manufacture. This is manifest in core reduction by the preparation of frontal and dorsal crests and the special attention which is given to the core platform edge. A particular hallmark is also the *talon à éperon* (Karlin in Leroi-Gourhan and Brézillon 1972), a characteristic blade butt attribute, found in lithic assemblages ranging from those of the Paris Basin to Belgium (Vermeersch *et al.* 1987), the Netherlands (Arts pers. comm.), N Germany (Veil pers. comm.) and the Central Rhineland (Bosinski and Hahn 1972).

Bone and antler equipment associated with the Late Magdalenian occurs over a wide area of NW Europe

and its characteristics may be shared with other technologies. For example bevelled-based bone and antler *sagaies* found at Trou de Chaleux, Grotte de Verlaine, Grotte de Goyet and Grotte de Coléoptère can be duplicated at the British cave sites of Fox Hole and Victoria Cave. The presence of a bevelled-based *sagaie* is also recorded from the Hamburgian level at Stellmoor (Rust 1943). Other widely distributed technological traits include the use of groove-and-splintering to obtain blanks for points of bone, antler and ivory. The technique is evidenced both in the Late Magdalenian (e.g. Dewez 1987; Veil 1979) and in the Hamburgian (Rust 1943; Bolus *et al.* 1988). Conversely, finished items of bone needles, needle cores or *bâtons percés* are very uncommon in the Hamburgian but this may be due to task specialisation or simply the result of poorer organic preservation at open-air locations in the North European Plain. Finally, the suggestion of long distance contacts between the Hamburgian and Late Magdalenian has sometimes been employed to explain likenesses in the decorated rods from Poggenwisch, N Germany and Isturitz in SW France (Bosinski 1978).

*Hamburgian*: Assemblages of this kind were first described in the Hamburg region of N Germany (Rust 1937, 1943). They have a more northerly distribution than those of the Late Magdalenian and, unlike the latter, are known exclusively from open-air locations. They can be shown to occupy a similar time range to Magdalenian sites (Table 4.32). Geographically, such assemblages cover a wide area of the North European Plain, extending as far east as Poland (Burdukiewicz 1981). Faunal remains from the German sites of Meiendorf and Stellmoor indicate a specialised reindeer hunting economy with the sites apparently occupied during the spring and autumn migration periods (Sturdy 1975; Bokelmann 1979). Such subsistence strategies have been contrasted with Magdalenian ones, where, in addition to horse and reindeer, smaller mammals such as the arctic hare were exploited. It has further been suggested that Magdalenian economic activities may have focused upon woodland areas on a year-round, rather than seasonal basis (Burdukiewicz 1981). However, data from the Paris Basin open-air sites and the caves of the Swabian Jura appear to contradict this model, indicating instead the importance of large seasonal kills in the Magdalenian economy (Audouze 1987).

The Hamburgian lithic assemblages display an important blade component with blades detached from single platform and opposed platform cores (Hahn in Leroi-Gourhan 1988). Like the Magdalenian, the blade cores often show signs of careful preparation. Blade butts apparently include a fairly high percentage of faceted types (Hartz 1987), but not enough studies of Hamburgian assemblages have yet been published to know whether this is part of a coherent pattern. For direct comparisons it would be interesting to see, for example, whether individual platforms were deliberately isolated (cf. Magdalenian *en éperon* technique) or simply whether faceting was employed mainly for adjusting the platform angle (cf. Hengistbury).

The most characteristic retouched tools in these assemblages are shouldered Hamburg(ian) points and *Zinken*, frequently with prongs at both ends of the blank (Hahn in Leroi-Gourhan 1988, also see Glossary this volume). Other tools within this inventory include end-of-blade scrapers, burins on truncations (usually outnumbering other burin types) and truncated bladelets. There are also non-geometric microlith forms (Rust 1937), but unlike Late Magdalenian assemblages straight-backed blades and bladelets are rare or absent. At Stellmoor and Poggenwisch the shouldered points sometimes show an additional proximal truncation forming a projecting 'spur' at the same extremity. This latter feature has parallels in some of the shouldered points from British cave assemblages (Jacobi pers. comm.), but is missing from the Hengistbury tools.

The bone and antler equipment from Hamburgian sites has been mentioned above. Apart from stylistic variation in some of the barbed material, the bone and antler artefacts show few essential differences with those of the Late Magdalenian. Amongst items not paralleled in Magdalenian assemblages are the antler slotted knife handles (*riemen schneide*) present at the site of Stellmoor (Rust 1943).

*Creswello-Tjongerian or Creswello-Hamburgian*: Another Late Glacial technology, believed to be wholly or partly contemporary with the Late Magdalenian and the Hamburgian, occurs in Belgium. The lithic technology is considered by some to have close taxonomic links with the British Creswellian and, depending upon present interpretation, with either the local Tjongerian (Dewez 1979, 1988) or the more geographically widespread Hamburgian (Otte 1984). The use of these equivalent terms underlines some of the current difficulties experienced with European Upper Palaeolithic nomenclature, but it also demonstrates the level of diversity apparent in technologies of this kind. Whatever the terminological problems, it is generally acknowledged that the Creswellian-like lithic assemblages are quite distinct from Magdalenian ones. These differences may be seen in the typology and technology, as well as the type of find location. Whereas Late Magdalenian material has been recovered from both caves and open-air sites in Belgium (Vermeersch 1979), Creswellian-like material seems to be more heavily restricted to caves and rockshelters (Dewez 1987).

The earliest dating evidence for the Creswello-Tjongerian comes from the site of Trou des Blaireaux, Vaucelles. Although emanating from a bulked sample, the radiocarbon date of 12,440±180 BP accords well with the rest of the dated sequence and there is no reason to doubt its integrity (Bellier and Cattelain 1984). A similarly early date has recently been produced for the Trou de l'Ossuaire (Léotard and Otte 1988) and these would seem to confirm a chronological overlap with the Late Magdalenian at the Grotte du Coléoptère (Dewez 1987). The Belgian Creswelloid assemblages differ from the Late Magdalenian ones in a number of important respects. First, unlike the Magdalenian, the retouched tools include many angle-backed blades of single truncated (Creswell) type as well as bi-truncated trapezoidal (Cheddar) forms. There are few if any straight-backed tools which are more usually associated with the Late Magdalenian. Further discordance may be recognised in the bone and antler equipment (Dewez 1987), which does not contain the same richness or diversity of artefacts or the same technological traits (e.g. the seeming absence of the groove and splinter technique). According to Dewez (1987) there are also fewer examples of engraved and decorated bone and antler items within the Creswello-Tjongerian, with a tendency towards the use of more schematic designs. Other possible cultural differences may be detectable in the less extensive use of red ochre in these assemblages and the presence of fossil marine shells of Atlantic origin (Dewez 1988).

*Final Magdalenian and contemporary technologies*: Another set of technologies, as yet ill-defined, may have co-existed or partially overlapped with those previously mentioned. On the strength of the very limited dating evidence available it would appear that this loosely-defined grouping becomes more predominant in the early Allerød stage of the Late Glacial Interstadial. Its appearance in the Pre-Allerød seems to reflect both the increasing technological diversity in the archaeological record of this period and a greater sense of fissioning and regionalisation in contemporary lithic technologies.

The appearance of *Nordic* elements within the Late Magdalenian is believed by various French authors (e.g. de Sonneville-Bordes 1963; Bordes *et al.* 1974; Allain 1976; Schmider 1979) to signify a final 'evolved' stage of the Magdalenian. Typically, these assemblages contain so-called North-European forms such as shouldered points, angle-backed points, *Zinken* and truncated bladelets (Allain 1976; Schmider 1981, 1987), but usually only in very small quantities or as minor components of much larger assemblages. Exceptionally, as in the case of the Paris Basin site of Cepoy (Allain 1974) shouldered points and angle-backed forms actually outnumber straight-backed blades and bladelets which is unusual for a Late Magdalenian lithic assemblage. Despite a greater similarity with the Hamburgian, this assemblage is considered atypical of the latter due to an absence of microlithic forms (cf. Rust 1943) and differences in the typology of endscrapers (Allain 1976; Kobusiewicz 1983). Unfortunately, secure dating evidence is presently lacking, but if the assemblage is homogeneous, as the excavators believe, it is possible that it represents a slightly later Magdalenian grouping. Such a suggestion has previously been made for the nearby site of Marsangy (Table 4.32), on the basis of so-called *Nordic* influences (Schmider 1979). It should be remembered, however, that potentially *Nordic* forms (e.g. *Zinken*-like becs) have also been recovered at earlier Late

Magdalenian sites such as Habitation 1 at Pincevent (Newcomer pers. comm., Table 4.32).

The appearance of *Nordic* forms in Late Magdalenian assemblages may be traceable to earlier phases of the Upper Palaeolithic in SW France, and they have been recorded for example in Magdalenian III contexts (Rigaud 1970, 1979). However, in central and eastern parts of the country, it could be argued that toolkits combining straight-backed blades, shouldered forms and angle-backed blades are more likely to belong to the Late Glacial and may be contemporary with pre-Allerød and Allerød assemblages further north. Thus, for example, recent excavations in the French Jura (David 1984) at the Cabones rockshelter (also known as Ranchot) have produced tools of this kind from within a level dating to between 12,620±250 BP and 11,520±191 BP, while just south of the Loire, at the Bourdois rockshelter (part of Roc-aux-Sorciers) a date of 11,265±130 BP (Guillien and Saint-Mathurin 1976) was obtained for the *Nordic* Magdalenian level, although the excavators believe the radiocarbon date to be erroneous. It is noteworthy that in both these cases, as with others in the Jura (Combier and Desbrosse 1964) and the Haute Loire (Alaux 1972), large tanged *Teyjat* points number among the flint artefacts. This tool is obviously of special relevance to Hengistbury, where potentially *Nordic* elements (large tanged points) are found in combination with shouldered points and backed pieces in a well-dated Late Glacial context.

The presence of large tanged points is of course not wholly restricted to the French or British Late Upper Palaeolithic. Similar examples are recorded in the Scandinavian Bromme assemblages but none so far can be shown to be of pre-Allerød age (Fischer and Mortensen 1977; Fischer and Nielsen 1987). Although most findspots of this kind are concentrated in S Scandinavia, the distribution does extend further south and east into Northern Germany (Taute 1968) and Poland (Chmielewski *et al.* 1975), where an Allerød dating is also considered acceptable (Schild 1988). Over most of its distribution area, Bromme assemblages are characterised by a very simplified lithic toolkit consisting of burins, end-scrapers and large tanged points (Andersen 1988). Structurally and technologically, there are few obvious parallels between the Bromme and British or French assemblages. For example, the Bromme assemblages lack a small blade and bladelet component. The blades are typically thick and detached from single-platform pyramidal cores using a predominantly hard-hammer technique (Madsen 1983; Barton 1986b; Andersen 1988). Absent from the Bromme inventory are tools such as shouldered points and straight-backed forms.

Across the North European Plain assemblages collectively referred to as 'Federmesser' (Schwabedissen 1954; Taute 1968) may have existed side by side with those of Late Hamburgian type. Part of the *Rissen group* of Federmesser industries has been described as having close typological affinities with the Late

Magdalenian (Schwabedissen 1954). At Rissen 14 this is exemplified by a toolkit combining straight-backed blades and a large tanged point. The assemblage is stratified above a band of organic mud dating to 11,930±290 BP and 11,500±280 BP (Schwabedissen 1957) and would therefore seem to be no earlier in age than Allerød. Similar assemblages, containing backed blades and shouldered points (Rissen 15) or combinations of these forms with tanged material (Rissen 15a), are identified as variants of the Rissen group but these collections are currently undated. Mace (1959) has already pointed to the apparent similarities between the material from Rissen and Hengistbury Head. However, not all of the N German assemblages with backed blades (non-Hamburgian) need neccessarily be of the same age. For example, Bokelmann (1983) has recently identified a pre-Allerød site in Schleswig-Holstein which appears to be neither Hamburgian nor Late Magdalenian and may instead belong to an early Federmesser or other technology. Finally, there is some suggestion in the Netherlands that the Hamburgian survives into the Allerød (Stapert *et al.* 1986) and overlaps substantially with the local Federmesser.

In the Southern Netherlands, although reliable dating evidence is still largely lacking, it is believed that Federmesser assemblages containing angle-backed material and straight-backed blades (Arts 1988) form a chronological continuum with Late Magdalenian settlement in the same area. Further south in Belgium technological developments in parallel with the Magdalenian have already been mentioned above. Recently excavated evidence suggests that the Creswello-Tjongerian continued to develop locally throughout the Allerød and possibly into the Youngest Dryas (Dewez pers. comm.). During the Allerød, however, assemblages with fewer angle-backed or shouldered forms occur. The appearance of thick curved-backed elements in them signifies the existence of the true Tjongerian (Lauwers 1988).

In the area of the Somme Valley in NW France exists another technology which seems to be restricted to that region and again may be broadly contemporary with the Latest Magdalenian. Recent work in this area (Fagnart 1984a, 1984b, 1988) has brought to light artefacts variously described by him as 'continental Creswellian' and 'Federmesser'. These assemblages are in fact structurally very similar to the ones from Hengistbury and Brockhill, which the present writer would prefer to separate from the British Creswellian by using the term 'straight-backed blade assemblages'. The best documented of the North French collections comes from three locations only a few hundred metres apart and close to the hamlet of Etouvie, near Amiens. Because of their apparent resemblance to the S English material they are described in some detail below.

The assemblages from Dreuil-lès-Amiens and the nearby gravel pits (la petite gravière and la gravière Jourdain) show a strong blade component and contain many opposed platform cores. The blades make up between 29.2% and 24.8% of the debitage and are

Table 4.32 Selected dates from Late Magdalenian and Hamburgian sites in NW Europe.

| Lab No | Sample | Findspot | Date (BP) | Ref. |
|---|---|---|---|---|
| **Late Magdalenian (France)** | | | | |
| OxA–138 | bone | Etiolles Foyer N20 | 12,990±300 | 1 |
| OxA–139 | bone | Etiolles Foyer N20 | 13,000±300 | 1 |
| OxA–173 | bone | Etiolles Foyer N20 | 12,800±220 | 1 |
| OxA–175 | bone | Etiolles Foyer N20 | 12,900±220 | 1 |
| OxA–148 | bone | Pincevent IV Upper level | 12,600±200 | 1 |
| OxA–149 | bone | Pincevent IV Upper level | 12,400±200 | 1 |
| OxA–177 | bone | Pincevent IV Upper level | 12,300±220 | 1 |
| Ly–3404 | charcoal | Verberie | 12,590±180 | 2 |
| OxA–730 | bone | Ville-St-Jacques C–151 | 12,300±160 | 3 |
| OxA–731 | bone | Ville-St-Jacques C–151 | 12,240±160 | 3 |
| OxA–740 | reindeer tooth | Marsangy C14–85 | 12,120±200 | 3 |
| OxA–178 | reindeer antler | Marsangy B12–35 | 11,600±200 | 4 |
| **Late Magdalenian (Belgium)** | | | | |
| LV–690 | bone fragments | Grotte de Verlaine | 13,780±220 | 5 |
| LV–1593 | bone fragments | Grotte de Walou | 13,120±190 | 6 |
| LV–1582 | bone fragments | Grotte de Walou | 13,030±140 | 6 |
| LV–1569 | bone fragments | Grotte de Chaleux | 12,990±140 | 6 |
| LV–1136 | bonefragments | Grotte de Chaleux | 12,710±150 | 6 |
| LV–1568 | bone fragments | Grotte de Chaleux | 12,370±170 | 6 |
| LV–717 | bone fragments | Grotte du Coléoptère | 12,400±110 | 5 |
| LV–686 | bone fragments | Grotte du Coléoptère | 12,150±150 | 5 |
| **Hamburgian (N Germany)** | | | | |
| K–4331 | reindeer bone | Poggenwisch | 12,440±115 | 7 |
| K–4332 | reindeer bone | Poggenwisch | 12,570±115 | 7 |
| K–4577 | reindeer bone | Poggenwisch | 12,440±115 | 7 |
| K–4329 | reindeer antler | Meiendorf | 12,360±110 | 7 |
| K–4261 | reindeer antler | Stellmoor | 12,190±125 | 7 |
| K–4328 | reindeer bone | Stellmoor | 12,180±130 | 7 |
| **Late Hamburgian (Netherlands)** | | | | |
| GrN–10274 | charcoal | Oldeholtwolde | 11,540±270 | 8 |

Laboratory: K= Copenhagen; OxA= Oxford; Ly= Lyon; LV= Louvain; GrN= Groningen.
References: 1= Gowlett et al. 1986a; 2= Audouze 1987; 3= Gowlett et al. 1986b; 4= Gowlett 1986; 5= Dewez 1988 (& Cordy pers. comm.); 6= Dewez 1987 (& Cordy pers. comm.); 7= Fischer & Tauber 1986; 8= Stapert et al. 1986.

Table 4.33    Selected dates from Final Magdalenian, Azilian, Federmesser & Tjongerian sites in NW Europe.

| Lab No | Sample | Findspot | Date (BP) | Ref. |
|---|---|---|---|---|
| **Final Magdalenian/Azilian (France)** | | | | |
| Ly–2296 | charcoal? | Abri des Cabones, Ranchot | 12,620±250 | 1 |
| Ly–3079 | charcoal? | Abri des Cabones, Ranchot | 11,520±191 | 1 |
| GrN–2916 | charcoal? | Roc-aux-Sorciers | 11,265±130 | 2 |
| Ly–1193 | bone | Rochedane, D1 | 11,060±470 | 3 |
| **Creswello-Tjongerian & Tjongerian (Belgium)** | | | | |
| LV–1386 | bulked bone | Trou des Blaireaux | 12,440±180 | 4 |
| LV–1472 | bulked bone | Trou de l'Ossuaire | 12,140±160 | 4 |
| OxA–942 | resin | Rekem | 11,350±150 | 5 |
| **Federmesser (N Germany)** | | | | |
| Kl–2124 | wood | Klein Nordende A | 12,035±110 | 6 |
| H–18/11 | charcoal | Rissen 14/14a | 11,450±180 | 7 |
| **Bromme (Denmark)** | | | | |
| K–2509 | wood | Trollesgave | 11,100±160 | 8 |

Laboratory: Ly= Lyon; GrN= Groningen; LV= Louvain; H= Hamburg; K= Copenhagen; Kl= Kiel.
Reference: 1= David 1984; 2= Guillien & Saint-Mathurin 1976; 3= Thévenin 1982; 4= Dewez 1987; 5= Gowlett et al. 1987; 6= Bokelmann 1983; 7= Schwabedissen 1957; 8= Fischer & Mortensen 1977.

mostly between 40–100 mm long, with the mean around 75 mm (Fagnart 1984a). Although the proportion of blades represented is slightly higher than at the English sites (Hengistbury= 16.9%), it is noteworthy that there is a remarkable similarity in the appearance of blade butt types (Table 4.34), with plain or puncti-

form butts being particularly well-represented and outnumbering all other forms.

Typologically, Dreuil-lès-Amiens and the adjacent sites at Etouvie (la petite gravière and la gravière Jourdain) are very similar. The most important elements in the assemblages are end-scrapers, burins and

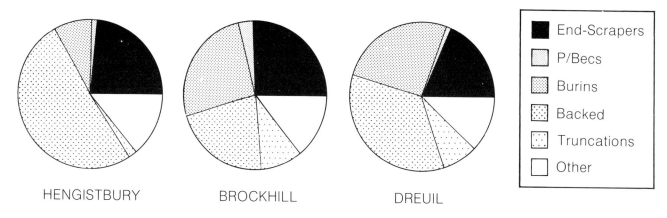

4.71 *Relative percentages of major retouched tool classes from Hengistbury Head, Brockhill and Dreuil.*

backed pieces (Table 4.35 and Fig. 4.71). Whereas the burins consistently outnumber the scrapers, the proportion of truncation to dihedral burins differs from site to site. The scrapers are dominated by short forms and the burins are typically thick and display areas of cortex like the Hengistbury and Brockhill examples. In all three of the French collections straight-backed blades and bladelets and shouldered points occur, which parallel finds made in the British assemblages, although the former also include many more backed points. There are marked similarities also in the the low proportions of piercers, becs and *Zinken*, as well as the relative paucity of truncated blades. A feature of potential chronological significance, however, is the presence of curved backed points. While finds of this sort are all but absent at Hengistbury and Brockhill, analogies may be found with the Late Upper Palaeolithic site of Crown Acres, Berkshire (Campbell 1977), presumed to be of somewhat younger age than Hengistbury (Barton 1986b). Also lacking from the French collections are any of the large tanged points which feature in the Hengistbury assemblage.

*Conclusions:* In most of the European areas bordering the North Sea Basin, and geographically closest to Britain, there is considerable evidence for Late Upper Palaeolithic activity from open-air sites, caves and rockshelters. Although some regions may not have been entirely deserted, even at the height of the last glaciation, signs of human occupation only begin to increase in NW Europe after 14,000 radiocarbon years ago. During the earlier period of re-colonisation (13–12,000 BP) it has been proposed that several discrete but contemporary flint technologies existed side by side (Fig. 4.72). The diversity seen in the archaeological record at this time may be explicable in terms of various adaptational responses to external stimuli including environmental and climatic change or, alternatively, simply due to regional variations in stylistic choice. The latter of course could be linked to the former, if some kind of regional demographic pressure was involved (Gamble 1986). Whatever the explanation in cultural terms, the most common technologies which appear to overlap both chronologically and spa-

tially are those with tool assemblages dominated by straight-backed blades (Magdalenian or related types) and others with many angle-backed forms (Creswellian and its variants).

Although the dating evidence is still relatively poor, at least two contemporary Late Upper Palaeolithic technologies are believed to overlap chronologically in Belgium (Creswello-Tjongerian/Late Magdalenian) and Northern Germany (Late Hamburgian/'Federmesser') and by inference also in the Netherlands and France. In Britain, a similar duality may be shown in the existence, on the one hand by the Creswellian sites (so far restricted mainly to caves and rockshelters), and on the other by assemblages from open-air locations such as Hengistbury and Brockhill. This picture is undoubtedly an oversimplification, since the closest parallels for Hengistbury come from non-Magdalenian assemblages in N France, rather than from typical Late Magdalenian ones. Secondly, it should also be borne in mind that the Final Magdalenian of Central and Eastern France has produced large tanged points and shouldered material individually very similar to the finds from Hengistbury. The pattern which seems to be emerging from the Late Glacial is one of much greater technological diversity than previously supposed. For the time being, it may thus be prudent to classify Hengistbury within the broad grouping of straight-backed blade technologies, which at one end of the range is represented by the Late Magdalenian and at the other by various early Federmesser groupings.

### 4.10.6 Aspects of functional variability and the Hengistbury Later Upper Palaeolithic open-air site

Efforts to interpret the British open-air assemblages in functional terms are considerably hampered by the lack of good organic preservation. This is particularly true of sites in sands such as Hengistbury and Brockhill where organic remains, in the form of bone and antler are entirely lacking. The reconstruction of functional evidence at Hengistbury is therefore heavily dependent upon information from the lithic artefacts and more general inferences drawn from other Late Palaeolithic

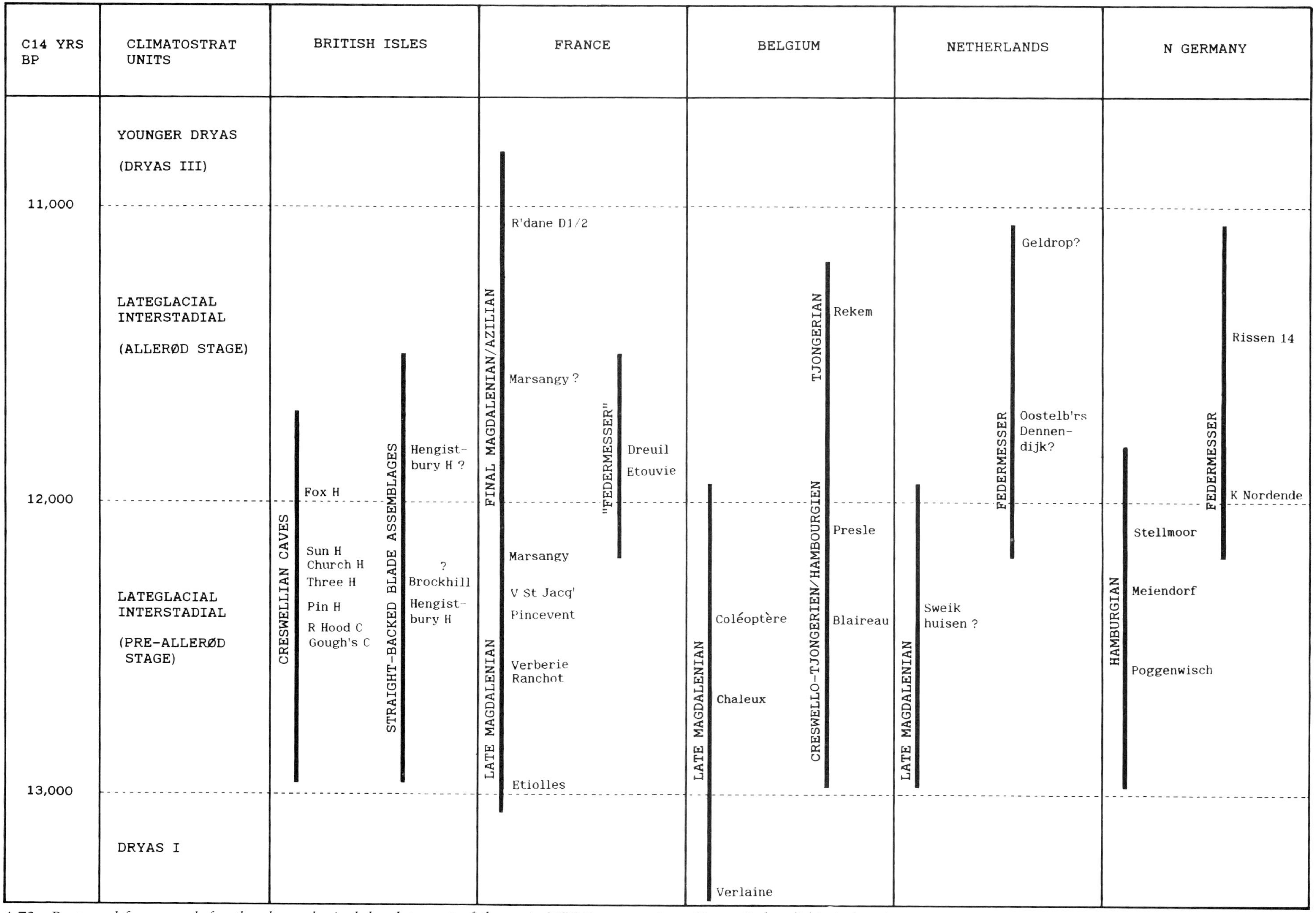

Figure 4.72 — Chronological framework chart

| C14 YRS BP | CLIMATOSTRAT UNITS | BRITISH ISLES | FRANCE | BELGIUM | NETHERLANDS | N GERMANY |
|---|---|---|---|---|---|---|
| 11,000 | YOUNGER DRYAS (DRYAS III) | | | | | |
| | LATEGLACIAL INTERSTADIAL (ALLERØD STAGE) | STRAIGHT-BACKED BLADE ASSEMBLAGES — Hengistbury H? / Brockhill / Hengistbury H | "FEDERMESSER" — Dreuil, Etouvie; FINAL MAGDALENIAN/AZILIAN — R'dane D1/2, Marsangy? | TJONGERIAN / CRESWELLO-TJONGERIEN/HAMBOURGIEN — Rekem, Presle, Blaireau | FEDERMESSER — Geldrop?, Oostelb'rs Dennendijk? | FEDERMESSER — Rissen 14, K Nordende |
| 12,000 | LATEGLACIAL INTERSTADIAL (PRE-ALLERØD STAGE) | CRESWELLIAN CAVES — Fox H, Sun H, Church H, Three H, Pin H, R Hood C, Gough's C | LATE MAGDALENIAN — Marsangy, V St Jacq', Pincevent, Verberie, Ranchot, Etiolles | LATE MAGDALENIAN — Coléoptère, Chaleux, Verlaine | LATE MAGDALENIAN — Sweik huisen? | HAMBURGIAN — Stellmoor, Meiendorf, Poggenwisch |
| 13,000 | DRYAS I | | | | | |

4.72  Proposed framework for the chronological development of the main NW European Late Upper Palaeolithic industries.

195

open-air sites on the European mainland, where the material evidence may be considerably better preserved.

Large open-air sites of Late Glacial age are relatively uncommon in Britain, so in seeking likely parallels for Hengistbury we must turn our attention to neighbouring areas of Northern France, Belgium and the Low Countries. Here, well-studied Late Magdalenian and Federmesser open-air contexts offer potentially the best opportunities for providing comparative data on aspects of site structure and settlement patterns in the Late Glacial landscape. The variables chosen for investigation are assemblage size, tool function and artefact spatial analyses (Audouze 1987; Julien *et al.* 1988; Arts and Deeben 1987; Deeben 1988).

Some of the best preserved Late Magdalenian sites occur in the Paris Basin, where faunal evidence indicates a hunting economy based on the exploitation of migrating reindeer and horse, in a relatively open landscape. Further northwards in the southern Dutch lowlands different subsistence strategies appear to have been adopted by Federmesser hunting groups, but these should not be regarded as being of a strictly contemporary age to the French sites. The Dutch evidence appears to indicate the exploitation of mixture of wooded and open environments where the hunting concentrated upon the pursuit of solitary species or those living in small herds including elk, roe deer, and aurochs (Deeben 1988).

The Late Magdalenian sites in the Paris Basin, now numbering 50 or so, mainly occur along rivers with many examples clustering within a few kilometres of river confluences or near suitable fording points (Audouze 1987). Most of the sites appear to concentrate on the low floodplain, but it is noteworthy that a major site with horse and reindeer (Ville-St-Jacques) is situated on the plateau overlooking the valley floor (Audouze *ibid.*). In general, the actual slaughter of animals seems to have occurred very close to all of the sites, as indicated by faunal body part representation. The faunal assemblages so far analysed in detail (Pincevent, Verberie) suggest mainly spring and/or autumn kills with occupation notably absent in winter (Leroi-Gourhan and Brézillon 1972; Baffier *et al.* 1982).

One hundred and twenty eight Federmesser sites have so far been recorded in S Holland (Arts 1988). Many of them are in the lowlying coversand areas where poor drainage and waterlogging has been responsible for creating extensive wetlands and they were probably damp places even in the Late Glacial. In consequence the Late Palaeolithic sites are often located on ridges slightly above the water table on the fen edges. According to Arts (*ibid.*), influential factors in site location seem to have been the local availability of water and natural shelter. For example, no site is further than 300 metres from open-water sources and many are located in the lee of the coversand ridges. On the basis of site size and related data these campsites are considered to have been occupied over relatively short periods, perhaps only seasonally (Deeben 1988).

Table 4.34 *Comparisons between Hengistbury and Late Upper Palaeolithic sites in N France: butt features of blade/bladelet debitage (after Fagnart 1984a)*

| | Plain/ punctiform | Faceted | Dihedral faceted | Cortical |
|---|---|---|---|---|
| Hengistbury | 85.4 | 11.5 | 2.4 | 0.6 |
| Dreuil-lès-Amiens | 84.6 | 10.6 | 2.9 | 1.9 |
| Etouvie petite gravière | 71.5 | 22.1 | 3.2 | 3.2 |

Table 4.35 *Comparisons between Hengistbury and Late Upper Palaeolithic sites in N France: tool indices (after Fagnart 1984a)*

| | No. | End-S | P/ becs | Burins | Backed pieces | Trunc | Others |
|---|---|---|---|---|---|---|---|
| Hengistbury | 649 | 22.7 | 0.6 | 10.2 | 51.4(1.2) | 2.1 | 12.9 |
| Brockhill | 194 | 25.9 | 3.6 | 25.2 | 22.8(2.1) | 9.8 | 12.8 |
| Dreuil-lès-Amiens | 86 | 17.4 | 1.2 | 27.9 | 34.9(5.8) | 8.1 | 10.5 |
| Etouvie petite grav. | 96 | 13.5 | 1.0 | 46.8 | 27.1(1.0) | 2.1 | 9.4 |

(Brackets indicate percentage contribution of shouldered points)

The position of Hengistbury, on a high ridge overlooking the confluence of two large rivers fits the expected pattern of a specialised hunting location. The site occupies an excellent strategic position, being relatively well-hidden and sheltered near the bottom of a dry stream valley but also affording maximum vantage over the landscape especially to the south. From this look-out point the approach of animal herds could be closely monitored from as far away as 10 kilometres.

*Spatial organisation*

The spatial distribution of artefacts in Late Magdalenian sites of the Paris Basin appears to conform to a remarkably consistent and regular pattern from site to site and throughout the region. Within each site or habitation area a series of hearths act as focal points for concentrations of lithic scatters and faunal remains (Julien *et al.* 1988). The hearths are of various types: they may be flat or dug-out basins, they may be lined with hearthstones or simply have a rough stone bordering. From the quantities of burnt and broken implements found either within emptied hearth waste (Julien in Leroi-Gourhan and Brézillon 1972) or next to undisturbed hearths (Leroi-Gourhan and Brézillon 1966, 1972) these places have been interpreted as major zones of human activity involving tool-use as well as artefact discard. On the basis of the distribution patterns of the tools and extensive refitting of production waste (mainly flint debitage), various distinctive patterns of movement can be discerned around each fireplace. In terms of the lithic materials,

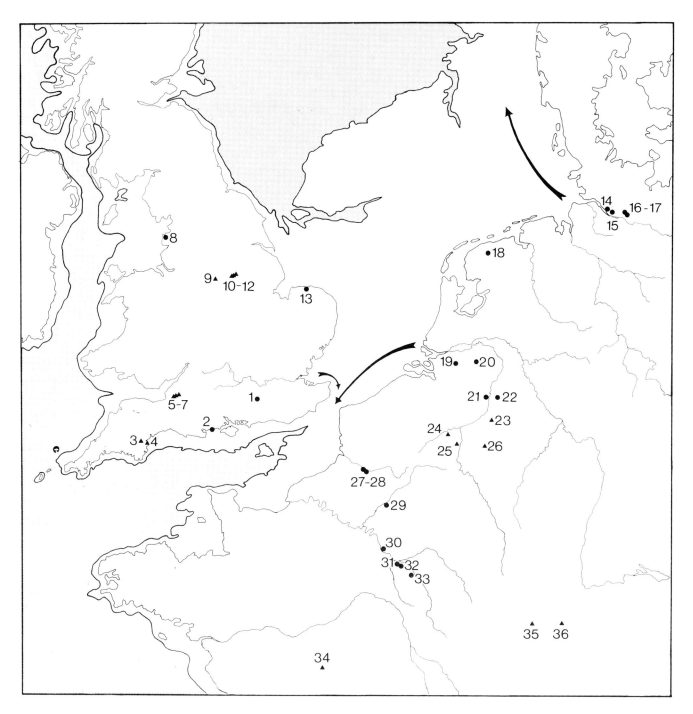

4.73  *Selected NW European Late Upper Palaeolithic findspots with stippled area marking the contemporary sea level and showing the major North Sea Basin drainage patterns (arrows); Triangles= caves and rockshelters; dots= open-air sites.*
*1= Brockhill; 2= Hengistbury Head; 3= Three Holes; 4= Kent's Cavern; 5-7= Gough's Cave, Sun Hole, Aveline's Hole; 8= Poulton-le-Fylde; 9= Fox Hole; 10-12= Pin Hole, Robin Hood's Cave, Church Hole; 13= Titchwell; 14= Klein Nordende; 15= Rissen 14; 16-17= Stellmoor, Meiendorf; 18= Oldeholtwolde; 19= Meer II; 20= Geldrop; 21= Rekem; 22= Sweikhuizen-Groene Paal; 23= Verlaine; 24= Grotte de l'Ossuaire, Presle; 25= Blaireau, Vaucelles; 26= Coléoptère; 27-28= Dreuil, Etouvie; 29= Verberie; 30= Etiolles; 31= Pincevent; 32= Ville St. Jacques; 33= Marsangy; 34= Roc-aux-Sorciers (Angles-sur-l'Anglin); 35= Ranchot (Cabone); 36= Rochedane.*

there appear to be two main kinds of movement. The first is described as *centrifugal* in type (Julien *et al.* 1988, 93): flint is knapped near the hearth and the waste is then removed *away* from the fire. This is the most common pattern observed at the sites of Pincevent, Verberie, Etiolles and Marsangy. The second (rarer) form involves the *centripetal* movement of artefacts *towards* the hearth. Here the debitage is left

where it was knapped (well away from the hearth) with only the best blanks being selected for further use in activities around the fire. This kind of behaviour has been inferred from the spatial evidence at Marsangy and Etiolles (Julien *et al.* 1988).

Other consistent patterns typically associated with Late Magdalenian open-air sites include the occurrence of thin ochre spreads in the habitation areas and the importation of various materials such as sandstone and limestone for hearth lining and non-local flint for tool-use. In some instances ready-made blanks of exotic flint were apparently brought to the habitation sites from locations as far away as 20–80 km (Mauger 1985).

Detailed analyses of site structure have been applied to only relatively few of the typical Federmesser sites. At a general level, however, it can be said that occurrences in S Netherlands typically cover a small area and contain low densities of retouched tools (Deeben 1988). This is a pattern which is repeated for Federmesser open-air sites in the Central Rhineland (Bosinski *et al.* 1982) in Northern Germany (Tromnau 1975) and as far east as Poland (Bokelmann 1983). Only very rarely are actual examples of hearth structures recorded at these locations but this may be due to preservation factors of sites in sands rather than to any genuine absence. In certain cases, as at Geldrop III–4 in the Netherlands, the presence of hearth material is inferred from the spatial distribution of burnt artefacts. At this site the excavator identified part of a flint production area close to the hearth with retouched tools discarded around the burnt area. In some ways this resembles the *centrifugal* pattern of debitage observable at the Late Magdalenian sites, except in so far as the waste was not obviously removed from the hearth zone. It may be relevant that at Geldrop III–4 there is also evidence for the long distance importation of lithic raw materials in the form of ready-prepared blanks (Deeben 1988).

At Hengistbury there is no clear evidence for hearths but there can be little doubt that these were present, judging by the scatter of thermally fractured stone slabs and burnt flints amongst the Late Upper Palaeolithic occupation debris. Thermoluminescence tests show that some of the sandstone slabs had been baked to temperatures in excess of 500° Celsius (see 2.4.3), a level of heat intensity typically generated by a small wood fire.

Aspects of the Hengistbury retouched tool and debitage distributions have been dealt with in previous sections (see esp. 3.2.7, 4.2.3 and 4.4) but it is worth recalling some of the main points regarding the spatial framework of finds at the site. Within the overall distribution of flint artefacts, at least two distinctive spatial patterns are identifiable (Fig. 4.74). In the NW of the 1981–4 area is a zone characterised by high proportions of backed tools, many of which are burnt and thermally fractured. Also identified as being present are quantities of burnt debitage and similarly affected sandstone fragments. About 5–7 m to the SE is a second zone (designated SC because it lies in the south central part of the Campbell area) displaying a higher than average density of blade debitage and blade cores. This zone is typified by low quantities of tools and an equal scarcity of burnt debitage. The majority of refitting artefacts come from this SC part of the site. A striking feature of some of the more completely reassembled cores is the occurrence of gaps in the reduction sequences which suggest that the better blades were transferred for use elsewhere.

Based on the European examples cited above it is possible to interpret the NW concentration of burnt tools and sandstone fragments as evidence of the remains of a hearth (Fig. 4.74). Some support for this model is provided by the type of tools making up the concentration. As observed at some of the French Late Magdalenian sites, there is marked tendency for backed tools to be associated with hearthside activities and in these contexts rejected broken and burnt examples often predominate. In the case of Hengistbury, the large number of burnt backed specimens could be regarded in similar terms as the residues of repair and

4.74 *'Activity' areas at the Hengistbury Late Upper Palaeolithic site. Blade manufacturing zone in the South Central area and the utilisation of backed tools concentrated around the remains of a possible hearth in the North-West area.*

retooling activities beside a fire. If the blade blanks for making these tools were supplied from the peripheral SC area, as we believe, then this would conform with the expected pattern of the *centripetal* movement of items from an outside knapping area to a position nearer the fireside (cf. Marsangy). It may also be relevant that fragments of rubbed ochre and engraved cortex were associated with the backed blades near the inferred hearth at Hengistbury.

*Tool function*
Backed blades and bladelets make up some of the most common tool classes in Late Magdalenian open-air assemblages. Various functional and microwear studies have shown these artefacts were parts of composite tools, serving as insets for weaponheads (Brézillon in Leroi-Gourhan and Brézillon 1966, 1972; Moss 1983) and meat knives (Moss and Newcomer 1982). At Pincevent the finding of pairs of backed tools foreshadowed the discovery of an antler projectile point with two bladelets set in grooves on either side of the tip (Leroi-Gourhan 1983). Alternative functional possibilities for such tools are suggested by antler knife handles at Blanchard (Allain and Descoutes 1957). Evidence for the use of mastic in fixing backed pieces has been reported from a number of sites (Leroi-Gourhan and Allain 1979). Preparation of the fixative would have involved softening by heating, and this interpretation may explain the association of backed pieces around hearths.

The recovery of ochre near hearths may also be linked with the hafting process if its application as a resin additive is correctly interpreted (Allain and Descouts 1957; Allain 1979). Other authors identify a more common usage in a range of hideworking activities either as a colorant, as a grease cleansing agent (Moss 1983) or even as a leather preservative (Keeley in Van Noten 1978; Audouin and Plisson 1982). Despite a multiplicity of potential uses, red ochre seems to have been employed by some Late Upper Palaeolithic groups and not by others. For example its ubiquitous appearance in the Late Magdalenian of France and Belgium is contrasted with a virtual absence in Belgian assemblages of Creswello-Tjongerian type (Dewez 1987). Such differences in the archaeological record are hard to explain but may be due to various factors including cultural choice, availability of raw material or even functional variation at a site level. At Hengistbury, there is a readily available supply of ochre in the Tertiary ironstones and, not surprisingly, this source was exploited fairly extensively.

In the Netherlands, the Federmesser assemblages are characterised by roughly equal proportions of end-scrapers and burins which individually may outnumber backed tools (Arts 1988). Red ochre also occurs at Federmesser sites such as Geldrop. Detailed analysis of Geldrop III–4 has shown a significant overlap in the distribution of end-scrapers and red-ochre fragments, some of which carry marks of intensive scraping (Deeben 1988). The presence of these tools and their association with ochre has been interpreted as evidence for specialised hideworking activities.

From the limited functional evidence available at Hengistbury (4.2 and 4.5.4) it would appear that the backed blades served as multipurpose tools. It is not clear whether they were primarily intended for use directly in the hand or as components of slotted equipment but, from their regularity of form and small size, some at least could have been hafted (cf. Bordes 1952). No traces of resin have been found on the backed pieces but one tool (Fig. 4.23, 11) shows signs of burning which vanish abruptly at the mid-point. It is possible that the unburnt portion of this blade was protected by some type of binding or mastic. Functional clues are also provided by damage patterns on the tools. For instance, scalariform damage on the unbacked edges of some tools (Fig. 4.22, 2) suggests they functioned as knives, while in other instances their use as disposable projectile equipment can be inferred from 'impact' fractures at the tips (Fig. 4.22, 4). The diversity of possible functions need not be surprising nor imply a separation of activities, especially in the context of a residential campsite, where meat processing tasks may have taken place side by side with the maintenance and repair of hunting equipment.

Abundant evidence for on-site processing and maintenance activities can also be inferred from the presence of other tool classes. Apart from damage patterns functional evidence may be deduced from particular features of the tool's working-edge. For example a recurrent feature of the Hengistbury end-scrapers is a pronounced overhang of the scraper edge, an attribute closely identified with hideworking (Nissen and Dittemore 1974). Study of the burins from the site shows them to be too thick for grooving bone or antler, but elsewhere practical experiments have illustrated the effectiveness of such artefacts as scraping tools (Bordes 1965, 1969; Rigaud 1972; Newcomer 1974). In this respect it is interesting to note that the heavy scalar damage reported on some of the Hengistbury burins is identifiable with whittling or scraping of hard materials such as bone or antler (4.5.5). The damage, mainly concentrated on the edge of the burin facet, shows these tools were used in a sideways or transverse motion rather than lengthwise as in grooving work. Similar wear patterns have been noted on long snapped blades from the site (e.g. Fig. 4.27, 3), and if not caused 'spontaneously' during breakage, may be related to a similar form of use (cf. Newcomer 1974). Heavy damage, possibly from chopping bone or antler, is also present on one of the cores (Fig. 4.50).

*Variation in settlement size*
During the Late Glacial, Upper Palaeolithic hunting strategies would inevitably have varied according to the nature and distribution of the game resources available. Wilmsen (1973) has argued convincingly that species that migrated seasonally in large herds, such as reindeer, would have been hunted most effectively by human groups aggregating temporarily for this pur-

pose. Conversely, a strategy for hunting solitary animals or ones living in smaller herds (e.g. elk, aurochs, roe deer) may have required less labour-intensive techniques and a more fragmented human presence across the landscape. If such differences are reflected as clearly in the structure of individual sites, then it would seem reasonable that the larger human collective units would be represented by denser accumulations of settlement evidence than those left by smaller highly mobile bands (Yellen 1977; Deeben 1988).

The application of this model to the Dutch site data shows that, in general, the Federmesser locations do not fit the pattern of the large aggregation units. Based on published site reports, Arts (1988) describes two categories of Federmesser site on the basis of flint scatter size. In the first, the artefacts come from more or less circular scatters covering an area of from four to 100 square metres and consisting of up to 3,000 artefacts. This is typical of the Dutch sites referred to above. Another category consists of oval scatters made up of 50,000–100,000 flints and covering an area of 2,000–25,000 square metres. This size of site is rarely seen in the Federmesser groups but does include exceptional cases like Milheeze-Hutseberg which may be interpreted as one site consisting of a series of contiguous activity areas. Arts proposes that these larger units would be characterised by a lithic toolkit of greater diversity (Arts 1988, 306–7).

Despite the fact that only a small proportion of the Hengistbury site has so far been investigated, survey work reveals a continuation of finds north of the excavated areas and along much of the length of the Eastern Depression. As artefacts do not occur in any number beyond the slopes of the dry stream valley, it is reasonable to suppose that this topographic feature provided a natural focus of occupation activity. Given that flints have been collected up to 100 m north of the main site (of *c.* 270 sq m) and across much of the 30 metre wide depression, it can be estimated that the site (or linked zones of activity) covered an area of some 2–3,000 square metres. This would place Hengistbury firmly in the same group of major aggregation camps as the rarer Federmesser examples, and within the likely range of the Late Magdalenian sites in the Paris Basin, although no comparative statistics appear to be available for the latter.

Ultimately, of course, the size model employed above provides only a very crude index of the actual dimensions of a site or the extent of site activity (cf. Foley 1981). Amongst other things, it does not, for example, take into account the potential for migrational shifts in a site caused by repeated visits to the same location, either on a seasonal basis or over much longer periods. An indication of the potential complexity of the record is illustrated at Pincevent and Etiolles where up to 12 separate occupation levels, with 15–21 overlapping domestic units have been recorded (Julien *et al.* 1988). In such cases, where the site evidence is well-articulated, it may possible to reach much closer approximations of the scale of occupation and even to calculate the duration of stay based on the sequential use of hearths. Notwithstanding the wealth of unprocessed site data yet to be analysed and fully published, the Paris Basin sites tend to corroborate the idea of relatively large hunting groups which probably came together on a seasonal rather than a permanent basis (Baffier *et al.* 1982).

*Conclusions*

This concludes the section on the Hengistbury Late Upper Palaeolithic site in its wider perspective. Some of the main conclusions of this section are as follows:

(1) At least two distinct lithic technologies can be identified in the Late Glacial Interstadial record of Britain (13,000–11,500 BP). On present evidence, however, it is uncertain whether they were fully or even partly contemporary or represent successive and independent adaptations. The two groupings are defined, respectively, as 'straight-backed blade' and 'angle-backed Creswellian' lithic assemblage types. The first grouping appears to be entirely restricted to open-air occurrences such as Hengistbury and Brockhill, in S England. Although the Creswellian toolkit may not prove to be entirely limited to caves and rockshelters it is currently best known from such locations, in limestone areas of England and Wales where no major evidence of Hengistbury-type assemblages has yet been found.

(2) Late Glacial human groups possessing the same bone and antler equipment and sharing a Creswellian lithic technology were exploiting a wide area of Britain extending from the Northern Pennines to the SW peninsula. Evidence from the associated faunal assemblages in caves and rockshelters suggests that these sites were used at least seasonally for food storage and/or equipment caching purposes.

(3) Based on continental parallels, open-air sites like Hengistbury can be interpreted as larger aggregation units that were occupied seasonally during the autumn and spring migrations of horse and reindeer. The residential camp at Hengistbury may cover an area of up to 2,000 sq m.

(4) Given the degree of dissimilarity in lithic technologies, it is highly unlikely that the straight-backed blade and Creswellian assemblage types belong to the same technological tradition. If the two groupings were contemporary, it may eventually be possible to demonstrate that these toolkits were used by peoples exploiting separate social territories but with some geographical overlap in range, especially in Eastern Britain and areas abutting the limestone massif.

# 5. The Powell Mesolithic Site

## 5.1 The finds: debitage and cores and the refitting evidence

### 5.1.1 *Raw material analysis*

Nearly all the artefacts from the site are of flint, the only exceptions being a quartzite hammerstone and two modified sandstone 'rubbers'. The non-flint material also includes a large block of 'sarsen' (a secondarily cemented sandstone) and several slabs of broken tabular ironstone. Since none of these materials occurs naturally within the archaeological deposits, it is reasonable to assume they were all humanly imported to the site.

The raw material used for making artefacts is typical of the Cretaceous flint found throughout S Britain and is highly suitable for flaking purposes. At Hengistbury, the flint varies in colour from a blue-black colour to a light tan brown, but many of the pieces are also grey or white patinated. The flint mostly occurs in the form of small water-worn cobbles with a thin, heavily weathered cortex; there are, for example, relatively few unrounded or angular flints. One exception is provided by a distinctive coarse speckled-grey flint which is well-represented in the collection. It appears to derive from a single large angular nodule with a relatively thick chalky cortex (Fig. 5.1). This flint varies greatly both in terms of texture and colour but towards the middle of the interior it grades into a high quality cream-coloured flint which was used for making several of the microliths.

The provenance of the flint worked at the site is unknown. Much of it would appear to derive from secondary geological sources, such as fluviatile or marine gravels, judging from the rounded appearance of the cobbles. Despite some superficial resemblances with the Hengistbury terrace gravels, there is little evidence to suggest that the local gravels were exploited to any great degree. In the first place, the nearby sources contain many examples of angular or sub-angular shaped nodules. Although these display a thin, often weathered cortex, their outer surfaces are heavily pitted with 'chattermarks', which are rarely present on the archaeological specimens. Secondly, the local gravels frequently show signs of frost-fracturing or partial desilicification. Such features would have made them unsuitable for flaking and not surprisingly they were largely ignored by the Mesolithic occupants. A further potential source of local flint exists in Tertiary deposits of the Headland. However, here again the flint with its olive-green appearance and very dense composition, is quite unlike the flint used at the site. It has been suggested by Gardiner (in Cunliffe 1987) that the post-Mesolithic occupants of the headland exploited raw material from 'clay-with-flints' deposits not far from Hengistbury. The clay-with-flints from Dorset and the Hampshire Basin often produces flint with a distinctive green or black staining on the cortex (Melville and Freshney 1982). My own samples taken from the Isle of Wight and Southern Dorset reveal a mixture of unworn and broken flints set in reddish brown clay. This flint also frequently displays a hardened cortex, with clay residues trapped in cavities or voids in the nodules. None of these distinctive features has been observed on the Mesolithic flints.

The most likely sources of raw material are locally-occurring river gravels in the Stour and Avon valley catchments, or possibly fluviatile deposits further west, nearer Poole (K. Jarvis pers. comm.). So far, limited attempts to match the Mesolithic flint with cobbles from riverine exposures have only proved moderately successful. The cobbles in gravel exposures near the present confluence of the Stour and Avon are much smaller than those at the site. It is possible, however, that an available gravel flint source existed next to the former 'Proto-Solent' river, but this area is likely to contain only traces of the former deposit as much of the submerged shelf has been intensively scoured by the sea.

A smaller percentage of flint from the site does not fit into this riverine category. It is identified by a slightly thicker chalky cortex which can be powdery to the touch. An example of this type is the speckled-grey flint recovered in the southern area of the site. Numerous flakes of this material have been refitted to form part of a nodule which weighs about 0.65 kg and is considerably larger than any of the naturally occurring flints seen at Hengistbury today. It seems likely that flint such as this was either quarried or collected from a freshly eroding chalk cliff. Efforts to find a provenance have centred on chalk quarries and exposures on the Isle of Wight, the Isle of Purbeck and at Tarrant Rushton in Dorset. Using micropalaeontological techniques, attempts have been made to link the archaeological finds with the geological sources. The details of the methodology are presented by Tocher (4.8.2). Unfortunately, none of the sampled material (including the speckled flint) was rich enough in dinoflagellates or other microfossils to provide conclusive links with any of the geological sources. Nevertheless, this technique seems to offer considerable potential for identifying primary flint sources.

Of the non-flint materials recovered, only the sandstone artefacts seem to have travelled any great distance to the site. They comprise two nearly identical elongated rectangular blocks of greyish sandstone (see 5.2.3 for a fuller description). From a petrological thin-section analysis, Mr D T Moore (Natural History Museum) identified one of the objects (Fig. 5.29) as being of a mixed tourmaline-bearing sandstone. The

5.1   A three core block in the speckled-grey flint. Key: 1-2= cores; 3= flake removals from missing core. 10 mm scale.

nearest known primary source of this material today is in Devon (Moore pers. comm.). The presence of rocks from the SW peninsula obviously raises the possibility of Mesolithic trade and exchange networks involving the transport of materials over relatively long distances during the Mesolithic. This is a question we shall return to in later sections of this chapter (5.2.3 and 5.5.5).

Another non-flint material seemingly absent in the geological deposits of the headland is sarsen. The lump of sarsen in the assemblage is large, weighing *c.* 4 kg and since it is not indigenous, it must have been humanly introduced to the site. Although not generally available in the area today, isolated large boulders of this cemented sandstone have been reported as coming from the Bournemouth area (Pleyder 1895; Solly 1910). It is possible therefore that a block of material was carried to the site from a relatively local source not more than a few kilometres away.

In conclusion, most of the artefacts appear to be made on flint from a derived geological context. Although, the gravels on the headland may occasionally have been exploited, they were clearly not the major source of raw material. A more likely origin would have been in river gravels which produce a better quality flint. Nodules of this material were probably brought up to the site for working. An additional source of material is indicated by the presence of nodules with a thicker chalk cortex. There are several chalk outcrops within 15–20 km of the site which could have been exploited during the Mesolithic. Apart from the sandstone rocks, which are of SW origin, the rest of the non-flint rocks (quartzite, sarsen, ironstone) occur in geological deposits either on or within easy reach of the headland (Pleyder 1895; Solly 1910; Melville and Freshney 1982). Notably absent from the assemblage is any of the dark grey/black, Jurassic rock commonly referred to as 'Portland Chert' (cf. Palmer 1977).

## 5.1.2 *Debitage and cores*

The unretouched waste or flint debitage from the 1980–3 excavations consists of 35,444 artefacts, of which approximately two-thirds are accounted for by small chips and flint debris less than 10 mm in size. Of the remaining 13,722 artefacts 6,312 are flakes, 5,699 are blades or bladelets while the rest (1,666) are unclassifiable. The totals do not include the 145 cores and 45 core fragments also from the excavations.

Alongside the excavation totals are presented the artefact counts from the surface collection. All the material derives from within a few metres of the site and was collected by Mr Ronald Powell, who was responsible for the site's initial discovery. It is a credit to his thoroughness that many millimetre size chips occur in his surface collected sample. The only slight discrepancy between the two collections is in the proportion of blades and bladelets to flakes. This may reflect actual differences in the spatial distribution of finds at the site.

*Table 5.1 Mesolithic Site: Debitage from the excavated and surface collections*

| Artefact Class | 1980-3 Excavations | | Powell Surface Coll. | |
|---|---|---|---|---|
| | n | % | n | % |
| Flakes | 6,312 | 17.8 | 637 | 49.6 |
| Blades/bladelets | 5,699 | 16.1 | 321 | 25.0 |
| Chips | 21,767 | 61.4 | 166 | 12.9 |
| Unclassified | 1,666 | 4.7 | 161 | 12.5 |
| Sub-Total | 35,444 | 100.0 | 1,285 | 100.0 |
| Cores | 140 | | 47 | |
| Core fragments | 45 | | 7 | |

*Flakes:* Flakes in the assemblage vary a great deal in terms of size. Like the blades they can occasionally reach up to 90 mm in length but are generally much smaller (Fig. 5.2). Overall, the majority of complete examples are between 10–20 mm long (54.1%), whilst most of the remainder occur in the 21–50 mm size class (42.8%), with a sharp fall-off above 51 mm The maximum dimensions of 294 unbroken flakes were measured from eight square metres. They reveal mean length, breadth and thickness measurements of 23.4 x 18.9 x 5.3 mm respectively. Each of the values displays a wide variation in the range, showing that flakes of many sizes are represented in the assemblage.

As can be seen in Table 5.3 over half the flakes in the collection are broken. Our taphonomic experiments have shown that potential contributory factors include anything from accidental breakage during manufacture to trampling damage following discard. Figure 5.3 illustrates the distribution of artefact break refits across the site. Apart from some of the longer distance conjoins, natural factors probably account for most of the dispersion (see Chapter 3). Relatively few artefacts are burnt (18%) and this is only a minor cause of breakage. Unlike the blade and bladelet blanks many flakes retain significant areas of cortex on their dorsal surfaces (50%), reflecting both the small size of flint nodules and the fact that many belong to the earlier stages of core reduction. The relatively low proportion of flakes with platform abrasion (24%) again contrasts with the blades and bladelets, and shows less need for preparation during the early reduction stages. A high proportion of the butts are large and show the blow was delivered well back from the core edge (i.e. non-marginal). The flake butts are not subdivided into separate types as they fall into only two categories: plain and cortical. The dorsal flake scar pattern indicates a high proportion (30%) of mixed or multidirectional removals; such flakes were probably associated with the earlier stages of reducing the core.

*Blades and bladelets:* A substantial proportion of the debitage consists of blades and bladelets (41.5%). Technically, most of them occur within the bladelet class (see Chapter 7 Glossary) with only 574 classifiable as true 'blades'. To a certain extent the distinction between the categories is an arbitrary one with one

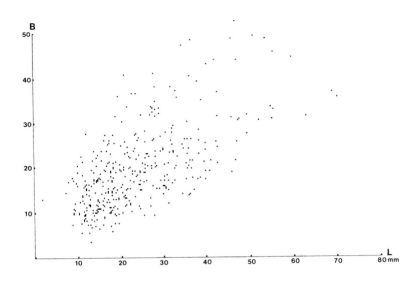

5.2 *Scatter diagram of flake length x breadth dimensions. Complete flakes from squares F12, G9, G11, G12, H10, H11, H12, I10, I12.*

Table 5.2 *Flakes: quantitative measurements*

Main dimensions (mm)

|  | | Length | Breadth | Thickness |
|---|---|---|---|---|
| Total | = | 294 | 294 | 294 |
| Range | = | 5.6-63 | 3.3-52.9 | 1-33.5 |
| Mean | = | 23.36 | 18.87 | 5.24 |
| Standard Deviation | = | 1.139 | 9.052 | 3.492 |

Butt dimensions (mm)

|  | | Length | Breadth |
|---|---|---|---|
| Total | = | 185 | 185 |
| Range | = | 1.2-44.1 | 1-33.5 |
| Mean | = | 8.95 | 3.24 |
| Standard Deviation | = | 6.37 | 3.399 |

Table 5.3 *Flakes: qualitative attributes*

|  | n | % |
|---|---|---|
| *Condition* (n=6,312) | | |
| (a) Complete | 2,651 (208) | 42.0 |
| (b) Proximal fragments | 1,343 | 21.3 |
| Mesial fragments | 1,048 | 16.6 |
| Distal fragments | 1,270 | 20.1 |
| Total broken | 3,661 | 58.0 |
| (c) Burnt | 1,122 | 17.7 |
| (d) Unburnt | 5,190 | 82.2 |
| (e) Broken & burnt | 914 | 14.5 |
| *Cortex* (n= 2,651) | 1,326 | 50 |
| *Platform Abrasion* (n=2,651) | 626 | 23.6 |
| *Dorsal scar pattern* (n=765) | | |
| (a) Unidirectional | 356 | 46.5 |
| (b) Opposed | 49 | 6.4 |
| (c) Crossed | 33 | 4.3 |
| (d) Multidirectional | 194 | 25.4 |
| (e) Unidentifiable | 133 | 17.4 |

group naturally grading into the other (Fig. 5.4). Because of this blurring of the size categories, we have decided to present the blade and bladelet data jointly.

A typical blade or bladelet from the Powell site is an artefact more than twice as long as it is wide, with an average length measurement of 31 mm. An observable feature, however, is that many of the blanks are quite broad and the mean dimension (11.3 mm) falls very close to the limit between blades and bladelets (12 mm) according to Tixier (1963). The blanks generally show an uncorticated dorsal surface (76%) with fairly straight dorsal ridges. The proximal ends are frequently characterised by platform abrasion (78%), but seldom show any other special signs of preparation. As with the flakes no statistics have been presented for the butt types as they divide naturally into two major categories (plain/punctiform and cortical types). The average butt sizes of bladelets are small (length x breadth= 4.3±2.06 x 1.3±0.84 mm) and most would be considered punctiform. The profiles of the blanks are generally straight or slightly curved, with very few examples of twisted debitage.

A high percentage of the blanks are broken (76%), but burning was probably not a major cause since only

22% of all broken pieces are also burnt. Since there is no evidence for deliberate snapping (see Glossary: intentional breakage), it seems more likely that fracturing was due to accidents of manufacture or trampling under foot. The marked differences between the numbers of broken flakes and the bladelets is probably accounted for by the shape of the latter which are longer and thinner and more susceptible to breakage.

A somewhat surprising feature is the low representation of bidirectional scars (16%) on the dorsal surfaces of blades and bladelets, as compared to unidirectional ones (53%). This might not be expected given the large

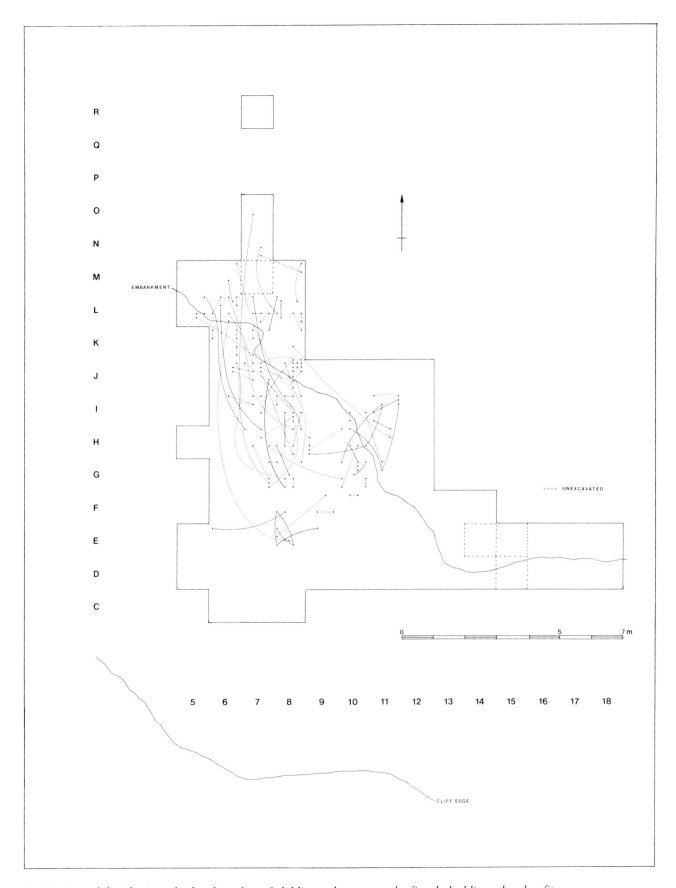

5.3  *Horizontal distribution of refitted artefacts. Solid lines= dorso-ventral refits; dashed lines= break refits.*

number of opposed platform cores in the assemblage. In fact, refits show that one platform was generally more heavily used than the other on opposed platform cores. In the later stages of reduction the second platform was often employed to correct mistakes or to remove obstacles on the flaking face. This might explain the apparent discrepancy between the bladelet and core data.

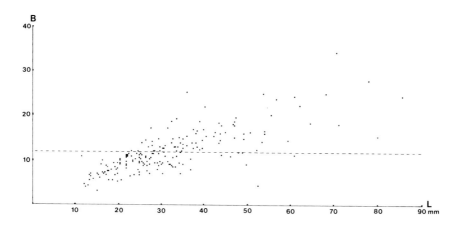

5.4 *Scatter diagram of blade and bladelet length x breadth dimensions. Complete artefacts from squares F12, G9, G11, G12, H10, H11, H12, I10, I12. Dashed line shows the 'division' between blades and bladelets.*

Table 5.4 *Blades and bladelets: quantitative measurements.*

Main dimensions (mm)

|  |  | Length | Breadth | Thickness |
|---|---|---|---|---|
| Total | = | 136 | 136 | 136 |
| Range | = | 11.4-64.4 | 4.2-24.9 | 1-10.4 |
| Mean | = | 30.57 | 11.3 | 3.6 |
| Standard Deviation | = | 12.257 | 4.182 | 1.881 |

Butt dimensions (mm)

|  |  | Length | Breadth |
|---|---|---|---|
| Total | = | 104 | 104 |
| Range | = | 1.2-11.1 | 1-6.5 |
| Mean | = | 4.34 | 1.29 |
| Standard Deviation | = | 2.061 | 0.843 |

*Crested pieces, core tablets and other rejuvenating flakes*: Three types of waste product have been identified from the various stages of core reduction: crested pieces, core tablets and *flancs de nucléus* (see Chapter 7 for definitions). Whereas the two latter are usually associated with the repair or rejuvenation of the core, the first may also be linked with the initial preparation stages.

Cresting preparation was not used in all cases but very much depended on the original shape of the nodule. For example, in preparing a cylindrical cobble, cresting of any kind was simply not necessary (Fig. 5.5). Instead, platforms were created at either end and flaking occurred down the unprepared (cortical) edges. In less regular specimens, however, such as angular blocks or flakes, unidirectional cresting could be used to 'regularise' one edge to guide the first removal. Unlike the Upper Palaeolithic cores, however, evidence for bidirectional cresting rarely occurs in preforming stage of the cores at the Mesolithic site. This may partly be a reflection of the small size of raw material.

Nearly all the core tablets are on flakes (Fig. 5.6, 7), the sole exception being a laminar blank which was converted into an end-scraper (Fig. 5.9, 15). The large number of core tablets found in the excavation confirms the existence of a primary manufacturing area. Several of the tablets can be refitted to nearby cores (Fig. 5.23, 3).

Table 5.5 *Blades and bladelets: qualitative attributes*

|  | n | % |
|---|---|---|
| *Condition* (n=5,699) |  |  |
| (a)  Complete | 1,346 (62) | 23.6 |
| (b)  Proximal fragments | 1,620 | 28.4 |
| Mesial fragments | 1,487 | 26.1 |
| Distal fragments | 1,246 | 21.9 |
| Total broken | 4,353 | 76.4 |
| (c)  Burnt | 1,054 | 18.5 |
| (d)  Unburnt | 4,645 | 81.5 |
| (e)  Broken & burnt | 992 | 17.4 |
| *Cortex* (n= 1,346) | 328 | 24.4 |
| *Platform Abrasion* (n=1,346) | 1,047 | 77.8 |
| *Dorsal scar pattern* (n=656) |  |  |
| (a)  Unidirectional | 348 | 53 |
| (b)  Opposed | 105 | 16 |
| (c)  Crossed | 3 | 0.5 |
| (d)  Multidirectional | 118 | 18 |
| (e)  Unidentifiable | 82 | 12.5 |

(brackets indicate nos. burnt)

Table 5.6 *Crested pieces, core tablets and flancs de nucléus*

|  | 1980–3 | | Surface coll. | |
|---|---|---|---|---|
|  | Complete | Broken | Complete | Broken |
| Crested pieces |  |  |  |  |
| Unidirectional | 90 | 137 | 9 | 7 |
| Bidirectional | 5 | 2 | 0 | 0 |
| Core tablets | 75 | 25 | 9 | 4 |
| *Flancs de nucléus* | 18 | 7 | 0 | 0 |

The method of removing part or all of the flaking face by detaching a *flanc de nucléus* was only used occasionally at the Mesolithic site. This is not surprising given the small size of nodules and the fact that mistakes could more easily be rectified from an oppo-

5.5  Opposed platform bladelet core with refits. The core is made on a waterworn flint cobble. 5 cm scale.

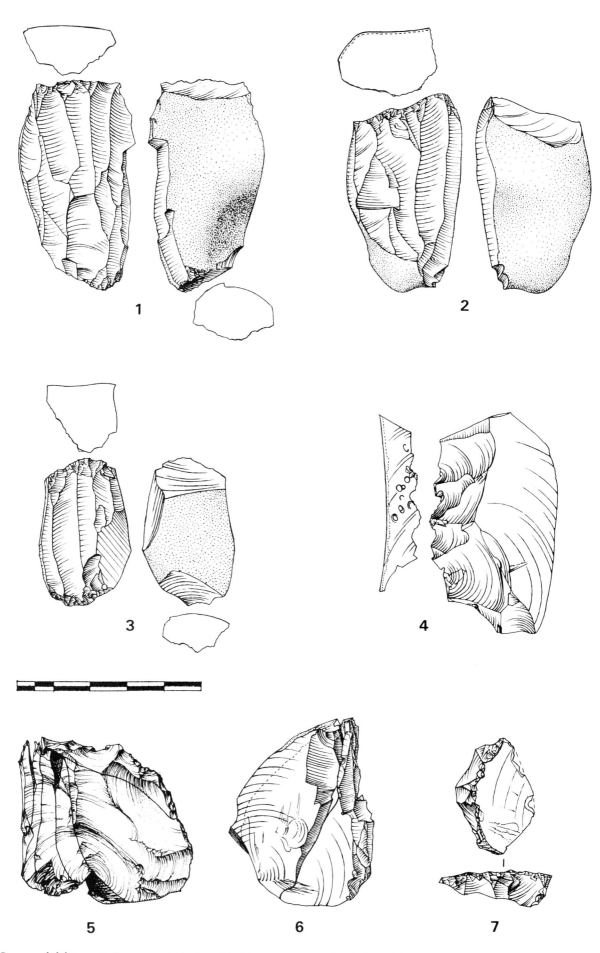

5.6 *Cores and debitage. 1, 3= opposed platform bladelet cores; 2= single platform bladelet core; 4= single platform flake core (note the incipient cones on the platform); 5-6= single platform bladelet cores on flakes, with refitting debitage; 7= core tablet. Centimetre scale.*

site platform. Some of the *flancs* have large platforms indicating that the percussion blow was delivered well away from the edge. A poorly aimed blow could have produced this type of debitage accidentally.

*Cores*: The total of 187 cores can be divided into blade and bladelet cores (99), flake cores (55) and unclassified examples (33). Most them come from the excavated sample (140), with only 47 from the surface collection. Excluded from the analysis are 52 core fragments, the majority of which also derive from the excavations (45). Amongst the blade and bladelet cores are 54 prismatic types (Fig. 5.6 and 5.7), with either one or two or double-opposed platforms. Single platform pyramidal cores (16) and irregular examples (29) make up the rest of the total. The length of the prismatic cores ranges from 36.4–65.4 mm, with the mean at 49.8±0.801 mm.

An interesting aspect of the Mesolithic assemblage is the presence of sixteen bladelet cores made on flakes or fragmented blocks. One of them with refitted bladelets and a unidirectionally prepared crest is illustrated in Fig. 5.6, 5. The reason for discarding a core can usually be attributed to some form of accident (e.g. a large hinge fracture or plunging removal), an irregularity in the raw material (e.g. crystalline inclusions) or the small size of material. In this case the core seems to have become too small and was therefore abandoned.

Although the prismatic cores are often significantly reduced, their mean weight of 41.4 gm in fact compares favourably with the mean weight of all the classified cores (46.06 gm, n=119). More than anything else, this similarity probably reflects a standardisation in the size of the raw material.

The presence of so many irregular examples amongst the blade and flake cores may also be partly attributable to the raw material. The Mesolithic flint-knappers generally selected either small cobbles or reduced larger blocks into more manageable fragments before flaking them.

Flake cores make up a significant proportion (29.4%) of the total core sample. Amongst them however are 15 which have had no more than 1–8 removals from one platform and may have been trial pieces which were subsequently rejected. The reason for their rejection is not always clear, except that some of the negative flake scars end in pronounced hinge fractures. Amongst the other cores represented are 26 multiplatform types many of which are probably fully worked-out bladelet cores, but without extensive refitting this is difficult to prove.

As a group, the cores are fairly evenly distributed across the whole site with a slight tendency towards an increased concentration in the north-eastern quadrant (Fig. 5.8). The fact that recent erosional processes (e.g. wind deflation) are unlikely to have greatly affected the spatial distribution of finds is indicated by similarities in the distribution of cores found deeply buried in the northern part of the site and those on the scoured surfaces of the cliff-top. The marginally greater density of

*Table 5.7  Classification of all Mesolithic blade and bladelet cores from the excavated and surface collections*

|  | Prismatic | Pyramidal | Irregular |
|---|---|---|---|
| One Platform | 13(4) | 9(7) | 15(3) |
| Two Platforms, opposed | 31(5) | – | 5(2) |
| Two Platforms, non-opposed | 1(-) | – | – |
| Multiplatform | – | – | 3(1) |

(Powell surface collection totals in brackets)

*Table 5.8  Prismatic blade and bladelet cores: quantitative data*

Main dimensions (mm) & weight (gm):

| Total (31) |  | Length | Breadth | Weight |
|---|---|---|---|---|
| Range | = | 36.4-65.4 | 21.4-47.5 | 14.7-84.6 |
| Mean | = | 49.84 | 31.6 | 41.37 |
| Standard Deviation | = | 8.018 | 6.85 | 17.983 |

*Table 5.9  Classification of flake cores and other cores from the excavated and surface collections*

|  | Pyramidal | Globular | Irregular |
|---|---|---|---|
| One Platform | 1(–) | – | 15(5) |
| Two Platforms, opposed | – | – | 5(–) |
| Two Platforms, non-opposed | – | 1(–) | 5(–) |
| Multiplatform | 1(–) | 4(4) | 9(6) |
| Unidentified (other) |  | 3(2) | 24(7) |

(Powell surface collection totals in brackets)

finds in the north-western zone closely matches the pattern displayed in the distribution of other artefacts (see below), identifying it as a particularly rich focus of site activity.

## 5.2  The retouched tool assemblage

Of the 626 Mesolithic retouched tools listed, 566 were recovered from the excavations and 60 from the surface collection. The retouched tools represent 1.7% of all the flaked material from the site. However, if the smaller chips and flakes unsuitable for tool blanks (e.g. <10 mm) are omitted from this total the proportion of retouched artefacts rises to 4.2% of the total sample.

The various tool categories presented below are based on the typology devised by Clark (1932, 1934a, 1934b) with some additional sub-groups provided from the type-list of de Sonneville-Bordes and Perrot (1953). The only slight divergence with Clark's typology is in the use of the term 'microdenticulate' (cf. Bocquet 1980) which is preferred here to the term 'saw'. The retouched tools consist of 390 microliths, 95 end-scrapers, 65 microdenticulates with lesser numbers of truncations (15), retouched blades and flakes (20), a

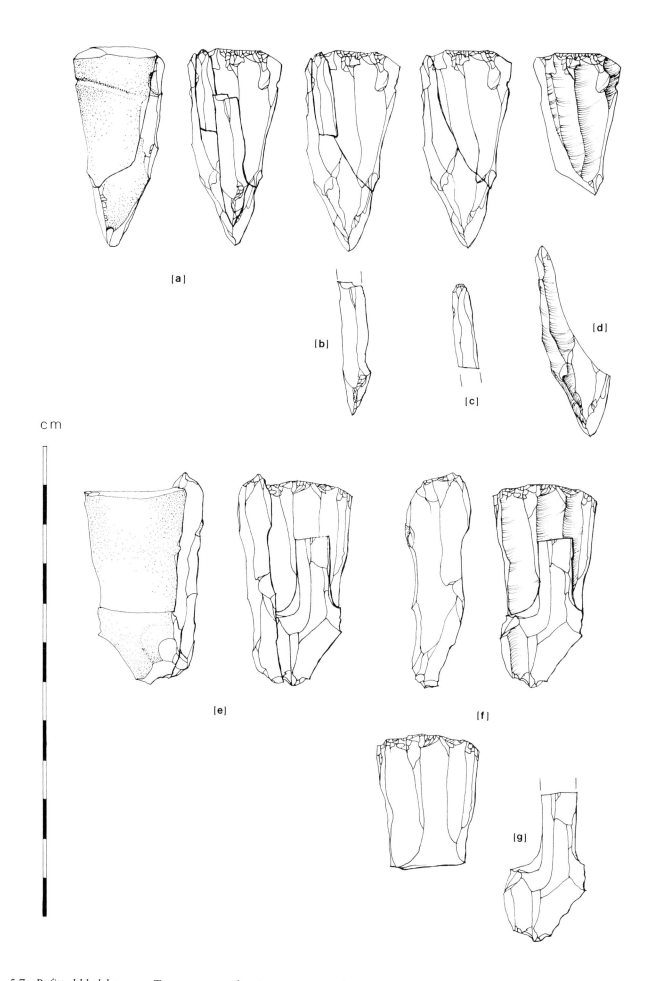

cm

5.7  *Refitted bladelet cores. Two sequences showing successive reduction stages a)-d)= opposed platform core which is reduced to a single platform core; e)-g)= opposed platform core discarded as a single platform core after a plunging blade removal.*

210

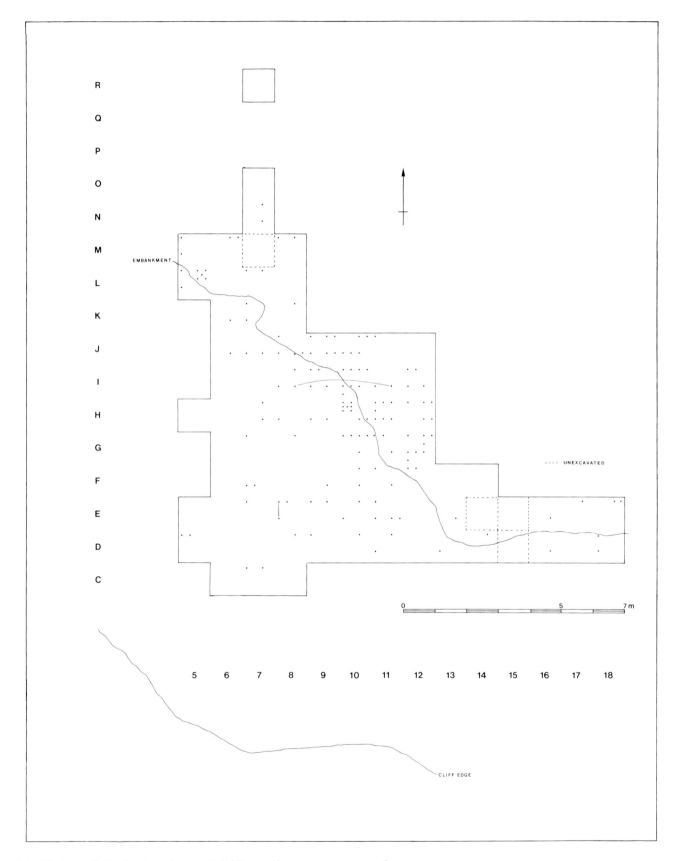

5.8 *Horizontal distribution of cores. Solid lines indicate core on core refits.*

possible fabricator and various miscellaneous retouched artefacts (40). Ample evidence for the on-site manufacture of tools, mostly microliths, occurs in the form of 273 microburins, 35 Krukowski microburins plus 16 unfinished forms and broken fragments. These

are considered under the retouched tool debitage (5.2.1).

*End-Scrapers:* Of 95 end-scrapers from the site, 85 come from the excavations and ten from the surface

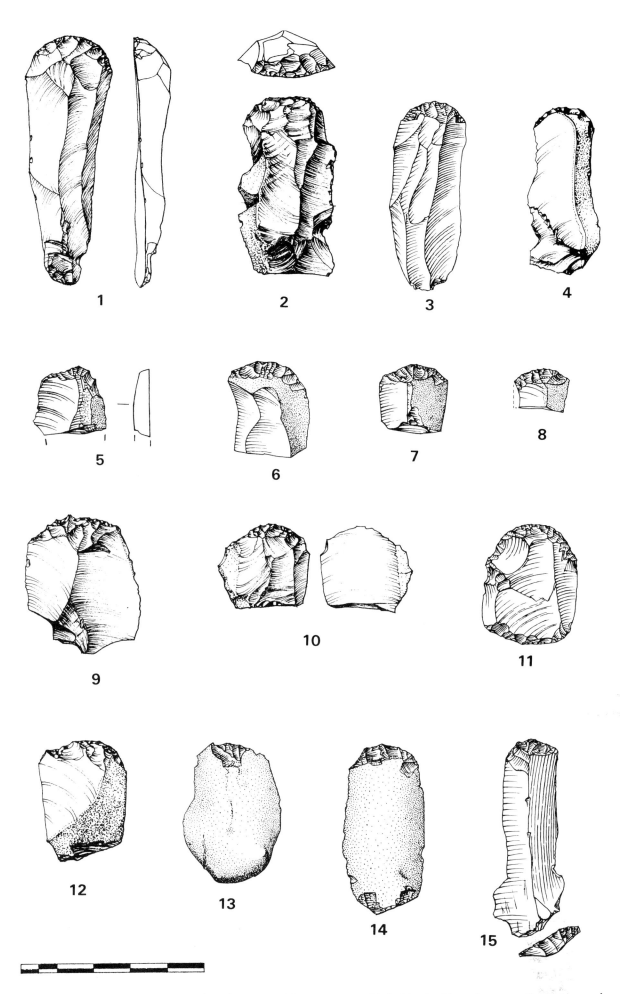

5.9 *End-scrapers. 1-10 and 12-15= simple end-scrapers (15 is on a core tablet); 11= double end-scraper. Centimetre scale.*

*Table 5.10 Retouched tools from the Powell Mesolithic site*

| | Excavations 1980-3 | Powell Collection | Total | % |
|---|---|---|---|---|
| End-scrapers | 85 | 10 | 95 | 15.2 |
| Microdenticulates | 64 | 1 | 65 | 10.4 |
| Microliths: | | | | |
|   A-type | 307 | 42 | 349 | 55.7 |
|   B-type | 6 | 2 | 8 | 1.3 |
|   C-type | – | 1 | 1 | 0.1 |
|   D-type | 1 | – | 1 | 0.1 |
|   unclassified | 27 | 4 | 31 | 4.9 |
| Truncations | 15 | – | 15 | 2.3 |
| Retouched flakes/blades | 20 | – | 20 | 3.2 |
| Miscellaneous retouch | 40 | – | 40 | 6.4 |
| ? Fabricator | 1 | – | 1 | 0.1 |
| | 566 | 60 | 626 | 99.7 |
| Post-Mesolithic: | | | | |
| Polished stone axe frag. | 4 | – | 4 | |
| Arrowhead | 1 | – | 1 | |
| Pot sherds | 5 | – | 5 | |

*Table 5.11 End-scrapers: classification (total= 95)*

| | Excavations 1980-3 | Powell Collection | Total | % |
|---|---|---|---|---|
| Simple end-scraper | 67 | 7 | 74 | 77.9 |
| Double end-scraper | 1 | – | 1 | 1.0 |
| Thumbnail scraper | 3 | 2 | 5 | 5.3 |
| Side scraper | 2 | 1 | 3 | 3.1 |
| Broken/unidentifiable | 12 | – | 12 | 12.7 |
| | 85 | 10 | 95 | 100.0 |

*Table 5.12 Simple end-scrapers: quantitative measurements*

Flake end-scrapers (n=39)

| | | Length | Breadth | Thickness |
|---|---|---|---|---|
| Range | = | 15.5–52.9 | 13.1–44.5 | 4.4–15.9 |
| Mean | = | 31.2 | 27.7 | 8.9 |
| Standard Deviation | = | 8.65 | 7.62 | 2.95 |

Blade end-scrapers (n=6)

| | | | | |
|---|---|---|---|---|
| Range | = | 39.3–65.3 | 19–23 | 5.3–9.1 |
| Mean | = | 48.9 | 20.9 | 6.4 |
| Standard Deviation | = | 9.13 | 1.58 | 1.36 |

collection. Typologically, the assemblage is dominated by simple end-scrapers, most of them short and made on flakes (62). Only 12 scrapers are made on blades. Amongst the other types is one double end-scraper (Fig. 5.9, 11), five thumbnail scrapers (*sensu* de Sonneville-Bordes and Perrot 1954) and three side-scrapers (Fig. 5.10, 2). There are 12 unclassifiable fragments.

Simple end-scrapers outnumber all other forms in the scraper class. They consist mainly of short forms with semi-abrupt retouch at the distal end, with only four tools retouched proximally. There are a few short atypical examples with retouch partially extending onto the lateral edges but not sufficiently to be considered as sub-circular types. Nearly all the simple end-scrapers have convex working edges; the one or two

exceptions have an irregular or slightly 'nosed' appearance (Fig. 5.9, 5).

The above measurements show that the blade end-scrapers are made on fairly broad blanks and are slightly thinner than the average flake end-scraper. Apart from this attribute they are in many other respects fairly similar. For example, the majority of simple scrapers are hooked in profile, with a marked curvature of the scraper front (Fig. 5.10, 1 and 3). This characteristic is also noticeable on the five thumbnail scrapers. No particular preference is indicated for the angle of the working edge. The retouch is generally semi-abrupt, but can produce angles ranging from as much as 80° to 40° or less. The actual inclination of the scraper edge varies from piece to piece, but seems to be largely independent of the overall thickness of the blank. It is probably closely linked to the degree of sharpening and usage of the tool.

The five thumbnail scrapers are all retouched distally and are characterised by their short, slightly splayed appearance (Fig. 5.10, 6–8). The only scrapers not retouched at their extremities are three side–scrapers. They are all made on broad flakes with a convex retouched lateral edge opposite a cortical one (Fig. 5.10, 2).

Overall, the scrapers do not appear to have been made on specially prepared blanks. Many of them have cortex on their dorsal surfaces (77%) which suggests the blanks came from the earlier stages of core reduction. In addition, four of the scrapers occur on core tablets (Fig. 5.9, 15), one is a crested blank and another is made on a heavily battered (hammerstone?) fragment. When combined, these features suggest that a high degree of expediency was exercised in the selection of pieces for scraper manufacture.

Just under half of the scrapers are broken (44%), the majority of which are on distal fragments (23). None of them displays the 'contact' or percussive features associated with deliberate fracture (cf. Bergman *et al.* 1983, 1987). On the other hand, the presence of thirteen flexional snaps (Fig. 5.9, 10) suggests that most of the breaks were accidental and probably produced when the scraper edge was retouched. Relatively few of the scrapers are burnt (22%) which contrasts, slightly, with the condition of some of the other tools such as the microliths.

Despite the fact that the majority of tools are extremely fresh-looking, a microscopic examination by Levi-Sala showed that they were nearly all affected by some form of post-depositional modification (Chapter 5.3). Occasionally, the morphology of a tool may give some clue of its former function. For example, J9/4a/30 (Fig. 5.9, 2) is noticeably thicker than many of the others and possesses a relatively flat profile, with no pronounced curvature at the distal end. Although end-scrapers are more usually linked with working soft materials such as hide, many authors have reported wood polish on scrapers (e.g. Moss 1983; Plisson 1982, 1985; Dumont 1983, 1987; Gendel 1982). It has also been suggested, most recently by Juel-Jensen

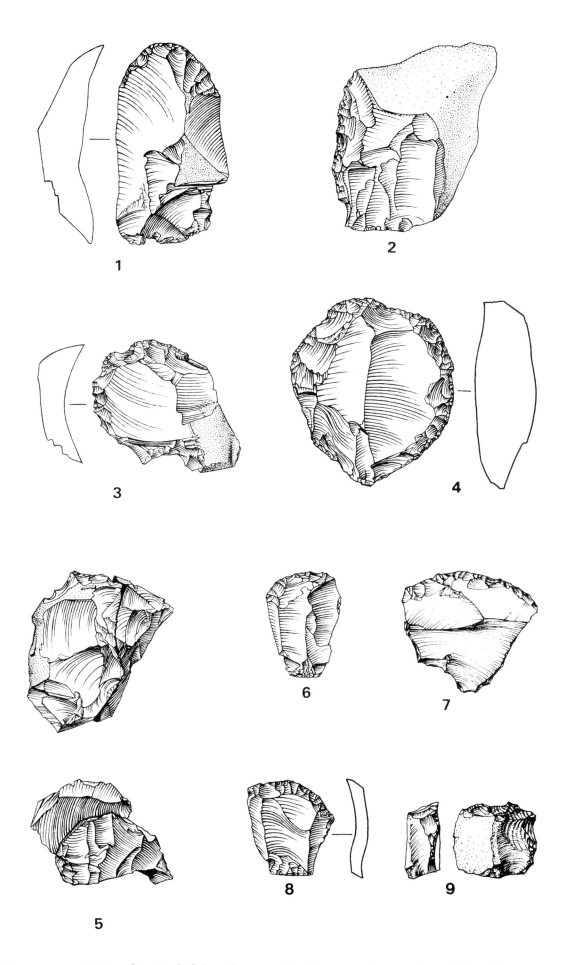

5.10   *Various scrapers. 1, 3-4 and 9= simple flake end-scrapers; 2= side scraper; 5= two refitting flake end-scrapers; 6-8= thumbnail end-scrapers. 1:1 scale.*

214

(1988), that a relevant factor in determining tool-use is the morphology of the scraper-edge. Thus according to her observations thick-edged scrapers were apparently used for woodworking, while those with flatter and thinner edges were preferred as hide tools. If this observation were to be extended to the Hengistbury examples, it would suggest that the majority (which have thin edges and curved profiles) were used in hide-working activities.

Some support for this idea is indicated by the scarcity of tools with visible signs of edge damage, sometimes regarded as diagnostic of working harder materials. When these macroscopic traces are (rarely) present, they are generally confined to the lateral edges of the tools and include minute 'crescentic' breaks. Damage of this type, however, need not necessarily develop as a result of utilisation. Similar breakage patterns have been observed on experimentally trampled artefacts as reported by Tringham and others in their experiments (1974). None of the Powell scrapers shows any signs of edge-rounding (cf. Bosinski and Hahn 1972) or scalar damage of the kind noted on scrapers from other British sites (Barton 1986a).

Although end-scrapers are widely dispersed across the site there is a tendency towards an increase in numbers in the NW sector of the excavated area (Fig. 5.11). An overlap in the distribution can be observed with other tools such as microlith points and it is reasonable to suppose this area formed a central focus of tool-making and tool-using activity. Two of the end-scrapers can be refitted (Fig. 5.10, 5) and since they were made on successive flakes and occur close together it is tempting to infer some pre-planning of activities or at least consecutive manufacture, use (?) and discard of these tools in more or less the same spot.

*Microdenticulates*.: Whereas 64 microdenticulates were found in the excavations, only one example comes from the surface collection. These tools are generally made on blanks with a concave or sinuous edge, with the edge displaying a series of tiny continuous notches (Fig. 5.12). The minute denticulations are usually restricted to a small area of the edge and rarely if ever extend along the entire length of the artefact. Only one tool from the site shows denticulations on both lateral margins.

The 32 unbroken specimens from the Powell site range in length from 31–63 mm with a mean measurement of 45.4±7.07 mm. Their widths vary between 10–24.6 mm with the mean at 14.6±3.51. The tools range in thickness from 2.2–9.3 mm and have a mean value of 4.4±1.66 mm. These measurements indicate that the microdenticulates are made on relatively broad blanks, which technically fall within the blade category, although many are in fact less than 50 mm long.

A common feature of nearly all the blanks is the presence of a concave edge. In profile the blanks are generally fairly straight, although a small number tend to be slightly curved or twisted. Relatively few of the

*Table 5.13 End-scrapers: qualitative data*

|  | No | % |
| --- | --- | --- |
| Condition | | |
| (a) Complete | 53 | 55.8 |
| (b) Broken | 42 | 44.2 |
| Proximal | 7 | 7.4 |
| Mesial | 12 | 12.6 |
| Distal | 23 | 24.2 |
| (c) Burnt | 21 | 22.1 |
| Unburnt | 74 | 77.9 |
| (d) Broken & burnt | 13 | 13.7 |
| (e) Cortex | 73 | 76.8 |

*Table 5.14 Microdenticulates: quantitative measurements*

| Main dimensions (mm) | | Length | Breadth | Thickness |
| --- | --- | --- | --- | --- |
| Total | = | 32 | 31 | 31 |
| Range | = | 31–63 | 10–24.6 | 2.2–9.3 |
| Mean | = | 45.4 | 14.6 | 4.4 |
| Standard Deviation | = | 7.07 | 3.51 | 1.66 |

tools (*c.* 20%) display extensive areas of cortex, and while several display partially cortical areas opposite the retouched edge (Fig. 5.12, 2), none exhibits true natural backing.

No obvious signs of 'handedness' of the maker can be inferred from the location of the denticulated edge. Instead, the choice seems to have been governed largely by the position of the curved edge. Out of 65 tools, 43 have serrations along the right edge and 21 on the left, with only one example displaying them on both. A particularly important criterion, then, seems to have been the morphology of the edge itself. Of the 48 tools complete enough for assessment, most (77%) displayed a concave edge, with the rest comprising sinuous (concave/convex and convex) edges (8%) or straight edges (14%). There is also a measure of consistency in the length of the edge chosen for notching. In 38 examples measured, the serrated portion ranges from 15–27 mm in overall length, with the mean at 18.6±3.13 mm. As a proportion of the average lengths of complete tools, this figure indicates that up to 40% of the blank's edge was denticulated.

The method of producing the microdenticulation appears to have been relatively simple. In all but two examples, the point of origin of the tiny notch scars (making up the denticulation) occurs on the dorsal side. The tiny notches are more or less continuous, with the intervening high points between them making up the saw-teeth. The notches can be produced in a number of different ways. According to Bocquet (1980) they can be made by a pressure technique using another stone tool as the 'compressor'. Alternatively, they can be produced by simply dragging a blade held at right angles gently across the edge of the intended tool. When executed in a dorso-ventral direction, the point of percussion in the notch scars originates from

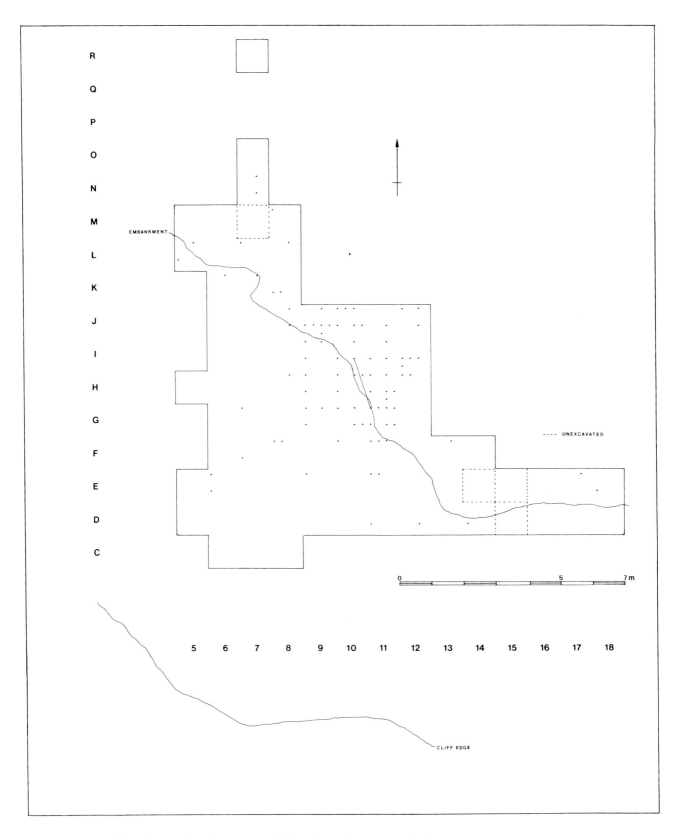

5.11 *Horizontal distribution of end-scrapers. Solid line shows dorso-ventral refit (Fig. 5.10,5).*

the dorsal surface. This is exactly as they appear on the Hengistbury implements. Bocquet also claimed that irregular notching frequently occurred on the 'compressor'. Interestingly, nothing matching this description was observed on any of the Hengistbury artefacts, nor could it be replicated in my experiments which left few visible traces on the notching tool.

Morphological changes in the nature of denticulation can be recognised between individual artefacts. Some tools show well-defined teeth, whilst others reveal only shallow continuous scars along the tool-edge. Such variation probably depends more on the thickness and angle of the edge, and the manufacturing technique used, than on actual use-wear. It is doubtful

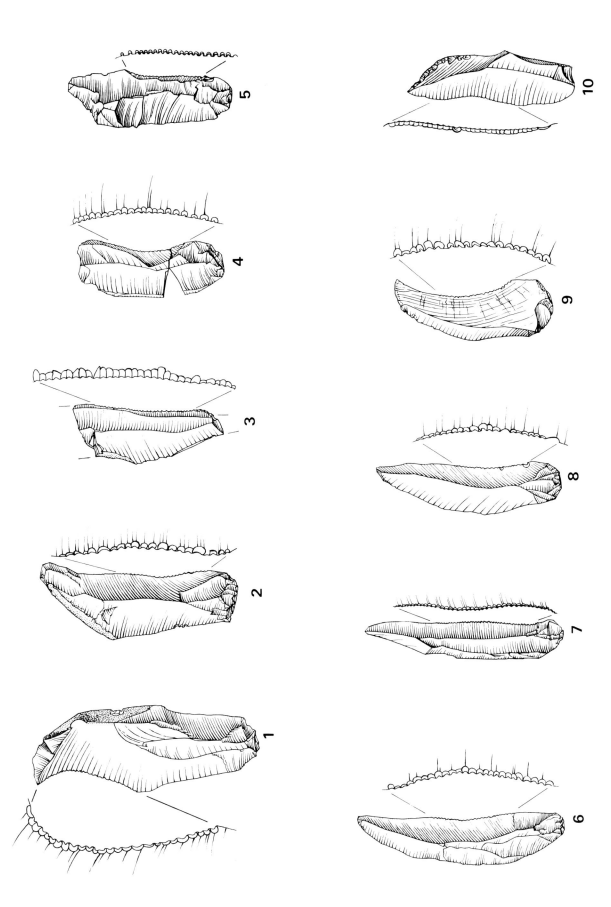

5.12 *Microdenticulates. Details of notched edges illustrated from ventral side at x2 scale. 1:1 scale.*

217

whether the regular denticulation could be a direct result of use.

Detailed experimentation into the function of microdenticulates has been carried out by Levi-Sala and the results are reported below (5.3.3). Her work shows that the tools were probably used for cutting (rather than scraping) soft plant materials, such as the stems of coarse ferns or the bark fibres of green wood. Several informal experiments carried out by the writer with A J Roberts (British Museum), serve to underline Levi-Sala's findings. Figure 5.13 shows an experimental microdenticulate first unused and then after 5 minutes cutting fresh reed stems. The degree of rounding apparent on the saw-teeth is less marked than on the archaeological specimen illustrated but it should be noted that the outlines of the retouch scars (as opposed to the saw-teeth), in both examples, are still sharply defined and unabraded by the working. As one might expect, this implies only superficial penetration of the saw edge into the material being processed. The scoring of slightly harder materials, such as birch bark, would be more consistent with the patterns of wear observed on the archaeological tools. The use of birch bark rolls for matting and basketry is, of course, well attested in the European Mesolithic record (Bokelmann 1986; Gramsch 1987).

Like the end-scrapers, the distribution of the microdenticulates suggests a slightly greater concentration of activity in the NW section of the site (Fig. 5.14). Further confirmation of the spatial organisation is provided by the fact that surface collecting in the southern and eastern areas yielded only one retouched tool of this type.

*Microliths*: Microliths comprise the single largest group of retouched tools, with 341 excavated examples and 49 tools collected from the surface. Amongst the most common types represented are the non-geometric microlith points, classified as A-type points or obliquely blunted points in Clark's typological scheme (1934a). The remainder consist of straight backed bladelets or B-type points, with only a few examples of the geometric tool classes. The list of types is presented below (Table 5.15). Excluded from the essential tool count are the waste products of microlith manufacture (microburins, Krukowski microburins) as well as unfinished tools (e.g. notched blanks). These are treated separately under the category of retouched tool debitage (see below).

A-type microliths constitute nearly 90% of the microlith assemblage. These are characterised by abrupt or semi-abrupt retouch forming a point at the proximal end of the blank (Fig. 5.15). The minor obliqueness of the truncation gives the microlith its distinctive pointed appearance, with the retouched tip either slightly offset or symmetrical to the main axis of the bladelet. Most of the A-types are retouched on the left side (that is, with the pointed end uppermost, as is the formal convention). Only eight out of 349 are retouched on the right hand side. The retouch is almost

*Table 5.15 Microliths: classification*

| | 1980-3 Excavations | Surface Collection | Total | % |
|---|---|---|---|---|
| A-Types (Obliquely blunted) | 307 | 42 | 349 | 89.5 |
| B-Types (Straight backed) | 6 | 2 | 8 | 2.1 |
| C-Types (Obliquely bi-truncated) | – | 1 | 1 | 0.2 |
| D-Types (Isosceles triangle) | 1 | – | 1 | 0.2 |
| Unclassified | 27 | 4 | 31 | 7.9 |
| Total | 341 | 49 | 390 | 99.9 |

always direct (from the ventral surface), although there is one inversely retouched example and 40 with bidirectional retouch scars. The latter are generally present on the thicker tools (Fig. 5.15, 3–7).

Normally, the A-type points possess a simple outline with retouch confined to part of one edge (270), but there are also a number of related sub-categories. A breakdown of the A-type class is illustrated in Figure 5.16. It shows that 35 examples have additional semi-abrupt or fine retouch opposite the main retouched edge. A similar refinement is sometimes seen at the distal (basal) end (14). In most cases, the retouch is of ancillary importance to the main oblique truncation. Its purpose was probably to streamline the tool by removing any irregularities of the edge. Such adjustment would no doubt have been important for hafting purposes.

The 59 complete microlith A-types have a mean length of 31.5 mm with a standard deviation of 7.47 mm. The total range represented in the sample is 16–50 mm. The breadths of the unbroken pieces vary between 6–13 mm, giving a mean dimension of 8.1 mm. The standard deviation is 1.71 cm. Broken pieces with breadth dimensions complete enough to be measured are much more numerous, but their inclusion would not significantly alter the statistics quoted above. The mean thickness is 2.5±0.8 mm. The range in size varies between 1–5 mm and again this compares well with the maximum thicknesses of broken points. As can be seen from these measurements, the Hengistbury microliths are predominantly made on blanks within the bladelet size class.

Out of a total of 349 classified A-types, only 59 are complete. The rest are made up of broken distal (35) or mesial fragments (108), with proximal retouched tips also being well-represented (141). Although distal fragments of microliths might be difficult to identify (due to the absence of retouch) the low proportion of distal ends is difficult to explain solely in these terms. The actual reason for low numbers of these pieces may be more closely linked to their suggested function as projectiles. This is discussed in greater detail below.

A fairly high proportion of broken tools show signs of burning (35%), which may have been a cause of breakage. Other observations show that, with few exceptions, none of the microliths has any cortex. The fact that the microlith blanks were carefully selected for tool-making is suggested by a general uniformity of appearance. For example, their profiles are generally straight and they have a tendency to end in a flat or feathered termination.

Among the broken A-types are 61 proximal tips displaying straight snaps; these are separated from other broken tips known as 'Krukowski microburins' (see 5.2.1). In practice, there is little to choose between the two types of fragment, except in the nature of the break facet. Many of the tips undoubtedly resulted from simple manufacturing accidents and it may be significant that a relatively high proportion of broken tips display bidirectional retouch scars (16%). The latter are often considered good indicators of anvil-use during manufacture (Tixier *et al.* 1980)

Apart from the A-types, there are eight straight-backed B-types (Fig. 5.15, 33), and single examples of the bi-truncated C-type (Fig. 5.15, 34) and isosceles triangle or D-type (Fig. 5.15, 35) microliths. The rest (31) are made up of unclassified fragments. None of microliths in the collection possesses the straight or concave truncation characteristic of the 'Hollow-based' F-types (also described as 'Horsham Points').

In terms of their horizontal distribution, the microliths appear to be heavily concentrated in the NW area of the site (Fig. 5.17). This pattern could reflect either a special focus of manufacturing activity or a particular discard pattern resulting from tool use or a combination of both. The overlap in the distribution of microliths and microburins (5.2.19) indicates that this was certainly a focus of microlith manufacturing activity. It has even been possible to refit microliths made on successive blades (Fig. 5.18). However, that this was not purely a tool manufacturing zone is implied by some of the tool breakages (see below). Moreover, it is likely that very many more refits of broken tools would have been possible if they were all simply manufacturing accidents.

Although there may be plenty of evidence for on site blank manufacture and tool-making it is often difficult to demonstrate actual examples of tool-use. In exceptional cases, however, as with certain of the microliths, it is possible to observe breakage patterns which are diagnostic of use. The nature of such damage patterns at Hengistbury and what they reveal in terms of tool function is discussed in the next section.

*Functional evidence for the use of microliths*: Despite no real consensus in the archaeological literature most authors would agree that because of their small size microliths were designed for use in a haft rather than being directly held in the hand (Bordes 1952). In consequence, microliths are generally interpreted as multifunctional tools serving as barbed insets in projectile equipment (Clark 1962, 1975) or as slotted components in plant knives (Clarke 1976) or as mounted drill-bits (Clark 1936, Fig. 69). The extremely fragile nature of bone, antler or wooden hafts means that associations between the tool and the handle or shaft are seldom capable of being demonstrated archaeologically.

Some of the best surviving examples of the use of microliths is in connection with Mesolithic archery equipment. The examples most widely referred to come from Scandinavia, North Germany and Eastern USSR where wooden bows and arrowshafts have been preserved in organic sediments (Becker 1945; Andersen 1951; Petersson 1951; Troels-Smith 1962; Clark 1975; Gramsch 1987; Nuzhnyi 1989). All the bows are wooden self-bows, either of pine (Gramsch 1987) or elm (Clark 1975; Andersen 1985). The arrowshafts are usually of birch, pine or hazel wood and consist of microlithic flint inserts (Petersson 1951), sometimes held with resin and set in a detachable foreshaft (Clark 1975). So far, the most convincing British Mesolithic example of this equipment comes from Seamer Carr, Yorkshire, where a series of small geometric microliths were found in association with a crushed wooden shaft of poplar or willow (Walker and Otlet 1988). One of the flints showed traces of a beeswax fixative (David pers. comm.). The remnant shaft gave a radiocarbon date of 8,210±150 BP (HAR-6498).

Indirect evidence for the use of flint projectile equipment derives from microliths embedded in animal bones for which there are plenty of European examples (Hartz and Winge 1906; Péquart *et al.* 1937; Strobel 1959; Clark 1975; Fischer *et al.* 1984). Only one British find of this type has so far been recorded (Jacobi 1980), although others will doubtless come to light with further study of museum faunal collections. The example quoted comes from Lydstep, Wales and was found in association with a pig's skeleton. Some supporting evidence for the use of microlith arrowheads, derives from excavated arrangements of these tools (Jacobi 1978; Myers 1987) or can be inferred from resin traces left on the artefacts (Clark 1954; Wymer 1962; Roberts, Barton and Evans in prep).

A further reason for identifying microliths as components of archery equipment comes from breakage patterns observed directly on the flints themselves. In particular, breaks known as 'impact fractures' have been described on a range of lithic projectile types from N America (Hester and Heizer 1973; Frison *et al.* 1976; Odell 1978; Whitthoft 1968) and from Europe and the Near East (Paulsen 1975; Moss and Newcomer 1982; Bergman and Newcomer 1983; Fischer *et al.* 1984). Similar breakages have been demonstrated experimentally to occur as the result of high velocity impact when the arrow strikes its target.

*Microliths and 'Impact Fractures'*: Amongst the microlith points from the Mesolithic site are at least six with breakages which have been identified tentatively as 'impact fractures' (Barton and Bergman 1982). Common examples of this type of breakage are 'burin-like' breaks or else simple flexional (bending) breaks, and sometimes they occur in combination (Fig. 5.19, 1-5). At Hengistbury, fractures of this type have been

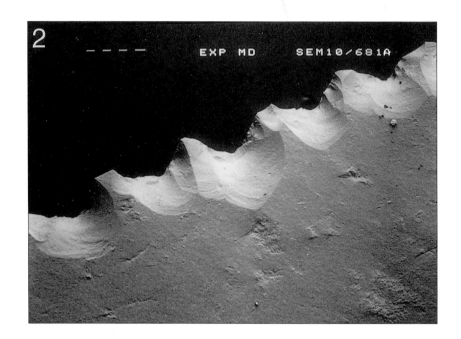

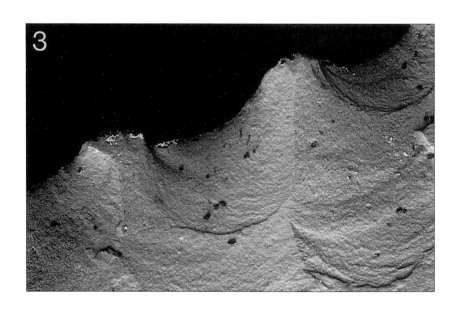

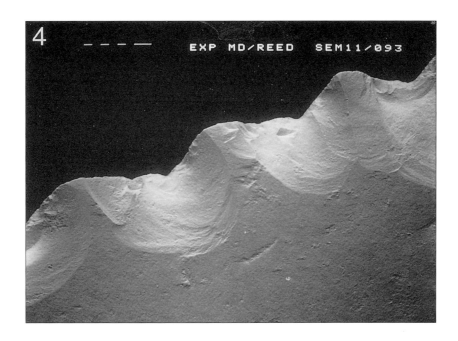

5.13  *SEM photomicrographs of experimental and archaeological microdenticulates. 1 and 3= archaeological (x30 and x50, respectively); 2= experimental (x30) before use; 4 and 5= experimental (x50 and x75, respectively) after 5 minutes cutting fresh reed. Right bar of each scale= 0.1 mm. (Photo: Natural History Museum)*

recognised on one B-type microlith and five A-type oblique points (Fig. 5.19). The breaks are thought to result from the high velocity impact of flint projectiles against a hard medium such as animal bone (cf. Bergman and Newcomer 1983).

In 1981, an experiment was carried out by the author and Christopher Bergman to test the efficiency of microliths as arrowheads and to see whether the damage on the archaeological pieces could be duplicated experimentally. It was also speculated that if microscopic polishes were to develop on the experimental arrowheads these should also be apparent on the Mesolithic specimens.

The experiment involved the firing of arrows into a suspended fallow deer carcass (Fig. 5.20) with the archer standing at close range (Barton and Bergman 1982). The bow was a yew wood replica of the Mesolithic Holmegaard self-bow and drew 40 lb. at 26 inches. All the arrowshafts were c. 800 mm long x 10 mm wide and made of softwood (Port Orford Cedar). Since, the target range was relatively short (4–8 m) most of the arrows were unfletched. The flint points themselves were all copies of the A-type microliths from the Hengistbury site. They were made out of Cretaceous flint from East Anglia and were all flaked with a soft antler hammer. Hafting consisted of insert-

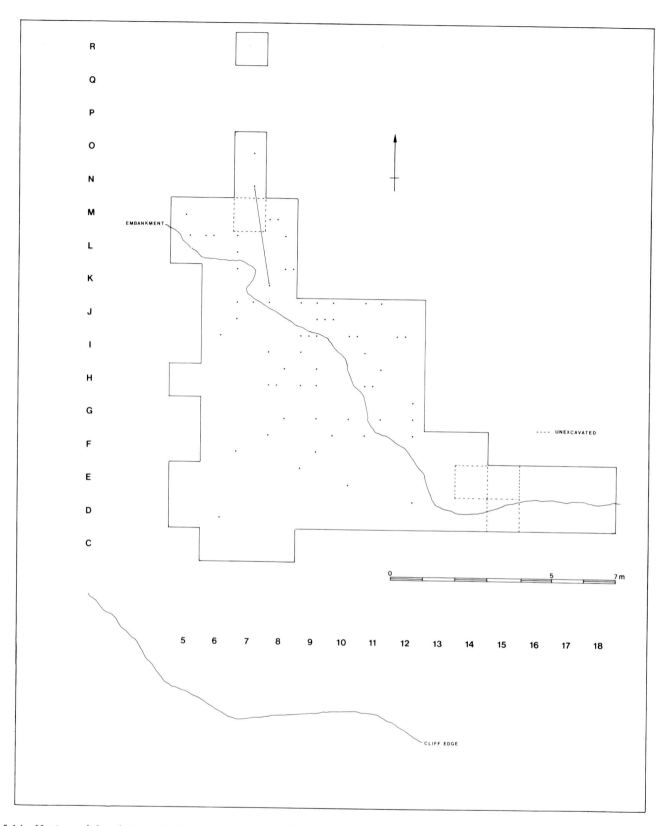

5.14 *Horizontal distribution of microdenticulates. Solid line shows break refit.*

ing the microlith into a pre-cut slot at one end of the arrowshaft. The flint point was then fixed in position using an organic resin (beeswax and pine) and sinew wrapping (Fig. 5.21).

The results have been reported in detail elsewhere (Barton and Bergman 1982). Briefly, they confirmed that the various breakages noted in the archaeological specimens could all be simulated experimentally (Fig. 5.19, 6-10), although the most common form of break was the simple flexional 'straight' snap. An unexpected result, which at the time surprised us, was the relatively high number of microliths with no outward signs of damage at all. We observed that although the tips had sliced through the thick skin and inner tissue, meat

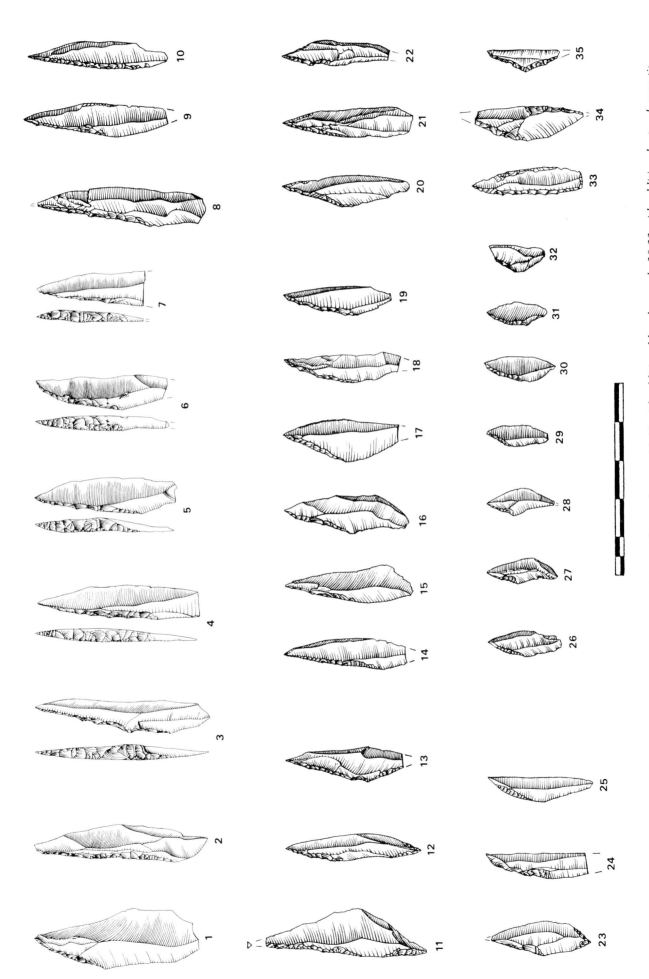

5.15  Microliths. 1-32= A-type obliquely blunted microliths (3-7 with bidirectional retouch scars, 11-12 with additional basal retouch, 20-22 with additional retouch near tip, 23-27 showing microburin facet); 33= B-type straight-backed bladelet; 34= C-type obliquely bi-truncated microlith; 35= D-type isosceles triangle. Centimetre scale.

223

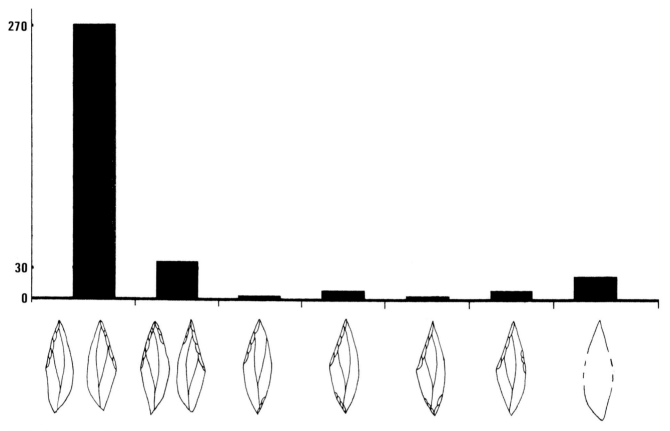

5.16 *A-type microliths and sub-categories. Y-axis= absolute numbers of microliths*

Table 5.17 *Microlith A-types: quantitative data*

| Main dimensions (mm) | | Length | Breadth | Thickness |
|---|---|---|---|---|
| Total | = | 59 | 59 | 59 |
| Range | = | 16–50 | 6–13 | 1–5 |
| Mean | = | 31.5 | 8.1 | 2.5 |
| Standard Deviation | = | 7.47 | 1.71 | 0.8 |

Table 5.18. *Hengistbury A-type microliths: qualitative attributes*

| | n | % |
|---|---|---|
| *Condition* | | |
| (n= 343) | | |
| (a)  Complete | 59 | 17.2 |
| (b)  Broken | | |
| Proximal (tips) | 141 | 41.6 |
| Mesial fragments | 108 | 31.5 |
| Distal (basal) | 35 | 10.2 |
| (c)  Burnt (n= 346) | 104 | 30.0 |
| *Dorsal scar pattern* | | |
| (n= 238) | | |
| (a)  Unidirectional | 180 | 75.6 |
| (b)  Opposed | 50 | 21.0 |
| (c)  Crossed | 4 | 1.7 |
| (d)  Multidirectional | 4 | 1.7 |
| *Retouch Type* | | |
| (a)  Abrupt/semi abrupt | 321 | 92.0 |
| (b)  Fine | 6 | 1.7 |
| (c)  Combination of above | 16 | 4.6 |
| (d)  Other | 6 | 1.7 |
| *Retouch Direction* | | |
| (a)  Direct | 301 | 86.2 |
| (b)  Bidirectional | 40 | 11.5 |
| (c)  Inverse | 1 | 0.3 |
| (d)  Unrecorded | 7 | 2.0 |
| *Retouch position* | | |
| (a)  Left | 326 | 93.4 |
| (b)  Right | 8 | 2.3 |
| (c)  Unrecorded | 15 | 4.3 |

alone was not enough to cause visible damage to the points. It was only when they struck bone (or missed the target altogether and hit the ground) that impact damage occurred. On the other hand the rapid cutting through skin, meat and cartilage suggested to us that in the absence of obvious damage, we might be able to investigate microscopic wear patterns caused by the flint entering the animal.

*Microwear analysis of the Mesolithic points* (By R Unger–Hamilton): Observations of experimental flint arrowheads by Peter Rasmussen (Fischer *et al.* 1984) suggested that it might be worth investigating the Hengistbury points for microwear traces. In the Danish experiments, microscopically visible striations were recorded near the tips of broken flint points. It was thought that these resulted from minute fragments breaking away on impact and striating the surface as the rest of the point followed through (Fischer *et al.* 1984). This is not the first time that projectile points

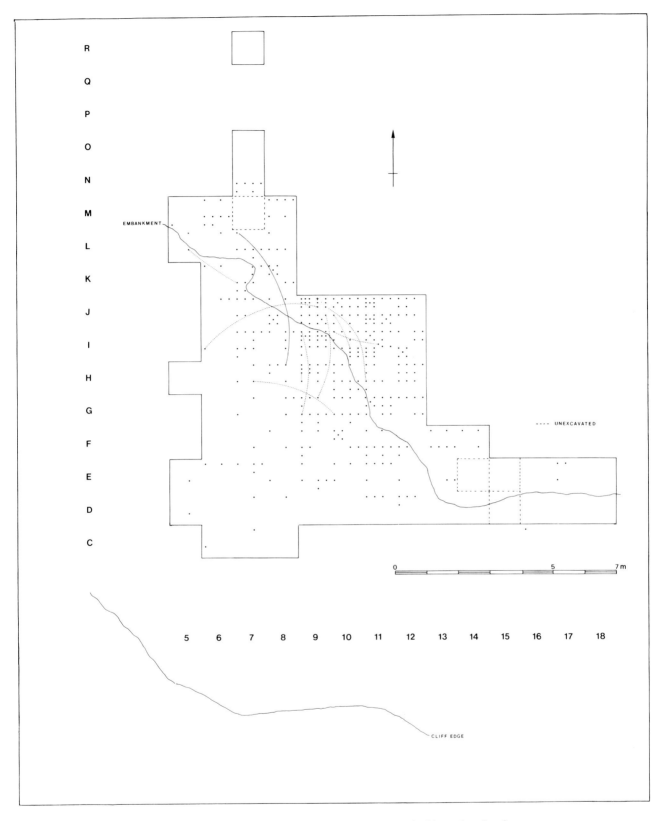

*5.17 Horizontal distribution of microliths. Solid line= dorso-ventral refit; dashed line= break refit.*

have been investigated for microwear. Earlier work was carried out by Ahler (1971) and Odell (1978). More recently, Anderson-Gerfaud (1983) using high-power studies has claimed that the type of target (animal tissue) could be recognised on microliths from the Near East. However, other researchers have not been able to confirm these findings (Moss 1983; Moss and Newcomer 1982), and generally report microscopic impact traces on much fewer artefacts.

Thirty of the microlith points from the Mesolithic site were selected for examination. They consisted of the six 'impact damaged' pieces as well as a selection of artefacts displaying 'straight' flexional breaks, either proximally or distally. Apart from one example (a B-

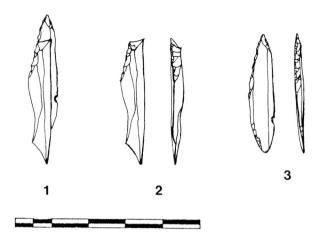

*5.18  Refitting A-type microliths. Centimetre scale.*

type microlith), all of them conformed to the characteristic A-types found at the site.

An initial analysis showed that despite their superficially fresh appearance, a relatively high proportion of the pieces were affected by post-depositional modification (see Chapter 5.3) which only became apparent once the artefacts had been microscopically examined. The analysis involved examination, both with the naked eye and using high-power microwear analysis based on the Keeley (1980) method, but modified for my own uses (Unger-Hamilton 1984a).

The comparative sample of experimental microliths was provided by Barton and Bergman (1982), as well as several flints from one of Newcomer's experiments. The latter consisted of flint-tipped arrows with side armatures which had been fired into a meat and bone target, whilst others were shot into dry sand and wet sand. Additionally, as an experimental control ten microlith copies were laid on a sand surface, or partially buried, and trampled for ten minutes.

*Results*: Various forms of microscopic damage were visible on the experimental pieces. These consisted of tiny flute-like fractures associated with the larger breaks, longitudinal striations, polish streaks and superficial scoring (cf. 'stone polish'), as well as oblique and randomly orientated striations. The results from the experimental sample may be summarised as follows:

(1) None of the trampled material showed any signs of micro-fracturing or other minute breakages. Aside from these pieces, the only other flints without obvious signs of damage were the side armatures used in Newcomer's experiments.

(2) Striations, scores and streaks appeared on many of the experimental pieces. Interestingly, some of these features were produced by factors other than the animal target. For example, multi-directional striations occurred on some of the trampled artefacts; deeper scores were also visible on microliths shot into the sand.

These results were then compared with observations made on the archaeological microliths. Unfortunately because of the condition of the Mesolithic artefacts it was not possible to draw any firm conclusions about the function of these tools, at least from the microscopic traces. Nevertheless, the following general observations could be made:

(A) Apart from one tool, multi-directional and random striations occurred on all of the microliths and these are most likely attributable to trampling or natural post-depositional processes, rather than tool-use.

(B) Microscopic damage on the lateral (unretouched) edges of the microliths might not be the result of use-wear especially if the flints had experienced movement in the sands (by trampling and so forth). Nevertheless, it is possible that the edges of some microliths could be used for meat cutting without leaving any discernible polish (Unger-Hamilton 1984a).

Although the findings from this study were inconclusive and largely negative in their implications, they do not contradict the main findings of Barton and Bergman (1982). In my own experience it is extremely unlikely that macroscopic damage of the the kind reported in the archery experiment could have resulted from trampling or from the range of post-depositional processes described above (Chapter 3). Unfortunately, it was not possible to demonstrate any microscopic striations or scores exclusively associated with forms of impact breakage.

*Truncations*: Amongst the retouched tools are a few artefacts with single, straight or oblique truncations. These tools are on broader and thicker blanks, are frequently cortical and do not resemble any of the microlith forms. They comprise six blanks with straight truncations and nine obliquely truncated pieces. The retouch is always direct and semi-abrupt to abrupt in type (Fig. 5.22, 4–5).

*Retouched flakes, blades and bladelets*: There are 20 implements which belong to this category. Nine of the tools are on flakes and eleven on blades or bladelets. Excluded from this class are four cortical blades with scalar retouch on their lateral edges (Fig. 5.23, 4–6); these are described with other miscellaneous tools in the next section.

None of the artefacts in this category are highly standardised, the only aspect they share in common is the continuous or near continuous retouch down one edge. Most of them display semi-abrupt, direct retouch; there are no inversely retouched examples. Although few tools have abrupt edges, the retouch may have served to blunt one side or one end to make a finger-hold (Fig. 5.22, 9). In some examples discontinuous shallow scars or small notches are clearly visible on the opposite edge which may be a form of use-wear. However, it should be cautioned that the edges are thin

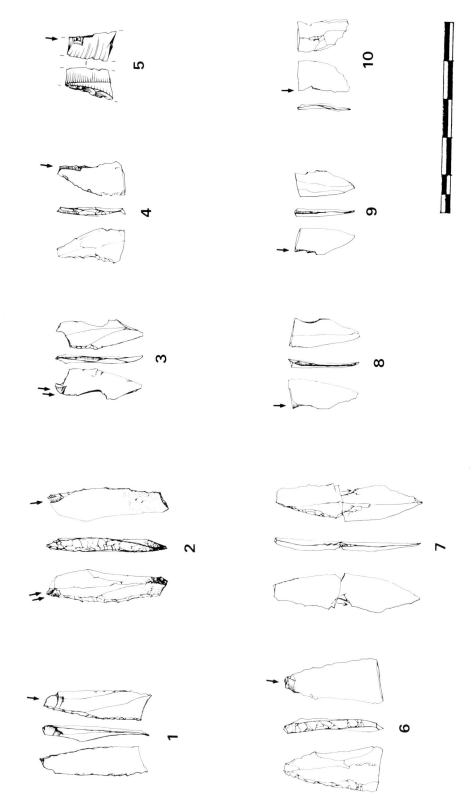

5.19  Microliths with 'impact fractures'. 1-5= archaeological (all on A-types except 2 which is a B-type microlith); 6-10= experimental examples. (Centimetre scale).

227

5.20 *Suspended fallow deer carcass in the arrow firing experiment. Any impact shattered debris was caught on the underlying plastic sheet.*

and are particularly susceptible to other forms of casual damage.

*Miscellaneous retouched tools*: Within this class are nearly all the retouched pieces which do not fall into any of the preceding categories. They include mainly broken flakes and blades with areas of discontinuous retouch. Most of it is semi-abrupt and direct, but there are five inversely retouched fragments. Also included, are four small blades with continuous invasive scalar retouch along one edge. Since the tools are naturally backed with cortex (Fig. 5.23, 4–5), it is possible that the scalar scars are the result of damage incurred during use.

This tool group highlights the extensive grey-area which undoubtedly exists between some forms of retouched blank. Besides the examples described above, accidental damage can also occur during flaking (see Chapter 7 'spontaneous retouch') or as a result of post-depositional processes (e.g. trampling, cf. Barton 1987). Due to these potential pitfalls, the count of miscellaneous pieces has necessarily erred on the cautious side and doubtless many more artefacts could have been included. For example, a quantity of flakes and blades with isolated retouched notches or crescentic breaks, which resemble accidental edge damage, were deliberately omitted from the essential tool count.

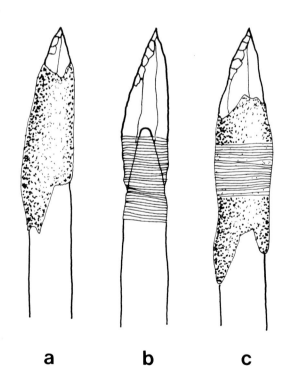

a          b          c

5.21 *Methods of hafting the experimental microlith points. a= resin; b= sinew; c= sinew and resin (practical experience proved that the sinew would have been more effective if covered by the resin) (Drawing by Spence Ingerson).*

228

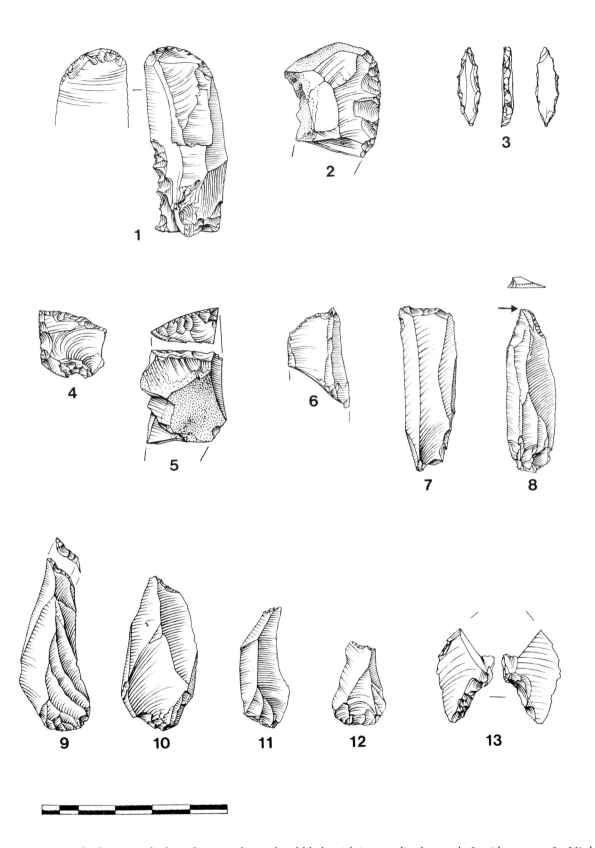

5.22  *Truncations and other retouched artefacts. 1= denticulated blade with inverse distal retouch; 2= side scraper; 3= Mèche de foret (drill-bit); 4-5 and 9-10= truncations; 6-7= 'pronged' pieces; 8= retouched flake with 'burin facet'; 11-12= examples of 'spontaneous retouch'; 13= petit tranchet derivative. Centimetre scale.*

Two artefacts display convergent semi-abrupt/abrupt direct retouch forming a slight projection at the distal end (Fig. 5.22, 6–7). Although, the 'prongs' are not pronounced, the tools bear some resemblance to awls or becs (cf. Brézillon 1977b).

Figure 5.22, 8 shows a related tool with a 'burin facet' at the distal end. Similar damage has been noted on experimental becs where too much lateral force has been exerted at the tip and a spall is detached. No obvious signs of damage accompany the retouch, but one

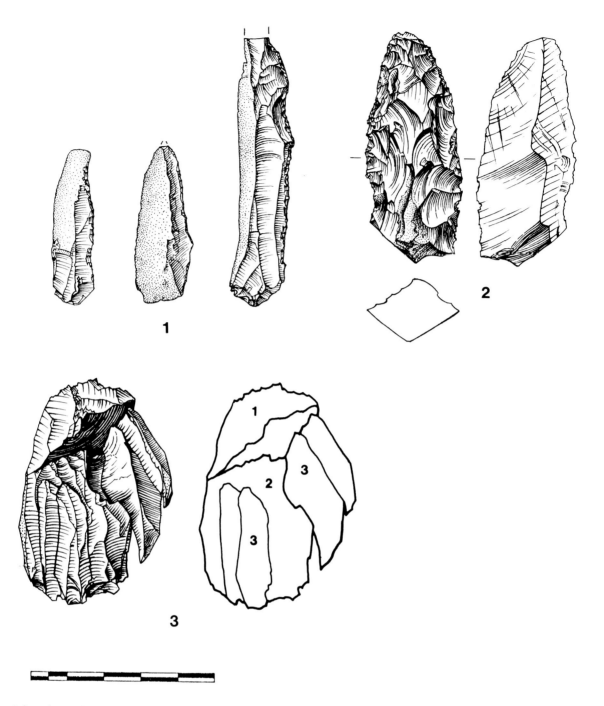

5.23 *Selected Mesolithic artefacts. 1= naturally backed blades with invasive scalar retouch; 2= fabricator ?; 3= refitted bladelet core (1= core tablet, 2= opposed platform core, 3-4 refitted artefacts detached from different ends of the core). Centimetre scale.*

tool has a flexion break which may indicate breakage during use.

The mèche de foret is also included in the miscellaneous class. The tool is abruptly retouched down its lateral edges and pointed at both ends (Fig. 5.22, 3). One of the extremities has a torsion snap visible on the ventral surface. According to a preliminary microwear study by Unger-Hamilton there is an undefined micropolish and a single longitudinal striation, associated with the torsion fracture near the tip. The combination of features strongly implies the tool had been used as a drill. There are no other examples of its kind at the site. Figure 5.24 shows photomicrographs of the

Hengistbury drill and an experimental example made and used by the author to bore a hole in a shale bead.

Several artefacts, not included in the miscellaneous group, appear to have 'spontaneous retouch' at their distal ends (cf. Newcomer 1976, also see Chapter 7 this volume) They all occur on thin flakes or bladelets and do not appear to be suitable as tool blanks (Fig. 5.22 11-12).

*Fabricator?*: One tool made on a thick flake, with a rhombic cross-section and flaked on two sides, may have served as a fabricator for retouching other tools. However, no marked damage occurs where it might be

5.24   *SEM photomicrograph of drill-bits. 1= archaeological (x16); 2= experimental (x18). Right bar on scale= 0.1 mm. (Photo: Natural History Museum)*

most expected, close to the robust tip (Fig. 5.23, 2). Experimental fabricators often have visible grinding and rounding on the utilised end (Bergman pers. comm.).

*Post-Mesolithic artefacts*: A small number of artefacts of clearly post-Mesolithic age have been recovered from the Powell site. These include four polished stone axe flakes, five fragments of pottery and at least one flake arrowhead abandoned in the early stages of manufacture. The latter is an example of a petit tranchet derivative arrowhead (Clark 1934c), and shows a lateral snap (Fig. 5.22, 13). The five sherds of pottery are highly fragmented and it is not possible to tell from their weathered state whether they are Neolithic or later in age, although they are probably linked with other Bronze Age finds made from the nearby barrow.

Like the arrowhead and two of the axe flakes, the pottery (which all derives from one square metre: D14), occurs on the fringes of the Mesolithic scatter. When all these extraneous artefacts are added together, they constitute no more than 2% of the retouched tool assemblage.

Another source of 'contamination' can be identified within the core debitage from the site. In these cases, features which help distinguish them from the bulk of Mesolithic products can be narrowed down to just two factors: the choice of raw material and the reduction methods used.

As has been mentioned above, the quality of raw material was of singular importance to the Mesolithic flintknappers. It is undoubtedly significant that only one of the bladelet cores seems to have been made on the poor-quality flint available in the headland gravels.

231

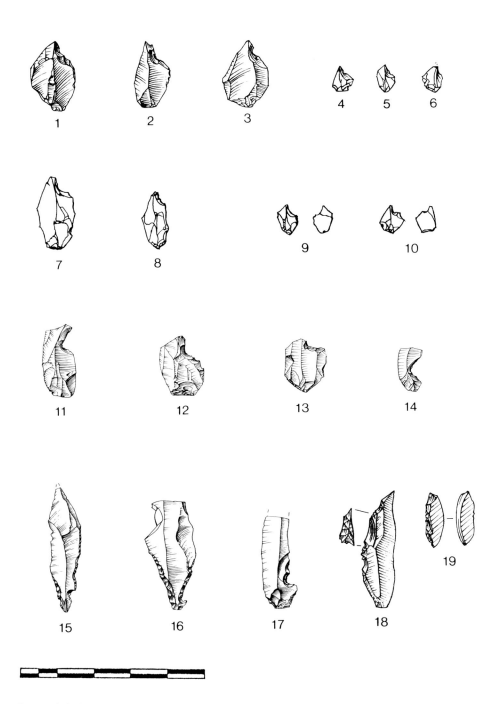

5.25 *Microburins and microlith debitage. 1-10= proximal microburins; 11-14= microburin miss-hits; 15-17= unfinished forms; 18= experimental microlith with lateral snap; 19= lateral edge fragment of microlith. Centimetre scale.*

This observation may be contrasted with features noted on a sample of artefacts from a Bronze Age barrow near the Mesolithic site. The barrow yielded large amounts of flake debris and cores made on small pebbles of the same low-grade flint which occurs locally on the headland.

The core reduction method used at the barrow site appears to be quite distinctive from the technique used at the Mesolithic site. For one thing it was aimed directly at the manufacture of short broad flakes; the type of blank used for scrapers and bifacially flaked arrowheads. In consequence the shapes of the cores are generally very different, at least in the final stages of abandonment. From a more subjective viewpoint, flaking of the Bronze age cores seems to have been fairly haphazard and involved little if any platform preparation. The barrow site sample contains a high proportion of non-cortical flakes; these are evidently hard-hammer struck with incipient cones on their butts. Groups of incipient cones are also clearly visible on the cores (Fig. 5.6, 4). In complete contrast, the cores from the Mesolithic site rarely if ever share these features; for example they never occur on bladelet cores or any of their refitting components. Seven cores made on smaller pebbles do, however, display such attributes and on these grounds are considered to be potentially intrusive elements. Recognition of these few post-Mesolithic artefacts indicates the contamination level is likely to be very low.

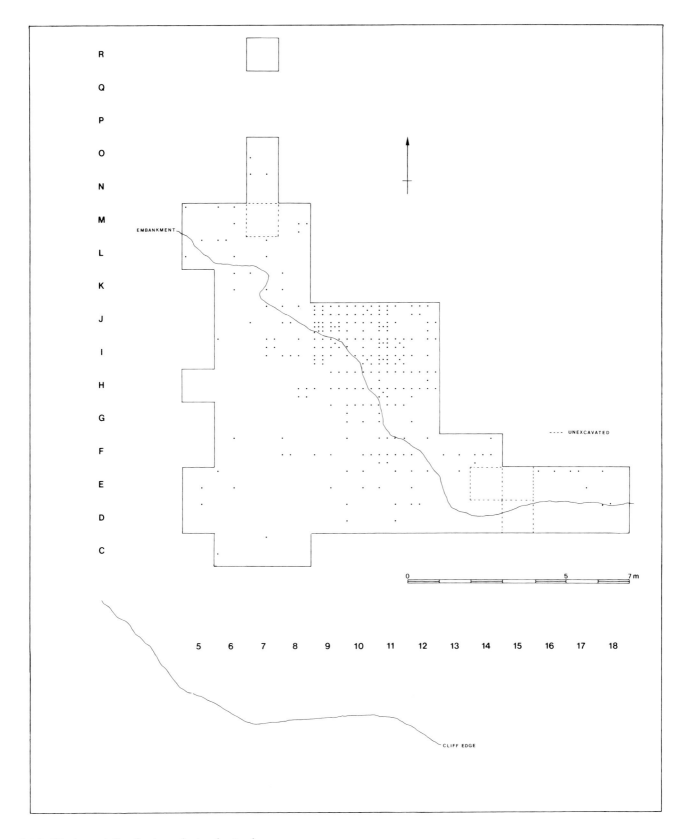

5.26 *Horizontal distribution of microburins by metre squares.*

### 5.2.1   *Retouched tool debitage*

*Microburins:* Originally identified by Siret (1893) as the by-product of flint trapeze manufacture (the *coup du trapèze*), the artefact-type suffered a reversal of fortunes at the hands of Henri Breuil who described them as a small form of burin or 'micro-burin' (1921).

Although he subsequently retracted this view (Breuil and Zbyszewski 1947), following the refitting work of Vignard (1931, 1934), the term entered the literature and has remained in use ever since. In Britain, Clark was one of the first to recognise the relationship between the tool and the waste product (1932).

233

The 273 microburins from the Powell site are all proximal examples (Fig. 5.25, 1–10). This is not particularly surprising given the absence of bi-truncated microlith forms (triangles and trapezes) and the fact that virtually all the Hengistbury microliths are retouched proximally. Evidence illustrating how the microliths were made is provided by a microburin which refits to the proximal section of a microlith (Fig. 5.27, 3). It shows that the blank was notched and then broken, removing the thicker proximal end. The proximal microburin displays the characteristic notch portion, intersected by an oblique break facet. In nearly all cases the break facet occurs on the ventral surface. The corresponding dorsal negative scars are sometimes visible on the tips of microliths (Fig. 5.15, 23–27).

The microburins range in size from a few millimetres to over 20 mm long. The other dimensions suggest they were made on fairly broad blanks of a highly standardised shape suitable for making microliths. The breadths of the microburins range from 4–17 mm with a mean measurement of 7.3±2.27 mm. Thicknesses of the pieces vary from 1–4 mm and have a mean of 2.3±0.65 mm.

A common characteristic of S English Early Mesolithic assemblages is the highly uniform technique of retouching microliths, with one edge repeatedly being modified in preference to the other. At Hengistbury, the microliths are invariably modified on the left side (proximal end uppermost) and this is reflected in the high proportion of left notched microburins (99%). Since there would appear to be no obvious advantage to be gained by retouching one or other edge, it is tempting to ask whether this stylistic choice was linked in any way to 'handedness'. Although the author holds no strong views on this matter it is worth noting that notching a blank (ventral side up) is more easily achieved with the blank supported in the left hand and the right hand doing the notching. In the case of a left-handed person this task is much more difficult (since only a tiny portion of the blank can be supported while notching). For this practical reason alone it seems quite likely that the makers of the Hengistbury microliths were all right-handed.

Not all microliths, however, were made by deliberately notching and snapping a bladelet. On some of the thinner blanks, for example, it appears that the retouch extends all the way down to the proximal end. This attribute has been noted on a number of snapped bulbar fragments (Fig. 5.27, 11–13) which show no signs of notching. Although, none of them has been refitted to a tool, these pieces were undoubtedly the by-products of microlith manufacture.

When the microburin break produces a straight snap it is known as a miss-hit (Fig. 5.25, 11–14). There are 44 such examples in the assemblage.

The distribution of microburins broadly reflects that of the microliths with the heaviest concentration occurring in the NW area (Fig. 5.26).

Table 5.19 *Microburins: quantitative data*

| Main dimensions (mm) | | Length | Breadth | Thickness |
|---|---|---|---|---|
| Total | = | 246 | 259 | 271 |
| Range | = | 5–22 | 4–17 | 1–4 |
| Mean | = | 11.08 | 7.33 | 2.31 |
| Standard Deviation | = | 3.40 | 2.27 | 0.65 |

*Unfinished forms:* Another category of waste comprises those pieces where the first stage of notching preparation was carried out but for some reason the microburin was never detached. Figure 5.25, 17 illustrates one such example where the reason for discard is relatively straightforward: the distal end is broken. In the second example (Fig. 5.25, 16), the explanation might be linked to the steepness of retouch on the edge opposite the notch, which made it unsuitable for continuing any further.

*Krukowski Microburins:* Thirty-five broken tips of microliths have been recovered which can be classified as 'Krukowski microburins' (Fig. 5.27, 4–8). This type of waste was first recognised in the Polish Mesolithic (Krukowski 1914) but the eponymous term does not appear to have been widely used until 1938 when it was coined by Giraud and others in describing French material (Tixier 1963). The choice of name is somewhat unfortunate because it implies a direct comparison with the artefact as well as the microburin technique. In fact, unlike the true microburin, the Krukowski variant is unlikely to be a deliberate by-product. According to François Bordes, the Krukowski microburin is a type of accidental waste flake which occurs when backing the edges of blades and bladelets. It often happens for example when the retouching blow is delivered too far onto the blank and the piece breaks, producing a fracture scar almost identical to the microburin facet (Bordes 1957, 580).

At Hengistbury, tips of this kind display retouch along one edge and a microburin-like facet on the ventral surface. Another form of fracture which commonly occurs during microlith manufacture is the straight or diagonal transverse snap at the proximal end. To remedy this mistake and produce a serviceable point the broken end must be further retouched. Occasionally, as illustrated in Figure 5.27, 1–2, this resulted in a second break at the tip.

All of the Krukowski microburins at the Powell site are proximal end examples, and so cannot easily be confused with distal microburins which sometimes occur in other Mesolithic assemblages.

### 5.2.2 Hammerstones

One quartzite cobble weighing 404.2 gm was found in the southern part of the site (Fig. 5.28, 3), in close proximity to the sandstone 'rubbers' (see below). In terms of its weight and shape, it would appear to be an ideal form of hard percussor, but there are no outward

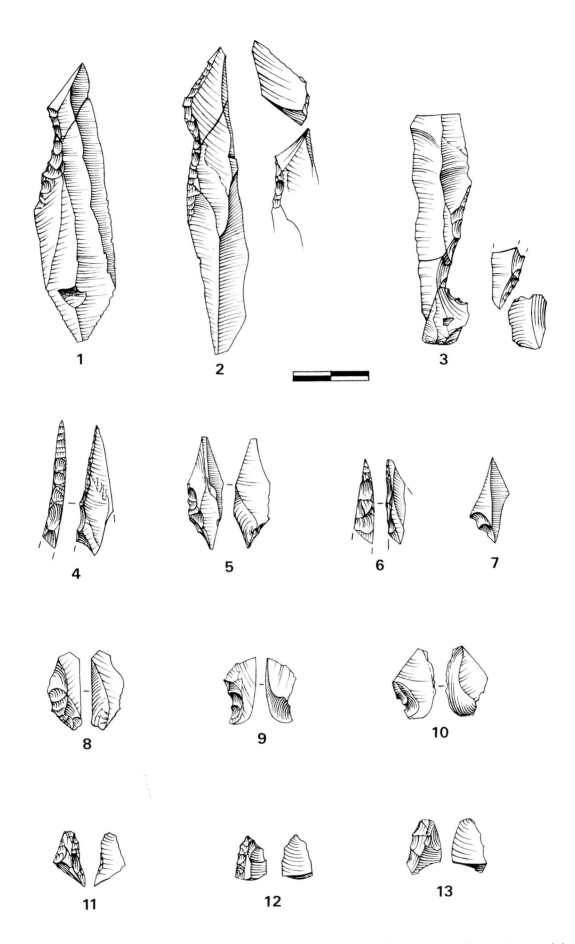

5.27  *Krukowski microburins and microlith debitage. 1-2= microliths with refitting Krukowski microburins; 3= microlith with proximal microburin refit, plus ventral views; 4-8= Krukowski microburins; 9-10= notch fragments; 11-13= retouched proximal end fragments. 2.5 cm scale.*

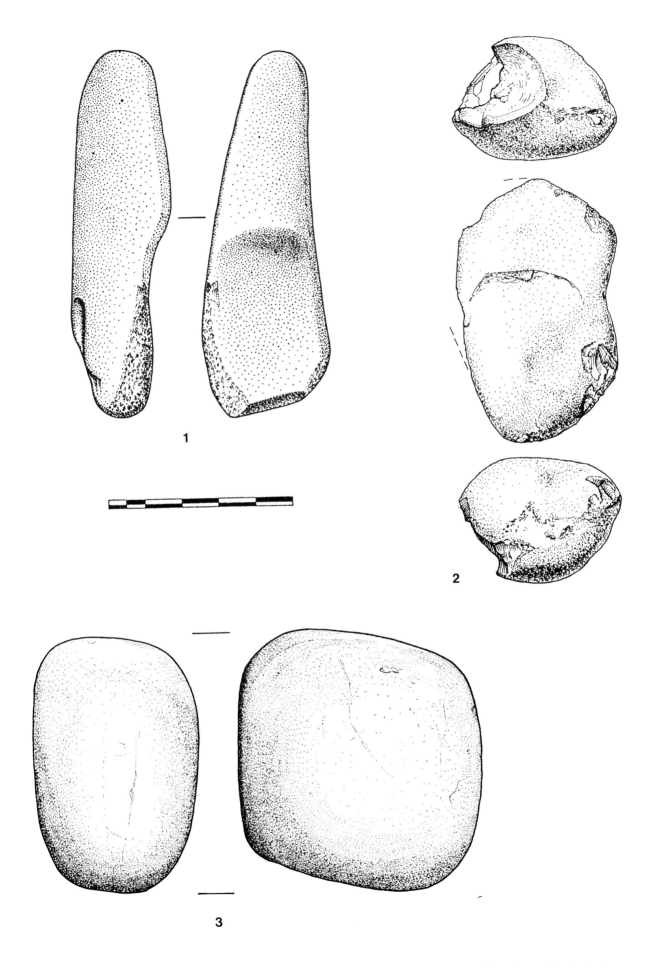

5.28 *Hammerstones. 1= sandstone; 2= flint; 3= quartzite (this example shows signs of polish and smoothing). Centimetre scale.*

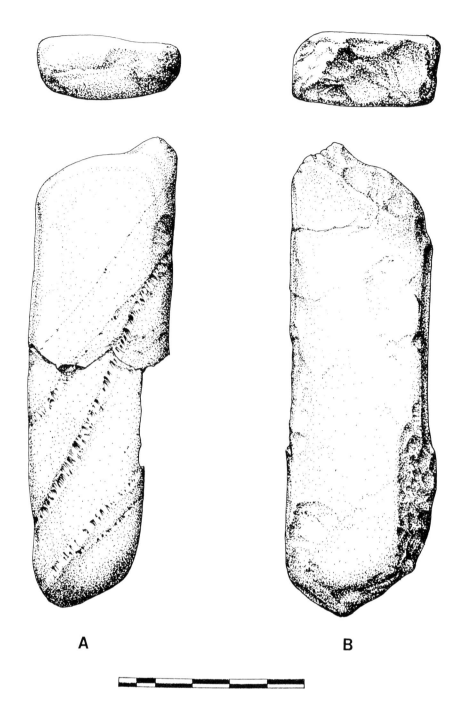

*5.29  Elongate sandstone cobbles. A= mixed tourmaline-bearing sandstone; B= unidentified sandstone. Centimetre scale.*

signs of battering or heavy percussive use. Indeed the edges of the object are very smooth and heavily worn as though the cobble had been used for rubbing or abrading a fine material. In addition to the quartzite, one elongated sandstone cobble and several slightly battered flint pebbles have been recovered which may have served as hammerstones. The sandstone cobble is sub-cylindrical in shape and measures 98 mm long (Fig. 5.28, 1). Signs of abrasion, possibly from flaking other rocks, are visible at one end. Although flint is not an ideal hammerstone material, because it shatters easily, the example illustrated (Fig. 5.28, 2) shows traces consistent with battering. Previous mention has also been made of two flint cores which display signs of similar

battering, as well as a scraper on a broken hammerstone fragment.

### 5.2.3   Non-Flint artefacts

*Elongate cobbles or 'rubbers'*: Two elongate cobbles of sandstone, each measuring about 120 x 40 mm were recovered from the Mesolithic site (Fig. 5.29). Similar artefacts have been described from other S British Mesolithic contexts as 'rubbers' (*sensu* Rankine 1952). However, not all such items are necessarily Mesolithic as shown by equivalent items from the Iron Age site below Warren Hill (Cunliffe 1987). The two artefacts from the Powell site were found less than a metre apart within the same level as the rest of the Mesolithic assemblage. One of them was fractured in two (and separated by several centimetres) but the surfaces were fresh enough to allow refitting across the break. When compared, it is clear that each of the complete 'rubbers' is in fact a mirror image of the other, being sub-rectangular in shape and possessing flat, regular sides. Although neither displays obvious traces of utilisation along the flat sides or edges, the extremities of both objects seem to show signs of slight modification. Evidence of rounding is present at one end of Cobble A (Fig. 5.29), while the corresponding end of Cobble B displays a marked angularity which is probably artificial.

Various functions might be envisaged for these objects if they are indeed of Mesolithic type. From their identical shape and close archaeological association it is possible that were intended for use together. Certain functions, however, can probably be ruled out. For example, because of the rocks' smoothness and the absence of grooves it is unlikely they functioned as arrowshaft abraders or 'shaft straighteners' (cf. Miles 1963). A more likely option, and one supported by the apparent modification of the extremities, is as an implement for grinding or stretching purposes. Elongate stones of similar type have been recorded from N American ethnographic contexts where they were used for grinding or pounding materials ranging from plant matter to red ochre. No such traces of ochre or other substances were found on the Hengistbury cobbles. Stone implements of this kind have also been identified with skin stretching and hideworking activities (Miles 1963; Osgood 1940).

Petrographic analysis of the cobbles by D T Moore of the Natural History Museum has confirmed that both are made of sandstone. As has been noted above, one of the 'rubbers' is of a mixed tourmaline bearing rock (Fig. 5.29, A), the nearest natural occurrence of which is in Devon. Although transport by longshore drift cannot be ruled out altogether (cf. Jacobi 1979), it is noteworthy that the Early Mesolithic coastline was perhaps 15–20 kilometres further south from its present position, and this implies movement of materials by man.

Evidence for the human importation of materials over much greater distances (either directly or via exchange networks) may occur further inland from Hengistbury. For example, elongate pebbles of Palaeozoic type and of SW English origin have been found at Oakhanger V and VII and Kingsley Common Y4 (Rankine 1949, 1952, 1961; Jacobi 1981c). Significantly the Oakhanger V and Farnham examples (the last being from a Later Mesolithic context) are of a tourmaline-bearing 'siltstone', geologically allied to the Hengistbury specimen. Such archaeological occurrences lie much further east of the Powell site and well inland of present-day or previous Mesolithic shorelines. If human movement of materials is involved, as seems likely, this would have considerable implications for studying links between hunter-gatherer groups occupying Central S England and the SW peninsular during the Early Holocene (cf. Jacobi 1979).

*Sarsen*

A large flat-topped sarsen boulder measuring 245 x 150 x 110 mm was uncovered from square J11 (Fig. 5.30). It was located near the centre of the microlith concentration and was deeply stratified in the Mesolithic horizon. There can be little doubt that the block was imported to the site, since no natural rocks of this size or type are known from the deposits of the Headland. The exact function of this block is unclear but it is possible that it served as an *ad hoc* working surface perhaps for retouching tools or preparing plant foods. The surfaces of the rock are smooth but there is no sign of a concavity or striations to suggest it was used as a grindstone.

## 5.3 Functional analysis and post-depositional alterations of microdenticulates

### 5.3.1 *Description*

The Hengistbury Head microdenticulates are made on bladelets, either curved or curved and twisted in profile. Of the 34 pieces examined 26 are denticulated on a concave edge, while the remainder are too broken to be characterised (see Fiche 1.B8). The edge angle of the denticulated edge varies between 30–45° and rarely exceeds the upper limit. The retouched edge normally consists of a series of small contiguous notches which are extremely regular and equally spaced, and give the tool its 'saw tooth' profile. The manufacturing technique as suggested by Bocquet (1980) involves the removal of tiny flakes along one edge of a blank using another artefact. The resulting notch scars are highly characteristic (Fig. 5.31) and occur on the ventral surface when the retouch is produced from the dorsal side (which is mostly the case here) or vice versa. Although use wear can affect the appearance of the teeth there is no question that the retouch is the result of use alone. Experiments with unretouched blanks on a range of materials failed to produce a single example with the kind of regular serration found on the Hengistbury artefacts (see Fiche 1.B9–14).

### 5.3.2 *Methods*

The functional analysis was (originally) undertaken using the method elaborated by Keeley (1980). The flint surfaces were observed by optical microscopy using an Olympus Vanox microscope at magnifications of up to x400 (more frequently at x100 and x200). All micrographs were taken with an Ilford FP4 film. The Keeley method relies upon the observation of polishes and striations on stone artefacts from which the materials used and the tasks performed can then be inferred. Unfortunately, problems are presently being encoun-

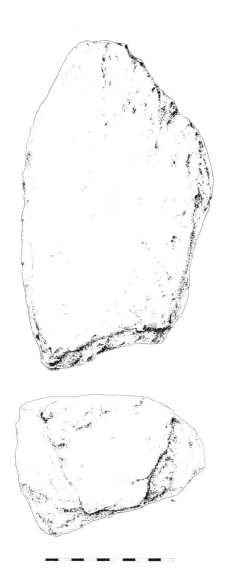

5.30 *Sarsen manuport. 10 cm scale.*

tered in the application of this method particularly with respect to identifying materials used from polish. This may be due in part to *post-depositional surface alteration* (PDSM) described below and in other recent publications (Levi-Sala 1986a, 1986b; Newcomer *et al.* 1986). A more realistic approach was therefore adopted which relies not only on polish identification but also on a combination of factors including, the recording of macroscopic edge morphology and edge scars, microscopic edge wear traces including polish when present, (Grace 1981; Grace *et al.* 1988) and on experimental replication as described in Moss and Newcomer (1982).

Prior to examination, all the artefacts both experimental and archaeological, were cleaned with warm water and detergent then immersed in distilled water in an ultrasonic tank. Occasionally spirit and/or acetone were used to remove finger prints. Only two archaeological pieces (I6/2a/I and E9/1b/4) were washed in 5% HCl to try and remove some spots of what looked like varnish but which, in the event, were not removed. A more detailed discussion of the reasons for abandoning

the Keeley method of cleaning in favour of the present method can be found in Levi-Sala (1988, 85).

### 5.3.3 *Experiments to determine tool function*

Experiments were carried out on a variety of materials in an attempt to match the rather perplexing traces observed on the archaeological pieces (see Microscopic Analysis below). Apart from experiment three in which an unretouched artefact was used, all the experimental pieces were microdenticulates. The examples were used both in the hand and hafted to test their efficiency. They were all of quarried East Anglian flint except experiment seven which was made from a beach cobble (see Raw materials Chapter 5.1). A detailed description of the individual experiments appears in the Fiche 1.B9–14, but they can be summarised as follows:

(1) Cutting fresh deer hide.
(2) De-hairing fresh hide.
(3) De-hairing and cutting hide using an unretouched flake.
(4) Cutting meat.
(5) Cutting cartilage and sinew.
(6) Cutting and whittling dry reed (*Phragmites*).
(7) Reaping green *Phragmites*.
(8) Reaping green bracken (*Pteridium*) stems.
(9) Whittling seasoned wood.
(10) Incising and cutting green birch (*Betula*).
(11) Sawing mollusc shell.
(12) Sawing bone.
(13) Cutting rushes (*Juncus*).

### 5.3.4 *Observations resulting from the experiments*

The small size of the tool, its thin cross section and low edge angle appeared to rule out a variety of heavy duty tasks and this observation was subsequently confirmed by the experimental work. On 24 out of 34 archaeological specimens, the individual teeth making up the serrated edge were worn down in a relatively even manner. Experiments again showed that this would exclude use on very hard materials such as stone, shell or bone.

*Hafting*

1. Experiments confirmed what was already suspected from the size and morphology of these tools: namely, that they were difficult to hold in the hand for long periods and in heavy tasks. The tools were too small and sharp for comfortable handling, for more than short periods. Despite the obvious advantages of using a handle, no diagnostic hafting traces were observed on any of the experimental implements. This is not surprising since an efficient haft would not allow the tool to move.

2. The likelihood that several implements were inserted in a row in a haft was rejected because: (a) the concave

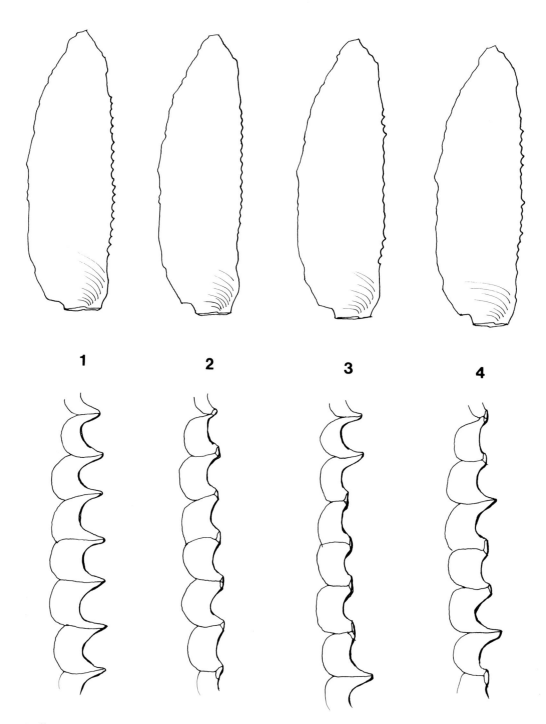

5.31 *Schematic illustration of microdenticulates showing various wear traces referred to in the text and in fiches 1.B8–14.*

edges of the microdenticulates would have made them impractical to use in a row, even in a crescentic haft; (b) the curved and sometimes twisted profile would likewise make them unsuitable for inserting in a handle; (c) there was no evidence for consistent modification of the tools in order to facilitate hafting. This might have been achieved by snapping both ends of the implement. In fact only four were broken in this way, the majority (24) were more or less complete.

3. The experimentally hafted tools did not develop microscopic traces similar to those observed on the archaeological specimens and tentatively supposed to be hafting traces (Fiche 1.B9–14).

4. At least one of the microdenticulates (K8/2b/1) was modified in such a way as to suggest handholding. The distal end of the tool was abruptly truncated which would have provided a comfortable finger grip for an unhafted tool (Fig. 5.12, 10).

*Functional efficiency*
Tixier (1963, 124) has suggested that fine denticulated saws from the Capsian have the same edge morphology as modern steak knives, and were probably used in much the same way. Considerable differences exist, however, in the overall shape of the North African and British Mesolithic artefacts. For example, whereas the Maghreb examples are long and straight-edged, the

Hengistbury tools are much shorter and have concave edges. They are also curved and sometimes slightly twisted.

Despite the differences, it is clear that the most obvious function of these tools is in cutting or sawing. This has been amply demonstrated in the experiments which showed that other actions, requiring a scraping motion (e.g. whittling, dehairing) are far less efficiently carried out than say with a high-angle unretouched edge.

A slightly surprising discovery, given the highly standardised nature of the tool, was the fact that denticulation did not seem to greatly improve the tools' performance in any of the experiments involved. In fact, a long straight edge performed much more efficiently, especially in the cutting of hide thongs and meat and detaching cartilage from bone. Likewise, experiments in reaping plants such as bracken proved slow and cumbersome and in any case these plants could be gathered using much simpler methods (e.g. uprooting). Although comments of this kind are inevitably subjective, they give some indication of how we might begin to evaluate the function of the microdenticulates.

*Materials used in the experiments*

*Hard Materials*
The experiments showed that in the case of use on dry reeds, seasoned wood and shell, the teeth were worn down in a manner which is not observed on the archaeological pieces. The central part of the edge completely lost its denticulation while the adjacent teeth were still very sharp (Fig. 5.13, 3). Even the 10 archaeological microdenticulates described as differentially worn (see Fiche 1.B8–14) did not present this pattern of wear. In these, a few teeth were occasionally worn down more than the rest. It was therefore concluded that the material(s) worked could not have been as hard as dry reed, seasoned wood or shell.

*Soft Materials*
The experiments suggest that the idea of use on hide, meat, cartilage and sinew should be discarded, on the grounds that work on these materials could be carried out just as easily using an unretouched edge. Furthermore, it was not possible to match the polish produced with that observed on the archaeological implements (Fig. 5.32, 1–4).

Dumont (1983, 143) put forward meat cutting as a possible use for microdenticulates from Star Carr. There were only two artefacts involved in his interim report and due to the lack of polish in the scars, he concluded "that the denticulation occurred after or shortly before the tool ceased being used to cut meat or fresh hide". It is my observation that cutting meat and fresh hide does not leave a well-developed polish (cf. Dumont 1983, Fig. 4) but rather a 'shine' which can be produced by a variety of soft materials as well as by soil (Fig. 5.32, 5). Many of the experimental tools used on both soft and hard materials have no polish in scars (Fig. 5.32, 11). It would seem that the function of

meat/fresh hide cutting does not fit the evidence from Hengistbury where the edge is concave and the wear on the teeth of the serration was greater than that produced experimentally by cutting meat. In my opinion the material/s used, was/were not as hard as dry reed, but not as soft as meat.

The presence of bracken (*Pteridium*) in the Early Flandrian (Scaife pers. comm.) together with its potential use as bedding material made it a reasonable candidate for study. The bracken was reaped from the vicinity of the site in early and late Summer. In June, after 10 minutes of use (Fig. 5.32, 6) the resulting polish showed some similarity with the polish observed on a few of the archaeological pieces. The slight resemblance might be due to the polish being not too well-developed. By September bracken is no longer very green and the cutting was carried on for 20 minutes (Fig. 5.32, 7). The polish was better developed but the similarity with the 'polishes' on the archaeological pieces was still doubtful.

The use of birch (*Betula*) bark vessels and mats is well known in the North European Early Mesolithic (Clark 1954; Bokelmann 1986). Experiments were carried out involving the cutting and incising of the outer bark prior to removing it from the tree. Although these tasks produced polish (Fig. 5.32, 8), it was not similar either in appearance or in distribution to the polish on the Mesolithic artefacts; the minimal edge damage caused plus the wear on the denticulations, however, were broadly comparable.

Microdenticulates were also used experimentally in basketry manufacture. An experiment was carried out cutting up dry rushes. After 30 minutes work no polish developed on the tool edge (Fig. 5.32, 9). After soaking the rushes (as is usually done in basketry) the polish which appeared in only 15 minutes was very well-developed (Fig. 5.32, 10) but unlike anything observed on the archaeological microdenticulates.

Reaping, cutting and whittling dry reeds (*Phragmites*) also produced the very well-developed macroscopic polish (Fig. 5.32, 11–12) commonly attributed to use on plants. Such polish, often referred to as a 'sickle gloss' generally survives even when the flint surfaces have been affected by post-depositional processes. The reason for this phenomenon is not yet very clear but has been empirically observed elsewhere (Unger-Hamilton 1984a, 266; Levi-Sala 1986b). If the Hengistbury microdenticulates had been used to reap *Phragmites*, it is very likely that the polish would have survived. While dry reeds wore down the teeth too heavily, reaping fresh reeds wore them only very lightly. As mentioned above, in both cases the polish was very well developed and distinctive, which is not the case with the archaeological specimens. The experimentally observed polish was in no way similar to the traces on the archaeological implements.

In conclusion, it is possible that the Hengistbury microdenticulates were used for incising or cutting green, but woody plant material for a relatively limited length of time. No one task is envisaged but it has been

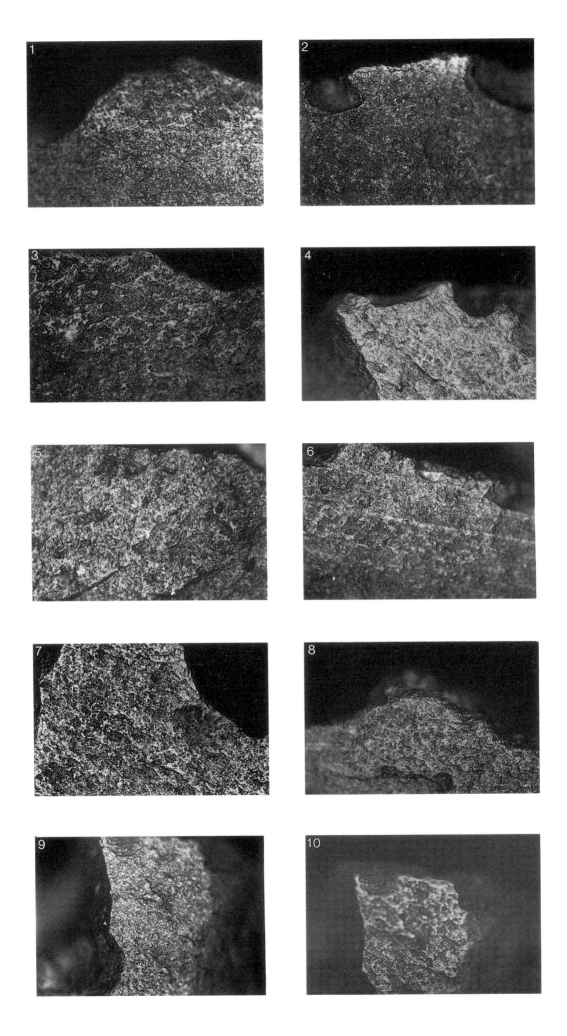

242

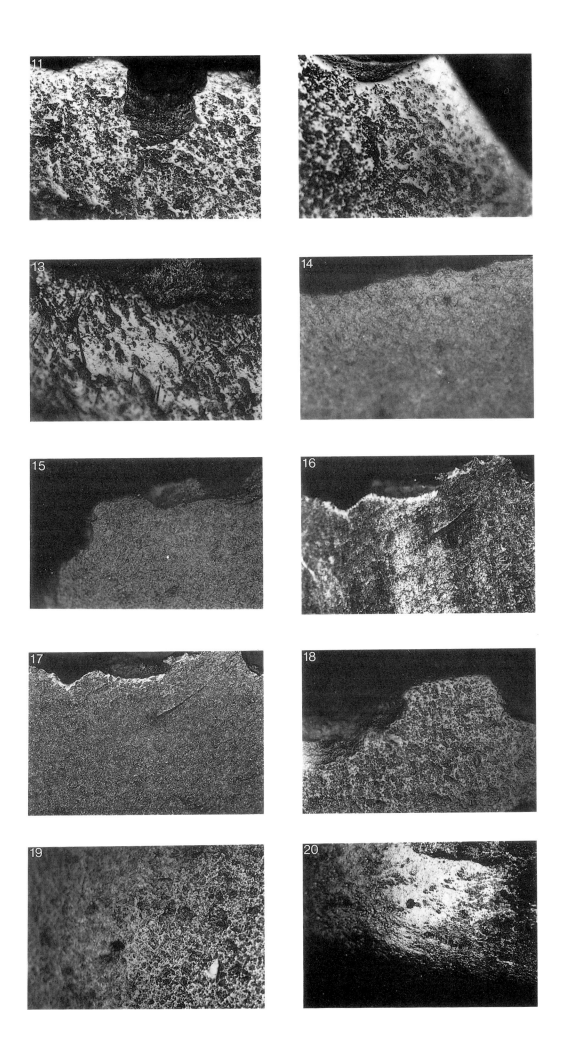

243

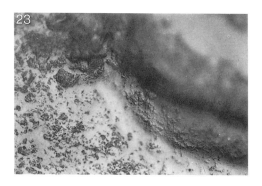

5.32 *Microscopic traces on the surfaces of experimental and archaeological microdenticulates. Key: 1= polish from cutting meat for 60 mins. (x200); 2= polish from cutting fresh hide for 25 mins. (x200); 3= polish on archaeological tool (x200), unlike 1 and 2; 4= polish on archaeological tool (E9/1b/4)(x100), unlike 1 and 2; 5= soil polish produced by 24 hour tumbling in sediment (x200); 6= polish from cutting fresh bracken for 10 mins. (x200); 7= polish from cutting dry 'woody' bracken for 20 mins. (x200); 8= polish from incising green birch for 10 mins.; 9= no polish after cutting dry rushes for 30 minutes (x200); 10= well-developed polish after cutting fresh wet rushes for 15 mins. (x200); 11= macroscopic polish after cutting green reeds for 60 mins. (x200). Note absence of polish in scar; 12= polish rounding the edge after cutting green reeds for 60 mins. (x200); 13= bright spot cluster with striations on edge of archaeological tool (L8/2b/IV)(x200); 14= macroscopic soil sheen on archaeological tool (F11/1a/38)(x200); 15= soil sheen on unused edge of experimental tool after tumbling for 50 hours in dry sand (x200); 16= polish and striations from whittling dry reeds for 10 mins. (x100); 17= same piece after tumbling (x100). Note polish still on edge but striations no longer present and most of surface scoured clean; 18= polish from tumbling in gravelly sand for 50 hours (x200). Compare with (1); 19= polish from tumbling in gravelly sand for 50 hours (x200). This polish compares well with polish originally identified as 'hafting traces' on archaeological tools; 20= bright spots produced by rubbing two wet flint flakes together for two minutes (x100); 21= bright spots on archaeological tool (x50); 22= bright spots similar to use wear on archaeological tool (J9/4a/30)(x100); 23= bright spots on archaeological tool similar to polish from cutting reeds (J9/4a/30)(x200). Also see (13).*

suggested that a particular function might have involved the 'roughening' of arrowshafts near the nock-end prior to attaching the feather flights (Bergman pers. comm.). Unfortunately, the limited experiments so far carried out (using a scraping motion for 30 minutes on soft wood) did not produce the same wear seen on the teeth of the Hengistbury tools. Despite the failure to find a precise parallel it seems that in the task(s), the convex shape of the working-edge clearly mattered and that the observed wear patterns are consistent with work on a material softer than stone, shell, bone or hardwood but harder than meat.

*Microscopic analysis*

As mentioned above the evidence from the microscope was rather confusing. Many implements seemed, at x100, to have a polish which could have been mistaken for use-wear. At higher magnifications (x200 and over) which are more useful for interpreting the function of the tool, the microsurface appeared too reflective and did not resemble any experimentally produced polish.

Although there seemed to be more polish along the edges, the whole surface of the tool was also polished. In many instances there was no clear cut evidence that the denticulated edges were the ones used since the 'polish' was more concentrated on the unserrated edge. Striations (i.e. linear indicators for direction of use) were rare and when present did not show a consistent pattern from which to infer the motion or direction of tool use.

### 5.3.5 *Post-Depositional Surface Modifications (PDSM)*

It soon became apparent that the conflicting evidence from the microscopic observation, was probably due to post-depositional processes. Their effect on flint tools has been observed from a variety of sites of many ages and geographic settings (Levi-Sala 1986b, 1989). The problem is much more widespread than can be inferred from the microwear literature. Flint surfaces and/or use-wear polish are altered in such a way as to render difficult, if not impossible, their interpretation according to the Keeley method. Even Keeley (1980, 29) observed that patination can alter "the light reflection qualities of the flint so that the microsurface and the microwear cannot be observed with light microscopes". The Hengistbury microdenticulates, when not white patinated, had a macroscopic sheen which has been attributed by many researchers to the effect of burial in the soil. This is sometimes called 'soil sheen' or 'glossy patina'. Most of the artefacts examined also had randomly distributed glossy bright spots. Microscopically they appear like a smooth highly reflective polish. They vary in size from the microscopic to the macroscopic occurring singly and in clusters, on cortical and non-cortical surfaces alike. Although bright spots often appear on artefacts affected by soil sheen, the two are in no way comparable in their appearance (Fig. 5.32, 13–14). A more detailed description of these and other features has been published elsewhere (Levi-Sala 1986b, 230–232).

## Soil sheen and bright spots

Soil sheen is often uniform over the whole surface of the flint implement. In certain cases it can be concentrated on the prominent areas of artefacts. There is not yet widespread agreement on the precise processes involved in its formation, but it is certainly clear that the traces are caused by natural rather than human action; its effect on use-wear polishes is being studied (Levi-Sala 1989).

Bright spots are a smooth, highly reflective polish localised on flint surfaces (Levi-Sala 1986b, 231). They have been observed on artefacts from many sites of varying ages and locations. Bordes (1950) and other researchers have described them and concluded that they were enigmatic. Shepherd (1972, 120–121) called them friction gloss and Stapert (1976, 29) disagreeing on their genesis uses the name within quotation marks. Microscopically there seems to be a variety of them and here too, though the exact cause of all these types is as yet unknown, there is agreement that they are post-depositional in nature. On many microdenticulates they occur on the serrated edge, inside the scars, and on the teeth.

## Condition of the Hengistbury artefacts

As mentioned above, the Hengistbury artefacts were often patinated and affected by soil sheen and bright spots. The Powell site is situated on an exposed hillside covered by windblown sands with a well-developed podzol formation. The Mesolithic artefacts are found in fine sands with pebbles occurring within the lower levels. There is evidence for vertical movement of artefacts on the site as shown by the conjoining of artefacts separated vertically by up to 39 cm (Barton 1981, 19). Similar observations have been made of Mesolithic material from other S. British sites in sands, which show a marked vertical dispersal of artefacts and surface alteration of the flint (Maher 1983; Dimbleby in Keef et al. 1965).

From a microscopic point of view, the effect of wind blown sands on flint artefacts has also been described extensively by Stapert (1976, 14–19) who concludes "it is not impossible that in places where windgloss is highly developed, microscopic traces of the use formerly present are completely or partly obliterated".

To test whether such effects could be observed under modern conditions, Barton and Bergman (1982) undertook a series of experiments involving freshly knapped flint scatters in sands. The artefacts were flaked onto a sand surface and lay exposed over several months. Even after a relatively short period of lying on the surface, being buried and then sometimes subsequently re-exposed, many of the flints were noticeably discoloured and patinated. No soil sheen or bright spots were, however, observed. It should be noted in passing that the experimental site was located on the sea shore in a highly alkaline environment and with conditions quite unlike those prevailing during the Mesolithic, when Hengistbury was essentially an inland location.

Another possibility considered was that the soil sheen resulted from mechanical polishing, for example by the abrasive action of sand on flint or flint on flint. This could have been produced by trampling, bioturbation, windblasting, or simply the settling of the sediment under pressure (Villa 1977; Cahen and Moeyersons 1977; Barton 1981; Villa 1982; Rowlett and Robbins 1982; Villa and Courtin 1983 and others). In fact it is likely that one or several of these processes influenced the Hengistbury site (see Chapter 3.1). Finally, it should be noted that the chemistry of the soil itself can affect flint surfaces, and although we were not able to carry out any detailed work, the effects of such processes should not be overlooked.

## Experiments concerning Post-Depositional Processes

To investigate the hypothesis of mechanical polishing, an experiment was set up to reproduce the movement of artefacts in sands. Since it was obviously impossible to simulate the length of time of burial (9,700 years), we were able to speed up the processes artificially by using a mechanical tumbling device (see also Levi-Sala 1986a, 1986b). The sands used were collected from Hengistbury and were exactly the same as those which occurred at the Mesolithic site. The results can be summarised as follows:

## Experiment 1

Shaking and tumbling individual experimental flint artefacts with known use-wear patterns at 60 revolutions per minute, in fine sand from the site, with and without water. The length of time and the speed were increased gradually, from 10 minutes to 50 hours after which: (a) soil sheen appeared on the artefacts (Fig. 5.32, 15), (b) striations present on artefacts used to whittle dry reeds and incise wood had completely disappeared (Fig. 5.32, 16–17), (c) the surface of the flint away from the edge was scoured clean (Fig. 5.32, 17).

*Experiment 2*
Experimental artefacts used on green birch, bracken, rushes, seasoned oak, fresh willow were tumbled in gravelly wet sand, for up to 50 hours at 60 rpm which resulted in:

(a) the appearance of varying degrees of sheen intensity,
(b) the disappearance of use wear striations,
(c) the addition of polish on the edges without any clues to indicate that there had been two consecutive polishing events (Fig. 5.32, 18),
(d) the appearance of a concentration of polish on either side of the serration (Fig. 5.32, 19).

*Discussion of experiments 1 and 2*
The presence of gravel in the sediment in the second set of experiments is undoubtedly the variable that accounts for the different results. It is significant that gravel was also present in the sands at the site. The concentration of polish on the edges after tumbling may mean that the original use-wear polishes were 'increased' by movement in the sediment. However, similar concentrations of polish were also noted on the unserrated (and unused) edges of the experimental pieces. This suggests that the edge is more vulnerable to polishing than the rest of the flint surface, a fact empirically observed by other experimenters (Moss pers. comm.). The fact that movement in the sediment can cause polish to concentrate on unused edges indicates that extreme caution should be exercised before automatically equating a concentration of polish on an edge with some form of use.

These observations are directly relevant to the artefacts from the Hengistbury site. During the original microscopic examination soil sheen was noted on many of the artefacts but these also showed a significant concentration of polish along the edges. It would appear to us that the above explanation might account for the occurrence of polish concentration along the edges. Likewise, the traces which appeared on either side of the serration and were first thought to be hafting traces are now believed to have a different origin. These bladelets are curved and twisted and on many of them the affected areas are quite prominent, and consequently more likely to be polished when moving in the sediment.

*Experiment 3*
This involved repeatedly rubbing flints together to produce macroscopically visible 'bright spots'. The bright spots appeared only when using water as a medium and rubbing for two minutes (Fig. 5.32, 20–21).

*Discussion of experiment 3*
Bright spots do not usually have any systematic relation to the edges and should not be confused with genuine signs of use-wear, although they can mask parts of the edge (Fig. 5.32, 13). In such cases it is important to understand the sequence of development; this can help

ascertain whether other traces on the edge are natural or not. When bright spots occur as large, very flat and isolated polish traces they are easily identified, but if they occur in clusters which are not circumscribed in area and taper off, they can look remarkably similar to use-wear polish.

A very appropriate example is the case of 6 scrapers from the Powell site which were examined to see whether the problems with the microdenticulates were related to function or due to post-depositional factors. In the case of a particular tool J9/4a/30, the traces on the retouched scraping edge could have been mistaken for use polish (Fig. 5.32, 22). However, examination of the other parts of the implement showed that bright spots on the proximal end of the ventral aspect were definitely not attributable to use. Interestingly, they appear very similar to the polish commonly described as 'sickle gloss' (Fig. 5.32, 23). Where these bright spots were less developed they closely resembled the 'use' polish on the scraping edge. It is therefore extremely likely that all the polish on this implement was post-depositional in nature.

### 5.3.6 Concluding remarks

The disappearance of microwear traces on artefacts with soil sheen has been demonstrated experimentally. The use of microwear analysis in these cases is likely to produce dubious results. Similar PDSM effects have been noted on the Hengistbury flints as well as others from sites in sands. For example, the artefacts from the open-air site of Meer II, in Belgium (Van Noten 1978) underwent extensive vertical and horizontal movement in the sediment and they are macroscopically so lustrous that they appear varnished. My examination of two of the Meer artefacts (Keeley 1978) under the microscope showed that in the previous analysis post-depositional traces may have been mistaken for use-wear.

In the cases where post-depositional surface modification (PDSM) occurs on artefacts, the number of tools which can be confidently analysed is often reduced to an almost unrepresentative sample and the detailed interpretation of microwear traces on such artefacts is clearly very doubtful. This does not mean, however, that functional analysis on such tools should be abandoned altogether. Tool and edge morphology can suggest possible uses; experimentation with observation of edge wear patterns can narrow down the number of tasks a tool is suitable for or is likely to have been used for. It is no doubt a more modest result than the first microwear studies may have led archaeologists to expect. On the other hand, while the results may be limited in scope they are at least placed on a more realistic footing.

In conclusion, therefore, it is only possible to suggest that the Hengistbury microdenticulates were used in a general cutting/sawing motion on a relatively soft material such as a bracken type plant or green wood. This interpretation is based on a study of the edge morphology and other characteristics coupled with the results of experimental work. In this instance the microwear polish on the tools could not be used to substantiate the above observations. It was not possible in the sample of 34 artefacts to differentiate with any degree of certainty, polish produced by use (if any) and by post-depositional processes.

*Acknowledgements*

I would like to thank various colleagues who have helped at different stages of my work: to the excavators of the Hampstead West Heath site (Hendon and District Archaeological Society) for allowing me access to artefacts for comparative purposes; to R N E Barton and C A Bergman for their co-operation, advice and for providing the experimental flints; to my supervisors, M H Newcomer and D Griffiths and finally to my fellow research students, K. Ataman and R. Grace who have read my manuscript, offered advice and made valuable suggestions to render my English more readily understandable.

## 5.4 Mesolithic findspots at Hengistbury and in the Bournemouth area

Apart from the Powell site, low concentrations of Mesolithic material have been recovered from several other locations on the headland. Palmer (1977) has drawn attention to Mesolithic finds in the private collections of Mr R Atkinson, Mr A Cotton, Mr C Draper (deceased), Mr B King and the Marchese A Nobili-Vitelleschi. The author is also aware of flints belonging to Mr Powell, Mr C Pepin (now deceased) and Mr and Mrs Mulholland. Although identifications have been recorded by the author, no detailed catalogue of these artefacts exists and the collections remain in the hands of the finders or their families. In many cases only the barest information is available concerning the provenance of artefacts (e.g. 'Warren Hill') so it is often difficult to obtain more than an overall impression of the distribution of known findspots.

A number of isolated Mesolithic finds have been collected from the surface near the Powell site. It is quite likely, therefore, that they originate from the same assemblage and in one instance it has even been possible to refit a microlith from the surface (Atkinson collection) to one of the excavated cores (Fig. 5.1). Not far from the summit of the Warren Hill, a small collection of Mesolithic flints (mainly debitage) came to light during the construction of the present Coastguards' Station (M Ridley pers. comm.), but the whereabouts of this collection is no longer known. Sporadic finds of microliths and bladelet debitage have been made on deflation surfaces and on the coastal footpath which runs along the southern edge of the headland (Atkinson, Powell, Vitelleschi pers. comm.). Further source areas are the footpaths near the Transverse Quarry (Rankine 1956 and Draper, Atkinson, Powell pers. comm.); along the northern margin of the headland; and at the SE end of the headland near the Upper

Palaeolithic site. Amongst the diagnostic flints are A-type microliths and occasional Late Mesolithic geometric forms (including several stray finds at the Upper Palaeolithic site, reported in 4.2).

Finds of Mesolithic type are not just confined to the upper areas of the Headland. For example, the digging of a lily-pond in the Nursery on the north side of the headland in 1980 produced several large A-type microliths (Barton 1981). Additional finds have been recovered along the Harbour Foreshore near the Iron Age site (Vitelleschi pers. comm.), while the North and South Fields outside the Iron Age Double Dykes have also been prolific collecting areas (Palmer 1977). Together these finds demonstrate widespread use of the headland throughout the Mesolithic, although Later Mesolithic finds are still considered relatively rare.

Beyond Hengistbury, Mesolithic flints have been recovered at Wick and at Tuckton, as well as on the opposite side of Christchurch Harbour at Mother Siller's Channel. This site, investigated by Susann Palmer (Palmer 1977), produced small geometric microliths and is one of very few Later Mesolithic findspots to have been positively identified. Further westwards, in Bournemouth, many isolated lithic finds were discovered during the 19th century expansion of the seaside town. The artefacts, which include tranchet axes (data from Wymer 1977), hint at a much more intensive settlement of the western Hampshire plain than is generally believed to be the case. It is interesting to note that tranchet axes, potentially attributable to exploitation of more heavily wooded environments, are all but absent in the Hengistbury collections and none has been recorded from the Powell site.

One location of probable relevance to the Early Mesolithic settlement of the Bournemouth area comes from Turbary Common on the NW outskirts of the town. The collection described by Sherwood (1974) contains examples of A-type microliths, microdenticulates and end-scrapers and would appear to compare very closely with the Powell assemblage. Perhaps significantly, the Common is situated on a sandy outcrop, on relatively high ground (*c*. 50m OD) overlooking a stream valley (a tributary of the Stour), in a strikingly similar topographic location to the Powell site. The author has not had the opportunity to examine the collection. Further signs of potential Early Mesolithic activity occur upstream of the Bournemouth conurbation, near Wimborne Minster. The small collection discovered by Marsh (1982) includes broad A-type microliths as well as bladelet debitage.

Mesolithic findspots can also be traced much further inland and northwards along the River Avon. The author's preliminary surface searches of sandy bluffs overlooking this river valley (between Fordingbridge and Christchurch) have yielded amounts of bladelet debitage, but so far few retouched tools. Judging by the rich assemblage of Early Mesolithic material from Downton (Higgs 1959, also Chapter 5.5), this stretch of river would seem to hold considerable potential for new discoveries and it may be relevant that flint-bearing chalk outcrops also occur in this area. Closer to Christchurch a number of bladelets, recorded as coming from St Catherine's Hill, are stored in the collections of the Red House Museum, Christchurch.

From this brief summary it is apparent that the Bournemouth area provides a relatively dense scatter of Mesolithic findspots, all of which should properly be regarded as inland locations, bearing little or no relation to the earlier Holocene coastline. Amongst the scatter of findspots are several which can be identified from their lithic components as being of Early Mesolithic type and therefore contemporaries of the Powell site. From the pattern of distribution it can be shown that potentially Early locations occur either at confluences (Hengistbury) or along main river courses (Downton) or their tributaries (Turbary Common, Wimborne Minster). This is a recurrent pattern which characterises much of the known Mesolithic settlement in this region and is a theme we shall return to in the final section of the chapter (5.5 below).

## 5.5 The Powell site within its wider Mesolithic context

### 5.5.1 Introduction and brief historical outline

Ever since Gordon Childe (1931), changes in the European earliest Postglacial archaeological record have been identified principally with major climatic and environmental shifts at the end of the last Ice Age. Indeed Childe regarded these new technologies as very specific adaptational responses to the development of Postglacial woodland landscapes and was the first to coin the term 'Forest Cultures' in this respect. Other authors recognised aspects of forest adaptation in the tool assemblages (e.g. flaked axes and antler tools) but saw advantages in adopting the term 'Mesolithic' (Clark 1932; Reboux 1874; Brown 1888).

Following some of the earliest Mesolithic discoveries in the Maglemose (literally 'big bog') near Mullerup in Denmark (Sarauw 1903), more finds were made which confirmed the widespread distribution of such material across N Europe (Breuil 1926). In reviewing the Mesolithic, Clark (1936) was able to draw comparisons between some of the S English and N European sites (on the one hand represented by Broxbourne, Kelling Heath, Thatcham and on the other the sites of Duvensee and Svaerdborg). In particular, he noted striking similarities in the occurrence of flint-types, including broad obliquely blunted points or A-type microliths (Clark 1932). These characteristics were not shared by other 'more evolved' industries of the Tardenoisian, which were typified by very small microliths (Clark 1936, 94). In consequence, Clark divided the Mesolithic of N Europe into two facies: the Maglemosian and the Tardenoisian. These industries were considered neither to overlap chronologically nor to occupy the same social territory: the Tardenoisian being identified with the sandy areas of Europe while the Maglemosian was associated with lakes and more open fenland (Clark 1936). Subsequent attempts were made to further sub-divide the Mesolithic according to regional variations in the bone, antler and lithic equipment (Schwabedissen 1944; Kozlowski 1973).

A very similar scheme to the one originally proposed by Clark is still in existence today, albeit in slightly modified form. Following Clark, Buckley (Petch 1924) divided the Mesolithic of N England into two separate industrial traditions which were termed 'broad blade' and 'narrow blade' respectively. Subsequently, Jacobi (1973, 1976) and Mellars (1974), introduced a formal separation of the British Mesolithic into 'Early' and 'Later' facies, according to typological characteristics of the flintwork and a limited number of radiocarbon dates then available. On the basis of these occurrences, Jacobi proposed that the Early Mesolithic assemblages were rapidly replaced around 8,500 BP, by ones containing a wider variety of small, 'geometric' microlithic tools. The main identifying feature of the Early Mesolithic facies was the very restricted range of microlith tool forms it contained. These included large isosceles triangles and trapezoids, but typically showing a predominance of large broad obliquely blunted points, with a mean width of of 8–12 mm (Jacobi 1973). Although this twofold scheme is undoubtedly an oversimplification and is coming increasingly under challenge (see for example Jacobi 1987), the basic division is still very widely accepted.

In terms of the English record, Jacobi (1978) has estimated a minimum total of 230 Early Mesolithic findspots, but this is only a rough approximation and the actual total may exceed this figure by several hundred (Jacobi pers. comm.). Some variation has been noted within the Early Mesolithic facies, particularly in relation to the relative frequencies of large isosceles triangles and short trapezoids to obliquely blunted points (Clark 1975; Jacobi 1976). Such variability might be due to simple functional differences between contemporary toolkits (see below) or to an evolutionary trend which would place assemblages with broad triangles and basally retouched microliths later than those in which these shapes are lacking (Jacobi 1987). Unfortunately until certain key assemblages are accurately dated these problems remain unresolved. Despite these and other subtle differences in typological variability, it is apparent that early Holocene assemblages over much of Northern Europe and the connected British peninsula are strikingly similar both in terms of their overall structure and tool components. Nowadays, the Scandinavian equivalents of the Early British facies would be most closely identified with the proto-Maglemosian (Clark 1954) or Maglemosian 0 (Brinch-Petersen 1973; Jacobi 1976). It is within this Early Mesolithic grouping that the Hengistbury assemblage belongs.

### 5.5.2 The Early Mesolithic chronology in Britain

Despite recent advances in radiometric and other dating techniques, the chronological evidence for this period is still remarkably poor. Most of the radiocarbon dates currently available from Pre-Boreal and Early Boreal contexts have been obtained using the conventional method (Shotton 1977 and Table 5.20) but increasing use is being made of Accelerator Mass Spectrometry (Table 5.21). The main advantage of the accelerator technique is that it allows smaller samples to be measured (Gillespie and Gowlett 1983), including portions of highly fragile specimens normally ruled out by the conventional radiocarbon method. A limiting factor in the existing conventional dates is that they mostly derive from bulked charcoal samples or wood fragments, which are more susceptible to various forms of contamination. So far no critical reappraisal of the conventional dates has been published but it is relevant that very few of the currently available measurements can be related unequivocally to human activity.

By contrast, all of the accelerator dates (in Table 5.21) were obtained directly from human bone or humanly modified organic materials (i.e. cut-marked bone, bone and antler artefacts and so forth) from Mesolithic contexts so there can be no ambiguity over the association. Application of these stricter criteria shows that the earliest currently acceptable evidence for postglacial Mesolithic activity comes from the Kennet Valley. The worked antler beam from Thatcham IV, which dates to around 9,700 BP, is probably associated with the lithic assemblage of Thatcham III on an adjacent dryland surface. This date is also closely matched by another on a barbed point from Essex, but for which there is no known lithic association. The new dates tie in very closely with the available radiocarbon evidence from the continent (Table 5.22), which would place the first Mesolithic settlement of Friesack in Germany approximately within the same period.

Although the radiocarbon record for this period should be treated with extreme caution (see for example Becker and Kromer 1986), it is clear that the AMS dates can be used to test the internal consistency of the conventional chronology. At present, for example, they show that the earliest evidence of clearly postglacial human activity does not occur in Britain much before 9,700 BP but that soon after this period Mesolithic settlement rapidly spreads over a major part of the country. This implies that the very high conventional dates from the Kennet Valley (both greater than 10,000 BP), which are not in accord with the rest of the British or the European Mesolithic evidence, should be treated very guardedly. As can be seen in Table 5.20, the two dates fall well outside the range of datings for the Pre-Boreal and Boreal assemblages. The fact that they deviate so markedly from the established pattern suggests they are not representative of the main Mesolithic occupation of this site and should therefore be rejected.

Independent support for a similar pattern of chronological development can be found in recently published radiocarbon dates from the European Mesolithic record. The results presented below (Table 5.22) were all obtained by means of conventional radiocarbon

measurements, but in the main come from reliably documented contexts. They show an upper age range of around 9,700 BP which is in keeping with the earliest 'Forest' Mesolithic settlement of Britain. The evidence from Friesack derives from the lowest occupation level (10a/Xe) of a multi-level site, for which more than fifty radiocarbon determinations now exist, and can be shown to occur in correct stratigraphic sequence (Gramsch 1987). These agree well with the early dates from Duvensee Wohnplatz 8 on worked birch bark matting (Bokelmann *et al.* 1981). Despite the relative paucity of reliable dates, the assemblages from Northern Germany (Friesack, Duvensee), Denmark (Klosterlund), S Sweden (Henninge Boställe) and Britain (Thatcham, Star Carr) are sufficiently similar to suggest that a shared technological mode was present over much of N Europe by the end of the Pre-Boreal.

In parallel with the anticipated continuation of the programme to radiocarbon date British Mesolithic sites is a separate programme to construct an early Holocene chronology using the Thermoluminescence (TL) technique. The TL method, which relies on analysing burnt stone, has been used to date flint artefacts from the Mesolithic assemblage at Hengistbury (see Chapter 2.4.4). The central date obtained of *c.* 9,750 BP is well in keeping with the expected Pre-Boreal age of the assemblage. Apart from Hengistbury, thermoluminescence dating has also been applied successfully to artefacts from Longmoor Inclosure (Hampshire). Here the dates agree closely with the radiocarbon evidence (Huxtable and Jacobi 1982) and indicate the great potential of applying this technique to sites which lack organic materials.

### 5.5.3 The Early Mesolithic and its environmental context

Botanical evidence from Britain and Northern Europe indicates a rather complex sequence of events at the end of the last glaciation. The traditional view that the Pleistocene-Holocene boundary (Younger Dryas III/Pre-Boreal) was marked by steady climatic improvement with a gradual transition from near arctic to temperate postglacial conditions is no longer universally accepted (Behre 1978).

An alternative view suggests that the end of the Pleistocene was in fact marked by a series of short lived climatic oscillations, of varying intensity. In Northern Europe the Postglacial is thought to begin around 10,200 BP with a relatively rapid warming attributable to the Friesland Oscillation (Behre 1978). This is immediately followed by a short cold phase (Rammelbeek Oscillation) at 10,000 BP when temperatures dropped to similar levels to those experienced during the coldest parts of Younger Dryas III. According to this hypothesis the return to temperate conditions only began at *c.* 9,600 BP (Behre 1967, 1978). Evidence for the Friesland warm episode has so far only been recognised (and then only tentatively) in pollen profiles from several parts of N Europe, but is not recorded from Britain or elsewhere in Europe south of the Alps (Frenzel 1966).

Table 5.20  *Selected British Pre-Boreal and Early Boreal Mesolithic radiocarbon dates (conventional technique).*

| Lab No | Sample | Findspot (County) | Date (BP) | Reference |
|---|---|---|---|---|
| | | S England | | |
| Q–658 | C (bulked) | Thatcham III (Berks) | 10,030±170 | 1 |
| Q–659 | C ('hearth') | Thatcham III | 10,365±170 | 1 |
| Q–652a | W pine | Thatcham V | 9,480±160 | 1 |
| Q–652b | W (repeat) | Thatcham V | 9,500±160 | 1 |
| Q–677 | W (bulked) | Thatcham V | 9,780±200 | 1 |
| Q–650 | W (bulked) | Thatcham V | 9,670±160 | 1 |
| Q–651 | W birch + pine | Thatcham V | 9,840±160 | 1 |
| Q–3033 | Bone (bulked) | Broxbourne 104 (Herts) | 9,350±120 | 9 |
| Q–1129 | C | Marsh Benham (Berks) | 9,300±150 | 4 |
| Q–1489 | Hazelnuts | Oakhanger VII (Hants) | 9,225±200 | 7 |
| Q–1491 | C | Oakhanger VII | 9,100±200 | 7 |
| Q–1493 | C | Oakhanger VII | 9,040±160 | 7 |
| Q–1490 | C | Oakhanger VII | 8,995±200 | 7 |
| Q–1492 | C | Oakhanger VII | 8,975±200 | 7 |
| BM–471 | Human bone | Aveline's Hole (Somer) | 9,114±110 | 8 |
| BM–1458 | Human bone | Aveline's Hole | 9,090±110 | 8 |
| BM–525 | Human bone | Gough's New Cave (Somer) | 9,080±150 | 8 |
| Q–973 | Bone (bulked) | Greenham D Farm (Berks) | 8,779±100 | 3 |
| | | N England | | |
| Q–14 | C | Star Carr (N Yorks) | 9,557±210 | 2 |
| C–353 | C | Star Carr | 9,488±350 | 2 |
| Q–1187 | C | Lominot III (W Yorks) | 9,560±350 | 4 |
| Q–1560 | C | Money Howe I (N Yorks) | 9,430±390 | 2 |
| Q–1300 | C | Waystone Edge (N Yorks) | 9,396±210 | 2 |
| Q–1185 | C | Warcock Hill S (N Yorks) | 9,210±340 | 4 |
| | | Wales | | |
| OxA–1495 | Hazelnut | Nab Head I (Dyfed) | 9,210±80 | 10 |
| OxA–1496 | Hazelnut | Nab Head I (Dyfed) | 9,110±80 | 10 |
| BM–671 | Hazelnut | Rhuddlan (Clwyd) | 8,739±86 | 5 |
| BM–822 | Hazelnut | Rhuddlan (Clwyd) | 8,528±73 | 5 |
| HAR–1194 | C | Aberffraw (Anglesey) | 8,590±90 | 6 |

Lab: BM= British Museum; Q= Cambridge; C= Chicago; HAR= Harwell. Sample key: C= Charcoal; W= Wood.
Bibliographic references: 1= Wymer 1962; 2= Jacobi 1978; 3= Switsur & West 1975; 4= Switsur & Jacobi 1975; 5= Miles 1972; 6= Jacobi 1976; 7= Jacobi 1981c; 8= Jacobi 1987; 9= Jacobi pers. comm.; 10= Hedges *et al.* 1989.

Table 5.21  *Selected British Pre-Boreal and Boreal Mesolithic radiocarbon dates (Oxford AMS)*

| Lab No | Sample | Findspot (County) | Date (BP) | Reference |
|---|---|---|---|---|
| OxA–1427 | Barbed point (antler) | Waltham Abbey (Essex) | 9,790±100 | 5 |
| OxA–732 | Worked antler (red deer) | Thatcham IV (Berks) | 9,760±120 | 1 |
| OxA–1176 | Worked antler | Star Carr (N Yorks) | 9,700±160 | 6 |
| OxA–1154 | Antler (red deer) | Star Carr | 9,500±120 | 6 |
| OxA–894 | Burnt antler (elk) | Thatcham IV (Berks) | 9,490±110 | 1 |
| OxA–500 | Barbed point (antler) | Earls Barton (Nthants) | 9,240±160 | 2 |
| OxA–799 | Human bone | Aveline's Hole (Somer) | 9,100±100 | 2 |
| OxA–800 | Human bone | Aveline's Hole | 8,860±100 | 2 |
| OxA–814 | Human bone | Gough's Cave (Somer) | 9,100±100 | 2 |
| OxA–376 | Hazelnut C | Longmoor (Hants) | 8,930±100 | 3 |
| OxA–377 | Hazelnut C | Longmoor | 8,760±110 | 3 |
| OxA–1160 | Antler mattock | Kew Bridge (Surrey) | 8,820±100 | 4 |

Sample key: C= Charcoal.
Bibliographic references: 1= Gowlett *et al.* 1987; 2= Gowlett *et al.* 1986b; 3= Gillespie *et al.* 1985; 4= Hedges *et al.* 1988; 5= Hedges *et al.* 1989; 6= Cloutman & Smith 1988.

Some of the best evidence for the Friesland-Rammelbeek succession comes from the Netherlands, where the phases were first formally identified. In the Puntbeek-Gele Beek valley for instance Van der Hammen and Wijmstra (1971) were able to demon- strate an early climatic amelioration beginning around 10,200 BP, being accompanied by a rapid spread of birch woodland. This episode was abruptly halted by the sudden catastrophic disappearance of the birch at around 10,000 BP to be replaced by open grassland (*ibid*, 204–5). An identical very sharp decline in birch after an early initial rise has also been observed in diagrams from the Dinkel Valley (Van der Hammen and Wijmstra 1971). Elsewhere in the Netherlands, similar changes are documented for the vegetation on the sandier soils of Friesland at Westrhauderfehn (Behre 1967) and Waskemeer (Casparie and Van Zeist 1960) but instead of the rapid early rise in birch there is a noticeable peak in pine pollen of this period. Outside the Netherlands, the mild Friesland oscillation has been identified at Stellmoor in Northern Germany (Schütrumpf 1943) and as far south as Belle-Croix, Belgium (Van der Hammen 1951).

Judging from the biochronological and radiocarbon evidence (Tables 5.22 and 5.23) it would seem that the earliest recognisable Mesolithic technologies in the European lowlands appear to coincide with the establishment of open pine and birch woodland in the post-Rammelbeek Pre-Boreal phase. According to Behre (1978) the onset of warm temperate conditions suitable for major forest growth took place only after 9,600 BP, but in more westerly locations it may have begun as early as 9,800 BP (Van der Hammen 1971). For the NW European mainland the slightly earlier date would be in much closer accord with the archaeological evidence from Friesack and Duvensee.

Despite an absence of evidence for any comparable climatic shifts in Britain, there is some indication of an early climatic warming prior to 10,000 BP. Evidence in the form of morainic retreats has been recorded in Scotland by 10,200 BP (Walker and Lowe 1980) and earlier retreats have been inferred elsewhere in Scotland (Lowe and Walker 1977) and in NW England. During the latest Glacial (terminal Zone III) the vegetation in many parts of the country was characterised by disturbed ground flora and open grassland communities. Such floral cover may have survived into the Postglacial period, persisting in some areas (e.g. the Eastern Chalklands) as late as 9,400 BP (Bennett 1983; Bush 1988). Elsewhere, there are indications of a relatively early rise in birch on the slopes of Cader Idris, N Wales (Lowe 1981) and in N England (Godwin *et al.* 1957) where a significant rise in juniper is also apparent by the early Postglacial. Nevertheless contemporary evidence from western parts of Britain shows that the mean summer temperatures were still depressed as low as 13°C at the beginning of the Postglacial (Taylor 1980) and this may have proved too cold for many trees.

In southern Britain, pollen and plant macrofossil remains reveal that soon after 10,000 BP most areas supported at least some open woodland, in which birch was the predominant species. The presence of this tree in East Kent has been documented by wood fragments dated to 9,960±120 (Kerney *et al.* 1980) while similar finds have been made from early Pre-Boreal contexts in the Kennet Valley, Berkshire (Clapham and Clapham 1939; Churchill in Wymer 1962). In central southern England contemporary floras show a rise in juniper at about 9,900 BP (Scaife 1982) which is closely followed by birch (Barber and Clarke 1987). Another important early coloniser in the south of the country is pine. This appears to have been widely present by approximately 9,600 BP, especially on the sandier soils of Dorset, Hampshire and Surrey (Haskins 1978). The establishment of such woodland has important implications for the the earliest Mesolithic dates from the south of the country. Dated pollen sequences from Hampshire indicate that hazel may also have been widely present in southern England well before 9,000 BP (Barber and Clarke 1987).

The initial rapid rise in temperature during the early Postglacial is also well-documented in the changing beetle faunas (Coope 1977). Somewhat surprisingly however, in view of the fact that coleoptera can respond with great rapidity to climatic shifts, is the general persistence and late disappearance of cold faunas typical of the 'open' environments of Younger Dryas III. For example, beetle assemblages of this kind have been recorded from south-east England near Croydon, Surrey at 10,130±120 BP (Osborne 1971) and in the Midlands from West Bromwich at 10,025±100 BP (Osborne 1976). If correct, such dates may indicate that the initial Postglacial warming might have been retarded in eastern parts of Britain. It is unlikely that the dates constitute sufficient proof of the European re-cooling episode (cf. Rammelbeek).

Supporting evidence for the general 'openness' of the early Postglacial landscape may be provided by large mammal faunas, although here the evidence is more contradictory. Occurrences of reindeer and horse (generally considered to be good indicators of open conditions) have been attributed to the earliest Postglacial (Clutton-Brock and Burleigh 1983). Recently, however, the dates on which this information is based have been recalibrated by the British Museum and are now shown to have been too young (Bowman *et al.* 1990 and Table 5.24). Apart from the specimen from Anston Stones Cave, S Yorkshire, all the reindeer are of Late Glacial age (Table 5.24). Nevertheless, the date from that cave may indicate environmental differences which enabled slightly later survival of these species in N Britain. It is perhaps relevant that no reindeer remains have been reported from any of the S British Pre-Boreal Mesolithic sites (Grigson 1978). Indeed, by the time the first Mesolithic toolkits appear in S Britain, the hunted fauna is largely dominated by woodland-preferring species such as the elk, roe deer, pig and beaver (Jacobi 1975; Grigson 1978). The occurrence of horse at this time is sporadic and limited to partial remains from a very few sites e.g. teeth from Thatcham II. Until properly dated, the presence of isolated horse teeth at this site could be explained by taphonomic factors with the possibility that the remains are intrusive (Jacobi pers. comm.).

### 5.5.4 *Mesolithic antecedence in Britain*

Of special relevance to the nature of the Early Mesolithic and its first occurrence in Britain is the question of whether or not there is any evidence for

251

continuity with the preceding technologies of the Palaeolithic. In answering this question it is necessary to turn to the European evidence, which although still only sparsely represented during the critical periods, seems to hint at a very late continuation of technologies with strong Upper Palaeolithic affinities into the earliest Postglacial.

One example of such a technology is the Ahrensburgian which occurs over a wide area of the North European Plain and can be seen to persist into the terminal Younger Dryas and, in some areas, probably into the earliest Pre-Boreal (Fagnart 1988). The Ahrensburgian lithic assemblages are clearly related to the Upper Palaeolithic blade tradition, but they also possess characteristics which anticipate developments in the Mesolithic, and could therefore be described as 'transitional'. For example, in addition to small tanged points, the retouched tools include many microlithic oblique forms (*Zonhoven points*), which are typologically similar to the British Early Mesolithic microliths. At Stellmoor in N Germany, small tanged points and *Zonhoven points*, form part of an assemblage associated with a massive reindeer kill, dating to around 10,200 BP (Fischer and Tauber 1986). Here flint-tipped arrowshafts provide the first unequivocal proof of the use of archery equipment in N Europe (Rust 1943). Also associated were finds of giant or long blades, with 'bruised' edges, which appear to have been used for butchery purposes or for massacring reindeer antler (Barton 1986a).

Material of the same age as Stellmoor has been excavated from the Somme Valley in N France (Commont 1913; Fagnart 1984a). Although the assemblages share elements in common with the Ahrensburgian (e.g. oblique points and 'bruised' blades), the backed material does not include small tanged points. These finds have been dated by an associated horse fauna to about 9,900 BP (Fagnart 1984a). Flint assemblages of a structurally similar nature to the French ones have now been identified over much of SE Britain (Barton 1986b). These are characterised by the combined presence of long 'bruised' blades and small backed material, sometimes including microliths (Barton 1989). Perhaps significantly, the British assemblages are nearly all located along river valleys which could have provided suitable locations for culling horse or reindeer during seasonal migrations (Barton 1986b).

The presence of small tanged points in the Kennet Valley, Berkshire (Jacobi 1980; Barton and Froom 1986) and from Risby Warren, Lincolnshire (Jacobi pers. comm.) indicates the probable maximum western extent of the Ahrensburgian technocomplex. It has been suggested elsewhere (Barton 1986b) that the assemblages without small tanged points but including various microlithic forms and large blades are the technological equivalents of the Ahrensburgian, but for cultural, stylistic or functional reasons lack the small tanged forms. So far none of the British sites has been satisfactorily dated, but the indications are that they belong within the same phase (Younger Dryas III/Early

Table 5.22 Selected Pre-Boreal and Boreal Mesolithic radiocarbon dates from N Europe

| Lab No | Sample | Findspot (Country) | Date (BP | Reference |
|---|---|---|---|---|
| Bln–3036 | C | Friesack (Germany) | 9,680±70 | 1 |
| Bln–3026 | C | Friesack | 9,670±60 | 1 |
| Bln–2756 | C | Friesack | 9,630±100 | 1 |
| Bln–2761 | C | Friesack | 9,560±100 | 1 |
| Kl–1818 | Bark mat (B) | Duvensee W8 (Germany) | 9,640±100 | 2 |
| Kl–1885.02 | Hazelnut | Duvensee W8 | 9,420±130 | 2 |
| Kl–1110 | Pinecone | Duvensee W6 | 9,300±180 | 2 |
| K–1466 | C | Draved 604 Syd (Denmark) | 9,390±120 | 3 |

Lab: Bln= Berlin; Kl= Kiel; K= Copenhagen. Sample key: C= Charcoal; B= Birch (*Betula*). Bibliographic references: 1= Gramsch 1987; 2= Bokelmann *et al.* 1981; 3= Jacobi 1976.

Table 5.23 Chronology of Late Glacial/early Postglacial environmental changes in NW Europe (after Behre 1967, 1978; Van der Hammen 1971)

| Radiocarbon dating kyr | Geological epoch | Pollen chronozone | European biochronology | |
|---|---|---|---|---|
| 9.4 | | Boreal V | | (warmer) |
| | | | Pre-Boreal | (warm) |
| | | | Rammelbeek | (cold) |
| 9.8-9.6 10.0 | Holocene | Pre-Boreal IV | Friesland | (warm) |
| c.10.3 | | | | |
| | Pleistocene | Dryas III | Younger Dryas | (cold) |

Table 5.24 Radiocarbon dates for Horse and Reindeer later than c. 10,300 BP

| Lab No | Species | Findspot | Radiocarbon Years BP | Ref. |
|---|---|---|---|---|
| OxA–1778 | wild horse | Uxbridge | 10,270±100 | 4 |
| OxA–1902 | wild horse | Uxbridge (Gtr London) | 10,010±120 | 4 |
| OxA–111 | wild horse | Kendrick's Cave (Clwyd) | 10,000±200 | 3 |
| BM–1619R | wild horse | Darent Gravels (Kent) | 9,840±120 | 2 |
| BM–2350 | wild horse | Seamer Carr (N Yorks) | 9,790±180 | 5 |
| BM–2249R | reindeer | Soldier's Hole (Somerset) | 10,090±230 | 2 |
| BM–1674R | reindeer | Darent Gravels (Kent) | 10,080±120 | 2 |
| Q–1581 | reindeer | Gough's Cave (Somerset) | 9,920±130 | 1 |
| BM–440B | reindeer | Anston Stones Cave (S Yorks) | 9,750±110 | 1 |

References:
1= Clutton-Brock & Burleigh 1983; 2= Bowman *et al.* 1990; 3= Gillespie *et al.* 1985; 4= Lewis 1989; 5= Ambers *et al.* 1987.

Pre-Boreal IV) as those on the European mainland. Given the marked concentrations of Early Mesolithic material in the Thames and its major tributaries (the Kennet, Colne, Lea) it would not be surprising if eventually some chronological continuity or overlap between early Postglacial and Late Glacial technologies could be demonstrated in these areas.

The replacement of Late Glacial toolkits may not have been altogether sudden but the increasing level of 'microlithisation' in the flintwork does reflect a major change of emphasis in toolmaking strategies. These appear to be related on the one hand to the (?re-)introduction of bow hunting and, on the other, to major environmental changes which caused some animals such as the reindeer to disappear altogether from the S British record. In S Britain, then, we might expect assemblages pre-dating the main forest development (c. 9,700 BP) to have certain 'transitional' features, sharing affinities with both the Late Palaeolithic Ahrensburgian and the 'Forest' Early Mesolithic. Such changes probably did not occur synchronously across the whole country, and may even have been delayed in eastern areas where the open grassland conditions seem to have continued longest.

In summary, the following observations may be made concerning the Early Mesolithic:

(1) Typological similarities exist between Early Mesolithic assemblages over a wide area of N Europe. Such toolkits contain microliths, particularly obliquely blunted points (Clark's A-types or 'Zonhoven points') but sometimes also large isosceles triangles and trapezoidal forms. A close resemblance can be seen between the assemblages of Northern Germany (Friesack, Duvensee), Denmark (Klosterlund), S Sweden (Henninge Boställe) and the British examples (Thatcham, Star Carr and Hengistbury).

(2) Apart from one or two radiocarbon dates, which show marked discordance with the established pattern (Table 5.20), the first recognisable 'Mesolithic' technology in Britain seems to occur around 9,700 BP. This is broadly confirmed by the radiocarbon record for similar occurrences in N Europe. The thermoluminescence dates from Hengistbury place the Powell site in this early phase.

(3) Environmental evidence from southern Britain demonstrates an open patchwork of birch woodland at the end of the last glaciation, but with apparently less forest cover especially on the eastern Chalklands. The vegetation is marked by a rise in pine in many areas in S Britain around 9,600 BP. Late Pleistocene faunas (horse and reindeer) may persist until just before the main pine expansion, when they are replaced by woodland species (roe deer, pig and beaver).

(4) Using continental analogies, the industries with Late Palaeolithic affinities (cf. Ahrensburgian) which already employed archery equipment probably continued to exist into the earliest Postglacial period. Around 9,700 BP changing environmental conditions had a major impact on human adaptive strategies. The emergent technologies, broadly identifiable with the Mesolithic, still relied upon archery hunting equipment but belonged to hunter-gatherers more fully adapted to living in forested environments.

### 5.5.5 Functional variability in the Early Mesolithic

*Introduction and research background*
Following the original discoveries in Denmark (Sarauw 1903), Early Mesolithic finds of a strikingly similar type were shown to occur over a very broad geographical range extending from Estonia and Latvia in the east to the British Isles in the west (Clark 1932). The flint, antler and bonework from such locations was of a very uniform nature, indicating a highly standardised and widely distributed toolkit. Despite such acknowledged similarities, however, it soon became apparent that considerable variability existed between Mesolithic assemblages especially in the flintwork. Such variability was exhibited not only in the proportion of tools recovered but also in the representation of tool-types from the different sites. Thus for example, the microlith triangles identified at the Zealand and Duvensee sites were noticeably absent in the British collections from Kelling Heath and Broxbourne (Clark 1936). At the same time, recognisable differences were observed between sites dominated by microliths and others where these forms were found with tools such as axes, adzes and picks (Clark 1936, 190).

In addition to the variation observed between assemblages, Grahame Clark was able to make some interesting observations concerning the patterns of Mesolithic activity, based on plotting the distribution of certain artefacts in relation to the major geological outcrops. He noted, for instance, that assemblages on sandier soils tended to show higher proportions of microliths to other tools. The microliths, regarded principally as projectile equipment, were considered to be the residue of hunting settlements in these areas. Using ecological models it was concluded that the sandier soils with their lighter vegetation cover and good drainage qualities offered considerable benefits for game hunting and settlement purposes (Clark 1936, 88). Out of this model was born the idea of the importance of geological controls over the human use of the landscape (Clark 1936, 190).

Since the 1930s Clark's ideas concerning geological controls, the landscape and Mesolithic hunter-gatherer settlement patterns have been further explored and elaborated upon by various authors (Clark and Rankine 1939; Rankine 1949, 1956; Draper 1968; Mellars 1976; Mellars and Rheinhardt 1978; Jacobi 1978). An example is the model of Mellars and Rheinhardt (1978) developed to explain the diversity of Mesolithic toolkits in S Britain, believed to be of a contemporary nature. Using the large database of sites catalogued in the CBA Gazetteer (Wymer 1977), they were able to show that when combinations of lithic tools (as opposed to individual tool-types of Clark) were mapped against the underlying geology, clear patterns emerged in the overall distribution of assemblages. On the basis of these locational data they proposed the following hypothesis, which is worth quoting in full:

"(...) when explained *in toto*, the individual tool assemblages recovered from the major sand-yielding geological formations of lowland Britain should reflect a significantly greater emphasis on hunting equipment than those recovered from clay or silt-yielding formations. In the assemblages from the latter areas one would expect to find a quantitatively weaker representation of hunting equipment, and a correspondingly stronger emphasis on tools associated with other economic activities -for example, the collection and processing of plant foods, or activities connected with the general 'maintenance' requirements of the human groups." (Mellars and Rheinhardt 1978, 287).

This provides a highly plausible explanation for the contemporary exploitation of two contrasting ecological zones. In addition to the specific toolkits of the sandier soils, the distribution of adzes and axes can be correlated with the heavier soils of river valleys, where one might envisage a greater emphasis on woodworking and other maintenance activities associated with water-edge occupations sites.

Similar ideas have been developed for the north of the country (Clark 1932, 1975; Jacobi 1978), where distinctive patterning of microlithic assemblages can be seen particularly in relation to topographic setting. For example, sites above 365 m have produced remarkably high concentrations of microliths, whilst lower-lying sites show a much greater diversity in tool-types (Jacobi 1978). The upland locations have been interpreted as summer hunting stands, connected with the seasonal movements of red deer populations (Clark 1972).

On the basis of some of the models described above, the following section examines the Hengistbury assemblage and several geographically related Mesolithic assemblages in terms of the structure and composition of the lithic toolkits as well as landscape features of site setting, topography and the underlying geology.

*Functional variability and inter-assemblage comparisons between Hengistbury and other Early Mesolithic sites in S Britain*
Hengistbury is just one of a number of Early Mesolithic sites identified in the Hampshire basin (Jacobi 1981c). The site lies on a Tertiary geological outcrop of the Bracklesham Series. It consists of a large concentration of microliths and the by-products of their manufacture (microburins). Apart from end-scrapers and microdenticulates, the toolkit has produced few other tools. For example, there are no axes, adzes or burins and only a single mèche de foret (drill-bit). The lithic assemblage would therefore appear to conform to the pattern previously predicted for a

Mesolithic hunting location on a sandy soil (Clark 1932).

To see how this toolkit might correlate with others of potentially similar age, six Mesolithic assemblages from central southern England were compared using two sets of variables. The analysis involved measuring quantitative attributes (shape and size of microliths) and qualitative data (observations on the main tool components in each assemblage). Because of constraints of time the latter could only be undertaken as an exercise in recording the presence or absence of certain tool-types. The study was thus divided into two parts:

(1) a morphometric analysis of A-type microliths
(2) an analysis of assemblage variability based on the presence or absence of various retouched tool-types.

The five Mesolithic sites selected for analysis are all open-air locations within a 100 km radius of Hengistbury. The distance was dictated by the availability and size of the study sample rather than by other considerations, such as site catchment or time/distance factors. In practice, however, only one of the locations lies anywhere near the outer 100 km limit; most occur a good deal closer (Fig. 5.33). The nearest of the sites, Downton, Wiltshire (Higgs 1959) is situated barely 30 km north of Hengistbury on the River Avon and is well within a day's walk of the headland. It is followed next by Winfrith Heath (Palmer and Dimbleby 1979) and Iwerne Minster (Summers 1941), Dorset, both just under 40 km distance away. Slightly further afield is the site of Iping Common, West Sussex (Keef *et al.* 1965) which is situated some 70 km to the east, while Thatcham III, Berkshire (Wymer 1962) 85 km to the north represents the furthest site from Hengistbury. Several other collections which could have been examined (e.g. the Oakhanger complex of sites, Hampshire) were omitted for reasons of time but it would be possible to include the results within the same format of the analysis presented below.

Each of the assemblages in the sample contain abundant quantities of non-geometric microliths, mainly of obliquely blunted type (Fig. 5.34). The rest of the flint toolkit conforms very closely with the highly standardised equipment already described for the Early Mesolithic. Apart from Iwerne Minster (which includes an admixture of post-Mesolithic artefacts), each of the collections comes from excavated contexts although not always with the same standard of recovery techniques. For example, systematic sieving procedures were not employed at any of the sites except Hengistbury and Iping Common. The dating evidence for Early Mesolithic sites has already been mentioned above (5.5.2 and Tables 5.21 and 5.22). Apart from Thatcham and Hengistbury, the four other occurrences are undated, their relative age being determined strictly on typological grounds.

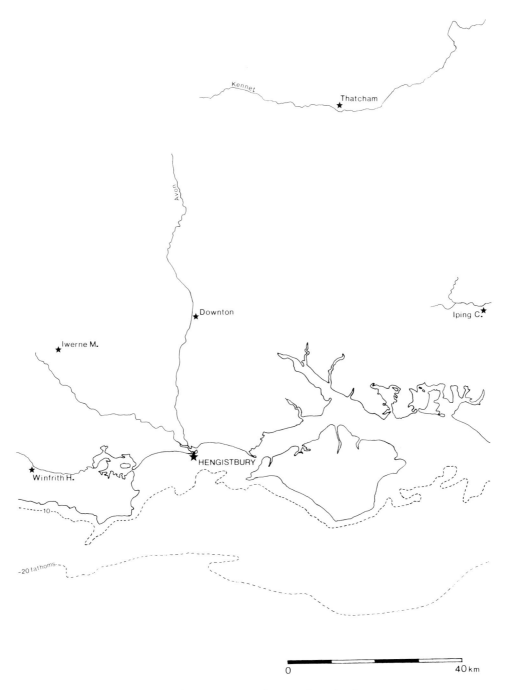

5.33  *Distribution of selected Early Mesolithic findspots in South Central England.*

*Morphometric analysis of A-type Microliths*: The length x breadth x thickness dimensions of 623 microliths (additional to those from Hengistbury) were measured according to the methods set out in Chapter 1. Only complete pieces were used for length dimensions, but because some of the assemblage samples were numerically small, it was decided to incorporate minimally broken microliths (i.e. only those with a few mm of the tip missing) into the breadth and thickness calculations. Apart from these artefacts a further 300 complete blades and bladelets were measured (Iwerne Minster, Thatcham III and Winfrith Heath) to provide comparative statistics between the debitage and the microliths.

*Results*: The results are presented in Tables 5.25 and 5.26. Despite the unevenness of the data samples, both in terms of size and collecting history, a high degree of uniformity is exhibited in the mean statistics for each of the six assemblages. They also match very closely the measurements presented in Pitts and Jacobi (1979) for Early Mesolithic assemblages (Fig. 5.35).

On statistical grounds it would appear that all six assemblages in our sample fall well within the expected range of Early Mesolithic microlith sizes. The fact that this feature may be more or less *independent* of raw material quality is indicated by the absence of major distinction between sites located near primary flint sources (Thatcham and Iwerne) and those situated

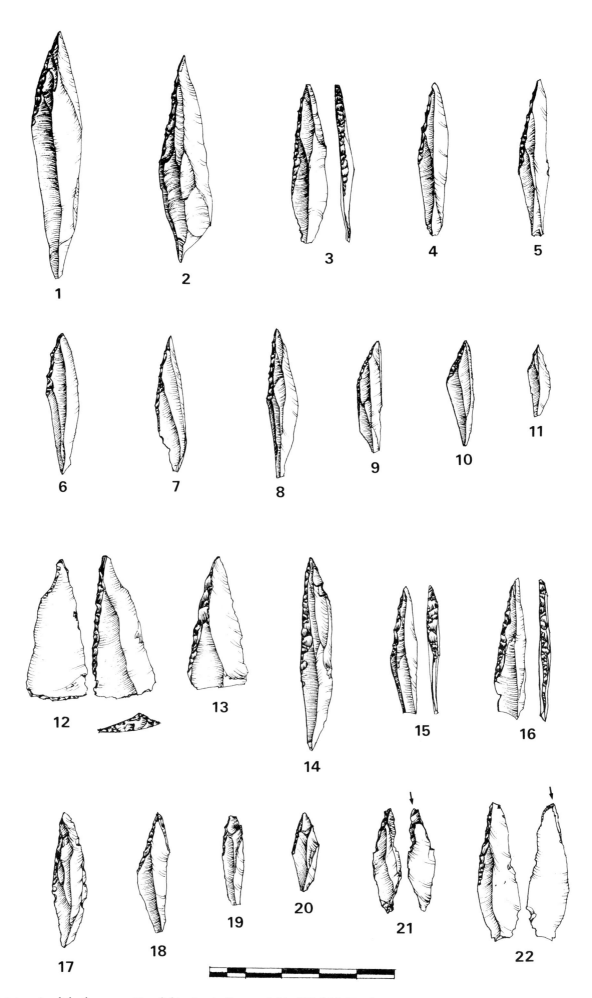

5.34   *A-type microliths from two Mesolithic sites in Dorset. 1–11= Winfrith Heath; 12–22= Iwerne Minster. Centimetre scale.*

Table 5.25 *Mean Measurements of A-type Microliths*

| Site | Length | Breadth | Thickness |
|---|---|---|---|
| HENGISTBURY | | | |
| Sample Size: | 90 | 90 | 90 |
| Range (cm): | 2.42 – 6.44 | 0.42 – 2.49 | 0.13 – 1.04 |
| Mean (cm): | 3.67 | 1.28 | 0.42 |
| Std Dev (cm): | ±1.05 | ±0.42 | ±0.19 |
| | | | |
| IWERNE MINSTER | | | |
| Sample Size: | 20 | 30 | 30 |
| Range (cm): | 2.91 – 5.31 | 0.47 – 1.61 | 0.19 – 0.54 |
| Mean (cm): | 3.962 | 1.066 | 0.330 |
| Std Dev (cm): | ±0.647 | ±0.251 | ±0.786 |
| | | | |
| THATCHAM III | | | |
| Sample Size: | 100 | 100 | 100 |
| Range (cm): | 2.15 – 6.00 | 0.59 – 1.98 | 0.12 – 0.53 |
| Mean (cm): | 3.875 | 1.182 | 0.285 |
| Std Dev (cm): | ±0.849 | ±0.271 | ±0.0885 |
| | | | |
| WINFRITH HEATH | | | |
| Sample Size: | 100 | 103 | 103 |
| Range (cm): | 2.19 – 8.20 | 0.58 – 1.95 | 0.12 – 0.75 |
| Mean (cm): | 4.062 | 1.119 | 0.312 |
| Std Dev (cm): | ±1.101 | ±0.281 | ±0.113 |

Table 5.26 *Mean Measurements of Unretouched Blades and Bladelets*

| Site | Length | Breadth | Thickness |
|---|---|---|---|
| DOWNTON | | | |
| Sample Size: | 11 | 93 | 26 |
| Range (cm): | 2.62 — 3.90 | 0.46 — 1.57 | 0.10 — 0.38 |
| Mean (cm): | 3.269 | 0.776 | 0.233 |
| Std Dev (cm): | ±0.415 | ±0.179 | ±0.0694 |
| | | | |
| HENGISTBURY | | | |
| Sample Size: | 59 | 316 | 326 |
| Range (cm): | 1.62 — 5.00 | 0.19 — 1.51 | 0.10 — 0.55 |
| Mean (cm): | 3.151 | 0.777 | 0.241 |
| Std Dev (cm): | ±0.747 | ±0.175 | ±0.067 |
| | | | |
| IPING COMMON | | | |
| Sample Size: | 72 | 77 | 77 |
| Range (cm): | 2.07 — 6.57 | 0.66 — 1.96 | 0.13 — 0.49 |
| Mean (cm): | 3.862 | 1.043 | 0.259 |
| Std Dev (cm): | ±0.751 | ±0.251 | ±0.0681 |
| | | | |
| IWERNE MINSTER | | | |
| Sample Size: | 14 | 32 | 32 |
| Mean (cm): | 3.607 | 0.842 | 0.288 |
| Std Dev (cm): | ±0.977 | ±0.174 | ±0.0658 |
| | | | |
| THATCHAM III | | | |
| Sample Size: | 40 | 47 | 47 |
| Range (cm): | 2.13 — 5.80 | 0.37 — 1.76 | 0.15 — 0.38 |
| Mean (cm): | 3.406 | 0.919 | 0.248 |
| Std Dev (cm): | ±0.859 | ±0.213 | ±0.0559 |
| | | | |
| WINFRITH HEATH | | | |
| Sample Size: | 44 | 48 | 48 |
| Range (cm): | 1.83 — 6.49 | 0.56 — 1.39 | 0.15 — 0.52 |
| Mean (cm): | 3.746 | 0.841 | 0.272 |
| Std Dev (cm): | ±0.909 | ±0.183 | ±0.0755 |

some distance from such raw materials (e.g. Winfrith Heath)(Table 5.25). This aspect is also reflected in the statistics for the unretouched debitage (Table 5.26 and Fig. 5.36).

The addition of the thickness attribute adds little to our understanding of comparative tool size. Most of the microliths are made on relatively thin blanks (1–5 mm), presumably to facilitate hafting. Although, not particularly informative in this case, the thickness variable can be a sensitive indicator of percussive mode (hard vs. soft hammer) which in turn might help detect changes in manufacturing technique over time or between different contemporary groups.

An interesting aspect revealed in the statistics is the striking similarity in size between the Hengistbury and the Downton microliths, and a further sample from Hampshire (Oakhanger V and Va, measured by Jacobi), which together form a tightly clustered statistical grouping. While it is possible that Hengistbury sample is skewed (the excavated collection contains tools as small as 16 mm), it is tempting to speculate that all of these sites may be genuinely connected in some way. For example, it is significant that both Hengistbury and Oakhanger contain artefacts made of exotic rocks (sandstone 'rubbers') which originate in SW England and cannot be paralleled elsewhere in the sample. From a geographical viewpoint, it is also noteworthy that Downton is located a relatively short distance upstream of Hengistbury on the River Avon. Neither of these factors constitute hard evidence in themselves but they may hint at successive occupation of sites by a single group (cf. Binford 1983, Fig. 52) or movement of materials via human exchange networks, as inferred from Mesolithic evidence in other parts of the country (Jacobi 1978).

In conclusion, it can be shown that the microlith measurements from the Dorset sites and adjacent localities correlate remarkably well with those of other representative Early Mesolithic collections (cf. Pitts and Jacobi 1979). This observation serves to underscore the very high degree of standardisation exhibited by the A-type microlith assemblages of this period throughout southern Britain. Not surprisingly, the degree of similarity is also reflected in the size of the bladelet blanks (debitage) used to manufacture the microliths.

*Lithic toolkit variability*: The analysis was limited to considering the presence or absence of six Mesolithic retouched tool-types in each of the collections concerned. In selecting these artefacts, the writer has followed previous studies concerning the intercomparison of Mesolithic assemblages (Mellars 1976; Mellars and Rheinhardt 1978), with only a few slight adjustments to the basic tool list. The interpretation of tool function is based on existing published data, some of which is discussed in earlier sections (5.2 and 5.3). For purposes of comparability, it assumes that for a given task, tools of the same type functioned in a similar manner. Finally, the six assemblages are compared from the point of view of their topographic context and geological setting.

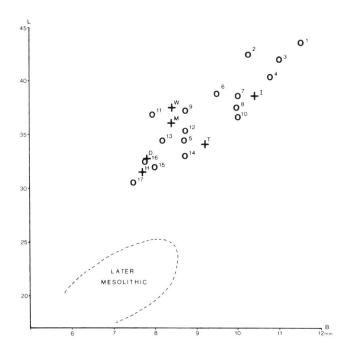

5.35 *Length x breadth dimensions of A-type microliths (after Pitts and Jacobi 1979, Figure 5). Key: 1= Thatcham V; 2= Lackford Heath; 3= Thatcham II; 4= Thatcham VII; 5=Kingsley Common Y4; 6= Kelling Heath; 7= Iping II (Fitzhall collection); 8= Greenham Dairy farm; 9= Thatcham I; 10= Thatcham IIIA; 11= Marsh Benham; 12= Oakhanger VII; 13= Downton; 14= Frensham Great Pond (North); 15= Oakhanger VA; 16= Oakhanger V; 17= Heath Common. Comparative sample (Barton): D= Downton; H= Hengistbury Head Powell site; I= Iping Common; M= Iwerne Minster; T= Thatcham III; W= Winfrith Heath.*

Table 5.27 summarises the main typological features of the six tool assemblages which serves to link them with others of Early Mesolithic type. The common features include the presence of broad A-type (obliquely blunted) points which are often numerous and outnumber other microlith types, plus end-scrapers and microdenticulates. Additional components of the tool-kit but which are not present in all of the assemblages are burins, axes or adzes and drill-bits. On the basis of this admittedly limited sample it is possible to divide the assemblages into two groupings: one with a relatively restricted tool inventory (oblique microliths, end-scrapers and microdenticulates) and a second displaying a wider range of tools (including the three tool-types mentioned above but with the addition of burins, axes and adzes and drill-bits). The sites of Hengistbury, Winfrith Heath and Iping Common can be identified with the first grouping, while Downton and Thatcham III are typical of the second. Apart from the occurrence of axes, Iwerne Minster shows a relatively low diversity of forms and therefore appears to be more closely related to the first group of sites than the second.

Except for Downton and Thatcham III, none of the other sites has the burin/axe or adze/drill-bit combination. It is true that single examples of either burins or axe/adzes do occur in three of the assemblages but their token presence is considered relatively insignificant. Burins, a tool class frequently misidentified, are totally absent from Hengistbury and Winfrith Heath (*pace* Palmer and Dimbleby 1979), while only one example is known from Iping Common (Keef *et al.* 1965, Fig 2.9)

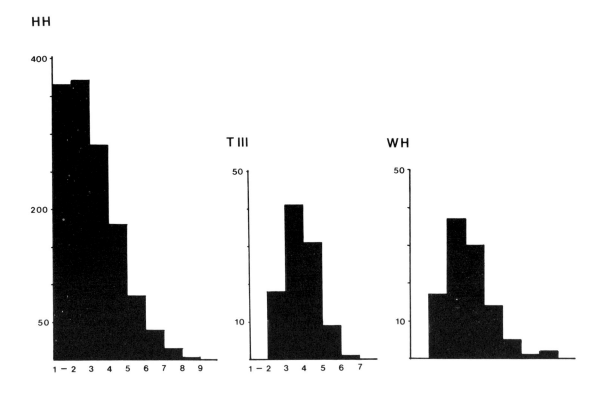

5.36 *Blades and bladelet debitage from Hengistbury, Thatcham III and Winfrith Heath: histogram of absolute length dimensions. X= measurements in cm. Y= absolute numbers of artefacts;*

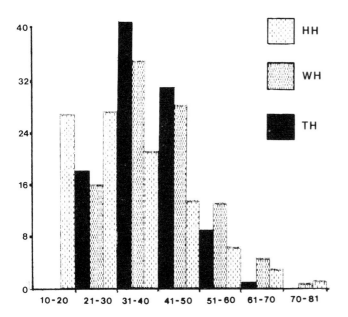

5.37 *Microliths from Hengistbury, Thatcham III and Winfrith Heath: histogram of relative length dimensions. X= measurements in mm; Y= relative percentages.*

Table 5.27 *Mesolithic inter-assemblages comparisons based upon the presence/absence of six retouched tool-types*

|  | Microlith A-types | End-scrapers | Microden-ticulates | Burins | Axes/ Adzes | Drill-bits |
|---|---|---|---|---|---|---|
| Hengistbury (Dorset) | X | X | X |  |  |  |
| Winfrith H (Dorset) | X | X | X |  |  |  |
| Iping C, Fitzhall Coll. (Sussex) | X | X |  |  |  |  |
| Iwerne Minster (Dorset) | X | X | X |  | X |  |
| Downton (Wiltshire) | X | X | X | X | X | X |
| Thatcham III (Berkshire) | X | X | X | X | X | X |

(X= ≥2 examples)

and Iwerne Minster (Summers 1941). Similarly, there are no published finds of tranchet axes or adzes at Hengistbury or Iping Common and only one example is recorded from Winfrith Heath. Another consistent feature is the more or less total absence of tranchet axe flakes or burin spalls, which might otherwise evidence the use of these tools in the sites concerned. Of the first group of sites (and using a simplified tool-list), only one stands out as being slightly anomalous. Despite a low diversity of tools, Iwerne Minster has produced large numbers of tranchet axes and axe sharpening flakes. The reason for this apparent discrepancy is discussed below.

*Topographic and geological contexts*: Landscape setting was also taken into account in the analysis of the six assemblages. The results are tabulated according to geological substrate, relative height and general topo-

Table 5.28 *Mesolithic inter-site comparisons: the geological substrate, relative heights and topographical locations of the six sites in the sample*

| Sites | Geological deposit | Relative ht. | Site topography |
|---|---|---|---|
| Hengistbury (Dorset) | Sands: Tertiary Bracklesham series | 30 m | High ground |
| Winfrith H (Dorset) | Sands: Tertiary Bagshot series | 50 m | High ground |
| Iping Common (Sussex) | Sands: Tertiary Lower Greensand | 30 m | High ground |
| Iwerne Minster (Dorset) | Clay-with-flints & Cretaceous chalk | 152 m | High ground |
| Downton (Wiltshire) | River gravels & Pleistocene alluvium | 7 m | Low, river edge |
| Thatcham III (Berkshire) | Silts and silty clays-Pleistocene | 2.5 m | Low, water edge |

graphic position of each site location. The potential importance of the geological deposit as a major influence on Mesolithic settlement patterns has been mentioned above (cf. Clark 1932, 1936; Mellars and Rheinhardt 1978). The relative height of each findspot refers to its altitude above the surrounding area, rather than the more general indications given by absolute height above present sea level. This enables a better appreciation of the site in its local context and is an aspect further summarised in the accompanying topographic description.

As indicated in Table 5.28, two groupings can be recognised with respect to general topographic setting: sites occupying low, water-edge positions and those situated on higher ground, generally away from standing water sources. With the exception of Iwerne Minster, the same twofold division may be identified in the nature of the underlying geological substrate. What gives these observations particular meaning is that they mirror precisely the same division between the first group (Hengistbury, Winfrith Heath and Iping Common) and the second group (Thatcham III and Downton) of tool assemblages.

### 5.5.6 Discussion and conclusions

Amongst the listed sets of variables, three common attributes appear to be shared by Hengistbury, Winfrith Heath and Iping Common: the composition of the lithic toolkit, the topographic situation and a broadly similar geological substrate. The lithic equipment from each of these sites is dominated by highly standardised microlith forms, here interpreted as hunting projectile equipment (Clark 1932; Jacobi 1976; Mellars and Rheinhardt 1978). The role of end-scrapers and microdenticulates, although not precisely determined, can nevertheless be seen as integral elements of a toolkit representing the activities of a temporary field camp (i.e. skinning, hide processing, repair and maintenance of hunting equipment etc.). Such an interpretation would be fully in accordance with the sites' settings which fulfill the predicted model of idealised hunting camp locations. As has previously been observed, higher ground and better drained subsoil would confer a number of distinct advantages on the hunter. These include aspects of concealment and ground cover (Clark 1936), and the ability to monitor distant game movements (Clark 1972; Jacobi 1978), as well as providing more comfortable site conditions in terms of dryness and heat insulation (Mellars and Rheinhardt 1978).

In contrast to the locations described above, both Thatcham III and Downton occupy lower-lying situations near the river edge and contain a greater variety of lithic tool equipment. The presence of burins, axes or adzes and drill-bits in addition to the more common tool forms seems to imply a significantly wider range of activities than were performed at the first group of higher ground sites. The greater heterogeneity of tool forms, of course, need not necessarily correlate with a "weaker representation of hunting equipment" (cf. Mellars and Rheinhardt 1978, 287). For example, microliths continue to be dominant elements in the lowland Downton assemblage and the burins from Thatcham III could have been important ancillary items in the manufacture and re-sharpening of antler weaponheads, also found at the same site (Wymer 1962, Fig. 13 and Plate L). From the presence of the extra tools, however, it may reasonably be inferred that a broader range of activities was practised at these locations. Thus at Thatcham, the expanded lithic inventory with its axes and adzes, could be identified quite plausibly with a local requirement for wood-working tools. This of course would not be surprising, especially in the context of a wooded, water-edge location where axes and adzes might have been relied upon in the manufacture of canoes (Kobusiewicz 1973), fishing leisters, traps and static fish weirs (Jacobi 1987).

The virtual absence of axes, adzes or their by-products in the first group of toolkits is an interesting phenomenon. Superficially, it could be argued that their absence in the upland record is more apparent than real and the fact that they did not enter the archaeological record owes more to the special value of these items than the frequency of their use (Binford 1976). That both types of toolkit were part of a 'curated technology' (cf. Binford 1976) is not here at issue but it is suggested that more relevant to the current discussion is the question of 'expediency' and the way the Mesolithic technology was organised. As we have seen, both at Hengistbury and the other typical upland assemblages, the lithic toolkit is dominated by microliths and their by-products. Many of the retouched pieces from these sites are broken and may have been manufactured for immediate use or as replacements for damaged tools. From the quantity of by-products (e.g. microburins) it is reasonable to suppose that a proportion of the finished tools were not used immediately but were removed for use elsewhere (e.g. as hafted weaponheads). Of particular relevance to the production work at these sites is the generally small size of the flint raw material. It is therefore frequently *unsuitable* for making axes or adzes and this is undoubtedly one of the reasons why these tools are rarely recovered at such sites.

An inference to be drawn from these observations is that the assemblages of the first group (Hengistbury, Winfrith Heath and Iping Common) reflect essentially 'non-curated' or 'expedient' components of a generalised technology (cf. Binford 1976), with more heavily 'curated' items of equipment occurring elsewhere. This factor might help explain the paucity of axe or adze finds since these are tools which would have been securely hafted in wooden or antler sleeves and were unlikely to have been intentionally discarded unless broken. Axes and adzes also require relatively large slabs of raw material for their manufacture (Care 1979). The fact that such tools were not necessarily made and used in the same places is demonstrated by the very occasional occurrence of axe tools (e.g. Winfrith Heath) or resharpening flakes (e.g. Iping Common) without any of the accompanying manufacturing debris. This contrasts markedly with the second group assemblages (Thatcham and Downton) where the collections reportedly include evidence of axe-use (re-sharpening flakes) and of axe and adze manufacture (primary and thinning flakes). It is clearly relevant that neither of these sites lies far away from good raw material sources. A similar observation can also be made at Iwerne Minster, the only first group assemblage which does not conform to the expected pattern. This high ground site, includes a very strong representation of axes, but perhaps significantly, few burins and no drill-bits. The simplest explanation is that the site is located on clay-with-flints, known to be a good source of superior quality and large-size raw material.

The absence of burins in the toolkits from Hengistbury, Winfrith Heath, Iping Common and Iwerne Minster, is more difficult to explain other than in purely functional terms. These tools do not appear to have been 'curated' in the same way as axes, but for some reason they do not seem to have played an important role in tasks undertaken at sites of the first group. This could be due to the fact that such implements were linked to maintenance tasks mainly associated with residential locations (e.g. bone and antler carving or woodworking). The same general observations may be valid for the drill-bits.

In summary, it seems likely that sites of the first group on sands were associated with a narrower range of activities than at the lower-lying second group. However, it should be noted that such an interpretation is difficult to prove without the preservation of organic materials and may need to be substantially qualified in the knowledge that some tools were more heavily curated (i.e. less visible in the archaeological record) than others. Based on general considerations of artefact type, technology and dating evidence, it is probable that all of the assemblages in the sample are of a broadly contemporary age. Given this information, it is interesting to speculate that the findspots described above could all lie within a projected lifetime's round of a single hunter-gatherer group (see for example Binford 1983, Fig. 52).

The purpose of this section was briefly to consider how the Powell site at Hengistbury might relate to other Mesolithic occurrences of potentially similar age in the same region. One can conclude that in a topographic situation where there are distinctive 'upland' and 'lowland' sites, Hengistbury represents a good example of the former and the functional suggestions made about these assemblages all apply to it.

# 6. Management of the Archaeological Resource

Like most sea promontories, Hengistbury has been subjected to the same general erosional processes which have helped winnow and shape the British coastline into its present form. A constant battle against the destructive forces of the sea has been waged over several centuries. This is illustrated by the implementation of numerous coastal protection schemes at Hengistbury Head, the earliest being documented in 1670 (Cunliffe 1978). Despite early attempts to bolster the sea wall defences, coastal erosion continues to eat away at the base of the cliff, causing slumping and major collapse of deposits. This has been exacerbated, in recent years, by vegetation loss and soil depletion along the cliff-top due to the combined effects of surface run-off and constant visitor pressure.

Both the Late Upper Palaeolithic site and the Powell Mesolithic site are especially vulnerable to damage, being situated on the south side of the headland along the cliff-top. Here, the effects of wind and soil erosion are particularly severe and in some areas cliff regression can be measured in metres rather than fractions of centimetres per year (Holloway and Lavender 1989, 12). As a consequence of the deteriorating conditions on the headland, the landowners, Bournemouth Borough Corporation, commissioned an archaeological feasibility survey of the areas most susceptible to erosional damage (Barton and Collcutt 1980). The report findings recommended that because of the advanced state of erosion, the worst affected areas of the cliff-top should be excavated immediately and that this should be coupled with investigations further inland to establish the fuller extent of archaeological deposits.

A key element of the work, therefore, was to assess the nature and distribution of the archaeological evidence with a view to finding practical solutions for the protection, maintenance and conservation of the surviving resource. Although there is a great deal still to learn about how archaeological sites are affected by the mechanics of site degradation, the present project has been effective in defining the limits of the archaeological deposits and in suggesting positive measures to improve the management of the resource. In executing these broad aims, the Hengistbury Project has benefited from the active involvement of English Heritage, in the person of Paul Gosling, one of its Ancient Monuments Inspectors. The whole of the headland is now a scheduled ancient monument (since 1986) and full management prescriptions have been determined for each of the sites concerned here.

The assessment of the sites included a detailed ground survey of the Eastern Depression, which established that the Upper Palaeolithic deposits extended well inland from the present coastal footpath. Artefacts of Late Upper Palaeolithic type were recorded as far as 120 m north of the coastal footpath, but the greatest densities of finds and deepest deposits occurred within 35 m of the present cliff-edge. These observations were confirmed by a small-scale excavation north of the footpath in 1984 which showed this to be one of the richest areas of the site. Since it supports undisturbed heathland vegetation, is relatively stable and is not undergoing active erosion, it was decided to leave the area for future archaeological analysis and investigation. Sufficient of the site had also been examined to fulfil the main aims of the project (Chapter 1.5) and no further work was envisaged for the time being.

Excavations at the Powell Mesolithic site demonstrated that the artefactual deposits also continued well inland of the cliff. Although much more of the site was excavated than at the Upper Palaeolithic area, it is estimated that at least a third of the main flint scatter remains intact and is preserved under a deep bank of deposits, roughly 15–20 m from the cliff-edge. With the immediate aims of the rescue work achieved, an undisturbed area of the site has been retained for future reference.

The future preservation of archaeological remains at both sites is dependent on several factors, some involving interim remedial measures at a local scale, others requiring much more major schemes to prevent further substantial cliff recession. Measures to combat the latter have already been put into effect and are laid out in the Hengistbury Head Management Plan (Holloway and Lavender 1989). Coastal protection works include the provision of groynes to bolster the south-eastern end of the headland to allow the build up of beach deposits at the base of the cliff. At the same time a stretch of cliff to the east of the Upper Palaeolithic site has been allowed to continue to erode, by removing talus material from the cliff base. Agreement has been reached with English Nature (formerly the Nature Conservancy Council) to facilitate the arrangement, but as there is some conflict of interest between those wishing to stabilise the cliffs and the NCC, who wish to leave sections exposed, this will need to be kept under regular review. In the meantime, the other areas will continue to erode slowly until the cliff regrades to an angle of approximately 35°. Depending on the rate of regression, further work may in due course be necessary further inland at both archaeological sites, but not in the foreseeable future.

In the shorter term, conservation measures at the top of the cliff will need to be implemented to stabilise erosion along paths and in adjacent areas. A particular threat is the heavy use made of the headland by the inhabitants of the rapidly burgeoning Christchurch and

Bournemouth conurbations. In 1981 it was estimated that the headland received one and a quarter million visitors annually (May and Osborne 1981) and this shows no immediate signs of diminishing. In consequence, one of the stated aims of the Management Plan is to organise public access of the headland so that "wear and tear is not more than can be repaired by the natural powers of regeneration by the vegetation" (1989, 33). It has also been acknowledged that any remedial action must take fully into account the needs of the archaeology.

On the basis of the Management Plan, various positive measures have been adopted to safeguard the archaeological deposits at both sites and combat soil erosion. This has taken the form of erecting fences and regravelling certain footpaths to convey visitor traffic away from the cliff-edge. At the Powell Mesolithic site archaeologically sterile gravels have been introduced to help stabilise exposed ground surfaces. In addition to covering the sandy sediments the gravels also provide suitable colonising habitats for communities of disturbed ground plants and grasses. Today, a firm matting of vegetation is beginning to be established in some areas and this has helped stem the constant loss of sand from higher areas of Warren Hill. Despite the slight risk of contamination from re-deposited flint or non-lithic artefacts, this strategy of gravel spreading seems to have been largely successful in the areas where it has been carried out. However, it is still too early to predict whether it will cushion the effects of more spectacular erosional damage at the cliff-edge.

At the Late Upper Palaeolithic site, fencing has been employed to cordon off the old cliff-path, while the refurbishment of other footpaths now redirects walkers further inland. The old excavation trenches have been lined with black plastic sheeting and then carefully backfilled using sediments of the spoil heap. Wherever possible the original grass and heath turves were also rebedded to minimise the risk of further erosion damage and help stabilise the soil. Additional protective measures at the LUP site have been recommended in consultation with Paul Gosling. These include covering the exposed north footpath section with clean sediments in order to encourage renewed plant growth and to reseed bare surfaces closer to the cliff-edge. Again, it will be several years before the results of this work can be seen and properly assessed.

Further routine monitoring of the archaeological sites is carried out on an informal but regular basis by Mr Mark Holloway, the Ranger of Hengistbury Head. He is also responsible for the day to day conservation management of the headland and, as one of the authors of the Management Plan, takes a keen interest in applying its recommendations. None of the archaeological site management prescriptions is particularly expensive to implement. A modest rolling programme with a budget of £3000 per annum is provided by Bournemouth Borough Council to deal with the effects of localised erosion. It is considered that the remedies proposed here could be integrated into this programme. Ultimately, it is this close local monitoring and control of the resource that will ensure the effective management of the site, and hence its longer term preservation.

# 7. Glossary of Archaeological Terms

*Abrasion* (see under Platform Abrasion)

*Anvil retouch* Anvil retouch is a technological term which describes a specific type of retouch generally found on backed blades and bladelets. It is characterised by opposed retouch scars originating from the dorsal and ventral surfaces. These may be formed when the blank is rested on an anvil and usually retouched by direct percussion. In percussion, the blow passes down through the surface of the blank in contact with the hammer and rebounds off the anvil resulting in opposed retouch scars (Fig. 1.7). Common accidents of this retouching technique are Krukowski microburins (see under Microburin).

*Backed blade/bladelet* A backed blade or bladelet usually has one edge which is totally covered with semi-abrupt or abrupt retouch. This retouch modifies the lateral edge in a major way and has the effect of 'blunting' it. The backed pieces at Hengistbury have a retouched edge which is usually straight in plan rather than convex (Fig. 4.22).

*Bec* see Piercer/Bec.

*Blade* A blade is a product of flaking whose length is twice or more than twice its width (Bordes 1961).

*Bladelet* A bladelet is a narrow blade with a width of less than 12 mm. In the case of retouched tools like backed blades and bladelets, those with a width greater than 9 mm are considered backed blades, while those examples under 9 mm are backed bladelets (Tixier 1963). These definitions are somewhat arbitrary and are used here for general descriptive purposes only.

*Blank* In this volume the word blank refers to any substantial product of debitage including flakes, blades and bladelets which might potentially be converted into one of the tool categories present at Hengistbury Head. Figure 7.2 illustrates the morphological terms used to describe the various parts of a blank.

*Break* refit (see under Dorso-ventral refit)

*Burin* A burin is a flake or blade which has been modified by the burin blow technique. This entails the removal, by percussion or pressure, of a narrow splinter of flint (the burin spall) from a lateral edge or either end of the blank. Burins are generally classified by the morphology of the surface from which the spall is detached (spall removal surface) as well as the position of the burin edge and the number of facets making up the edge (Fig. 7.3). Two

major groups of burins are recognised by de Sonneville-Bordes and Perrot (1956a). The first group, known as truncation burins, have a spall removal surface formed by retouch which may occur at either end of a blank or on a lateral edge. The second type of burin has burin spalls detached from one of the following surfaces: a break, an unmodified natural surface (e.g. an unretouched lateral edge) or another burin facet. This second type of burin is referred to as a dihedral burin.

*Burin spall* The burin spall is the part of the blank detached by the burin blow. The spall itself is normally a narrow sliver of flint with a triangular or trapezoidal cross-section. At Hengistbury Head it was almost always regarded as a waste product (Fig. 4.16, 4); in only a few cases did spalls serve as blanks for tool manufacture.

*Butt* The butt of a flake, blade or bladelet is the part of the core's striking platform detached by the blow of the hammer. In the case of a burin spall it is the part of the spall removal surface (see under Burin) detached as the burin blow is delivered. The butt is found at the proximal end of a blank, and, the following terms are often used to describe its morphology: (1) plain, (2) dihedral, (3) faceted, (4) cortical. The main butt types which occur at Hengistbury are illustrated in Figure 7.4 (see also under striking platform).

*Chip* For the purposes of this volume a chip (cf. Newcomer and Karlin 1987) is any complete artefact which measures less than 5 mm in length. The small size of these pieces clearly indicates that they are waste products not intended for use or modification into tools. Chips can be produced in a variety of ways including retouching a blank to make a tool or abrading the edge of a core (see Platform abrasion).

*Composite tool* This is an artefact which combines tools of two or more tool groups (e.g. scrapers, burins, piercers etc.) on the same blank. One possible example from the Late Upper Palaeolithic site combines a retouched tang and a burin on a concave truncation (Fig. 4.18, 6). A more typical example is of a combined truncation burin and end-scraper illustrated by Mace (1959, Fig. 6, 44).

*Core* A core is the block of raw material from which flakes, blades or bladelets are detached. Figure 7.5 illustrates the terms used to describe the various parts of the core.

*Core tablet* This term refers to a characteristic by-product of rejuvenating a core's striking platform. A core tablet usually removes the whole of the platform; its butt almost always displays remnants of the upper part of the core's

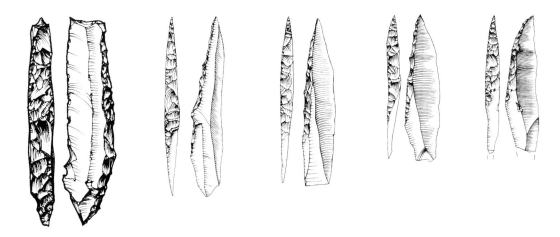

7.1  *Bidirectional (anvil) retouch.*

distal end

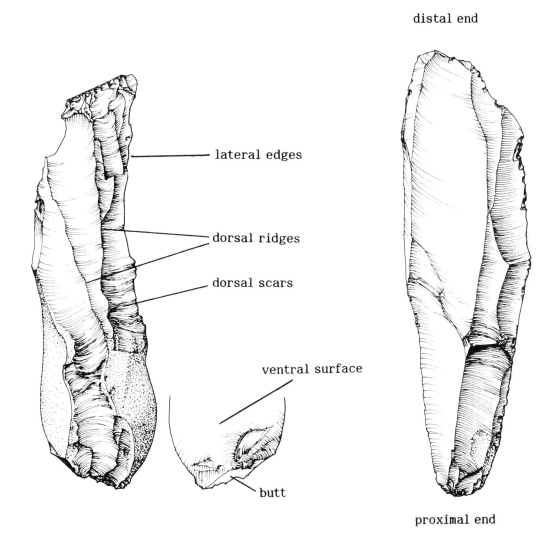

— lateral edges

— dorsal ridges

— dorsal scars

ventral surface

butt

proximal end

7.2  *Morphological attributes of a blank.*

flaking face. The technique of detaching a core tablet is used to remove damaged platforms as well as for correcting faulty flaking angles (Fig. 7.6).

*Cresting* Cresting is a term which applies to the preparation of a core, usually for the production of blades or bladelets. It involves the creation of a longitudinal ridge to guide the first removal and set up parallel ridges on the flaking face. The crested blade is generally triangular in cross-section and has either uni- or bidirectional removals, originating from the central ridge, which are perpendicular to the axis of percussion

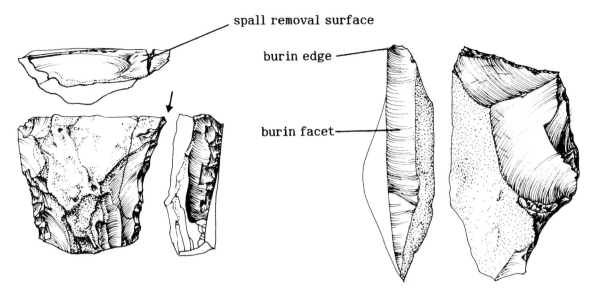

7.3  *Burin.*

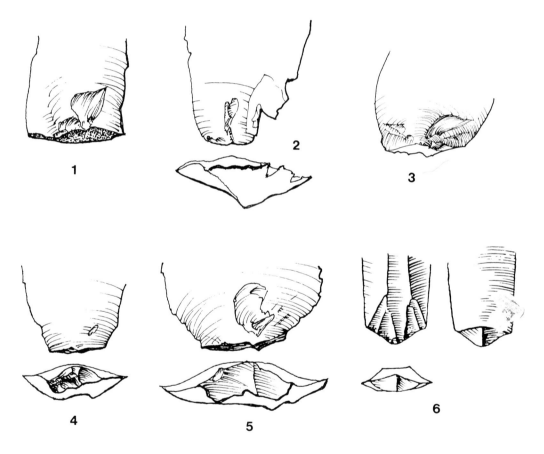

7.4  *Butt types: 1= cortical; 2= linear; 3= plain; 4= faceted; 5= dihedral (faceted); 6= en éperon (after Tixier et al. 1980).*

of the blade. It should also be noted that cresting can be used at any stage of core reduction for such purposes as removing hinge fractures or maintaining the curvature of the flaking face (Fig. 7.7).

*Debitage* The term debitage (derived from the French 'débitage') refers to the deliberate act of flaking a block of raw material in order to obtain the by-products. It is also the name given to all the by-products of this action, including cores, blanks, chips and other debris.

*Denticulate* A denticulate is a tool with at least three contiguous notches on one edge (Fig. 4.12, 8).

*Distal end* The distal end is the part of the blank opposite the proximal or bulbar end (Fig. 7.2).

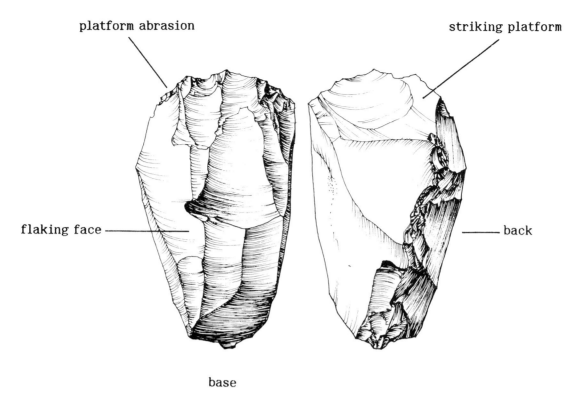

platform abrasion

striking platform

flaking face ——————

—————— back

base

7.5 *Morphological attributes of a core.*

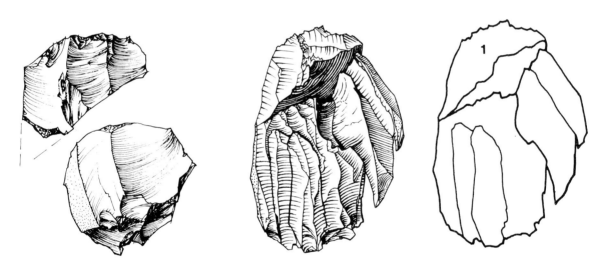

7.6 *Core tablet and a core with a refitting core tablet (1).*

*Dorsal surface* The dorsal surface is the upper side of a flake, blade or bladelet which carries the ridges and scars of previous removals, and/or cortex (Fig. 7.2).

*Dorso-ventral refit* This term refers to two artefacts which can be fitted together by dorsal/ventral contact. In contrast, a *break refit* consists of two or more refitting fragments from a single broken artefact.

*Drill-bit* A tool of narrow lanceolate shape with parallel abruptly retouched edges converging to a point at one or both ends. It is sometimes known by the french term *mèche* or *mèche de foret*. There is only one example in the Hengistbury Mesolithic assemblage

(Fig. 5.22, 3).

*End-Scraper* The term end-scraper refers to a tool made on a flake or blade with one or both ends retouched into a semi-circular (convex) edge. This retouch is generally semi-abrupt in angle but can become abrupt through sharpening (Fig. 4.11).

*Faceting* (see under Butt; also Platform Preparation)

*'Flanc de nucléus'* A flake which removes all or part of the core's flaking face. This can be the result of an accident, as when the blow is delivered too far back from the edge or deliberately to rejuvenate the core (Fig. 7.8).

267

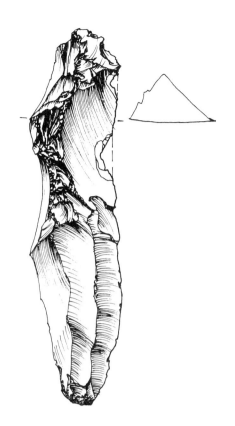

7.7  *Crested blade.*

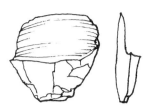

7.9  *Languette fracture.*

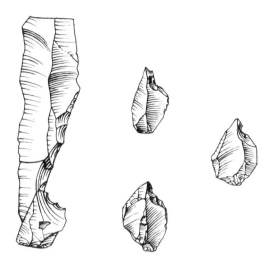

7.10  *Microburins (proximal examples).*

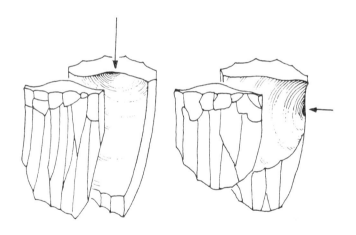

7.8  *Flanc de nucléus (after Brézillon 1977b).*

*Flake* A flake is a product of debitage that has a length to width ratio of less than 2:1.

*Flaking face* This term is used to describe the part of the core which is the focus of flaking and from which most blanks are detached (Fig. 7.5).

*Flexion break* When a flint is flexed or 'bent' one surface is subjected to tensile stress, the other to compressive forces. The break is initiated at the surface under tensile stress. Flexion breaks can be caused in a number of ways, both accidental and intentional. One of the most common types occurs as a blank snaps into one or more pieces as it is detached from the core.

*Flintknapping* Flintknapping is used here as a synonym for 'flaking' or the deliberate act of detaching flakes from an object of raw material.

*Hammer types* The tools used to flake by percussion are normally divided into two major categories: hard hammers and soft hammers. A hard hammer is usually made of stone (e.g. a quartzite pebble), while soft hammers include a variety of materials such as wood, antler and softer stones (e.g. limestone; Ohnuma and Bergman 1982). Different hammer types are chosen to do different kinds of tasks: for general flaking where the blow will land in from the core's edge a hard hammer will often be used, whereas for marginal flaking a softer hammer may be preferred (Newcomer 1971, 1975). The term percussor is sometimes used as an alternative for the word hammer, while billet usually refers to a soft hammer of antler.

*Intentional break* An intentional break is a percussion-induced fracture which produces two substantial pieces (Bergman *et al.* 1983, 1987). The break surfaces are usually transverse to the long axis of the blank and have no pronounced concavity. Intentionally broken flakes and blades are occasionally used as blanks to make tools such as burins. In some cases it also appears that the break surface was utilised without further modification. This may be due to the fact that the break surface creates edge angles similar to those which occur on burin facets (Fig. 4.26).

*Krukowski microburin* (see under Microburin).

*Languette fracture* This feature results from a flexion break and takes the form of a pronounced lip or negative lip on the break edge (Bordes 1970) (Fig. 7.9).

*Mèche de foret* (see drill-bit)

*Microburin* A microburin is a waste product of microlith manufacture characterised by a relatively small notch contiguous with an oblique break facet. The microburin technique involves the notching of a blade or bladelet until the piece fractures obliquely. This action results in two pieces: the microburin and the generally larger pointed blank (or *piquant trièdre* according to the french terminology). If the microburin removes the butt, it is known as a proximal microburin (Fig. 7.10), while a microburin which removes the opposite end is referred to as a distal microburin. In this monograph a 'miss-hit' describes an unsuccessful microburin blow, which results in a transverse, straight snap instead of the desired oblique break. Unlike the true microburin, the Krukowski microburin is an accidental by-product of retouch (Fig. 5.27).

*Microdenticulate* This class of tool, found at the Hengistbury Mesolithic site, is generally made on a bladelet blank with concave or sinuous (concave-convex) lateral edges. The retouched edge is usually concave and has a series of miniscule notches which are contiguous (Fig. 7.11).

*Microlith* Strictly speaking, this term only applies to bladelets which have had their proximal ends removed by semi-abrupt or abrupt retouch (Clark 1934a). However, a broader definition is accepted here, which also includes rarer examples of tools with a similar morphology but with the bulb left intact. In England, microliths have been divided into two classes (Clark 1932; Jacobi 1976): Geometric (e.g. triangles, trapezes, rhombic forms) and non-geometric (obliquely blunted points, backed points). At Hengistbury the most commonly occurring microliths are non-geometric forms, such as the tools illustrated in Figure 7.12 below.

*Miscellaneous* This term is used to describe retouched tools which for reasons of breakage or atypical character cannot be placed in any of the existing tool classes.

*Multiple tools* A multiple tool combines at least two tools of the same class on a single blank (Fig. 4.15, 5).

*Notch* A notch is a tool with a pronounced concavity on a lateral edge produced by a single blow or by the removal of a series of small retouch flakes.

*Percussion flaking* Percussion flaking involves the use of a hammer of stone or any suitable organic material such as wood or antler to strike a blow to detach a flake. In the case of direct percussion, the hammer lands on the striking platform, while indirect percus-

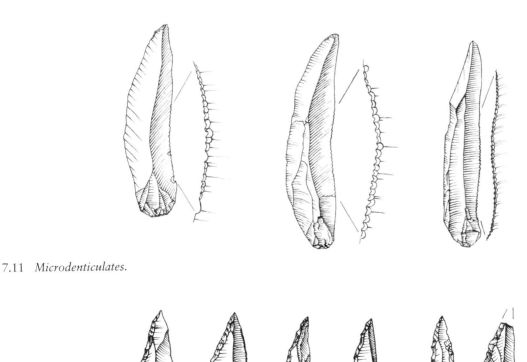

7.11   *Microdenticulates.*

7.12   *Microliths. A-types, B-type (second from right) and C-type (extreme right).*

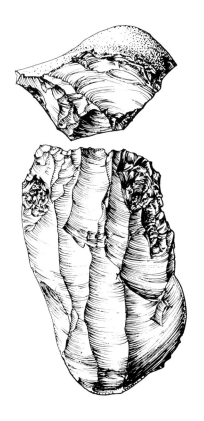

7.13 *Core with partially faceted platform.*

sion utilises a 'punch' or some other intermediary device between the core and hammer.

*Piercer/Bec* These types of tools are rare at Hengistbury Head and are therefore grouped together. At the Late Upper Palaeolithic site a piercer/bec has a relatively narrow pointed tip formed by two lines of converging retouch (Fig. 4.15, 1–3).

*Platform abrasion* This core preparation technique involves the removal of a series of small chips ((Fig. 4.8, 5) from the intersection of the striking platform and the main flaking face; the scars of these removals occur on the flaking face. It is most often done to remove the overhang (a point of weakness) which results from previous removals. It is essential to abrade the platform when striking close to its edge in order to avoid crushing. In the Hengistbury Late Upper Palaeolithic assemblage the abrading of core platforms is sometimes quite heavy and may best be described as grinding.

*Platform preparation* At Hengistbury two main forms of core platform preparation occur: core tablet removal (see Core tablet) and faceting. Both involve the removal of flakes to prepare the platform and correct faulty

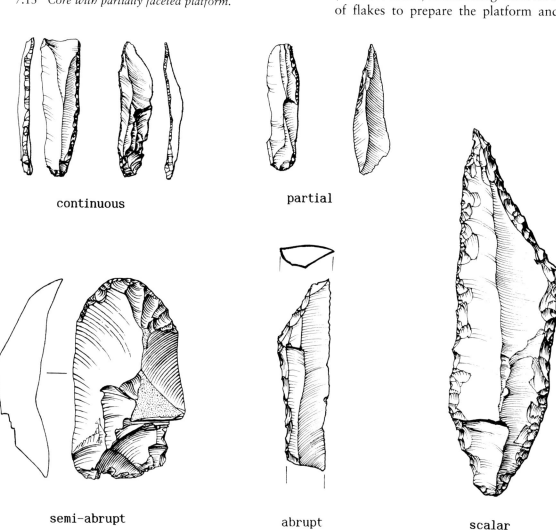

continuous

partial

semi-abrupt

abrupt

scalar

7.14 *Retouch classification.*

270

angles. In the Late Upper Palaeolithic assemblage minor adjustments are often made near the front of the platforms (Fig. 7.13); this may best be described as partial faceting (cf. Bordes 1967). The method is not used at the Mesolithic site. Core tablets are common forms of debitage at both sites.

*Pressure flaking* Pressure flaking is a technique of knapping which involves the removal of flakes by pressure rather than percussion. In Britain, this technique is found most often in later stone age industries with bifacially flaked projectiles (e.g. Neolithic leaf-shaped arrowheads). A few end-scrapers at Hengistbury appear to have edges made by pressure (Fig. 4.11, 5).

*Proximal end* The proximal end is the part of a flake, blade or bladelet with the butt and bulb of percussion (Fig. 7.2).

*Retouch* A tool is created by the act of retouching a blank, either by percussion-or pressure-flaking. Retouch is the trace left by this action (Newcomer 1972). While the term is mainly used to describe deliberate modification, it can also be applied to accidental traces left on a blank which has been utilised. A variety of terms are used to describe the position, angle and type of retouch and some of these are illustrated in Figure 7.14. Almost all of the tools at Hengistbury are made by direct retouch which originates from the ventral surface leaving retouch scars on the dorsal surface.

*Retouched tool* An artefact modified by retouch and conforming to a recognisable type. Retouched tools may be classified according to a group or class of tools (e.g. end-scrapers, burins, composite tools etc.) or to individual types (e.g. dihedral symmetrical burin, parrot-beaked burin etc.). The total collection of tools is referred to as the retouched tool assemblage.

*Shouldered points* These tools are sometimes also known as Hamburgian points (cf. Rust 1937, 1943), and, at Hengistbury are characterised by partial, abrupt retouch forming a shoulder towards the proximal end of the piece. The distal end often has an oblique truncation (Fig. 4.25, 7–10).

*Spontaneous retouch* This term, introduced by Newcomer (1976), describes the accidental retouching of a blank as it is being detached from the core. In this monograph the term has been expanded to include similar accidents of flaking (*spontaneous effects*) which can also result in the formation of features like burin facets.

*Striking platform* The striking platform is the part of the core which receives the blow of the hammer during flaking (Fig. 7.5).

*Tanged point* This kind of point has an axial tang, defined by abrupt or semi-abrupt retouch. The examples from Hengistbury are made on blades, with a long, broad tang usually at the proximal end. The distal end is often retouched to make the pointed tip more acute (Fig. 4.25, 1–2).

*Truncation* A truncation is a tool with semi-abrupt or abrupt retouch truncating either the proximal or the distal end of the blank. Depending on the shape and position of the retouch, the truncation can be classified as straight, oblique, concave or convex (Fig. 4.12, 9).

*Ventral surface* The ventral surface is the side of the blank which has the bulb of percussion (Fig. 7.2).

*Zinken* A type of bec made on a thick blank (de Sonneville-Bordes and Perrot 1955). The bec or prong is well-defined by direct abrupt retouch with additional lamellar removals running back from the tip. The tool may be either single or double, with the prong(s) being offset rather than symmetrical to the long axis of the blank.

# 8. Summary

Hengistbury Head is a conspicuous promontory located on the south coast of England eight kilometres east of Bournemouth in Dorset (50° 43" N, 1° 45" W; NGR SZ 175905). The headland juts out into the Solent Channel and overlooks the Isle of Wight to the south-east. Geologically, the headland is composed of a succession of Tertiary marine and sub-littoral beds overlain, in places, by Pleistocene terrace gravels. The whole sequence is capped by fine and medium sands of windblown origin which contain archaeological evidence of Late Glacial and Holocene age.

Over the years the headland has continued to be affected by coastal erosion but more recently there has been a visible increase in cliff-regression, threatening archaeological deposits along its southern edge. Following a preliminary survey commissioned by the landowners, full-scale rescue excavation work was undertaken at two sites on the cliff top between 1980–1984. The excavations, directed by the author, were funded principally by Bournemouth Corporation and English Heritage.

The first site is a Late Upper Palaeolithic (LUP) open-air site located at the south-eastern end of the headland, in an area known as the Eastern Depression (14 m OD). The U-shaped depression probably formed the head of a dry stream valley now truncated by the sea-cliff. The site had been known for many years and was previously investigated in 1957 by Angela Mace and in 1968-9 by John Campbell. The second site lies about 650 m further west, close to the summit of Warren Hill (35 m OD), the highest point on Hengistbury Head. It is of Early Mesolithic age and is named the Powell site after its discoverer. The two excavations are fully described in Chapter 1.

The new investigations in the Eastern Depression took the form of excavation near the cliff-edge and a ground survey of the deposits further inland. An area of 96 sq m was uncovered in the excavations as compared with c. 71 sq m and 136 sq m by Mace and Campbell, respectively. It was confirmed that the deepest and richest Upper Palaeolithic deposits are concentrated near the cliff edge but that lower densities of material continue well inland. The survey also enabled study of a Late Bronze Age/Early Iron Age bank and ditch boundary feature which cuts diagonally across the Depression. Environmental evidence from this feature covers the later vegetational history of the headland and shows that land clearance and ditch construction were followed by a period of oak woodland regeneration. Intensive podzolisation of the sands seems to have been initiated prior to the development of the heathland vegetation which exists on the headland today (Chapter 2).

The LUP site is situated in sands overlying gravels. The sediments consist of moderately well sorted, windblown sands overlying soliflucted deposits. The sands are now heavily podzolised and the artefacts occur in a band 40–50 cm thick in the lower Ea and upper Bh horizon of the gley podzol. The new excavations provided an opportunity to obtain fresh dating evidence for the LUP occupation and to analyse a large body of artefactual material from the point of view of typological, technological and spatial studies. They also allowed a reappraisal of geological and contextual data which had led the previous excavator, John Campbell, to identify Mesolithic and Upper Palaeolithic levels at this one site. New interpretation shows that the site consists of only one, homogeneous LUP assemblage and is based partly on the following evidence:

(1) Thermoluminescence dating of burnt artefacts resulted in six determinations with an average age of 12,500±1150 years BP (OXTL 707a), fully in accordance with the expected time range for an assemblage of LUP type.

(2) No significant breaks could be recognised in the vertical distribution of finds. Various post-depositional processes may account for the vertical dispersal of artefacts (Chapter 3.1), but the most likely cause of movement is small-scale biological activity within the soil. This view was supported by experimental models which predicted certain patterns in the weight distribution and orientation of the artefacts, some of which are observable in the archaeological data.

(3) Refitting evidence established that significant numbers of artefacts previously identified as 'Mesolithic' by Campbell could be conjoined with 'Upper Palaeolithic' artefacts.

The LUP assemblage is fully described in Chapter 4. It is composed mainly of flint artefacts, with a scattering of sandstone blocks and red ochre fragments. One flint core has an engraving on its cortex. A combined total of 649 retouched tools, from the three excavations, includes 147 end-scrapers, 66 burins and 324 backed blades and bladelets. Also contained in the tool inventory are tanged points and tanged point fragments (19), shouldered points (8) and truncations (8). Piercers and becs are very scarce. There is only one composite tool (a burin on truncation/end-scraper). One of the more unusual aspects of the assemblage is the occurrence of intentionally broken artefacts (176), of which 30 have subsequently been converted into tools.

Raw material analysis indicates that the flint is of a non-local variety and must have been humanly transported to the site from at least 12 km away. Refitting has shown that the nodules were brought in whole and not preformed elsewhere. All stages of the core reduction process are represented at the site.

A technological study of the debitage recovered by Campbell and in the recent excavations revealed that out of a total of 13,419 artefacts, there are 3815 flakes and 2266 blades or bladelets. The remainder consists of unidentified pieces (4078) and chips ≤ 5 mm (3260). The blades vary considerably in size, ranging in length from 44–138 mm in the case of one very large refitted core. Average dimensions from a sample of 307 complete blades give a mean measurement of 55 x 19 x 6 mm. The blade butts are generally plain (85%) and the larger butts tend to be heavily abraded. Although some blades have faceted butts (11%) none can be described as *en éperon* in type. The strong blade component in the collection is reflected in the large number of blade cores (63 out of 88). From the refitting evidence it can be shown that blades were usually detached from opposed platform cores, prepared by a frontal and a dorsal crest. Chapter 4.3 describes individual refitting sequences.

A spatial analysis was made of 29 refitted core reduction episodes (Chapter 4.4). The plotted data showed two discrete groups of refitting clusters, the largest occurring in the south central area of the site. Here the artefacts consist mainly of blade debitage and have produced the most complete blade-to-core refitting sequences. In contrast, an area a few metres to the north west, containing large numbers of retouched tools, notably backed blades, many of them burnt, exhibits very few refits. Taken together, it is possible to infer a spatial separation of activities represented, on the one hand by tool activity around the remains of a hearth and, on the other, by a peripheral zone where the primary production of tool blanks occurred. A similar division of activities, with flint-knapping being performed away from the hearth, was noted at the French Late Magdalenian sites of Marsangy and Etiolles.

A use-wear analysis of the flint artefacts from Hengistbury proved inconclusive, due to post-depositional alteration of the flint surfaces. The macroscopic study of tools, however, showed that some of the burins had been heavily utilised along their edges and had undergone frequent resharpening (Chapter 4.5.4). In addition, the backed blades appear to have served various functions, some of them for cutting while others were apparently projectile points. Experimental work, supported by Scanning Electron Microscopy, has also established that flint was used to engrave an abstract design on the corticated surface of a core, although the engraving tool itself was not identified (Chapter 4.6). Wear traces consistent with heavy abrading and rubbing were also identified on a red ochre 'crayon' (Chapter 4.2.3).

The LUP site at Hengistbury would appear to have been used as a residential hunting location. It occupies an excellent vantage point over a flat landscape and is well-sheltered and concealed in the dry stream valley. Based on Upper Palaeolithic continental parallels, Hengistbury is fairly typical of the larger hunter-gatherer aggregation site, occupied seasonally during the period of autumn and spring migrations of animals such as horse and reindeer (Chapter 4.10.6).

The Hengistbury LUP assemblage can be paralleled at only one other location in Britain (Brockhill, Surrey), and then only incompletely. As noted by previous authors, it appears to bear no resemblance to the Creswellian cave assemblages, which are characterised by angle-backed tools and show different features in the debitage. According to the available dating evidence, it is quite conceivable that the timespan of the two technologies coincided or partly overlapped in the Late Glacial Interstadial. The continental evidence of this period shows a similar diversity. The best continental parallels for Hengistbury are to be found in the straight-backed blade technologies of NW Europe, represented at one end of the spectrum by Late Magdalenian assemblages and at the other by various Early Federmesser groups (Chapter 4.10.5).

The second site investigated at Hengistbury provides rich evidence of Early Mesolithic activities on the headland. It was discovered in 1977 by Mr Ronald Powell who collected large quantities of artefacts eroding out of a deflation surface on the cliff-top. Fieldwork, begun in 1980, concentrated on areas near the cliff-edge immediately under threat and later extended inland to try to define the northern limit of the main artefact scatter. In all, 78 sq m were excavated, with a further 50 sq m being covered by surface collection.

The Powell Mesolithic site consists of a dense concentration of flint artefacts occupying a band 50–70 cm thick in the upper (Ea2 horizon) of the present-day podzol, just above a very compact iron-manganese pan (Bh horizon). The sands are finer and better sorted than in the Eastern Depression, implying a wholly windblown origin. The existing podzol also shows pedogenic modification from earlier brown sand soils, believed to be contemporary with the Mesolithic occupation of the site (Chapter 2.2.3).

Sufficient of the occupation area has now been investigated to show that the main artefact scatter is sub-circular or slightly oval in shape with a maximum diameter of some 12 m, although there is a denser concentration of finds about 5 m across within this area. The scatter consists mostly of flint artefacts but amongst the non-flint materials are two sandstone 'rubbers' and a large block of sarsen. Virtually all of the flint and non-flint materials are believed to be of local origin, except the rubbers which are of rock-types found in SW England.

Within the main scatter of flint artefacts were burnt specimens which have provided five thermoluminescence determinations giving an average age of 9750±950 years BP (OXTL 707c) for the Mesolithic horizon. This indicates that the site was occupied during the Pre-Boreal or Boreal when Hengistbury was still an inland location, with the contemporary coastline perhaps lying as far away as 20 km.

The excavations yielded some 35,444 flint artefacts, of which two-thirds are accounted for by small chips and flint debris less than 10mm in size. Amongst the identifiable debitage are 6312 flakes and 5699 blades or bladelets, plus 145 cores. The retouched tools contain a high proportion (62%) of microliths, mostly non-geometric types. Out of 626 tools from the excavated and surface collections (described in Chapter 5.2) there are 95 end-scrapers, 65 microdenticulates and 390 microliths with the remainder consisting of truncations, retouched flakes and blades and miscellaneous retouched types. The microliths from the site are almost all A-types (oblique points) and come from the denser part of the concentration. The presence of large numbers of proximal microburins (273) indicate that this was a primary tool production zone.

Microwear studies (Chapter 5.3) of the flints have shown them to be largely unsuitable for analysis because of post-depositional surface modifications. However, study of the edge morphology and other characteristics coupled with experimental work suggests that one of the tool groups (the microdenticulates) was probably used for cutting softer plant materials, such as the bark fibres of green wood. Visible damage to the tips of some of the microliths has also been interpreted as evidence of tool-use and may indicate that re-tooling of projectile equipment took place at the site.

From the refitting of various artefacts (Chapters 3.2.3 and 5.1) it is possible to identify individual flaking episodes within the main occupation scatter. One of the refitted blocks (which includes a microlith) is of a distinctive speckled-grey flint and covers a roughly oval area of 400 x 300 cm. The horizontal spread of this material appears to reflect some post-depositional displacement of the artefacts.

The Powell Mesolithic site is one of several Early Mesolithic sites in the Hampshire basin, dating to the Pre-Boreal and Boreal. They belong to the earliest group of Mesolithic assemblages known in NW Europe, although they lack the microlithic triangles typical of the Star Carr-Duvensee complex. According to the microlith morphology (analysed in Chapter 5.5.5), Hengistbury compares closely with other sites in the region, including Downton, 30 km to the north and Winfrith Heath, 38 km to the west.

In terms of actual tool types (Chapter 5.5.5) Hengistbury displays a narrow range characterised by microliths, end-scrapers and small denticulates but with no burins, axes or adzes. Similar toolkits have been identified at other upland locations in the region and are believed to reflect a highly specialised range of activities associated with game hunting. Lower lying, water-edge sites with a wider selection of tools, including burins and adzes, may have functioned as contemporary residential locations where more intensive maintenance and processing activities were performed. The proximity of both these types of site within the same region and the regularity of the toolkits could fit the pattern of a social territory exploited by a single hunter-gatherer community during an annual round of settlement.

Conservation and preservation of unexcavated parts of the Palaeolithic and Mesolithic sites, as well as others on Hengistbury Head, is regarded as a high priority for safeguarding future research needs. Currently there is a management scheme to stabilise cliff recession and to replant areas of the cliff-top which are undergoing active erosion.

## Resumé

L'important promontoire de Hengistbury Head se situe sur la côte sud de l'Angleterre à huit kilomètres à l'est de Bournemouth (Dorset) (50°43" N, 1°45" W; NGR SZ 175905). Il s'avance dans le Solent et fait face au sud-est à l'Ile de Wight. Au point de vue géologique, le promontoire se compose d'une succession de dépôts marins et sub-littoraux du Tertiaire, recouverts par endroits de graviers de terrace du Pléistocène. Le tout est surmonté de sables éoliens fins et moyens, de source strictement locale, qui contiennent des restes archéologiques du Tardiglaciaire et de l'Holocène.

Le promontoire est sujet à l'érosion côtière mais recemment la regression de la falaise s'est accélérée de façon visible, mettant en danger les dépôts archéologiques situés sur le côté sud. Après une étude préliminaire, commandée par les propriétaires, d'importantes fouilles de sauvetage étaient entreprises en 1980–1984 sur deux sites au sommet de la falaise. Ces fouilles, dirigées par l'éditeur, ont été financées en majeure partie par le Conseil Municipal de Bournemouth et par English Heritage.

Le premier gisement, du Paléolithique supérieur tardif (angl. 'Late Upper Palaeolithic' ou 'LUP'), est un site de plein-air situé à l'extrémité sud-est du promontoire dans un endroit appelé la Dépression Est (14 m au-dessus de la mer). Cette dpression était sans doute le départ d'une petite vallée sèche tronquée aujourd'hui par la falaise. Ce site, connu depuis longtemps, avait été partiellement fouillé en 1957 par Angela Mace et en 1968–69 par John Campbell. Le deuxième site, 650 m plus à l'ouest, se trouve près du sommet de Warren Hill (35 m), point le plus élevé de Hengistbury Head. Ce site du Mésolithique inférieur a été découvert par Mr. Powell. Les anciennes fouilles sont décrites en détail dans le chapitre 1.

Les nouvelles recherches dans la Dépression Est ont inclus des fouilles en haut de la falaise et un relevé de couches plus au nord. Une surface de 96 m$^2$ a été fouillée, à comparer aux 71 m$^2$ par Mace et aux 136 m$^2$ fouillés par Campbell. Nous avons confirmé que les dépôts du Paléolithique supérieur les plus riches et les plus profonds se trouvent près de la falaise mais que le matériel à des densités inférieures continue vers le nord. Ces recherches nous ont permis aussi d'étudier un élément de périmètre (fossé et talus) de l'Age du Bronze supérieur/Age de Fer inférieur qui traverse diagonalement la dépression. Les données palynologiques et pédologiques provenant de ce pèrimètre révèlent l'histoire de la végétation du promontoire à ces époques et démontrent que la phase de défrichement et de construction du périmètre a été suivie par une période de régénération de la chénaie. La podzolisation intense des sables semble avoir commencé avant le développement de la lande actuelle (Chapitre 2).

Le site du LUP se trouve dans les sables éoliens assez bien classés recouvrant d'abord des dépôts soliflués puis des graviers. Ces sables sont aujourd'hui très podzolisés et les artéfactes se trouvent dans une bande de 40 à 50 cm d'épaisseur qui chevauche la limite entre les horizons éluviaux et illuviaux du podzol gléifié. Les fouilles récentes ont permis d'obtenir de nouveaux éléments de datation de l'occupation du LUP et d'analyser un ensemble important d'artéfactes au point de vue typologique, technologique et spatial. Ces fouilles ont aussi permis une réévaluation de la géologie et du contexte physique. Auparavant, Campbell avait cru identifier des niveaux et mésolithiques et paléolithiques dans ce même gisement. Cependant, nous avons pu démontrer qu'il ne s'agit que d'une seule industrie homogène du LUP grâce aux raisonnements suivants.

(1) La datation par thermoluminescence de silex brûlés a donné six déterminations avec une moyenne de 12 500 ± 1150 BP (OXTL 707a), un résultat parfaitement en accord avec la durée connue des industries du LUP.

(2) Nous n'avons pas trouvé de lacunes dans la distribution verticale des artéfactes. L'épaisseur de la bande peut être due à une variété de processus postérieurs au dépôt (Chapitre 3.1) mais la cause la plus probable est l'activité biologique du sol à l'échelle millimétrique donnant un mouvement cummulatif important. Cette conclusion est soutenue par des modèles théoriques prévoyant certaines caractéristiques de la distribution des artéfacts d'après leur poids et leur orientation individuels, caractéristiques qui paraissent souvent dans l'ensemble archéologique.

(3) Le remontage a établi qu'un nombre important d'artéfactes qui avaient été auparavant identifiés en tant que 'mésolithiques' par Campbell pouvaient en fait être raccordés à ceux de son 'Paléolithique supérieur'.

L'industrie du LUP est décrite dans le chapitre 4. Elle se compose en majeure partie d'artéfactes en silex, avec de rares blocs de grès et quelques fragments d'ocre rouge. Un nucléus de silex présente une gravure sur le cortex. Le nombre total d'outils retouchés (provenant des trois fouilles) est de 649, dont 147 grattoirs, 66 burins et 324 lames et lamelles à dos. On trouve aussi des pointes et des fragments de pointes à pédoncule (19), des pointes à cran (8), et des pièces tronquées (8). Les perçoirs et les becs sont très rares. Il n'y a qu'un seul objet composite (un burin sur troncature/grattoir). L'un des aspects les plus insolites de cette industrie est la présence de 176 pièces à fracture volontaire, dont 30 ont été converties en outils par la suite.

L'analyse de la matière première indique que le silex n'est pas d'origine locale et a dú être transporté par l'homme d'une douzaine de kilomètres au moins. Le remontage a démontré que les blocs ont été amenés entiers et non préformés ailleurs. Toutes les étapes de la chaine opératoire sont représentées sur le gisement.

Une étude technologique du débitage receuilli par Campbell et par nous-mêmes a révélé que, sur un total de 13,419 artéfactes, il y a 3,815 éclats et 2,266 lames et lamelles. Le restant consiste en 4,078 pièces non identi-

fiées et aussi 3,260 débris de ≤ 5 mm. Les lames, élément important de l'industrie, sont de tailles très variées allant de 44 mm à 138 mm dans un seul cas d'un très grand nucléus remonté. Les dimensions moyennes d'un échantillon de 307 lames complètes sont: 55 x 19 x 6 mm. Les talons de lames sont généralement lisses (85%) et les plus grands portent souvent de fortes traces d'abrasion sur l'angle de chasse. Bien que certaines lames aient des talons facetés (11%) aucunes d'entre elles sont en éperon. La haute teneur en lames de la collection est reflétée dans le grand nombre de nucléus à lames (63 sur 88). A partir du remontage on peut démontrer que les lames étaient en général détachées de nucléus à deux plans de frappe opposés, préparés à partir de deux crêtes, l'une frontale et l'autre dorsale. Les séquences de remontage individuelles sont décrites dans le chapitre 4.3.

Une étude spatiale de 29 épisodes de réduction de nucléus a été entreprise (Chapitre 4.4). Le plan de distribution sur le terrain montre deux groupes dinstincts d'éléments remontables, le plus important se situant dans la zone centrale sud du gisement. Là, les artéfactes sont en majorité des produits de débitages de lames et ont donné les remontages les plus complets jusqu'au bloc originel. Par contre, les raccords sont fort rares dans une zone quelques mètres plus au nord-ouest qui contient un grand nombres d'outils retouchés, très souvent brûlés, en particuliers des pointes à dos. Donc, il est possible de déduire une séparation spatiale des activités, d'une part, production des supports dans une zone périphérique et, d'autre part, fabrication et utilisation d'outils autour d'un foyer. Les sites du Magdalénien supérieur de Marsangy et d'Etiolles présentent une division similaire d'activités, avec l'aire de débitage du silex loin du foyer.

L'analyse des traces d'utilisation sur les artéfactes en silex s'est avérée inefficace à cause de l'altération de la surface des silex survenue après dépôt. Cependant, l'étude macroscopique des outils a révélé que certains burins avaient été fortement utilisés le long de leurs bords et avaient subi de fréquents ravivages (Chapitre 4.5.4). De plus, les lames à dos semblent avoir eu des fonctions diverses; certaines d'entre elles étaient utilisées pour couper alors que d'autres étaient apparemment des projectiles. L'expérimentation, soutenue par une étude au MEB, a établi qu'un silex avait été utilisé pour graver le dessin abstrait sur une plage de cortex d'un nucléus, bien que nous n'ayons pas identifié l'outil de gravure (Chapitre 4.6). Des traces d'utilisation compatibles avec une abrasion ont aussi été identifiées sur un 'crayon' d'ocre rouge (Chapitre 4.2.3).

Le gisement du LUP à Hengistbury semble avoir été utilisé en tant que campement de chasse. Il occupe une excellente position au-dessus d'un paysage plat, bien à l'abri et caché dans sa petite vallée sèche. Si l'on se base sur des sites du Paléolithique supérieur comparables sur le continent, Hengistbury est assez typique des plus importants lieux de rassemblement de chasse-ceuillette, occupés au printemps et en automne lors du passage des animaux migrateurs tels le cheval et le reine (Chapitre 4.10.6).

Le seul autre gisement en Grande Bretagne qui présente une industrie ayant certains traits en commun avec celle de Hengistbury est Brockhill. Comme l'ont déjà remarqué plusieurs auteurs, l'industrie ne ressemble pas à celle des grottes creswelliennes, charactérisées par des outils à dos anguleux et dont le débitage est différent. Selon les datations connues, les deux technologies ont pu être totalement ou partiellement contemporaines pendant le principal interstade tardiglaciaire. On observe une diversité similaire sur le continent où les meilleurs parallèles sont les technologies de lames à dos droit de l'Europe du nord-ouest, représentées par toute une gamme allant des industries du Magdalénien tardif aux divers groupes federmesser (Chapitre 4.10.5).

Le deuxième gisement fouillé à Hengistbury témoigne amplement des activités du Mésolithique inférieur sur le promontoire. Il a été découvert en 1977 par Ronald Powell qui a ramassé d'importantes quantités d'artéfactes qui apparaissaient sur une surface de déflation en haut de la falaise. Les fouilles, commencées en 1980, ont été concentrées d'abord dans les zones de danger immédiat, près de la falaise, puis ont été agrandies vers le nord pour essayer de déterminer l'étendue de la concentration principale des artéfactes. Il y a eu 78 m$^2$ de fouilles en tout, en plus 50 m$^2$ de collection de surface.

Le gisement mésolithique de Powell a une haute densité d'outils en silex qui occupent une bande de 50 à 70 cm d'épaisseur dans l'horizon éluvial du podzol actuel juste au-dessus d'un horizon très compact d'accumulation ferro-manganique. Les sables sont plus fins et mieux classés que dans la Dépression Est, ce qui implique une origine totalement éolienne mais toujours locale. Le podzol actuel a subi une modification pédogénétique à partir d'un sol lessivé sableux, sol qui pourrait être contemporain de l'occupation mésolithique du gisement (Chapitre 2.2.3).

La zone d'occupation qui a été étudiée est suffisamment grande pour démontrer que la répartition principale des artéfactes est de forme presque circulaire ou légèrement ovale, d'un diamètre maximum de 12 m. Cependant, la plus haute concentration d'objets se trouve dans un noyau d'un diamètre de 5 m à l'intérieur de cette zone. Cet ensemble consiste en majeure partie d'artéfactes en silex, avec aussi deux polissoirs de grès et un gros bloc de 'sarsen', un grès régional bien caractéristique. A peu près toutes ces matières premières, y compris le silex, seraient d'origine locale, à part les polissoirs en grès qui proviennent du sud-ouest de l'Angleterre.

La datation par thermoluminescence de silex brûlés provenant de la concentration principale a donné cinq déterminations avec une moyenne de 9,750 ± 950 BP (OXTL 707c), ce qui signifie que le gisement était occupé durant le Pré-Boréal or Boral quand la côte se situait jusqu'à 20 km de Hengistbury.

On a receuilli 35,444 artéfactes en silex dont les deux tiers sont des débris et des éclats de moins de 10 mm de longueur. Parmi les produits de débitage, on compte 6,312 éclats, 5,699 lames et lamelles et 145 nucléus. La classe des outils retouchés contient une forte proportion (62%) de microlithes, principalement de type non géométrique. Sur les 626 outils provenant de la fouille et de la collection de surface (décrites au chapitre 5.2) on décompte 95 grattoirs, 65 microdenticulés et 390 microlithes, le reste étant des pièces tronquées et divers autres objets retouchés y compris des éclats et des lames. Les microlithes sont presque tous à troncature oblique et proviennent de la partie la plus dense de la concentration. La présence d'un grand nombre de microburins proximaux (273) indique qu'il s'agissait là d'une zone importante de production d'outils.

L'analyse des traces d'utilisation (Chapitre 5.3) s'est avérée insatisfaisante, dans l'ensemble, à cause des modifications de surface après dépôt. Cependant, l'étude de la morphologie des bords et d'autres caractéristiques, soutenue par les résultats d'expérimentation, suggère que l'un des groupes d'outils, les microdenticulés, étaient utilisés pour couper le matériel végétal souple tel que les fibres de l'assise cambiale du bois vert. Un certain nombre de microlithes ont leur pointe visiblement endommagée, caractère que l'on interpète comme traces d'utilisation; l'abandon de ces pièces abîmées laisse supposer une remise à neuf des projectiles sur le gisement même.

A partir du remontage de plusieurs artéfactes (Chapitres 3.2.3 et 5.1), provenant de la zone principale de répartition, il est possible d'identifier les épisodes individuels de taille. Les éléments (y compris un microlithe) de l'un des blocs, d'un silex gris moucheté caractéristique, couvrent une surface plus ou moins ovale de 400 x 300 cm. La légère dilatation de ce matériel semble refléter un déplacement après dépôt.

Dans le bassin du Hampshire il existe plusieurs sites du Mésolithique inférieur comme celui du gisement de Powell, datant du Pré-Boréal et du Boréal. Ils appartiennent au plus vieux groupe d'industries mésolithiques connues en Europe du nord-ouest, malgré leur manque de triangles microlithiques typiques du complexe Star Carr-Duvensee. D'après l'analyse morphologique des microlithes (Chapitre 5.5.5), Hengistbury est fort comparable à d'autres sites de la région tels que Downton à 30 km au nord et Winfrith Heath à 38 km à l'ouest.

Quant aux types d'outils à Hengistbury (Chapitre 5.5.5), l'industrie est peu variée. Elle se caractérise par l'absence de burins, de haches et d'herminettes aussi bien que par la présence de microlithes, de grattoirs, et de petits denticulés. Des outillages similaires ont été identifiés dans d'autres sites sur les collines de la région; ils semblent refléter une gamme restreinte d'activités spécialisées, associées à la chasse. Les gisements de vallée, avec un outillage plus varié comprenant des burins et des herminettes, ont pu servir de campements de base où avaient lieu les activités d'entretien et de traitement, de plus longue durée. La proximité de ces deux types de gisement dans la même région et l'uniformité des outillages correspondants pourraient signifier le territoire exploité par une seule communauté de chasse-ceuillette durant leur routine annuelle.

La conservation des parties non fouillées des gisements du Paléolithique et du Mésolithique, ainsi que d'autres sites à Hengistbury Head, est une priorité absolue si l'on veut sauvegarder les futures recherches. Un projet de gestion a déjà été mis en place pour stopper le recul de la falaise et pour replanter les zones près du bord les plus sujettes à l'érosion.

## Zusammenfassung

Hengistbury Head ist ein deutlicher Geländesporn an der Südküste Englands, 8km östlich von Bournemouth in Dorset (50° 43" N, 1° 45" W: NGR SZ 175905). Die Landzunge springt in den Solent Channel vor und gibt Blick auf die Isle of Wight im Südosten.

Geologisch besteht die Landzunge aus einer Folge mariner und littoraler tertiärer Schichten, die stellenweise von pleistozänen Terrassenschottern überlagert werden. Auf dieser Sequenz liegen äolische Fein-und Mittelsande, in denen die spätglazialen und holozänen archäologischen Funde liegen.

Seit langem ist die Landzunge der Küstenerosion ausgesetzt, doch in neuerer Zeit nahm die Zurückverlegung des Kliffs sichtbar zu und bedrohte die archäologischen Schichten an seiner Südkante. Nach einem vorläufigen Survey im Auftrag der Geländeeigentümer wurden in den Jahren 1980 –1984 an zwei Stellen des Kliffs groß angelegte Rettungs-Ausgrabungen durchgeführt. Die vom Verf. geleiteten Ausgrabungen wurden finanziell vor allem von der Bournemouth Corporation und der English Heritage unterstützt.

Bei der ersten Fundstelle handelt es sich um einen spätjungpaläolithischen (LUP) Freilandfundplatz am Südostende der Landzunge in einem als Eastern Depression (14 m NN) bezeichneten Gebiet. Die U-förmige Depression bildete möglicherweise das Kopfende eines Trockkentales, das heute durch das See-Kliff gekappt ist.

Der Fundplatz war seit vielen Jahren bekannt und ist zuvor von Angela Mace (1957) und John Campbell (1968–1969) untersucht worden.

Die zweite Fundstelle liegt etwa 650 m weiter westlich, dicht beim Gipfel von Warren Hill (35 m NN) dem höchsten Punkt von Hengistbury Head. Dieser Fundplatz gehört in das frühe Mesolithikum und wird nach seinem Entdecker Powell Fundplatz genannt.

Die beiden Ausgrabungen werden in Chapter 1 ausführlich beschrieben.

Die neuen Untersuchungen in der Eastern Depression beinhalteten Ausgrabungen an der Kliff-Kante und Geländebegehungen weiter landeinwärts. Es wurde eine Fläche von 96 m² freigelegt; A. Mace hatte 71 m² und J Campbell 136 m² untersucht.

Es bestätigte sich, daß die tiefsten und reichsten jungpaläolithischen Ablagerungen an der Kante des Kliffs konzentriert sind. Eine geringere Funddichte setzt sich jedoch landeinwärts fort.

Die Geländebegehung erlaubte auch kie Untersuchung eines spätbronzezeitlichen/früheisenzeitlichen Wall und Grabensystems, das quer durch die Depression läuft.

Umweltdaten aus diesem Befund betreffen die spätere Vegetationsgeschichte der Landzunge und belegen, daß auf die Rodung und Anlage der Grabenkonstruktion eine Phase der Regeneration des Eichenwaldes folgte.

Die intensive Podsolbildung in den Sanden hat anscheinend vor der Entwicklung der Heide-Vegetation auf der Landzunge, wie sie heute existiert, begonnen (Chapter 2).

Der spätjungpaläolithische (LUP) Fundplatz liegt in den Sanden, die die Schotter überlagern. Die sedimente bestehen aus annähernd gut sortierten, äolischen Sanden auf Solifluktionsschichten. Die Sande sind heute stark podsoliert und die Artefakte befinden sich in einem 40-50 cm mächtigen Streifen im unteren Ea- und oberen Bh-Horizont des Gley-Podsols.

Die neuen Ausgrabungen gaben Möglichkeiten für neue Datierungshinweise und zur Analyse eines umfangreichen Artefaktmaterials in typologischer, technologischer und räumlicher Hinsicht. Sie erlaubten ferner eine Neubewertung der geologischen und stratigraphischen Faktoren, die den früheren Ausgräber John Campbell zur Unterscheidung mesolithischer und jungpaläolithischer Horizonte an diesem Fundplatz geführt hatten. Die Neuinterpretation zeigt, daß der Fundplatz nur aus einem einzigen, homogenen spätjungpaläolithischen Ensemble besteht und basiert teilweise auf folgenden Beobachtungen:

(1) Thermolumineszenz-Datierungen verbrannter Artefakte ergaben sechs Bestimmungen mit einem Durchschnittsalter von 12,500±1,150 Jahren BP (OXTL 707a). Dies stimmt völlig mit der erwarteten Zeitstellung eines spätjungpaläolithischen (LUP) Inventars überein.

(2) In der vertikalen Verteilung der Funde waren keine signifikanten Lücken zu erkennen. Für die vertikale Verlagerung der Artefakte mögen verschiedene post-sedimentäre Prozesse verantwortlich sein (Chapter 3.1); der wahrscheinlichste Grund für diese Bewegung ist jedoch geringfügige biologische Aktivität innerhalb des Bodens. Diese Auffassung wird durch experimentelle Modelle gestützt, die gewisse Muster in der Gewichtsverteilung und Orientierung der Artefakte ergaben, die sich teilweise im archäologischen Befund wiederfinden.

(3) Zusammenpassungen zeigten, daa eine signifikante Zahl von zuvor von Campbell als 'mesolithisch' klassifizierten Artefakten mit 'jungpaläolithischen' Artefakten zusammengesetzt werden konnten.

Das spätjungpaläolithische (LUP) Fundmaterial wird in Chapter 4 ausführlich beschrieben. Außer einer Streuung von Sandsteintrümmern und roten Ockerstücken besteht es vor allem aus Feuersteinartefakten. Ein Feursteinkern trägt auf seiner Rinde eine Gravierung.

Die Gesamtzahl von 649 retuschierten Werkzeugen aus den drei Grabungen enthält 147 Kratzer, 66 Stichel und 324 rückengestumpfte Klingen und Lamellen. Außerdem beinhaltet das Werkzeugspektrum Stielspitzen und Stielspitzenbruchstcke (19), Kerb-spitzen (8) und Endretuschen (8). Bohrer und Zinken (Bec) sind sehr selten. Es gibt nur ein Kombination-swerkzeug (Stichel an Endretusche/Kratzer).

Einer der ungewöhnlichsten Aspekte des Fundmaterials ist das Auftreten von intentionell gebrochenen Artefakten (176), von denen 30 anschließend zu Werkzeugen umgeformt wurden.

Die Untersuchung des Rohmaterials ergab, daß der verwendete Feuerstein ortsfremd ist und vom Menschen von mindestens 12 km entfernten Vorkommen zum Fundplatz gebracht wurde. Die Zusammenpassungen zeigten, daß die Knollen vollständig, ohne andernorts durchgeführte Vorpräparation zum Fundplatz gelangten. Am Fundplatz sind alle Stadien der Kern-Abarbeitung belegt.

Eine technologische Untersuchung des von Campbell und während der neuen Grabungen geborgenen Artefaktmaterials ergab, daß unter den insgesamt 13,419 Artefakten 3,815 Abschläge und 2,266 Klingen oder Lamellen sind. Der Rest besteht aus unklassifizierbaren Stücken (4,078) und Absplissen ≤ 5 mm (3,260).

Einen bedeutenden Teil des Materials bilden Klingen. Durchschnittswerte einer Probe von 307 vollständigen Klingen ergaben einen Mittelwert von 55 x 19 x 6 mm.

Die Schlagflächenreste der Klingen sind meist glatt (85%) und die größeren Schlagflächenreste sind häufiger stark verschliffen. Auch wenn einige Klingen einen facettierten Schlagflächenrest haben (11%), zeigt keine Klinge den *en éperon*-Typ. Die starke Klingenkomponente des Ensembles spiegelt sich in der großen Zahl der Klingenkerne (63 von 88) wider.

Die Zusammensetzungen zeigten, daß die Klingen meist von Kernen mit gegenständigen Schlagflächen gewonnen wurden, die mit einem zentralen Grat präpariert waren.

In Chapter 4.3 werden die zusammengepaßten Sequenzen individuell beschrieben. Von 29 zusammengepaßten Kernabbausequezen wurde eine räumliche Analyse erstellt (Chapter 4.4). Die Kartierungen zeigen zwei diskrete Gruppen von Zusammenpassungs-Clustern. Das größere Clauster liegt im südlich zentralen Bereich des Fundplatzes. Hier bestehen die Artefakte vor allem aus Abfallmaterial der Klingenherstellung und ergaben die vollständigsten Zusammenpassungen von Kern-Klingen-Sequenzen. Dagegen enthielt ein einige Meternordwestlich gelegenes Areal viele retuschierte Werkzeuge, vor allem rückengestumpfte und häufig verbrannte Klingen, und lieferte nur sehr wenige Zusammenpassungen.

Zusammengenommen kann eine räumliche Trennung der belegten Tätigkeiten erkannt werden: Einerseits durch Werkzeug-Verwendung um die Reste einer Feuerstelle herum, zum andern durch eine periphere Zone, in der Primärproduktion von Grundformen belegt ist. Eine ähnliche Trennung der Tätigkeitsbereiche, mit Feuersteinbearbeitung abseits der Feuerstalle, wurde and den französischen Spätmagdalénien-Fundplätzen Marsangy und Etoilles beobachtet.

Eine Gebrauchsspurenuntersuchung der Feuersteinartefakte von Hengistbury erwies sich wegen der post-sedimentären Oberflächenveränderung der Artefakte als ergebnislos. Makroskopische Untersuchungen der Werkzeuge zeigten jedoch, daß einige Stichel mit ihren Kanten intensiv benutzt und häufig nachgeschärft wurden (Chapter 4.5.4). Außerdem scheinen die rückengestumpften Klingen für unterschiedliche Arbeiten gedient zu haben, einige zum Schneiden, andere waren offensichtlich Projektilspitzen.

Experimentelle Arbeiten, unterstützt durch rasterelektronische Mikroskopie, ergaben, daß Feuerstein für die Gravierung des abstrakten Zeichens auf dem Rindenrest an einem Kern verwendet wurde, auch wenn das Gravierinstrument nicht identifiziert werden konnte (Chapter 4.6).

An einem 'crayon' aus rotem Ocker finden sich ferner Gebrauchsspuren durch starkes Abschleifen und Abreiben (Chapter 4.2.3).

Der spätjungpaläolithische Fundplatz Hengistbury könnte als länger bewohnte Jagdstation (residential hunting location) gedient haben. Er bietet einen hervorragenden Aussichtspunkt über die flache Landschaft und ist in dem Trockental gut geschützt und verborgen. Verglichen mit jungpaläolithischen Parallelen vom Kontinent ist Hengistbury recht typisch für einen größeren Jäger-Sammler-Treffpunkt (aggregation site), der saisonal während der Herbst- und Frühjahrswanderungen der Tiere (Pferd, Ren) benutzt wurde (Chapter 4.10.6).

Der spätjungpaläolithische (LUP) Fundstoff von Hengistbury kann in England nur mit einem einzigen Fundplatz verglichen werden (Brockhill) und dies auch nur eingeschränkt. Wie frühere Autoren bereits bemerkten, gibt es keine Ahnlichkeit mit den Creswellian-Höhlenfunden, die durch geknickte Rückenspitzen gekennzeichnet sind und eine unterschiedliche Bearbeitungstechnik zeigen. Nach den vorliegenden Datierungen scheint es gut vorstellbar, daß beide Technologien gleichzeitig oder in teilweiser Uberlappung während des spätglazialen Interstadials bestanden. Die Funde vom Kontinent zeigen in dieser Zeit eine ähnliche Diversität. Die besten Parallelen zu Hengistbury finden sich in den Rückenmesser-Technologien (straight-backed blade technologies) Nordwesteuropas, zu denen einerseits Spätmag-dalénienfunde und andererseits verschiedene frühe Federmessergruppen gehören (Chapter 4.10.5).

Der zweite in Hengistbury untersuchte Fundplatz lieferte ein umfangreiches Material für frühmesolithische Aktivitäten auf der Landzunge. Der Fundplatz wurde 1977 von Ronald Powell entdeckt, der hier große Mengen von Artefakten an durch Winderosion freigelegten Stellen auf der Kliff-Spitze sammelte. Die 1980 begonnene Feldarbeit konzentrierte sich auf das unmittelbar gefährdete Areal an der Kliff-Kante und wurde später landeinwärts ausgedehnt, um die Nordgrenze der Artefaktkonzentration zu erfassen.

Insgesamt wurden 78m$^2$ ausgegraben; weitere 50 m$^2$ wurden durch Oberflächenfunde erfaßt.

Der mesolithische Powell-Fundplatz besteht aus einer dichten Konzentration von Feuersteinartefakten, die in einer 50–70 cm mächtigen Schicht im oberen Teil (Ea2-Horizont) des heutigen Podsol, direkt oberhalb einer sehr kompakten Eisen-Mangan-Schwarte (Bh-Horizont) liegen. Die Sande sind feiner und besser sortiert als in der Eastern Depression und insgesamt äolisch abgelagert.

Der vorhandene Podsol zeigt auch pedogene Veränderungen durch ältere braune Sandböden, von denen wir annehmen, daß sie zeitgleich mit der mesolithischen Besiedlung waren (Chapter 2.2.3).

Der Siedlungsplatz wurde ausreichend erfaßt, um zu zeigen, daß die zentrale Artefaktstreuung rundlich oder leicht oval mit einem maximalen Durchmesser von etwa 12 m war. Innerhalb dieses Areals gibt es eine 5 m breite, dichtere Fundkonzentration.

Die Fundstreuung besteht vor allem aus Feuersteinartefakten. Unter dem übrigen Material sind zwei Reibsteine aus Sandstein und ein groaer Block aus verkieseltem Sandstein (Sarsen). Außer den Reib-steinen, die aus einem in Sdwestengland vorkommenden Gestein sind, dürften alle Feuersteinvarietäten und sonstigen Materialien lokaler Herkunft sein.

Innerhalb der zentralen Streuung der Feuersteinartefakte befanden sich verbrannte Stücke, deren Thermolumineszenz-Datierung ein Durch-shnittsalter des mesolithischen Horizontes von 9,750 ± 950 BP ergab (OXTL 707c). Dies weist darauf hin, daß der Fundplatz während des Präboreals oder Boreals bewohnt war, als Hengistbury noch im Inland, vielleicht 20 km von der damaligen Küstenlinie entfernt lag.

Die Ausgrabungen lieferten 35,444 Feuer-steinartefakte, darunter 2/3 kleine Absplisse und Trümmer kleiner als 10 mm. Unter dem klassifizierbaren Material sind 6,312 Abschläge und 5,699 Klingen oder Lamellen, dazu 145 Kerne. Die retuschierten Werkzeuge beinhalten einen hohen Prozentsatz (62%) von meist nicht-geometrischen Mikrolithen. Unter den 626 Werkzeugen aus Grabung und Oberflächenfunden (Beschreibung in Chapter 5.2) sind 95 Kratzer, 65 mikrolithische gezähnte Stücke und 390 Mikrolithen. Der Rest besteht aus Endretuschen, retuschierten Abschlägen und Klingen und sonstigen retuschierten Formen.

Die Mikrolithen des Fundplatzes sind fast sämtlich A-Typen (Spitzen mit schräger Endretusche) und stammen aus dem dichteren Teil der Konzentration. Die große Anzahl (273) proximaler Kerbreste (Mikrostichel) weist darauf hin, daß hier eine primäre Herstellungszone von Werkzeugen lag.

Gebrauchsspurenuntersuchungen (Chapter 5.3) der Feuersteine ergaben, daß die Stücke wegen post-sedimen-tärer Oberflächenveräderungen für diese Untersuchungen weitgehend ungeeignet sind. Die Untersuchung der Kantenmorphologie und anderer Merkmale, verbunden mit experimentellen Arbeiten, macht jedoch wahrscheinlich, daß eine Werkzeuggruppe (die mikrolithischen gezähnten Stücke) vermutlich zum Schneiden weicheren Pflanzenmaterials wie z. B. Bastfasern von frischem Holz dienten.

Sichtbare Beschädigungen der Spitzen einiger Mikrolithen werden auch als Hinweis auf den Gebrauch gewertet und könnten darauf hinweisen, daß am Fundplatz Projektile ausgewechselt wurden.

Durch das Zusammenpassen zahlreicher Artefakte (Chapter 3.2.3. und 5.1) lassen sich innerhalb der zentralen Fundstreuung individuelle Episoden der Steinbearbeitung aufzeigen. Eine Zusammenpassung, darin ein Mikrolith, besteht aus einem besonderen, grau-gesprenkelten Feuerstein und bedeckt eine annähernd ovale Fläche von 4 x 3m. Die horizontale Verteilung dieses Materials scheint eine post-sedimentäre Verlagerung der Artefakte anzudeuten.

Der mesolithische Powell-Fundplatz gehört zu mehreren frühmesolithischen Fundplätzen im Hampshire Becken aus dem Präboreal und Boreal. Auch wenn an diesen Fundplätzen die für die Star Carr-Duvensee-Gruppe typischen Dreiecksmikrolithen fehlen, gehören sie zu der ältesten Gruppe mesolithischer Funde in Nordwesteuropa.

Hengistbury läßt sich gut mit anderen Fundplätzen des Gebietes wie Downton 30 km nördlich und Winfrith Heath 38 km westlich vergleichen.

Nach den tatsächlichen Werkzeugformen (Chapter 5.5.5.) gehört Hengistbury zu einer kleinen Gruppe von Fundplätzen, die durch Mikrolithen, Kratzer und kleine gezähnte Stücke sowie das Fehlen von Sticheln und Kernbeilen charakterisiert ist. Ahnliche Werk-zeugspektren gibt es an anderen, höher gelegenen Fundplätzen des Gebietes und es wird angenommen, daß diese Inventare einen hoch spezialisierten Tätigkeitsbereich im Zusammenhang mit der Jagd widerspiegeln. Tieferliegende Fundplätze mit einem größeren Werkzeugspektrum einschließlich Sticheln und Kernbeilen könnten zeitgleiche Wohnplätze darstellen, an denen längerfristige Arbeiten (maintenance and processing activities) durchgeführt wurden. Die Nachbarschaft beider Fundplatztypen innerhalb der gleichen Region und die Beständigkeit der Werkzeugspektren könnte zu der Modellvorstellung eines Gruppenterritoriums, das von einer Jäger-Sammler-Gemeinschaft im jahreszeitlichen Wechsel der Siedlungsplätze genutzt wurde, passen.

Schutz und Erhaltung der nicht ausgegrabenen Teile der paläolithischen, mesolithischen und sonstigen Fundplätze von Hengistbury Head ist von hoher Priorität für die Belange zukünftiger Forschung. Gegenwärtig besteht ein Verwaltungs-Projekt zur Stabilisierung der Kliff-Erosion und zur Bepflanzung von der aktiven Erosion ausgesetzten Arealen auf dem Kliff.

# Bibliographic references

AHLBRANDT, T.S., ANDREWS, S. AND GWYNNE, D.T. 1978: Bioturbation in aeolian deposits *Journal of Sedimentary Petrology* 43, 8, 839–48.

AHLER, S.A. 1971: *Projectile Point Form and Function at Rodgers Shelter, Missouri.* (Columbia, University of Missouri, Missouri Archaeological Society, Research Series 8).

AITKEN, M.J. AND ALLDRED, J.C. 1972: The assessment of error limits in thermoluminescent dating. *Archaeometry*, 14: 257–267.

ALAUX, J.F. 1972: L'industrie magdalénienne de l'abri de Blassac II, commune de Blassac. *Bull. Soc. Préhistorique Française*, 69, 2, 499–507.

ALBRECHT, G. 1979: *Magdalénieninventare vom Petersfels. Siedlungsarchäologische Ergebnisse der Ausgrabungen 1974–1976.* (Tubingen, Tubinger Monogr. zur Urgeschichte 6).

ALLAIN, J. 1974: Informations Archéologiques. Circonscription du Centre. *Gallia Préhistoire* 17, 465–485.

ALLAIN, J. 1976: Les civilisations du Paléolithique supérieur dans le sud-ouest du Bassin Parisien. In Lumley, H. de (editor), *La Préhistoire Française*, 1315–1320.

ALLAIN, J. 1979: L'industrie lithique et osseuse de Lascaux. In Leroi-Gourhan, A. and Allain, J. (editors), *Lascaux Inconnu* XIIe supplément à Gallia Préhistoire (Paris, CNRS) 87–120.

ALLAIN, J. AND DESCOUTS, J. 1957: A propos d'une baguette à rainure armée de silex découverte dans le magdalénien de Saint-Marcel. *L'Anthropologie* 61, 503–512.

ALLISON, J., GODWIN, H. AND WARREN, S.H. 1952: Late Glacial deposits at Nazeing in the Lea Valley, North London. *Phil. Trans. Roy Soc.* London B 236, 169–240.

AMBERS, J., MATHEWS K. AND BURLEIGH, R. 1985: British Museum natural radiocarbon measurements XVIII. *Radiocarbon* 27, 3, 508–24.

ANDERSEN, K. 1951: Hytter fra maglemosetid. Danmarks aeldste boliger. *Fra Nationalmuseets Arbejdsmark* (Copenhagen) 69–76.

ANDERSEN, S.H. 1985: Tybrind Vig. A preliminary report on a submerged Ertebølle settlement on the west coast of Fyn. *Journal of Danish Archaeology* 4, 52–70.

ANDERSEN, S.H. 1988: A survey of the Late Palaeolithic of Denmark and Southern Sweden. In Otte, M. (editor), *De la Loire à l'Oder: Les civilisations du Paléolithique final dans le nord-ouest européen* (Oxford, British Archaeological Reports International Series 444ii) 523–566.

ANDERSON-GERFAUD, P. 1983: A consideration of the uses of certain backed and lustred stone tools from late mesolithic and natufian levels of Abu Hureyra and Mureybet (Syria). In Cauvin, M.C. (editor), *Traces d'Utilisation sur les Outils Néolithiques du Proche Orient* (Lyon, Travaux de la Maison de l'Orient) 77–106.

ANDERTON, R., BRIDGES, P.H., LEEDER, M.R., AND SELLWOOD, B.W. 1979: *A Dynamic Stratigraphy of the British Isles: a study in crustal evolution* (London, George Allen and Unwin).

ANON 1862: *The Norfolk Chronicle and Norwich Gazette* (February 1)

ARTS, N. 1988: A survey of final Palaeolithic archaeology in the Southern Netherlands. In Otte, M. (editor), *De la Loire à l'Oder, les civilisations du Paléolithique final dans le nord-ouest européen* (Oxford, British Archaeological Reports International Series 444 i) 287–356.

ARTS, N. AND DEEBEN, J. 1987: On the northwestern border of Late Magdalenian territory: ecology and archaeology of early Late Glacial band societies in Northwestern Europe. In Burdukiewicz, J.M. & Kobusiewicz, M. (editors), *Late Glacial in Central Europe. Culture and Environment* (Wroclaw, Ossolineum) 25–66.

ATKINSON, R.J.C. 1957: Worms and weathering. *Antiquity* 31, 219–33.

ATKINSON, T.C., BRIFFA, K.R. AND COOPE, G.R. 1987: Seasonal temperatures in Britain during the past 20,000 years, reconstructed using beetle remains. *Nature* 325, 587–592.

AUDOUIN, F. AND PLISSON, H. 1982: Les ochres et les témoins au paléolithique en France: enquête et expériences sur leur validité archéologique. *Cahiers du Centre de Recherches Préhistoriques* 8, 33–80.

AUDOUZE, F. 1987: The Paris Basin in Magdalenian times. In Soffer, O. (editor), *The Pleistocene Old World: Regional Perspectives* (New York, Plenum Press) 183–200.

AUDOUZE, F., CAHEN, D., KEELEY, L.H. AND SCHMIDER, B. 1981: Le site Magdalénien du Buisson Campin à Verberie (Oise). *Gallia Préhistoire* 24, 1, 99–143.

AVERY, B.W. 1980: *Soil Classification for England and Wales* (Harpenden, Soil Survey Monograph 14).

AVERY, B.W. AND BASCOMB, C.L. (editors) 1974: *Soil Survey Laboratory Methods* (Harpenden, Soil Survey Technical Monograph 6).

AZOURY, I. AND HODSON, F.R. 1973: Comparing Palaeolithic assemblages: Ksar Akil, a case study. *World Archaeology* 3–4, 292–306.

BABEL, U. 1975: Micromorphology of soil organic matter, In Gieseking, J.E. (editor), *Soil Components. Vol I. Organic Components.* (Berlin-Heidelberg-New York, Springer) 369–473.

BAFFIER, D., DAVID, F., GAUCHER, G., JULIEN, M., KARLIN, C., LEROI-GOURHAN, A. AND ORLIAC, M. 1982: Les occupations magdaléniennes de Pincevent -problèmes de durée. In *Les Habitats du Paléolithique supérieur* (Unpublished Actes du colloque international en hommage à Professeur Leroi-Gourhan, Roanne-Villerest, June 1982) 243–271.

BAGNOLD, R.A. 1941: *The Physics of Blown Sand and Desert Dunes* (London, Methuen).

BAKER, C.A., MOXEY, P.A. AND OXFORD, P.M. 1978: Woodland continuity and change in Epping Forest. *Field Studies* 4, 645–669.

BAL, L. 1982: *Zoological Ripening of Soils* (Wageningen, Pudoc. Centre for Agricultural Publishing and Documentation Agricultural Research Reports 850).

BALAAM, N.D., SMITH, K. AND WAINWRIGHT, G.J. 1982: The Shaugh Moor Project IV. *Proc. Prehistoric Society*, 48, 203–278.

BALL, D.F. 1975: Processes of soil degradation: a pedological point of view. In Evans, J.G., Limbrey, S. and Cleere, H (editors) *The Effect of Man on the Landscape: the Highland Zone* (Council for British Archaeology Research Report 11) 20–27.

BARBER, K.E. AND CLARKE, M.J. 1987: Cranes Moor, New Forest: Palynology and macrofossil stratigraphy. In Barber, K.E. (editor), *Wessex and the Isle of Wight Field Guide* (Cambridge, Quaternary Research Association) 33–43.

BARKER, P. 1977: *Techniques of Archaeological Excavation* (London, Batsford).

BARTON, R.N.E. 1981: Some conjoined artifacts from a new Mesolithic site at Hengistbury Head, Dorset. *Proc. Dorset Natural History and Archaeological Society* 103, 13–20.

BARTON, R.N.E. 1983a: Hengistbury Head, Dorset. Excavation report summaries. *Proc. Prehistoric Society* 49, 383.

BARTON, R.N.E. 1983b: Hengistbury Head: Palaeolithic and Mesolithic Project. Dorset Archaeology in 1983. *Proc. Dorset Natural History and Archaeological Society* 105, 137–139.

BARTON, R.N.E. 1986a: Experiments with long blades from Sproughton, near Ipswich, Suffolk. In Roe, D.A. (editor), *Studies in the Upper Palaeolithic of Britain and Northwest Europe* (Oxford, British Archaeological Reports International Series 296) 129–141.

BARTON, R.N.E. 1986b: *A Study of Selected British and European Flint Assemblages of Late Devensian and Early Flandrian Age* (Oxford University, Unpublished D.Phil thesis).

BARTON, R.N.E. 1987: Vertical distribution of artefacts and some post depositional factors affecting site formation. In Rowley-Conwy, P., Zvelebil, M. and Blankholm, H.P. (editors), *Mesolithic Northwest Europe: recent trends* (Sheffield, Department of Archaeology & Prehistory University of Sheffield) 55–62.

BARTON, R.N.E. 1989: Long blade technology in Southern Britain.

In Bonsall, C. (editor), *The Mesolithic in Europe*. Papers presented at the third international symposium, Edinburgh 1985, (Edinburgh, John Donald) 264–271.

BARTON, R.N.E. AND BERGMAN, C.A. 1982: Hunters at Hengistbury: some evidence from experimental archaeology. *World Archaeology* 14, 237–248.

BARTON, R.N.E. AND COLLCUTT, S.N. 1980: The Late Pleistocene and Early Holocene deposits of Hengistbury Head, Dorset, and their associated archaeology. *Hengistbury Head Report HH/5* (Bournemouth, Bournemouth Corporation).

BARTON, R.N.E. AND FROOM, F.R. 1986: The long blade assemblage from Avington VI, Berkshire. In Collcutt, S.N. (editor), *The Palaeolithic of Britain and Its Nearest Neighbours: recent trends* (Sheffield, Department of Archaeology and Prehistory University of Sheffield) 80–84.

BARTON, N. AND HUXTABLE, J. 1983: New dates for Upper Palaeolithic and Mesolithic occupations at Hengistbury Head, Dorset. *Antiquity* 220, 133–135.

BASCOMB, C.L. 1968: Distribution of pyrophosphate-extractable iron and organic carbon in soils of various groups. *Journal of Soil Science* 19, 2, 251–268.

BAXTER, F.P. AND HOLE, F.D. 1967: Ant (*Formica cinerea*) pedoturbation in prairie soil. *Proc. Soil Science Society of America* 31, 425–8.

BEASLEY, M.J. 1987: A preliminary report on incremental banding as an indicator of seasonality in mammal teeth from Gough's Cave, Cheddar, Somerset. *Proc. Univ. Bristol Spelaeological Society* 18, 1, 116–129.

BECKER, C.J. 1945: En 8000-Arig Stenalderboplads. Forelobig Meddelelse. Fra *Nationalmuseets Arbejdsmark* (Kobenhavn).

BECKER, B. AND KROMER, B. 1986: Extension of the Holocene dendrochronology by the preboreal pine series, 8,800 to 10,100. *Radiocarbon* 28, 2b, 961–967.

BEHRE, K.E. 1967: The late glacial and early postglacial history of vegetation and climate in Northwestern Germany. *Review of Palaeobotany and Palynology* 4, 149–161.

BEHRE, K.E. 1978: Die Klimaschwankungen im europäischen Präboreal. Festschrift in honour of Prof. H. Kliewe's 60th birthday. *Petermann's Geographische Mittellungen* 2, 97–102.

BELLIER, C. AND CATTELAIN, P. 1984: Occupation paléolithique au Trou de Blaireaux à Vaucelles. In *2e Congrès de l'Association des Cercles Francophone d'Histoire et d'Archéologie de Belgique à Nivelles* 1, 62–63.

BENNETT, K.D. 1983: Devensian late-glacial and Flandrian vegetational history at Hockham Mere, Norfolk, England. I: Pollen percentages and concentrations. *New Phytologist* 95, 457–487.

BERGMAN, C.A. 1987a: *Ksar Akil, Lebanon. A technological and typological analysis of the Later Palaeolithic levels of Ksar Akil. Volume II: levels XIII–VI* (Oxford, British Archaeological Reports, International Series 329).

BERGMAN, C.A. 1987b: Hafting and the use of bone and antler tools from Ksar Akil, Lebanon. In Stordeur, D. (editor), *La main et l'outil. Manches et emmanchements préhistoriques* (Lyon, Travaux de la Maison de l'Orient Méditerranéen) 117–126.

BERGMAN, C.A., BARTON, R.N.E., COLLCUTT, S.N. AND MORRIS, G. 1983: La fracture volontaire dans une industrie du Paléolithique suprieur tardif du sud de l'Angleterre. *L'Anthropologie* 87, 3, 323–337.

BERGMAN, C.A., BARTON, R.N.E., COLLCUTT, S.N AND MORRIS, G. 1987: Intentional breakage in a Late Upper Palaeolithic assemblage from Southern England. In Sieveking, G. de G. AND NEWCOMER, M.H. (editors), *The Human Uses of Flint and Chert* Proc. Fourth International Flint Symposium, Brighton 1983 (Cambridge University Press) 21–32.

BERGMAN, C. and NEWCOMER, M.H. 1983: Flint arrowhead breakage: examples from Ksar Akil, Lebanon. *Journal of Field Archaeology* 10, 238–243.

BERGMAN, C.A. AND ROBERTS, M.R. 1988: The Lower Palaeolithic site at Boxgrove (West Sussex, England). In Tuffreau, A. (editor), Cultures et industries lithiques en milieu loessique. *Revue Archéologique de Picardie*, 1–2 (numéro spécial) 105–114.

BINFORD, L.R. 1976: Forty seven trips: a case study in the character of some formation processes of the archaeological record. In Hall, E.S. (editor), *Contributions to Anthropology: The interior peoples of Northern Alaska* (Ottawa, National Museum of Canada, Mercury series) 49, 299–351.

BINFORD, L.R. 1983: *In Pursuit of the Past* (London, Thames and Hudson).

BISHOP, W.W. AND COOPE, G.R. 1977: Stratigraphical and faunal evidence for Lateglacial and early Flandrian environments in south-west Scotland. In Gray, J.M. and Lowe, J.J. (editors), *Studies in the Scottish Lateglacial Environments* (Oxford, Pergamon) 61–88.

BOCQUET, A. 1980: Le Microdenticulé un outil mal connu. *Bull. Soc. Préhistorique Française* 77, 76–85.

BOËDA, E. AND PELEGRIN, J. 1985: Approche expérimentale des amas de Marsangy. *Archéologie Expérimentale* (Association pour la Promotion de l'Archéologie de Bourgogne, Archéodrome) 19–37.

BOHMERS, A. 1960: Statistiques et graphiques dans l'étude des industries préhistoriques. V. Considérations générales au sujet du Hambourgien, du Tjongerien, du Magdalénien et de l'Azilien. *Palaeohistoria* 8, 15–37.

BOKELMANN, K. 1979: Rentierjäger am Gletscherrand in Schleswig-Holstein ? Ein Diskussionsbeitrag zur Erforschung der Hamburger Kultur. *Offa* 36, 12–22.

BOKELMANN, K. 1983: Fundplätze des Spätglazials am Hainholz-Esinger Moor, Kreis Pinneberg. *Offa* 40, 199–239.

BOKELMANN, K. 1986: Rast Unter Bäumen: Ein Ephemerer Mesolithischer Lagerplatz aus dem Duvensee Moor. *Offa* 43, 149–163.

BOKELMANN, K., AVERDIECK, F-R. AND WILLKOMM, H. 1981: Duvensee Wohnplatz 8, Neue Aspekte zur Sammelwirtschaft im frühen Mesolithikum. *Offa* 38, 21–40.

BOLUS, M., BOSINSKI, G., FLOSS, H., HUSMANN, H., STODIEK, U., STREET, M., TERBERGER, T. AND WINTER, D. 1988: La séquence Bölling-Dryas III en Rhénanie. In Otte, M. (editor), *De la Loire à l'Oder: Les civilisations du Paléolithique final dans le nord–ouest européen* (Oxford, British Archaeological Reports International Series 444ii) 475–511.

BONSALL, C. 1977: Woking: near Parley Bridge, Horsell. *Surrey Archaeological Society Bulletin* 139, 4.

BONSALL, C. AND SMITH, C. 1989: Late Palaeolithic and Mesolithic bone and antler artefacts from Britain: first reactions to accelerator dates *Mesolithic Miscellany* 10, 33–8.

BORDES, F. 1950: Du poli particulier de certains silex tailles *L'Anthropologie* 54, 161–3.

BORDES, F. 1952: A propos des outils à bord abattu. Quelques remarques. *Bull. Soc. Préhistorique Française* 49, 645–7.

BORDES, F. 1957: La signification du microburin dans le Paléolithique supérieur. *L'Anthropologie* 61, 578–582.

BORDES, F. 1961: *Typologie du Paléolithique Ancien et Moyen* (Bordeaux, Delmas) 2 Vols.

BORDES, F. 1965: Utilisation possible des côtés des burins. *Fundberichte aus Schwaben* 17, 3–4.

BORDES, F. 1967: Considérations sur la typologie et les techniques dans le Paléolithique. *Quartär* 18, 25–55.

BORDES, F.B. 1969: Les Chasseurs. In *La France au temps de mammouths* (Paris, Hachette) 93–131.

BORDES, F. 1970: Réflexions sur l'outil au Paléolithique. *Bull. Soc. Préhistorique Française* 67, 7, 199–202.

BORDES, F. AND FITTE, P. 1964: Microlithes du Magdalénien supérieur de la Gare de Couze (Dordogne). *Miscelanea en Homenaje al Abate Henri Breuil* (Barcelona, Instituto de Prehistoria y Arqueologià) 259–267.

BORDES, F., GRAINDOR, M.J. AND MARTIN, P. 1974: L'industrie de la grotte ornée de Gouy (Seine Maritime). *Bull. Soc. Préhistorique Française* 71, 115–118.

BOSINSKI, G. 1978: Der Poggenwischstab. *Bonner Jahrbücher* (Festschrift R. Von Uslar) 178, 83–92.

BOSINSKI, G. 1979: *Die Ausgrabungen in Gönnersdorf 1968–1976 und die Siedlungsbefunde der Grabung 1968* (Wiesbaden).

BOSINSKI, G. AND HAHN, J. 1972: Der Magdalénien-Fundplatz Andernach (Martinsberg). Beiträge zum Paläolithikum in Rheinland, *Rheinische Ausgrabungen* 11, 81–257.

BOSINSKI, G., BRAUN, R., TURNER, E., AND VAUGHAN, P. 1982: Ein spätpaläolithischen Retuscheurdepot von Niederbieber/Neuwied Becken. *Archäologisches Korrespondenzblatt* 12, 295–311.

BOSINSKI, G. AND FISCHER, G. 1974: *Die Menschen-darstellungen von Gönnersdorf der Ausgrabung von 1968* (Wiesbaden).

BOULTON, G.S., JONES, A.S., CLAYTON, K.M. AND KENNING, M.J. 1977: A British ice sheet model and patterns of glacial erosion and deposition in Britain. In Shotton, F.W.

(editor), *British Quaternary Studies. Recent Advances* (Oxford, Clarendon Press) 231–247.

BOWERS, P.M., BONNICHSEN, R. AND HOCH, D.M. 1983: Flake dispersal experiments: noncultural transformation of the archaeological record. *American Antiquity* 48, 3, 553–572.

BOWMAN, S.G.E., AMBERS, J.C. AND LEESE, M.N. 1990: Re-evaluation of British Museum radiocarbon dates issued between 1980 and 1984. *Radiocarbon* 32, 59–79.

BRADLEY, B. AND SAMPSON, C.G. 1986: Analysis by replication of two Acheulian artefact assemblages from Caddington, England. In Bailey, G.N. and Callow, P. (editors), *Stone Age Prehistory. Studies in memory of Charles McBurney* (Cambridge University Press) 29–46.

BRAMWELL, D. 1977: Archaeology and palaeontology. In Ford, T.D. (editor), *Limestones and Caves of the Peak District* (Norwich, Geo Abstracts) 263–291.

BRESSOLIER, C. AND THOMAS, Y.-F. 1977: Studies on wind and plant interactions on French Atlantic coastal dunes. *Journal of Sedimentary Petrology* 47, 1, 331–338.

BREUIL, H. 1921. Note sur la communication de E. Cartailhac: Observations sur l'Hiatus et le Néolithique. *L'Anthropologie* 31, 349–354.

BREUIL, H. 1926: Harpon Maglemosien trouvé à Bethune en 1849. *L'Anthropologie*, 309–312.

BREUIL, H. AND ZBYSZEWSKI, G. 1947: Révision des industries mésolithiques de Muge et de Magos. *Communicaçoes dos Serviços Geologicos de Portugal* 28, 149–196.

BRÉZILLON, M. 1977a: Informations archeologiques-Circonscription d'Ile de France. *Gallia Préhistoire* 20, 2, 350.

BRÉZILLON, M 1977b: *La Dénomination des Objets de Pierre Taillée* (Paris, CNRS IVe supplément à Gallia Préhistoire).

BRINCH–PETERSEN, E. 1973: A survey of the Late Palaeolithic and Mesolithic of Denmark. In Kozlowski, S.K. (editor), *The Mesolithic in Europe* (Warsaw, Warsaw University Press) 77–127.

BRINK, J. 1978: *An Experimental Study of Microwear Formation on Endscrapers* (Ottawa, National Museum of Man, Mercury Series, Archaeological Survey of Canada 83).

BROADBENT, N.D. AND KNUTSON, K. 1975: An experimental analysis of quartz scrapers. Results and applications. *Forvännen* 70, 113–128.

BROWN, J.A. 1888: On some small highly specialised forms of stone implements found in Asia, N. Africa and Europe. *Journal Roy. Anthropological Institute of Gt. Britain and Ireland* 18, 134–9.

BRUSSAARD, L. AND RUNIA, L.T. 1984: Recent and ancient traces of scarab beetle activity in sandy soils of the Netherlands. *Geoderma* 34, 3/4, 229–50.

BULLOCK, P., FEDEROFF, N., JONGERIUS, A., STOOPS, G. AND TURSINA, T. In Press: *Handbook for Soil Thin Section Description* (Wolverhampton, Waine Research Publications).

BURDUKIEWICZ, J.M. 1981: Creswellian and Hamburgian. The Shouldered Point Technocomplex. In Kozlowski, J.K. and Kozlowski, S.K. (editors), *Archaeologia Interregionalis* (Warsaw University and Krakow, Jagiellonian University) 43–57.

BURLEIGH, R., JACOBI, R.M. AND JACOBI, E.B. 1985: Early human resettlement of the British Isles following the last glacial maximum, new evidence from Gough's Cave, Cheddar. *Quaternary Newsletter* 45, 1–6.

BUSH, M.B. 1988: Early Mesolithic disturbance: a force in the landscape. *Journal Archaeological Science* 15, 453–462.

CAHEN, D. 1987: Refitting stone artefacts: why bother? In Sieveking, G. de G. and Newcomer, M.H. (editors), *The Human Uses of Flint and Chert* (Cambridge University Press) 1–11.

CAHEN, D. AND MOEYERSONS, J. 1977: Subsurface movements of stone artefacts and their implications for the prehistory of Central Africa. *Nature* 266, 812–815.

CAHEN, D., KARLIN, C., KEELEY, L.H. AND VAN NOTEN, F. 1980: Méthodes d'analyse technique, spatiale et fonctionelle d'ensembles lithiques. *Helinium* 20, 209–259.

CALKIN, J.B. 1960: *Prehistoric Bournemouth and Christchurch; with a reference to the Roman occupation* (Christchurch, Red House Museum).

CALKIN, J.B. 1966: *Discovering prehistoric Bournemouth and Christchurch* (Christchurch, Red House Museum).

CALKIN, J.B., AND GREEN, J.F.N. 1949: Palaeoliths and terraces near Bournemouth. *Proc. Prehistoric Society* 15, 21–37.

CAMPBELL, J.B. 1977: *The Upper Palaeolithic of Britain: a study of man and nature in the Late Ice Age* (Oxford, Clarendon Press)

2 vols.

CARE, V. 1979: The production and distribution of Mesolithic axes in Southern England. *Proc. Prehistoric Society* 45, 93–102.

CARPENTER, C.P. AND WOODCOCK, M.P. 1981: A detailed investigation of a pingo remnant in western Surrey. *Quaternary Studies* 1, 1–26.

CASPARIE, W.A. AND VAN ZEIST, W. 1960: A late glacial lake deposit near Waskemeer (Prov. of Friesland). *Acta Bot. Neerl.* 9, 191–196.

CATT, J.A. 1979: Soils and Quaternary geology in Britain. *Journal of Soil Science* 30, 607–642.

CHARLES, R. 1991: Note sur la découverte de nouvelles incisions rythmiques du Paléolithique supérieur provenant de Gough's Cave, Somerset, Angleterre. *Bull. Soc. Préhistorique Française* 88, 2, 45–48.

CHILDE, V.G. 1931: The Forest Cultures of Northern Europe: a study in evolution and diffusion. *Journal of the Royal Anthropological Institute* LXI, 325–48.

CHEPIL, W.S. AND WOODRUFF, N.P. 1963: The physics of wind erosion and its control. *Advances in Agronomy* 15, 211–302.

CHMIELEWSKI, W., SCHILD, R. AND WIECKOWSKA, H. 1975: *Prahistoriaziem Polskich I. Paleolit i Mezolit* (Wroclaw, Polska Akademia Nauk).

CHOLLOT, N. 1964: *Collection Piette, Art Mobilier Préhistorique* (Ministère d'Etat d'Affaires culturelles, Editions des Musées nationaux).

CLAPHAM, A.R. AND CLAPHAM, B.N. 1939: The Valley Fen at Cothill, Berkshire. Data for the study of Post-Glacial history. II. *New Phytologist* 38.

CLARK, J.G.D. 1932: *The Mesolithic Age in Britain* (Cambridge University Press).

CLARK, J.G.D. 1934a: The classification of a Microlithic culture: the Tardenoisian of Horsham. *Archaeological Journal* 90, 52–77.

CLARK, J.G.D. 1934b: A late Mesolithic site at Selmeston, Sussex. *The Antiquaries Journal* 14, 2, 134–158.

CLARK, J.G.D. 1934c: Derivative forms of the petit tranchet. *Archaeological Journal* 91, 32–58

CLARK, J.G.D. 1936: *The Mesolithic Settlement of Northern Europe* (Cambridge University Press).

CLARK, J.G.D. 1954: *Excavations at Star Carr* (Cambridge University Press).

CLARK, J.G.D. 1962: *World Prehistory: An Outline.* (Cambridge University Press).

CLARK, J.G.D. 1972: *Star Carr: a case study in bioarchaeology* (USA Addison-Wesley Publishing Company) Module 10, 1–42.

CLARK, J.G.D. 1975: *The Earlier Stone Age Settlement of Scandinavia* (Cambridge University Press).

CLARK, J.D.G. AND RANKINE, W.F. 1939: Excavations at Farnham, Surrey (1937–38): The Horsham Culture and the question of Mesolithic dwellings. *Proc. Prehistoric Society* 5, 61–118.

CLARKE, D. 1976: *Mesolithic Europe: The Economic Basis* (London, Duckworth).

CLARKE, R.F.A. AND VERDIER, J-P. 1967: An investigation of mesoplankton fauna from the chalk of the Isle of Wight, England. *Verhandelingen der Koninklijke Nederlansche Akademie van Wetenschappen, Afdeeling Natuurkunder, Eerste Reeks* 24, 1–96.

CLIFFORD, M.H. 1936: A Mesolithic flora in the Isle of Wight. *Proc. Isle of Wight Natural History Society* 2, 582–594.

CLOUTMAN, E.W. AND SMITH, A.G. 1988: Palaeoenvironments in the Vale of Pickering. Part 3: Environmental history of Star Carr. *Proc. Prehistoric Society* 54, 37–58.

CLUTTON-BROCK, J. AND BURLEIGH, R. 1983: Some archaeological applications of the dating of animal bone by radiocarbon with particular reference to post-Pleistocene extinctions. In Mook, W.G. and Waterbolk, H.T. (editors), *1st International Symposium on 14C and Archaeology, Groningen 1981.* PACT 8, 409–419.

COLLCUTT, S.N. 1979: Notes sur le "LUP" (Creswellien, Cheddarien etc.) de la Grande Bretagne. In Sonneville-Bordes, D. de (editor), *La Fin des temps glaciaires en Europe* (Paris, CNRS, Colloques Internationaux No 271) 783–789.

COLLCUTT, S.N. 1984: *The Analysis of Quaternary Cave Sediments and its bearing upon Palaeolithic Archaeology* (University of Oxford, unpublished D.Phil thesis) 3 Vols.

COMBIER, J. AND DESBROSSE, R. 1964: Magdalénien final à pointe de Teyjat dans le Jura méridional. *L'Anthropologie* 68, 190–194.

COMMONT, V. 1909: L'industrie moustérienne dans la région du Nord de la France. *Congrès Préhistoriques de France* Beauvais, 120.

COMMONT, V. 1913: Les hommes contemporains du renne dans la vallée de la Somme. *Mémoire de la Soc. des Antiquaires de Picardie* 37, 207–646.

COMMONT, V. 1916: Les terrains quaternaires des tranchées du nouveau canal du Nord. *L'Anthropologie* 28, 3–323.

CONACHER, A.J. AND DALRYMPLE, J.B. 1977: The nine unit landsurface model. *Geoderma* 18, 1/2, 1–154.

CONINCK, F. DE 1980: Major mechanisms in formation of spodic horizons. *Geoderma* 24, 101–128.

COOK, J. AND BARTON, R.N.E. 1986: Dating Late Devensian/Early Flandrian barbed points. In Gowlett, J.A.J. and Hedges, R.E.M. (editors), *Archaeological Results from Accelerator Dating* (Oxford: Committee for Archaeology, Monograph 11) 87–90.

COOK, J. AND DUMONT, J. 1987: The development and application of microwear analysis since 1964. In Sieveking, G. de G. and Newcomer, M.H. (editors), *The Human Uses of Flint and Chert* (Cambridge University Press) 53–61.

COOPE, G.R. 1977: Fossil coleopteran assemblages as sensitive indicators of climatic change during the Devensian (last) cold stage. *Phil. Trans. R. Soc. London*, B 280, 313–40.

COOPE, G.R. AND BROPHY, J.A. 1972: Late-glacial environmental changes indicated by a coleopteran succession from North Wales. *Boreas* 1, 97–142.

COOPE, G.R. AND JOACHIM, M.J. 1980: Lateglacial environmental changes interpreted from fossil Coleoptera from St Bees, Cumbria, NW England. In Lowe, J.J., Gray, J.M. and Robinson, J.E. (editors), *Studies in the Lateglacial of North-West Europe* (Oxford, Pergamon) 55–68.

COOPE, G.R. AND PENNINGTON, W. 1977: The Windermere Interstadial of the Late Devensian. *Phil. Trans. Roy. Soc. London*, B 280, 337–9.

COOPE, G.R. AND LISTER, A.M. 1987: Late-glacial mammoth skeletons from Condover, Shropshire, England. *Nature* 330, 472–4.

CORNWALL, I.W. 1958: *Soils for the Archaeologist* (London, Phoenix House Ltd.).

COURTY, M.A., GOLDBERG, P. AND MACPHAIL, R.I. 1989: *Soil and Micromorphology in Archaeology.* (Cambridge University Press, Manuals in Archaeology).

COX, N. 1976: Woking: Brockhill, near Parley Bridge, Horsell. *Surrey Archaeological Society Bulletin.* 126.

CULLING, W.E.H. 1963: Soil creep and the development of hillside slopes. *Journal of Geology* 71, 2, 127–61.

CUNLIFFE, B.W. 1978: *Hengistbury Head* (London, P. Elek).

CUNLIFFE, B.W. 1987: *Hengistbury Head, Dorset. Volume 1: The Prehistoric and Roman Settlement 3500 BC to 500 AD.* (Oxford, Oxford University Committee for Archaeology, Monograph 13).

CURRANT, A.P. 1986: The Lateglacial mammal fauna of Gough's Cave, Cheddar, Somerset. *Proc. Univ. Bristol Spelaeol. Soc.* 17, 3, 286–304.

CURRANT, A.P. 1987: Late Pleistocene Saiga antelope *Saiga Tatarica* on Mendip. *Proc. Univ. Bristol Spelaeol. Soc.* 18, 1 74–80.

CURRANT, A.P., JACOBI, R.M. AND STRINGER, C.B. 1989: Excavations at Gough's Cave, Somerset 1986–7. *Antiquity* 63, 238, 131–6.

CURRY, D. 1965: The Palaeogene beds of south-east England. *Proc. Geologists' Association* 76, 2, 151–73.

CURRY, D. 1976: The age of the Hengistbury Beds (Eocene) and its significance for the structure of the area around Christchurch, Dorset. *Proc. Geologists' Association* 87, 401–7.

DALRYMPLE, J.B. 1962: Some micromorphological implications of time as a soil–forming factor, illustrated from sites in S.E. England. *Zeitschrift für pflanzenernährung Düngung und Bodenkunde* 98, 143, 3, 232–239.

DARWIN, C. 1883: *The Formation of Vegetable Mould Through the Action of Worms With Observations on Their Habits* (London, Murray).

DAVID, F. 1972: Temoins osseux. In Leroi-Gourhan, A. and Brézillon, M. (editors), *Fouilles de Pincevent: Essai d'analyse éthnographique d'un habitat Magdalénien* (Paris, CNRS, VIIe supplément à Gallia Préhistoire) 295–320.

DAVID, S. 1984: Pointes de type nord-europeén dans le Magdalénien final et l'epipaléolithique de Franche-Comté. *Revue Archéologique de l'Est et du Centre-Est* 35, 2, 144–149.

DEEBEN, J. 1988: The Geldrop sites and the Federmesser occupation of the Southern Netherlands. In Otte, M. (editor), *De la Loire à l'Oder: Les civilisations du Paléolithique final dans le nord-ouest européen* (Oxford, British Archaeological Reports International Series 444i) 357–398.

DELPECH, F. 1975: *Les Faunes du Paléolithique Supérieur dans le Sud-Ouest de la France* (Bordeaux, Université de Bordeaux I, Thèse de Doctorat d'Etat ès Sciences naturelles).

DESBROSSE, R. AND KOZLOWSKI, J.K. 1988: Le paléolithique final entre Atlantique et Vistule: comparaisons entre les civilisations de la plaine et celles des plateaux. In Otte, M. (editor), *De la Loire à l'Oder: Les civilisations du Paléolithique final dans le nord-ouest européen* (Oxford, British Archaeological Reports International Series 444ii) 655–682.

DEVOY, R.J.N. 1982: Analysis of the geological evidence for Holocene sea-level movements in South-East England. *Proc. Geologists' Assoc.* 93, 65–90.

DEVOY, R.J.N. 1987: The estuary of the western Yar: sea-level changes in the Solent region. In Barber, K.E. (editor), *Wessex and the Isle of Wight Fieldguide* (Cambridge, Quaternary Research Association).

DEWEZ, M. 1979: Problématique de l'étude des groupes culturels du Paléolithique final en Belgique. In Sonneville-Bordes, D. de (editor), *La Fin des temps glaciaires en Europe* (Paris, CNRS, Colloques Internationaux No 271) 791–799.

DEWEZ, M. 1987: *Le Paléolithique Supérieur Récent dans les Grottes de Belgique* (Court-St-Etienne, Oleffe, Publications d'histoire de l'art et d'archéologie de l'Université Catholique de Louvain).

DEWEZ, M. 1988: Ahrensbourgien, Creswellien et Magdalénien en Belgique. In Otte, M. (editor), *De la Loire à l'Oder: Les civilisations du Paléolithique final dans le nord-ouest européen* (Oxford, British Archaeological Reports International Series 444i) 179–189.

DICKINSON, N.M. 1982: Investigation and measurement of root turnover in semi-permanent grassland. *Revue d'Ecologie et de Biologie du Sol* 19, 3, 307–14.

DIMBLEBY, G.W. 1961: Soil pollen analysis. *Journal of Soil Science* 12, 1–11.

DIMBLEBY, G.W. 1962: The development of British heaths and their soils. *Oxford Forestry Memoirs No. 23* (Oxford, Clarendon Press).

DIMBLEBY, G.W. In Evans, J.G. and Limbrey, S. 1974: The experimental earthwork at Morden Bog, Wareham, Dorset, England. *Proc. Prehistoric Society* 40, 171–2.

DIMBLEBY, G.W. AND GILL, J.M. 1955: The occurrence of podzols under deciduous woodland in the New Forest. *Forestry* 28, 96–106.

DIMBLEBY, G.W. AND BRADLEY, R.J. 1975: Evidence of pedogenesis from a Neolithic site at Rackham, Sussex. *Journal of Archaeological Science* 2, 179–186.

DORAN, J. AND HODSON, F. 1975: *Mathematics and Computers in Archaeology* (Edinburgh University Press).

DRAPER, J.C. 1962: Upper Palaeolithic type points from Long Island, Langstone Harbour, Portsmouth. *Proc. Hampshire Field Club* 22, 105–106.

DRAPER, J.C. 1968: Mesolithic distribution in South-east Hampshire. *Proc. Hampshire Field Club* 23, 110–119.

DREWETT, P. 1976: The excavation of four round barrows of the second millenium BC at West Heath, Harting, 1973–75. *Sussex Archaeological Collections* 114, 126–150.

DUCHAUFOUR, P. 1982: *Pedology* (London, George, Allen and Unwin).

DUMONT, J.V. 1983: An interim report of the Star Carr microwear study. *Oxford Journal of Archaeology* 2, 2, 127–145.

DUMONT, J.V. 1987: Mesolithic microwear research in Northwest Europe. In Rowley-Conwy, P., Zvelebil, M. and Blankholm, H.P. (editors), *Mesolithic Northwest Europe: recent trends* (Sheffield, Department of Archaeology & Prehistory University of Sheffield) 82–89.

DUPLESSY, J.C., DELIBRAS, G., TURON, J.L., PUJOL, C. AND DUPRAT, J. 1981: Deglacial warming of the northeastern Atlantic Ocean: correlation with the palaeoclimatic evolution of the European continent. *Palaeogeography, Palaeoclimatology, Palaeoecology* 35, 121–144.

EDWARDS, K.J. AND HIRONS, K.R. 1984: Cereal pollen grains in pre-elm decline deposits: implications for the earliest agriculture in Britain and Ireland. *Journal of Soil Science* 11, 71–78.

EMBLETON, C. AND KING, C.A.M. 1975: *Periglacial Geomorphology* (London, Edward Arnold).

283

ERLANDSON, J.M. 1984: A case study in faunalturbation: delineating the effects of the burrowing pocket gopher on the distribution of archaeological materials. *American Antiquity* 49, 4, 785–90.

EVERARD, C.E. 1954: The Solent River: a geomorphological study. *Transactions and Papers of the Institute of British Geographers* 20, 41–58.

FAEGRI, K. AND IVERSEN, J. 1974: *Textbook of Pollen Analysis* (Oxford, Blackwell) 3rd edition.

FAGNART, J.P. 1984a: Le Paléolithique supérieur dans le Nord de la France et le Bassin de la Somme (Lille, Université des Sciences et Techniques de Lille, thèse de doctorat d'université).

FAGNART, J.P. 1984b: Le Paléolithique supérieur dans le Nord de la France: un état de la question. *Bull. Soc. Préhistorique Française* 81, 10–12, 291–301.

FAGNART, J.P. 1988: *Les Industries Lithiques du Paléolithique Supérieur dans le Nord de la France* (Amiens, Revue Archéologique de Picardie, Numéro spécial).

FAIRBRIDGE, R.W. 1961: Eustatic changes of sea-level. *Phys. Chem. of the Earth* 5, 99–185.

FEDOROFF, N. 1982: Soil fabric at the microscopic level. In Bonneau, M. and Souchier, B. (editors), *Constituents and properties of soil* (London, Academic Press) 13: 288–303.

FISCHER, A. AND MORTENSEN, B.N. 1977: *Trollesgave-bopladsen. Et eksempel på anvendeise af EDB inden for arkaeologien* (Copenhagen, Nationalmuseets Arbejdsmark).

FISCHER, A., GRONNOW, B., JONSSON, J.H., NIELSEN, F.O. AND PETERSEN, C. 1979: *Stone Age Experiments at Lejre* (Copenhagen, National Museum of Denmark, Working Papers 8).

FISCHER, A., HANSEN, P.V. AND RASMUSSEN, P. 1984: Macro and microwear traces on lithic projectile points: experimental results and prehistoric examples. *Journal of Danish Archaeology* 3, 19–46.

FISCHER, A. AND TAUBER, H. 1986: New C–14 datings of Late Palaeolithic cultures from Northwestern Europe. *Journal of Danish Archaeology* 5, 7–14.

FISCHER, A. AND NIELSEN, F.O.S. 1987: Senistidens bopladser ved Bromme. *Aarbøger for Nordisk Oldkyndighed og Historie* (1986) 5–69.

FISHER, P.F. AND MACPHAIL, R.I. 1985: Studies of archaeological soils and deposits by micromorphological techniques. In Feiller, N.R.J., Gilbertson, D.D. and Ralph, N.G.A. (editors), *Palaeoenvironmental investigations.* (Oxford, British Archaeological Reports, International Series 258) 93–125.

FOLEY, R. 1981: *Off-site Archaeology and Human adaptation in East Africa* (Oxford, British Archaeological Reports, International Series 97).

FRENCH, H.M. 1976: *The Periglacial Environment* (London and New York, Longman).

FRENZEL, B. 1966: Climatic change in the Atlantic/Sub-Boreal transition in the Northern Hemisphere: botanical evidence. In Sawyer, J.S. (editor), *Proc. of the International Symposium on World Climate 8,000–0 B.C.* (London, Royal Meteorological Society) 99–123.

FRISON, G.C. 1979: Observations of the use of stone tools: dulling of working edges of some chipped stone tools in bison butchering. In Hayden, B. (editor), *Lithic Use-Wear Analysis* (New York, Academic Press) 259–268.

FRISON, G.C., WILSON, M. AND WILSON, D.J. 1976: Fossil bison and artifacts from an Early Altithermal Period arroyo trap in Wyoming. *American Antiquity* 1, 28–57.

GAMBLE, C. 1986: *The Palaeolithic Settlement of Europe* (Cambridge University Press).

GALLAGHER, J.P. 1977: Contemporary stone tools in Ethiopia: implications for archaeology. *Journal of Field Archaeology* 4, 407–414.

GARROD, D.A.E. 1926: *The Upper Palaeolithic Age in Britain* (Oxford, Clarendon Press).

GENDEL, P. 1982: Functional analysis of scrapers. In Lauwers, R. and Vermeersch, P.M. (editors), *Un site Mésolithique Ancien à Neerharen De Kip. Studia Praehistorica Belgica* 1 49–51.

GIBBARD, P.L. AND HALL, A.R. 1982: Late Devensian river deposits in the Lower Colne Valley, West London, England. *Proc. Geologists' Assoc.* 93, 291–9.

GIFFORD, D.P. AND BEHRENSMEYER, A.K. 1977: Observed depositional events at a modern human occupation site in Kenya. *Quaternary Research* 8, 245–266.

GIFFORD-GONZALEZ, D.P., DAMROSCH, D.B., DAMROSCH, D.R., PRYOR, J. AND THUNEN, R.L. 1985: The third dimension in site structure: an experiment in trampling and vertical dispersal. *American Antiquity* 50, 4, 803–818.

GILLESPIE, R. AND GOWLETT, J.A.J. 1983: Archaeological sampling for the new generation of radiocarbon techniques. *Oxford Journal of Archaeology* 2, 3, 379–382.

GILLESPIE, R., HEDGES, R.E.M. AND WAND, J.O. 1984: Radiocarbon dating of bone by Accelerator Mass Spectrometry. *Journal of Archaeological Science* 11, 165–170.

GILLESPIE, R., GOWLETT, J.A.J., HALL, E.T., HEDGES, R.E.M. AND PERRY, C. 1985: Radiocarbon dates from the Oxford AMS system: Archaeometry datelist 2. *Archaeometry* 27, 2, 237–246.

GODWIN, H. 1964: Late Weichselian conditions in south-eastern Britain: organic deposits at Colney Heath, Herts. *Proc. Roy. Soc. London B* 150, 199–215.

GODWIN, H. 1975a: *The History of the British Flora* (Cambridge University Press, 2nd edition).

GODWIN, H. 1975b: History of the natural forests of Britain: establishment, dominance and destruction. *Phil Trans R Soc. B* 271, 47–67.

GODWIN, H. WALKER, D. AND WILLIS, E.H. 1957: Radiocarbon dating and postglacial vegetational history: Scaleby Moss. *Proc. Roy. Soc. London, B* 147, 352–366.

GOULD, R.A., KOSTER, D.A. AND SONTZ, A.H.L. 1971: The lithic assemblage of the Western Desert aborigines of Australia. *American Antiquity* 36, 2, 149–169.

GOWLETT, J.A.J. 1986: Radiocarbon accelerator dating of the Upper Palaeolithic in Northwest Europe: a provisional view. In Collcutt, S.N. (editor), *The Palaeolithic of Britain and Its Nearest Neighbours: recent trends* (Sheffield, Department of Archaeology and Prehistory University of Sheffield) 98–102.

GOWLETT, J.A.J., HALL, E.T., HEDGES, R.E.M. AND PERRY, C. 1986a: Radiocarbon dates from the Oxford AMS system: Archaeometry datelist 3. *Archaeometry* 28, 1, 116–125.

GOWLETT, J.A.J., HEDGES, R.E.M., LAW, I.A. AND PERRY, C. 1986b: Radiocarbon dates from the Oxford AMS system: Archaeometry datelist 4. *Archaeometry* 28, 2, 206–221.

GOWLETT, J.A.J., HEDGES, R.E.M., LAW, I.A. AND PERRY, C. 1987: Radiocarbon dates from the Oxford AMS system,: Archaeometry datelist 5. *Archaeometry* 29, 1, 125–155.

GRACE, R. 1981: *Attribute Analysis as a Method of Studying Functional Variability in Palaeolithic Assemblages* (University of London, Institute of Archaeology, unpublished BA dissertation).

GRACE, R., ATAMAN, K., FABREGAS, R. AND HAGGREN, C.M.B. 1988: A multi-variate approach to the functional analysis of flint tools. In Beyries, S. (editor), *Industries Lithiques Tracéologie et Technologie.* (Oxford, British Archaeological Reports International Series 411 ii) 217–230.

GRADWELL, M.W. 1954: Soil frost studies at a high country station. *New Zealand Journal of Science and Technology* 36, B, 240–57.

GRAMLY, R.M. 1982: *The Vail Site: A Palaeo-Indian Encampment in Maine* (Buffalo, Bulletin of the Buffalo Society of Natural Sciences).

GRAMSCH, B. 1987: Ausgrabungen auf dem mesolithischen Moorfundplatz bei Friesack, Bezirk Potsdam. *Veröffentlichungen des Museums für Ur-und Frühgeschichte Potsdam* 21, 75–100.

GREEN, J.F.N. 1946: The terraces of Bournemouth, Hants. *Proc. Geologists' Association* 57, 2, 82–101.

GRIGSON, C. 1978: The Late Glacial and Early Flandrian ungulates of England and Wales: an interim review. In Limbrey, S. and Evans, J.G. (editors), *The Effect of Man on the Landscape: the Lowland Zone* (CBA Research Report 21) 46–56.

GROSE, F. 1779: A description of ancient fortifications near Christchurch, Hampshire. *Archaeologia* 5, 237–40.

GUILLIEN, Y. AND SAINT-MATHURIN S. DE 1976: Le gisement du Roc-aux-Sorciers et la séquence climatique du Magdalénien. *Bull. Soc. Préhistorique Française* 23, 1, 15–21.

GUILLET, B. 1982: Study of the turnover of soil organic matter using radio-isotopes (C14). In Bonneau, M. and Souchier, B. (editors), *Constituents and properties of soil* (London, Academic Press) 10, 238–255.

HAHN, J. 1979: Essai sur l'écologie du Magdalénien dans le Jura souabe. In de Sonneville-Bordes, D. (editor) *La Fin des Temps Glaciares en Europe* (Paris, CNRS) 203–14.

HALLAM, J.S., EDWARDS, B.J.N., BARNES, B. AND STUART, A.J. 1973: The remains of a Late Glacial elk with associated barbed points from High Furlong, near Blackpool, Lancashire.

*Proc. Prehistoric Society* 39, 100–128.

HANSEN, P.V. AND MADSEN, B. 1983: Flint axe manufacture in the Neolithic. An experimental investigation of a flint axe manufacture site at Hastrup Vaenget, East Zealand. *Journal of Danish Archaeology* 2, 43–60.

HARRISON, C.J.O. 1986: Bird remains from Gough's Cave, Cheddar, Somerset. *Proc. Univ. Bristol Spelaeological Society* 17, 3 305–310.

HARRISON, C.J.O. 1989: Bird remains from Gough's Old Cave, Cheddar, Somerset. *Proc. Univ. Bristol Spelaeological Society* 18, 3, 409–11.

HARTZ, S. 1987: Neue spätpaläolithische fundplätze bei Ahrenshoft, Kreis Nordfriesland. *Offa* 44, 5–52.

HARTZ, N. & WINGE, H. 1906: Om uroxen fra Vig, saaret og draebt med flintvaaben. *Aarbøger for nordisk Oldkyndighed og Historie* (Copenhagen) 225–236.

HASKINS, L.E. 1978: *The Vegetational History of South-East Dorset* (University of Southampton, Unpublished PhD thesis).

HAYDEN, B. 1979a: *Palaeolithic Reflections* (Canberra, Australian Institute of Aboriginal Studies and New Jersey, Humanities Press Inc.).

HAYDEN, B. 1979b: Snap, shatter and super-fractures: use wear on stone skin scrapers. In Hayden, B. (editor), *Lithic Use-Wear Analysis* (New York, Academic Press) 207–229.

HEDGES, R.E.M., HOUSLEY, R.A., LAW, I.A., PERRY, C. AND GOWLETT, J.A.J. 1987: Radiocarbon dates from the Oxford AMS system: Archaeometry datelist 6. *Archaeometry* 29, 2, 289–306.

HEDGES, R.E.M., HOUSLEY, R.A., LAW, I.A. AND PERRY, C. 1988: Radiocarbon dates from the Oxford AMS system: Archaeometry datelist 7. *Archaeometry* 30, 1, 155–164.

HEDGES, R.E.M., HOUSLEY, R.A., LAW, I.A. AND BRONK, C.R. 1989: Radiocarbon dates from the Oxford AMS system: Archaeometry datelist 9. *Archaeometry* 31, 2, 207–234.

HESTER, T.R. & HEIZER, R.F. 1973: Arrow points or knives ? Comments on the proposed function of "Stockton Points". *American Antiquity* 38, 2, 220–1.

HIGGS, E.S. 1959: The excavation of a late Mesolithic site at Downton, near Salisbury, Wilts. *Proc. Prehistoric Society* 25, 209–232.

HODGSON, J.M. 1974: *Soil Survey Field Handbook* (Harpenden, Soil Survey Technical Monograph 5).

HOLE, F.D. 1981: Effects of animals on soils. *Geoderma* 25, 1/2, 75–112.

HOLLOWAY, M. AND LAVENDER, J. 1989: *Hengistbury Head Management Plan* (Bournemouth Borough Council).

HOOPER, W. 1933: The pigmy flint industries of Surrey. *Surrey Archaeological Collections* 41, 50–78.

HOOKER, J.J. 1975: Report of field meeting to Hengistbury Head and adjacent areas, Dorset; with an account of published work and some new exposures. *Tertiary Times* 2, 3, 109–21.

HOOKER, J.J. 1977: A mammal from the Upper Eocene of Hengistbury, Dorset. *Tertiary Research* 1, 3, 91–4.

HUNTLEY, D.J., GODFREY-SMITH, D.I. AND THEWALT, M.L.W. 1985: Optical dating of sediments. *Nature* 313, 105–7.

HUYGE, D. AND VERMEERSCH, P.M. 1982: Late Mesolithic settlement at Weelde-Paardsdrank. In Vermeersch, P.M. (editor), *Studia Praehistorica Belgica*. Contributions to the study of the Mesolithic of the Belgian Lowland (Tervuren, Musée Royal de l'Afrique Centrale) 1, 115–203.

HUXTABLE, J. AND JACOBI, R.M. 1982: Thermoluminescence dating of burned flints from a British Mesolithic site: Longmoor Inclosure, East Hampshire. *Archaeometry* 24, 2, 164–169.

HYLLEBERG, J. 1975: Selective feeding by *Abarenicola pacifica* with notes on *Abarenicola vagabunda* and a concept of gardening in lugworms. *Ophelia* 14, 113–37.

ISAAC, G. 1971: Whither archaeology? *Antiquity* 45, 123–9.

JACOBI, R.M. 1973: Aspects of the "Mesolithic Age" in Great Britain. In Kozlowski, S.K. (editor), *The Mesolithic in Europe* (Warsaw University Press) 237–65.

JACOBI, R.M. 1975: Aspects of the Postglacial Archaeology of *England and Wales* (University of Cambridge, Unpublished Ph.D. thesis).

JACOBI, R.M. 1976: Britain inside and outside Mesolithic Europe. *Proc. Prehistoric Society* 42, 67–84.

JACOBI, R.M. 1978: Northern England in the eighth millennium bc: an essay. In Mellars, P.A. (editor), *The Early Postglacial settlement of Northern Europe* (London, Duckworth) 295–332.

JACOBI, R.M. 1979: Early Flandrian hunters in the South-West. *Proc. Devon Archaeological Society* 13, 48–93.

JACOBI, R.M. 1980: The Upper Palaeolithic of Britain, with special reference to Wales. In Taylor, J.A. (editor), *Culture and Environment in Prehistoric Wales* (Oxford, British Archaeological Reports, British Series 76) 15–99.

JACOBI, R.M. 1981a: Late glacial settlement in Essex. In Buckley, D.G. (editor), *Archaeology in Essex to AD 1500* (London, CBA Research Report No. 34) 12–13.

JACOBI, R.M. 1981b: The Late Weichselian peopling of Britain and North-West Europe. In Kozlowski, J.K. and Kozlowski, S. (editors), *Archaeologia Interregionalis I* (Warsaw, Universitas Varsoviensis) 57–76.

JACOBI, R.M. 1981c: The Last Hunters in Hampshire. In Shennan, S.J. and Shadla-Hall R.T. (editors), *The Archaeology of Hampshire. From the Palaeolithic to the Industrial Revolution* (Hampshire Field Club and Archaeological Society, Monograph No. 1).

JACOBI, R.M. 1986: The lateglacial archaeology of Gough's Cave, Cheddar. In Collcutt, S.N. (editor), *The Palaeolithic of Britain and its nearest neighbours: recent trends* (Sheffield, Department of Archaeology and Prehistory, University of Sheffield) 75–80.

JACOBI, R.M. 1987: Misanthropic miscellany: musings on British Early Flandrian archaeology and other flights of fancy. In Rowley-Conwy, P., Zvelebil, M & Blankholm, H.P. (editors), *Mesolithic Northwest Europe: recent trends* (Sheffield, Department of Archaeology & Prehistory, University of Sheffield) 163–8.

JACOBI, R.M. 1988: Gough's Cave. In Leroi-Gourhan, A. (editor) 1988: *Dictionnaire de la Préhistoire* (Paris, Presses Universitaires de France) 439.

JACOBI, R.M. AND MARTINGELL, H.E. 1980: A late-glacial shouldered point from Cranwich, Norfolk. *Norfolk Archaeology* 37, 3, 312–314.

JELGERSMA, S. 1979: Sea level changes in the North Sea basin. In Oele, E., Schuttenhelm, R.T.E. and Wiggers, A.J. (editors), *The Quaternary History of the North Sea* (Stockholm, Almqvist and Wiksell) 233–48.

JOHNSON, D.L. AND HANSEN, K.L. 1974: The effects of frost-heaving on objects in soils. *Plains Anthropologist* 19, 81–98.

JOHNSON, D.L. AND HESTER, N.C. 1972: Origin of stone pavements on Pleistocene marine terraces in California. *Proc. Association of American Geographers* 4, 50–3.

JOHNSON, D.L., MUHS, D.R. AND BARNHARDT, M.L. 1977: The effects of frost-heaving on objects in soils. II: laboratory experiments. *Plains Anthropologist* 22, 133–47.

JUEL-JENSEN, H. 1988. Functional analysis of prehistoric flint tools by high–power microscopy: a review of west european research. *Journal of World Prehistory* 2, 1, 53–88.

JULIEN, M., AUDOUZE, F., BAFFIER, D., BODU, P., COUDRET, P., DAVID, F., GAUCHER, G., KARLIN, C., LARRIRE, M., MASSON, P., OLIVE, M., ORLIAC, M., PIGEOT, N., RIEU, J.L., SCHMIDER, B. AND TABORIN, Y. 1988: Organisation de l'espace et fonction des habitats magdaléniens du bassin Parisien. In Otte, M. (editor), De la Loire à l'Oder. *Les civilisations du Paléolithique final dans le nord-ouest européen* (Oxford, British Archaeological Reports International Series 444i) 85–125.

KALISZ, P.J. AND STONE, E.L. 1984: Soil mixing by scarab beetles and pocket gophers in North-Central Florida. *Journal of the Soil Science Society of America* 48, 169–72.

KAMMINGA, J. 1978: *Journey into the Microcosms: a Functional Analysis of Certain Classes of Prehistoric Australian Stone Tools* (University of Sydney, unpublished PhD thesis, 2 volumes).

KARLIN, C. AND NEWCOMER, M. 1982: Interpreting flake scatters: an example from Pincevent. In Cahen, D. (editor), *Tailler! Pour quoi faire: Préhistoire et technologie lithique II. Studia Praehistorica Belgica* 2 (Tervuren, Musée royal de l'Afrique centrale) 159–166.

KEEF, P.A.M., WYMER, J.J. AND DIMBLEBY, G.W. 1965: A Mesolithic site on Iping Common, Sussex, England. *Proc. Prehistoric Society* 31, 85–92.

KEELEY, L.H. 1978: Preliminary microwear analysis of the Meer Assemblage. In Van Noten, F. (editor), *Les Chasseurs de Meer* (Brugge, de Tempel, Dissertationes Archaeologicae Gandenses 18) 78–86.

KEELEY, L.H. 1980: *Experimental Determination of Stone Tool Uses: a microwear analysis* (Chicago, University of Chicago Press).

KERNEY, M.P., BROWN, E.H. AND CHANDLER, T.J. 1964: The lateglacial and postglacial history of the Chalk escarpment near

Brook, Kent. *Phil. Trans. Roy. Soc.* B 248, 135–204.

KERNEY, M.P., PREECE, R.C. AND TURNER, C. 1980: Molluscan and plant biostratigraphy of some late Devensian and Flandrian deposits in Kent. *Phil. Trans. Roy. Soc.* B 291, 1–43.

KIRKBY, A.V.T. AND KIRKBY, M.J. 1974: Surface wash at the semi-arid break of slope. *Zeitschrift für Geomorphologie* SB 21, 151–76.

KOBUSIEWICZ, M. 1973: Les outils du groupe des haches tailles dans le Mésolithique en Pologne. In Kozlowski, S.K. (editor), *The Mesolithic in Europe* (Warsaw University Press) 267–74.

KOBUSIEWICZ, M. 1983: Le problème des contacts des peuples du Paléolithique final de la plaine européenne avec le territoire français. *Bull. Soc. Préhistorique Française* 80, 10–12, 308–321.

KOZLOWSKI, S.K. (editor) 1973: *The Mesolithic in Europe* (Warsaw University Press).

KOZLOWSKI, J.K. AND KOZLOWSKI, S.K. 1979: *Upper Palaeolithic and Mesolithic in Europe: Taxonomy and Palaeohistory* (Polska Akademia Nauk).

KRA, R.R. AND STUIVER, M. (editors) 1986: 12th International Radiocarbon Conference, Trondheim, Norway, 1985. *Radiocarbon* 28, 2.

KRUKOWSKI, S. 1914: Nowy odpadek microlitu neolitycznego. *Comptes rendus de la soc. scientifique de Varsovie* 7, 1.

LAUWERS, R. 1988: Gisement Tjongerien de Rekem (Belgique), premier bilan d'une analyse spatiale. In Otte, M. (editor), *De la Loire à l'Oder: Les civilisations du Paléolithique final dans le nord-ouest européen* (Oxford, British Archaeological Reports International Series 444i) 217–235.

LAUWERS, R. AND VERMEERSCH, P.M. 1982: Un site du Mésolithique ancien à Neerharen-De Kip. In Vermeersch, P.M. (editor), Contributions to the study of the Mesolithic of the Belgian Lowland. *Studia Praehistorica Belgica* 1 (Tervuren, Musée royal de l'Afrique centrale) 15–55.

LEE, K.E. AND WOOD, T.G. 1971: *Termites and Soils* (London, Academic Press).

LEONARDI, P. 1988: Art Paléolithique mobilier et pariétal en Italie. *L'Anthropologie* 92, 1, 139–202.

LÉOTARD, J.M. AND OTTE, M. 1988: Occupation Paléolithique Final aux grottes de Presle fouilles de 1983–84 (Aiseau-Belgique). In Otte, M. (editor), *De la Loire à l'Oder: Les civilisations du Paléolithique final dans le nord-ouest européen* (Oxford, British Archaeological Reports International Series 444i) 189–217.

LEROI-GOURHAN, A. 1983: Pointe de sagaie de Pincevent. *Bull. Soc. Préhistorique Française* 80, 5, 154–156.

LEROI-GOURHAN, A. 1988: *Dictionnaire de la Préhistoire* (Paris, Presses Universitaires de France).

LEROI-GOURHAN, A. AND BRÉZILLON, M. 1966: L'habitation Magdalénienne no. 1 de Pincevent près Montereau (Seine-et-Marne). *Gallia Préhistoire* 9, 2, 263–385.

LEROI-GOURHAN, A. AND BRÉZILLON, M. 1972: *Fouilles de Pincevent: Essai d'analyse éthographique d'un habitat Magdalénien* (Paris, CNRS, VIIe supplément à Gallia Préhistoire).

LEROI-GOURHAN, AR. AND ALLAIN, J. 1979: *Lascaux inconnu* (Paris, CNRS, XII supplément à Gallia Préhistoire).

LEVI-SALA, I. 1986a: Experimental replication of post-depositional surface modifications on flint. *Early Man News* 9/10/11, 103–108.

LEVI-SALA, I. 1986b: Use wear and post-depositional surface modification: a word of caution. *Journal of Archaeological Science* 13, 3, 229–244.

LEVI-SALA, I. 1988: Processes of polish formation on flint tool surfaces. In Beyries, S. (editor), *Industries Lithiques Tracéologie et Technologie* (Oxford, British Archaeological Reports International Series 441 ii) 83–96.

LEVI-SALA, I. 1989: *A study of microscopic polish on flint implements* (University of London, Institute of Archaeology, unpublished PhD dissertation).

LEWIN, J. 1966: Fossil ice-wedges in Hampshire. *Nature* 211, 5050, 728.

LEWIS, J.S.C. 1989: The Late Glacial/early Flandrian site at Three Ways Wharf, Uxbridge, Middlesex, England. *Mesolithic Miscellany* 10, 2, 7–9.

LINDQUIST, S. 1918: Nordens benalder och en teori om dess stenaldersraser. *Rig* 65.

LINELL, K.A. AND TEDROW, J.C.F. 1981: *Soil and Permafrost Surveys in the Arctic* (Oxford, Clarendon Press).

LOFTUS, J. 1982: Ein verzierter Pfeilschaftglatter von Fläche 64/74–73/78 des spätpaläolithischen Fundplatzes Niederbieber/Neuwieder Becken. *Archäologisches Korrespondenzblatt* 12, 313–316.

LOWE, S. 1981: Radiocarbon dating and stratigraphic resolution in Welsh lateglacial chronology. *Nature* 293, 210–212.

LOWE, J.J. AND WALKER, M.J.C. 1977: The reconstruction of the lateglacial environment in southern and eastern Grampian Highlands. In Gray, J.M. and Lowe, J.J. (editors), *Studies in the Scottish Late Glacial Environment* (Oxford, Pergamon Press) 101–118.

LOWE, J.J. AND WALKER, M.J.C. 1984: *Reconstructing Quaternary Environments* (London and New York, Longman).

LUTZ, H.J. AND GRISWOLD, F.S. 1939: The influence of tree roots on soil morphology. *American Journal of Science* 237, 389–400.

MACE, A. 1959: An Upper Palaeolithic open-site at Hengistbury Head, Christchurch, Hants. Proc. *Prehistoric Society* 25, 233–59.

MACKAY, J.R. AND MATHEWS, W.H. 1974: Movement of sorted stripes, the Cinder Cone, Garibaldi Park, BC, Canada. *Arctic and Alpine Research* 6, 347–59.

MACKNEY, D. 1970: *Podzols in lowland England* (Welsh Soils Discussion Group) 11, 64–87.

MACPHAIL, R.I. 1979: *Soil variation on selected Surrey heaths* (Kingston Polytechnic, C.N.A.A., unpublished PhD thesis).

MACPHAIL, R.I. 1982: *Preliminary Soil Report on Hengistbury Head, Bournemouth, Dorset* (Ancient Monuments Laboratory Report No. 3811).

MACPHAIL, R.I. 1983a: Surrey heathlands and their soils. In Burnham, C.P. (editor), *Seesoil* 1, 57–69.

MACPHAIL, R.I. 1983b: The micromorphology of podsols in catenary sequences on lowland heathlands in Surrey, England. In Bullock, P. and Murphy, C.P. (editors), *Soil Micromorphology* (Berkhamsted, A.B. Academic Publishers) 2, 647–654.

MACPHAIL, R.I. 1985: *Review of Dr. I. Cornwall's thin sections from Caesar's Camp, Keston, Kent* (Ancient Monuments Laboratory Report No. 4798).

MACPHAIL, R.I. 1986: Paleosols in archaeology; their role in understanding Flandrian pedogenesis. In Wright, V.P. (editor), *Paleosols* (Oxford, Scientific Publications) 9, 263–284.

MACPHAIL, R.I. 1987a: A review of soil science in archaeology in England. In Keeley, H.C.M. (editor), *Environmental archaeology, a regional review* 2 (Historic Buildings & Monuments Commission for England, Occasional Paper No 1) 332–379.

MACPHAIL, R.I. 1987b: *Soil Report on the Cairn and Field System at Chysauster, Penzance, Cornwall* (Ancient Monuments Laboratory Report No. III/87).

MACPHAIL, R.I., ROMANS, J.C.C. AND ROBERTSON, L. 1987: The application of micromorphology to the understanding of Holocene soil development in the British Isles. In Fedoroff, N., Bresson, L.M. and Courty, M.A. (editors), *Soil Micromorphology* (Association Française pour l'Etude du Sol, Plaisir, Proceedings VII International Congress, July 1985, France) 647–656.

MADSEN, B. 1983: New evidence of Late Palaeolithic Settlement in East Jutland. *Journal of Danish Archaeology* 2, 12–31.

MAHER, M. 1983: *Knapping areas at the Mesolithic site, West Heath, Hampstead* (University of London, Institute of Archaeology, unpublished BA dissertation).

MARKS, A.E. (editor) 1976: *Prehistory and palaeoenvironment in the Central Negev, Israel* (Dallas, Southern Methodist University Press).

MARSH, A.W. 1982: A new Mesolithic site at Wimborne. *Proc. Dorset Natural History & Archaeological Society* 104, 169–70.

MARTIN, Y. 1972: *L'Art paléolithique de Gouy* (St. Etienne-du-Rouvray, Imprimerie Buquet).

MAUGER, M. 1985: *Les Matériaux Siliceux Utilisés au Paléolithique Supérieur en île de France* (Paris, Université de Paris I, unpublished thesis).

MAY, V.J. AND OSBORNE, K.A. 1981: *Recreational Use of Hengistbury Head* (Dorset Institute of Higher Education).

MELLARS, P.A. 1974: The Palaeolithic and Mesolithic. In Renfrew, C. (editor), *British Prehistory* (London, Duckworth) 41–99.

MELLARS, P.A. 1976: Settlement patterns and industrial variability in the British Mesolithic. In Sieveking, G. de G., Longworth, I.H. and Wilson, K.E. (editors), *Problems in Social and Economic Archaeology* (London, Duckworth) 375–399.

MELLARS, P. AND RHEINHARDT, S.C. 1978: Patterns of Mesolithic land–use in southern England: a geological perspective. In Mellars, P. (editor), *The Early Postglacial Settlement of Northern Europe* (London, Duckworth) 371–396.

MELVILLE, R.V. AND FRESHNEY, E.C. 1982: *The Hampshire Basin and Adjoining Areas* (London, HMSO, British Regional Geology) 4th edition.

MILES, C. 1963: *Indian and Eskimo Artifacts of North America* (New York, American Legacy Press).

MILES, H. 1972: Excavations at Rhuddlan, 1969–71: Interim report. *Flintshire Historical Society Publications* 25 (1971–2), 1–8.

MOEYERSONS, J. 1978: The behaviour of stones and stone implements, buried in consolidating and creeping Kalahari Sands. *Earth Surface Processes* 3, 115–28.

MOHR, E. 1971: *The Asiatic Wild Horse* (London, J.A. Allen and Co.).

MOIR, J.R. 1932: Further Solutré implements from Suffolk. *Antiquaries Journal* 12, 257–261.

MOKMA, D.L. AND BUURMAN, P. 1982: *Podzols and Podzolisation in Temperate Regions* (Netherlands, International Soil Museum, Wageningen, Monograph 1)

MOORE, P.D. 1980: Resolution limits of pollen analysis as applied to archaeology. *MASCA Journal* 1(4), 118–120.

MOORE, P.D. AND WILLMOT, A. 1976: Prehistoric forest clearance and the development of peatlands in the uplands and lowlands of Britain. *VI International Peat Congress* (Poznan, Poland) 1–15.

MOSS, E.H. 1983: *The Functional Analysis of Flint Implements. Pincevent and Pont d'Ambon: two case studies from the French Final Palaeolithic* (Oxford, British Archaeological Reports International Series 177).

MOSS, E.H. AND NEWCOMER, M.H. 1982: Reconstruction of tool use at Pincevent: microwear experiments. In Cahen, D. (editor) *Tailler! Pour Quoi Faire: Préhistoire et Technologie Lithique II. Recent Progress on Microwear Studies* (Tervuren, Musée Royal de L'Afrique Centrale) 289–313.

MURPHY, C.P., McKEAGUE, J.A., BRESSON, L.M., BULLOCK, P., KOOISTRA, M.J., MIEDEMA, R AND STOOPS, G. 1985: Description of soil thin sections: an international comparison. *Geoderma* 35, 15–37.

MUNCK, E. DE, 1893: Observations nouvelles sur le Quaternaire de la région de Mons-Saint-Symphorien-Spiennes et nucléi de l'époque paléolithique sur lesquels se rappliquent plusieurs éclats. *Bull. Soc. Anthrop. Bruxelles* 11, 198–210.

MYERS, A. 1987: All shot to pieces ? Inter-assemblage variability, lithic analysis and mesolithic assemblage 'types': some preliminary observations. In Brown, A.G. & Edmonds, M.R. (editors), *Lithic Analysis and Later British Prehistory: some problems and approaches* (Oxford, British Archaeological Reports 162) 137–154.

NEWCOMER, M.H. 1971: Un nouveau type de burin à Ksar Akil (Liban). *Bull. Soc. Préhistorique Française* 68, 267–272.

NEWCOMER, M.H. 1972: *An Analysis of a Series of Burins from Ksar Akil (Lebanon)* (University of London, unpublished PhD thesis).

NEWCOMER, M.H. 1974: Study and replication of bone tools from Ksar Akil. *World Archaeology* 6, 2, 138–153.

NEWCOMER, M.H. 1975: "Punch Technique" and Upper Palaeolithic Blades. In Swanson, E.H. (editor), *Lithic Technology: making and using stone tools* (The Hague, Mouton Publishers) 97–102.

NEWCOMER, M.H. 1976: Spontaneous Retouch. In Engelen, F.H.G. (editor), *Second International Symposium on Flint, Staringia 3* (Maastricht: Nederlandse Geologische Vereiniging) 62–64

NEWCOMER, M.H. 1981: Stone carving with flint: experiments with a Magdalenian lamp. *Staringia* 6, 77–9.

NEWCOMER, M.H. AND HIVERNEL-GUERRE, F. 1974: Nucléus sur éclat: technologie et utilisation par différentes cultures préhistoriques. *Bull. Soc. Préhistorique Française* 71, 4, 119–128.

NEWCOMER, M.H. AND SIEVEKING, G. DE G. 1980: Experimental flake scatter patterns: a new interpretative technique. *Journal of Field Archaeology* 7, 345–352.

NEWCOMER, M.H., GRACE, R. AND UNGER-HAMILTON, R. 1986: Investigating microwear polishes with blind tests. *Journal of Archaeological Science* 13, 3, 203-217.

NEWCOMER, M.H. AND KARLIN, C. 1987: Flint chips from Pincevent. In Sieveking, G. de G. and Newcomer, M.H. (editors), *The Human Uses of Flint and Chert* (Cambridge University Press) 33–37.

NEWELL, R.R. 1981: Mesolithic dwelling structures: fact and fantasy. In Gramsch, B. (editor) *Mesolithikum in Europa* 2. Internationales Symposium, Potsdam, April 1978 (Berlin, VEB Deutscher Verlag der Wissenschaften) 235–84.

NEWEY, W.W. 1970: Pollen analysis of Late Weichselian deposits at Corstorphine, Edinburgh. *New Phytologist* 69, 1167–1177.

NISSEN, K. AND DITTEMORE, M. 1974: Ethnographic data and wear pattern analysis: a study of socketed eskimo scrapers. *Tebiwa* 17, 1, 67–88.

NUZHNYI, D. 1989: L'utilisation des microlithes géométriques et non-géométriques comme armatures de projectiles. *Bull. Soc. Préhistorique Française* 86, 3, 88–96.

NYE, P.H. 1955: Some soil-forming processes in the humid tropics. IV The action of soil fauna. *Journal of Soil Science* 6, 73–83.

ODELL, G.H. 1978: Préliminaires d'une analyse fonctionelle des pointes microlithiques de Bergumermeer (Pays-Bas). *Bull. Soc. Préhistorique Française* 75, 2, 37–49.

ODELL, G. AND ODELL-VEREECKEN, F. 1980: Verifying the reliability of lithic use-wear assessments by "blind-tests": the low power approach. *Journal of Field Archaeology* 7, 1, 87–120.

OHNUMA, K. 1988: *Ksar Akil, Lebanon. A Technological and Typological Analysis of the Earlier Upper Palaeolithic Levels of Ksar Akil. Volume III: levels XXV–XIV* (Oxford, British Archaeological Reports, International Series 426).

OHNUMA, K. AND BERGMAN, C.A. 1982: Experimental Studies in the Determination of Flaking Mode. *Bulletin of the Institute of Archaeology, London* 19, 161–170.

OSBORNE, P.J. 1971: Appendix on the insect fauna of the organic deposit within the Wandle gravels. In Peake, D.S. The age of the Wandle gravels in the vicinity of Croydon. *Proceedings and Transactions of the Croydon Natural History and Scientific Society* 14(7), 147–175.

OSBORNE, P.J. 1972: Insect faunas of Late Devensian and Flandrian age of Church Stretton, Shropshire. *Phil. Trans. Roy. Soc. B* 263, 327–67.

OSBORNE, P.J. 1974: An insect assemblage of early Flandrian age from Lea Marston, Warwickshire and its bearing on the contemporary climate and ecology. *Quaternary Research* 4, 471–486.

OSBORNE, P.J. 1976: Evidence from the insects of climatic variation during the Flandrian period: a preliminary note. *World Archaeology* 8, 2, 150–158.

OSGOOD, C. 1940: *Ingalik Material Culture* (Yale University Publications in Anthropology 22).

OSWALT, W.H. 1976: *An Anthropological Analysis of Food-getting Technology* (New York, John Wiley and Sons).

OTTE, M. 1980: Le couteau de Kostienki. *Helinium* 20, 54–8.

OTTE, M. 1984: Paléolithique supérieur en Belgique. In Cahen, D. and Haesaerts, P. (editors), *Peuples Chasseurs de la Belgique Préhistorique dans leur Cadre Naturel* (Brussels, Institut Royal des Sciences Naturelles de Belgique) 157–181.

OTTE, M. 1988: Le Paléolithique final: bilan d'une rencontre. In Otte, M. (editor), *De la Loire à l'Oder: Les civilisations du Paléolithique final dans le nord-ouest européen* (Oxford, British Archaeological Reports International Series 444ii) 723–731.

PALMER, S. 1977: *Mesolithic Cultures of Britain* (Dorset, Dolphin Press).

PALMER, S. AND DIMBLEBY, G. 1979: A Mesolithic habitation site on Winfrith Heath, Dorset. *Proc. Dorset Natural History and Archaeological Society* 101, 27–49.

PARKIN, R.A., ROWLEY-CONWY, P. AND SARJEANTSON, D. 1986: Late Palaeolithic exploitation of horse and red deer at Gough's Cave, Cheddar, Somerset. *Proc. Univ. Bristol Spelaeological Society* 17, 3, 311–330.

PAULSEN, H. 1975: Oberflachenretuschierte Pfeilspitzen in Schleswig-Holstein. *Die Heimat* 4–5.

PEARSON, R.G. 1962: The Coleoptera from a detritus deposit of full-glacial age at Colney Heath near St Albans. *Proc. Linn. Soc. London* 173, 37–55.

PENNINGTON, W. 1975: A chronostratigraphic comparison of Late-Weichselian and Late-Devensian subdivisions, illustrated by two radiocarbon-dated profiles from western Britain. *Boreas* 4, 157–71.

PENNINGTON, W. 1977a: Lake sediments and the Lateglacial environment in northern Scotland. In Gray, J.M. and Lowe, J.J. (editors), *Studies in the Scottish Lateglacial Environment* (Oxford, Pergamon) 119–41.

PENNINGTON, W. 1977b: The Late Devensian flora and vegetation of Britain. *Phil. Trans. Roy. Soc. B* 280, 247–71.

PEPIN, C. (editor) 1979: *Hengistbury Head: an environmental study*

(Bournemouth, Roman Press) 3rd edition.

PEPIN, C. (editor) 1985: *Hengistbury Head* (Bournemouth, Roman Press) 4th (revised) edition.

PÉQUART, M., PÉQUART, ST J., BOULE, M. & VALLOIS, H. 1937: Téviec, station necropole mésolithique de Morbihan. *Archives de l'Institut de Paléontologie Humaine 18* (Paris).

PERRIN, R.M.S., WILLIS, E.H. AND HODGE, C.A.H. 1964: Dating of humus podzols by residual radio-carbon activity. *Nature* 202, 165–166.

PETCH, J.A. 1924: *Early Man in the District of Huddersfield* (Huddersfield: Tolson Memorial Museum Handbook No 3).

PETERSSON, M. 1951: Microlithen als Pfeilspitzen: Ein Fund aus dem Lilla Loshult Moor, Ksp. Loshult, Skåne. *Meddelanden fran Lunds Universitets Historiska Museums* 123–137.

PETTERSEN, S. 1958: *Introduction to Meteorology* (New York, McGraw-Hill).

PITTS, M.W. AND JACOBI, R.M. 1979: Some aspects of change in flaked stone industries of the Mesolithic and Neolithic in Southern Britain. *Journal of Archaeological Science* 6, 163–177.

PLEYDER, J.C.M. 1895: Plateau and valley gravels, sarsen stones at Little Bredy and elsewhere in the county. *Dorset Natural History and Antiquarian Field Club* 16, 75–80.

PLINT, A.G. 1983a: Facies, environments and sedimentary cycles in the Middle Eocene, Bracklesham Formation of the Hampshire Basin: evidence for global sea-level changes? *Sedimentology* 30, 625–53.

PLINT, A.G. 1983b: Liquefaction, fluidization and erosional structures associated with bituminous sands of the Bracklesham Formation (Middle Eocene) of Dorset, England. *Sedimentology* 30, 525–35.

PLISSON, H. 1982: Analyse fonctionelle de 95 micro-grattoirs "Tourassiens" In Cahen, D. (editor), *Tailler! pour quoi faire. Préhistoire et Technologie Lithique II* Recent Progress on Microwear Studies (Tervuren, Musée Royal de l'Afrique Centrale) 279–287.

PLISSON, H. 1985: *Etude Fonctionelle d'Outillages Préhistoriques par l'Analyse des Micro-usures: recherches méthodologique et archéologique* (University of Paris I, unpublished thesis).

POMEROY, D.E. 1976: Some effects of mound-building termites on soils in Uganda. *Journal of Soil Science* 27, 3, 377–94.

POPLIN, F. 1976: *Les grands vertébrés de Gönnersdorf. Fouille 1968. Der Magdalénien-Fundplatz Gönnersdorf, 2* (Wiesbaden, Fr Steiner Verlag).

PRESTWICH, J. 1849: On the position and general characters of the strata exhibited in the coast section from Christchurch Harbour to Poole Harbour. *Quarterly Journal of the Geological Society of London* 5, 43–9.

RANKINE, W.F. 1949: Pebbles of Non-Local Rock from Mesolithic Chipping Floors. *Proc. Prehistoric Society* 15, 193–194.

RANKINE, W.F. 1952: A Mesolithic Chipping Floor at the Warren, Oakhanger, Selborne, Hants. *Proc. Prehistoric Society* 18, 21–35.

RANKINE, W.F. 1956: The Mesolithic of Southern England. *Research Papers of the Surrey Archaeological Society* 4, 1–63.

RANKINE, W.F. 1961: Mesolithic Folk Movements in Southern England: Further Evidence from Oakhanger, Hants. Phase II. *Archaeological Newsletter* 7, 3, 63–65.

RANKINE, W.F. AND DIMBLEBY, G.W. 1960: Further excavations at a Mesolithic site at Oakhanger, Selborne, Hampshire. *Proc. Prehistoric Society* 26, 246–262.

REBOUX, M. 1874: Des trois poques de la pierre. *Bull. Soc. Anthropologie de Paris,* 5 June 1873.

REID, C. 1898: *The Geology of the Country Around Bournemouth* (London, HMSO Memoir of the Geological Survey of Great Britain 1st edition).

REID, C. 1902: *The Geology of the Country Around Ringwood* (London, HMSO Memoir of the Geological Survey of Great Britain).

REID, E.M. 1949: The late-glacial flora of the Lea Valley. *New Phytologist* 245–252.

REID, E.M. AMD CHANDLER, M.E.J. 1923: The Barrowell Green (Lea Valley) Arctic flora. *Quarterly Journal of the Geological Society of London* 79, 604–605.

REINECK, H.-E. AND SINGH, J.B. 1980: *Depositional Sedimentary Environments* (Berlin, Heidelberg & New York, Springer-Verlag, 2nd Edition).

RHOADES, D.C. AND STANLEY, D.J. 1965: Biogenic graded bedding. *Journal of Sedimentary Petrology* 35, 4, 956–63.

RHODES, E.J. 1988: Methodological considerations in the optical dating of quartz. *Quaternary Science Reviews* 7, 395–400.

RICK, J.W. 1976: Downslope movement and archaeological intrasite spatial analysis. *American Antiquity* 41, 133–44.

RIGAUD, A. 1972: La technologie du burin appliquée au matériel osseux la Garenne (Indre). *Bull. Soc. Préhistorique Française* 69, 104–8.

RIGAUD, J.P. 1970: Etude préliminaire des industries magdaléniennes du Flageolet, commune de Bezenac, Dordogne *Bull. Soc. Préhistorique Française* 67, 2, 456–474.

RIGAUD, J.P. 1979: A propos des industries magdaléniennes du Flageolet. In Sonneville-Bordes, D. de (editor), *La Fin des temps glaciaires en Europe* (Paris, CNRS, Colloques Internationaux No 271) 467–471.

RIGHI, D. AND GUILLET, B. 1977: Datations par le Carbonne-14 naturel de la matière organique d'horizons spodiques de podzols des Landes du Médoc (France). *Soil Organic Matter Studies I* (Vienna, Atomic Energy Agency) 187–192.

RODDA, J.C. 1967: A countrywide study of intensive rainfall for the United Kingdom. *Journal of Hydrology* 5, 58–69.

ROE, D.A. 1981: *The Lower and Middle Palaeolithic periods in Britain* (London, Routledge & Kegan Paul).

ROE, D.A. 1985: Some recent research involving microwear analysis. *Quarterly Review of Archaeology* 4–6.

ROLFSEN, P. 1980: Disturbance of archaeological layers by processes in the soil. *Norwegian Archaeological Review* 13, 2, 110–118.

RONEN, A. 1965: Observations sur l'Aurignacien. *L'Anthropologie* 69, 5/6, 465–486.

ROMANS, J.C.C., STEVENS, J.H. AND ROBERTSON, L. 1966: Alpine soils of North-East Scotland. *Journal of Soil Science* 17, 184–199.

ROMANS, J.C.C. AND ROBERTSON, L. 1974: Some aspects of the genesis of alpine and upland soils of the British Isles. In Rutherford, G.K. (editor), *Soil Microscopy* (Canada, Kingston, Limestone Press) 498–510.

ROMANS, J.C.C., ROBERTSON, L. AND DENT, D.L. 1980: The micromorphology of young soils from south east Iceland. *Geografiska Annaler* 62A, 1–2, 93–103.

ROTTLAENDER, R. 1975: The formation of patina on flint. *Archaeometry* 17, 106–110.

ROWLETT, R.M. AND ROBBINS, M.C. 1982: Estimating original assemblage content to adjust for post-depositional vertical artefact movement. *World Archaeology* 14, 73–83.

RUDDIMAN, W.F. AND McINTYRE, A. 1981: The North Atlantic during the last deglaciation. *Palaeogeogr. Palaeoclimatol. Palaeoecol.* 35, 145–214.

RUHE, R.V. 1959: Stone lines in soils. *Soil Science* 87, 223–31.

RUST, A. 1937: *Das altsteinzeitliche Rentierjägerlage Meiendorf* (Neumünster, Karl Wachholtz).

RUST, A. 1943: *Die alt-und mittelsteinzeitlichen Funde von Stellmoor* (Neumünster, Karl Wachholtz).

SAINT-MATHURIN, S. DE AND PINCON, G. 1986: Gravure sur cortex de silex du Magdalénien Final du Roc-aux-Sorciers. In *IIIe Congrès national des Sociétés savantes, Poitiers, 1986, Préet Protohistoire* (Poitiers) 187–192.

SALAZAR-JIMÉNEZ, A., FREY, R.W. AND HOWARD, J.D. 1982: Concavity orientations of bivalve shells in estuarine and nearshore shelf sediments, Georgia. *Journal of Sedimentary Petrology* 52, 2, 565–86.

SALOMONSSON, B. 1964: Découverte d'une habitation du Tardiglaciaire à Segebro, Scanie, Suède. *Acta Archaeologica* 35 (2–4), 1–28.

SALTER, C.J. 1987. The lithic material of possible metallurgical significance. In Cunliffe, B.W. 1987: *Hengistbury Head, Dorset. Volume 1: The Prehistoric and Roman Settlement 3500 BC to 500 AD* (Oxford, Oxford University Committee for Archaeology, Monograph 13) 196.

SARAUW, G.F.L. 1903: En stenalders Boplads i Maglemose ved Mullerup sammenholdt med beslaegtede Fund. *Aarbøger* 148–315.

SATCHELL, J.E. (editor) 1983: *Earthworm Ecology* (London, Chapman and Hall).

SCAIFE, R.G. 1980: *Late-Devensian and Flandrian Palaeo-ecological Studies in the Isle of Wight* (University of London, King's College, unpublished PhD dissertation).

SCAIFE, R.G. 1982: Late-Devensian and early Flandrian vegetation changes in southern England. In Limbrey, S. and Bell, M. (editors), *Archaeological Aspects of Woodland Ecology* (Oxford, British Archaeological Reports, International Series 146) 57–74.

SCAIFE, R.G. 1987: A review of later Quaternary plant microfossil and macrofossil research in Southern England: with special reference to environmental archaeological evidence. In Keeley, H.C.M. (editor), *Environmental Archaeology: a regional review, Vol II* (Historic Buildings & Monuments Commission for England, Occasional Paper No 1) 125–204.

SCAIFE, R.G. 1988: The "Elm Decline" in the pollen record of south-east England and its relationship to early agriculture. In Jones, M. (editor), *Archaeology and the Flora of the British Isles* (Oxford, Oxford University Committee for Archaeology, Monograph 14), 21–33.

SCAIFE, R.G. AND MACPHAIL, R.I. 1983: The post-Devensian development of heathland soils and vegetation. In Burnham, C.P. (editor), *Soils of the Heathlands and Chalklands* (South East Soils Discussion Group-SEESOIL) 1, 70–99.

SCHICK, K.D. 1986: *Stone Age Sites in the Making: experiments in the formation and transformation of archaeological occurrences.* (Oxford, British Archaeological Reports, International Series 319).

SCHIFFER, M.B. 1987: *Formation Processes of the Archaeological Record* (Albuquerque, University of New Mexico Press).

SCHILD, R. 1988: Processus de changement dans le Paléolithique final au sud de la Loire. In Otte, M. (editor), *De la Loire à l'Oder: Les civilisations du Paléolithique final dans le nord-ouest européen* (Oxford, British Archaeological Reports International Series 444ii) 595–614.

SCHMIDER, B. 1979: Un nouveau faciès du Magdalénien final du Bassin Parisien: l'industrie du gisement du Pré-de-Forges à Marsangy (Yonne). In Sonneville-Bordes, D. de (editor), *La Fin des temps glaciaires en Europe* (Paris, CNRS, Colloques Internationaux No 271) 763–771.

SCHMIDER, B. 1981: Les particularités dans le développement du Magdalénien du Centre du Bassin Parisien et ses relations avec les cultures de la Plaine de l'Europe du Nord. In Kozlowski, J.K. and Kozlowski, S.K. (editors), *Archaeologia Interregionalis* (Warsaw University and Krakow, Jagiellonian University) 117–131.

SCHMIDER, B. 1987: Environment and culture in the Seine Basin during the Late Glacial period. In Burdukiewicz, J.M. and Kobusiewicz, M. (editors), *Late Glacial in Central Europe: culture and environment* (Warsaw, Polska Akademia Nauk) 11–24.

SCHMIDER, B. AND CROISSET, E. DE 1985: La structure centrale (N19) du campement Magdalénien de Marsangy (Yonne): données archéologiques. *Archéologique Expérimentale* (Association pour la Promotion de l'Archéologie de Bourgogne, Archéodrome) 3–19.

SCHÜTRUMPF, R. 1943: Die pollenanalytische Untersuchung der Rentierjägerfundstätte Stellmoor in Holstein. In Rust, A. (editor), *Die alt-und mittelsteinzeitlichen Funde von Stellmoor* (Neumünster, Karl Wachholtz) 6–45.

SCHWABEDISSEN, H. 1944: *Die mittelere Steinzeit im westlichen Nord-Deutschland* (Neumünster, Karl Wachholtz).

SCHWABEDISSEN, H. 1954: *Die Federmesser-Gruppen des nordwesteuropäischen Flachlandes. Zur Ausbreitung des spät-Magdalénien* (Neumünster, Karl Wachholtz).

SCHWABEDISSEN, H. 1957: Das Alter der Federmesser-Zivilisation auf Grund neuer naturwissenschaftlicher Untersuchungen. *Eiszeitalter und Gegenwart* 8, 200–209.

SEAGRIEF, S.C. 1956: *A Pollen-analytic Investigation of the Quaternary Period in Britain* (University of Cambridge, unpublished PhD dissertation).

SEAGRIEF, S.C. 1959: Pollen diagrams from Southern England: Wareham, Dorset and Nursling, Hampshire. *New Phytologist* 58, 316–325.

SEAGRIEF, S.C. 1960: Pollen diagrams from Southern England: Cranes Moor, Hampshire. *New Phytologist* 59, 73–83.

SEAGRIEF, S.C. AND GODWIN, H. 1960: Pollen diagrams from Southern England: Elstead, Surrey. *New Phytologist* 599, 84–91.

SEDDON, B. 1962: Late-glacial deposits at Llyn Dwythwch and Nant Ffrancon, Caernarvonshire. *Phil. Trans. Roy. Soc. B* 244, 459.

SEITZER, D.J. 1978: Forms vs. function: microwear analysis and its application to Upper Palaeolithic burins. *Meddelanden fran Lund universitets historiska museum (New Series)* 2, 5–20.

SEMENOV, S.A. 1964: *Prehistoric Technology* Translated by M.W. Thompson (London, Cory, Adams and Mackay).

SHARP, R.P. 1966: Kelso Dunes, Mojave Desert, California. *Bulletin of the Geological Society of America* 77, 1045–74.

SHELLEY, P.H. AND NIALS, F.L. 1983: A preliminary evaluation of aeolian processes in artefact dislocation and modification: an experimental approach to one depositional environment. *Proceedings of the New Mexico Archaeological Council* 5, 1, 50–56.

SHEPHERD, W. 1972: *Flint* (London, Faber & Faber).

SHERWOOD, R.G. 1974: *A Mesolithic site on Turbary Common, Bournemouth.* (Bournemouth Teacher's Centre, unpublished manuscript).

SHOTTON, F.W. 1977: British dating work with radioactive isotopes. In Shotton, F.W. (editor) *British Quaternary Studies: recent advances* (Oxford University Press), 17–30.

SIEVEKING, A. 1987: *Engraved Magdalenian plaquettes* (Oxford, British Archaeological Reports: International Series 369).

SIEVEKING, A. 1981: Continuité des motifs schématiques, au Paléolithique et dans les périodes postérieures en Franco-Cantabrie. In *The Proceedings of the Altamira Symposium* (Madrid, Departamento de Prehistoria de la Universidad Complutense de Madrid) 319–337.

SIMMONS, I.G. AND TOOLEY, M. 1981: *The environment in prehistory* (London, Duckworth).

SIRET, L. 1893: L'Espagne préhistorique. *Revue des Questions Scientifiques.*

SMITH, A.G. AND PILCHER, J.R. 1973: Radiocarbon dates and the vegetational history of the British Isles. *New Phytologist* 72, 903–914.

SMITH, R.A. 1924: Stone Age site near Woking, *The Antiquaries Journal* 4, 415.

SMITH, W.G. 1884: On a Palaeolithic floor at North East London. *Journal of the Anthropological Institute of Great Britain and Ireland* 12, 357–384.

SMITH, W.G. 1894: *Man the primeval savage: his haunts and relics from the hill-tops of Bedfordshire to Blackwall* (London, Stanford).

SOLLY, H.S. 1910: Note on a large boulder found at Branksome, Upper Parkstone. *Dorset Natural History and Antiquarian Field Club* 31, 161–4.

SONNEVILLE-BORDES, D. DE 1960: *Le Paléolithique Supérieur en Périgord* (Bordeaux, Delmas).

SONNEVILLE-BORDES, D. DE 1963: Le Paléolithique supérieur en Suisse. *L'Anthropologie* 67, 205–268.

SONNEVILLE-BORDES, D. DE 1969: Pointes à cran (Kerbspitzen) du Magdalénien supérieur de Petersfels. *Quartär* 20, 175–181.

SONNEVILLE-BORDES D. DE AND PERROT, J. 1953: Essai d'adaptation des méthodes statistiques au Paléolithique supérieur. Premiers résultats. *Bull. Soc. Préhistorique Française* 50, 6, 323–333.

SONNEVILLE-BORDES, D. DE AND PERROT, J. 1954: Lexique typologique du Paléolithique supérieur. *Bull. Soc. Préhistorique Française* 51, 7, 327–335.

SONNEVILLE-BORDES, D. DE AND PERROT, J. 1955: Lexique typologique du Paléolithique supérieur. Outillage lithique: III Outils composites, perçoirs *Bull. Soc. Préhistorique Française* 52, 76–79.

SONNEVILLE-BORDES, D. DE AND PERROT, J. 1956a: Lexique typologique du Paléolithique supérieur. *Bull. Soc. Préhistorique Française* 52, 7/8, 408–412.

SONNEVILLE-BORDES, D. DE AND PERROT, J. 1956b: Lexique typologique du Paléolithique supérieur. *Bull. Soc. Préhistorique Française* 53, 9, 547–559.

SONNEVILLE-BORDES, D. DE AND DEFFARGE, F. 1974: Lames retouchées magdaléniennes du Morin. *Zephyrus* 25, 95–105.

SOUTH, S. 1977: *Method and theory in historical archaeology* (New York, Academic Press).

SPAN, A. 1983: Een geornamenteerde shrabbe uit de Drunense Duinen. *Archaeologische Berichten* 13, 113–114.

SPURRELL, F.C.J. 1880: On implements and chips from the floor of a Palaeolithic workshop. *The Archaeological Journal* 37, 249–99.

STAPERT, D. 1976: Some natural surface modifications on flint in the Netherlands. *Palaeohistoria* 18, 8–41.

STAPERT, D., KRIST, J.S. AND ZANDBERGEN, A.L. 1986: Oldeholtewolde, a Late Hamburgian site in the Netherlands. In Roe, D.A. (editor), *Studies in the Upper Palaeolithic of Britain and Northwest Europe* (Oxford, British Archaeological Reports International Series 296) 187–227.

STEIN, J.K. 1983: Earthworm activity: a source of potential disturbance of archaeological sediments. *American Antiquity* 48, 2, 277–89.

STOCKTON, E.D. 1973: Shaw's Creek Shelter: human displacement of artefacts and its significance. *Mankind* 9, 112–117.

STROBEL, R. 1959: Tardenoisspitze in einem Bovidknochen von Schwenningen am Nechar. *Fundberichte aus Schwaben* Neue Folge, 15, 103–6.

STUART, A.J. 1977: The vertebrates of the Last Cold Stage in Britain and Ireland. *Phil. Trans. R. Soc. London* B 280, 295–312.

STUART, A.J. 1982: *Pleistocene Vertebrates in the British Isles* (London and New York, Longman).

STURDY, D.A. 1975: Some reindeer economies in prehistoric Europe. In Higgs, E.S. (editor), *Palaeoeconomy* (Cambridge University Press) 55–95.

SUMMERS, P.G. 1941: A Mesolithic site, near Iwerne Minster, Dorset. Notes. *Proc. Prehistoric Society* 7, 145–164.

SUMMERFIELD, M.A. 1979: Origin and palaeoenvironmental interpretation of sarsens. *Nature* 281, 5727, 137–9.

SWITSUR, V.R. AND JACOBI, R.M. 1975: Radiocarbon dates for the Pennine Mesolithic. *Nature* 256, 32–34.

SWITSUR, V.R. AND WEST, R.G. 1975: University of Cambridge natural radiocarbon measurements XIV. *Radiocarbon* 17, 3, 301–312.

TAUTE, W. 1968: *Die Stielspitzen-Gruppen im nördlichen Mitteleuropa. Ein Beitrag zur Kenntnis der späten Altsteinzeit.* (Köln, Böhlau, Fundamenta Reihe A, Band 5).

TAYLOR, J. 1980: Environmental changes in Wales during the Holocene period. In Taylor, J. (editor), *Culture and Environment in Prehistoric Wales* (Oxford, British Archaeological Reports British Series 76), 101–130.

THÉVENIN, A. 1982: *Rochedane* (Strasbourg, Mémoires de la Faculté des Sciences sociales).

THOMPSON, M.W. AND ASHBEE, P. 1957: Excavation of a barrow near the Hardy Monument, Black Down, Portesham, Dorset. *Proc. Prehistoric Society* 23, 6, 124–136.

TIXIER, J. 1963: *Typologie de l'Epipaléolithique du Maghreb.* (Algers and Paris, Mémoires du Centre de Recherches Anthropologiques, Préhistoriques et Ethnographiques).

TIXIER, J. 1972: Obtention de lames par débitage "sous-le-pied". *Bull. Soc. Préhistorique Française* 69, 5, 134–9.

TIXIER, J. 1980: Expériences de taille. In, *Préhistoire et technologie lithique.* (Valbonne, CNRS cahier 1 de l'URA 28 du CRA) 47–49.

TIXIER, J., INIZAN, M.L. AND ROCHE, H. 1980: *Préhistoire de la Pierre taillée. 1. Terminologie et technologie.* (Valbonne, Cercle de Recherches et d'Etudes Préhistoriques).

TOSI, M. AND PIPERNO, D. 1973: Lithic technology behind the ancient lapis lazuli trade. *Expedition.* 16, 1, 15–23.

TRATMAN, E.K. 1976: A Late Upper Palaeolithic calculator (?), Gough's Cave, Cheddar, Somerset. *Proc. Univ. Bristol Spelaeol. Soc.* 14, 2, 123–129.

TRINGHAM, R.G., COOPER, G., ODELL, G., VOYTEK, B. AND WHITMAN, A. 1974: Experimentation in the Formation of Edge Damage: A new approach to Lithic Analysis. *Journal of Field Archaeology* 1, 171–196.

TROELS-SMITH, J. 1962: Et Pileskaft fra Tidlig Maglemosetid. *Aarbøger,* 122–146.

TROMNAU, G. 1975: Neue Ausgrabungen im Ahrensburger Tunneltal. Ein Beitrag zur Erforschung des Jungpaläolithikums im nordwesteuropäischen Flachland. *Offa* Band 33.

TUDHOPE, A.W. AND SCOFFIN, T.P. 1984: The Effects of Callianassa bioturbation on the preservation of carbonate grains in Davies Reef Lagoon, Great Barrier Reef, Australia. *Journal of Sedimentary Petrology* 54, 4, 1091–6.

TURNER, J. 1962: The Tilia decline: an anthropogenic interpretation. *New Phytologist* 61, 328–41.

TURNER, J. AND KERSHAW, A.P. 1973: A Late-and Post-glacial pollen diagram from Cranberry Bog, near Beamish, County Durham. *New Phytologist* 72, 915–28.

UNGER-HAMILTON, R. 1984a: *Method in Microwear Analysis: sickles, blades and other tools from Arjoune, Syria.* (University of London, Institute of Archaeology, unpublished PhD thesis).

UNGER-HAMILTON, R. 1984b: The formation of use-wear polish on flint: beyond the "deposit versus abrasion" controversy. *Journal of Archaeological Science* 11, 91–8.

UNGER-HAMILTON, R., GRACE, R., MILLER, R. AND BERGMAN, C.A. 1987: Experimental replication, use and microwear analysis of spindle-tipped borers from Abu Salabikh, Iraq. In Stordeur, D. (editor), *La main et l'outil. Manches et Emmanchements Préhistoriques* (Lyon, Travaux de la Maison de l'Orient Méditerranéen) 269–285.

VALENSI, L. 1960: De l'origine des silex protomagdaléniens de l'Abri Pataud, Les Eyzies (Dordogne). *Bull. Soc. Préhistorique Française,* 57: 80–84.

VALENTINE, K.W.G. AND DALRYMPLE, J.B. 1975: The identification, lateral variation and chronology of two burial palaeocatenas at Woodhall Spa and West Runton, England. *Quaternary Research* 5, 551–590.

VAN DER HAMMEN, T. 1951: Late-glacial flora and periglacial phenomena in the Netherlands. *Leidse. Geol. Meded.* 17, 71–184.

VAN DER HAMMEN, T. 1971: The Upper Quaternary stratigraphy of the Dinkel Valley. In Van der Hammen, T. and Wijmstra, T.A. (editors), Upper Quaternary of the Dinkel Valley. *Mededelingen Rijks Geologische Dienst* Neuwe Serie 22, 59–72.

VAN DER HAMMEN, T. AND WIJMSTRA, T.A. 1971: Upper Quaternary of the Dinkel Valley. *Mededelingen Rijks Geologische Dienst* Nieuwe Serie 22.

VAN DER LEE, 1977: Versierde Laat-Paleolithische stenen werktuigen Noord-Brabant. In Roymans, N., Biemans, J., Slofstra, J., & Verwers, W.J.H. (editors), *Brabantse Oudheden* (Einhoven, Stichting Brabants Heem) 27–32.

VAN NOTEN, F. 1978: *Les Chasseurs de Meer* (Brugge, de Tempel, Dissertationes Archaeologicae Gandenses 18).

VAN VLIET, B., FAIVRE, P., ANDREUX, F., ROBIN, A.M. AND PORTAL, J.M. 1983: Behaviour of some organic components in blue and ultra-violet light: application to the micromorphology of podzols, Andosols and Planosols. In Bullock, P. and Murphy, C.P. (editors), *Soil Micromorphology* (Berkhamsted, A.B. Academic Press) 91–100.

VAUGHAN, P.C. 1981: *Lithic microwear experiementation and the functional analysis of a Lower Magdalenian stone tool assemblage* (University of Pennsylvania, unpublished PhD thesis).

VERHEYLEWEGEN, J. 1956: Le Paléolithique final de culture périgordienne du gisement préhistorique de Lommel. *Bull. Soc. roy. Belge d'Anthropologie et Préhistoire* 67, 179–257.

VERMEERSCH, P. 1979: Een jongpaleolitische nederzetting te Kanne. *Conspectus MCMLXXVIII, Archaeologia Belgica* 213, 12–16.

VERMEERSCH, P.M. 1981: Magdalénien à Kanne et à Orp. Extrait des Actes du Congrès de Comines 1980, 2. *Fédération Archéologique et Historique de Belgique* 205–213.

VERMEERSCH, P.M., SYMENS, N., VYNCKIER, P., GIJSELINGS AND LAUWERS, R. 1987: Orp, site magdalénien de plein air (comm. de Orp-Jaunche). *Archaeologia Belgica* III, 7–56.

VERMEERSCH, P. AND SYMENS, N. 1988: Le Magdalénien de plein air en Belgique. In Otte, M. (editor), *De la Loire à l'Oder: Les civilisations du Paléolithique final dans le nord-ouest européen* (Oxford, British Archaeological Reports International Series 444i) 243–259.

VEIL, S. 1979: Neue Ausgrabungen auf dem Magdalénien-Fundplatz Andernach, Martinsberg (Rheinland–Pfalz). *Archäologisches Korrespondenzblatt* 9, 251–260.

VIGNARD, E. 1931: Les microburins tardenoisiens du Sébilien. Fabrication. Emplois. *Congrès Préhistorique de France* (Nìmes-Avignon, 10e session) 66–106.

VIGNARD, E. 1934: Triangles et trapèzes du Capsien en connexion avec leurs microburins. *Bull. Soc. Préhistorique Française* 31, 457–9.

VILLA, P. 1977: Sols et niveaux d'habitat du Paléolithique Inférieur en Europe et au Proche Orient. *Quaternaria* 19,107–134.

VILLA, P. 1982: Conjoinable pieces and site formation processes. *American Antiquity* 47, 276–290.

VILLA, P. AND COURTIN, J. 1983: The interpretation of stratified sites: a view from underground. *Journal of Archaeological Science* 10, 267–281.

VISHER, G.S. 1969: Grain size distributions and depositional processes. *Journal of Sedimentary Petrology* 39, 1077–1106.

WALKER, M.J.C. AND LOWE, J.J. 1980: Pollen analysis, radiocarbon dates and the deglaciation of Rannoch Moor, Scotland, following the Loch Lomond Advance. In Cullingford, R.A., Davidson, D.A. and Lewin, J. (editors), *Timescales in Geomorphology.* (J. Wiley and Sons) 247–259.

WALKER, A.J. AND OTLET, R.L. 1988: Harwell radiocarbon measurements. VI *Radiocarbon* 30, 3, 297–317.

WARME, J.E. 1967: Graded bedding in the Recent sediments of Muga Lagoon, California. *Journal of Sedimentary Petrology* 37, 2, 540–7.

WARREN, A. 1979: Aeolian processes. In Embleton, C. and Thornes, J. (editors), *Process in Geomorphology* (London, Edward Arnold) 325–51.

WASHBURN, A.L. 1979: *Geocryology: A Survey of Periglacial*

*Processes and Environments* (London, Edward Arnold) 2nd edition.

WATON, P.V. 1982a: Man's impact on the chalklands: some new pollen evidence. In Limbrey, S. and Bell, M. (editors), *Archaeological aspects of Woodland Ecology* (Oxford, British Archaeological Reports, International Series 146) 75–91.

WATON, P.V. 1982b. *A palynological study of the impact of man on the landscape of central southern England, with special reference to the chalklands.* (University of Southampton, Department of Geography, Unpublished PhD dissertation).

WEST, R.G. 1977: Early and Middle Devensian flora and vegetation. *Phil. Trans. Royal Soc. London* B 280, 229–46.

WHITE, H.J.O. 1917: The geology of the country around Bournemouth. *Memoirs of the Geological Survey of Great Britain* (2nd Edition) 48, 53–54 & 70.

WHITE, H.J.O. 1921: *A short account of the geology of the Isle of Wight* (London, HMSO).

WHITTOFT, J. 1968: Flint arrowpoints from the Eskimo of Northwestern Alaska. *Expedition* 10, 2, 30–37.

WHITTLE, A.R. 1978: Resources and population in the British Neolithic. *Antiquity* 52, 34–42.

WIKEN, E.B., BROERSMA, K., LAVKULICH, L.M. AND FARSTAD, L. 1976: Biosynthesis alteration in a British Columbia soil by ants (*Formica fusca* Linné). *Soil Science Society of America Proceedings* 40, 422–26.

WILLIAMS, M.A.J. 1968: Termites and soil development near Brooks Creek, Northern Territory. *Australian Journal of Science* 31, 4, 153–4.

WILLIAMS, R.B.G. 1973: Frost and the works of man. *Antiquity* 47, 19–31.

WILMSEN, E.N. 1968: Functional analysis of flaked stone artifacts. *American Antiquity* 33, 2, 156–161.

WILMSEN, E.N. 1973: Interaction, spacing behaviour and the organisation of hunting bands. *Journal of Anthropological Research* 29, 1–31.

WOOD, W.R, AND JOHNSON, D.L. 1978: A survey of disturbance processes in archaeological site formation. In Schiffer, M.B. (editor), *Advances in Archaeological Method and Theory: Volume 1* (New York, Academic Press) 315–81.

WOODCOCK, A.G. 1978: The Palaeolithic in Sussex. In Drewett, P.L. (editor), *Archaeology in Sussex to AD 1500* (CBA Research Report No. 29) 8–14.

WOODMAN, P.C. 1978: The chronology and economy of the Irish Mesolithic: some working hypotheses. In Mellars, P.A. (editor), *The early postglacial settlement of Northern Europe* (London, Duckworth) 333–370.

WOODMAN, P.C. 1985: *Excavations at Mount Sandel 1973–77* (Belfast, HMSO Northern Ireland Archaeological Monographs No.2).

WOOLDRIDGE, S.W. AND LINTON, D.L. 1933: The loam terraces of South East England and their relation to its early history. *Antiquity* 7, 297–310.

WOOLDRIDGE, S.W. AND LINTON, D.L. 1955: *Structure, surface and drainage in South-East England* (London, G. Phillip and Son).

WOUTERS, A.M. 1984: "De Fransman". Een Jongpaleolithische vindplaats, behorend tot een der componenten van het "Gravettien" (Perigordien). *Archaeologische Berichten* 15, 70–124.

WYMER, J.J. 1962: Excavations of the Maglemosian sites at Thatcham, Berkshire, England, and the stratigraphy of the Mesolithic sites III and V at Thatcham, Berkshire, England. *Proc. Prehistoric Society* 28, 329–370.

WYMER, J.J. 1971: A possible Late Upper Palaeolithic site at Cranwich, Norfolk. *Norfolk Archaeology* 35, 259–263.

WYMER, J.J. (editor) 1977: *Gazetteer of Mesolithic sites in England and Wales.* With a Gazetteer of Upper Palaeolithic sites in England and Wales edited by C.J. Bonsall. CBA Research Report No. 22. (Norwich, Geo Abstracts).

YELLEN, J.E. 1977: *Archaeological Approaches to the Present: Models for Reconstructing the Past* (New York, Academic Press).

YONG, R.N. AND WARKENTIN, B.P. 1975: *Soil Properties and Soil Behaviour* (Amsterdam, Elsevier).

# Index

Note on page numbering with examples:
*132F* refers to Figure/s on page 132
T64 refers to Table/s on page 64
The above are generally omitted if there is a text reference
on the same page
84..86 means that other matter intervenes
193–7 *passim* indicates one mention at least on each of the pages
*Abbreviations:*   LUP:   Late Upper Palaeolithic
Meso:   Mesolithic
PM site:   Powell Mesolithic site

*Compiled by Freda Wilkinson*